Medical Terminology

Connecting through Language

W9-AAW-831

Ebony S. Lawrence

PARADIGM
EDUCATION SOLUTIONS

St. Paul

Senior Vice President: Linda Hein
Editor in Chief: Christine Hurney
Managing Editor: Brenda M. Palo
Senior Editor: Carley Bomstad Fruzzetti
Developmental Editor: J. Trout Lowen
Director of Production: Timothy W. Larson
Senior Production Editor: Lori Michelle Ryan
Production Editor: Elizabeth Mathews
Cover and Text Designer and Senior Design and Production Specialist: Jaana Bykonich
Copy Editor: Mary Byers
Proofreader: Kristin Melendez
Indexer: Beverlee Day
Vice President and Director of Digital Projects: Chuck Bratton
Digital Projects Manager: Tom Modl
Director of Marketing: Lara Weber McLellan
Product Marketing Specialist: Shealan Eldredge

Care has been taken to verify the accuracy of information presented in this book. However, the authors, editors, and publisher cannot accept responsibility for web, email, newsgroup, or chat room subject matter or content, or for consequences from the application of the information in this book, and make no warranty, expressed or implied, with respect to its content.

Trademarks: Some of the product names and company names included in this book have been used for identification purposes only and may be trademarks or registered trade names of their respective manufacturers and sellers. The authors, editors, and publisher disclaim any affiliation, association, or connection with, or sponsorship or endorsement by, such owners.

Cover Image: © iStock.com/iLexx; © wawritto/Shutterstock.com

  A.D.A.M. Imagery Copyright © 2016 A.D.A.M., a business unit of Ebix, Inc. All rights reserved. Images may not be reproduced in any manner without express written consent of A.D.A.M., a business unit of Ebix, Inc.; 1 Ebix Way, Johns Creek, GA 30097 USA

We have made every effort to trace the ownership of all copyrighted material and to secure permission from copyright holders. In the event of any question arising as to the use of any material, we will be pleased to make the necessary corrections in future printings.

ISBN 978-0-76386-826-0 (print)
ISBN 978-0-76386-827-7 (digital)

© 2017 by Paradigm Publishing, Inc.
875 Montreal Way
St. Paul, MN 55102
Email: educate@emcp.com
Website: http://ParadigmCollege.com

Printed in the United States of America

25 24 23 22 21 20 19 18 17 16   1 2 3 4 5 6 7 8 9 10

Brief Contents

Contents

Preface

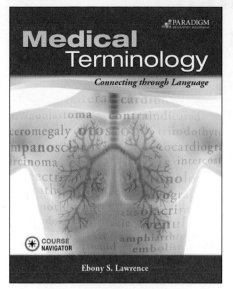

Medical Terminology: Connecting through Language is written for students who are preparing for a variety of professional and paraprofessional careers in the medical field, particularly for careers related to direct patient care and support services. A healthcare professional must be familiar with human anatomy and be able to convey information to multiple parties, including administrative and clinical colleagues, healthcare providers, and patients. Meeting this challenge requires a thorough understanding of the terminology related to anatomy, physiology, and medical procedures. Importantly, it also requires the ability to communicate accurately and effectively. This course integrates anatomy, physiology, and pathology information for each body system with exercises and activities designed to ensure that healthcare careers students build a strong foundation in medical terminology.

Studying medical terminology requires patience, practice, and critical thinking skills. *Medical Terminology: Connecting through Language* is developed so that each chapter immediately presents the most essential information in an easy-to-understand format. Students will learn the most important information first. The textbook is organized so that students encounter word structure fundamentals in the first chapter and learn the skills necessary to analyze and understand new words. Students are then prepared to apply these skills throughout the program. Chapter 2 introduces essential body organization and healthcare terminology that will play a role within all subsequent chapters. Chapters 3-16 focus on body systems and necessary anatomy and physiology concepts, conditions, clinical tests and examinations, and treatments, offering students ample practice and application opportunities.

Text Features

Translation Challenge

Chapter-openers include topic-specific medical scenarios or questions that challenge students to accurately translate medical information.

Learning Objectives

Chapter learning objectives are clearly declared at the start of each chapter.

Tables and Figures

Tables provide essential terminology in a clear and easy-to-understand format. Colorful and accurate figures are engaging and thoroughly illustrate anatomical and physiological concepts.

Margin and Sidebar Features

Each chapter includes additional information in either brief margin notes or helpful sidebars. Topics include:

- **What's in a Word?** Quickly identifies terminology-related information, such as word definitions, etymology, or word pronunciations.
- **Did You Know?** Highlights brief tips and intriguing facts.
- **To Note!** Reiterates important or noteworthy details.
- **Soft Skills for Health Care** Introduces the many soft-skills required to succeed in the healthcare professions.
- **In The Know** Presents additional information, terms, or concepts related to chapter content.
- **Beyond Words** Provides fun facts and games related to the chapter content.

Checkpoints and Exercises

Students can quickly assess their understanding by completing the assessment questions appearing at the end of each major content section and by working through the exercises offered within the chapters.

Chapter Review

Each chapter ends with a chapter review containing self-assessment questions. Answers are provided at the end of the textbook (Appendix A) so that students can check their work and determine whether to revisit and review any of the chapter content. Chapter Review content includes knowledge-based questions delivered as matching, spelling, and word building exercises, as well as higher-order questions such as application and evaluation activities.

Appendixes

In addition to the many helpful in-text and in-margin features, *Medical Terminology: Connecting through Language* presents three appendixes to enhance student comprehension and learning: Checkpoint, Exercise, and Chapter Review Answer Keys; Abbreviation Lists; and Word Part Lists.

Index

A comprehensive index.

eBook

For students who prefer studying with an **ebook**, the *Medical Terminology: Connecting through Language* textbook is available in an electronic format. The web-based, password-protected ebook features dynamic navigation tools, including bookmarking, a linked Table of Contents, and study tools such as highlighting and note-taking. The student ebook is available online at Paradigm.bookshelf.emcp.com

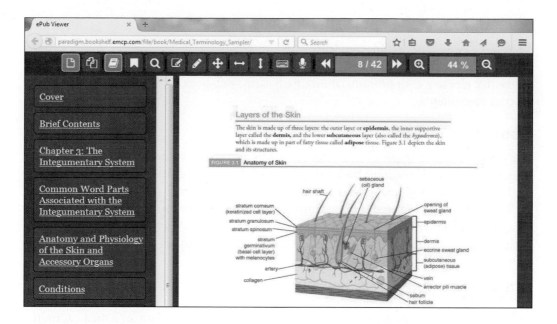

Course Navigator Learning Management System

Integrated with the *Medical Terminology: Connecting through Language* textbook is the *Course Navigator* learning management system. This rich, web-based system offers students a rich variety of learning and practice opportunities related to course content.

Students will observe that the *Course Navigator* logo is tucked into the margins of the book. This logo alerts students to go to the *Course Navigator* for related learning activities.

Student Practice Opportunities

The *Course Navigator* provides students with a variety of engaging activities to support their learning of chapter concepts. These activities include end-of-chapter exercises, an interactive glossary with pronunciations, flash cards, web projects, interactive games, and practice assessments.

Instructor Support

The *Course Navigator* enables instructors to access and review students' work and to track students' progress throughout the course. Most of the provided student resources are automatically gradable and final grades can be exported to instructors' grade books.

The **instructor resources** that accompany this textbook are located on the *Course Navigator* and are visible only to instructors. These resources offer instructors a number of tools such as course-planning guidelines and chapter lessons as well as control of the PowerPoints.

Supplemental Resources

Lastly, the *Course Navigator* provides a variety of resources to supplement a medical terminology course. Resources located on the *Course Navigator* or offered separately include:

- Pronunciation Coach: Students can practice and perfect their pronunciation of medical terms using this exciting interactive tool.

- BioDigital™ Human: Access is provided within the *Course Navigator* to view and interact with three-dimensional human anatomy images for enhanced study of anatomy and physiology.

- Paradigm's *Pocket Drug Guide* print book, ebook, and the new *Drugs & Terms* mobile application.

About the Author

Ebony S. Lawrence, BS, MHA

Ebony S. Lawrence received a Bachelor of Science degree in Community Health Education from Virginia Commonwealth University in 2001 and a Master of Science degree in Health Administration (MHA) from The University of North Carolina at Charlotte in 2003. At the time of publication, she was in the dissertation phase of completing a Doctorate in Public Health (DrPH) from Capella University with a specialization in Epidemiology.

Ebony began her career working in the area of Corporate Health and Safety for one of the largest supermarket chains in the nation, Publix Super Markets, Inc. As an executive-level manager, she led the organization's health and safety program, created written programs to ensure OSHA Compliance specific to First Aid and Safety, and conducted facility safety assessments. During her tenure with Publix, she became an Instructor-Level Trainer with the American Red Cross. In 2006, Ebony relocated back to Charlotte, NC and worked as an Occupational Safety Instructor with Cintas First Aid and Safety and became Training Center Faculty with the American Heart Association. She has since certified over 12,300 adults in Heartsaver First Aid/CPR/AED or Basic Life Support.

Ebony has a wealth of experience in both traditional and distance education settings, with a focus in allied health programs. In 2009, her passion for teaching and education led her to an Adjunct Faculty position at Johnson C. Smith University in Charlotte, NC.

She became a full-time educator in higher education the following year as she joined ECPI University's Medical Career Institute (MCI) as an Instructor in the Medical Assisting and Medical Administration programs. Ebony's experience in distance education began in 2010 as an Instructor for Kaplan University Online. She has since led virtual classrooms for Ameritech College, Bryant & Stratton College, and PIMA Medical Institute. While she has spent most of her academic career in Instruction and Curriculum Development, Ebony has an extensive background in program evaluation. She is currently vetted as an Evaluator in several specialized areas with Accrediting Council for Independent Colleges and Schools (ACICS) and Distance Education Accrediting Commission (DEAC). Over the course of her career, she has also served on numerous advisory boards for allied health programs. Ebony lives with her family in Lakeland, Florida.

Acknowledgments

The quality of this body of work is a testament to the many contributors and reviewers who participated in the creation of *Medical Terminology: Connecting through Language.* We would like to thank Alice G. Ettinger and Pamala F. Burch for their generosity in contributing material from Paradigm's original medical terminology program, *Medical Terminology for Health Careers.* In addition, we offer a heartfelt thank-you to all contributors listed in the following sections for their commitment to producing high-quality instructional materials for allied health students.

Expert Content-Reviewers

Sabrina N. Adams, MSIT, MPH, RHIA

James S. Dunnick, MD, FACC, CHCQM, CPCA, CMDP

Loxie E. Kistler, EdD, RN, CMA (AAMA)

Marilyn M. Turner, RN, CMA (AAMA)
Ogeechee Technical College
Statesboro, GA 30458

Contributing Writers, Course Navigator Learning Management System

ansrsource
5440 Harvest Hill Road
Suite 234
Dallas, TX

Patti Isaacs
45th Parallel Maps and Infographics

Loxie E. Kistler, EdD, RN, CMA (AAMA)

Dasantila Sherifi, MBA, RHIA
DeVry University

Interactive Image Programs, Course Navigator Learning Management System and eBook

Aaron Oliker
BioDigital Systems
594 Broadway
Suite 1101
New York, NY

Dan Johnson, MSMI
Ebix, Inc./A.D.A.M.
1 Ebix Way
Johns Creek, GA

Shawn McPartland, MD, JD
Azure College - School of Nursing
Boca Raton, FL

Survey Respondents

Carolyn Gaarder, MLA, RHIA
Minnesota State Community
and Technical College

Amie Mayhall, MBA, CCA
Olney Central College

Marla R. Phillips, MPH, RHIT

Health Information Technology Advisory Board

An additional special acknowledgment of gratitude goes out to the members of Paradigm's Health Information Technology Advisory Board for sharing their insights and advice throughout the development of this text:

Catherine Bell, BS, RHIT, CCS
Milwaukee Area Technical College

Ruth Berger, MS, RHIA
Florida Gateway College

Amy Bledsoe, MS, RHIA, CHPS,
CHTS-PW, CHTS-IM
Spokane Community College

Sue Biedermann, MSHP, RHIA, FAHIMA
Texas State University, Emerita

Hertencia Bowe, EdD, RHIA
Fisher College

Christine Bushaw, MEd, RHIT, CTR
Rochester Community and Technical
College

Jerrie S. Cleaver, MS, RHIA
Central Texas College

Darline Foltz, RHIA
University of Cincinnati— Clermont
College

Lynnette Hessling, MSHI, RHIA,
CHTS-PW, CHTS-TR
Ultimate Medical Academy

Karen Lankisch, PhD, RHIA, CPC
University of Cincinnati— Clermont
College

Jorell Lawrence, BSHA, MSA-HR, CPC
Stratford University

Christi Lower, MS, RHIA

Yvonne Morrissey, BAS, CCS-P
Harrison College

Marla Phillips, MPH, RHIT

Sandra K. Rains, MPA, MBA, RHIA
DeVry University

Terri Randolph, MBA/HCM
Stratford University

Sabine Simmons, PhD, RHIA, CHPS, CPAR
Alabama State University

Word Structures

"Observe, record, tabulate, communicate. Use your five senses. Learn to see, learn to hear, learn to feel, learn to smell, and know that by practice alone you can become expert."

—William Osler, physician

Translation Challenge

A new mother frantically calls your office after receiving the following letter:

> Dear Mrs. Smith,
>
> Our efforts to reach you at the telephone number on file have been unsuccessful. We received your message regarding the Tx of your newborn son's circumcision. The neonatologist and urologist on staff have recommended you D/C the use of Neosporin with the presence of erythema and irritation. If the CC of pain remains, acetaminophen can be given as long as NKA exist. Please feel free to RTO immediately if the infant becomes febrile in order to R/O a possible UTI.
>
> Thank you,
> Lincoln Pediatrics

Although a pediatric clinic is unlikely to send a letter like this, this letter does include many terms and abbreviations you will find in the medical record. Can you accurately "translate" this letter?

Learning Objectives

1.1 Describe the parts of words used to create medical terms.

1.2 Determine the meaning of medical terms by identifying and defining word parts.

1.3 Recognize the meanings of common root words, combining forms, suffixes, and prefixes.

1.4 Utilize the rules provided to form the plural and adjective forms of medical terms.

1.5 Explain the importance of the proper phonetic pronunciation of medical terms.

1.6 Recognize and recall abbreviations commonly used in the healthcare industry.

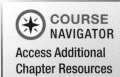

COURSE NAVIGATOR

Access Additional Chapter Resources

Medical terminology is a language in and of itself. If you understand from the beginning that you are learning a new language, you will be better prepared to approach this challenge. This chapter marks the start of your journey toward the mastery of this language by introducing you to the parts of words that combine to create medical terminology. Rather than setting out to memorize thousands of words and phrases, you will begin by building a vocabulary of word parts. You will also learn various medical abbreviations and become familiar with how to transition terms to their plural and adjective forms.

Learning the meanings of basic medical word parts will serve as an important tool for mastering the language of medicine, but the process still requires a significant amount of memorization. You will need to practice and review the content persistently and patiently. Use each and every tool provided by this text, the digital program that accompanies it, and suggestions from your instructor to facilitate your learning. Once you have mastered a core vocabulary of word parts, you will be well on your way to understanding and using the language of health professionals.

The Origins of Our Medical Language

We owe most of the development of early medical language to the ancient Greeks and Romans. Hippocrates (460–370 BC), the Greek physician recognized as the "Father of Western Medicine," was among the first to study anatomy, physiology, and disease processes. Prior to his work, myths and superstition dominated teachings about healing and the human body. Hippocrates and other early Greek anatomists dissected cadavers (human corpses) and attempted to treat disease in living humans.

As they worked, they named body structures using terms familiar to them. For example, the thyroid gland reminded them of a shield, and they named it with the Greek word for shield, *thyreos*. The eardrum looked to them like a tambourine, and they named it accordingly with the Greek word *tympanon*, which is the source for our term *tympanic membrane*.

During the Roman Empire, Latin became the dominant language, and many new anatomy terms were based on Latin words. For example, the term *bowel* (intestine) originated from the Latin *botulus*, meaning "sausage." In ancient times, as now, sections of animal intestines were used as sausage casings.

Over subsequent centuries, German, French, and English researchers and physicians tended to dominate medicine in the Western world and gave names based in those languages to new discoveries about the body, diseases, and therapies. For example, the Middle English *drogge* gave us the word *drug*; French terms yielded *fontanel* (the soft spot in an infant's skull) and *tourniquet* (a band pressed against an artery to stop bleeding); and Trendelenburg position (a position for treatment of shock) is named after the German physician who first used it. The result is a medical language that is 90 percent Greek and Latin in origin, with influences from several other cultures.

Understanding the Structure of Medical Terms

As a future healthcare professional, it is important that you build a solid foundation of medical terminology to communicate effectively in the workplace. You will be expected to exhibit competency in medical terminology as you listen, read, write, and speak to others. You will need to use these terms accurately in daily interactions with both patients and other healthcare professionals.

Most medical terms are composed of two to three basic word parts: a prefix, a root word or the combining form of a root word, and a suffix. The parts can be joined to form a complete term that conveys a specific idea. For example, the word parts *intra-* (a prefix meaning "inside"), *muscul/* (a root word meaning "muscle"), and *-ar* (a suffix meaning "pertaining to") combine to form the word *intramuscular*, which means "pertaining to the inside of a muscle."

Each word part can be easily identified by the format in which it is presented in this text. Prefixes are followed by a hyphen as shown above. The root word/combining form is followed by a slash (/) and a combining vowel (when a vowel applies), and the suffix is preceded by a hyphen. Keep this in mind as you are tasked with identifying word parts in the exercises and activities throughout this chapter.

Note that the majority of medical terms are built by combining individual word parts, as the preceding example shows. As you move forward in this text, you will find that there are exceptions to the rule. We will refer to these terms as "undecodable," as they cannot be broken into word parts.

Soft Skills for Health Care: Communication

Clear and accurate communication is important in any job; in the healthcare industry, however, it is essential. Safe and effective patient care relies on the ability of health professionals to communicate with each other and with the patient. *Communication* is a process by which information is exchanged between individuals. Communication has verbal (what you say and hear), nonverbal (how you deliver and receive messages), and written (what you write) components. As a healthcare professional, your job depends on your ability to communicate using the correct medical terminology in verbal and written communication. Knowing the correct pronunciation, meaning, and spelling of words used in your profession requires practice. These skills, however, are invaluable to your career in the medical field.

A **root word** (also known as a *root*) is just what its name implies: the word part that forms the basis or "root" of a term's meaning. Sometimes a combining vowel is added to the root word to connect it to a suffix or another root word. When a root word has a combining vowel attached to it, we call it the **combining form**. More often than not, the addition of the vowel makes a word easier to pronounce. A **prefix** is a word part that comes before the root word or combining form and adds to or changes the meaning of the root word. A **suffix** is a word part that follows the root word and adds to or changes the meaning of the root word.

Mastering word parts is similar in some ways to learning how to ride a bicycle. No one knows how to ride a bike until they have tried. They must learn how to balance on the bike, to steer, and to pedal. In the same way, you must learn how to deconstruct and construct words using your growing knowledge of word parts. Like learning to ride a bike, learning the basic structure of words and the meanings of word parts requires practice and patience. Once you get the basic concepts down (balancing, steering, pedaling or prefixes, root words, and suffixes), you will be able to use these skills again and again, no matter what bike you ride or what word you encounter.

In the Know: Learning Medical Terminology

Today's medical dictionaries contain more than 100,000 entries. Fortunately, learning to use medical language correctly does not require you to memorize every word in the dictionary. Approach the study of medical terminology with the idea of dividing the work into smaller, more manageable tasks:

- Memorize the root words and combining forms associated with each body system.
- Learn the most commonly used terms that apply when discussing the whole body, since you will encounter these terms with each of the body systems.
- Learn the ways different word parts are combined into the major terms associated with each body system.
- Memorize the meanings and spellings of common prefixes and suffixes.
- Apply the standard rules for spelling the plural forms of nouns and memorize the unusual plural spellings.
- Listen to the pronunciation of medical terms and practice saying them correctly.

Root Words and Combining Forms

Most medical terms are formed by joining a root word or a combining form with a suffix. The next two sections address the identification and use of root words and combining forms.

Root Words

Each body system has a set of root words. For example, many terms used to describe the cardiovascular system (the heart and blood vessels) derive from the root words *cardi/* (heart) and *angi/* (vessel). Many terms relating to the respiratory system (the lungs and airways) use the root words *pneum/* (air or lung), *pulmon/* (lung), or *bronch/* (airway). Many words related to the nervous system (the brain, spinal cord, and nerves) are formed from the root words *neur/* (nerve) or *cerebr/* (brain).

Table 1.1 lists some examples of root words and meanings related to the body systems. Sometimes two or three root words have the same meaning. You will use one root word in some contexts, and a different root word in other contexts. When we have two or more root words with the same meaning, they are not interchangeable. You do not get to pick which root word you wish to use for which meaning. Certain root words make specific words. Why do we have more than one root word with the same meaning? Because medical terminology grew in several places at once. The most common example is the existence of a Latin root word and a Greek root word for the same meaning. For the meaning "kidney," for example, we have the Latin root word *ren*, as in *renal*, and the Greek root word *nephr*, as in *nephron*. There are no rules regarding which root word is used to build specific terms. You will learn some of these as you read this text, while others will simply come from exposure to the correct form in the workplace. Concentrate on learning the root words in Tables 1.1 and 1.2, and pay close attention to the body system with which each root word listed is associated.

What's in a Word?

Stand-alone root words are traditionally followed by a hyphen (e.g., *muscul-*). In this text, however, root words will be discussed as combining forms and presented with a slash followed by the combining vowel (e.g., *muscul/o*).

To Note!

Remember that sometimes two or three root words have the same meaning.

TABLE 1.1 Root Words Associated with Specific Body Systems

Root Word	Meaning	Body System
bronch/	bronchus	respiratory
cardi/	heart	cardiovascular
dermat/	skin	integumentary
gastr/	stomach	digestive
hyster/	uterus	female reproduction
muscul/	muscles	musculoskeletal
nephr/	kidneys	urinary
neur/	nerve	nervous
orchid/	testis	male reproduction
thalam/	thalamus	endocrine

Note that not all root words are associated with a specific body system. Some root words are used more broadly and can be applied to multiple body systems. For example, the root words in Table 1.2 can be combined with prefixes, suffixes, and combining vowels to produce terms that describe something (adjectives, adverbs) or name something (nouns). These root words are often used in terms that describe *conditions* or *diagnoses*.

TABLE 1.2 Common Root Words Associated with Various Body Systems

Root Word	Meaning
abdomin/	abdomen
bacter/	bacteria
bas/	base
carcin/	cancer
cephal/	head
corp/	body
cost/	ribs
electr/	electric
fibrin/	fiber
lip/	fat
necr/	death
sarc/	tissue
thromb/	clot
viscer/	organs

Checkpoint **1.1**

Answer the following questions to identify any areas of the section that you may need to review.

1. Name and briefly describe the three parts of a medical term.

   _____

   _____

   _____

2. Explain how two different root words could have the same meaning, yet cannot be used interchangeably.

   _____

   _____

3. From what two languages are 90 percent of medical terms derived?

   _____

   _____

Exercise 1.1 Matching Root Words and Meanings

Read the root word carefully, paying attention to its spelling, and match the root word in column 1 with its meaning in column 2. Write the letter of the meaning beside the root word.

1. _____ *nephr*   a. fiber
2. _____ *necr*   b. ribs
3. _____ *fibrin*   c. kidneys
4. _____ *thromb*   d. death
5. _____ *cost*   e. clot

Combining Forms

Adding a *connecting* or *combining* vowel to a root word creates a word part called a *combining form*. As described before, connecting vowels make medical terms easier to spell and pronounce, but they can also connect a root word with another root word when more than one root word is used to form a term. For example, in the word *musculoskeletal*, the root word *muscul* adds the connecting vowel *o* to make the combining form *muscul/o* so that the two root words (*muscul* and *skelet*) can be combined. In addition, a combining vowel may be used to join a root word and a suffix. The most commonly used combining vowel is *o*; the second most common is *i*.

Note that when combining forms are shown, a slash separates the root word and the connecting vowel, as in *carcin/o*, which is the root word *carcin* plus connecting vowel *o*. This pattern is shown in Table 1.3.

TABLE 1.3 Common Combining Forms Associated with Diseases and Conditions

Combining Form	Meaning
bacteri/o	bacteria
carcin/o	cancer
fibrin/o	fiber
necr/o	death
onc/o	tumor
path/o	disease
thromb/o	clot

Tables 1.4 and 1.5 contain additional combining forms related to anatomy and colors, respectively.

Why learn combining forms related to colors? These combining forms are used in many areas of medicine. Dermatologists apply them to skin lesions, cytologists use them to discuss cell types, and all physicians use them to describe a variety of conditions.

TABLE 1.4 Common Combining Forms Associated with Anatomy

Combining Form	Meaning
abdomin/o	abdomen
angi/o	vessel
cardi/o	heart
cephal/o	head
cyst/o	sac or cyst containing fluid (also urinary bladder)
cyt/o	cell
enter/o	intestines
gynec/o	woman; female
hem/o	blood
hemat/o	blood
hepat/o	liver
lip/o	fat
mamm/o	breast
nephr/o	kidney
pelv/io	basin; pelvis
sarc/o	flesh
trache/o	trachea
uter/o	uterus

TABLE 1.5 Combining Forms Associated with Colors

Combining Form	Meaning
cyan/o	blue
erythr/o	red
leuk/o	white
melan/o	black
xanth/o	yellow

Checkpoint **1.2**

Answer the following questions to identify any areas of the section that you may need to review.

1. Explain the difference between a combining form and a root word.

_____

_____

2. What is the purpose of the combining vowel?

_____

3. What is the most common combining vowel?

_____

Exercise 1.2   Identify Combining Forms

Read each sentence and circle the medical term that contains the combining form(s). Write the definition of the combining form on the lines provided. If the term has more than one combining form, write the definition for each of them.

1. Leeann sees the gynecologist once a year. _____

2. The lab test revealed that the child had leukocytosis. _____

3. A tracheostomy was necessary to allow the patient to breathe. _____

4. Dr. Lee performed the cardiogram. _____

5. Dr. Raney is a hematologist. _____

6. Martin wants to be a gastroenterologist. _____

7. This patient will undergo a cystoscopy. _____

8. Cardiomegaly can sometimes be identified by a chest X-ray. _____

Suffixes and Prefixes

Now that you have an understanding on root words and combining forms, take a closer look at prefixes and suffixes. To build your foundation of medical terminology, you will need to thoroughly understand how suffixes and prefixes can shape and alter word roots.

Suffixes

Many medical terms are formed by adding a suffix to a root word or combining form. You already know that a root word is the foundation of the medical term and is the source of a term's meaning. You may also recall that the suffix is an ending that adds information or modifies the meaning of the root word or combining form.

> **To Note!**
>
> Suffixes add information to the root word by adding a description such as *-megaly* (enlarged) or *-itis* (inflammation).

Sometimes a root word is used with a suffix to form a word, and sometimes the combining form of that same root word is used with a suffix to form a word. Whether a root word is used or its combining form is used depends on the suffix, its spelling, and the meaning it conveys. For example, a root word meaning "head" is *cephal*. A combining form for *cephal* is *cephal/o*. The root word (*cephal*) plus suffix (*ic*) gives us the word *cephalic*; the combining form (*cephalo*) plus another root word (*pelv*) plus suffix (*ic*) gives us *cephalopelvic*; and the combining form *electr/o* plus prefix (*en*) plus combining form (*cephal/o*) plus suffix (*graph*) gives us *electro-encephalograph*.

Study the way combining forms and suffixes are joined in the following examples:

> **Example: abdominocentesis (*abdomin/o* + *-centesis*)**
>
> *abdomin/o* = combining form for abdomen
>
> *-centesis* = puncture for withdrawal of fluid
>
> Abdominocentesis is the puncture of the abdomen for withdrawal of fluid.

Example: cardiogram (*cardi/o* + *-gram*)

cardi/o = combining form for heart

-gram = record

A cardiogram is a record of the activity of the heart.

When you are studying or examining suffixes, pay particular attention to their spelling, since changing a single letter may change the meaning.

The following examples use the suffixes *-logy* and *-logist* to show how changing the suffix alters the meaning of the term.

Example: *nephr/o* (combining form meaning kidneys)

Adding the suffix *-logy* (study of) to *nephr/o* creates nephrology (study of the kidneys).

Example: *nephr/o* (combining form meaning kidneys)

Adding the suffix *-logist* (one who studies) to *nephr/o* creates nephrologist (one who studies the kidneys).

Example: *cardi/o* (combining form meaning heart)

Adding the suffix *-logy* (study of) to *cardi/o* creates cardiology (study of the heart).

Example: *cardi/o* (combining form meaning heart)

Adding the suffix *-logist* (one who studies) to *cardi/o* creates cardiologist (one who studies the heart).

Table 1.6 provides common combining forms and gives examples of how the suffixes *-logy* and *-logist* can be used to form the names of body systems, medical specialties, and medical specialists. Study Table 1.6 to familiarize yourself with some of the combining forms used with *-logy* and *-logist* to name medical specialty areas and physician practitioners. Can you find the specialty and practitioner terms that use two combining forms in one term?

TABLE 1.6 Suffixes Used in the Names of Specialties and Practitioners

Combining Form	Meaning	Term for Specialty (Using Suffix *-logy*)	Term for Practitioner (Using Suffix *-logist*)
arthr/o-	joints	arthrology	arthrologist
cardi/o-	heart	cardiology	cardiologist
dermat/o-	skin	dermatology	dermatologist
enter/o-	intestines	gastroenterology	gastroenterologist
gastr/o-	stomach	gastroenterology	gastroenterologist
immun/o-	immune	immunology	immunologist
nephr/o-	kidney(s)	nephrology	nephrologist
neur/o-	nerve	neurology	neurologist
oste/o-	bones	osteology	osteologist
path/o-	disease	pathology*	pathologist
pulmon/o-	lung(s)	pulmonology	pulmonologist

*Note that, like so many English words, *pathology* has two definitions. One is the study of disease; the other refers to the manifestations of a disease or a deviation from what is normal. When we say that something is "pathological," we mean that it is not normal.

The term in Table 1.6 that uses two combining forms plus a suffix is *gastroenterologist.* Two or more suffixes can have the same meaning. In some cases, a group of suffixes may have related meanings. The language of medicine uses a large number of suffixes, and studying them in meaning groups can help you learn them. Tables 1.7, 1.8, and 1.9 present groups of suffixes with the same or related meanings. Note that the suffixes in Table 1.7 form adjectives, but the suffix *-e* forms nouns.

TABLE 1.7 Suffixes Meaning "Related to" or "Pertaining to"

Suffix	Example
-ac	cardiac (pertaining to the heart)
-al	caudal (pertaining to the tail)
-ar	vascular (related to or containing blood vessels)
-e (noun marker)	melanocyte (pigment-producing cell)
-eal	congeal esophageal (pertaining to the esophagus)
-ic	pelvic (pertaining to the pelvis)
-ose	glucose (pertaining to the final product of carbohydrate digestion, sugar in the blood)
-ous	callous (relating to a callus)
-ry	secretory (relating to secretion)
-tic	arthritic (relating to arthritis)

Many of the suffixes in Table 1.8 can indicate a disease process or some type of pathology that adds further description to the root word, but a few of the suffixes indicate only a condition. A condition can be something that is pathological or something that is an abnormality without any associated disease.

TABLE 1.8 Suffixes Indicating a Condition or Process

Suffix	Meaning	Example
-emia	condition of the blood	glycemia (condition in which there is glucose [sugar] in the blood)
-ia	condition or process	insomnia (inability to sleep)
-ism	condition or process	hyperthyroidism (overactivity of the thyroid)
-itis	inflammation	phlebitis (inflammation of a vein)
-lysis	breakdown or dissolution process	hemolysis (dissolution/destruction of red blood cells)
-oma	tumor or neoplasm	sarcoma (cancer of the connective tissue)
-osis	abnormal condition	necrosis (abnormal condition of death)
-y	condition or process of	ambulatory (able to walk about, referring to a patient who is not confined to a bed or hospital)

The suffixes in Table 1.9 indicate shape, form, or size. These suffixes are important because medical language needs to communicate the size and shape of wounds, tumors, or abnormal formations. Note the similarities in the spelling of suffixes that mean "small."

TABLE 1.9 Suffixes Indicating Shape, Form, and Size

Suffix	Meaning	Example
-asis	formation, presence of	lithiasis (formation of calculi)
-cle	small	ossicle (tiny bone found in the middle ear)
-form	shape or resembling	vermiform (resembling a worm, worm-shaped)
-megaly	enlargement	hepatomegaly (enlargement of the liver)
-ole	small	arteriole (small artery)
-penia	abnormal reduction or lack of	cytopenia (a reduction or lack of cellular elements in the blood)
-plasia	formation	achondroplasia (without cartilage formation, a common cause of dwarfism)
-poiesis	formation	hematopoiesis (the process of formation and development of blood cells)
-trophy	development	dystrophy (abnormal growth or development of a tissue or organ)
-ula	small	fistula (a small channel or passageway that develops between organs)
-ule	small	pustule (a small raised area of skin containing pus, such as acne)

Most medical procedures are either diagnostic (identifying what the problem is) or therapeutic (curing or treating the problem). The suffixes in Table 1.10 describe diagnostic procedures.

TABLE 1.10 Suffixes Describing Diagnostic Procedures

Suffix	Meaning	Example
-gram	record	arteriogram (imaging test that uses X-rays and dye to view the arteries)
-graph	record or instrument used for making a record	electrocardiograph (an instrument used to record electrical currents of the heart)
-graphy	process of recording	amniography (recording of the amniotic cavity and fetus)
-meter	measure or measurement	sphygmometer (instrument used to measure arterial blood pressure)
-metry	process of measuring	spectrometry (the process of measuring wavelengths of light)
-scope	instrument used for viewing	arthroscope (an instrument used to view the interior of a joint)
-scopy	process of viewing with an instrument	colonoscopy (process of viewing the colon with a colonoscope)

Table 1.11 lists suffixes that describe some type of treatment or therapeutic procedure. Many of these suffixes indicate a procedure that is surgical in nature, because surgery is frequently used to treat or restore damaged areas of the body.

TABLE 1.11 Suffixes Indicating Therapeutic Procedures

Suffix	Meaning	Example
-centesis	puncture to withdraw fluid or tissue	abdominocentesis (puncture to withdraw fluid or tissue from the abdomen)
-desis	stabilization or binding	arthrodesis (surgical stabilization of a joint)
-iatric	treatment	geriatric (treatment relating to old age)
-plasty	repair	angioplasty (surgical repair of a blood vessel)
-rrhaphy	suturing	hepatorrhaphy (suturing of a wound in the liver)
-stomy or -ostomy	creation of an artificial opening	tracheostomy (creation of an artificial opening in the trachea)
-tomy	cut or incision	keratotomy (surgical cut or incision into the cornea)
-tripsy	crushing	lithotripsy (the crushing of a kidney stone by force or sound waves)

The suffixes listed in Table 1.12 are widely used in describing procedures, actions, or structures.

Some suffixes in medical terminology are technically compound suffixes; that is, one suffix with a second suffix added on. These suffixes are often found in terms relating to medical specialties, diagnoses, or procedures. The second suffix is usually only one letter and may simply function as a noun marker (a visual sign that the word is a noun), as in:

Example: erythrocyte (*erythr/o* + *-cyt* + *-e*)

erythr/o = red + *-cyt* = cell + *-e* = noun marker

An erythrocyte is a red blood cell.

In the following example, part of the suffix is another single letter, *y*:

Example: urology (*ur/o* + *-log* + *-y*)

ur/o = urine or the urinary tract + *-log* = to know (a derivative of the Greek word *logos*) + *-y* = condition or process of

Urology is the process of knowing urinary function and disease.

An analysis of the word *urology* points out a practice that occurs frequently in the formation of medical words: when two suffixes are combined, the resulting meaning is usually a shortened version of the two separate suffix meanings. Thus, *-logy* becomes "the study of" (shortened from "the process of knowing"). You will encounter many of these compound suffixes and usually learn the combined meaning. However, being aware of the meaning of individual suffixes may help you decipher new combinations of those suffixes in unfamiliar words.

TABLE 1.12 Commonly Used General Suffixes

Suffix	Meaning	Example
-algia	pain	neuralgia (severe, stabbing nerve pain)
-ate	make, use, subject to	intubate (insertion of a tube into a canal, hollow organ, or cavity)
-blast	immature cell	osteoblast (an immature cell that forms into bone)
-cele	pouch	cystocele (hernia of the bladder)
-cyte	cell	leukocyte (white blood cell)
-dynia	pain	arthrodynia (pain in the joints)
-emesis	vomiting	hematemesis (vomiting blood)
-eum	tissue or structure	periosteum (the membrane around bone)
-genesis	origin	lysogenesis (the production of lysins)
-genic	origin	carcinogenic (causing cancer)
-ium	tissue or structure	pericardium (the membrane around the heart)
-ize	make, use, subject to	anesthetize (to produce loss of sensation)
-malacia	softening	cardiomalacia (softening of the walls of the heart)
-oid	like, resembling	ovoid (resembling an egg, oval-shaped)
-oma	tumor	lymphoma (cancer of the lymphatic system)
-phage	eat, swallow	bacteriophage (eater of bacteria)
-phagia	process of eating or related to eating	dysphagia (difficulty swallowing)
-phile	affinity for	halophile (organisms that thrive in high salt concentrations)
-phobia	fear	photophobia (fear of light due to pain and sensitivity)
-pnea	breathing	apnea (the suspension of normal breathing)
-ptosis	drooping	blepharoptosis (drooping of the upper eyelid)
-rrhage	bursting forth or rapid flow	hemorrhage (an escape of blood through a ruptured or unruptured blood vessel)
-rrhagia	bursting forth or rapid flow	menorrhagia (an abnormally heavy and prolonged menstrual period)
-rrhea	drainage, discharge	diarrhea (an abnormally frequent discharge of fecal matter from the bowel)
-spasm	abrupt, forceful contraction	bronchospasm (contraction of smooth muscle in the walls of the bronchi)
-stasis	stop, stand	hemostasis (a process which causes bleeding to stop)

Checkpoint **1.3**

Answer the following questions to identify areas of the section that you need to review.

1. What do suffixes provide to root words and combining forms?

_____

_____

2. Describe the difference between the following two suffixes: -logy and *-logist*.

_____

_____

3. Is it possible for two or more suffixes to have the same meaning? If so, provide an example.

_____

_____

Exercise 1.3   Word Analysis

Circle the medical term in each sentence, underline the suffix, and write the definition of the suffix on the line provided.

1. The doctor said Joan's grandfather had carditis. _____

2. He was concerned about pulmonary complications. _____

3. Rheumatic heart disease is often coded incorrectly. _____

4. The arthrosis has gotten worse. _____

5. Cardiomegaly can cause some distressing symptoms. _____

6. The laboratory studies identified renal disease. _____

7. Anemia is often related to a poor diet. _____

8. Hypertrophy of the prostate sometimes requires surgery. _____

Exercise 1.4   Word Building

Select the suffix that best fits the blank. Write it on the line to complete the word, then write the definition of the suffix.

centesis	_graphy_	_plasty_	_stomy_
desis	_iatric_	_rrhaphy_	_tomy_
gram	_meter_	_scope_	_tripsy_
graph	_metry_	_scopy_	

1. During the first or second prenatal visit, the doctor performs a pelvi_____. The doctor measures the pelvis.

   _____

2. A gluco_____ measures glucose in the blood.

   _____

3. Russell underwent gastro_____ this morning. The technician looked into his stomach.

   _____

Continues

4. The test results of the electrical activity of Julie's heart, her electrocardio_____, were normal.

_____

5. The procedure that uses X-rays to view the arteries of the heart, also called angio_____, can help identify problems in the heart.

_____

6. Jones-Swanson Hospital is for treatment of mental disorders. This psych_____ hospital will soon expand.

_____

7. The needle passed between Andrew's ribs to withdraw fluids. This procedure is called thora_____.

_____

8. Louann's spine required arthro_____ to fuse some vertebrae after the auto accident.

_____

Exercise 1.5   Word Building

Using the list of combining forms and the list of suffixes, create the word that best completes the following sentences. Write the word on the line provided. The meaning for the desired word is provided in brackets after each sentence.

Combining Forms: *arthr/o, cephal/o, cyst/o, derm/o, erythr/o, hem/o, osteo-*
Suffixes: *-algia, -blast, -cele, -cyte, -dynia, -ic, -pnea, -um*

1. Several _____ were found in the fluid. [immature cells associated with bone production]

2. The _____ ruptured when it was placed in the solution. [a red blood cell]

3. _____ had to be achieved before the surgery could proceed. [procedure of stopping the flow of blood]

4. The patient required medication for severe _____. [headache]

5. _____ described the way the patient's knee felt. [pain in a joint]

6. A _____ often requires surgery. [herniation of the bladder]

Prefixes

A prefix is a word part that comes before (*pre-* = before) the root word or combining form and usually begins the term. Prefixes modify the root word or combining form; they often give an indication of direction, time, orientation, size, or number.

Example: prenatal (*pre* + *natal*)

pre- = prefix meaning "before"

natal = root word meaning "birth"

Prenatal means before "birth."

Example: intra-abdominal (*intra* + *abdominal*)

intra- = prefix meaning "within"

abdomin = root word meaning "abdomen"

-al = suffix meaning "pertaining to"

Intra-abdominal means "pertaining to the inside of the abdomen."

As with suffixes, there can be several prefixes associated with one meaning. A few prefixes have more than one related meaning. Watch the spelling as you study Tables 1.13–1.15.

TABLE 1.13 Prefixes Associated with Numbers or Amounts

Prefix	Meaning	Example
a-	without	anemia (lack of blood)
ambi-	both	ambivalent (simultaneous existence of conflicting attitudes)
an-	without	anaerobic (living without oxygen)
bi-	two, both	bilateral (pertaining to or having two sides)
brady-	slow	bradycardia (slow heartbeat)
di-	two	diplopia (double vision)
hemi-	half (usually right/left halves)	hemisphere (half of a spheric structure)
mega-	large, excessive	megalgia (very severe pain)
micro-	very small	microscopy (viewing of small objects via a microscope)
mono-	one	monochromatic (containing or using only one color)
multi-	many, several	multiphasic (characterized by many stages or phases)
olig-	few, scant	oliguria (minimal urine production)
pan-	all	pandemic (an infectious disease that has spread across regions, countries, or continents)
poly-	many	polycythemia (condition plagued by an increased number of red blood cells)
quadri-	four	quadriplegia (paralysis of both arms and both legs)
semi-	part of a whole	semicanal (half canal)
tachy-	fast	tachycardia (fast heartbeat)

Continues

Prefix	Meaning	Example
tetra-	four	tetralogy (made up of four distinct parts)
tri-	three	trivalent (containing three strains of microorganisms)
uni-	one, single	unilateral (confined to one side)

TABLE 1.14   Prefixes That Indicate Amount or Position/Direction

Prefix	Meaning Amount	Example Amount	Meaning Position/Direction	Example Position/Direction
hyper-	more, excessive, increased	hypertension (increased blood pressure)	above	hyperflexion (flexion of a limb beyond the normal limit)
hypo-	less, deficient	hypoglycemia (low blood sugar)	below	hypodermic (beneath the skin)
infra-	less than	infrasonic (frequencies that lie below the range of human hearing)	under, below	infrared (portion of the electromagnetic spectrum with wavelengths between 770 and 1000 nm)
meta-	change	metastasize (to pass into or invade)	behind	metacarpus (the five bones making up the posterior portion of the hand)
sub-	less than	subnormal (lower or smaller than normal)	under, below	substernal (under the sternum)
super-	excessive, more	supernumerary (exceeding the normal number)	above	superimpose (place or lay one thing over another)
supra-	excessive, outside	supraliminal (existing above the threshold of consciousness)	beyond	suprarenal (above the kidney)
ultra-	excessive	ultraviolet (electromagnetic rays at higher frequency than violet)	beyond	ultrasound (sound having a frequency beyond 30,000 Hz)

TABLE 1.15   Prefixes That Indicate Position/Direction

Prefix	Meaning	Example
ab-	away from	abduction (to move a body part away from the midline)
ad-	toward, to, near	adduction (to move a body part toward the midline)
anti-	against, opposed to	anticoagulant (an agent that prevents clotting)
circum-	around, circular motion	circumcision (cutting around an anatomic part)
contra-	against, opposed to	contraindicated (a specific situation in which a drug or treatment should not be used because of risk of harm)
de-	not, from, down	descending (moving or falling downward)
dia-	across or through	diapedesis (the passage of blood through the intact walls of blood vessels)
dis-	separate, apart	distal (situated away from the center of the body)
epi-	upon, above	epiglottis (a flap attached to the top of the larynx)
para-	along, beside	parathyroid (adjacent to the thyroid gland)
peri-	around	periosteum (thick, fibrous membrane around the bones)
trans-	across or through	transverse (lying across the long axis of the body)

Some prefixes can indicate position or direction, or they can indicate time. Table 1.16 shows some of these versatile prefixes.

Prefixes in Table 1.17 represent commonly used prefixes. Many of these prefixes share the same meaning. For example, the prefixes *e-*, *ec-*, *ex-*, *ecto-*, and *extra-* all mean "out, outside, away." The prefixes *en-*, *endo-*, *in-*, and *intra-* all mean "inside or in." Knowing these pairings may help you more easily recognize new terms.

Additional details to consider when studying these prefixes include the differences and similarities in spelling. For example, the prefixes indicating *out* or *outside* all begin with *e*, and most have only one to three letters. The prefixes that mean "with" all contain either *n* or *m*. Noticing these types of details can help you remember the prefixes and their spellings.

To Note!

Many prefixes share the same meaning and knowing these pairings may help you more easily recognize new terms.

TABLE 1.16 Prefixes That Indicate Time or Position/Direction

Prefix	Meaning	Example Time	Example Position/Direction
per-	through	perforated (pierced through with one or more holes)	percutaneous (the passage of substances through unbroken skin)
post-	after	postsurgical (after surgery)	posterior (near the back or end)
pre-	before	precursor (one that precedes and indicates the onset of another)	preaxial (situated in front of the axis of the body or limb)
re-	again, back	revive (to restore life or consciousness)	recline (lean or lie back in a position with the back supported)
retro-	backward or behind	retrospective (a study that collects past information on individuals to explain a current illness)	retrobulbar (situated or occurring behind the eyeball)

TABLE 1.17 Commonly Used Prefixes

Prefix	Meaning	Example
ante-	before	anterior (in reference to position: front surface; in reference to time: before)
anti-	against	antibacterial (a substance that fights against bacteria)
auto-	self	autoimmune (against the person's own tissues)
bio-	life	biology (the study of life and living organisms)
con-	with	conjugated (joined or paired with)
dys-	faulty, painful, difficult	dyspepsia (upset stomach)
e-	out, outside, away	elevate (to raise or lift up to a higher position, away from the body)
ec-	out, outside, away	eclabium (turning a lip inside out)
ecto-	out, outside, away	ectosteal (pertaining to the external surface of the bone)
en-	inside or in	endermic (through the skin)
endo-	inside or in	endocardium (inner surface of the heart muscle)
eu-	normal	eupeptic (digesting well)
ex-	out, outside, away	external (on the outside)
exo-	out, outside, away	exogenous (originating or produced outside of an organism)
extra-	out, outside, away	extraction (surgical removal by pulling out)
hyper-	excessive, above	hyperglycemia (excessive sugar in the blood)
hypo-	below, deficient	hypogastric (below the stomach)

Continues

Prefix	Meaning	Example
in-	inside or in	interior (located on the inside)
inter-	between	interspace (any space between two similar objects)
intra-	inside or in	intramuscular (within a muscle)
mal-	bad, abnormal	malocclusion (the misalignment or incorrect relation between the teeth)
neo-	new	neonatology (study of conditions related to newborns)
pachy-	thick	pachycephaly (abnormal thickness of the skull)
peri-	surrounding, around	periosteum (structure surrounding the bone)
post-	after, behind	postpartum (period immediately following childbirth)
pre-	before	premature (occurring before the usual or expected time)
pro-	before	prophylactic (an agent that acts to prevent disease)
sym-	with	symbiosis (the biological association of two or more species with one another, state of living together)
syn-	with	synthesis (process of building up, putting together, or composing with)

Checkpoint 1.4

Answer the following questions to identify any areas of the section that you may need to review.

1. Define the two different meanings for the prefix *sub-*.

   _____

   _____

   _____

2. Provide two examples of words containing prefixes related to numbers or amounts.

   _____

   _____

3. Provide two examples of words containing prefixes related to position or direction.

   _____

   _____

Exercise 1.6   Comprehension Check

Study the sentences below. Write the appropriate prefix for the medical term related to the word or phrase in italics on the line.

1. The patient could perceive only *one*-color images. _____chromatic

2. He had a hearing loss in *both* ears. _____lateral

3. Some individuals are able to use *both* hands equally well. _____dextrous

4. The patient experienced several episodes of cardiac dysrhythmia in which heartbeats occur in *groups of three.* _____geminy

5. Advances in technology have produced hope for paralysis of *all four limbs.* _____plegia

6. There is a new treatment for the condition marked by an *abnormally large number* of red blood cells in the circulatory system. _____cythemia

7. Teams with members from *several various* disciplines are common in health care. _____disciplinary

8. *Abnormally large* nucleated red blood cells are easily identified. _____blasts

Exercise 1.7 Word Building

Study the following sentences. From the list, select the appropriate prefix to fill in the blank in each sentence. The definition of the target word is given for each item. Write the prefix on the line provided.

ab-	*de-*	*para-*	*super-*
ad-	*epi-*	*post-*	*trans-*
circum-	*hyper-*	*re-*	*ultra-*
supra-	*hypo-*	*sub-*	

1. The patient's _____kalemia was dangerous to his heart. (high levels of potassium)

2. The pain was located in the _____gastric area. (lower part of the abdomen)

3. Some medications are intended for _____lingual use. (below the tongue)

4. The injuries were _____ficial. (on the surface; not deep)

5. The _____clavicular tumors were easily felt. (situated above the clavicle)

6. _____sound helped identify the condition of the fetus. (a diagnostic technique that uses high-frequency sound waves)

7. _____duction of the leg caused pain. (moving a limb toward the body midline)

8. The patient had only 10 degrees of _____duction at the shoulder. (moving a limb away from the body)

Exercise 1.8 Matching

Match the prefix in column 1 with its meaning in column 2. Write the letter of the meaning on the line next to the prefix.

1. _____ *ex-*   **a.** life
2. _____ *intra-*   **b.** self
3. _____ *pre-*   **c.** with
4. _____ *sym-*   **d.** before
5. _____ *auto-*   **e.** inside
6. _____ *bio-*   **f.** outside

Five Ways to Combine Parts to Create Words

A medical term consists of a combination of several word parts. Although some terms are simply the root words (or combining forms) paired with a single suffix, others consist of multiple root words, a prefix, and one or more suffixes. The following word constructions illustrate standard ways to combine word parts into terms. Study the examples and flag each example for future reference.

1. combining form + suffix (that begins with a vowel) = drop the combining vowel

Example: *arthr/o* + *-algia* = arthralgia (joint pain)

gastr/o + *-itis* = gastritis (inflammation of the stomach)

col/o + *-ectomy* = colectomy (removal of all or part of the colon)

2. combining form + suffix (that begins with a consonant) = keep the combining vowel

Example: *spir/o* + *-metry* = spirometry (process of measuring breathing)

ophthalm/o + *-scope* = ophthalmoscope (instrument used to view the eye)

rhin/o + *-plasty* = rhinoplasty (surgical repair of the nose)

3. two or more combining forms + suffix = keep the combining vowel between the two combining forms

Example: *gastr/o* + *enter/o* + *-itis* = gastroenteritis (inflammation of the stomach and small intestine)

oste/o + *myel/o* + *-itis* = osteomyelitis (inflammation of the bone and bone marrow)

oophor/o + *cyst/o* + *-ectomy* = oophorocystectomy (removal of an ovarian cyst)

4. prefix + combining form + suffix

Example: *anti-* + *bacteri/o* + *-al* = antibacterial (pertaining to against bacteria)

hyper- + *glyc/o* + *-emia* = hyperglycemia (condition of excessive sugar in the blood)

poly- + *neur/o* + *-itis* = polyneuritis (inflammation of many nerves)

5. root word (that ends with the same vowel as the start of the suffix) + combining vowel + suffix (that begins with the same vowel as the end of the root word) = drop the final vowel in the root word as well as the combining vowel

Example: *cardi* + *o* + *-itis* = carditis (inflammation of the heart)

oste + *o* + *-ectomy* = ostectomy (removal of a bone)

crani + *o* + *-ium* = cranium (structure enclosing the brain or head)

In the Know: Nondecodable Terms

As with most languages, there are exceptions to the rules that describe how medical terms are formed. In this case, there are no rules to memorize, but being aware of them will help you determine the meanings of words that seem to stray from the typical patterns. One example of this exception is an **eponym**, which is a term named after a person or place. Amyotrophic lateral sclerosis (ALS), is one such term, as it is often referred to as "Lou Gehrig's disease." ALS is "a progressive neurodegenerative disease that affects nerve cells in the brain and the spinal cord."[1] Another example is the Achilles tendon, which is named after an area of weakness written about for a warrior hero in Greek mythology (Achilles). As you can see, these terms cannot be defined by word parts and therefore must be learned and deposited into memory.

[1]ALS Association. "What Is ALS?" http://www.alsa.org/about-als/what-is-als.html. Accessed March 5, 2015.

Checkpoint 1.5

Answer the following questions to identify any areas of the section that you may need to review.

1. When combining word parts, what do you do if the suffix begins with a vowel?

   _____

   _____

2. When combining word parts, what do you do if the suffix begins with a consonant?

   _____

   _____

3. Provide an example of an eponym.

   _____

   _____

Beyond Words: Word Play

Learning terminology does not have to be all work and no play. In fact, playing with words can help you learn them. See how you do with the following exercise. Use your knowledge of word parts to answer the following questions. You might need a dictionary for some of them.

1. Why do we call an elephant a pachyderm?

2. While we're on the subject, what's a pachycephalosaur?

3. What do these words have in common: *clavicle*, *clavichord*, *conclave*, and *corn*?

4. Can you use the words *epidemic*, *epidermal*, and *hypodermic* in the same sentence? Try it.

(Possible) Answers

1. An elephant is called a *pachyderm* because it has thick skin. Does that mean that because Uncle Joe is thick-skinned he's a pachyderm?

2. It's a medium-sized dinosaur that has a beaked mouth, rows of bumps on its head, and a *thick skull* (10 inches thick!) shaped like a dome. Met any lately?

3. The Latin word *clavus* means "key." The clavicle bone is shaped like a key . . . well, somebody long ago thought so. A clavichord is a keyboard instrument that makes sounds. (So's your computer. Hmm.) *Conclave* uses the prefix *con*, meaning "with," and the root word *clav-*, meaning "key." So a conclave is a gathering together in a place or room that is locked *with a key* . . . although nowadays we don't lock people up when there's a conclave. And *corn*? We're talking about the medical term *corn*, the kind you get on your toes when your shoes don't fit. What's the connection? Yup. The other word for *corn* is, you guessed it, *clavus*.

4. Yes, of course the possibilities are limited only by your imagination. But here's one to get you started: The epidemic of epidermal spiderosis (OK, name your own favorite skin thing) could be treated only by hypodermic injections of antispiderosis serum.

Exercise 1.9   Word Building

Using the prefixes, root words, combining forms, and suffixes from the following list, create a term that matches the definition. You may use the same word parts in more than one term. Some terms use two parts; others use three parts. Write the term you create on the line.

Prefixes: *neo-, pre-, dys-, peri-*
Suffixes: *-ectomy, -al, -ia, -rrhaphy, -osis, -ic, -oma, -ologist*
Root words and combining forms: *sarc/o, hepat/o, nat, phag, cephal/o, mast/o, cardi/o, necr*

1. Removal of a breast _____

2. Heart specialist _____

3. Around the heart _____

4. Connective tissue tumor _____

5. Difficulty swallowing _____

Learning to Pronounce Medical Terms

When you work in a medical setting, you will be expected to recognize and understand the most common medical terms by sound and by sight. Most of the terms you encounter will be ones you have seen or used before and are familiar with, but occasionally you will discover a new term. When you hear an unfamiliar word, repeat it aloud and listen for familiar word parts to help you determine the meaning of the entire term.

Pronunciation in the Workplace

In the medical workplace, you will need to pronounce medical terms clearly and correctly so that others understand your meaning precisely. Be particularly attentive to your pronunciation if you are speaking on the telephone, recording a voicemail message, or dictating for someone else to transcribe.

You will need to listen carefully to others; their pronunciation may be influenced by an accent or inflection. Some terms may even be pronounced differently based on the region of the country. Listening to someone on the telephone or to voicemail or dictation may take practice and concentration. You will need to learn how others pronounce medical terms so that you do not misunderstand what they are saying.

Pronunciation Keys

The tables in this text provide pronunciation keys for new and difficult terms. The pronunciation is given in phonetic or "sounds like" syllables (see Table 1.18). When you encounter a new word, say the word out loud or to yourself several times; then if you are using the digital program that accompanies this book, listen to the term and practice pronouncing it. Being able to speak the language you are learning is just as important as being able to spell the words correctly.

Consider the medical term *pathology*. It is constructed from the combining form (*patho*) of the root word *path/* (meaning "disease") plus the suffix *-logy* ("study of"). The resulting word, *pathology*, means the study of disease. Using the same combining form *patho* with the suffix *-logist*, which means "one who specializes in the study or treatment of," results in the word *pathologist*, which is the name for the physician who specializes in the study of diseases. Notice that using the pure root for these words yields words that would be more difficult to pronounce—pathlogy and pathlogist.

To help you with vocabulary words that might be difficult to pronounce, this textbook uses a phonetic pronunciation. The words are separated into syllables (indicated by hyphens), and **boldface** indicates which syllable should receive the emphasis when you say the word aloud. Note also that the word's plural spelling is shown only when it does not conform to the described rules for forming plurals. The following letters and letter combinations represent specific sounds in the phonetic pronunciations.

TABLE 1.18 Pronunciation Key

Letter or Symbol	Pronounced Like
a	the short *a* as in can
ay	the long *a* as in cane
ah	*ah* as in father
ai	*ai* as in fair
ar	*ar* as in far
aw	*aw* as in fall
e	the short *e* as in pen
ee	the long *e* as in me
i	the short *i* as in pin
I	the long *i* as in pine
o	the short *o* as in not
O	the long *o* as in note
oo	*oo* as in food
or	*or* as in for
ow	*ow* as in cow
oy	*oy* as in boy
u	the short *u* as in run
yoo	the long *u* as in cube
zh	*s* as in casual

Learning How to Form Plurals and Adjectives

In medical terminology, plural word forms can be confusing. Some plural terms are formed based on Greek and Latin rules, while others are formed using English language rules. English usually forms plurals by adding *s* or *es* to the singular form (the plural of *vein* is *veins*). Latin- and Greek-based words form plurals by adding an ending based on the ending of the singular form. For example, many singular words ending in *a* add the letter *e* to create the plural form (*stria*, meaning a discolored stripe on the skin, becomes *striae* as a plural). Singular words ending in *um* replace the *um* with an *a* to create the plural form (*diverticulum*, a pouch or sac that has developed within the gut or bladder, becomes *diverticula* in the plural). Words ending in *nx* change the *nx* to *nges* in the plural (*larynx,* part of the throat, becomes *larynges*).

Unfortunately, the rules do not apply consistently, and for that reason the best strategy is to memorize the plural spelling for each new word you learn. This text provides the plural spelling of terms in the tables only if the plural spelling differs from the guidelines described here. Whenever you are uncertain of the correct plural form of a term, consult your medical dictionary. Table 1.19 lists some of the common plural forms.

TABLE 1.19 Frequently Used Plural Forms

Singular	Ending	Plural
apex	-ex/-ices	apices
appendix	-ix/-ices	appendices
bacterium	-ium/-ia	bacteria
cardiopathy	-y/-ies	cardiopathics
condyloma	-a/-ata	condylomata
diagnosis	-is/-es	diagnoses
fungus	-us/-i	fungi
phenomenon	-on/a	phenomena
thorax	-ax/-aces	thoraces
vertebra	-a/-ae	vertebrae

Earlier sections of this chapter introduced a group of adjective suffixes (*-ac*, *-al*, *-ar*, *-ary*, *-eal*, *-ic*, *-ous*, and *-tic*) that, when added to the end of a noun, create the adjective form of a word. These suffixes generally mean "pertaining to," although they are not necessarily interchangeable. Other adjective suffixes include *-genic* (producing), *-genous* (produced by or from), *-oid* (resembling), and *-ole* or *-ule* (little). Creating adjectives from nouns often involves more than just adding an ending, however. Usually, the final letter in the noun is either dropped or changed to another letter. To help you learn the adjective forms of some common body system terms, the word tables in later chapters of this text sometimes include the adjective spelling.

Sound-alikes

The correct spelling of a word can be critical in patient care. In some instances, two or more words may sound alike but be spelled differently and have different meanings. The difference of even one letter can make a dramatic difference in meaning. Consider the words *ilium* (a pelvic bone) and *ileum* (the terminal portion of the small intestine). These two words, very different in meaning, are pronounced the same and only differ by one letter in their spelling. Surgery to repair an ilium would be very different from that done to repair an ileum! Think about the words *osteal* (bony or bonelike) and *ostial* (relating to an ostium, an opening, as in the ostium of the Eustachian tube). *Viscous* (sticky) and *viscus* (a hollow, multilayered, walled organ such as the heart) are two more terms that sound alike but are spelled differently and have different meanings.

Whenever you are uncertain about the spelling of a term, consult a reliable medical dictionary or other reference book. If you are not sure how to spell a drug name, look it up in the *Physicians' Desk Reference* (*PDR*) or a similar drug reference book.

Checkpoint 1.6

Answer the following questions to identify any areas of the section that you may need to review.

1. Generally, in the English language, the plural form of a word is created by adding _____ or _____ to the end of the term.

2. Per the information provided in Table 1.19, what is the plural form of the term *digitus*?

   _____

3. Per the information provided in Table 1.19, what is the plural form of the term *cortex*?

   _____

Exercise 1.10   Spelling Check

Read the sentences below, paying special attention to the medical terms. Some of the terms are spelled incorrectly. Identify the correctly spelled terms by writing "correct" on the line. If the term is spelled incorrectly, write the correct spelling on the line.

1. Larry will undergo a nephrectomy next week. _____

2. The physician performed a tracheaottomy. _____

3. Vanessa is studying to become a cardiolologist. _____

4. An abbonimoocentesis will remove the fluid. _____

5. Trachycardis is a condition of rapid heart rate. _____

Using a Medical Dictionary

Even with the best deciphering skills, your analysis of an unfamiliar term can sometimes produce a strange-sounding definition. If your word analysis result doesn't seem right, consult a reliable medical dictionary.

Looking up new terms in a medical dictionary is a smart strategy in general. Comparing definitions among different dictionaries takes your knowledge one step further. You may understand one definition better than another, or the combination of definitions may provide a more complete meaning. You may notice some minor differences among medical dictionaries. Sometimes the term you seek is not in one dictionary, but can be found in another.

If you have an idea of the correct spelling, of course, you can find the correct page easily. If you are uncertain of the spelling, concentrate on the sound of the first part of the word and look at the words that begin with that sound. Remember that *c* and *s* (and *ps* as in psychology) can sound alike, as can *ph* and *f* and a number of other letters and letter combinations. If you are working with a new or unfamiliar term and you do not know the spelling, try to visualize all the different possible spellings of the term and check your dictionary for each one.

A medical dictionary can be a great help even if you only need to confirm your understanding of a term's meaning. You may find some additional information that you were unaware of, or you may learn that your understanding of the meaning was inaccurate. Remember, if you cannot find your term in the first medical dictionary you try, switch to a different one. Your time will be well spent because you will have looked up many different terms in the process of trying to find the one you need.

Become familiar with and use resources on the Internet. Here are a few online medical dictionaries:

- http://dictionary.webmd.com
- http://medical-dictionary.com
- http://nlm.nih.gov/medlineplus/mplusdictionary.html

The Internet changes frequently, so use a search engine such as Google.com to find new or additional reference tools.

Exercise 1.11 Word Analysis

Study the following terms. Use a diagonal line to break each word into its parts: prefix, suffix, and root word or combining form. (Remember that not all medical terms have all word parts.) Identify the meaning of each word part and try to combine those meanings into a definition of the term. Write your answer on the first line, then look up the term in a medical dictionary and write the dictionary's definition on the second line.

Term	Your definition	Dictionary's definition
1. urologist	_____	_____
2. thrombocytosis	_____	_____
3. cephalic	_____	_____
4. pathology	_____	_____
5. gastrorrhaphy	_____	_____

Abbreviations

In both written and oral communication, medical personnel use a large number of abbreviations to save time as well as to save space on forms. "HPI," for example, is much quicker and shorter to write than "history of present illness." Some abbreviations are immediately obvious or make sense; others are not. Personal medical history, for example, is often abbreviated "hx."

Provider-patient interactions within a clinical environment are documented using medical charts. Historically, a patient's information was tracked on a paper medical record. As technology has advanced, so has the process of medical charting. Medical charting is now transitioning to an electronic forum.

Some common charting abbreviations are listed in Table 1.20, but other common medical abbreviations will be presented in Chapter 2. Moreover, each body system chapter includes a list of the abbreviations generally associated with that specialty. Remember that each hospital, clinic, or other healthcare setting has its own list of charting abbreviations. Be sure to request a list of accepted abbreviations for your particular workplace and use it accordingly. If you make decisions regarding charting in a setting that does not have an abbreviation list, prevent confusion and miscommunication by establishing a list for everyone to follow.

The abbreviations in Table 1.20 are widely used in the healthcare industry.

TABLE 1.20 Common Charting Abbreviations

Abbreviation	Meaning
ad lib	as desired
b.i.d.	twice daily
BP	blood pressure
CC	chief complaint
CBC	complete blood count
CCU	coronary care unit
c/o	complains of (patient's report of a symptom)
CP	chest pain
D/C	discontinue or discharge
↓	decrease or decreasing
Dx	diagnosis
ETOH	ethyl alcohol (beverage alcohol)
♀	female
HEENT	head, eyes, ears, nose, throat
H&P	history and physical
HPI	history of present illness
HTN	hypertension, high blood pressure
hx	medical history
IM	intramuscular
IMP	impression (related to diagnosis)
↑	increased or increasing
IP	inpatient
IV	intravenously
Ⓛ	left
Ⓡ	right
♂	male
NKA	no known allergies
NKDA	no known drug allergies

Continues

Abbreviation	Meaning
n.p.o.	nothing by mouth
OP	outpatient
P	pulse
PAR	postanesthesia recovery
PERRLA	pupils equal, round, reactive to light and accommodation
PMH	past medical history
p.o.	by mouth
p.r.n.	as needed
pt	patient
q.2h.	every two hours
q.4h.	every four hours
R	respirations
R/O	rule out
ROM	range of motion
ROS	review of systems
RRR	regular rate and rhythm (refers to heart)
RTC	return to clinic
RTO	return to office
SOB	shortness of breath
stat.	at once, immediately
T	temperature
t.i.d.	three times daily
Tx	treatment
VS	vital signs
WNL	within normal limits

Exercise 1.12 Matching

Read the following list of abbreviations and definitions. Match the abbreviation in column 1 with the correct definition in column 2 by writing the letter for the definition on the line beside the abbreviation.

1. _____ SOB
2. _____ RRR
3. _____ CP
4. _____ WNL
5. _____ PAR
6. _____ NKA
7. _____ c/o
8. _____ hx

a. within normal limits
b. regular rate and rhythm
c. personal medical history
d. chest pain
e. complains of
f. shortness of breath
g. no known allergies
h. postanesthesia recovery

Chapter Review

After successfully completing this chapter, you should be able to correctly answer the following review questions. Answers are provided in the back of the text. This self-assessment opportunity allows you to check your understanding of the content and determine whether you need to revisit any of the chapter's content.

Matching

Match the following terms to their proper definitions.

1. _____ hemiplegia
2. _____ neonatal
3. _____ rhinoplasty
4. _____ renal
5. _____ gastralgia
6. _____ ostectomy
7. _____ hematology
8. _____ cephalic
9. _____ endoscopy
10. _____ pericardium

a. the study of blood and blood-forming tissues
b. process of viewing within
c. pain in the stomach
d. surgical removal of bone
e. structure surrounding the heart
f. paralysis of one side of the body
g. pertaining to the kidneys
h. surgical repair of the nose
i. pertaining to the head
j. new birth (newborn)

Abbreviations

Identify the appropriate abbreviation for the bold term(s) and write your answer(s) on the line provided.

1. A **patient** presents to the office presenting classic signs of **high blood pressure**.
   _____

2. Physician orders a **complete blood count** for a **patient** whose **chief complaint** is frequent urination to **rule out** a kidney infection. _____

3. Antibiotic drops are to be administered to the patient's right eye **three times a day**.
   _____

4. **Patient's chief complaint involves chest pain** and **shortness of breath**. An EKG is ordered **immediately**. _____

5. A 13-year-old **male** requests an athletic physical in order to play recreational soccer. His form requires **vital signs within normal limits**, a record of **past medical history**, as well as a **diagnosis** of any conditions that may prohibit participation. _____

Spell-Check

On the line beside each term, write the correct spelling of the medical term. If no change is required, write "no change" in the space provided.

1. biology _____
2. tracheotomi _____
3. cardiologisst _____
4. amneocentesis _____
5. tachicardia _____
6. gastralgia _____
7. pleural _____
8. card _____
9. lukeocytes _____
10. cyanosas _____

Word-Building Challenge

Review the following sentences. Apply what you have learned in this chapter by identifying the meaning of each underlined term. Write your answer on the line provided and then check your definition against the answer provided in the appendix..

1. Post-Zumba <u>arthralgia</u> is generally the result of participation in the first few classes. _____

_____

2. Toddlers are known to have frequent episodes of <u>logorrhea</u>, also known as "diarrhea of the mouth." _____

3. Instructors insist that the key to success in this course is the creation and utilization of index cards. Students who neglect to follow this advice are assumed to suffer from <u>cephalosclerosis</u>.

_____

4. <u>Hypersomnia</u> is a condition common to students pulling "all-nighters" before exams. _____

_____

5. College students often experience <u>hypersalivation due to polyphagia</u> upon returning home for break and smelling a home-cooked meal. _____

_____

Extension Activity

Complete the following activity as assigned by your instructor.

Historically, success in this course is dependent on the retention of information learned and stored in your long-term memory. The terms covered in this textbook will be utilized throughout your career; therefore, the short-term memorization of word parts in order to pass a test or quiz is counterproductive to your success in the healthcare industry. It is recommended that you build a personalized library of flashcards (e.g., notecards) throughout this course to use as a reference tool as you move forward. You may find that actively creating hard-copy flashcards for each term helps you remember the terms better than seeing them on a screen. In addition, those with smartphones are advised to search the app store for additional resources. Many medical terminology applications are free to download. The applications offer help with phonetics and use games, quizzes, and activities to give users repetitive practice. To learn more about these free apps, go to http://MedTerm.ParadigmCollege.net/FreeApps.

Student eResources

The Course Navigator learning management system that accompanies this textbook offers multiple opportunities to master chapter content, including end-of-chapter exercises, a glossary of key terms with audio pronunciations, games, pronunciation coach, and additional activities such as engaging with the BioDigital® Human.

2 Body Organization and Healthcare Terminology

> "I tend to think that the best face of humanity is that we learn. We explore, we study, we think."
>
> —**Kurt Busiek**, American comic book writer

Translation Challenge

On your way home from work, you witness an automobile accident. As one of the first people to arrive at the scene, you immediately call 911 and offer assistance to those who have been injured. When emergency medical services arrive, you overhear the paramedics having the following conversation:

"Driver in vehicle 1 has several lacerations to the anterior portion of the head. The airbag has also caused superficial burns to the superior surface of the chest. Passenger in vehicle 2 was not wearing a seat belt and has hyperextended cervical vertebrae C2 and C3. Let's stabilize both and transport them to the hospital for AP X-rays of the spine and head."

The question of the hour: What's in a term? Can you accurately "translate" this dialogue and describe this scene using terminology you know?

Learning Objectives

2.1   List and describe the various levels of organization of the human body.

2.2   Describe the functions of cells.

2.3   Identify the four types of tissue present in the human body.

2.4   Name the body systems and corresponding medical specialties.

2.5   Identify the most commonly used directional and positional terms on the human body.

2.6   Describe the three planes of the body.

2.7   List and define the terms related to body cavities, regions, and quadrants.

2.8   Identify commonly used medical imaging methods and associated terminology.

2.9   Define commonly used general lab, pathology, surgery, and pharmacology terms.

2.10 Distinguish among chemical, generic, and trade names of drugs.

2.11 Interpret correctly the abbreviations commonly used in prescriptions.

2.12 List and describe the various routes of drug administration.

2.13 Correctly spell and pronounce terminology related to body areas and directions, and general terms related to medical imaging, medical records, laboratory tests, and pharmacology.

2.14 Explain the importance of knowing and understanding correct medical terminology.

✦ COURSE NAVIGATOR
Access Additional Chapter Resources

Much of your work learning medical terminology will pertain to the separate contexts of the body systems (also known as *organ systems*). This chapter, however, offers an overview of the body from the smallest unit of matter to the overall functioning of the organism as a whole. At the conclusion of this chapter, you will have a basic understanding of how the medical profession "organizes" its thinking about the human body.

In this chapter you will develop a foundation for your study of body systems. You will learn the general, whole-body terminology that you need to build your vocabulary of individual body system words. As you read this chapter, note the presence of terms that do not combine as elegantly as the word parts introduced in the previous chapter. We will refer to them as nondecodeable words and—although not constructed of word parts—they will make up a significant portion of your medical vocabulary. A list of common noncombinable terms has been provided for you in the appendix. Consider adding to that list and referring to it as you study combinable terms.

Table 2.1 contains a set of terms you will encounter often as you learn about the organization of the human body.

TABLE 2.1 Key Terms for Body Organization

Term	Meaning
cell	the basic unit of all living things
tissue	similar cells grouped together
organ	a collection of different tissues that work together
organ (body) system	groups of organs that work together to perform a specific function
organism	Any living individual; the compilation of cells, tissues, organs, and organ systems working together as a whole

Levels of Organization

When Anton van Leeuwenhoek invented the microscope in the mid-1600s, the study of anatomy and physiology changed forever. The Dutchman's early search for a way to evaluate woven cloth had led him to experimentation that eventually produced a working, but crude, microscope. He refined his invention, and when he discovered "animalcules" (little animals) in almost everything he viewed, the science of microbiology (the study of very small living things) was born. Van Leeuwenhoek's discovery made it possible to study cells, the basic unit of life in the human body. His work revolutionized the science of medicine. Researchers could now see how groups of cells make up a tissue, a group of tissues make up a body organ, and organs make up functional systems such as the nervous system, the gastrointestinal system, and the urinary system. This concept is known as "levels of organization" (see Figure 2.1).

FIGURE 2.1 Levels of Organization

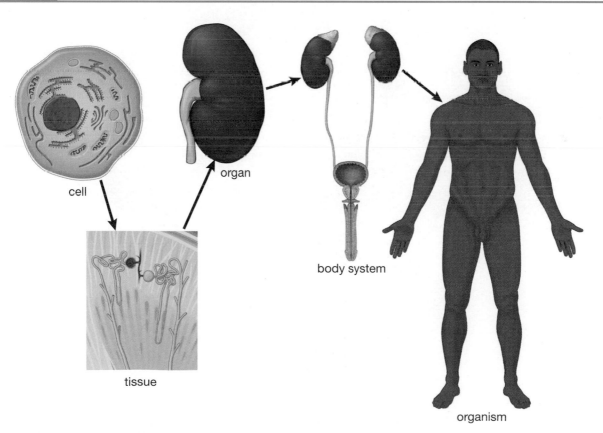

cell

tissue

organ

body system

organism

Note that each level becomes larger and more complex than the one before it. The concept of levels of organization provides scientists with a useful tool for thinking about how all parts of the body function and how the functions are interrelated.

How do these individual levels work together to perform the functions of the body? We will now take a glance at each one and discuss its unique role in the process.

Cells

Cytology is the study of cells, including their origin, structure, functions, and pathology. (Recall that the combining form *cyt/o* means "cell" and the suffix *-ology* means "study of.") The **cell** is the basic unit of all living things, the smallest unit capable of independent life and reproduction (see Figure 2.2). All cells have three basic parts: the cell membrane, a nucleus, and the cytoplasm. The membrane is a distinct outer layer that separates the cell from its environment. It permits the flow of molecules in and out and contains receptors that influence the cell's activity. The nucleus is the "control center" of the cell. It contains the cell's DNA and/or genetic information. The cytoplasm, made up mostly of water and salt, is the fluid that fills the cell. It contains various particles and organelles inside the cell membrane and outside the nucleus.

FIGURE 2.2   **Cell Structure**

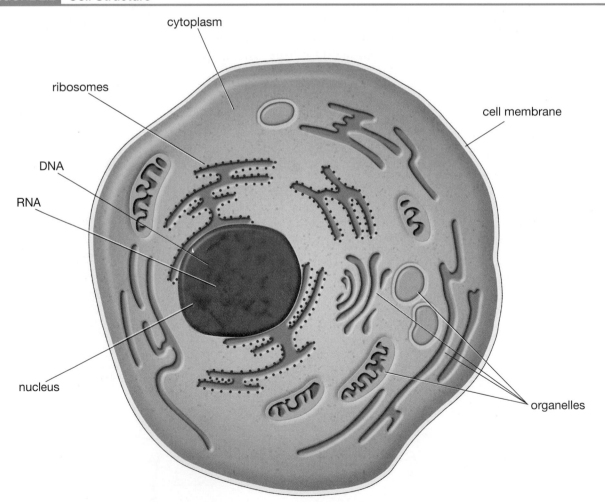

Cells perform many important functions that are vital to the survival of living things. They play a role in the following functions: oxygen exchange, energy conversion, digestion of foods, reproduction, and the excretion of waste.

Oxygen Exchange

Breathing, or respiration, occurs when oxygen enters the cells through a process called diffusion, during which carbon dioxide (waste) is removed from the cells. Both oxygen and carbon dioxide are transported throughout the body in the blood by means of arteries, veins, and capillaries. This process will be covered in greater detail in Chapter 7.

Energy Conversion/Digestion of Foods

As food is consumed, cells produce enzymes that break down food and convert it into energy. This energy can be used to keep all the body's organs (and their many functions) running. The process of consuming and processing food is called digestion and is discussed in Chapter 11.

Reproduction

Cells duplicate using a process called mitosis (cell division). This process allows a dying cell to replace itself in an organism. This important type of reproduction is vital to the survival of all living things, further characterizing the cell as the fundamental unit of life. The continuous division of skin cells to maintain a protective barrier against infection is an example of mitosis. The outer layer of skin, made up largely of dead cells, contains a protective coating called keratin. As skin cells divide and new cells are produced, the skin sheds cells, replacing the old cells with a new layer of protection.

The most common cells in the body, red blood cells (RBCs), also known as *erythrocytes*, do not reproduce using mitosis. These cells are produced in the bone marrow. The body produces about 2 million RBCs per second. Red blood cells make up approximately a quarter of the cells in the human body. Their job is to carry oxygen throughout the body. If these cells failed to replicate and reproduce, then humans would have a life span averaging about 115 days. You will learn more about the cardiovascular system in Chapter 8.

When cells grow and divide at an abnormal or uncontrolled rate, they are considered cancerous. **Cancer** refers to a large group of diseases that have malignant properties—that is, a tendency to grow and spread. Cancer cells differ in size, shape, and function (from normal cells and also from one another).

In most normal cells, a substance found within the cell will stop the division of cells. Cancer cells have the ability to divide and invade surrounding tissues (this is known as metastasis). Each type of cancer is identified by the site and/or cell type from which it begins. For example, colon cancer starts in the colon; breast cancer starts in the breast. Cancer may result from exposure to carcinogens, a damaged immune system, or a genetic predisposition (an inherited trait increasing an individual's susceptibility to a particular condition).

> **Did You Know?**
>
> Enzymes are proteins that speed up a chemical reaction. Proteins are large molecules that are essential to the structure and function of living cells.

In the Know: Tumor Staging

Once a confirmed cancer diagnosis is made, the next step in the treatment process is to obtain information on the amount of cancer present and its exact location in an individual's body. This information is critical to one's treatment plan and ultimately the prognosis (predicted outcome) of the individual being treated. The recommended treatment plan for an early-stage cancer may be the surgical removal of a tumor or use of radiation therapies, while an individual with an advanced stage cancer may need to be treated with chemotherapy. **Grade** (typically ranging from 1 to 4) refers to the description of a tumor based on how abnormal its cells appear under a microscope. Generally, grading is an indication of how quickly a tumor will grow and spread throughout the body. **Stage** refers to the extent to which cancer cells have already spread within the body. Several tumor classification systems are used, depending on the body area affected. For example, Dukes' staging is used for colon cancer, and Jewett's staging is used for bladder cancer. The most widely used classification is based on three factors and is called the TNM (primary Tumor, lymph Node, and Metastasis) system:

T (T1–T4) Describes the size of the original (primary) tumor, T is for TUMOR

N (N0–N3) Describes the extent to which the cancer cells have spread to nearby lymph nodes, N is for NODES

M (M0–M1) Describes the extent to which the cancer cells have metastasized or spread from one part of the body to another, M is for METASTASIS

Did You Know?

The waste product urea is a chemical compound of carbon, hydrogen, nitrogen, and oxygen.

Excretion of Waste

The process of exhaling, or breathing out, is one example of cells' ability to eliminate waste. Another example would be digestion and the utilization of energy. As cells work hard to break down proteins and carbohydrates, waste products (e.g., urea) are formed. An accumulation of such waste within the body could be harmful, so the kidneys filter out the waste stored in the blood cells. This process is discussed in greater detail in Chapter 12.

Although cells play a role oxygen exchange, energy conversion, digestion of foods, reproduction, and the excretion of waste; they also have special characteristics that perform unique tasks depending on their location and purpose. A very general list of some cell types would include bone cells, blood cells, and fat cells (these three are all associated with one general category), as well as skeletal and smooth muscle cells, nerve cells, and intestinal tract lining cells (of several types), sperm, ova, and many, many more. When similar cells are grouped together, they form the next level of organization, known as *tissue*.

Beyond Words: Word Parts & Fun Facts

The term *nucleus* is created with the combining form *nucle/o*, meaning "nucleus," and the suffix *-us*, meaning "structure." The term *cytoplasm* is created using the combining form *cyt/o*, meaning "cell," and the suffix *-plasm*, meaning "formation." Recall that the cytoplasm, which is made up mostly of water and salt, is the fluid that fills the cell.

Fun Facts:

- Adult bodies are made up of about 50%-65% water.
- A child's body is made up of about 75% water.
- The human brain is made up of about 75% water.

Tissues

Human bodies consist of billions of cells that are grouped together and arranged to form tissues. A tissue is a collection of specialized cells with similar structures and functions.

Histology is the branch of science specializing in the microscopic study of tissues. (Note that the combining form *hist/o* means "tissue" and the suffix *-ology* means "study of.") Tissues are grouped into four basic types—epithelial, connective, muscle, and nerve—and the entire body is made up of combinations of these tissues.

> **To Note!**
>
> Tissue is made up of specialized cells with similar structures and functions.

Epithelial Tissue

Epithelial tissue, which is found throughout the body, covers internal and external surfaces of organs. The skin and the linings of the digestive system, urinary system, and respiratory system are covered by epithelial tissue.

Connective Tissue

Connective tissue includes blood, bones, cartilage, tendons, ligaments, and fat. The human body has more connective tissue than any other tissue type. Connective tissue provides a framework for the body, holds organs in place, connects body parts, and allows for the movement of joints. It is supportive and also plays an important role in the body's immune system. Fat, or **adipose** tissue, is a type of connective tissue that cushions, stores energy, and insulates against heat loss.

Muscle Tissue

Muscle tissue is categorized into three types: *smooth*, *skeletal* (or striated), and *cardiac*. All three types share the two primary muscle tissue activities: contraction and relaxation. Smooth muscle and cardiac muscle are considered **involuntary**, meaning the individual has little or no control over the muscle's movement. Skeletal or striated muscle is considered **voluntary**, which means such muscles are under the conscious control of the individual.

Smooth muscle is found in the walls of hollow internal structures, such as the bladder, intestines, blood vessels, and uterus. Skeletal muscles are attached to and move bones and joints. This muscle tissue is also called striated muscle because when viewed through a microscope it appears to have stripes, or *striae*. Chapter 4 presents more detail on muscle tissue.

Found only in the heart, cardiac muscle is responsible for pumping blood throughout the body. Cardiac muscle makes up the bulk of the heart's mass and is known to have incredibly high contractile strength and endurance, two characteristics vital to the heart's ability to beat continuously over a person's lifetime. We will discuss cardiac tissue in greater detail in Chapter 8.

Nerve Tissue

Nerve tissue makes up the nervous system and is specialized to conduct nerve impulses, which are tiny electrical signals responsible for the transmission of information throughout the body. Nerve tissue comes in a variety of cell types, often referred to as *neurons*, including cells that support, maintain, and repair the nerves. Nerve tissue comprises the brain and spinal cord, as well as nerves throughout the body. See Chapter 5 for more about nerve tissue.

Organs

To Note!
When an organ is referred to as *visceral*, that means that is located within the body (and usually within a body cavity).

The four tissue types—epithelial, muscle, connective, and nerve—combine in various ways to form organs. An **organ** is an essential body structure that works in harmony within body systems to perform a specialized function. Examples of organs include the small and large intestines, heart, liver, pancreas, lungs, stomach, and spleen. The body's internal organs are called visceral organs, or *viscera*. They are soft and are generally located in one of the body cavities.

Not all organs are viscera. Some are not internal and are not as localized as the heart or liver. For example, sweat glands, hair, and skin are all considered body organs, but they are not internal viscera.

Body Systems

A **body system** is composed of several related organs that work together to perform a complex function. Body systems include the integumentary, musculoskeletal, nervous (including the special senses), respiratory, cardiovascular, lymphatic, digestive, urinary, endocrine, and male and female reproductive systems. Figure 2.3 illustrates the body systems and lists the major structures and the corresponding medical specialties.

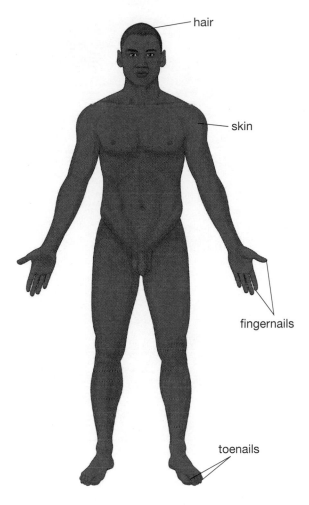

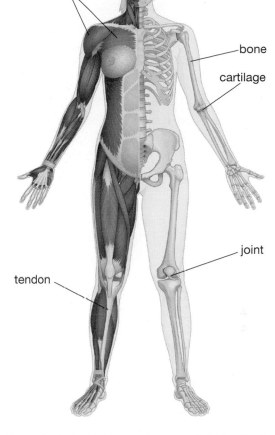

A. Integumentary System (responsible for the protection of the body from the outside world and maintenance of homeostasis)

Major structures:
    skin, sweat glands, sebaceous (oil) glands, hair, fingernails, toenails

Medical field/specialists:
    dermatology/dermatologist

B. Musculoskeletal System (responsible for the body's overall support and movement)

Major structures:
    muscles, tendons, bones, joints, cartilage

Medical field/specialists:
    orthopedics/orthopedic surgeon, physical therapist chiropractic/chiropractor

Beyond Words: Facts about Skin

Skin is the human body's largest organ. It accounts for around 15 percent of your body weight. Every minute, your skin sheds more than 30,000 dead cells. Over 50 percent of the dust in your home is dead skin.

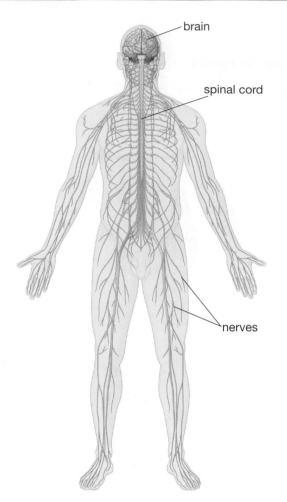

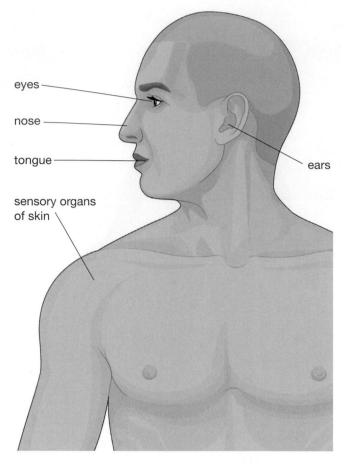

C. Nervous System (responsible for receipt and processing of information)

Major structures:
brain, spinal cord, nerves

Medical field/specialists:
neurology
neurologist
neurosurgeon

D. Nervous System: Special Senses

Major structures:
eyes, ears, nose, tongue, sensory organs of the skin

Medical field/specialists:
ophthalmology
ophthalmologist
optometry
optometrist
otolaryngology
otolaryngologist

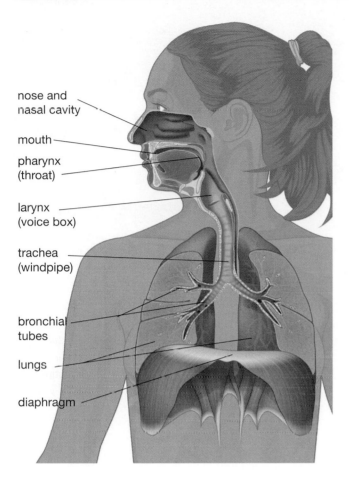

nose and
nasal cavity

mouth

pharynx
(throat)

larynx
(voice box)

trachea
(windpipe)

bronchial
tubes

lungs

diaphragm

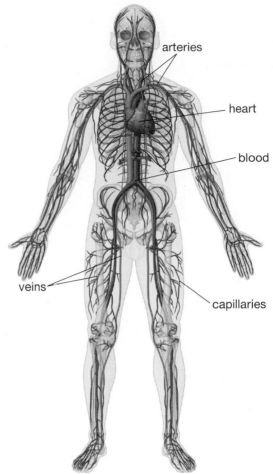

arteries

heart

blood

veins

capillaries

E. Respiratory System (responsible for the delivery of oxygen to all vital organs and the removal of carbon dioxide)

Major structures:
  nose, pharynx, larynx, trachea, bronchial tubes, lungs, mouth, diaphragm

Medical field/specialists:
  pulmonology/pulmonologist
  thoracic surgery/thoracic surgeon
  internal medicine/internist
  immunology/allergist

F. Cardiovascular or Circulatory System (responsible for the circulation of blood)

Major structures of the cardiovascular system:
  heart, blood vessels (arteries, veins, and capillaries), blood

Medical field/specialists:
  cardiology/cardiologist
  hematology/hematologist
  internal medicine/internist
  thoracic surgery/thoracic surgeons

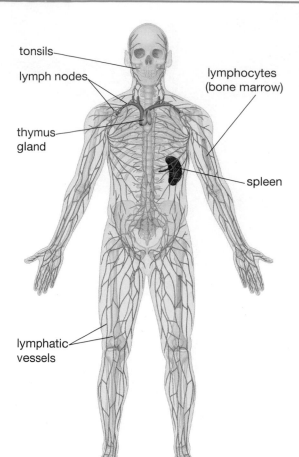

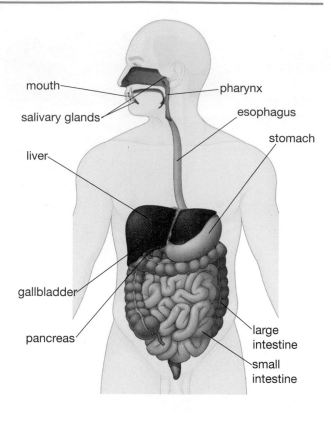

G. Immune or Lymphatic System (responsible for the protection of the body from disease)

Major structures of the immune system:
   lymphatic nodes, thymus gland, tonsils, spleen, lymphocytes (white blood cells), lymphatic fluid, lymph nodes, lymphatic vessels

Medical field/specialists:
   immunology/allergist, immunologist

H. Digestive or Gastrointestinal System (responsible for the digestion and absorption of nutrients from foods)

Major structures:
   mouth, pharynx, esophagus, stomach, small intestine, large intestine, anus

Accessory organs of digestion:
   liver, gallbladder, and pancreas

Medical field/specialists:
   gastroenterology/gastroenterologist
   proctology/proctologist

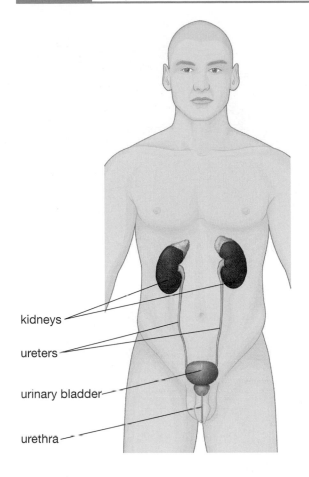

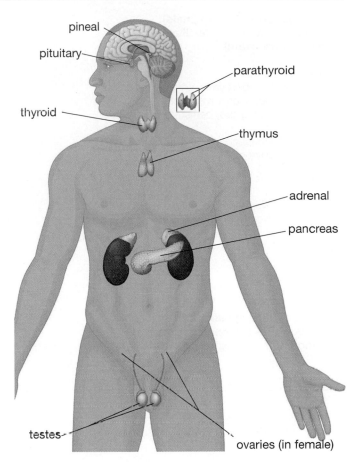

I. Urinary System (responsible for elimination of waste from the body)

Major structures:
kidneys, ureters, urinary bladder, urethra

Medical field/specialists:
urology/urologist
nephrology/nephrologist

J. Endocrine System (responsible for the secretion of hormones that control the actions of organs)

Major structures:
thyroid gland, pituitary gland, testes and ovaries, adrenal glands, pancreas, parathyroid glands, pineal gland, thymus gland

Medical field/specialists:
endocrinology/endocrinologist
internal medicine/internist

K. Reproductive System (male) (responsible for the fertilization of a woman's ovum)

Major structures:
testes, epididymis, seminal vesicle, ductus (vas) deferens, prostate gland, penis

Medical field/specialists:
urology/urologist

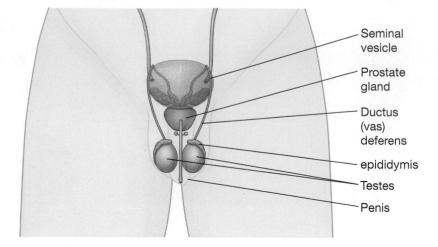

Seminal vesicle

Prostate gland

Ductus (vas) deferens

epididymis

Testes

Penis

L. Reproductive System (female) (responsible for reproduction from conception to pregnancy and childbirth)

Major structures:
ovaries, fallopian tubes, uterus, vagina, vulva, mammary glands (breasts)

Medical field/specialists:
obsterics/obstetrician gynecology/gynecologist

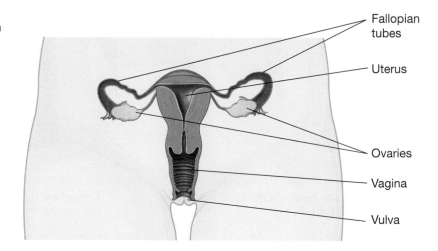

Fallopian tubes

Uterus

Ovaries

Vagina

Vulva

In the Know: What Is Homeostasis?

What is homeostasis? Let's examine the parts of the word to determine what it means. The combining form *home/o* means "same," and the suffix *-stasis* means "controlling a state of equilibrium." **Homeostasis** describes the body's constant effort to maintain balance. The process can be compared to that of the job of a thermostat. For example, sweating is the body's way of cooling itself when overheated (trying to maintain a healthy temperature). Alongside heat cramps, sweating often serves as an early sign that the body can no longer compensate for the imbalance. Once the body's efforts to cool itself have been exhausted, a person stops sweating, and he or she enters into a state called "heat stroke," which is life-threatening if untreated. That, in effect, is the loss of homeostasis.

In the Know: Where Did That Term Originate?

Early Greek and Roman anatomists came up with the names for many body parts and diseases. For inspiration, they often turned to the natural world around them, as illustrated in the examples below.

Cochlea

Root word: *Cochlea* (Latin for "snail shell")

Named after the spiral structure of a snail's shell, this tube forms part of the inner ear. It is filled with fluid and houses the organ of Corti, a group of cells that convert sound vibrations into nerve impulses, which are then translated by the brain as sounds.

Ichthyosis

Root word: *Ichthys* (Greek for "fish")

Ichthyosis is the term for any one of a group of skin disorders characterized by a skin texture resembling fish scales. Most ichthyoses are hereditary.

Lupus

Root word: *Lupus* (Latin for "wolf")

A term dating to the thirteenth century, lupus originally denoted a type of localized skin lesion that resembled a wolf bite. Today, the term is paired with a range of modifiers to refer to a class of connective tissue disorders, each of which has a typical skin lesion.

Muscle

Root word: *Musculus* (Latin for "little mouse")

A muscle is a group of fibers that can contract and produce movement. Early anatomists thought the small mass moving under the skin when a person flexed an arm looked like a mouse scurrying back and forth; hence, they named this mass *musculus*.

Checkpoint 2.1

Answer the following questions to identify any areas of the section that you may need to review.

1. List the levels of organization of the human body from least complex to most complex.

   _____

   _____

   _____

   _____

2. Which type of muscle tissue is classified as voluntary?

   _____

3. What is the name of the control center of a cell that contains the cell's DNA?

   _____

Exercise 2.1   Matching

Match the terms in the first column with the meanings in the second column. Write the letter of the meaning in the blank beside the term.

1. _____ cell
2. _____ tissue
3. _____ cytoplasm
4. _____ nucleus
5. _____ connective tissue
6. _____ cytology
7. _____ histology
8. _____ organs

a. collection of specialized cells with similar structures and functions

b. provides framework for the body; holds organs in place; connects body parts; allows for movement of joints

c. study of cells

d. essential body structures; work in harmony within body systems; carry on specialized functions essential to a human being

e. branch of science specializing in the microscopic study of tissues

f. cell substance; collection of organelles in fluid-like matrix

g. basic unit of living things; smallest unit capable of independent life and reproduction

h. structure that controls activities of cell; contains genetic material necessary for its reproduction

Directional and Positional Terms

Most people have used a map to establish directions, and most people know that when the map is held in the correct position, the top of the map represents north. However, the reference point of "north" can only be established if the map is held in the appropriate position. Like map readers and mapmakers who use commonly understood reference points and positions to make map reading easier, medical personnel use certain positions and reference points to ensure accurate and quick communication about the human body. For example, read the following sentence, taken from a surgeon's report on a lung procedure. The surgeon uses three directional terms (italicized) that convey instantly and precisely to healthcare staff where the chest tubes were placed.

> "Two 32 French chest tubes were then placed *inferior* to the incision, directed both *anteriorly* and *posteriorly* toward the apex."

Using directional terms that are common knowledge among healthcare personnel gives the surgeon confidence that everyone who reads the report comes away with the same information. You will learn the meaning of these and other terms in the sections that follow.

Anatomical Position

A specific position, called "anatomical position," is used as a reference position in medical communication. Anatomical position assumes that the patient is standing, facing forward, with arms at the sides, palms facing forward, legs straight, and feet flat on the floor with toes pointing forward. Imagining a person in anatomical position provides uniform reference points for anyone describing areas of the body.

Positional Terms

With the anatomical position as a base, a comprehensive range of terms has been developed to describe the location of structures and **lesions** (damage to an organ or tissue due to disease or injury), as well as the direction of movements during a surgical procedure or physical exam. These terms are usually in pairs that have opposite meanings, such as terms that mean front and back, inside and outside, top and bottom. Directional terms are part of the core medical vocabulary that is used to communicate about every body system. To learn the meaning of the directional terms, read the information provided in Table 2.2 and then look at Figures 2.4(a) and 2.4(b) to locate the anatomical parts mentioned and note how their locations relate to one another.

TABLE 2.2 Positional Terms of the Human Body

Directional Term	Meaning	Example	Word Analysis	
superior or cranial or cephalic	toward the head or upper portion of the body	The heart is superior to the stomach.	*super/o* *-ior*	upward pertaining to
inferior or caudal	toward the feet or lower portion of the body	The ankles are inferior to the knees.	*infer/o* *-ior*	downward pertaining to
anterior or ventral	toward the front of the body ("ventral" is frequently used in veterinary anatomy to indicate the underside of an animal)	The sternum is anterior to the spine.	*anter/o* *-ior*	front pertaining to
posterior or dorsal	toward the back ("dorsal" is frequently used in veterinary anatomy to indicate the top of an animal)	The shoulder blades are posterior in relation to the breasts.	*post/o* *-ior*	back pertaining to
medial	toward the middle or center of the body or body part	The nose is medial in relation to the cheekbone.	*medi/o* *-al*	middle pertaining to
lateral	on or closer to the side	In anatomical position, the thumb is on the lateral aspect of the hand.	*later/o* *-al*	side pertaining to
proximal	nearer the point where a limb attaches to the body (toward the point of movement)	The proximal aspect of the femur is near the hip joint.	*proxim/o* *-al*	near pertaining to
distal	farther from the point where a limb attaches to the body (away from the point of movement)	The elbow is distal in relation to the shoulder.	*dist/o* *-al*	far pertaining to
bilateral	pertaining to both sides of the body or structure	The patient had lesions on his nose, bilaterally.	*bi-* *later/o* *-al*	two side pertaining to

Continues

Directional Term	Meaning	Example	Word Analysis	
unilateral	pertaining to only one side of the body or structure	A stroke may cause unilateral paralysis (affecting only the right or the left).	*uni-* *later/o* *-al*	one side
deep	away from the surface of the body	The heart is deep to the ribcage.		
superficial	near the surface	The skin is superficial to the bone.		
parietal	the wall of a cavity	The parietal pleura lines the chest cavity and adheres to the chest wall.		
visceral	refers to the internal organs	The visceral pleura covers the lungs within the thoracic cavity.	*viscer/o* *-al*	organ pertaining to

FIGURE 2.4 Anatomical Position (a) Frontal; (b) Side

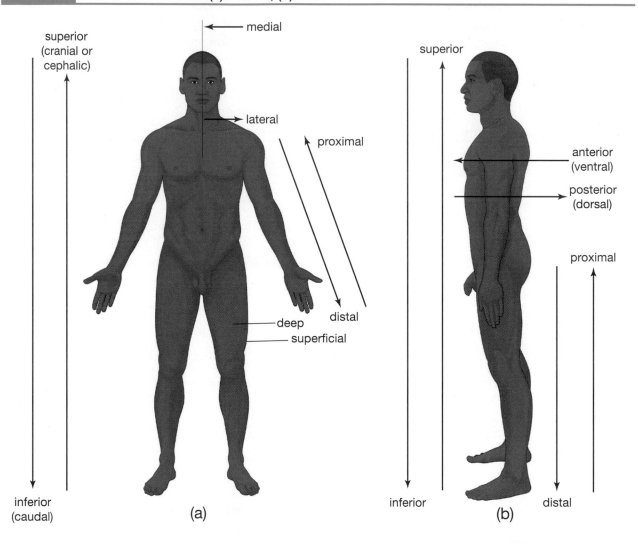

Beyond Words: Positional Term Analogies

Try to find creative ways to remember positional terms and word parts. Consider the following two statements and how they can help you remember the meanings of the prefixes *super-* and *uni-*.

- Superman flies high in the sky above, superior to all others.
- A bicycle has two wheels, while a unicycle has one wheel.

The following questions should help you identify other analogies you can use to remember positional terms:

1. In the chain of command, where do those with superiority rank among others?
2. Those who feel inferior to those around them place themselves in what position?
3. How are postdated checks written in relation to today's date?
4. How is a median number computed in basic math?
5. If someone lives in "near proximity" to his or her job, how would you define that person's location?
6. If someone must travel a great distance to work, how would you define his or her location?

Answers

1. above, 2. below, 3. after/behind today's date, 4. in the middle, 5. close to, 6. distal

Body Positions

Patients are placed on a bed, examining table, or operating table in positions that make treatment, examination, or surgery easier. Ten commonly used positions are listed below and shown in Figures 2.5-2.14. Study each illustration along with the description and the examples of when the position is used.

Supine—The patient lies on the back with knees straight and arms at sides.

The supine position may be used for examination of the anterior (front) body surfaces, breast examinations, X-rays, and some surgical procedures.

Prone—The patient lies on the stomach, with knees straight; forearms may be under the head or at sides.

The prone position may be used for examination of the posterior (back) body surfaces and for some operations.

FIGURE 2.5 Supine Position

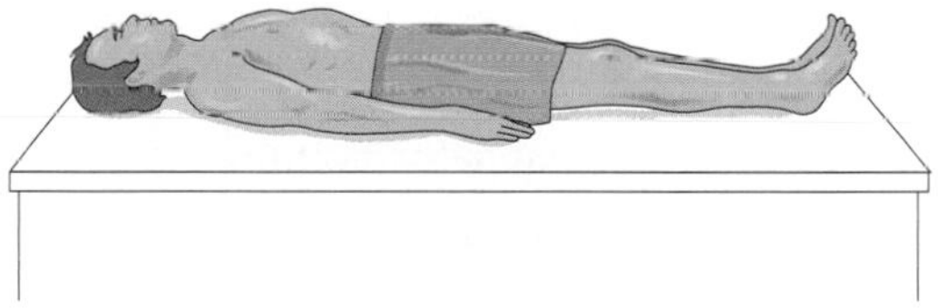

FIGURE 2.6 Prone Position

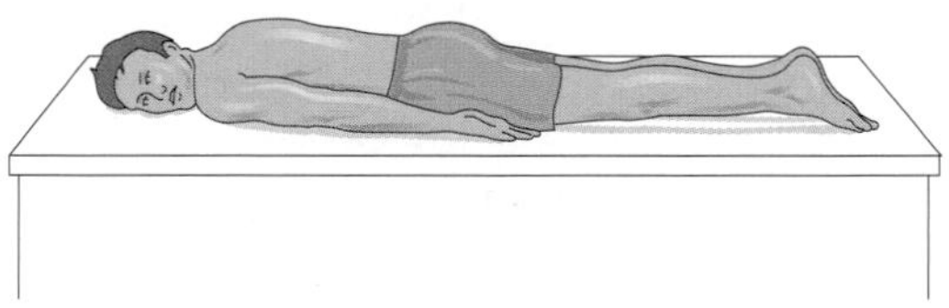

Dorsal recumbent—The patient lies on the back, with knees bent and feet flat on the examination table, arms at sides.

The dorsal recumbent position may be used for examination of the abdomen, occasionally for vaginal or rectal examinations, for childbirth, and for some surgical positions. Recall that *dors/o* means "back" and *-al* means "pertaining to."

Lithotomy—The patient lies on the back, with knees bent, thighs abducted (apart) and feet resting in stirrups.

The lithotomy position may be used for female pelvic examinations, rectal examinations, some operations, and sometimes in childbirth.

Knee-chest—The patient's head, chest, and knees are flat against the examining table, knees are bent, and weight is resting primarily on the knees and chest.

The knee-chest position may be used for rectal examinations, artificial insemination, and some surgical procedures. In some instances, the examination table may be contoured to facilitate positioning and to support the patient in this position.

Sims' (or left lateral position)—The patient lies on the left side, with left arm behind the back; left knee is slightly bent, and right knee is flexed rather sharply.

Sims' position may be used for administering rectal suppositories and enemas, and for certain examinations and surgical procedures.

Trendelenburg—The patient lies supine at an angle with the head lower than the trunk, knees bent, and feet below the level of the knees.

The Trendelenburg position may be used to prevent and treat shock, for radiological examinations and procedures, and for some types of surgery.

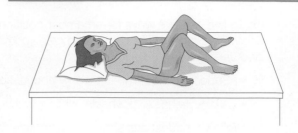

FIGURE 2.7   Dorsal Recumbent Position

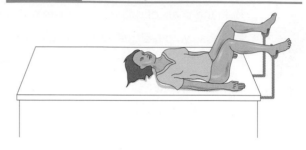

FIGURE 2.8   Lithotomy Position

FIGURE 2.9   Knee-Chest Position

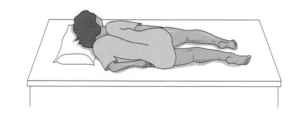

FIGURE 2.10   Sims' Position

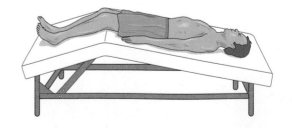

FIGURE 2.11   Trendelenburg Position

Modified Trendelenburg—The patient lies supine, with the head lower than the trunk, and the knees straight.

The modified Trendelenburg position may be used to prevent and treat shock in trauma patients, for radiological examinations, or during some operations.

Sitting—The patient sits on the examining table, with knees bent; feet are often supported on a footrest.

The sitting position may be used for auscultation of the heart and lungs, or for taking blood pressure readings; for head, eyes, ears, nose, and throat (HEENT) examinations, and for portions of a neurological exam.

Fowler's—The patient is sitting, with legs extended, and the trunk at a 90-degree angle; the back is supported, and sometimes the knees are elevated.

Fowler's position may be used for examination of the heart and lungs, to promote respiration in patients who have shortness of breath, and for examination of the feet and lower legs.

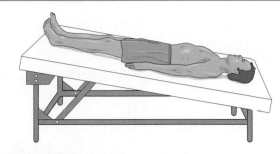

FIGURE 2.12 Modified Trendelenburg Position

FIGURE 2.13 Sitting Position

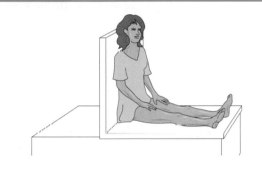

FIGURE 2.14 Fowler's Position

Directional Planes

Another set of terms that describes the body and its parts is directional planes. The directional planes are imaginary slices through the body at specific points and in specific directions. Figure 2.15 illustrates the three planes.

1. The **sagittal plane** divides the body into two parts lengthwise, right and left, though not necessarily into halves. The term *midsagittal plane* refers to the sagittal plane dividing the body into equal parts, or halves.

2. The **frontal** (or **coronal**) **plane** divides the body into front and back sections from top to bottom. The front side is referred to as anterior, or ventral, and the back side is referred to as posterior, or dorsal.

3. The **transverse plane**, also called the *horizontal plane*, divides the body into upper and lower portions. The upper portion is called superior or cephalic; the lower portion is referred to as inferior or caudal.

FIGURE 2.15 Body Planes

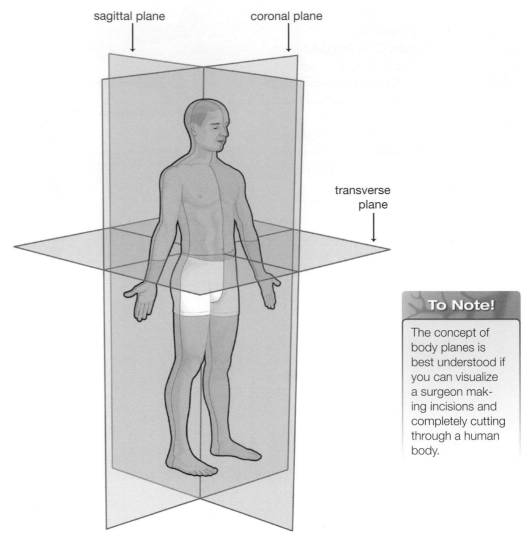

sagittal plane

coronal plane

transverse plane

To Note!

The concept of body planes is best understood if you can visualize a surgeon making incisions and completely cutting through a human body.

Movement Terms

The terms in Table 2.3 describe actions or movements of body parts. The terms are paired; that is, for almost every movement term, we have a term for the opposite movement. Read the terms, their descriptions, and the sentences using the terms in context. As you do so, examine the related illustration in Figure 2.16.

TABLE 2.3 Movement Terms

Movement Term	Meaning	Example	Word Analysis	
flexion	bending a joint	With the hand on the chest, the elbow joint is flexed.	*flex/o* *-ion*	bending process of
extension	straightening (stretching) a joint	When the hand is resting beside the thigh, the elbow is extended.	*ex-* *tens/o* *-ion*	out stretching process of
abduction	moving a limb away from the midline of the body	When the left leg moves away from the right leg, and to the side of the body, the thigh is abducted.	*ab-* *duct/o* *-ion*	away from carrying process of

Continues

Movement Term	Meaning	Example	Word Analysis	
adduction	moving a limb toward the midline of the body	When you "add" the leg back to the midline of the body.	*ad-* *duct/o* *-ion*	toward carrying process of
circumduction	moving around, circular movement	Circumduction involves moving a body part (arm, leg, finger, etc.) to trace a circle.	*circum-* *duct/o* *-ion*	around carrying process of
eversion	turning out, turned outward	When the feet are everted, they turn outward. This term is used to describe turning the upper eyelid outward, to expose the inner side.	*e* *vers/o* *-ion*	out turning process of
inversion	turning in, turned inward	When a foot is turned inward, as to look at the thumbtack you stepped on, it is inverted.	*in-* *vers/o* *-ion*	in turning process of
supination	turning the palm of the hand or the medial edge of the foot upward	If you wanted to hold soup in your hand, you would supinate your hand.		
pronation	turning the palm of the hand downward or raising the lateral edge of the foot	You may think of your hand in the prone position when you pronate your forearm.		
dorsiflexion	bending back, movement (rotation) of the foot upward	To get a good look at your toenails, you would dorsiflex your foot.	*dors/i* *flex/o* *-ion*	back bending process of
plantar flexion	bending/planting the sole, movement (rotation) of the foot downward	Putting just your toes into the water may involve a plantar flexion of your foot.	*plant/o* *-ar* *flex/o* *-ion*	sole pertaining to bending process of

FIGURE 2.16 Directional Terms

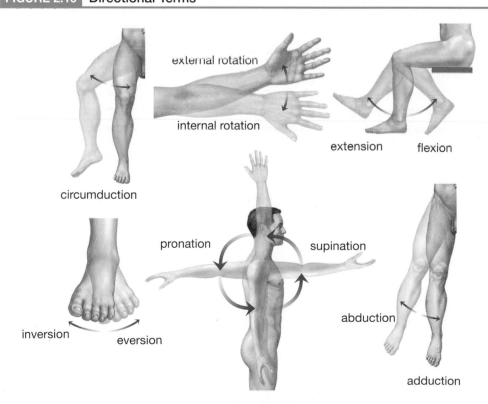

Beyond Words: Mnemonic Devices for Movement Terms

Mnemonic devices are hints, word associations, and analogies you can use to help you remember the meanings of terms. Try to find creative ways to remember movement terms and word parts. Consider the following two statements and how they can help you remember the meanings of terms. Can you think of any other ways to remember these terms?

- Abduction—to abduct/kidnap, take away
- Adduction—to add, move toward
- Circumduction—*circum*ference describes measuring the distance around a *circ*le
- Inversion—introverts tend to keep to themselves; they are private people who keep feelings inside
- Supination—my palm would need to be facing up to hold a cup of soup in my hand

Checkpoint 2.2

Answer the following questions to identify any areas of the section that you may need to review.

1. Provide a detailed description of the "anatomical position."

   _____

   _____

   _____

2. Use the positional term *distal* to describe the relationship between two body parts.

   _____

   _____

3. While watching your 10-year-old nephew's middle school basketball game, you witnessed a teammate "roll" his ankle coming down from a layup. What movement terminology best describes the direction of this type of injury?

   _____

   _____

Exercise 2.2   Spelling Check

Read the following sentences and correct the spelling of the underlined term (if necessary) by writing the correct spelling on the line provided at the end of the sentence. Then write the term's meaning in the line provided beneath each sentence.

1. To test the range of motion of the hip joints, the patient's thighs were <u>abducted</u>. _____

   _____

2. The <u>dorsal</u> aspect of the body was covered with second-degree burns. _____

   _____

3. The <u>mediam</u> aspect of the left thigh was swollen. _____

   _____

4. The patient's injury was <u>superfecial</u>. _____

   _____

5. The wrists were swollen <u>bilaterally</u>. _____

   _____

6. The patient has a tattoo <u>distal</u> to his elbow. _____

   _____

7. The <u>parietal</u> layer of the peritoneum was torn during surgery. _____

   _____

8. Surgery was performed with the patient in the <u>pone</u> position. _____

   _____

Body Cavities, Regions, and Quadrants

Medical language includes sets of terms to identify both general and specific areas of the body. Some general areas include body cavities, body regions, and spinal column divisions. These terms are commonly used in both oral and written communication, and in diagrams.

Body Cavities

Body cavities are areas that hold organs. The cranial cavity holds only the brain, and the spinal cavity holds only the spinal cord. The other three cavities—the abdominal/abdominopelvic cavity, the pelvic cavity, and the thoracic cavity—hold various other organs. Study Figure 2.17 and Table 2.4. Figure 2.17 illustrates body cavities, and Table 2.4 lists the major body cavities and the organs or structures they contain.

FIGURE 2.17 | Body Cavities

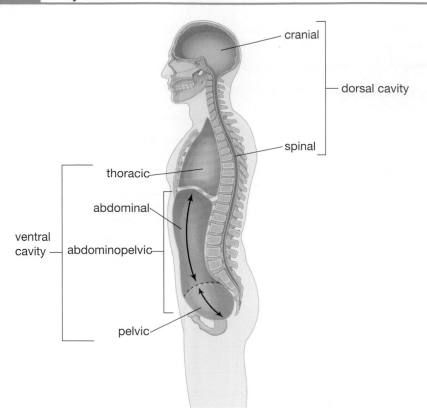

TABLE 2.4 | Body Cavities and Contents

Body Cavity	Organs
abdominal cavity	stomach, liver, gallbladder, spleen, pancreas, part of small and large intestines
pelvic cavity	portions of small and large intestines; ureters; urinary bladder; urethra; female: uterus, ovaries, fallopian tubes, vagina; male: prostate gland, seminal vesicles, ejaculatory duct, vas deferens
abdominopelvic cavity	combination of both abdominal and pelvic cavities
cranial cavity	brain
thoracic cavity	esophagus, trachea, bronchi, lungs, thymus gland, aorta, heart
spinal cavity	spinal cord

Abdominopelvic Regions or Quadrants

The abdominopelvic region includes the abdominal cavity and the pelvic cavity. It is separated from the thoracic cavity by the diaphragm. Because the abdominopelvic area is quite large, we need to be able to indicate smaller areas so we can communicate more precisely. There are two separate division strategies for doing this: a division of nine regions and a division of four regions, or quadrants. Figures 2.18 and 2.19 show the abdominopelvic regions and the quadrants, respectively. Table 2.5 lists the regions and describes them. The abbreviations for the quadrants are shown in Table 2.6.

FIGURE 2.18 Abdominopelvic Regions

FIGURE 2.19 Body Quadrants

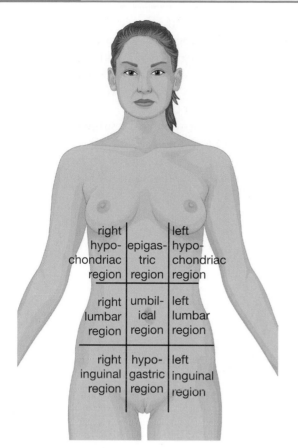

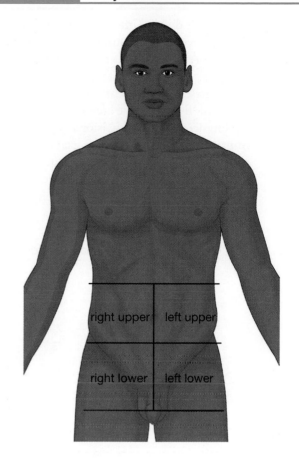

TABLE 2.5 Abdominopelvic Regions and Quadrant Terms

Term	Location
right hypochondriac	upper right, beneath the ribs
left hypochondriac	upper left, beneath the ribs
epigastric	upper middle, over the stomach
right lumbar	right middle, near the waist
left lumbar	left middle, near the waist
umbilical	around the navel
right inguinal	right side, near the groin
left inguinal	left side, near the groin
hypogastric	lower middle, under the navel

TABLE 2.6 Abdominopelvic Regions and Quadrant Abbreviations

Abbreviation	Location
RUQ	right upper quadrant
RLQ	right lower quadrant
LUQ	left upper quadrant
LLQ	left lower quadrant

Divisions of the Spinal Columns

The back is divided into five regions. These five regions correspond to the divisions of the spinal, or vertebral, column: cervical, thoracic, lumbar, sacral, and coccygeal (or coccyx) (see Figure 2.20). The vertebral column consists of a series of 24 irregularly shaped bony structures called vertebrae (the singular form is *vertebra*) that encase and protect the spinal cord. These bones start at the neck and extend down to the tailbone. Two sets of vertebrae are fused: five vertebrae are fused in the sacrum and four are fused in the coccyx.

Physicians use the divisional terms to identify problems with the spine and resulting impairments in function. For example, a major spinal cord lesion or injury in the cervical region (C1-C7) might lead to quadriplegia (paralysis in all four limbs), while a similar lesion or injury in the lower thoracic area might produce paraplegia (paralysis in the lower part of the body). Table 2.7 lists the spinal divisions, their location, number of vertebrae, and abbreviations.

FIGURE 2.20 Spinal Column Regions

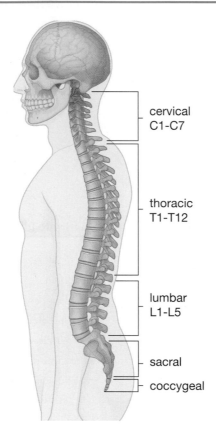

cervical
C1-C7

thoracic
T1-T12

lumbar
L1-L5

sacral

coccygeal

TABLE 2.7 The Vertebrae

Spinal Division	Region of the Back	Number of Vertebrae	Abbreviation
cervical	neck	7	C (C1-C7)
thoracic	chest	12	T (T1-T12)
lumbar	loin	5	L (L1-L5)
sacral, sacrum	lower back	5 fused bones	S (S1-S5)
coccygeal, coccyx tailbone	4 fused bones		

Other Body Regions

Many regions of the body are named according to the underlying bones or structures. For example, the femur is the bone in the upper thigh, and the entire upper thigh area is referred to as the femoral area. This is not a rule, however. Some regions are named for a blood vessel that passes through the area; others are named for a prominent muscle or muscle group. For example, the brachial area refers to the upper arm. The brachial artery and brachial vein can be traced through the upper arm.

Study Table 2.8 to familiarize yourself with terms for other areas of the body. Some of the terms and their regions are shown in Figure 2.21.

FIGURE 2.21 **Body Regions**

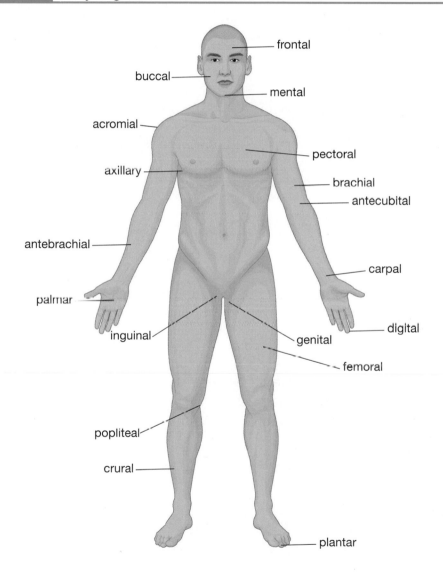

TABLE 2.8 Body Regions

Region Name	Description	Word Analysis	
cranium	superior aspect of skull	*cran/o*	skull
		-ium	structure
cephalic	head	*cephal/o*	head
		-ic	pertaining to
frontal	forehead	*front/o*	front
		-al	pertaining to
otic	ear	*ot/o*	eye
		-ic	pertaining to
orbital	eye cavity	*orbit/o*	orbit
		-al	pertaining to
nasal	nose	*nas/o*	nose
		-al	pertaining to
buccal	cheek	*bucc/o*	cheek
		-al	pertaining to
cervical	neck	*cervic/o*	neck
		-al	pertaining to
occipital	posterior of the head	*occipit/o*	occipital
		-al	pertaining to
mental	chin	*ment/o-al*	chin
			pertaining to
acromial	point of shoulder	*acrom/o*	acromion
		-ial	pertaining to
thoracic	chest	*thorac/o*	chest
		-ic	pertaining to
pectoral	front of chest	*pector/o*	chest
		-al	pertaining to
sternal	anterior of rib cage	*stern/o*	sternum
		-al	pertaining to
axillary	armpit	*axill/o*	armpit
		-ary	pertaining to
brachial	arm	*brach/o*	arm
		-ial	pertaining to
cubital	elbow	*cubit/o*	elbow
		-al	pertaining to
antecubital	front of elbow	*ante-*	front
		cubit/o	elbow
		-al	pertaining to
antebrachial	forearm	*ante-*	front
		brach/i	arm
		-al	pertaining to
carpal	wrist	*carp/o*	wrist
		-al	pertaining to
palmar	palm	*palm/o*	palm
		-ar	pertaining to
digital	finger or toe	*digit/o*	finger or toe
		-al	pertaining to
coxal	hip	*cox/o*	hip
		-al	pertaining to

Continues

Region Name	Description	Word Analysis	
inguinal	groin	*inguin/o* *-al*	groin pertaining to
genital	external reproductive organs	*genit/o* *-al*	genital pertaining to
perineal	between the thighs, the anus, and the external reproductive organs	*perin/o* *-eal*	perineum pertaining to
gluteal	buttocks	*glut/o* *-eal*	gluteus pertaining to
femoral	thigh	*femor/o* *-al*	thigh pertaining to
popliteal	back of knee	*poplit/o* *-eal*	back of knee pertaining to
crural	shin	*crur/o* *-al*	leg pertaining to
sural	calf of the leg	*sur/o* *-al*	calf pertaining to
plantar	sole of the foot	*plant/o* *-ar*	sole of foot pertaining to

Checkpoint 2.3

Answer the following questions to identify any areas of the section that you may need to review.

1. The female reproductive organs lie in which body cavity?

   _____

2. Name two abdominopelvic regions located near the groin.

   _____

   _____

3. Name the vertebrae located in the neck and identify how many vertebrae are encased in this section of the vertebral column.

   _____

Exercise 2.3   Matching

Write the letter of the related definition in column 1 on the line next to each item in column 1.

1. _____ cephalic   a. hip
2. _____ coxal   b. wrist
3. _____ popliteal   c. head
4. _____ carpal   d. back of knee
5. _____ sternal   e. buttocks
6. _____ gluteal   f. front of ribs

Exercise 2.4 Identification

Label the illustration by placing the corresponding letter (A-J) on the line provided beside each body area.

1. _____ antecubital
2. _____ brachial
3. _____ carpal
4. _____ crural
5. _____ digital

6. _____ femoral
7. _____ frontal
8. _____ palmar
9. _____ pectoral
10. _____ popliteal

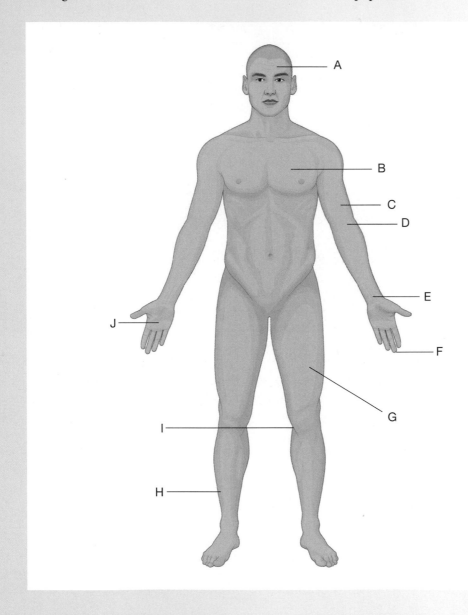

Exercise 2.5 Word Maps

The grid below represent the abdominopelvic regions. Write the name of each region in the appropriate cell.

Medical Imaging Terms

Medical imaging is the visualization of internal body parts, tissues, or organs hidden by the skin and bones. These tests are used to give physicians a better understanding of a patient's condition in order to effectively diagnose, treat, and monitor disease. Although they are often used for diagnostic purposes, these techniques may also be used to guide surgery or other procedures. Advances in medical imaging have made it possible for physicians to view refined, detailed pictures of the body's interior without a single cut or incision. The new equipment and techniques have revolutionized medicine and have made diagnosis safer, more accurate, more timely, and more comfortable for the patient. The written results from medical imaging often appear in medical records, in the form of reports written by radiologists. While most paper-based chart formats have a separate section for radiology reports, with the images stored elsewhere, electronic medical records (EMRs) can accommodate both the reports and the images. These reports and images can be printed as often as necessary, eliminating the problem of original films being lost, damaged, or destroyed by exposure to chemicals or environmental conditions.

New imaging technology is continually being developed, and older techniques are frequently updated to make them more effective. In some workplaces, the term *nuclear medicine* denotes the branch of medicine that uses radioactive emissions (radiation) to produce images of the body for diagnosing and treating various illnesses. Also, some institutions group electrocardiograms, electroencephalograms, and similar image-producing techniques with X-rays and computerized scans under a single department referred to as *medical imaging*. The following is a description of the most common tests used in medical imaging as well as when and why they are used.

X-Rays

Radiology includes the study of X-rays and other imaging modalities used to screen for or diagnose abnormalities. X-rays are a painless procedure that uses radiation to allow physicians to take still images of the inside of the body. Although X-rays are an older imaging technique, they are still useful for a number of applications (e.g., during dental exams and to determine whether a patient has a broken bone). X-ray images are less detailed than many types of computerized scans, but they are less expensive, often more available, and can be a screen to determine if more detailed imaging is needed. X-rays are often more comfortable for the patient, and they carry less risk than some of the more advanced imaging procedures. Since X-rays depend on radiation to create the black-and-white images, patients are generally required to wear protective material on the areas of their body that are not being X-rayed. Pregnant women, or those who may be pregnant, are advised to avoid X-ray procedures as they are more sensitive to the potential risks of exposure.

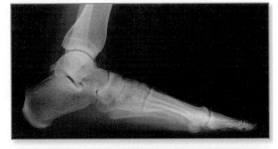
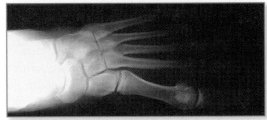

Normal foot X-ray

X-ray films are usually taken by a radiologic technologist and interpreted by a radiologist, a physician who specializes in radiology. These technicians (and any healthcare workers who work with radiology diagnostic imaging) must be aware of their own exposure to radiation. In addition to following established safety protocols, workers typically wear a badge that records their personal exposure to raditation.

Fluoroscopy

Fluoroscopy is an imaging technique that uses X-rays to display current images on a monitor. The images are shown on-screen in real time, and allow physicians to monitor the movement of internal body parts, contrast dyes, and instruments during a procedure. When compared to the traditional X-ray, fluoroscopy has an added benefit of moving images.

Fluoroscopy is particularly useful in diagnosing problems of the gastrointestinal system (the esophagus, stomach, intestines, and colon) and other passageways (such as the coronary arteries). Fluoroscopy images can be recorded as either still pictures or moving images.

Sonography

Sonography, or ultrasound imaging, is a diagnostic procedure that uses high-frequency sound waves, also known as *ultrasound*, to capture real-time images from within the body. Similar to fluoroscopy, sonography produces a moving image that can be recorded as a moving picture or printed as a still image (such as with fetal ultrasounds).

A sonograph is created when an ultrasound wave bounces (or echoes) off an internal organ. These waves also allow the imaging of tissues and blood flow. During the procedure, a device that produces ultrasound waves, such as a *transducer*, is placed directly over or into the area being imaged. If the transducer is placed outside the body, a layer of gel is applied to the patient's skin. This gel aids in the transmission of the waves through the skin. Ultrasounds are used in multiple specialties by primary care physicians, surgeons, emergency physicians, and specialists. In obstetrics it is used as a tool to evaluate fetal growth and health status, and to determine gestation dates. In vascular imaging, ultrasounds are generally the initial diagnostic tool to test for lower extremity obstructions, imaging of the carotid arteries, as well as imaging of the abdominal aorta to evaluate aneurysm potential. In the abdomen, ultrasound is used as a routine test to detect conditions affecting the gall bladder, pancreas, and kidney. Echocardiography is the form of ultrasound used to investigate cardiac problems (e.g. heart's ability to pump, status of heart valves, fluid present around the heart, and clots).

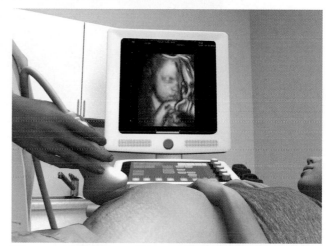
Ultrasound imagery used in pregnancy

Computed Tomography (CT)

Computed tomography (CT) is a medical imaging technique that uses computer interpretation of X-rays to produce images of structures inside the body. The scan produces images that represent individual slices of the body, which are beneficial in reaching an accurate diagnosis. CT scans are performed while the patient is lying on a table and placed in a tunnel-shaped scanner. An X-ray beam within the scanner then rotates around the patient and collects several images of the targeted area. Viewed together, these images provide a 3-D sample that physicians can assess and use to support the next steps in treatment. This particular procedure lasts a few minutes but can last up to 45 minutes. It is painless to the patient. CT scans are generally used to identify and diagnose disease, identify internal injuries (such as those caused by motor vehicle accidents), and create a plan of action for future medical care (e.g., surgery). See Figure 2.22 for a simplified diagram of a CT scan.

> **To Note!**
>
> Typically, CT scans are the medical imaging procedure utilized to identify trauma following motor vehicle accidents.

FIGURE 2.22 CT Scan

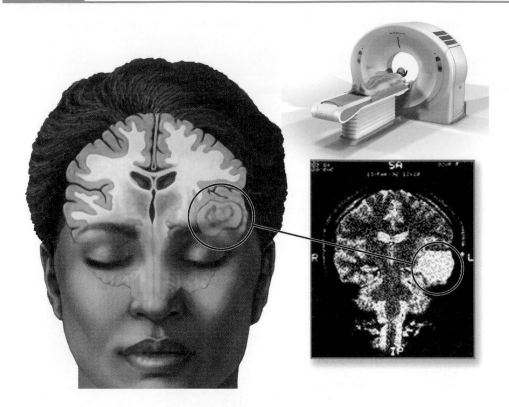

Positron Emission Tomography (PET)

Another medical imaging technique is a PET scan. A **positron emission tomography (PET)** scan utilizes a radioactive substance and a special scanner to produce three-dimensional images of vessels, organs, and tissues within the body. The radioactive substance, called a tracer, is injected into the body by way of a vein. This substance disperses throughout the body into vessels, organs, and tissue. After it has been absorbed, usually one hour post-injection, the PET scan can begin.

The PET scanner is similar to the MRI scanner (described in the next section). It is used to detect signals from the tracer and translate them into 3-D images. These images are displayed on a monitor for the physician to read. PET scans are commonly used to check brain function, diagnose and assess the spread of cancer, and less often to identify areas of poor blood flow to the heart.

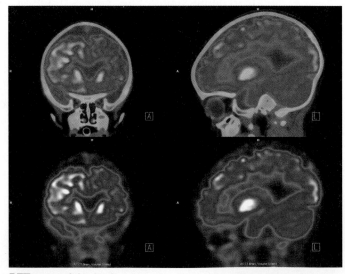

PET scan of the brain

Magnetic Resonance Imaging (MRI)

Another type of imaging is **magnetic resonance imaging (MRI)**, also called nuclear magnetic resonance (NMR). An MRI scanner uses magnets and radio waves to produce computerized images of organs and tissues in the body.

Jewelry and other metal objects are *not* allowed in the room during the procedure, as magnets are used to create the images. The presence of metal objects during an MRI could result in blurry images. In addition to objects that patients may have on their persons or in their pockets, metal or electronic devices *within* the body (e.g., a pacemaker or cochlear implants) can also compromise the test results. In addition, the strong magnetic field could cause the implanted device to move within the body. Manufacturers are working to develop devices that are unaffected by MRI scanners. That means patients' medical histories should be known and explains why patients are advised to alert their technicians of any implants before conducting the procedure. The use of non-magnetic headphones is common during an MRI to help protect the patient's hearing as the scan can be very loud.

Physicians can use MRI scans to diagnose or monitor treatments for a variety of medical conditions (e.g., tumors, cysts, certain heart problems, liver disease, fibroids, endometriosis, infertility, joint injuries, and abnormalities of the brain and spinal cord). See Figure 2.23 for a diagram of an MRI scan.

FIGURE 2.23 | MRI Imaging

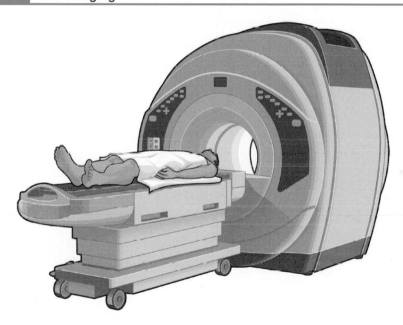

Medical Imaging and Potential Risks

Medical imaging has many known benefits as well as some risks.

X-rays and CT scans expose patients to some radiation. Although radiation is naturally present all around us (in the food we eat, the water we drink, and the air we breathe), patients should speak with their physicians to weigh potential risks and benefits of imaging that uses radiation. A chest X-ray typically results in an exposure equivalent to 10 days in our environment, while a CT scan exposes patients to a year's worth of radiation.

In certain instances, a contrast dye may be used in an X-ray, CT scan, or MRI to give physicians a better view of the area being imaged. This dye is ingested or injected intravenously. There is a risk of allergic reaction to the contrast dye used during these procedures, especially if the patient is allergic to shellfish or iodine.

Claustrophobia, or the fear of closed, small spaces, is another risk patients face during certain medical imaging procedures. CT scans and MRIs can be uncomfortable for those with this condition. Although both tests are performed inside a scanner, CT scans are generally a better option as patients are not fully enclosed and the procedure can be completed in just a few minutes, whereas an MRI can last an hour or more and the patient is fully enclosed in the scanner.

Table 2.9 lists common terms associated with radiology, nuclear medicine, and diagnostic imaging. Notice that most of the procedural and diagnostic testing terms contain the suffixes *-graphy* ("process of recording") or *-gram* ("record").

TABLE 2.9 Terms Associated with Radiology

Materials and Equipment Terms	Meaning
barium	contrast medium or dye, frequently used to provide enhanced images of body structures of the digestive system
film	thin sheet of cellulose or plastic, coated with chemicals, used to take photos or X-rays
radioactive	emitting radiation energy
radiogram	image on X-ray film
roentgen	unit of exposure to radiation
shield	device used to protect against radiation
transducer	device for converting energy from one form to another
radiopaque (radiolucent)	property of blocking the passage of X-rays
Diagnostic Procedure Terms	
angiocardiography	process of viewing the heart and blood vessels by injecting radiopaque dye into circulating blood and exposing the chest to X-rays
angiography	process of recording a vessel through the use of radiopaque dye and X-rays
bronchography	process of viewing the bronchus by x-ray examination
cholangiogram	X-ray examination of the bile ducts
cholecystogram	X-ray examination of the gallbladder
echocardiogram	ultrasound that records the function of the valves and flow of blood through the heart
echogram	examination of body structures using ultrasound imaging techniques
fluoroscopy	examination of body tissues and deep structures by use of fluoroscope
lymphangiography	X-rays of lymphatic vessels

Continues

Materials and Equipment Terms	Meaning
Diagnostic Procedure Terms	
myelography	X-rays of the spinal cord
pyelography	X-rays of the kidneys and ureters
radiography	X-rays
radioimmunoassay	measurement of antigen-antibody interaction using radioactive substances
radiotherapy	treatment of disease using radioactive emissions; treatment for cancer
salpingography	X-rays of fallopian tubes
sonogram	image produced by sound waves reflected off body structures (examination of a part of the body using sound waves)
tomography	X-ray exam in which the X-ray device is moved to view areas of the body
ultrasonography	imaging technique that uses sound waves to study a portion of the body
Directional Terms in Medical Imaging	
anteroposterior	front to back (direction of X-ray passing through the body when the patient is in a standard X-ray examination position)
posteroanterior	back to front (direction of X-ray passing through the body when the patient is in a standard X-ray examination position)
axial	around an axis
lateral	on or closer to the side (X-rays passing through the body from the side when the patient is in a standard X-ray position)
decubitus	lying down (describes patient position for an X-ray examination)
Medical Imaging General Terms	
radiologist	physician who specializes in the use of X-rays and other imaging techniques; interprets X-rays
roentgenology	alternate term for X-ray technology
scan	repeated recording of emissions from radioactive substances onto a photographic film for one area of the body
scintiscan	image created by gamma radiation, indicating concentration within the body; an imaging technique that requires the injection of radioactive substances
sonolucent	permitting the passage of ultrasound waves
tagging	attachment of radioactive material to a substance that can be found as it moves through the body
technologist	one who is trained in the science and practice of using a technology
therapeutic	treatment of disease; curative
uptake	absorption of radioactive substance into tissue

Checkpoint 2.4

Answer the following questions to identify any areas of the section that you may need to review.

1. Which imaging procedure uses an X-ray beam to create an image of moving body parts, similar to a movie?

_____

2. How is sonography utilized in prenatal care?

_____

_____

3. Which of the medical imaging procedures uses a tracer to create 3-D images for clinical diagnosis and treatment?

_____

Exercise 2.6   Comprehension Check

Read the definition provided and write the term it defines on the corresponding line. See if you can do it without looking up the answers in the table.

Definition	Term
1. process of recording a vessel (through the use of radiopaque dye and X-rays)	_____
2. process of viewing the bronchus (by X-ray examination)	_____
3. examination of body structures using ultrasound imaging techniques	_____
4. X-rays of the spinal cord	_____
5. measurement of antigen-antibody interaction using radioactive substances	_____

General Laboratory Terms

Lab reports generally contain terms from the sciences of microbiology, microscopic analysis, and biochemistry, all of which use their own highly specialized language. For example, many of the terms microbiologists use are best learned in the context of the specific ways microbes survive, grow, flourish, and die. The other sciences have similar themes. Some frequently used general laboratory terms are defined in Table 2.10. Some of these terms have a common usage definition, but also have specialized meanings in the healthcare environment.

TABLE 2.10 General Laboratory Terms

Term	Meaning	Word Analysis	
asepsis	freedom from infection	*a*	not
		sepsis	putrefaction
CBC	complete blood count; calculation of numbers of red blood cells, white blood cells, and platelets (clotting cells)		
culture	a medium that encourages the growth of micro-organisms, tissues, or cells	*cultura*	to till
differential	refers to white blood cell count; procedure that determines quantities of various types of white blood cells (WBCs)	*differo*	to carry apart
hematology	the study of blood and its components	*hemat/o*	blood
		-logy	study
incubation	maintenance of near-ideal conditions for the growth of micro-organisms	*incubo*	to lie upon
morphology	study of shape	*morph/o*	form, shape
		-logy	study
pathogens	disease-causing organisms	*path/o*	disease
		gen/o	to produce
resistant	refers to microbes that are completely or relatively unaffected by certain antibiotics	*resisto*	to stand back, withstand
sensitivity	state of being sensitive to a particular substance; refers to ability of certain drugs to inhibit the growth of a particular micro-organism	*sensus*	to feel
serology	the study of serum (fluid portion of blood)	*ser/o*	serum
		-logy	study
sterile	free from living organisms	*sterilis*	barren
urinalysis	laboratory study of the urine	*urin/o*	urine
		ana	up, apart, away
		-lysis	loosening, breaking down, dissolving

In the Know: Laboratory Sciences

Microbiology—the study of living micro-organisms (algae, bacteria, fungi, protozoa, and viruses)

Microscopic—visible only with the aid of a microscope

Biochemistry—the chemical, molecular, and physical changes of living organisms

Microbiologist—one who specializes in the study of living micro-organisms

General Pathology Terms

Although pathologists specialize in the study of disease processes, all health-care practitioners need to know pathology to some degree. Much of pathology's language is specialized and best learned in relationship to diseases. There are many terms that are important to know at every level of expertise. Some examples are included here in Table 2.11.

What's in a Word?

Pathologist and *pathology* both contain *path/o* ("disease"); but the suffix *-ologist* means "one who specializes in" and *-ology* means "the study of."

TABLE 2.11 Terms Associated with General Pathology

Term	Meaning	Word Analysis	
endemic	disease or condition that exists within a particular region or population of people	*end-* *demos*	within people
epidemic	disease or illness afflicting many people in a geographical area at the same time	*epi -* *demos*	upon people
etiology	the cause of an illness or disease	*etio-* *-logy*	cause study of
hyperplasia	uncontrolled overgrowth of tissue	*hyper-* *-plasia*	excessive formation
infection	invasion and growth of disease-causing micro-organisms in body tissues	*in-*	inside
inflammation	response by the body to injury or disease	*in-*	inside
lesion	area of pathological process or traumatic injury to a body part		
pandemic	widespread epidemic	*pan-* *demos*	widespread, all people
pathogenesis	origin of pathology; beginning of a disease process	*path/o* *-genesis*	disease origin

General Surgery Terms

In the early days of surgery, just as many patients died as a result of surgery as were cured; the high rate of surgery-related deaths was due to dangerous and unsanitary practices. Surgery has truly evolved from its earliest days of amputations without the benefit of painkillers, or the general practice of hand washing by healthcare providers. Over the years, tools for cutting, grasping, and connecting have been developed to meet the needs of specific situations, and technology has introduced new methods and techniques by which computers assist with clinical procedures. The art and science of surgery continue to change and evolve, increasing the overall rate of success and lessening the time required for patients to recover. Some of the common terms that describe surgery are shown in Table 2.12.

In the Know: The Savior of Mothers

Ignaz Semmelweis, a physician at a small maternity clinic in Vienna, introduced germ theory in the late 19th century. His work identified the fatal relationship between poor hygiene in medical facilities and the spread of infection and disease. He has historically been known as "the savior of mothers," because his discoveries drastically reduced the number of deaths due to puerperal fever (childbed fever). Thanks to Mr. Semmelweis, the world of health care truly understands the importance of hand washing.

TABLE 2.12 | Terms Associated with Surgery

Term	Meaning	Word Analysis	
anesthesia	substance used to render a patient insensitive to pain	*an-* *esthesi/o*	not feeling/sensation
anesthetize	render a patient insensitive to pain	*an-* *esthesi/o*	not feeling/sensation
bandage	material used to cover dressing, to protect the dressing and hold it in place		
biopsy	procedure to remove tissue for diagnosis and/or treatment	*bi/o* *-opsy*	life (process of viewing)
cyberknife	combination of MRI and CT imaging technology that uses precisely aimed radiation to treat cancers		
drain	device that establishes a channel for drainage of fluid or material from a cavity, wound, or infected area		
drainage	material that exits a wound, cavity, or infected area		
dressing	material used to cover a wound, protect it, and enhance healing		
excise	remove by cutting	*ex-* *-cision*	out to cut
forceps	instrument with two blades, used for holding or grasping tissues, supplies, or other instruments		
hemostat	small surgical instrument used for clamping blood vessels	*hem/o* *-stat*	blood stand
incision	surgical wound produced by cutting	*-in* *-cision*	into cut
intubation	insertion of a tube into the nose or mouth to provide for artificial breathing with the aid of a ventilator.	*in-* *tub/o* *-tion*	into tube process of
laparoscope	endoscope used to examine the abdomen that frequently includes capability of grasping and cutting; used for performing surgery of the gallbladder, appendix, uterus, and others	*lapar/a* *-scope*	abdominal walls instrument to view
reduction	correction of a fracture; realignment of bone fragments	*re-* *duct/o* *-tion*	back to carry/carrying process of
resection	to surgically remove	*re-* *sect/o* *-tion*	back cut process of
retractor	instrument used to separate or hold tissues apart during surgery	*re-* *tract/o* *-tion*	back pull/pulling process of
scalpel	cutting instrument, usually consisting of a blade and a handle		
sponge	porous, absorbent material used to soak up fluids during surgery		
suction	aspiration of gas or fluid by mechanical means		

General Pharmacology Terms

Every medical record contains pharmaceutical terms, either as part of the patient's history, the plan of treatment, or within a prescription. In addition to drug names, the vocabulary of pharmacology is filled with abbreviations and symbols for drug doses and regimens. Doctors, nurses, pharmacists, and pharmacy or medication technicians must know this language in detail so their communications to one another are accurately understood.

Drug Measurement Systems

To Note!

The metric system has become the standard for the prescribing, preparation, and administration of medications.

Medical records use two drug measurement systems: the apothecary system (see Table 2.13) and the metric system (see Table 2.14). The apothecary system, developed by the earliest chemists and pharmacists (or apothecaries), bases liquid measurements on one drop and weight measurements on one grain of wheat. For example, one aspirin tablet (325 mgs) is 5 grains. This system is rapidly giving way to the metric system, which has the advantages of being internationally recognized, easier to use, and more accurate. The metric system is a 10-based decimal system that uses the units shown in Table 2.15.

TABLE 2.13 The Apothecary System and Its Abbreviations

Unit	Abbreviation	Typical Measurement
dram	dr	liquid medications
drop	gt (sing.) or gtt (pl.)	liquid medications for infants and medications applied to the eye and ear
fluid ounce	fl oz	liquid medications
grain	gr	dry medications by weight
ounce	oz	liquid medications
minim-	min or m	liquid medications
pint-	pt	liquid measurement
pound (16 oz)	lb or #	weight of patient
quart (32 oz)	qt	measurement of irrigation fluid

TABLE 2.14 Metric Units of Measure

To Be Measured	Metric Unit	Abbreviation	Common US Unit Equivalent
length	meter	m	39.37 inches
volume	liter	L	1.0567 quarts
weight	gram	g	0.036 ounce

TABLE 2.15 The Metric System and Its Abbreviations

Unit	Abbreviation	Equivalent	Typically Used to Measure
cubic centimeter	cc	1 cc = 1 mL	liquid medications
centimeter	cm	2.54 cm = 1 inch	wound size
cubic millimeter	cu mm	1 cu mm = 0.001 cu m	laboratory measurement
gram	g or gm	1,000 gm = 2.2 lb	weight
kilogram	kg	1 kg = 2.2 lb	weight of an infant
liter	L	1 L = 1.05 quarts	intravenous fluid measurement, intake or output
milligram	mg	1 mg = 0.001 gm	dry medications
milliliter	mL	1 mL = 1 cc	liquid medications
millimeter	mm	1 mm = 0.001 m	size of skin lesion

Prescriptions and Medication Orders

Physicians, nurse practitioners, and physician assistants write prescriptions and medication orders; healthcare team members dispense or administer the medication. No prescription is necessary if the physician administers the medication on a one-time basis in a medical facility or physician's office, although an entry regarding the medication must be made in the patient's record. The prescription given to the pharmacist gives the name of the drug, the amount of drug per dose, the total number of doses, how many doses to take per day, the route of administration, and the number of refills permitted. For example:

> Ampicillin 500mg, 1 PO TID for 7 days, total 21 tablets, refill X1.

This will be translated to the patient as Ampicillin 500 mg tablets, take 1 tablet 3 times per day for 7 days. One refill is authorized. The pharmacist will include "instruction or warning information" on the bottle. This will provide information specific to the medicine prescribed (e.g., take with food or avoid sun exposure). Prescriptions given to a nurse are placed on a physician order sheet in the individual patient's chart. The language used will be the same as the language used for the pharmacy.

Soft Skills for Health Care: Integrity

Integrity is a necessary characteristic for the success of a healthcare professional. It is common for pharmaceutical drug representatives to visit medical practices frequently and leave product samples for medications they would like prescribed to patients.

Imagine that as an employee of a busy OB-GYN office, you notice a coworker taking birth control samples out of the most recent delivery. When confronted, she states that she is trying to save herself the cost of her copay for prescription drugs. She goes on to explain that the physicians do not charge patients for these medications since they are provided as free samples. The employee's behavior is unethical, unprofessional, and also illegal. She could be terminated, and her actions could also result in both criminal and civil prosecution.

Elements of a Prescription

Federal regulations require that a prescription follow a specific format. The prescription must contain the following elements: doctor's or clinic's name, address, telephone number, and drug license or registration number (issued by the federal Drug Enforcement Administration [DEA]); name of the patient, date, drug name and strength, amount to be dispensed, instructions for administration, signature of the physician, permission for refills, and whether generic substitution is allowed (see Figure 2.24). The transition from paper to electronic medical records has also affected the use of handwritten prescriptions. Today's healthcare system has evolved over the past decade, and handwritten prescriptions are less often used. Prescriptions can be phoned directly to the pharmacy. Medicines that have an abuse potential often must be done by hand as pharmacies may not accept computer orders nor phone orders for these classes of drugs. Technology now allows providers direct access to pharmacy ordering systems to fill patient prescriptions via an electronic medication administration record (e-mar) or electronic prescription form (e-script), although the use of electronic prescriptions for controlled substances varies from state to state.

FIGURE 2.24 Prescription Form

```
R̶x      MT. HOPE MEDICAL PARK
         5678 Medical Center Drive
         St. Paul, MN 12345    325-555-0112

    #_____   DEA #_____
    PT. NAME_____  DATE _____
    ADDRESS_____




    FILLS ____TIMES  (NO REFILL UNLESS INDICATED)

    _____M.D.  _____M.D.
    DISPENSE AS WRITTEN       SUBSTITUTE  PERMITTED
```

In the Know: The Drug Enforcement Administration

The DEA is a federal agency that regulates the prescribing of controlled substances by healthcare practitioners. Healthcare providers are tracked by the DEA number that is assigned when they initially register with the state government to write prescriptions.

Drug Names

Drug names are written in one of three ways: the chemical name, the generic name, or the trade name.

Chemical Name

A chemical name is the chemical formula for the drug written precisely according to its chemical structure. A chemical name can contain many syllables and numbers, which are often separated by commas or hyphens. A physician or pharmacist can use the chemical name to determine the composition of the drug.

Generic Name

A generic name is a name assigned by the manufacturer and generally accepted as a substitute for the chemical name. The generic name often indicates the drug classification, or general type. For example, phenobarbital is a generic name, and the compound phenobarbital is classified as a barbiturate drug. Drug classifications are important because most drugs in a given classification have similar actions, side effects, and precautions. Generic medications are generally offered at significantly lower cost to patients. Insurance companies often will only reimburse for generic medications unless physicians have specified exactly which medication must be used. To help with identification, generic names are never capitalized.

Trade Name

A trade name is the name under which the drug is marketed, usually a trademark. When a new drug is first developed, it has only a chemical name. The manufacturer gives the drug its generic name and a trade name. When the original manufacturer's patent on the drug expires, other drug companies can market the drug under brand names they provide. Consequently, one generic drug can have many trade or brand names. Trade names and brand names are always capitalized.

Accuracy in Drug Names

Although they may be difficult to spell, drug names must be recorded accurately. If you do not know how to spell or record the name accurately, find out. *The Physicians' Desk Reference (PDR)*, published by the Medical Economics Company, contains detailed information on prescription drugs and is probably the most widely accepted drug reference book.

Medication Administration Terms

When a pharmacist fills a prescription, he or she translates the abbreviations into words the patient can understand. Doctors use the same abbreviations and symbols when they write medication orders for hospitalized patients, although in a hospital setting, a nurse usually administers the medication. Table 2.16 gives some common abbreviations and symbols related to medications. Note that the abbreviation letters often derive from the first letters of the Latin terms. Some of the abbreviations below are pronounced letter-by-letter. Those are marked with an asterisk (*). You may remember some of these abbreviations from Chapter 1, Table 1.20.

It is important to note that in many hospitals, medical and pharmacologic abbreviations are no longer allowed. Some abbreviations may be confusing to the practitioner and can lead to inadvertent mistakes or near errors. The Joint Commission, a non-profit organization that accredits and certifies health care organizations and programs in the US, publishes a "Do Not Use" list of abbreviations. Examples are provided in Table 2.17.

> **Did You Know?**
>
> Individual hospitals often have their own list of acceptable abbreviations for their institution.

TABLE 2.16 Common Abbreviations in Prescriptions

Abbreviation	Meaning	Latin Term
$\bar{a}$	before	*ante*
a.c.	before meals	*ante cibum*
ad lib	as desired	*ad libitum*
a.m.	before noon	*ante meridiem*
amt.	amount	
aq	water	*aqua*
Ⓑ	bilateral	
C	Celsius, centigrade	
$\bar{c}$	with	
d.	day	*die*
F	Fahrenheit	
h.	hour	*hora*
h.s.	hour of sleep	*hora somni*
i	one	*uni*
ii	two	*bis*
iii	three	*ter*
OD	right eye	*oculus dexter*
ss	one-half	*semissem*
OS	left eye	*oculus sinister*
OU	both eyes	*oculi unitas*
$\bar{p}$	after	*post*
$\bar{p}$.c.	after meals	*post cibum*
per	by or through	*per*
p.m.	after noon	*post meridiem*
* p.o.	by mouth	*per os*
* p.r.	by rectum	*per rectum*
* p.r.n.	as needed	*pro re nata*
* q.	each or every	*quaque*
* q.s.	quantity sufficient	*quantum sufficiat*
Rx	prescription	*recipe, take*
sig.	label; instructions	*signa*
stat	immediately	*statim*
* t.i.d.	three times a day	*ter in die*
$\bar{s}$	without	*sine*
wk	week	
yr	year	
$\bar{x}$	times or for	
>	greater than	
<	less than	

TABLE 2.17 "Do Not Use" Abbreviations

Abbreviation	Could Be Confused with	Recommended Notation
IU (International Unit)	IV (intravenous) or 10	"International Unit"
$MgSO_4$	MSO_4 or morphine sulfate	"magnesium sulfate"
MS, MSO_4	$MgSO_4$ or magnesium sulfate	"morphine sulfate"
Q.D., QD, q.d., qd (daily)	Q.O.D., QOD, q.o.d, qod (every other day)	"daily"
Q.O.D., QOD, q.o.d, qod (every other day)	Q.D., QD, q.d., qd (daily)	"every other day"
U, u (unit)	0 (zero), 4, or cc	"unit"
X.0 mg (trailing zero)	X0 mg (decimal point may be missed)	"X mg"
.X mg (missing leading zero)	X mg (decimal point may be missed)	"0.X mg"

Routes of Medication Administration

Recommendations exist to reduce medication errors and harm to patients during the administration process. While some regulatory bodies address these components in further detail, the overall expectation is that the following "Rights of Medication Administration" be practiced: the right patient, right drug, right dose, right route, right time, and right documentation. While many facilities are still adopting these rights, two more rights are recommended for use: right reason and right response. Table 2.18 provides a list of the various routes by which medication is commonly administered. These terms and abbreviations often appear in physicians' prescriptions. Table 2.19 further identifies the various types of parenteral routes of administration. (See also Figure 2.25 for an illustration of parenteral administration.)

TABLE 2.18 Routes of Medication Administration

Route	Description
inhalation	vapor or gas is inhaled through the nose or mouth and absorbed into the bloodstream through the lungs
oral	drug is taken by mouth and is absorbed into the bloodstream through the stomach or small intestine (may also be called enteral administration)
parenteral	drug is administered by injection using a needle and syringe or a needle and intravenous (IV) tubing
rectal	drug is in the form of a suppository or liquid and is inserted into the rectum
sublingual	drug is placed under the tongue and is absorbed into the blood vessels there
topical	drug is applied to a particular area for local action (generally lotions, ointments, eyedrops, and eardrops)
transdermal	drug is absorbed into the bloodstream through the skin by means of a controlled release patch

TABLE 2.19 Types of Parenteral Injections

Types of Parenteral Injections	Where Injected
intradermal	within the layers of the skin
intramuscular (IM)	into a muscle
intravenous (IV)	into a vein
subcutaneous (SQ)	beneath the skin

FIGURE 2.25 Routes of Parenteral Administration

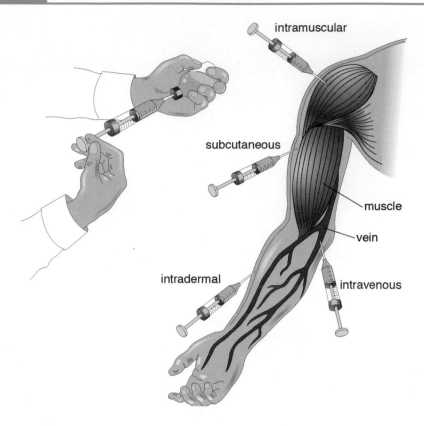

intramuscular

subcutaneous

muscle

vein

intradermal

intravenous

Beyond Words: Word Play

1. If *intubation* means "to put a tube in," why doesn't *incubation* mean "to put a cube in"?

2. If *hypo* means "under," and *chondros* means "cartilage," and *hypochondriac* means "under the ribs," why do we call a person who imagines illnesses a hypochondriac?

3. Long ago, persons who listened to gossip might have been in danger of having their left ears cut off. Can you guess why?

Answers

1. The root for the word *incubation* isn't "cube." It is from a Latin word *(incubo)* that means "to hatch" or "to lie down."

2. The term *hypochondriac* first was used to describe persons with depression or melancholy without identifiable cause. Earlier beliefs held that the viscera of the hypochondriac region were the location or source of melancholy.

3. The Latin for left ear will tell you—*auricle sinister*. Our derivative of *sinister* means evil or harmful.

Checkpoint **2.5**

Answer the following questions to identify any areas of the section that you may need to review.

1. Which two drug measurement systems are commonly used in medical records?

   _____

   _____

2. What does the abbreviation sig. stand for?

   _____

3. Define sublingual.

   _____

   _____

Exercise **2.7**   Word Building

Write the medical term for each definition.

1. analysis of urine to determine presence of abnormal substances _____

2. emitting radiation energy _____

3. cause of an illness or disease _____

4. response by the body to injury or disease _____

5. image on X-ray film _____

6. widespread epidemic _____

7. unit of exposure to radiation _____

8. encourage growth of bacteria _____

The Significance of Medical Terms in Health Care

You will use the medical terms you have learned in this chapter again and again in your healthcare career, and they will be part of your vocabulary for the rest of your life. Healthcare workers rely on medical terminology to convey important information about patient care, health statistics, billing and reimbursement information, and research. In time, you will find yourself using this language, or parts of it, every day. Even if you are not working in health care, you will hear a word or a phrase that once was foreign, and you will understand its meaning.

The terminology you are learning is the English version of the medical language; other languages have different versions. Since many of the terms are derived from Greek and Latin (and the Greek/Latin influence is almost universal), many medical terms are recognizable in other languages. In addition, there are other vocabularies, or terminologies, in the language of medicine. The medical coding systems **ICD-9-CM** (International Classification of Diseases—ninth version—Clinical Modification) and **CPT** (Current Procedural Terminology, revised every year) make up a type of language that is used primarily for gathering statistics and for healthcare reimbursement. The World Health Organization has completed work on creating **ICD-10** and it has been widely adopted over the last 20 years. ICD 9 has 4,000 procedure codes and 14,000 diagnostic codes, while ICD 10 has 87,000 procedure codes and 68,000 diagnostic codes. The code increase is in part new diseases and new procedures, but in larger part the tremendous specificity required in physician documentation. Originally, the U.S. Department of Health and Human Services (DHHS) mandated implementation by October 1, 2014. A bill, called H.R. 3402, stopped the DHHS from enforcing ICD-10 as the standard code set before October 1, 2015.

SNOMED (Systematized Nomenclature of Medicine), or *SNOMED CT* (SNOMED Clinical Terms), is a clinical reference terminology that bridges the communication gaps among healthcare workers, researchers, and patients through a common language. In some instances, SNOMED is almost like a translator, allowing the exchange of information among many different languages. The core vocabulary of SNOMED includes over 364,400 healthcare concepts and 984,000 descriptions. Combined with meanings and definitions, these are organized in ways that make SNOMED especially useful for electronic health records (EHRs). Given that the Affordable Care Act mandates the transition to EHRs, SNOWMED CT will be frequently utilized for such applications as ordering drugs and diagnostic tests, telemedicine, public health reporting, and clinical research.

Like the ICD coding systems, electronic health records, and the medical terminology you have been studying, SNOMED is an exciting part of health care. As your knowledge expands, watch for developments and changes in medical communication systems and be alert for the opportunities they provide. You can learn more about SNOMED at the International Health Terminology Standards Development Organisation website, http://ihtsdo.org.

Abbreviations

In the medical field, information is generally recorded in medical charts and provided to healthcare workers in medical shorthand. As a healthcare professional, you will be expected to be familiar with the appropriate utilization of various medical abbreviations. Table 2.20 lists common abbreviations that apply to anatomy.

TABLE 2.20 Anatomical Abbreviations and Their Meanings

Abbreviation	Meaning
ant-	anterior
AP	anteroposterior
inf-	inferior
Lat	lateral
Pos	posterior
Sup	superior

After successfully completing this chapter, you should be able to correctly answer the following review questions. Answers are provided in the back of the text. This self-assessment opportunity allows you to check your understanding of the content and determine if you need to revisit any of the chapter's content.

Crossword

Use the clues provided to fill in the puzzle with the correct terms. Enter one letter per square.

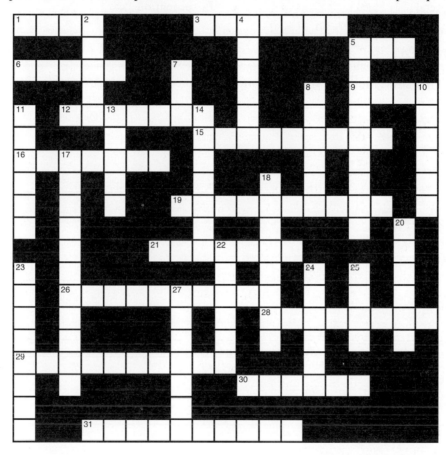

Across

1. toward the interior
3. cavity that holds the brain
5. coxal area
6. cubital area
9. position used for enemas
12. toward the front
15. straightening of a joint
16. side of the body
19. study of shape
21. internal organs
26. upper middle abdominopelvic region
28. groin area
29. tissue covering internal and external surfaces
30. toward the back
31. plane dividing the body into upper and lower

Down

2. lying on stomach
4. axillary area
5. microscopic study of tissues
7. deoxyribonucleic acid
8. far
10. pertaining to the lower back
11. cavity that holds the urinary bladder
13. a basic tissue type
14. injuries or defects
17. curative
18. cavity that holds the lungs
20. stripes
22. wrist
23. inside wall of a body cavity
24. essential body structures
25. mental
27. striae

Matching

Match the following terms to their antonyms (opposites).

1. _____ flexion
2. _____ supination
3. _____ proximal
4. _____ anterior
5. _____ lateral

A. distal
B. medial
C. posterior
D. extension
E. pronation

Identification

Correctly label the illustrations by writing the position name on the line that follows each figure.

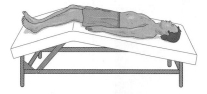

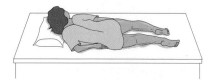

1. _____

2. _____

3. _____

4. _____

5. _____

6. _____

7. _____

8. _____

9. _____

10. _____

Abbreviations

Write the correct abbreviation for each of the following words and phrases on the line provided.

1. drop _____
2. as needed _____
3. immediately _____

4. fluid ounces _____
5. anteroposterior _____
6. bilateral _____

Word-Building Challenge

Review the following list of new terms. Apply your knowledge of word parts to accurately identify the meaning of each new term. Write your answer on the line provided and then check your definition against the answer provided in the appendix.

1. abdominopelvic _____

2. sternoclavicular _____

3. lumbosacral _____

4. contralateral _____

5. unilateral _____

Extension Activities

Complete the following activities as assigned by your instructor.

1. Consider the role of radiologists with respect to patient protection and the Affordable Care Act (ACA), also known as "Obamacare." As this legislation continues to roll out, various components of the healthcare service industry are affected. Historically, medical imaging services have been authorized and provided according to the permissions and limitations of the health insurance company approving reimbursement. Use the Internet to obtain information regarding the impact of ACA legislation on the radiology profession. Research the changes taking place in the following areas and identify your findings in a two-page informative essay:
   - transition from fee-for-service to bundled payments
   - quality versus quantity
   - involvement in the patient-care process
   - identification of appropriate imaging tests
   - standardization of data reporting (information provided)

2. Research low-cost generic prescription drug programs in your area. Identify three different programs in your area and compare the programs by presenting information on the following topics for each program:
   - eligibility requirements for participation
   - individual drug costs (30-, 60-, 90-day supplies)
   - specific medications offered through each program

Student eResources

The Course Navigator learning management system that accompanies this textbook offers multiple opportunities to master chapter content, including end-of-chapter exercises, a glossary of key terms with audio pronunciations, games, pronunciation coach, and additional activities such as engaging with the BioDigital® Human.

The Integumentary System

"Your skin is the fingerprint of what is going on inside your body, and all skin conditions, from psoriasis to acne to aging, are the manifestations of your body's internal needs."

—Dr. Georgiana Donadio,
National Institute of Whole Health founder

Translation Challenge

Read this excerpt from a dermatology office note and try to answer the questions that follow.

Skin: Comedo formations on the nose. Several pustular lesions on the forehead. Smooth, erythematous rash over the neck and back. A small hyperpigmented nevus on the right breast.

1. What is a comedo?
2. What type of fluid is within a pustular lesion?
3. What color is the rash on the neck and back?
4. What do you think a hyperpigmented nevus is?

Learning Objectives

3.1 Identify and define word parts most commonly used to describe the integumentary system.

3.2 Identify structures of the integumentary system.

3.3 Describe the functions of the skin.

3.4 Recognize and describe common conditions of the skin, hair, and nails.

3.5 Name tests and treatments for major integumentary abnormalities.

3.6 State the meaning of abbreviations related to the integumentary system.

3.7 Use integumentary system vocabulary correctly in written and oral contexts.

3.8 Correctly spell and pronounce integumentary system terminology.

COURSE NAVIGATOR

Access Additional Chapter Resources

The largest and most visible organ of the body is the skin. The skin and accessory organs (hair, nails, and sweat glands) make up the **integumentary system**. The integumentary system accounts for about 15 percent of the body's weight. The name comes from the Latin *integumentum*, meaning "cover." The integumentary system's primary role is to protect the body from physical damage as well as from exposure to elements present in the environment. The medical specialty concerned with the integumentary system is **dermatology**, and the physician who diagnoses and treats diseases and disorders of the skin, hair, and nails is a **dermatologist**. (Recall that the combining form *dermat/o* means "skin" and the suffix *-ology* means "study of," while the suffix *-ologist* means "one who specializes in.")

Treatments include topical creams, oral medications such as antibiotics or retinoids, surgeries, and specialty light treatments. Besides treating skin disorders and diseases, dermatologists also perform procedures to improve the skin, most commonly on the face. They also remove the disfiguring varicose veins, which generally present in the legs. Laser technology has advanced skin care treatment options. Cosmetic surgery choices continue to increase and often involve dermatologists and facial skin treatments.

Integumentary System Word Parts

As with other body systems, a core of combining forms serves as the source for most of the medical words associated with the integumentary system. Table 3.1 lists common combining forms and their meanings. Additional word parts related to the integumentary system include the prefixes *a-* (no, not, without), *epi-* (above), and *hypo-/sub-* (under, below, or upon). The suffix *-cyte* (cell) is a also commonly used in this system.

TABLE 3.1 Combining Forms Associated with the Skin, Hair, and Nails

Combining form	Meaning	Example
aden/o	gland	adenitis (inflammation of lymph node or gland)
adip/o	fat	adipose (pertaining to fat)
bas/o	base, bottom	basal (cell at the deepest level of skin tissue)
cutane/o	skin	cutaneous (pertaining to skin)
derm/o	skin	epidermis (structure above the skin)
dermat/o	skin	dermatology (study of the skin)
follicul/o	follicle	folliculitis (inflammatory reaction of hair follicles resulting in papules or pustules)
hidr/o	sweat glands	hidrosis (the production and excretion of sweat)
ichthy/o	fish (scales)	ichthyosis (abnormal condition of dry, scaly skin)
kerat/o	horny tissue (also refers to the cornea of the eye)	keratosis (abnormal growth of keratin on the skin)
lip/o	fat	liposuction (method of removing unwanted fat using suction tubes)
melan/o	black, dark	melanocytes (a cell in the basal layer of skin that produces melanin)
onych/o	nail	paronychia (infection of the skin beside the nail)
papill/o	papilla	papillectomy (surgical removal of a papilla)
pil/o	hair	pilonidal (presence of hair in a cyst or other opening on the skin)
seb/o	pertaining to secretion from the sebaceous glands (sebum)	seborrhea (excessive sebum as a result of an overactive gland)
squam/o	pertaining to scales	squamous cells (a flat, scale-like skin cell)
sudor/o	sweat	sudoriferous (glands that carry sweat)
ungu/o	nail	subungual (beneath the finger or toe nail)
vascul/o	vascular	vascular (relating to or containing blood vessels)

Anatomy and Physiology

The skin serves many functions, one of which is to aid in identification. Facial features, hair, skin color, and fingerprints are all characteristics unique to each individual. Another important role the skin plays in the body is that of a communicator. We rely heavily on the skin to express our emotions, such as when a person blushes from embarrassment or pales in fear. The sensory areas for touch, pain, temperature, and pressure that lie within the skin are vital to the body's reaction to external stimuli. Another function of skin is the production of vitamin D, produced using ultraviolet light from the sun, and essential to healthy-looking skin. The most important function of skin is protection, as the skin is the body's first line of defense against the elements present in the outside world.

The skin is waterproof and tough, a nearly impervious barrier as long as there are no disruptions to its **integrity** (soundness or firmness of a structure). The outermost layer of skin protects the body from pathogens and chemicals. Skin also contains a waterproofing agent that protects the body from losing fluids and cells that specifically prevent ultraviolet rays from penetrating and harming the skin.

Temperature regulation is a critical function of the skin (see Table 3.2). Subcutaneous insulation stores heat. The sweat glands of the skin release heat, and, on a humid day, the skin can release enough calories of body heat to boil more than 20 liters of water. Such heat dissemination is achieved by regulation of sweat secretions and the blood flow close to the skin. As sweat evaporates on the skin, heat is lost.

TABLE 3.2 Skin Functions

Function	Description
protection	acts as a physical barrier preventing bacterial or viral entry to organs or blood stream
thermoregulation	maintains homeostasis by raising or lowering body temperature
sensation	houses millions of sensory receptors (nerve endings) for pain, touch, heat, cold, and pressure
secretion	excretes water, perspiration (sweat), and oil as needed via designated glands
water retention	responsible for hydration to prevent the loss of excess water through evaporation

Table 3.3 lists anatomy and physiology terms relating to the skin, hair, and nails.

TABLE 3.3 Anatomy and Physiology Terms Associated with the Skin, Hair, and Nails

Term		Meaning	Word Analysis	
adipose	[**ad**-ih-pOs]	fatty tissue	*adiplo* *-ose*	fat pertaining to
anagen	[**an**-ah-jen]	the growth phase of hair cells	*ana-* *-gen[ous]*	up, back produced
apocrine	[**ap**-O-krin]	relating to sweat glands; the cells separate and become part of the secretion	*aplo* *-crine*	separate secrete
arrector pili	[ah-**rek**-tor **pI**-lI]	muscles that cause the hair to raise when stimulated	*rectus* *pil/o [pil/i]*	to raise up hair
circumscribed	[**ser**-kum-skrIbd]	having a boundary; confined	*circum* *-scribe*	surrounding write
collagen	[**kol**-ah-jen]	a major protein within the body	*koila* *-gen*	glue producing
confluent	[kon-**floo**-ent]	merging together	*con-* *-fluent*	with flowing

Continues

Term		Meaning	Word Analysis	
cutaneous	[kyoo-**tay**-nee-us]	relating to the skin	*cutane/o*	skin
cuticle	[**kyoo**-tih-kul]	the outer layer of skin that covers the root of the nail	*cutis*	skin
depilatory	[deh-**pil**-ah-tor-ee]	an agent that removes hair	*de-*	away
			pil/o	hair
dermatology	[der-mah-**tol**-ah-jee]	the study of skin and its appendages	*dermat/o*	pertaining to skin
			-logy	the study of
dermis	[**der**-mis]	the skin	*derm/o*	pertaining to skin
eccrine	[**ek**-rin]	denoting the flow of sweat	*ec-*	out of; away from
			-crine	secrete
ephelis ephelides (pl)	[eh-**fee**-lis] [eh-**fel**-ih-deez]	freckle; small, flat area of brown melanin-producing cells	*ephelis*	freckle
epidermis	[ep-ih-**der**-mis]	the uppermost layer of skin	*epi-*	upon
			-dermis	pertaining to skin
follicle	[**fol**-ih-kul]	a spherical portion of cells that form a cavity	*follicle*	a small sac
integrity	[in-**teg**-rit-ee]	soundness or firmness of a structure; as in skin integrity	*integritas*	wholeness, entirety
integument	[in-**teg**-yoo-ment]	body's covering, which includes the skin, hair, and nails	*integument*	covering
keratin	[**ker**-ah-tin]	the protein present in hair and nails	*kerat/o*	horny
lunula	[**loo**-nyoo-lah]	the crescent-shaped white area at the proximal end of the nail	*lunar*	pertaining to the moon
melanin	[**mel**-ah-nin]	the pigment within the skin	*melan/o*	black; dark hue
nevus nevi (pl)	[**nee**-vus] [**nee**-vI]	a circumscribed, hyperpigmented area of the skin caused by a local overgrowth of melanin-forming cells	*nevus*	mole, birthmark
papilla	[pa-**pil**-ah]	a small, nipple-like projection	*papilla*	nipple
root		the area where new cells are produced		
sebaceous gland	[sih-**bay**-shus gland]	gland that produces oily secretion	*seb/o*	sebum
			-aceous	pertaining to
sebum	[**see**-bum]	the secretion of the sebaceous glands	*seb/o*	sebum
shaft (hair)		the portion of hair that protrudes above the skin		
stratum corneum	[**strat**-um **kor**-nee-um]	the outer layer of skin	*stratum*	layer
			corne/o	horny
stratum germinativum	[**strat**-um jer-min-ah-**tih**-vum]	the layer of skin that produces new cells	*stratum*	layer
			germinativum	bud
subcutaneous	[sub-kyoo-**tay**-nee-us]	beneath the skin	*sub*	under; beneath
			cutane/o	skin
			-ous	pertaining to
sudoriferous	[soo-dur-**if**-uh-rus]	gland that produces sweat	*sudor/i*	meaning sweat
			-ferous	suffix meaning pertaining to
telogen	[**tel**-O-jen]	the resting phase of hair growth	*tel/o*	distance; end
			-gen	producing

Layers of the Skin

The skin is made up of three layers: the outer layer or **epidermis**, the inner supportive layer called the **dermis,** and the lower **subcutaneous** layer (also called the *hypodermis*), which is made up in part of fatty tissue called **adipose** tissue. Figure 3.1 depicts the skin and its structures.

FIGURE 3.1 Anatomy of Skin

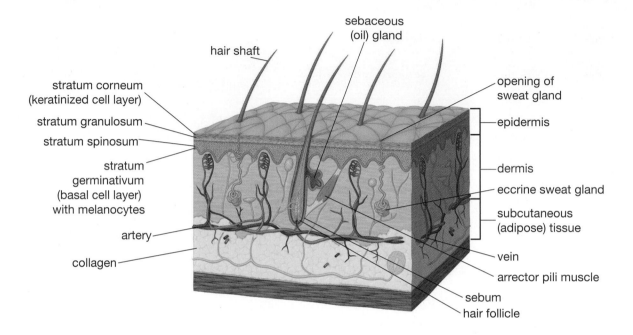

hair shaft

sebaceous
(oil) gland

stratum corneum
(keratinized cell layer)

stratum granulosum

stratum spinosum

stratum
germinativum
(basal cell layer)
with melanocytes

artery

collagen

opening of
sweat gland

epidermis

dermis

eccrine sweat gland

subcutaneous
(adipose) tissue

vein

arrector pili muscle

sebum

hair follicle

Epidermis

The epidermis, or outer layer of the skin, consists of five layers of epithelial tissue, from the innermost basal cell layer that forms new skin cells, called the **stratum germinativum**, to the outermost layer, known as the **stratum corneum**, sometimes referred to as the *horny cell layer*. The term *epidermis* is created by the prefix *epi-*, meaning "above or upon," the combining form *derm/o*, meaning "skin," and the suffix *-is*, meaning "structure."

New skin cells contain a protein called **keratin**, which provides tough, waterproof protection and adds moisture to the body. Within the stratum germinativum are **melanocytes**, cells that produce the pigment **melanin**, which is what gives brown tones to the skin and hair and protects skin from harmful ultraviolet light. Exposure to ultraviolet light (e.g., the sun) results in the skin's secretion of more melanin. All people have the same number of melanocytes, so genetics, hormones, and the environment are responsible for the wide variation in human skin color.

New cells move from the basal (innermost) layer to the stratum corneum (top layer) as older cells die. Thus the top layer of skin is composed of dead cells that are continuously being shed and replaced by new cells. A person's skin is replaced about every four weeks, and about 1 pound of skin is shed per year. Millions of skin cells must reproduce daily to replace the millions that are shed.

In the Know: Freckles

Where do freckles come from? Melanocytes are cells responsible for the skin's protection from sunlight. Melanocytes that are evenly distributed will produce an even tan when exposed to sunlight. Freckles are the result of the clumping (or close collection) of melanocytes. These dark spots, containing melanin, are generally found on people with fair skin.

Dermis

The upper region of the dermis is composed of peg-like projections called **dermal papillae**. Dermal papillae help keep the skin layers together and form the ridges and grooves that make fingerprints. The term *dermis* is created using the combining form *derm/o*, meaning "skin" and the suffix *-is*, meaning "structure."

The connective tissue, or **collagen** (from the Greek word meaning "glue"), in the dermis is a tough protein substance that prevents the skin from tearing. This elastic tissue within the skin allows it to stretch when the body moves, and it supports the blood vessels and nerves that pass through the dermis. Collagen is loose and delicate in the infant and hardens as the body ages. The dermis also contains the nerves, sensory receptors, blood vessels, lymphatics, and appendages of the skin: hair follicles and sebaceous and sweat glands (see subsequent paragraphs for more details).

Beyond Words: Fingerprints

Did you know the following facts about fingerprints?

- No two fingerprints are alike.
- Fingerprints are designed to assist in the gripping of objects.
- The fingerprints of babies are developed in month 3 of growth (gestation) in the mother's womb.
- Advances in technology have allowed the use of fingerprints as password protection in accessing smartphones.

Subcutaneous (Hypodermis) Layers

Also known as the *hypodermis*, the subcutaneous (bottom) layer of dermis serves as a point of attachment between the skin, muscles, and bones. The hypodermis is made up of adipose tissue, which is the main storage site for body fat. The hypodermis plays a large role in temperature control and acts as a cushion for the body. The blood vessels and nerves in this layer of skin are much larger than those found in the dermis. The term *hypodermis* is created by the prefix *hypo-*, meaning "under," the combining form *derm/o*, meaning "skin," and the suffix *-is*, meaning "structure." The word *subcutaneous* includes the prefix *sub-*, meaning "under," the combining form *cutane/o*, meaning "skin," and the suffix *-us*, meaning "structure."

Skin Glands

The dermal layer also contains glands (see Figure 3.2). The **sebaceous glands** secrete an oily substance, called **sebum**, into an area between each hair follicle and its hair shaft to make the hair soft and pliable. While offering lubrication to the hair and skin, sebum also prevents bacterial growth. The **sudoriferous glands**, also located in the dermis, are commonly known as *sweat glands*. The human body has approximately 2 million sweat glands. As outlined earlier, temperature regulation is a critical function of the skin. Such heat dissemination is achieved by regulation of sweat secretions and the blood flow close to the skin. Perspiration, or sweat, is secreted to the skin via skin ducts. As sweat evaporates on the skin, heat is lost. Figure 3.3 illustrates temperature regulation of the skin via blood vessel constriction and dilation (vasoconstriction and vasodilation).

FIGURE 3.2 Sweat Glands

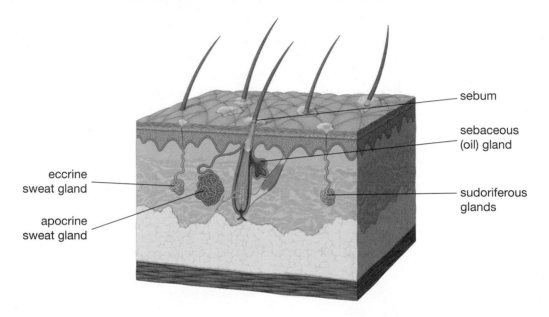

FIGURE 3.3 Temperature Regulation of the Skin

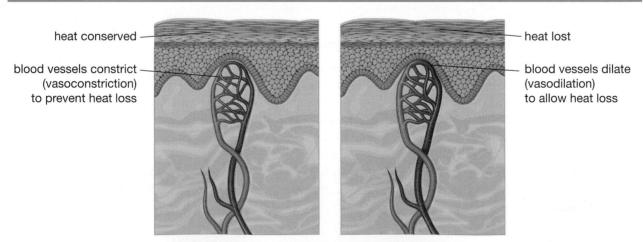

The sweat glands are classified into two categories: eccrine and apocrine. **Eccrine sweat glands** have ducts, or pores, that open directly onto the surface of the skin and are located all over the body (see Figure 3.2). The watery fluid they secrete is controlled by the sympathetic nervous system and is a method that helps eliminate waste products from the body and maintain body temperature. Approximately three thousand eccrine sweat glands occupy one square inch of the palm of the hand. **Apocrine sweat glands**, found in the axilla, or arm pit, and in the pigmented skin surrounding the genitals, become active during puberty. The sweat secreted by these glands is cloudy or milky in color and produces an odor when it is broken down by bacteria.

In the Know: Why Do I Sweat More during Exercise?

Skeletal muscles produce heat during movement, which in turn increases the body's core temperature. The body responds to the increase in temperature by trying to cool down. One of the ways in which the body can control temperature is by producing more sweat. The evaporation of sweat on the body's surface helps to cool the body. Another method of controlling the body's temperature is by bringing more of the warm core blood to the surface of the skin for cooling. This causes the skin to appear redder when people exercise or get overheated.

Sweat production increases during exercise as the three million sweat glands throughout the skin produce more sweat to achieve this result. It is important to replace the fluids lost during exercise (up to about 3 liters per hour) to prevent dehydration.

Hair

Hair covers almost every part of the human body. Hair is anchored into the skin by its **follicle**, a small tube-like structure within the dermis that develops early in fetal life. The lips, the palms of the hands, and the soles of the feet are the only areas of the body that do not have any hair. Examine Figure 3.4, which depicts the hair follicle and related structure. As shown, the part of the hair we see is called the hair shaft. Hair growth begins in a cluster of cells called the hair **papilla**, found at the base of the follicle. The root is located within the follicle, and is nourished by blood vessels in the skin. New hair will replace any hair that is removed as long as cells in the papilla are alive. Each hair is either in the growing phase, called **anagen**, or the resting phase, called **telogen**. About 80 percent of the hair on the scalp is in the anagen phase at any given time.

> **Did You Know?**
>
> Gray hair is the result of dying melanocytes.

Hair Removal

Although it may appear that hair grows faster and thicker after it is cut or shaved, that is not the case. That is because the area of growth is deeply embedded within the dermis and not at the epidermis. A **depilatory** is an agent (usually a cream) used to remove unwanted hair by dissolving the protein in the hair shafts. As with cutting, this process does not prevent hair from growing back because the follicle is not affected.

> **Did You Know?**
>
> The rate of hair growth differs from one person to another. The average rate of growth is approximately one-half inch per month.

Muscles within the Dermal Layer

Did You Know?

The mechanism that creates goosebumps is similar to what causes a dog's fur to rise when they are frightened or overstimulated.

Muscles within the Dermal Layer

There is a tiny smooth (involuntary) muscle attached to the base of the dermal papilla called the **arrector pili** muscle (see Figure 3.4). When a person is frightened or cold, this muscle causes goose bumps by pulling straight up on the hair follicle and down on the skin.

FIGURE 3.4 Hair Follicle and Related Structures

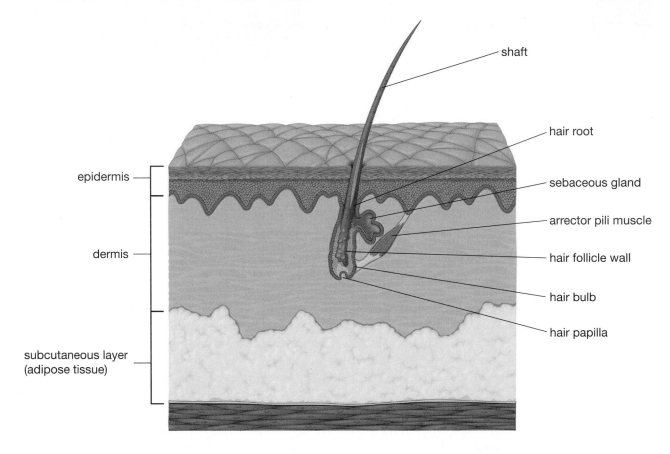

Nails

The nails, which are located on the dorsal side of the fingers and toes, are composed of hard keratin. Figure 3.5 depicts the nail, which is clear-colored but appears pink because the underlying nail bed of highly vascular epithelial tissue shows through. Pressing on a nail and then releasing will cause the nail to "blanche" or become white as the blood is expressed out of the vessels of the nail bed. This technique may be used to observe how quickly the nail bed returns to its normal color. This is called capillary refill. The visible portion of the nail is called the nail body. Fine ridges run longitudinally the length of the nail body. The lunula is an opaque, white, crescent-shaped area at the proximal end of the nail. The lunula lies over the root, where new keratinized cells are formed. The cuticle is the fold of skin that covers the root. Nail folds overlap the nail borders.

Did You Know?

Onychophagia is a common "nervous" habit of nail biting shared by roughly half of children aged 10 to 18.

FIGURE 3.5 The Fingernail

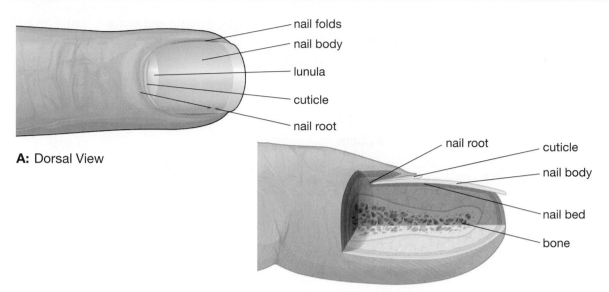

A: Dorsal View

B: Sagittal View

Checkpoint **3.1**

Answer the following questions to identify any areas of the section that you may need to review.

1. Which of the three layers of skin contains the sweat glands, responsible for maintaining body temperature and homeostasis?

_____

2. What is the name of the pigment in skin responsible for the wide variation in skin color among human beings?

_____

3. What is the medical term for the visible portion of hair?

_____

Exercise 3.1 Word Analysis

Practice using root words. Identify the root words or combining forms in the following terms by drawing a box around them. Then define the root word on the line provided.

Example: dermatology   skin

1. sebaceous   _____

2. cutaneous   _____

3. dermatitis   _____

4. epidermis   _____

5. hidrosis   _____

Exercise 3.2   Comprehension Check

Determine word meaning using your knowledge of the integumentary terms and context clues. Circle the most appropriate word choice in each sentence.

1. The adipose/exposed tissue underlying the dermis was damaged.

2. There were four confluent/congruent lesions on the left thigh.

3. The tuberculin skin test was given dermatitis/intradermally.

4. The young man's apocrine/eccrine glands became active at puberty.

5. Microbiology/Dermatology is the medical specialty concerned with skin disorders.

Exercise 3.3   Matching

Read the following anatomical terms and identify their meanings. Write the correct letter on the line provided.

1. _____ melanin   a. skin structure

2. _____ keratin   b. rigid shiny protein

3. _____ subcutaneous   c. cooling gland

4. _____ dermis   d. inner skin

5. _____ eccrine   e. pigment

Exercise 3.4   Word Building

Build words to match the definitions provided. Use the root words (or combining forms) presented in this chapter plus prefixes and suffixes. Write the term on the line provided, with hyphens between the word parts.

Definition	Term
1. pertaining to the skin	_____
2. specialist in the skin and its appendages	_____
3. the uppermost or outermost layer of skin	_____
4. pertaining to innermost layer of skin	_____
5. dissolution or breakdown of fat	_____

Exercise 3.5   Spelling Check

Practice editing for correct usage and meaning. Circle the correct singular or plural form for each word.

1. Several hyperpigmented nevus/nevi were noted on the right anterior chest.

2. The hair follicles/follicle on the entire right forearm were destroyed by burn injury.

3. Melanocytes/Melanocyte are dark-colored pigmentation cells.

4. Numerous papilla/papillae were noted along the right breast.

5. Ephelis/Ephelides are areas of brown melanin-producing cells.

Exercise 3.6   Identification

Label the illustration by placing the corresponding letter (A–H) on the line provided beside each anatomical label.

1. _____ basal layer of epidermis   2. _____ collagen

3. _____ dermis   4. _____ epidermis

5. _____ follicle   6. _____ hair shaft

7. _____ sebaceous gland   8. _____ subcutaneous tissue layer

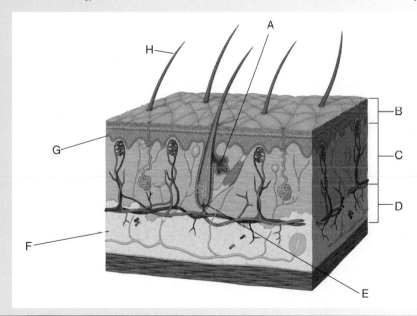

Conditions

Throughout one's life, skin appearance reflects the general health of the body. The physician's assessment of the skin involves the entire body and is usually accomplished during a complete physical examination. The examiner first inspects and palpates (examines by touch) the patient's skin, mucous membranes, hair, and nails to determine appearance, color, temperature, and turgor (an assessment of fluid loss and dehydration). The patient's general hygiene is noted alongside the skin's vascularity, and a thorough inspection for abnormalities or lesions is performed. After the overall inspection, any area of special concern is viewed under high-intensity lighting. Table 3.4 describes some of these common skin conditions; Table 3.5 identifies cancers of the integumentary system.

TABLE 3.4 Common Skin Conditions

Condition	Meaning	Word Analysis	
atopic dermatitis	chronic inflammation of the skin usually caused by an allergy (e.g., psoriasis)	*a-* *top/o* *-ic* *derm/o* *-itis*	no, not, without place, location pertaining to skin inflammation
contact dermatitis	inflammation of the skin as a result of contact with an allergen (e.g., through the ingestion of food or a drug)		
dermatitis	one of the most common disorders of the skin	*derm/o* *-itis*	skin inflammation
hemangioma	a collection of blood vessels near the epidermis that give a red appearance	*hemangi/o* *-oma*	blood vessel tumor, mass
nevi	skin lesions commonly known as *birthmarks* or *beauty marks*	*nevus/o*	birthmark
ringworm	infectious disorder caused by fungus, named after the circular rash it forms		
seborrheic dermatitis	a flattened, greasy patch on the scalp of infants (cradle cap)	*derm/o* *-itis*	skin inflammation

TABLE 3.5 Cancers of the Integumentary System

Condition	Meaning
basal cell carcinoma	common skin cancer; usually begins as a skin-colored papule and can spread if not removed promptly
malignant melanomas	skin cancer that usually results from a preexisting nevus; lesions are dark, raised, and may have scaling, often difficult to cure. This cancer metastasizes and is the most deadly form of skin cancer.
squamous cell carcinoma	less common skin cancer; has a scaly appearance; often found in areas susceptible to the sun (e.g., hands, nose, and ears)

Burns

One type of skin condition is a burn. The word **burn** describes the damage done to the skin as a result of exposure to heat, chemicals, and electricity. The type of burn (first degree, second degree, or third degree) is determined based on the severity of the damage (see Table 3.6).

TABLE 3.6 Burn Types and Symptoms

Burn	Definition	Symptoms
first-degree burn	damages only the first layer of skin; surface layers of epidermis may peel, but there is minimal tissue destruction; can be a sunburn	pain and redness of skin
second-degree burn, also known as *partial thickness*	extends to the deep epidermal layers; causes injury to upper layers of dermis; damages sweat glands, hair follicles, and sebaceous glands	forms blisters; involves severe pain, edema, fluid loss, and scarring; debridement may be necessary
third-degree burn, also known as *full thickness*	involves complete destruction of the epidermis and dermis; tissue death extends into the subcutaneous tissue and may involve muscle and bone	may not cause immediate pain because of the damage to nerve fibers; serious fluid loss; excision of dead tissue and surgery with skin grafts are usually required

Burns are treated with agents that offer pain relief, encourage healing, and provide antibacterial protection. Some agents, including iodine-based products or other antimicrobial solutions, are used for cleaning and sterilizing the skin. Antiseptic solutions are also used in the operating room to sterilize the skin before a surgical procedure.

In patients with severe burns, and when a restorative skin graft type procedure is performed, often plastic surgeons become involved. They can take layers of noninvolved skin and use it over burn damaged areas to restore some skin function and minimize scarring.

Serious burns are described based on the amount of skin involved and the depth of skin damaged. The **Wallace rule of nines** is used to determine the extent of a burn injury. In adults, body surface area is divided into 11 areas of 9 percent each, with the genitals representing the final 1 percent (see Figure 3.6). Another burn estimate uses the person's palm. The palm is approximately 1 percent of the body surface area. Therefore you can estimate how many palms it would take to cover the burned area. Five palms would be 5 percent.

> **Did You Know?**
>
> Skin cancer may develop from overexposure to the sun and ultraviolet rays. Avoid this risk by limiting time spent outdoors and/or by using protective sunscreen and covering exposed skin.

FIGURE 3.6 Rule of Nines

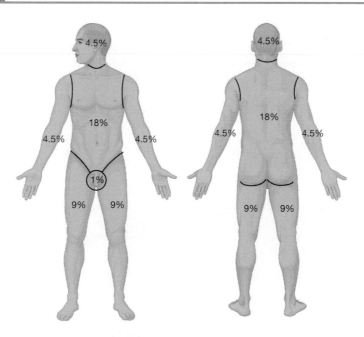

Skin Lesions

Various skin lesions are described by specific terms. Early lesions that have not been changed by manipulation or natural development are called *primary* lesions. When primary lesions change or are manipulated, they become *secondary* lesions. Table 3.7 describes primary skin lesions and lists examples of infectious and noninfectious diseases and associated abnormalities.

TABLE 3.7 Primary Skin Lesions and Associated Abnormalities

Lesion		Description	Infectious type	Noninfectious type	
bulla	[**bul**-lah]	a fluid-filled lesion larger than 1 cm that is thin-walled and ruptures easily		blister, contact dermatitis	
cyst	[**sist**]	an encapsulated, fluid-filled area in the dermis or subcutaneous layer	MRSA boil, staph infection	sebaceous cyst	
macule macular	[**mak**-yool] [**mak**-yoo-ler]	a round, flat, pigmented area	measles, scarlet fever	freckles, petechiae	
nodule nodular	[**nod**-yool] [**nod**-yoo-ler]	a solid, raised node-like lesion larger than 1 cm		xanthoma, fibroma	
papule papular	[**pap**-yool] [**pap**-yoo-ler]	a palpable lesion (something that can be felt) that is rounded, solid, and raised (less than 1 cm)	molluscum rubella (German measles)	elevated nevus (mole)	
plaque plaques (pl)	[**plak**] [plaks]	an area of papules that are merged to form a lesion larger than 1 cm		psoriasis, lichen planus	
pustule pustular	[**pust**-yool] [**pust**-yoo-ler]	a small, round, raised, pus-filled lesion	impetigo	acne	
urticaria urticarial	[er-tih-**kayr**-ee-ah] [er-tih-**kayr**-ee-ahl]	an intensely itchy (pruritic) area of wheals that have merged		severe allergic reaction	
vesicle vesicular	[**ves**-ih-kul] [ve-**sik**-yoo-ler]	a raised, clear fluid-filled lesion up to 1 cm in size	varicella (chickenpox), herpes zoster (shingles), herpes simplex	contact dermatitis, poison ivy	
wheal	[**hweel**]	a raised, erythematous, irregularly shaped area that is transient		allergic reaction, mosquito bite	

Secondary skin lesions are primary lesions that have changed as a result of manipulation (scratching) or natural and/or pathologic progression. Table 3.8 describes these lesions and the diseases or conditions associated with them.

TABLE 3.8 Secondary Skin Lesions and Associated Abnormalities

Lesion		Description	Infectious type	Noninfectious type	
crust		a thickened, dried area from broken pustules or vesicles	impetigo, varicella (at the end of the infection)	scab	
erosion	[ee-**rO**-zhun]	a superficial, scooped-out area that does not extend into the dermal layer	herpesvirus	pemphigus	
excoriation	[ek-skO-ree-**ays**-hun]	reddened abrasions, usually from itching	scabies	poison ivy reaction	
fissure	[**fish**-er]	a linear crack that extends into the dermis	athlete's foot	cheilosis (cracks in the corners of the mouth)	
keloid	[**kee**-loyd]	excess scar tissue; most commonly seen in African Americans			
lichenifica-tion	[lI-**ken**-ih-fi-**kay**-shun]	thickened area of skin that forms most commonly after intense scratching			
scale		a flaky, dry, silvery or white form of shedding keratin cells	tinea corporis (ringworm of the body), tinea capitis (ringworm of the head), tinea pedis (ringworm of the foot)	eczema, seborrheic dermatitis, psoria-sis, ichthyosis	
scar		connective tissue that remains after a skin lesion has healed	varicella (almost always leaves at least one pitted scar from a healed lesion)	acne	
ulcer	[**ul**-ser]	a deep depression that extends into the dermis	chancre (syphilitic lesion)	decubitus ulcers (pressure sores/bed sores)	

General Conditions of the Hair and Nails

Hirsutism is an abnormal growth of hair, particularly in areas where there is usually very little hair. Affected areas include the face (particularly in women), arms, back, and chest. **Alopecia** is the opposite of hirsutism: the absence of hair, or baldness. Alopecia can occur in men and women, and both hirsutism and alopecia may have psychological implications for the affected individual.

The nails and surrounding tissue are subject to inflammation and infection. A **paronychia** is a painful, red, swollen inflammation of the skin surrounding the nail. These inflammations can be caused by an infectious organism entering through the skin because of an improper removal of or damage to the cuticle. Herpetic paronychias also can develop when a person with a herpetic lesion of the lip bites his or her fingernails. Any opening in the skin can allow the herpes virus to enter the system in another location. **Onycholysis** is the loosening of the nail plate, beginning at the tip and progressing toward the root. Table 3.9 lists the major disease terms associated with the integumentary system.

TABLE 3.9 Terms Associated with the Conditions of the Integumentary System

Term		Meaning	Word Analysis	
acne	[**ak**-nee]	an inflamed papular and/or pustular eruption	*akme*	blossoming
acrochordon	[ak-rO-**kor**-don]	a papillomatous skin tag	*acr/o*	extremity; tip
			chord/o	cordlike structure
			-on	noun ending
acrocyanosis	[**ak**-rO-sI-ah-**nO**-sis]	a condition in which the hands and feet are	*acr/o*	extremity; tip
acrocyanotic	[**ak**-rO-sI-ah-**not**-ik]	cyanotic (blue-colored) because of the cold or decreased circulation; common in newborns	*cyan/o*	pertaining to the color blue
			osis	condition
actinic keratosis	[ak-**tin**-ik ker-ah-**tO**-sis]	a pre-malignant lesion	*actin/o*	pertaining to rays or radiation or parts that radiate out
			kerat/o	horny
			-osis	condition
alopecia	[al-O-**pee**-shee-ah]	baldness; hair loss	*alopecia*	fox mange
alopecia areata	[al-O-**pee**-shee-ah ahree-**ah**-tah]	baldness in a circumscribed pattern, most commonly on the head	*areat/o*	pertaining to an area
angioma	[an-jee-**O**-mah]	a tumor caused by increased filling of the blood vessels	*angi/o*	pertaining to blood or lymph vessels
			-oma	pertaining to a tumor
atopic dermatitis	[a-**top**-ik der-mah-**tI**-tis]	an inflammation of the skin caused by an allergic response	*atopy-*	strange; without a place
			dermat/o	pertaining to skin
			-itis	inflammation
basal cell carcinoma	[**bay**-sul sel kahr-sih-**nO**-mah]	a malignant tumor of the basal cell layer of skin	*basal*	relating to a base
			cella	chamber
			carcin/o	cancer
			-oma	pertaining to a tumor
café au lait spot	[caf-fay-O-**lay** spot]	a type of light brown lesion on the skin that resembles coffee with cream	*café*	coffee
			au	with
			lait	milk
carotenemia	[kar-ah-teh-**nee**-mee-ah]	an orange pigment transported via the blood that results in change in skin color; produced by ingesting carrots or other foods high in carotene	*carotene*	an orange pigment found in plants and animals
			-emia	pertaining to the blood
chloasma	[klO-**az**-mah]	brownish, irregularly shaped patches, particularly on the faces of pregnant women	*chloasma*	to become green

Continues

Term		Meaning	Word Analysis	
comedo comedones (pl)	[**kom**-eh-dO] [**kom**-eh-dO-nes]	blackheads (open); whiteheads (closed)	*comedo*	glutton
condyloma acuminatum condylomata (pl)	[kon-deh-**lO**-mah ah-kyoo-min-**ay**-tum] [kon-deh-**lO**-meh-tah]	a contagious wart that appears on the external genitalia; genital warts	*kondyloma* *accumino*	knob pointed
dermatitis	[der-mah-**tI**-tis]	inflammation of the skin	*derm/o* *-itis*	pertaining to skin inflammation
ecchymosis	[ek-im-**O**-sis]	black-and-blue mark caused by leakage of blood from the vessel	*ec-* *chyme* *-osis*	out of juice condition
eczema	[**ek**-zeh-mah]	a type of atopic dermatitis characterized by a rash that first is vesicular, then changes to an erythematous, papular, swollen rash; finally it becomes a scaling, crusted lichenification	*eczema*	to boil over
erythema toxicum	[er-ih-**thee**-mah **toks**-ih-kum]	a red rash commonly seen on the newborn at about 3 or 4 days; there is no known cause and it disappears without treatment	*erythema* *toxic/o*	flush, redness of skin poison
eschar	[**es**-kar]	a thick crust that forms on the skin after a burn	*eschar*	fireplace
exanthem exanthema	[eg-**zan**-them] [eg-zan-**thee**-mah]	a rash, usually of viral origin	*exanthem*	eruption
folliculitis	[fol-lik-yoo-**lI**-tis]	an inflammation of the hair follicles	*folliculus* *-itis*	a small sac inflammation
hematoma	[hee-mah-**tO**-mah]	an area of blood that has extravasated from the vessel and is confined in a space	*hemat/o* *-oma*	blood tumor
hidrosis	[hI-**drO**-sis]	excessive sweating	*hidr/o* *-osis*	pertaining to the sweat glands condition
hirsutism	[**her**-soot-iz-em]	excessive hair growth	*hirsutism*	shaggy
impetigo	[im-peh-**tI**-gO]	contagious rash caused by *Staphylococcus aureus* (group Λ) streptococci that consists of vesicles that rupture and then form a crust	*impetigo*	an eruption that forms a scab
keratosis	[ker-eh-**tO**-sis]	lesion formed from an overgrowth of the horny layer of skin	*kerat/o* *-osis*	horny cells condition
lanugo	[lan-**oo**-gO]	the fine, downy hair covering the fetus from the end of the first trimester	*lanugo*	down; wool
lentigo lentigines (pl)	[len-**tI**-gO] [len-**tI**-jen-ees]	a brownish spot on the skin; a freckle	*lentigo*	lentil
linea nigra lineae nigrae (pl)	[**lin**-ee-ah **nI**-grah] [**lin**-ee-ah **nI**-gree]	the vertical line that appears on the abdomen of a pregnant woman	*linea* *nigra*	line black
melanoma	[mel-eh-**nO**-mah]	a malignancy formed from the cells that produce melanin	*melan/o* *-oma*	black; extremely dark a malignancy
melanocyte	[mah-**lan**-O-sIt]	the pigment-producing cells within the skin	*melan/o* *-cyte*	black; dark hue denoting a cell
milia (pl)	[**mil**-ee-ah]	tiny white papules present on the face of the newborn; whiteheads	*milium*	millet
Mongolian spot	[mon-**gO**-lee-an spot]	a variation of pigment often found on the sacrum and buttocks of African Americans, Asians, Native Americans, and Latinos	Mongolian	relating to a native of Mongolia

Continues

Term		Meaning	Word Analysis	
nevus flammeus	[**nee**-vus **flam**-ee-us]	a congenital nevus, bright red in color, found on the head	*nevus* *flammeus*	mole; birthmark flame
nodule nodular	[**nod**-yool] [**nod**-yoo-ler]	a solid, raised node-like lesion larger than 1 cm	*nodule*	node
onycholysis	[on-ih-**kol**-ih-sis]	a loosening of the fingernail	*onych/o* *-lysis*	pertaining to the nail to kill
papule papular	[**pap**-yool] [**pap**-yoo-ler]	a palpable lesion (something that can be felt) that is rounded, solid, and raised (less than 1 cm)	*papule*	pimple
paronychia paronychial	[par-O-**nik**-ee-ah] [par-O-**nik**-ee-ahl]	a red, inflamed area around the nail, usually from an infection of the nail	*para-* *onych/o* *-ia*	around nail condition
petechia petechiae (pl)	[peh-**tek**-ee-ah] [peh-**tek**-ee-ee]	small, round hemorrhagic spot	*petechia* *petecchie*	based on Italian
psoriasis	[sO-**rI**-eh-sis]	condition characterized by round, reddish lesions with silvery scales	*psoriasis*	the itch
purpura	[**per**-pyoo-rah]	areas of hemorrhage into the skin; they first appear red, then turn purplish	*purpura*	purple
pustule	[**pus**-tyool]	a small, round, raised, pus-filled round lesion	*pustule*	pustule
seborrhea	[seb-O-**ree**-ah]	overactivity of the sebaceous glands; lesions usually appear on the scalp	*seb/o* *-rrhea*	sebum flowing
squamous cell carcinoma	[**skway**-mus sel kar-sih-**nO**-mah]	a scaly, cancerous lesion of the skin	*squam/o* *carcin-* *-oma*	scale tumor; cancer tumor
stria striae (pl)	[**strI**-eh] [**strI**-ee]	a stripe on the skin different in color from the area on which it appears	*stria*	channel
telangiectasia telangiectasis telangiectases (pl)	[tel-**an**-jee-ek-**tay**-see-ah] [tel-**an**-jee-ek-**tay**-sis] [tel-**an**-jee-ek-**tay**-sees]	a condition characterized by the enlargement of small vessels, making them appear red	*tel/o* *angi/o* *-asis*	distance pertaining to blood condition
turgor	[**ter**-ger]	the motility, elasticity, and texture of the skin	*turgeo*	to swell
vernix caseosa	[**ver**-niks kay-see-**O**-sah]	the cheese-like substance covering the skin of the newborn	*vernix* *caseose*	varnish product resulting from digestion of casein in cheese
verruca	[ve-**roo**-kah]	a wart; a small virus-induced lesion of the epidermal layer	*verruca*	wart
vitiligo	[vit-i-**lI**-gO]	white patches (depigmented) on the skin; without melanocytes	*vitiligo*	blemish
xanthoma	[zan-**thO**-mah]	a yellowish nodule of the skin	*xanth/o* *-oma*	yellowish tumor
xerosis	[**zee**-rO-sis]	dry skin	*xer/o* *-osis*	dry condition

Infants

The newborn is covered with a moist, white, cheese-like substance called the **vernix caseosa**, which protects its thin skin. The skin is covered with a fine, downy hair called **lanugo**. This hair, along with the hair on the head, may be lost in the first few weeks of life.

Newborns' skin color is typically lighter than it will eventually become because the pigment function in their skin is not fully developed. The infant's full melanotic color is noted in the nail beds and, for males, in the scrotal folds. Infants of African, Asian, Latin, and Native American descent commonly have a hyperpigmented blue-black to purple area on the sacrum or buttocks called a **Mongolian spot**. It is formed from the deep melanocytes and gradually fades during the first year of life.

Other types of birthmarks may appear on infants. Some may remain for their lifetimes, and others may fade or disappear. **Café au lait spots** are round or oval areas of light brown pigmentation present at birth. A person with more than about five of these spots may have a condition called **neurofibromatosis**.

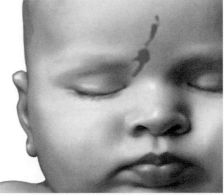

Stork bites, or **nevus simplex**, are common birthmarks caused by the dilation of certain blood vessels. They are present in about one-third of all newborns and are often temporary. They are generally found on the forehead, nose, lip, or back of the newborn's neck. A portwine stain, or **nevus flammeus**, may also be present at birth in some infants. It appears as a large, flat, red area sometimes covering the scalp or face. The area consists of capillaries and may darken with crying or exercise. This lesion will not fade with time, but may be diminished or removed with laser surgery.

Stork bites are present in about one-third of all newborns.

Erythema toxicum is a common rash of infancy that appears within the first four days of life as a red, macular, papular rash of tiny bumps on the cheeks, trunk, back, and buttocks. There is no known cause and no treatment is necessary. **Acrocyanosis** is a bluish color around the lips, hands, fingernails, feet, and toenails. It may last for a few hours after birth but disappears when the newborn is warmed.

A common occurrence in newborns is **jaundice**, characterized by a yellowing of the skin, sclera, and mucous membranes because of the increased numbers of red blood cells that are broken down after the third or fourth day of life.

Soft Skills for Health Care: Conflict Negotiation

Conflict negotiation, sometimes called mediation, is an important skill in the medical profession. You will be faced with conflict over the course of your career, and having the ability to resolve various situations will be beneficial to your success.

With the varying number of communicable illnesses/conditions present in today's environment, many medical practices have elected to designate separate waiting areas for sick and nonsick patients, especially in the specialty of pediatrics.

Consider the following scenario: After a young patient suspected to have chicken pox virus checks in, the parent of a child being seen for a sports physical approaches the desk. This parent is visibly upset that the potentially "contagious" child and his guardian have elected to sit in the area designated for nonsick patients. To maintain a harmonious environment in which all patients feel safe, comfortable, and respected, you will be expected to enforce the policies and procedures of the office with compassion and precautions to safeguard confidentiality.

Acne (technically called *acne vulgaris*) is the most common skin problem of adolescence, occurring to some degree in nearly all teenagers. Sebaceous glands become more active during the early teenage years and produce excess oil. Acne usually appears on the face, but sometimes manifests on the chest, back, and shoulders. The two most common types of blemish are **open comedones** (blackheads) caused by a sebum plug partially blocking the pore, and **closed comedones** (whiteheads), when the pore becomes completely blocked. Severe cases of acne occur when blocked pores become so irritated that their walls break. Types of severe acne include papules (large pimples that are hard to touch), pustules (pimples filled with a yellowish-pus), and nodules (large pimples that lie deep in the skin, harden, and cause pain).

Atopic eczema is a condition common in childhood, and 75 percent of all diagnoses occur in the first year of life. Although not exclusive to children, eczema affects 12–15 percent of school-aged children compared with 2–10 percent of the adult population. Patients generally experience dry, cracked, itchy skin in areas with creases (e.g., inside elbows, behind knees, and along the neck line). Efforts to prevent flare-ups include limiting exposure to scented soaps, lotions, and laundry detergents, metal jewelry, and pets.

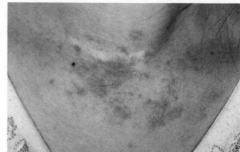

Atopic eczema

Psoriasis is another common skin condition that affects more than 5 million people in the United States. This chronic autoimmune disease is a direct result of the overproduction of skin cells. Dead cells appear scaly and become inflamed patches, causing intense itching. Unlike eczema, psoriasis is commonly present on thicker areas of skin (e.g., knees, elbows, palms of hands, and soles of feet).

Several skin changes appear as individuals age. **Angiomas**, known as both *cherry angiomas* and *senile angiomas*, are small, punctate (marked by spots or tiny holes), slightly raised bright-red dots that appear on the trunk. They are not malignant but may be profuse and cause the individual to feel self-conscious. Skin tags, or **acrochordons**, are overgrowths of normal skin that form on a stalk and have a small projection. They commonly appear on the eyelids, cheeks, neck, axillae, and trunk.

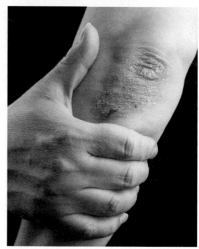

Psoriasis

The growth rate of hair and nails slows during middle age, and the amount of hair in axillary and pubic areas decreases.

In the Know: ABCD's of Melanoma

It is important to be aware of the ABCD's of melanoma. The ABCD rule is used to evaluate changes in the appearance of a mole that may indicate the presence of a melanoma, the deadliest form of skin cancer. A medical evaluation of the mole is recommended if any of the following apply:

Asymmetry (if a line is drawn through the middle of the mole, would the sides differ?)

Border (are edges uneven or irregular?)

Color (are varying shades or colors present?)

Diameter (is the mole raised and experiencing growth?)

Menopausal women may develop hairs on the chin from a decrease in female hormones that allows the male hormones to produce these secondary male characteristics. Men may develop more hair in the ears, nose, and eyebrows but lose hair on the head. Male-pattern balding, or alopecia, is an inherited trait. In both men and women, the hair gradually turns gray due to the reduction in the number of cells within hair follicles producing melanin. The decrease in pigment results in gray, silver, or white hair.

Pregnant Women

Pregnancy causes many changes. The skin stretches, and **striae**, or stretch marks, appear on the abdomen, the breasts, and sometimes the thighs. Striae result when the elastic collagen fibers break down. Striae usually fade after the delivery but do not disappear. A brownish-black line, the **linea nigra**, appears down the midline of the abdomen. A brownish hyperpigmented patch called **chloasma** may appear on the face. These markings disappear after the mother gives birth. Many pregnant women develop **vascular spiders**, tiny red lines with radiating branches, on the face, neck, upper chest, and arms.

Striae, or stretch marks, on an abdomen.

The linea nigra appears down the midline of the abdomen.

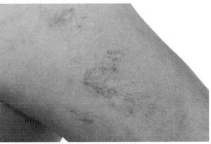

Vascular spiders (spider veins) have a radiating branch appearance.

Seniors

Age-related changes occur to the skin. Daily exposure to the environment contributes to the skin's gradual breakdown. Aging skin loses elasticity and begins to sag. The stratum corneum and the dermis thin and flatten, causing wrinkling. The progressive loss of elastin, collagen, and subcutaneous fat coupled with decreased muscle tone increase wrinkling and decrease protection. Sebaceous and sweat glands secrete less (a condition called **xerosis**), leaving the skin dry and diminishing its ability to maintain normal body temperature. This decreased temperature regulation can make the individual hypersensitive to heat; at the same time, loss of subcutaneous fat often makes the older person more sensitive to cold.

These changes cause the skin to become more fragile and break down more easily. Any trauma can produce senile purpura, purplish discolorations. Senile **lentigines**, or liver spots, appear as speckling in areas that were exposed to the sun, usually on the arms and hands. Some areas of the skin may appear yellowish and leathery. **Keratoses** are thick lesions with raised areas of pigmentation that usually appear on the trunk but may also be seen on the face. They rarely become cancerous. The risk of skin cancer increases with aging, particularly if there was significant sun exposure in childhood or young adulthood. One type of lesion that can become cancerous is **actinic keratosis**, which appears as a rough, raised, reddish-tan area, often with a silvery-white scale attached to the plaque. These lesions can develop into **squamous cell carcinoma** see Table 3.5).

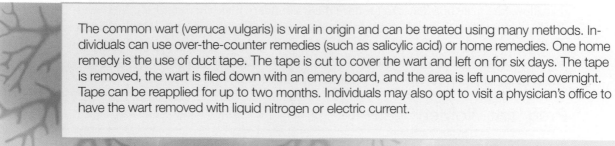

In the Know: The Common Wart

The common wart (verruca vulgaris) is viral in origin and can be treated using many methods. Individuals can use over-the-counter remedies (such as salicylic acid) or home remedies. One home remedy is the use of duct tape. The tape is cut to cover the wart and left on for six days. The tape is removed, the wart is filed down with an emery board, and the area is left uncovered overnight. Tape can be reapplied for up to two months. Individuals may also opt to visit a physician's office to have the wart removed with liquid nitrogen or electric current.

Checkpoint **3.2**

Answer the following questions to identify any areas of the section that you may need to review.

1. What is the name of the atopic dermatitis caused by an allergy?

_____

2. What is the most common form of skin cancer?

_____

3. What is the medical term often used in reference to birthmarks?

_____

Exercise **3.7** Word Analysis

Practice using root words. Break each word into parts, analyze the parts, and define the term.

Example:

| angioma | *angi* = blood vessel | tumor composed of blood vessels |
| | *-oma* = tumor | |

Term	**Analysis**	**Definition**
1. melanocyte	_____	_____
	_____	
2. ecchymosis	_____	_____
	_____	
3. cyanosis	_____	_____
	_____	
4. chronic	_____	_____
	_____	
5. pustule	_____	_____
	_____	

Exercise 3.8   Comprehension Check

Circle the correct term in each sentence.

1. Physiologic jaundice/Linea nigra was observed in three of four infants in the neonatal intensive care nursery.

2. The capillary/erythema toxicum rash on the infant's cheeks will not require treatment.

3. We will recommend laser surgery to remove the nevus flammeus/Mongolian spot.

4. Ephelides/Striae, also called *stretch marks*, are common during pregnancy.

5. Increased activity in the sebaceous glands/stratum corneum frequently produces acne during the teenage years.

Exercise 3.9   Matching

Match the terms in column 1 with the definitions in column 2. Write the letter of the definition on the line provided.

1. _____ dermatoses   **a.** wart

2. _____ angioma   **b.** blue color of the extremities

3. _____ acrocyanosis   **c.** vessel tumor

4. _____ nevus flammeus   **d.** bright red, congenital nevus found on the head

5. _____ verruca   **e.** conditions of the skin

Exercise 3.10   Word Building

Build words from combining forms, prefixes, and suffixes to fit the definitions given. Write the correct term on the line provided. Then write the meaning of the root word or combining form, the prefix, and/or the suffix for each term.

1. inflammation of the skin _____

   _____

2. pertaining to flow of oil _____

   _____

3. condition of blueness of the extremities _____

   _____

4. tumor of vessels _____

   _____

5. skin condition from orange pigment in the blood _____

   _____

Exercise 3.11 Spelling Check

On the line beside each term, write the correct spelling.

1. zerosis   _____
2. senilepurpera _____
3. exzema   _____
4. lineanagra   _____
5. impetago   _____

6. nodlue   _____
7. purtule   _____
8. vewruca   _____
9. xantoma   _____
10. villigo   _____

Exercise 3.12 Identification

Identify the relationship between anatomical and diagnostic terms. Label the pictures with the term that corresponds to the description of the abnormality.

_____ _____ _____ _____ _____

1. round, flat, pigmented area

2. palpable lesion that is rounded, solid, and raised < 1 cm

3. deep depression that extends into the dermis

4. area of papules merged to form lesion >1 cm in diameter

5. linear crack that extends into the dermis

Diagnostic Tests and Examinations

Various tests and equipment are used to diagnose skin problems. The most common include biopsies, patch tests, scratch tests, intradermal injections, and Wood's lamp.

The most important tool for determining the diagnosis of a skin lesion is a procedure called a biopsy. A **biopsy** involves removing a sample of the affected tissue and examining it under the microscope. The physician administers a local anesthetic to numb the area and uses a surgical scalpel to remove the specimen. A hole-punch-type instrument is used to perform a **punch biopsy**. Often, special immunofluorescent tests are performed to assist with the diagnosis. A dye stains the specimen, and a diagnosis is made based on how the lesion absorbs the dye (see Table 3.10).

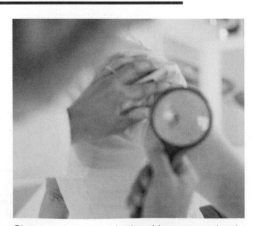

Changes that occur in the skin are examined by a physician.

TABLE 3.10 Integumentary Tests, Examinations, and Equipment

Test or Equipment	Description
biopsy	removing a sample of tissue to examine under a microscope
dermatome	instrument used to remove split-skin grafts
intradermal injection	suspected allergens are placed just below the epidermis using a needle
patch test	suspected allergens are placed on the skin's surface and covered for several days
punch biopsy	type of biopsy that uses a hole-punch type of instrument to remove a sample of tissue
scratch test	suspected allergens are scratched into the skin using an instrument
Wood's lamp	produces ultraviolet light to diagnose different species of tinea

A physician might perform a patch test to identify a patient's particular allergies. In a **patch test**, the suspected allergens are placed on the surface of the skin and covered for several days to determine the reaction. A **scratch test** involves scratching the surface of the skin with an instrument coated with different serums that contain the essence of various allergens. Similarly, **intradermal injections** of allergens can be placed just below the epidermis using a tiny needle. Any area that has a local inflammatory response is considered an allergen for that individual.

Equipment is also used for diagnosing skin conditions. A **Wood's lamp** is used to view skin or hair samples under an ultraviolet light to diagnose different species of tinea manus (ringworm) and other bacterial or fungal infections.

In the Know: Is Indoor Tanning Safe?

Tanned skin has been popular in the United States for decades, but sunlight contains dangerous ultraviolet rays—ultraviolet A (UVA) and ultraviolet B (UVB)—that can do long-term damage to the skin. Agents, such as sunscreen, can decrease the damage caused by these rays if they are used properly. Many people choose to tan using tanning booths, but does tanning in a booth produce the same harmful effects as tanning on the beach?

According to the Food and Drug Administration (FDA), indoor tanning salons use both UVA and UVB rays.[1] UVA rays penetrate deeply and can break down the connective structures deep within the skin. It is believed that UVA exposure causes increased wrinkling in a person's later years because of the damage to the deeper layers. UVB rays burn the outer layers of the skin and may be even more dangerous.

Although they are required by the FDA to offer protective glasses to customers, some tanning salons may not comply. Without the special glasses, UVA rays can penetrate and harm the retinas of the eyes. It is important that the tanning salon program the lights to shut off automatically at a time appropriate for the client's skin type to minimize exposure.

Just as sun exposure increases the risk of skin cancer, liver spots, and other disorders later in life, so can exposure to UV rays within a tanning booth.

[1]"Indoor Tanning: The Risks of Ultraviolet Rays," FDA. http://www.fda.gov/ForConsumers/ConsumerUpdates/ucm186687.htm (May 22, 2015).

Checkpoint 3.3

Answer the following questions to identify any areas of the section that you may need to review.

1. Identify three tests used to diagnose skin problems.

_____

2. Which test involves removing a sample of the affected tissue and examining it under the microscope?

_____

3. What is the name of equipment used to view skin or hair samples under an ultraviolet light to diagnose different species of tinea?

_____

Treatments

Healthcare practitioners use predetermined guidelines to direct patient care. These guidelines, known as clinical practice guidelines and evidence-based practices, have been developed by the specialty societies based on past clinical research. They represent the treatment pathways that have achieved the best outcomes. Treatment decisions generally fall into three categories: surgical, clinical, and pharmacological.

Surgical treatments are generally invasive as they involve a puncture or an incision into the skin. *Clinical treatments* are generally noninvasive and involve nonsurgical techniques (e.g., physical therapy). *Pharmacological treatments* involve the utilization of medicines (drugs) to treat specific illnesses or diseases. Medication therapies are regulated by the Food and Drug Administration (FDA). To be approved by the FDA for use in the United States, every medicine must be backed by research studies that have shown the medication to be effective in its treatment of a given disease and has a tolerable safety profile. The following sections provide an overview of treatments common to the integumentary system.

Surgical Treatments

Did You Know?

Tattoo removal requires surgical procedures to remove ink from beneath the surface of the skin. These procedures include laser surgery, surgical removal, and dermabrasion.

Some surgical procedures involving the skin are intended to improve or preserve the appearance of the individual. Applying the Mohs technique, for example, a surgeon removes a cancer layer by layer and tests each layer before removing the next. When a layer's test finally shows no cancer, no more layers are removed. The technique minimizes the amount of skin removed while working to ensure the cancer is completely removed. Several techniques are used to perform reconstructive surgery.

Burn victims undergo procedures to remove the burned skin, known as **debridement** (from the French word débrider, meaning "unbridle"). A piece of skin tissue that has been removed from the body (by burns or other conditions) is called **eschar**.

One of the most common procedures today is **laser treatment**, which uses a focused beam of light to remove skin lesions, unwanted hair, varicose veins, and other undesirable lesions. The procedure produces little pain or discomfort, and the area remains red for only a short period of time.

Dermabrasion is a procedure that rubs an abrasive device against the skin, similar to sanding a piece of wood to make it smooth. The rubbing can remove the upper layers of the skin and some scars, such as acne scars or tattoos. Another procedure is called a **chemical peel**. An acidic chemical is put on the skin of the face to burn the area. A new epidermis forms, and the burned skin is sloughed away. A chemical peel can remove small lines and scars on the face. Table 3.11 describes procedures and surgeries related to the skin. Cosmetic surgery uses several methods to improve a person's physical appearance.

TABLE 3.11 Surgical Treatments Associated with the Skin

Treatment		Description
allograft (homograft)	[**al**-uh-grahft]	the surgical graft of tissue from one human donor to another
autograft	[**ah**-tO-grahft]	the surgical graft of one's own skin from one part of the body to another
blepharoplasty	[blef-ar-O-**plas**-tee]	procedure to alter the appearance of the eyelids
breast augmentation	[og-men-**tay**-shun]	procedure that utilizes breast implants to increase or restore the size of breast volume
breast reduction		procedure to remove breast tissue to decrease the size of breast volume, also known as *reduction mammoplasty*
buttock augmentation (Brazilian butt lift)	[og-men-**tay**-shun]	procedure involving the transfer of fat to increase the size and roundness of the buttocks
debridement	[day-**breed**-mon]	procedure to remove dead skin
dermabrasion	[der-mah-**bray**-shun]	procedure using an abrasive device to remove scarring
micropigmentation (permanent makeup)	[my-cro-pig-men-**tay**-shun]	procedure involving a handheld device that punctures the skin with a thin needle to place a permanent pigment into the intended location; generally used to outline the eyes, or add color to the lips and cheeks
rhytidectomy (facelift)	[rih-tih-**deck**-tuh-mee]	procedure to remove excess fat, tighten muscles, and redrape skin across face
skin graft (SG)		skin transplant performed to replace skin loss due to burns, infections, trauma (damaged skin is removed and then replaced)
xenograft (heterograft)	[**ze**-no-grahft]	the surgical graft of tissue from one species to another, generally a pig, used in place of an autograft

Clinical Treatments

In today's society, how we look and what we wear are important to our own and other's perceptions of us. Although wrinkles can reveal much of our life history—laughing, worrying, frowning, too much sun, cigarette smoking—we don't want others to use them when forming an opinion about us. There are many medical treatments for facial wrinkles in an industry that's trying to keep up with our aging society. Many of these fall into the categories of topicals and injectables.

Dermal fillers (injectables) are often used to address wrinkles and scars in the skin as a result of aging, sun exposure, heredity, and lifestyle. Fillers are also used to plump thin lips via injections. The FDA approves fillers as medical devices. The injections are prescribed and administered by a physician.

Topicals are also prescribed by a physician, but are applied to the surface of the skin. These include chemical peels and creams. Table 3.12 describes several facial cosmetic treatments that may reduce the appearance of wrinkles.

TABLE 3.12 | Clinical Treatments Associated with the Skin

Type of Treatment	Treatment (Drug Name)	What Is It?	How Does It Work?
Fillers and Injectables	*botulinum* toxin type A (Botox, Dysport)	purified, low-dose form of toxin released by the bacterium that causes botulism	blocks nerve signals to muscles that cause wrinkles
	bovine collagen (Zyderm, Zyplast)	protein that forms skin, bones, and cartilage (purified from cow's tissue)	replaces depleted collagen under wrinkles
	fat transplantation (microlipoinjection)	involves the removal of fat from thigh, abdomen, or buttock, and its injection into wrinkles	fills in wrinkles
	human-based collagen (Cosmoderm, Cosmoplast)	identical to bovine collagen, but made from human sources	replaces depleted collagen in wrinkles
	hyaluronic acid (Captique, Restylane, Hylaform)	natural sugar molecule that adds volume and shape to skin	filler that draws water to the skin's surface to restore volume and elasticity
Topicals (available by prescription) and Skin Resurfacing	tretinoin (Retin-A, Renova)	vitamin A cream	lightens skin and replaces old skin with new skin
	chemical peels (chemexfoliation)	chemicals ranging from mild (glycolic acid) to harsh (phenol)	remove damaged epidermis to reveal new, smoother skin
	laser resurfacing	high-energy light beam lasers	removes epidermis, while heating dermis to stimulate the growth of new skin that grows back smoother and tighter
	microdermabrasion	sandblaster	gently sands the epidermis to remove the thicker outer layer and stimulate collagen production; treats scarring, discoloration, and stretch marks

Pharmacological Treatments

The pharmacological treatments used for the integumentary system are mostly topical agents. Abradants contain substances that act as an abrasive to remove dry, calloused skin. Several acne preparations, primarily applied to the skin to dry lesions, are available over the counter or by prescription. Severe acne may be treated with varying combinations of retinoids, antibiotics, and/or steroid injections.

Topical antibacterial and antifungal creams and ointments are used to prevent infections and kill bacteria and fungi. The salves are usually rubbed into the wound and can be covered to provide a protective barrier in the case of small burns or cuts and scrapes. Atopic dermatitis is treated with anti-inflammatory agents, which decrease inflammation, control itch, and help to soothe the tissue.

Dandruff, seborrhea, and psoriasis can be treated with coal tar, zinc, and emollient (moistening) preparations. Oral medications are now available to shorten the duration of symptomatic outbreaks of Herpes Simplex 1 (commonly called fever blisters). They also can decrease the chances of infecting a partner. A great deal of research is in the area of vaccine development. Table 3.13 lists a number of commonly prescribed pharmacological treatments.

TABLE 3.13 **Pharmacological Treatments Associated with the Skin**

Type of Treatment	Treatment	How Does It Work?
anesthetics	lidocaine	topical agents used to reduce pain and discomfort; *an-* (not, without), *-esthetic* (pertaining to feeling or sensation)
antibacterials (antibiotics)	bacitracin (topical), erythromycin (oral)	topical agents used to treat skin infections and prevent bacterial growth, oral agent used to treat acne; *anti-* (against)
antifungals	Lotrimin	topical agents used to treat skins conditions such as ringworm and athlete's foot
antihistamines	Claritin, Zyrtec	oral agents used to reduce symptoms triggered by allergens (i.e. itching)
anti-inflammatories/NSAIDS (nonsteroidal anti-inflammatory drugs) [**en**-saids]	aspirin, ibuprofen, Tylenol	oral agents used to reduce inflammation and pain
antipruritic	hydrocortisone	topical agent used to relieve itching
antiseptics	hydrogen peroxide	topical agent used to prevent germ growth around a wound
corticosteroids	prednisone	lotions, creams, or ointments used to treat eczema
emollients	Lubriderm	lotions, creams, ointments, or gels used to soften the skin
immunosuppressants	methotrexate	topical agents used to treat severe cases of eczema and psoriasis
keratolytics	salicylic acid, Oxy-10	topical agents used to treat warts, corns, calluses; *kerat/o* (hard, horny), *-lytic* (pertaining to breaking down)
pediculicides	Nix	topical agents used to destroy lice; *pedicul/o* (lice), *-cide* (killing)
protectives	sunscreen	topical agents used to protect the skin from ultraviolet sunlight
retinoids	Retin-A, Tazorac	gels or creams derived from vitamin A, used to treat acne and psoriasis

In the Know: Future Directions of Medical Tourism

Medical tourism (health tourism) is the practice of healthcare consumers who travel to a country outside their country of residence for the purpose of obtaining medical treatment. The Centers for Disease Control and Prevention estimates that approximately 750,000 US citizens travel abroad for medical treatment annually. Although a large portion of these individuals are immigrants returning to their home countries for treatment, the majority of medical tourists are simply seeking alternatives for cheaper care. Cosmetic surgery, dentistry, and heart surgery are the most common surgical procedures performed.[1]

An estimated 415,000 medical tourists were documented to visit Turkey in 2014. Revenues were reported to reach approximately $1 billion, up 75 percent from 2013. The majority of medical tourists in Turkey obtained medical treatment in areas related to hair transplants, liposuction, and cancer.

This trend carries a high risk for medical error and death as a result of complications attributed to poor communication and lack of follow-up care. Healthcare consumers must carefully research these "medical tourism resorts" to ensure they have regulations in place for infection control, physician credentialing, and the purchasing/administration of prescription medications.

[1] http://www.cdc.gov/features/medicaltourism/

Checkpoint 3.4

Answer the following questions to identify any areas of the section that you may need to review.

1. Which topical cosmetic treatment uses a sandblaster to remove the thicker outer layer of skin and stimulate the growth of collagen?

_____

2. What surgical cosmetic procedure involves the utilization of a thin needle to apply permanent makeup?

_____

3. What surgical cosmetic procedure alters the appearance of the eyelids?

_____

Abbreviations

In the medical field, information is generally recorded in medical charts and in the electronic medical record and provided to healthcare professionals in medical shorthand. It is important that healthcare professionals become familiar with the abbreviations utilized on a daily basis and to avoid abbreviations that cause confusion. Table 3.14 provides a list of common abbreviations used in reference to the integumentary system.

TABLE 3.14 Abbreviations Associated with the Integumentary System

Abbreviation	Meaning
BCC	basal cell carcinoma
b.i.d.	twice a day
bx	biopsy
derm.	dermatology
dx	diagnosis
FS	frozen section
H	hypodermic
H&P	history and physical
hx	history
I&D	incision and drainage
ID	intradermal
KOH	potassium hydroxide
p.c.	after a meal
PPD	purified protein derivative (utilized as a skin test for tuberculosis)
SCC	squamous cell carcinoma
STSG	split-thickness skin graft
subq; SQ	subcutaneous
ung.	ointment
UV	ultraviolet

Exercise 3.13 Word Analysis

Read each sentence and break each underlined word into its individual parts, using lines or slashes to divide the parts. Write a definition for the term on the line provided.

1. The infant has insufficient <u>adipose</u> tissue. _____

2. A 15-year-old male presents with <u>dermatitis</u> on his hands. _____

3. The patient was <u>cyanotic</u> after exposure to the 18 degree temperature. _____

4. This 30-year-old male displays a <u>squamous cell carcinoma</u>. _____

5. A 5-year-old female has a large <u>nevus</u> covering the right side of her face, neck, and shoulder. _____

_____

Exercise 3.14 Comprehension Check

Read each sentence. Answer the question after each statement. Then write the meaning of the underlined words. You may need to use a medical dictionary for this exercise, but keep your answers brief.

1. The <u>debridement</u> procedure, although painful, was necessary for healing. Is debridement removal of hair or removal of dead tissue?

_____

2. The burn wounds were covered with a thick <u>eschar</u>. Is eschar a crust or an ointment?

_____

3. A chemical peel causes <u>sloughing</u> of damaged skin and formation of new epidermis. Does sloughing refer to dissolving or separating?

_____

4. The child received <u>first degree burns</u> when she played in the sun too long. Is sun exposure harmful?

_____

5. The <u>rule of nines</u> helps assess burn injury. Does the rule refer to depth or the area of a burn?

_____

Exercise 3.15 Matching

Match the procedure or treatment listed in column 1 with the definition or goal listed in column 2. Write the corresponding letter on the line provided.

1. _____ biopsy

2. _____ debridement

3. _____ dermabrasion

4. _____ laser treatment

5. _____ chemical peel

a. remove eschar

b. diagnose skin lesion

c. acid burn; remove fine lines and scars

d. remove unwanted lesions and hair

e. rub; remove some lines and scars

Exercise 3.16   Word Building

Practice building words by combining roots, prefixes, and suffixes. Find word parts in your text and construct medical terms for the definitions that follow. Write the term on the line provided.

1. study of the skin _____

2. condition of numbness (without sensation) _____

3. flow of oil _____

4. within the skin _____

5. using an abrasive device to remove scars on the skin _____

Exercise 3.17   Spelling Check

Write the correct plural form for each term on the line provided.

1. angioma _____   3. comedo _____

2. keratosis _____   4. condyloma_____

Exercise 3.18   Word Maps

Categorize the following conditions by the general age span during which they occur: newborns, pregnant women, and seniors. Then define each term and draw a box around its root(s).

alopecia	chloasma	erythema toxicum
milia	acrocyanosis	senile purpura
melanoma	vascular spiders	linea nigra

Newborns

_____

_____

_____

Pregnant Women

_____

_____

_____

Seniors

_____

_____

_____

Chapter Review

After successfully completing this chapter, you should be able to correctly answer the following review questions. Answers are provided in the back of the text. Use this self-assessment opportunity to check your understanding of the content and determine whether you need to revisit any of the chapter's content.

Crossword Puzzle

Use the clues provided to fill in the puzzle with the correct terms. Enter one letter per square.

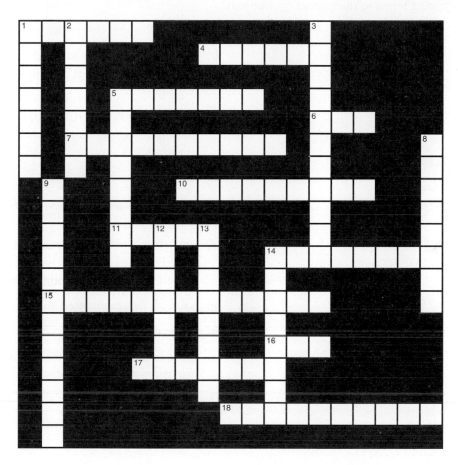

Across

1. small round elevation on the skin

4. a solid, raised area larger than 1 cm

5. dry skin

6. incision and drainage

7. the vertical line that appears on the abdomen of a pregnant woman

10. above the skin; outermost layer of skin

11. tiny white papules present on the face of the newborn; whiteheads

14. white patches (depigmented) on the skin; without melanocytes

15. surgical repair of the skin

16. abbreviation for ointment

17. on the surface of the body (skin)

18. a red, inflamed area around the nail, usually from an infection

Down

1. areas of hemorrhage into the skin
2. small round lesion containing pus
3. procedure to remove dead skin
5. a yellowish nodule of the skin

8. a malignancy formed from the cells that produce melanin
9. face lift
12. a brownish spot on the skin; a freckle
13. baldness; hair loss
14. pertaining to vessels

Matching

Match the following terms to their proper definitions.

1. _____ bulla
2. _____ macule
3. _____ tinea pedis
4. _____ Wood's lamp
5. _____ alopecia
6. _____ patch test
7. _____ cuticle
8. _____ chemical peels
9. _____ hirsutism
10. _____ collagen

a. fold of skin that covers the root

b. the connective tissue in the dermis; a tough protein substance that prevents the skin from tearing

c. used to view skin or hair samples under an ultraviolet light to diagnose different species of tinea

d. the absence of hair; baldness

e. an abnormal growth of hair, particularly in areas where there is usually very little hair

f. procedure in which suspected allergens are placed on the surface of the skin and covered for several days to determine the reaction

g. a round, flat, pigmented area

h. ringworm of the foot

i. procedure that removes the surface layer of skin using an acidic chemical

j. a fluid-filled lesion larger than 1 cm that is thin-walled and ruptures easily

Identification

Correctly label the illustration using the provided terms. Write the correct term on the line provided for each of the corresponding locations in the figure.

Terms:

opening of sweat gland   stratum corneum   sebaceous gland
dermis   subcutaneous (adipose) tissue   arrector pili muscle
epidermis   sebum
stratum germinativum   hair follicle

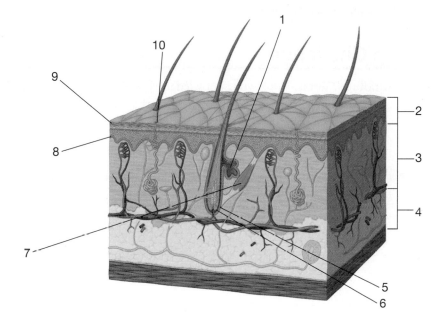

1. _____	6. _____
2. _____	7. _____
3. _____	8. _____
4. _____	9. _____
5. _____	10. _____

Abbreviations

Answer the following questions using abbreviations.

1. Meg was contacted by the local health department following prolonged contact with a coworker recently diagnosed with tuberculosis (TB). She was scheduled to come in for a screening to test for active or dormant TB. What is this screening commonly called? _____

2. Joyce is scheduled to have allergy testing today. During this particular allergy test, a small amount of allergen is injected into the skin to trigger a response. What are the name and abbreviation for this type of procedure? _____

3. This particular procedure, most commonly performed by a dermatologist, involves the removal of a small sample of skin for examination under a microscope. What is the name and abbreviation for this type of procedure? _____

4. Jasmine arrives at her physician's office complaining of severe pain from a pus-filled area on her inner thigh. She is diagnosed with an abscess and the boil is then removed by means of an outpatient process that includes cutting and removing the pus. What is the name and abbreviation for this type of procedure? _____

5. The sudden onset of the winter cold has resulted in a large number of pediatric patients with uncontrolled patches of eczema. What abbreviation will more than likely be found on prescription tabs to provide these patients with some relief?_____

Word-Building Challenge

Review the following list of new terms. Apply your knowledge of integumentary word parts to accurately identify the meaning of each new term. Write your answer on the line provided and then check your definition against the answer provided in the appendix.

Term   **Definition**

1. transcutaneous _____

_____

_____

2. hyperhidrosis _____

_____

_____

3. lipoma _____

_____

_____

4. onychomalacia _____

_____

_____

5. dyschromia _____

_____

_____

Extension Activities

Complete the following activities as assigned by your instructor.

1. Research the importance of the daily utilization of sunscreen on the skin. Write a brief informative essay that identifies the following: What is its intended purpose? What role does SPF (sun protection factor) play in the efficacy of its use? Is it designed for use in all populations or more beneficial to certain skin types?

2. You have been appointed as a preceptor to a medical assisting intern in your medical office. Today's assigned task is the introduction to the "rule of nines." Create a short presentation (using PowerPoint or your own visuals) that describes how the rule of nines is used in the process of healthcare reimbursement. Be prepared to present your work.

3. Historically, the presence of decubitis ulcers, bedsores, in patients of skilled nursing facilities has been attributed to staff negligence. Identify an example of a recent medical malpractice suit related to this particular area of care. Provide a one-page summary of the background of the case and the outcome.

Student eResources

The Course Navigator learning management system that accompanies this textbook offers multiple opportunities to master chapter content, including end-of-chapter exercises, a glossary of key terms with audio pronunciations, games, pronunciation coach, and additional activities such as engaging with the BioDigital® Human.

The Musculoskeletal System

> " Just as we develop our physical muscles through overcoming opposition, such as lifting weights, we develop our character muscles by overcoming challenges and adversity. "

—**Stephen R. Covey,** American businessman

Translation Challenge

Read this excerpt from an orthopedist's records and answer the questions that follow.

CHIEF COMPLAINT Right knee pain.

SUBJECTIVE A 17 y/o male patient presents today with pain in right knee. Patient states that pain has worsened over last few days and that he has had no prior injury to the area. Patient describes the pain as achy and more intense during track practice, especially when running long distances. Patient states the knee makes a crackling noise upon movement.

OBJECTIVE Patient has tenderness upon full extension of knee joint. Crepitus present upon extension. Patient has pain when applying resistive pressure to knee joint and upon palpation.

ASSESSMENT X-ray of right patella shows misalignment of bone. No fracture or dislocation.

PLAN Will order MRI to r/o chondromalacia. Follow-up scheduled with patient next week. He will continue to use ice and OTC medication for pain.

1. What is chondromalacia?

2. What is crepitus?

3. How could an MRI reveal an injury to the knee joint that was not identified by the initial X-ray?

Learning Objectives

4.1 List and define word parts most commonly used to describe the musculoskeletal system.

4.2 Use word parts to correctly analyze vocabulary related to the musculoskeletal system.

4.3 Identify structures of the musculoskeletal system.

4.4 Describe the function and physiology of bones and joints.

4.5 Describe the function and physiology of muscles and muscle tissue.

4.6 Recognize and describe common conditions of the musculoskeletal system.

4.7 Name tests and treatments for musculoskeletal system abnormalities or pathologies.

4.8 State the meaning of abbreviations related to the musculoskeletal system.

4.9 Use musculoskeletal system vocabulary correctly in written and oral contexts.

4.10 Correctly spell and pronounce terminology related to the musculoskeletal system.

COURSE NAVIGATOR

Access Additional Chapter Resources

The musculoskeletal system gives the body strength, structure, and the capability of movement. Think of the skeleton as being similar to the framework of a house. The function of this framework is to support the internal components and to protect the contents from outside forces. The human skeleton consists of 206 bones bound together by ligaments (*ligament/o*). **Ligaments** are tissues that serve as points of connection where two pieces of the structure (bones) meet; these points of connection are also called **joints**.

Bone movement is controlled by the contraction of skeletal muscles, which are attached to each other by bands of tissue called **tendons** (*tend/o*). Bone is also the site of blood cell formation and the storage place for minerals, such as calcium. This process is formally called hematopoiesis (*hemat/o*, meaning "blood" and *-poiesis*, meaning "formation").

The descriptions of the musculoskeletal system and its parts are separated into sections. The first section describes the structure and function of the skeleton, the second section describes the structure and function of the muscles, and the third section details the combined functions, and the conditions, tests, and treatments related to this body system.

> **What's in a Word?**
>
> The suffix *-algia* is commonly used in this body system and means "pain." For example, the term *neuralgia* means "nerve pain."

In the Know: Specialists of the Musculoskeletal System

The field of medicine concerned with the musculoskeletal system is **orthopedics**, and the physician who specializes in the musculoskeletal system is an **orthopedist**. Another health-care professional in this specialty is the **chiropractor**, who practices **chiropractic medicine**, an area of care devoted to restoring health by treating diseases and injuries of the body as a whole. Chiropractic medicine focuses on treating health problems through the theory that the body is better able to heal itself when the bones are in proper alignment and the body is in a good nutritional state. An **osteopathic physician** is a doctor of osteopathy (DO). The DO is trained and educated as an MD, but with an emphasis on primary care and lifestyle interventions. **Rheumatologists** are physicians who treat patients suffering from diseases of the joints, connective tissues, and collagen, among other structures. A **podiatrist** (doctor of podiatry, DP) specializes in diagnosing and treating disorders of the foot. Conditions of the musculoskeletal system can also be diagnosed by non-specialists (e.g. Family Practitioners and Internal Medicine physicians).

Musculoskeletal System Word Parts

As with other body systems, a core of combining forms serves as the source for most of the medical words associated with the musculoskeletal system. Table 4.1 lists the common combining forms and suffixes for the skeletal system, and Table 4.2 lists the most common combining forms for the muscular system.

TABLE 4.1 Word Parts Associated with the Skeletal System

Combining Form	Meaning	Example
arthr/o	joint	arthritis (inflammation of the joints)
cervic/o	neck	cervical spine (pertaining to the neck region of the spinal column)
crani/o	head	craniospinal (pertaining to the head and spine)
dactyl/o	fingers or toes	polydactyly (condition of more than five fingers or toes on one hand or foot)
ili/o	ilium; hip	iliosacral (pertaining to the ilium and sacrum)
lumb/o	lower back	lumbar (pertaining to the lower back and sacrum)
mandibul/o	lower jaw	submandibular (pertaining to the region below the lower jaw)
orth/o	straight	orthopedics (field of medicine, surgery, concerned with conditions of the musculoskeletal system)
osse/o	bony	osseous (porous, calcified substance from which bones are made)
oste/o	bone	osteoarthritis (inflammation of the bones and joints)
pelv/o	pelvis	pelvimetry (assessment of the female pelvis in relation to the birth of a baby)

Continues

Combining Form	Meaning	Example
pod/o	foot	podiatry (branch of medicine concerned with the diagnosis, medical, and surgical treatment of disorders of the foot, ankle, and lower extremity)
sacr/o	sacrum	sacroiliac (pertaining to the sacrum and the ilium)
scapul/o	scapula	scapulopexy (surgical fixation of the scapula to the chest wall)
spondyl/o	vertebrae	spondylosis (abnormal condition characterized by stiffening of the vertebral joints)
stern/o	chest	sternocostal (pertaining to the chest and rib)
tars/o	tarsal bones in the foot	tarsoclasis (surgical fracture of the tarsus)
tempor/o	temporal (a skull bone)	temporoauricular (pertaining to the temple and the ear)
vertebr/o	vertebra	vertebrocostal (pertaining to the vertebra and rib)
zyg/o	a yoke; a type of joining; the cheek bone	zygomatic bone (cheek bone)

Suffixes	Meaning	Example
-clasia	surgically break	osteoclasia (surgical fracture of a bone to fix a deformity)
-desis	stabilize, fuse, bind	spondylosyndesis (the immobilization of an unstable portion of the spine into a body cast)
—osis	diseased condition	porosis (formation of the callus in repair of a fractured bone)
-malacia	softening, decalcification	osteomalacia (softening of bones, generally attributed to a deficiency of vitamin D or calcium)

TABLE 4.2 Combining Forms for the Muscular System

Combining Form	Meaning	Example
ankyl/o	crooked, fusion, stiffness	ankylosis (stiffness or fixation of a joint by surgery)
arthr/o	joint	arthritis (inflammation of the joints)
articul/o	joint	articulation (joint, junction)
asthen/o	loss of strength	myasthenia gravis (loss of control of voluntary muscle)
chondr/o	cartilage	chondritis (inflammation of cartilage)
fibr/o	fiber	fibrosis (formation of excessive fibrous tissue)
kinesi/o	pertaining to movement	kinesthesia (sense of body position)
muscul/o	muscle	musculature (the arrangement of muscles in the body)
my/o	muscle	myofilament (muscle filaments constructed from proteins)
tend/o; tendin/o	tendon	tendinitis (inflammation of the tendon)

Anatomy and Physiology of the Skeletal System

The skeleton (see Figure 4.1) consists of 206 bones divided into four types based on their shape: (1) the long bones, such as the **humerus** in the arm or **femur** in the leg; (2) the short bones, such as the **carpals** in the hand or **tarsals** in the feet; (3) the flat bones, such as the **sternum** in the chest and the **scapulae** (shoulder blades); and (4) the irregular bones, such as the **vertebrae** in the spine. Table 4.3 identifies the anatomy and physiology terms associated with the skeletal system.

FIGURE 4.1 Skeletal System: Anterior View (A)

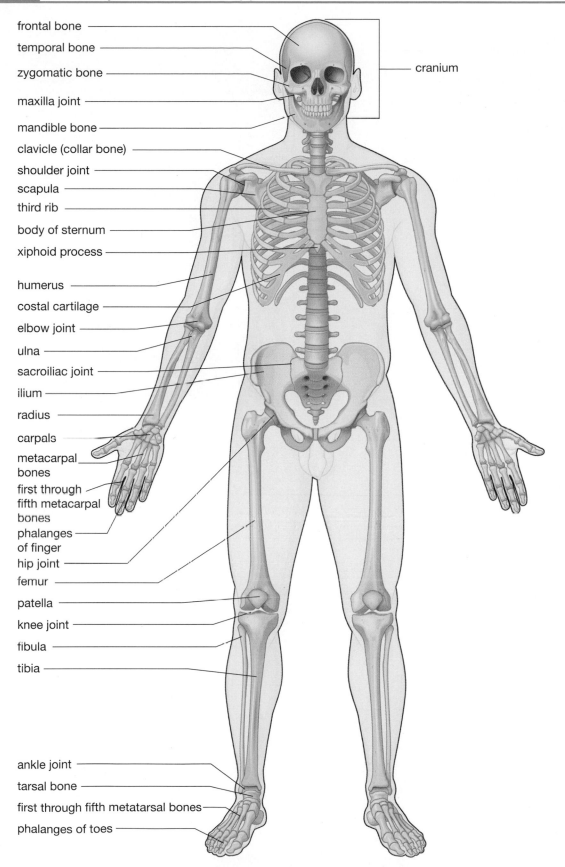

frontal bone

temporal bone

zygomatic bone

maxilla joint

mandible bone

clavicle (collar bone)

shoulder joint

scapula

third rib

body of sternum

xiphoid process

humerus

costal cartilage

elbow joint

ulna

sacroiliac joint

ilium

radius

carpals

metacarpal bones

first through fifth metacarpal bones

phalanges of finger

hip joint

femur

patella

knee joint

fibula

tibia

ankle joint

tarsal bone

first through fifth metatarsal bones

phalanges of toes

cranium

FIGURE 4.1 Skeletal System: Posterior View (B)

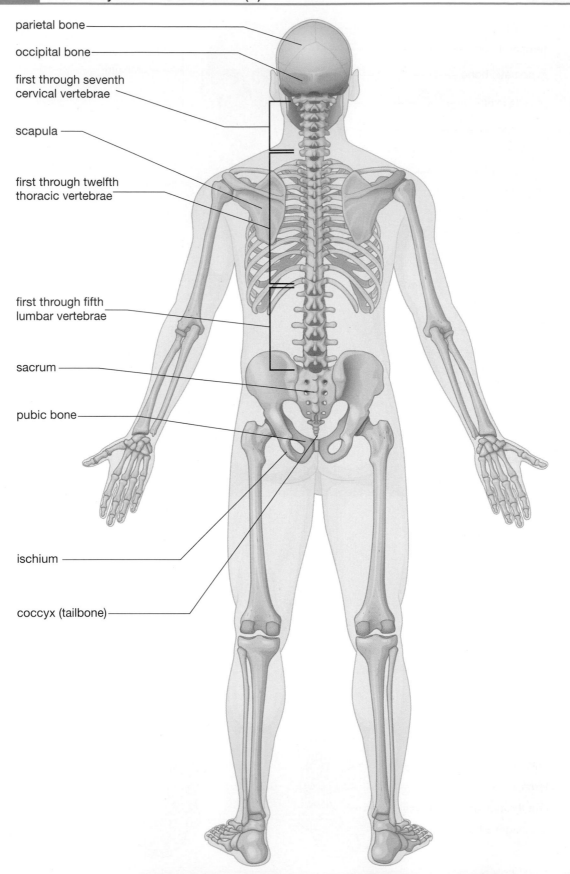

parietal bone

occipital bone

first through seventh cervical vertebrae

scapula

first through twelfth thoracic vertebrae

first through fifth lumbar vertebrae

sacrum

pubic bone

ischium

coccyx (tailbone)

TABLE 4.3 Anatomy and Physiology Terms Associated with the Skeleton

Term		Meaning	Word Analysis	
amphiarthrosis	[**am**-fee-ar-thrO-sis]	a fibrocartilaginous joining of two bones	amph/ arthr/o -osis	on both sides; around joint condition
articular cartilage	[ar-**tik**-yoo-lar **kar**-tih-lij]	firm connective tissue covering the bone surface in a synovial joint	articular cartilage	relating to a joint or joints connective tissue that covers the ends of bones at a joint
articulate	[ar-**tik**-yoo-layt]	to join or meet loosely in a way that allows motion	articulate	relating to a joint or joints
bone marrow		fatty tissue found within bones, responsible for the production of red blood cells in long bones	mearh	marrow
bursa	[**ber**-sah]	a closed sac containing synovial fluid found in areas of the most friction	bursa	purse
carpal	[**kar**-pul]	relating to the wrist bones	carpus	term
cartilage	[**kar**-tih-lij]	a nonvascular, firm connective tissue	cartilage	connective tissue that covers the ends of bones at a joint
chiropractic	[kI-rO-**prak**-tik]	medical practice that teaches manipulation of the musculoskeletal system to restore health to bodily functions	chir/o practic/o	hand efficient
chiropractor	[kI-rO-**prak**-tor]	the professional who practices chiropractic medicine		
chondrocyte	[**kon**-drO-sIt]	a cartilage cell within the matrix of cartilage	chondr/o -cyte	cartilage cell
condyle	[**kon**-dial]	the rounded projection at the end of a bone, often used for articulation with another bone for the purpose of motion		
crest	[**kress**]	ridge of bone		
diaphysis	[dI-**af**-ih-sis]	shaft of a bone	dia- -physis	through growth, growing between
diarthrosis	[dI-ar-**thrO**-sis]	synovial joint	diarthrosis	joint
diffusion	[dih-**fyoo**-zhun]	movement of molecules from one area to another to produce a uniform population in both	diffusion	moving in different directions
endochondral	[en-dO-**kon**-dral]	within the cartilage	end/o chondr/o	within cartilage
endosteum	[en-**dos**-tee-um]	layer of cells lining the inner bone structure	end/o oste/o	within bone
epiphyseal line	[eh-pih-**fiz**-ee-al]	an area of the long bone that remains after bone growth has ceased and epiphyseal plates are gone	epi- -physis linea	upon growth string
epiphyseal plate	[eh-pih-**fiz**-ee-al]	area of the long bone where growth takes place; it becomes the epiphyseal line after growth has ceased	epi- -physis plate	upon growth flat, broad

Continues

Term		Meaning	Word Analysis	
epiphysis	[eh-**pif**-eh-sis]	area of the long bone where growth takes place	*epi-* *-physis*	upon growth
femur	[**fee**-mer]	thigh bone	*femur*	thigh
foramen	[for-**ah**-men]	round or oval opening through a bone		
fossa	[**fah**-sah]	shallow, depression in a bone		
humerus	[**hyoo**-mer-us]	bone in the arm between the shoulder and elbow	*humerus*	shoulder
joint	[joynt]	area where two bones meet	*joint*	point of contact
joint capsule	[joynt **kap**-sul]	area surrounding the joint that provides the fluid for movement and acts as a shock absorber	*joint* *capsule*	point of contact box
ligament	[**lig**-ah-ment]	band of strong, fibrous tissue that connects the bones and provides support	*ligament*	band
matrix	[**may**-triks]	inner area of the bone where new cells are produced to form bone (including teeth or nails)	*matrix*	womb
meatus	[mee-**ay**-tis]	the external opening of a canal or passageway	*meat/o* *-us*	meatus structure, thing
medullary cavity	[**med**-yoo-lar-ee **kav**-ih-tee]	area inside bone that contains bone marrow	*medull/o* *cavity*	marrow hollow
orthopedics (orthopaedics is the spelling some practitioners prefer)	[or-thO-**pee**-diks]	medical practice concerned with the form and function of the musculoskeletal system	*orth/o* *ped/o*	straight; normal child
orthopedist	[or-thO-**pee**-dist]	physician who specializes in the musculoskeletal system		
ossification	[os-sih-fih-**kay**-shun]	natural process of bone formation, also known as *osteogenesis*	*oste/o* *-genesis*	bone production
ossify	[**os**-sif-I]	process of forming bone from cartilage	*osse/o*	bony
osteoblast	[**os**-tee-O-blast]	cell that produces bone	*oste/o* *-blast*	bone immature cell
osteoclast	[**os**-tee-O-klast]	cell that resorbs bone to help shape new bone	*oste/o* *-clast*	bone broken
osteocyte	[**os**-tee-O-sIt]	bone cell	*oste/o* *-cyte*	bone cell
periosteum	[per-ee-**os**-tee-um]	outer covering of bone	*peri/o* *oste/o*	around bone
phalanges	[fah-**lan**-geez]	long bones of the hands (fingers) and feet (toes); plural for phalanx		
resorb	[ree-**sorb**]	to absorb (as in an excretion)	*re-* *sorb*	again; back Latin for "to suck back"
rheumatologist	[**roo**-mah-**tol**-ah-jist]	physician who specializes in the diagnosis and treatment of conditions related to joint disorders	*rheum/a* *-logist*	flux (a movement of fluid from a cavity) practitioner
rheumatology	[**roo**-mah-**tol**-ah-jee]	study of conditions related to musculoskeletal movement or joint disorders	*rheum/a* *-logy*	flux (a movement of fluid from a cavity) the study of

Continues

Term		Meaning	Word Analysis	
ribs	[**ribbs**]	long, curved bones that surround and protect the chest		
sinus	[**sigh**-nus]	cavity within a bone		
sternum	[**ster**-num]	chest bone	*stern/o*	sternum
			-um	structure, thing
synarthrosis	[sin-ar-**thrO**-sis]	fibrous joint	*syn-*	together
			arthr/o	joint
synovial fluid	[sih-**nO**-vee-al **floo**-id]	fluid that bathes the joints to prevent friction	*syn-*	together
			ovum	egg
synovial membrane	[sih-**nO**-vee-al **mem**-brayn]	membrane that surrounds the synovial capsule	*syn-*	together
			ovum	egg
trabecula	[trah-**bek**-yoo-la]	spongy area inside bone	*trabecula*	beam
trochanter	[troh-**can**-tur]	large, irregular-shaped projection located on the femur bone		
tubercle	[**two**-bur-kal]	small, rounded projection on a bone	*tubercul/o*	tubercle
vertebra	[**ver**-teh-brah]	bone of the spine	*vertebr/o*	to turn

Structure of Long Bones

Because of their size and location, the long bones play a major role in supporting the body and facilitating movement. Studying the structure of the long bones provides insight into the makeup of all bones (see Figure 4.2). With the exception of any joint area, the outer surface of a long bone is covered by a dense, fibrous membrane called the **periosteum**, which contains nerves, as well as blood and lymph vessels (*peri-* means "surrounding," *oste/o* refers to "bone," and the suffix *-um* means "structure"). The **diaphysis** is the long shaft of the bone; it is tube-shaped and made of hard, compact bone. It is strong but light, which allows for easy movement. Within the bone is the **medullary cavity**, which is lined with a fibrous membrane called the **endosteum** and contains **bone marrow**—a gritty, fatty substance that produces blood cells. (The function of bone marrow will be described further in Chapter 15.) Recall that *endo-* is the prefix for "within," *oste/o* refers to "bone," and the suffix *-um* means "structure."

The **epiphysis**, found at either end of the bone, is composed of spongy bone that is more porous than compact bone. It is the area where the bone **articulates**, or meets, with another bone or bones. Covering each epiphysis is a thin layer of cartilage called the **articular cartilage**, which functions as a cushion at the joint where two bones meet. Underneath the epiphyses are areas known as the **epiphyseal plates**, in which normal bone growth occurs. Together, the epiphysis and epiphyseal plates form the **metaphysis** (*meta-* means "change" and *-physis* means "growth"), commonly referred to as the *growth plate*.

FIGURE 4.2 | Structure of Long Bones

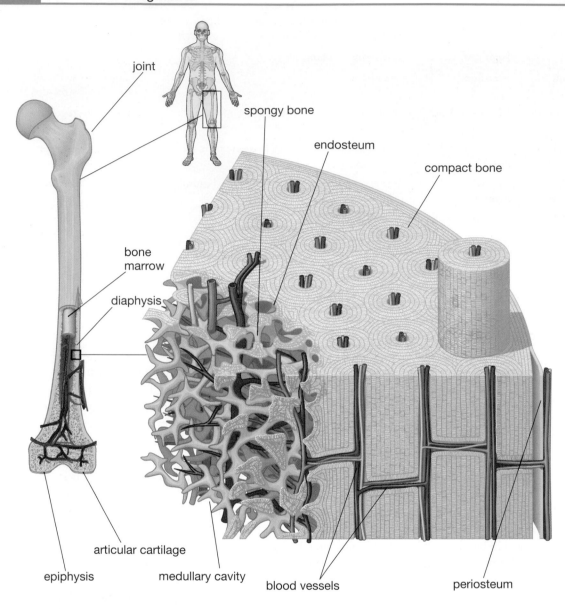

joint

spongy bone

endosteum

compact bone

bone marrow

diaphysis

articular cartilage

epiphysis

medullary cavity

blood vessels

periosteum

Bone Cells

A closer look at bone reveals an ever-changing, dynamic structure (see Figure 4.3). **Osteocytes** are the living cells of bone. They continually produce new bone, formed by cells known as **osteoblasts**, and resorb bone with cells called **osteoclasts**. Osteocytes produce and resorb bone in response to exercise, activity, and hormonal stimulation to lay down the calcium salts needed to strengthen bone. Within spongy bone are the **trabeculae**, which provide the network of spaces that surround the open area filled with marrow. Blood vessels feed the bone and move blood cells in and out of the bone marrow.

FIGURE 4.3 Microscopic View of Bone

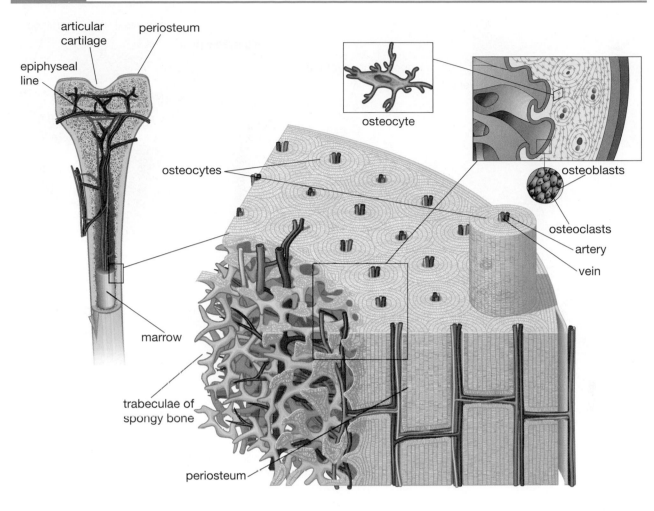

articular cartilage

periosteum

epiphyseal line

osteocyte

osteocytes

osteoblasts

osteoclasts

artery

vein

marrow

trabeculae of spongy bone

periosteum

Cartilage

Cartilage covers the ends of bones and provides protection and flexibility for the bones. Cartilage cells are called **chondrocytes**. Since cartilage does not contain blood vessels, nutrients pass through the **matrix** to the cells by a process called **diffusion**. This lack of blood supply causes cartilage to repair itself slowly after injury.

Bone Growth

Bone formation begins in the fetus, when the skeleton is composed of cartilage (see Figure 4.4 A). The cartilage is bone-shaped and gradually becomes bone by a process called **endochondral ossification**. During ossification, the osteoblasts lay down calcium salts in the cartilage to form hardened bone (B-E). Osteoclasts resorb some of the hardened bone, which gives the bone its adult structure. As bone becomes ossified, the epiphyseal plate (F) gradually decreases and eventually leaves an epiphyseal line, indicating that bone growth is complete and the person has attained adult height (G). A similar process, intramembranous ossification, takes place within connective tissue and also results in the formation of bone.

FIGURE 4.4 Bone Growth

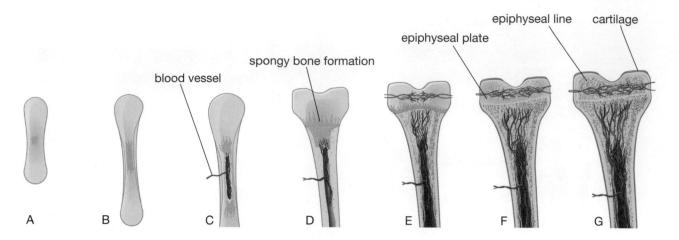

epiphyseal line cartilage

epiphyseal plate

spongy bone formation

blood vessel

A   B   C   D   E   F   G

In The Know: Predicting an Individual's Adult Height

A formula commonly used to predict height uses gender and parental height to predict the adult height (in inches) of individuals as follows:

For men: $\dfrac{\text{(height of mother in inches + height of father in inches + 5 inches)}}{2}$

For women: $\dfrac{\text{(height of mother in inches + height of father in inches − 5 inches)}}{2}$

For most people, this formula will accurately predict your height within 2 or 3 inches. Utilize this formula to predict your projected adult height. Is it accurate?

Joints

Every bone in the human body, except the hyoid bone in the neck (to which the tongue is attached), meets with another bone and forms a joint. There are three types of joints, classified according to the movement they can achieve. **Synarthorosis** is a joint formed between the bones of the skull. It allows no movement. **Amphiarthroses** connect the vertebrae and provide slight movement. **Diarthroses** (synovial joints) allow free movement and connect most bones in the body.

To provide a smooth motion, diarthroses have a **joint capsule** made of a strong, fibrous tissue (see Figure 4.5). The capsule is lined with a synovial membrane, which secretes **synovial fluid**, a smooth, slippery substance that prevents rubbing between the

FIGURE 4.5 Diarthrotic Joint

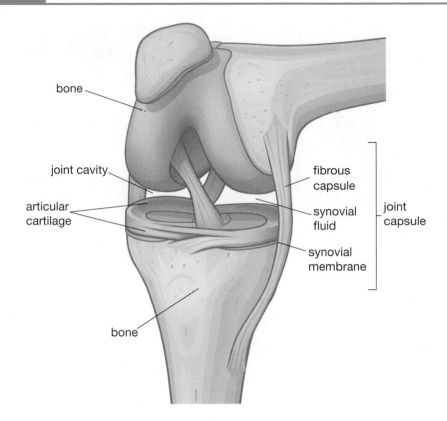

bone

joint cavity

articular
cartilage

fibrous
capsule

synovial
fluid

joint
capsule

synovial
membrane

bone

bone and the joint. Areas that support the most impact contain small sacs called **bursae** that are filled with synovial fluid. A joint cavity provides the space for the motion, and the articular cartilage covers the ends of the bones where it absorbs bumps and jolts. Bursae help to provide a cushion for joints as they move.

There are several types of diarthroses: ball and socket, hinge, pivot, saddle, gliding, and condyloid. Figure 4.6 shows each type and its movement, and illustrates one or more examples of that type of joint in the body.

Tendons are similar to heavy cords that attach muscles to bones. They are composed of dense regular connective tissue that provides great strength at their attachment sites. The Achilles tendon, also known as the *calcaneal tendon*, is the thickest in the body. Located at the back of the lower leg, it attaches the muscles responsible for plantar flexion of the foot and ankle and flexion of the knee. Ligaments are fibrous bands of dense regular connective tissue that run from one bone to another to support and strengthen joints and to prevent movement in the wrong direction. The anterior cruciate ligament (ACL) is one of four major ligaments in the knee. Tears to the ACL are one of the most common knee injuries in sports involving landing, planting, pivoting, or cutting movements that challenge the stability of the knee joint.

FIGURE 4.6 Types of Diarthroses and Their Functions

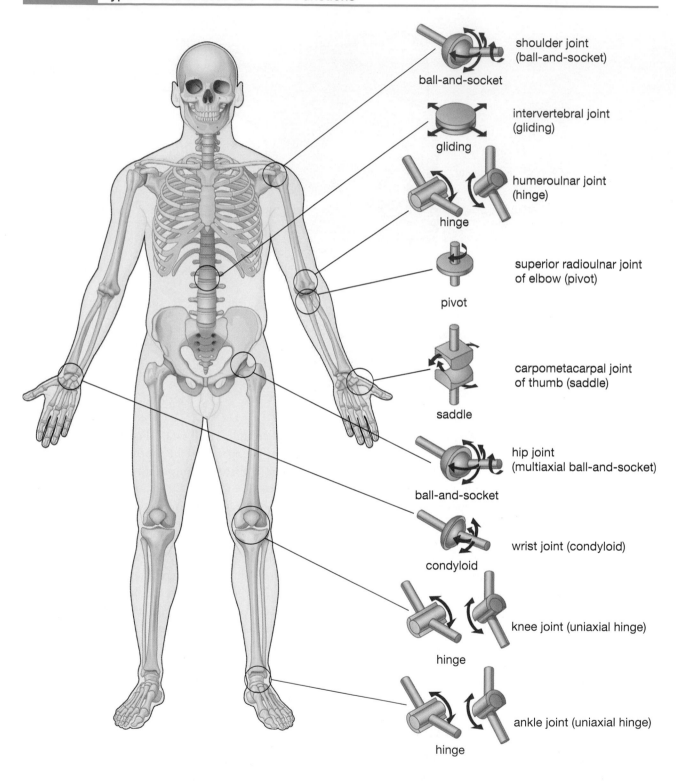

Checkpoint **4.1**

Answer the following questions to identify any areas of the section that you may need to review.

1. What makes up the central portion of a long bone?

   _____

2. Which physician specialty focuses on primary care and lifestyle interventions when treating diseases and injuries of the body?

   _____

3. Which type of cell is responsible for the continuous formation of new bone?

   _____

Exercise 4.1   Identification

Label the illustration by placing the corresponding letter (A-J) on the line provided beside each anatomical label.

1. _____ femur
2. _____ fibula
3. _____ humerus
4. _____ ilium
5. _____ mandible
6. _____ radius
7. _____ sternum
8. _____ tarsal bones
9. _____ tibia
10. _____ zygomatic bone

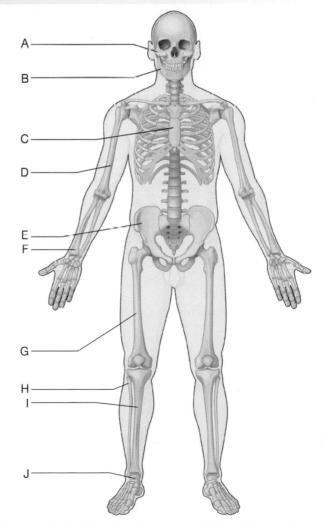

Exercise 4.2 Matching

Match the list of terms in column 1 with the definition in column 2. Write the letter of the definition in the space beside the term.

1. _____ humerus
2. _____ scapula
3. _____ sternum
4. _____ periosteum
5. _____ osteocyte

a. outer covering of bone
b. bone cell
c. shoulder blade
d. breastbone
e. bone of the upper arm

Exercise 4.3 Word Building

Use word parts to construct a medical term to match each definition. Separate the parts of the term with a slash (/).

1. study of rheumatic conditions

   _____

2. field of medicine concerned with the musculoskeletal system

   _____

3. examination of a joint using an instrument

   _____

4. process of becoming ossified

   _____

5. pertaining to the epiphysis

   _____

Exercise 4.4 Spelling Check

Using contextual clues to determine meaning, circle the correct singular or plural form in each word pair.

1. Ligamenti/Ligaments are fibrous bands between bones.
2. The vertebra/vertebrae are poorly aligned.
3. Osteoblastum/Osteoblasts are immature bone cells.
4. Both scapula/scapulae are fractured.
5. Several phalanges/phalange on the right hand are missing.

Anatomy and Physiology of the Muscular System

A muscle is elastic tissue made up of tens of thousands of small fibers banded together. Muscle has the ability to contract and relax, and ultimately controls the body's movement and functioning. The human body has more than 600 muscles, all of which can be classified by their specific function. The three types of muscle tissue are skeletal, smooth, and cardiac. The key to learning the muscles of the body is to understand the ways in which they are named. Most muscles are named according to one or more of the following characteristics: shape (deltoid), point of origin and insertion (sternocleidomastoid), size (vastus lateralis), location (tibialis anterior), length (adductor longus), or the number of "heads" (biceps). Table 4.4 identifies common anatomy and physiology terms of the muscular system.

Did You Know?

More than 40 percent of the body's weight comes from skeletal muscle.

TABLE 4.4 Anatomy and Physiology Terms Associated with the Muscles

Term		Meaning	Word Analysis	
cardiac muscle	[**kar**-dee-ak **mus**-sul]	muscle fibers found in the walls of the heart, involuntary muscle		
fasciculus	[fah-**sik**-yoo-lus]	a bundle of muscle fibers	*fasciculus*	bundle
homeostasis	[ho-meo-**sta**-sis]	state of having all body functions in balance	*home/o*	alike
			-stasis	stop
insertion	[in-**ser**-shun]	attachment of a muscle to a more movable part	*insertion*	a planting
involuntary muscle	[in-**vol**-un-tar-ee **mus**-sul]	muscle that cannot be controlled by the person; smooth muscle	*in-*	not
			voluntas	will
			-ary	relating to
lactic acid	[lak-tik as-id]	a chemical substance released by muscle cells during increased activity	*lact/o*	milk
			acid	sour
ligament	[**lig**-ah-ment]	band of strong, fibrous tissue that connects the bones and provides support	*ligament*	band
myofilaments	[mI-O **fil**-ah-ments]	microscopic threads that make up striated muscle	*my/o*	muscle
			filament	thread
origin	[**or**-ih-jin]	the less movable area of the points of attachment of bones	*origin*	source, beginning
sarcomeres	[**sar**-kO-meers]	units of muscle fiber that help an entire muscle contract, or shorten, when stimulated	*sarc/o*	muscular substance
			-mere	part
skeletal muscle	[**skel**-eh-tl **mus**-sul]	striated muscle fibers connected to the bones of the body, voluntary muscle		
smooth muscle		muscle fibers of the internal organs; involuntary muscle		
striated muscle	[**strI**-ay-ted **mus**-sul]	voluntary skeletal muscle with striations	*stria*	channel
voluntary muscle	[**vol**-un-tar-ee **mus**-sul]	muscle that can be controlled (moved) by the person	*voluntas*	will
			-ary	relating to

Types of Muscle Tissue

Skeletal muscle, also called **voluntary muscle**, is under the person's direct control. More than 40 percent of the body's weight comes from skeletal muscle. Skeletal muscles help to make up the musculoskeletal system (see Figure 4.7). The musculoskeletal system provides for movement, helps maintain the body's posture, and produces heat necessary to maintain the body's temperature.

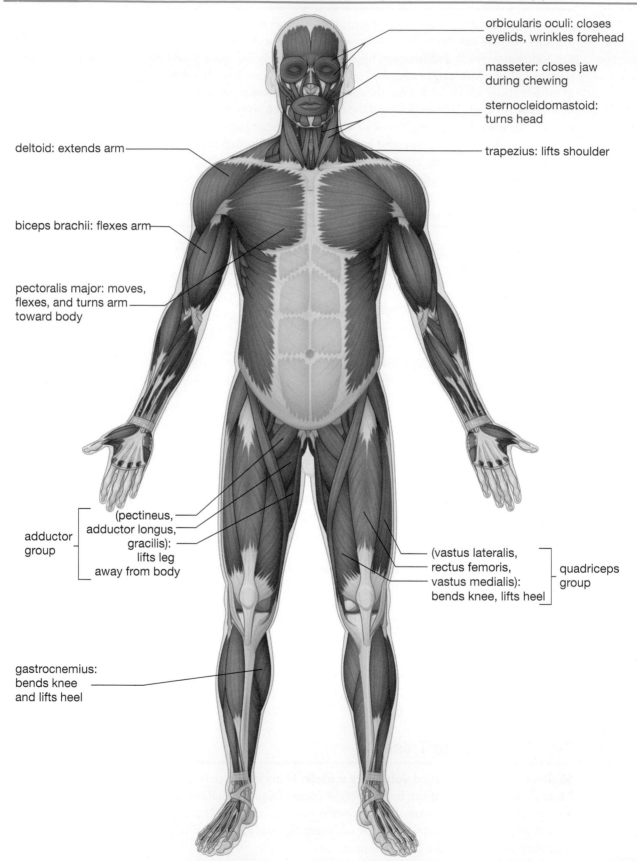

orbicularis oculi: closes eyelids, wrinkles forehead

masseter: closes jaw during chewing

sternocleidomastoid: turns head

deltoid: extends arm

trapezius: lifts shoulder

biceps brachii: flexes arm

pectoralis major: moves, flexes, and turns arm toward body

adductor group

(pectineus, adductor longus, gracilis): lifts leg away from body

(vastus lateralis, rectus femoris, vastus medialis): bends knee, lifts heel

quadriceps group

gastrocnemius: bends knee and lifts heel

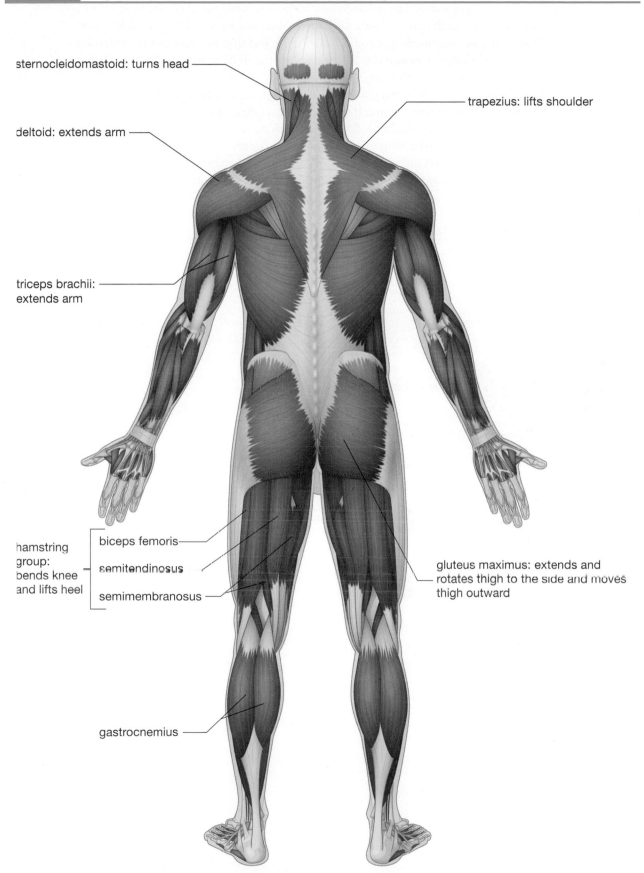

sternocleidomastoid: turns head

trapezius: lifts shoulder

deltoid: extends arm

triceps brachii: extends arm

hamstring group: bends knee and lifts heel

biceps femoris

semitendinosus

semimembranosus

gluteus maximus: extends and rotates thigh to the side and moves thigh outward

gastrocnemius

Skeletal muscle is composed of striated muscle (muscle with stripes called **striations**) and connective tissue. The striated muscle tissue is made up of contracting cells called muscle fibers, as shown in Figure 4.8. These fibers are arranged in layered bundles called **fasciculi** and composed of proteins called thick and thin **myofilaments**, which are grouped into units called **sarcomeres**. Sarcomeres are the units of muscle fiber that help an entire muscle contract, or shorten, when stimulated.

Smooth muscle, or **involuntary muscle**, is found in organs, such as the stomach, and throughout the digestive system. The involuntary contraction and relaxation of these muscles move food through the body. Specific smooth muscles are described throughout this textbook in chapters related to their particular functions.

Cardiac muscle, found only in the heart, is described more fully in Chapter 7. Also known as *myocardium*, cardiac muscle is responsible for the involuntary movement of blood throughout the body by the contraction of the heart.

FIGURE 4.8 Structure of Skeletal Muscle

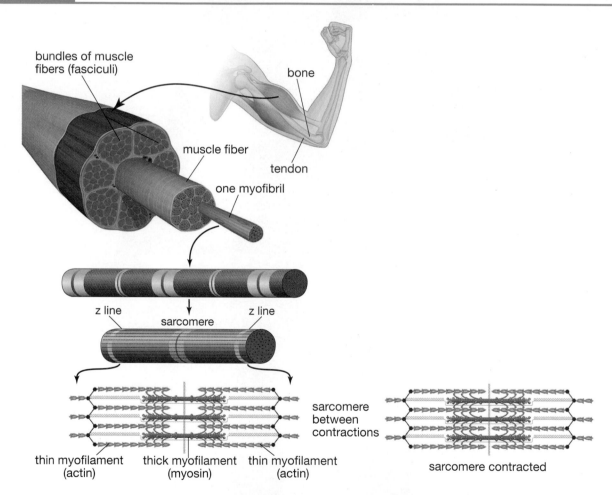

Skeletal Muscle Functions

Skeletal muscle connects two or more bones and is divided into three parts: (1) the **origin**, which is attached to the proximal end of the bone; (2) the **insertion**, or the area where the muscle attaches to the more movable bone (distal end), and (3) the body of the muscle (see Figure 4.9). Muscles move bones by pulling them or forcing a contraction. Usually, the insertion bone moves toward the origin bone, producing a coordinated, smooth motion. Posture is a kind of movement maintained by the musculoskeletal system pulling just enough to overcome the force of gravity. In proper posture, the head is held high, with the chin parallel to the ground in a tucked position. The shoulders are pulled back, the stomach and buttocks are pulled in, and the knees are slightly bent. Correct posture decreases the risk of deformities and provides adequate working space for the heart, lungs, and other internal organs.

Heat production is another function of muscle. Muscle contraction releases energy stored in the muscles and generates the heat required to maintain the normal body temperature of approximately 98.6°F (37°C).

FIGURE 4.9 Skeletal Muscle Attachments

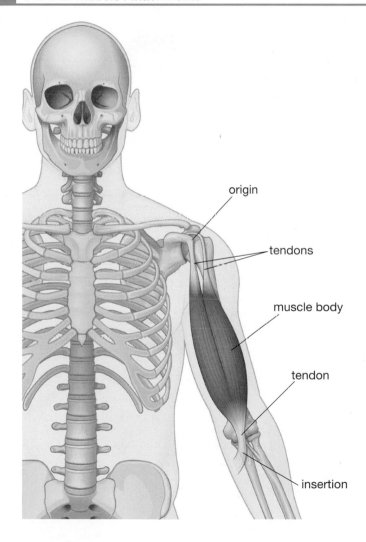

In the Know: About Exercise

Muscles contract during exercise, using stored energy and oxygen. The increase in activity increases the heart rate, which in turn increases blood flow, bringing additional oxygen to the muscle tissues. The rate and depth of respiration increase to maintain a balance between the amount of oxygen inhaled and absorbed in the blood and the amount of carbon dioxide eliminated as waste. The entire process is an example of how the body continually tries to maintain homeostasis. During exercise, oxygen supply becomes limited resulting in a buildup of lactic acid, which causes muscle pain. Lactic acid is moved to the liver by blood flow, converted to glucose, and used by the body for muscle movement (exercise).

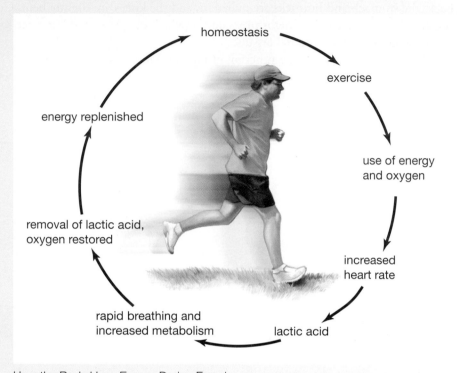

homeostasis

exercise

energy replenished

use of energy and oxygen

removal of lactic acid, oxygen restored

increased heart rate

rapid breathing and increased metabolism

lactic acid

How the Body Uses Energy During Exercise

Checkpoint 4.2

Answer the following questions to identify any areas of the section that you may need to review.

1. Which part of skeletal muscle is attached to the proximal end of the bone?

_____

2. Provide an example of a voluntary muscle composed of striated muscle fiber.

_____

3. What medical term refers to muscle fibers grouped in layered bundles?

_____

Exercise 4.5 Comprehension Check

This exercise provides practice in determining word meaning according to context. Circle the most appropriate word choice in each sentence.

1. The periosteum/pericardium was dissected away from the bone.

2. The metatarsal/medullary cavity was found to contain minimal marrow.

3. It is apparent that much of the articular cartilage/atrial cartilage is worn away.

4. The humerus and the ulna articulate/fibrillate.

5. The symbiotic membrane/synovial membrane was torn, and synovial fluid/syntactical fluid was absent.

Exercise 4.6 Name That Term

Write the medical term for the underlined word, phrase, or abbreviation in each sentence.

1. Nearly all persons over the age of 60 have signs of a noninflammatory, progressive disorder that eventually causes deterioration of the articular cartilage in the hands, feet, hips, spine, and other places.

   _____

2. The physician indicated that the bundle of muscle fibers was inflamed.

   _____

3. Establishing and maintaining a state of equilibrium among body systems is always a goal of treatment.

   _____

4. This connective tissue is like a heavy cord that attaches muscles to bones.

   _____

5. The uterus is composed of smooth muscle.

   _____

Exercise 4.7 Word Maps

The following chart is designed to group muscles by type, location, and type of nerve control. Fill in the blank spaces with the appropriate terms.

Muscle Type	skeletal		smooth
Location		heart	
Type of Nerve Control		involuntary	

Exercise 4.8   Word Puzzle

Use these misspelled clues to write the correctly spelled terms in the puzzle.

Across
- 2. ostoclast
- 7. epifisi
- 9. tirations
- 10. femor
- 12. carnium
- 14. sinoviul
- 16. dharthrosis
- 18. chartalige
- 19. sarchomires
- 20. facsiculous

Down
- 1. perinostiume
- 3. scalpula
- 4. joynt
- 5. stermun
- 6. reumotology
- 8. boen
- 11. miofilaments
- 13. bhurssa
- 15. illeum
- 17. ostify
- 18. karpl

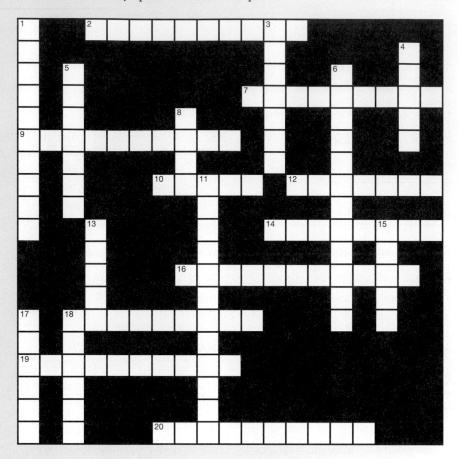

Conditions

A person with a problem or complaint such as a fracture, pain, swelling in a joint or muscle, or a skeletal malformation is referred to a specialist in the field. The physical examination of the musculoskeletal system includes an assessment of the patient's posture, standing and walking movements, and mobility of the joints and extremities. The examiner conducts and observes full range of motion (ROM) activities from each muscle group. Asymmetry of an area's range of motion indicates a problem, and obvious spinal malformations such as scoliosis and kyphosis are noted. All joints are inspected for pain, swelling, heat, or redness, any of which would indicate a problem. Table 4.5 provides an overview of the most common types of fractures and Figure 4.10 illustrates these fractures.

During the physical examination, the health professional palpates, or feels, for certain landmarks that can be touched and identified through the skin. These landmarks, called bone markings, are specific locations on different bones and each provides reference points for the examiner and may be noted in the patient's chart. Table 4.6 describes these landmarks and their associated structures. Figure 4.11 shows the location of each palpable bony landmark.

TABLE 4.5 | Common Fracture Types

Fracture Type	Description
displaced (complete)	bone snaps into two or more parts and shifts, misaligned
nondisplaced (incomplete)	bone is cracked, no movement or misalignment present
closed (simple)	bone breaks, but not through the skin
open (compound)	bone breaks through the skin
Subtypes	
buckled (impacted)	broken ends of bone are driven into each other, producing a bulge or buckle; often seen in children in the arm
comminuted	bone breaks into several pieces
greenstick (incomplete)	one side of bone is broken while the other side is bent; often seen in children
oblique	break has a curved or sloped pattern
pathologic	caused by a disease that weakens the bones (e.g., osteoporosis)
transverse	broken piece of bone is at a right angle to the bone's axis
spiral (torsion)	occurs when the body is in motion (twisted) while the extremity (e.g., leg/foot) is planted
stress (hairline)	small crack in the bone, caused by overuse and repetitive activity

FIGURE 4.10 · Common Fracture Types

closed
(simple) fracture

open
(compound) fracture

comminuted
fracture

greenstick
(incomplete) fracture

oblique fracture

transverse fracture

spiral
(torsion) fracture

TABLE 4.6 Palpable Bony Landmarks

Landmark	Location
various bones of the skull	example: zygomatic bone
acromion process of scapula	the highest point of the shoulder
spinous processes	vertebrae
medial and lateral epicondyles of the humerus	area where the upper arm and forearm connect
styloid process of the radius	projection on the bone on the thumb side of the lower arm
styloid process of the ulna	projection on the bone on the medial side of the lower arm
anterior superior iliac crest	upper portion of hip bone on anterior aspect of body
posterior iliac crest	upper portion of hip bone on posterior aspect of body
patella	kneecap
anterior crest of the tibia	shinbone
lateral malleolus of fibula	outside bone of fibula; lateral projection at ankle bone
medial malleolus of tibia	inside bone of the tibia; medial projection at ankle bone
calcaneus	heel bone

FIGURE 4.11 Palpable Bony Landmarks

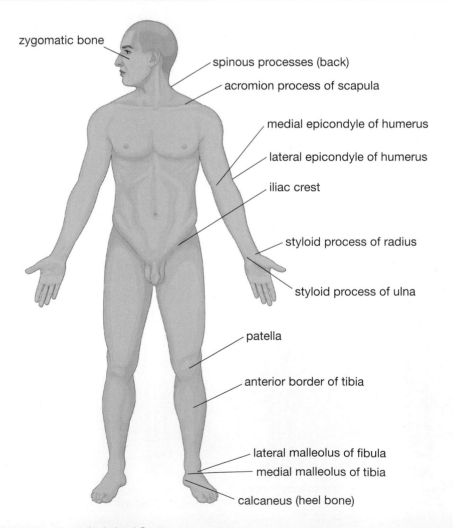

zygomatic bone

spinous processes (back)

acromion process of scapula

medial epicondyle of humerus

lateral epicondyle of humerus

iliac crest

styloid process of radius

styloid process of ulna

patella

anterior border of tibia

lateral malleolus of fibula

medial malleolus of tibia

calcaneus (heel bone)

Because of the current emphasis on physical fitness, many people are active and exercise regularly. Injuries due to exercise are treated by orthopedists; the field of sports medicine has also developed to treat such patients.

One of the most typical musculoskeletal problems is **epicondylitis**. The common name "tennis elbow" is an inaccurate designation, since it is possible to develop epicondylitis from any activity that involves excessive and repeated pronation and supination of the forearm with the wrist extended. The injury includes chronic pain at the lateral epicondyle of the humerus; the pain may radiate down the arm.

Carpal tunnel syndrome (CTS) is a repetitive motion injury seen in people who do the same activities daily. It is historically common in typists, carpenters, and other such workers who use their hands in the same manner all day. According to the Bureau of Labor Statistics, CTS accounts for 50 percent of all work-related injuries in the United States.[1]

Characterized by an inflammation of the tendon sheath, **tenosynovitis** produces pain and swelling that can limit the movement of the affected part. Although tenosynovitis can occur in any tendon, carpal tunnel syndrome involves the tendon sheath around the tendons in the wrist, limiting the movement of the wrist, hand, and fingers. Edema puts pressure on the median nerve, and pain radiates to the thumb and up the arm. Anti-inflammatory agents, such as corticosteroids, are injected into the area, but it is often necessary to surgically remove the swollen tissue pressing on the nerve.

The tendon sheath near the ankle can become inflamed and produce **Achilles tenosynovitis**, named for its presence in the Achilles tendon. Swelling and tenderness along the route of the tendon make movement painful and limited.

Bunions are a common deformity appearing on the first metatarsophalangeal joint (the base of the great toe). The bunion is an inflamed bursa that forms at the point of most pressure. The stress of walking (often in improperly fitted shoes or high heels that force the foot forward) puts pressure on the great toe, which pushes off to produce each step and contribute to bunion formation. Bunions are characterized by redness, swelling, and pain.

Chondromalacia patella is a condition in which the cartilage of the knee joint deteriorates and softens, causing inflammation, pain, and grinding (also called *runner's knee*). Patients often complain of the presence of crepitus, a cracking or popping sound in a joint. Note the combining form *chondr/o* (cartilage) and the suffix *-malacia* (softening).

Hammertoes are deformities usually found in any or all of the second, third, fourth, and fifth toes. They are characterized by hyperextension of the metatarsophalangeal joint, the joint between bones of the foot and toes, and flexion of the proximal interphalangeal joint, the joint nearest to the body that moves the toes.

Other common musculoskeletal conditions include the following:

Dislocations, which are injuries that cause the displacement of a bone from the joint. A **subluxation** is an incomplete dislocation, in which some articulation between the bone and the joint is present.

Bursitis, which is an inflammation (either acute or chronic) of a bursa, caused by trauma, chronic overuse, or infection. It can occur in any joint that has a bursa and involves swelling, pain, tenderness, and inflammation of the area.

Fibromyalgia is a disorder characterized by chronic musculoskeletal pain as well as abdominal pain, headaches, muscle soreness, and stiffness lasting for more than six months. The American College of Rheumatology has strict criteria for diagnosis. There must be 11 of 18 tender or trigger points on the body that are painful under pressure. Often the

---

[1]http://www.repetitive-strain.com/national.html

diagnosis is made after exclusion of several other conditions, such as depression, hypothyroidism, growing pains, chronic fatigue syndrome, and other systemic illnesses. Treatment includes medication, physical and occupational therapy, and behavior modification using techniques such as hypnosis, exercise, relaxation training, and/or biofeedback.

A **ganglion cyst**, which is a fluid-filled sac (a rounded nodule) that appears over a tendon, most commonly in the wrist. Ganglion cysts have no known cause, vary in size, and generally appear and disappear spontaneously.

Table 4.7 lists common conditions associated with the musculoskeletal system.

TABLE 4.7 Conditions Associated with the Musculoskeletal System

Term		Meaning	Word Analysis	
Achilles tenosynovitis	[a-**kil**-eez ten-O-sI-nO-**vI**-tis]	inflammation of the heel and the surrounding tissue and tendons	*Achilles*	the mythical Greek warrior who was defeated when wounded in the heel—his only weak spot
			ten/o	tendon
			synovia	fluid surrounding the joint
			-itis	inflammation
ankylosing spondylitis	[an-kih-**lO**-sing spon-dih-**lI**-tis]	stiffening and later fixation of the bones of the spine	*ankyl/o*	crooked; fusion
			-os	bone
			spondyl/o	vertebra
			-itis	inflammation
ankylosis	[an-kih-**lO**-sis]	stiffening and later fixation of a joint caused by fibrosis	*ankyl/o*	crooked; fusion
			-os	bone
			-osis	condition
arthritis	[ar-**thrI**-tis]	inflammation of a joint; usually a chronic condition	*arthr/o*	joint
			-itis	inflammation
avascular necrosis	[ah-**vas**-kyoo-lar neh-**krO**-sis]	condition resulting from lack of blood supply, which leads to erosion and destruction of a joint	*a-*	without
			vascul/o	blood vessel
			necr/o	death
			-osis	condition
bunion	[**bun**-yun]	inflammatory condition of the bursa of the first metatarsophalangeal joint	*bunion*	bump on the head
bursitis	[ber-**sI**-tis]	inflammation of a bursa	*bursa*	purse
			-itis	inflammation
carpal tunnel syndrome carpus carpi (pl)	[**kar**-pul **tun**-nul **sin**-drOm]	condition of weakness, pain, or numbness resulting from pressure on the median nerve in the carpal tunnel (wrist)	*carpal*	relating to the wrist
chondromalacia patella	[**chon**-droh-mah-lay-zea]	condition in which the cartilage of the knee joint deteriorates and softens, causing inflammation, pain, and grinding ("runner's knee")	*chondr/o*	cartilage
			-malacia	softening
dislocation	[dis-lO-**kay**-shun]	displacement of a body part	*dis-*	separation
			location	place
epicondylitis	[ep-ih-kon-dih-**lI**-tis]	inflammation of the projection on a long bone near the articulation	*epi-*	upon
			condyle	knob
			-itis	inflammation
fibromyalgia	[**fI**-bro-my-**al**-gee-ah]	condition characterized by chronic musculoskeletal pain, abdominal pain, headaches, muscle soreness, and stiffness lasting more than 6 months	*fibr/o*	fiber
			my/o-	muscle
			-algia	pain

Continues

Term		Meaning	Word Analysis	
fibrosis	[fĬ-**brO**-sis]	reparative or reactive tissue	*fibr/o*	fiber
			-osis	condition
fontanel	[fon-tan-**el**]	membranous area between the cranial bones of an infant	*fontanel*	fountain
fracture	[**frak**-cher]	a break	*fracture*	break
ganglion cyst	[**gang**-lee-on]	cyst usually found in the dorsal aspect of the wrist	*ganglion*	swelling; knot
ganglia (pl)	[**gang**-lee-ah]			
ganglions (pl)				
genu valgum	[**jee**-nyoo **val**-gum]	knock-knee	*genu*	knee joint
genus (sing)			*valgum*	turned outward
genua (pl)				
genu varum	[**jee**-nyoo **vay**-rum]	bowleg	*varum (varus)*	bent inward
gout		disorder characterized by an increase in uric acid, resulting in crystal formation in the articular cartilage; causes pain and inflammation; may be inherited (usually found in men)	*gout*	drop
greenstick fracture		incomplete fracture of a bone; bending of the bone	*green stick*	like the bending of young, green wood
kyphosis	[kih-**fO**-sis]	spinal deformity characterized by an extreme flexion; humpback	*kyphosis*	bent
Legg-Calvé-Perthes disease	[leg-cal-**vay-per**-tez]	aseptic necrosis of the epiphysis of the femur; named for the surgeons who identified the problem concurrently	*Legg*	US surgeon
			Calvé	French surgeon
			Perthes	German surgeon
lordosis	[lor-**dO**-sis]	anteroposterior curvature of the lumbar spine	*lordosis*	bending backward
metatarsus valgus	[met-ah-**tar**-sus **val**-gus]	deformity of the foot that causes the toes to face outward	*meta-tars/o*	behind bones of the instep
metatarsus (sing)	[met-ah-**tar**-sus]		*valgus*	turned outward
metatarsi (pl)	[met-ah-**tar**-sI]			
metatarsal	[met-ah-**tar**-sal]			
metatarsus varus	[met-ah-**tar**-sus **vay**-rus]	deformity of the foot that causes the toes to face inward	*meta-tars/o*	behind bones of the instep
			varus	bent inward
Osgood-Schlatter disease	[**oz**-good-**shlah**-ter]	aseptic necrosis of the tibial tubercle; named for the surgeons who identified the condition concurrently	*Osgood*	US orthopedic surgeon
			Schlatter	Swiss surgeon
osteoarthritis	[os-tee-O-ar-**thrI**-tis]	arthritis characterized by destruction of the articular cartilage	*oste/o*	bone
			arthr/o	joint
			-itis	inflammation
osteomyelitis	[**ahs**-tee-oh-mye-lye-tis]	inflammation of bone caused by infection that is generally found in the arms, legs, or spine	*oste/o*	bone
			myel/o	bone marrow
			-itis	inflammation
osteoporosis	[os-tee-O-pah-**rO**-sis]	reduction in the thickness of bone	*oste/o*	bone
			por/o	pore
			-osis	condition
pes planus	[pes **play**-nus]	flatfoot	*pes*	foot
pedes (sing)	[**pee**-deez]		*plan/o*	flat; level
pedi (pl)	[**pee**-dI]			

Continues

Term		Meaning	Word Analysis	
physique	[fih-**zeek**]	the physical body type; the build	*physi/o*	physical
podagra	[pO-**dag**-rah]	severe pain in the foot	*pod/o*	foot
			-agra	sudden pain
polydactyly	[pol-ee-**dak**-tih-lee]	extra fingers or toes	*poly-*	many
			dactyl/o	fingers (digits)
rhabdomyo-sarcoma	[**rab**-dO-mI-O-sar-**cO**-ma]	malignant tumor of striated muscle	*rhabd/o*	rod-shaped
			myo/o	pertaining to muscle
rheumatoid arthritis	[**roo**-mah-toyd ar-**thrI**-tis]	painful condition affecting articulations; immunologic disorder causing pain and inflammation of the joints	*rheuma*	flux
			arthr/o	joint
			-itis	inflammation
sarcoma	[sar-**cO**-ma]	type of cancer derived from connective and supportive tissue	*sarc/o*	denoting muscular substance denoting flesh
			-oma	tumor
scoliosis	[skO-lee-**O**-sis]	abnormal lateral curvature of the spine	*scoliosis*	crookedness
sprain		injury to a ligament		
strain		injury to a muscle or tendon		
subluxation	[sub-luks-**ay**-shun]	dislocation	*sub-*	below
			luxation	dislocation
suture lines	[**soo**-chur]	a fibrous joint between two bones that was formed in a membrane	*suture*	seam
syndactyly	[sin-**dak**-tih-lee]	webbed or fused fingers or toes	*syn-*	together
			dactyl/o	fingers or toes (digits)
talipes equin-ovarus	[**tal**-ih-peez ee-**kwI**-nO-**vay**-rus]	clubfoot; the foot is plantar flexed, inverted, and adducted	*talipes*	ankle
			equine	horse
			varus	bent inward
tenosynovitis	[ten-O-sI-nO-**vI**-tis]	inflammation of the tendon and its covering	*ten/o*	tendon
			synovia	fluid surrounding the joint
			-itis	inflammation
tibial torsion	[**tib**-ee-al **tor**-shun]	a twisting of the tibia (shinbone)	*tibi/o*	tibia
tibia	[**tib**-ee-ah]		*torsion*	twist
tibiae (pl)	[**tib**-ee-ee]			
tibial	[**tib**-ee-al]			

In the Know: Gaming and Carpal Tunnel Syndrome

"Gamers" of all ages should be aware of the risk of carpal tunnel syndrome as a result of the excessive time spent playing computer and video games. Diagnosis of CTS in children is on the rise because of the repetitive motion activities involved in "gaming." To avoid CPS, gamers and guardians of gamers should:

- Monitor and limit the total amount of time spent gaming weekly.
- Schedule regular breaks during gaming sessions and computer use.
- Be aware of signs of CTS (i.e., numbness and tingling sensation in the hands, wrist, and arms).[1]

[1]http://www.sierraneurosurgery.com/education/kids-and-carpal-tunnel

Fetal and Infant Development

By about two months gestation, the fetal skeleton resembles a miniature version of its final form, but is composed of cartilage. As the fetus develops, the cartilage begins to ossify (to become hardened bone) and grow into the shape of the true bone. After birth, the infant grows rapidly. The bones are soft, and the newborn seems almost foldable. When an infant breaks a bone, the fracture does not extend completely through the bone but has the appearance of the bend or break of a young, or green, piece of wood, and is therefore called a greenstick fracture. These fractures most often occur as a result of trauma to the newborn.

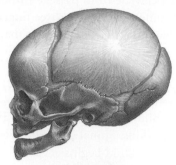

The bones of the skull also change from fetal to infant life. At birth the newborn's head measures between 32 and 38 cm and is about 2 cm larger than the chest circumference. The newborn head has palpable **suture lines**, the areas where the bones meet. Spaces, called **fontanels**, between the posterior sutures and the anterior sutures are called the posterior and anterior fontanels, respectively. The posterior fontanel may be palpable at birth but completely closes within one to two months. The anterior fontanel is larger and usually does not close until almost one year later, and possibly as long as two years. The fontanels provide space for the growing brain and are more commonly referred to as "soft spots."

Skull of a Newborn

Infants cannot control the movement of their heads at birth. In about two weeks, they can turn their heads from side to side, but they are unable to hold their heads upright until after about four months. Muscle movement is involuntary and uncoordinated at birth. Newborn movements are a result of reflexes, described more fully in Chapter 5.

The infant's cranial bones may become molded during the passage through the birth canal. This molding, which may result in an initial asymmetry of the infant's head, is caused by the cranial bones overlapping each other. When palpated, the infant's skull will feel like irregularly shaped ridges and often appear to be cone-shaped. Once the cranial bones have moved into place, the infant's head will return to a normal shape.

At birth the musculoskeletal development of the newborn is assessed by the healthcare team, beginning at the feet and working upward. Some deformities may originate from the fetus's position in the womb, and it is important to determine whether these deformities are positional (i.e., are correctable) or permanent. The first assessment also reveals whether the infant has **metatarsus varus** (an adduction and inversion of the forefoot), **metatarsus valgus** (in which the feet are turned outward), or neither.

The hips are checked for congenital dislocation by performing the Ortolani maneuver. This procedure involves abduction of the infant's knees apart and downward until the lateral aspects of the knees touch the examining table. The motion should feel smooth and be noiseless. The Allis test checks for hip dislocation by comparing leg lengths. The examiner checks the appearance of the folds of the legs: the anterior and posterior folds of the knees, and the symmetry of the gluteal folds.

Congenital malformations, such as **syndactyly** (webbed or fused fingers or toes) and **polydactyly** (extra digits on the hands or feet), are also noted. These deformities may be corrected by reconstructive surgery. **Talipes equinovarus**, or clubfoot, is a congenital, rigid malposition of the foot and a common birth defect present in one to three out of every thousand live births. Clubfoot affects twice as many males as females. This deformity can be corrected with casting in infancy or may require surgical intervention.

The newborn should have full ROM of the arms. A frequent birth injury is a fractured clavicle from passage through the birth canal. The examiner traces the length of the spine with two or three fingers to detect spinal deformities. There is a normal "C" curve of the newborn's spine that remains until the infant can lift his or her head, at about two months.

Toddlers and School-Age Children

The child develops length from the skeletal system, and muscles grow as the child gains motor skills. Spinal curvature development continues from 12 to about 18 months, when the child begins to walk, and develops an anterior curve in the lumbar region.

Common conditions during childhood may include **genu varum** (bowleg) or **genu valgum** (knock-knee). These abnormalities should disappear by the age of about three years. Children of this age often display **pes planus**

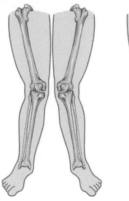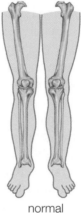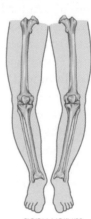

genu valgum   normal   genu varum

(flatfoot) because of the wide-based stance they must use to maintain balance. Young children may also appear to have pigeon toes, or intoe, a condition that usually corrects itself by the time they are about three years old.

Tibial torsion is the twisting of the tibia. This condition can be present at birth and is the result of the baby's position in the uterus. It becomes problematic when the child sits so that the buttocks are flat on the floor and the lower legs are positioned behind and outward.

Legg-Calvé-Perthes disease occurs most commonly in males between 3 and 12 years of age (with most cases occurring at six years). Inflammation leads to limited blood flow to the femoral head (hip joint), which in turn leads to the death of bone tissue, a condition called **avascular necrosis**. Although the decreased blood flow is only temporary, the bones tend to break easily and heal poorly.

Adolescents

The period of adolescence is characterized by a growth spurt, resulting from rising hormone levels (to be discussed further in Chapter 7), which cause significant linear (height) and muscular growth. Bones continue to expand until the epiphyseal plates close, generally at around 20 years of age.

Adolescents frequently have poor posture, in part because they are self-conscious about their changing bodies. Girls may be uncomfortable about developing breasts or, if they mature later than their peers, not developing breasts. Boys may feel that their thin, lanky shape is not attractive. Carrying heavy books in front of the body can lead to poor posture. Therefore, it is not uncommon to see **kyphosis**, a spinal deformity sometimes called *humpback*, in teenagers. Adolescence is the period when **scoliosis**, an abnormal S-shaped curvature of the spine, is most commonly diagnosed. A familial trait, scoliosis is most commonly seen in girls and can lead to spinal deformity if not surgically corrected.

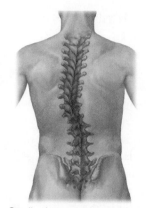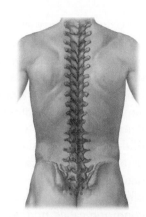

Scoliosis

To Note!

Scoliosis, an abnormal curvature of the spine, is most commonly diagnosed during adolescence.

Osgood-Schlatter disease occurs during the growth spurt, particularly in males, as a result of stress on the patellar tendon. It is characterized by painful swelling of the tibial tubercle, just below the knee, and may be brought on by biking, bending, kneeling, or climbing stairs. It is self-limiting and resolves with rest.

Sports injuries are common in the adolescent. Approximately 30 million children and adolescents participate in organized sports in the United States. Nearly 3 million injuries occur annually. In fact, musculoskeletal complaints account for 20 percent of the visits to primary care physicians and 80 percent of the visits to sports medicine clinics.

Fractures, sprains, ligament tears, and other injuries, most commonly to the knees and ankles, are part of the active teenager's life. Low back pain in adolescent athletes is a commonly seen problem in both sports medicine and general pediatrics and should be taken seriously.

Adults

Inflammatory conditions of the joints, bones, and surrounding connective tissues usually begin in young adults, although children and adolescents can have these conditions (e.g., juvenile rheumatoid arthritis, or JRA). **Arthritis** and **rheumatoid arthritis** are **chronic** (i.e., constant and continuous), although there may be periods where symptoms regress or subside. Healthcare professionals are not certain of the cause of rheumatoid arthritis (RA). RA is known as an autoimmune disease leading to severe pain and swelling as the body's immune system attacks its own joints. A thickening of the synovial membranes leads to **fibrosis** (the excessive formation of connective tissue), resulting in limited and painful motion. **Ankylosis** (joint stiffness) is often the result.

Ankylosing spondylitis is a chronic, progressive, inflammatory disease of the spine, sacroiliac, and larger joints of the extremities. The process leads to ankylosis and eventually deformity. Males are affected by ankylosing spondylitis more often than females by a ratio of ten to one.

Osteoarthritis is a noninflammatory, progressive disorder that eventually causes deterioration of the articular cartilage, with formation of new bone, at these joints. Osteoarthritis is the result of wear and tear of the body's joints over time. It is also the most commonly diagnosed form of arthritis. Nearly all persons over the age of 60 have signs of osteoarthritis in the hands, feet, hips, spine, and other places. The symptoms include pain, redness, swelling, stiffness, and often, decreased range of motion.

Gout, or **gouty arthritis**, is a disorder caused by hyperuricemia, an excess of uric acid in the blood. Uric acid is one of the body's necessary chemicals, but when it accumulates in the joints and surrounding tissues it can cause damage to and even the destruction of the articular cartilage or synovial membrane. This damage leads to sudden, severe pain and inflammation most often affecting the great toe, causing a condition called **podagra**, pain in the foot. Although gout can affect anyone, it is most common in men over the age of 40.

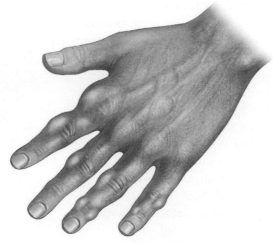

Gout in the hand

Soft Skills for Health Care: Professionalism

Professionalism is the behavior exhibited in the workplace. It is shaped by standards of etiquette and ethics. Although most healthcare facilities have various employee policies and procedures in place to safeguard the quality of a patient's care and experience, often the patient's first impression of the healthcare provider and staff is the most important. The communication style, demeanor, level of competence, and overall image of a healthcare professional can be built on the foundation of a first encounter. As a rule, employees should refrain from inappropriate language, personal phone use, and participation in office gossip.

Consider the following scenario:

A professional football player is seen in your orthopedic practice to obtain a second opinion regarding his ability to play in Sunday's game. The entire staff recognizes him on arrival and a few approach him for autographs and pictures during his office visit. Standards of professionalism would view this behavior as negative and unwelcome.

All patients should be treated with the same level of respect and privacy while in the medical office. Consider the patient's perspective in every situation and be cautious when faced with issues of privacy and confidentiality.

In addition, the Health Insurance Portability and Accountability Act of 1996 (HIPAA) is an integral part of the delivery of healthcare services. HIPAA's Privacy Rule safeguards the unauthorized release and disclosure of identifiable patient health information.

Pregnant Women

Pregnancy leads to increased levels of the hormones estrogen, relaxin, and corticosteroids (discussed more fully in Chapter 14). These hormones cause an increase in the mobility of the joints of the pelvic bones, allowing the pelvic outlet to expand during labor and delivery. A woman's posture changes during pregnancy, with a gradual **lordosis** or swayback, to compensate for the growing fetus. Consequently, the pregnant woman must shift her center of gravity.

Male and female pelvic bones have some significant differences, as depicted in Figure 4.12. The female pelvis is structured to carry a fetus; it is broader and shallower, and the inlet and outlet are wider than the male's. A wider pubic angle in women allows for childbirth.

FIGURE 4.12 Comparison of Male and Female Pelvises

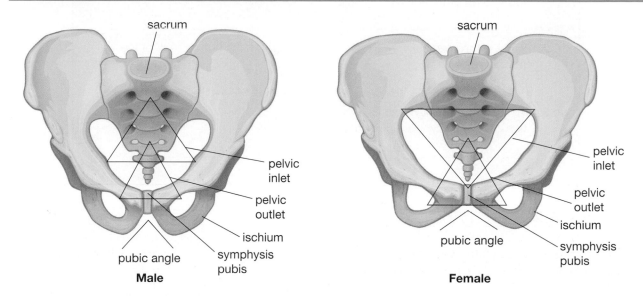

Male

Female

Seniors

The aging adult shows changes in **physique**, the physical, structural body, including a decrease in height. The shortening of the trunk makes the arms appear longer in comparison. It is common to see **kyphosis**, with the head protruding forward and the hips and knees flexing for balance.

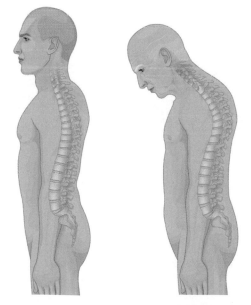

Typical spine   Kyphosis

Osteoporosis is a condition in which bones become fragile and brittle. It occurs when the decrease of bone mass and density results in an increased risk of fracture. The bone becomes weak, and fractures in the hip and vertebrae are common. Postmenopausal women are most commonly affected by osteoporosis, because of the decrease in the female hormones estrogen and progesterone.

The most common orthopedic operation performed in the older adult population is the **total hip replacement (THR)**, with more than 332,000 performed annually in the United States. The procedure has continued to advance since 1953, when it was introduced. Today, a THP involves the surgical removal of the ball and socket joint and replacement with an artificial prosthesis made of metal or ceramic.

Checkpoint **4.3**

Answer the following questions to identify any areas of the section that you may need to review.

1. What is the name of the process that occurs during pregnancy to allow for the growth of the fetus?

   _____

2. What is the medical term for the spaces between the suture lines of the newborn's skull?

   _____

3. What is the repetitive motion injury seen in people who do the same activities daily (e.g., typists and carpenters)?

   _____

Exercise 4.9   Word Analysis

Read each sentence carefully, then break each underlined word into its parts and write a definition for the medical term. Separate the parts of the term with a slash (/).

Example: arthroscopy   arthro / scopy   examination of interior of a joint using an instrument

1. The <u>fibrosis</u> of the muscle tissue in the shoulder girdle was widespread.

   _____   _____

2. The patient's <u>arthritis</u> limits her ability to use the telephone.

   _____   _____

3. Mr. Kelly has severe <u>bursitis</u> in his left hip.

   _____   _____

4. <u>Necrosis</u> in the head of the femur required a prosthetic replacement.

   _____   _____

5. The <u>dislocation</u> of the knee required surgery.

   _____   _____

Exercise 4.10   Comprehension Check

Circle the most appropriate word choice in each sentence.

1. Carpal tunnel syndrome/Genu varum is an example of a repetitive motion injury.
2. The fontanels/suture lines are palpable in an infant's head and are areas where the bones of the skull meet.
3. We will recommend surgery to correct the calcaneus/syndactyly.
4. Tibial torsion/Tendinitis is a twisting of the tibia.
5. In bursitis/osteoporosis there is a decrease in bone mass.

Exercise 4.11   Name That Term

Write the medical term for the underlined word, phrase, or abbreviation in each sentence.

1. <u>Stiffening and later fixation of a joint</u> may be associated with aging.   _____

2. An <u>inflamed bursa on the side of the great toe</u> may be aggravated by poorly fitting shoes.   _____

3. The child displayed severe <u>humpback</u>.   _____

4. A 70-year-old woman is referred for treatment of a <u>decrease in bone mass</u>.   _____

5. The patient is a 30-year-old carpenter with a fracture of the <u>heel bone</u>, the result of a fall.   _____

Exercise 4.12   Word Building

Use word parts to create medical terms for the definitions given. Write the term in the space beside the definition.

1. inflammation of a bone and bone marrow   _____

2. pertaining to the femur   _____

3. pertaining to the skeleton   _____

4. bone tumor   _____

5. bone pain   _____

Exercise 4.13   Spelling Check

Correct each sentence by providing the correct spelling, including singular and plural form, of each word on the line provided.

1. Several <u>bioppsy</u> will be necessary to accurately diagnose the problem.   _____

2. An <u>antigens</u> is a protein.   _____

3. Archer, a two-year old child, has a condition commonly known as tibial torsion, as it affects both <u>tibias</u>.   _____

4. The <u>metatarsus</u> of the left ankle were crushed in the accident.   _____

5. The two <u>fontenel</u> in the child's head were closed.   _____

Exercise 4.14   Identification

For each condition listed below, write a one- or two-sentence explanation of the cause. Then circle the area of the body where the condition occurs. Write the number of the condition in the circle, and also indicate if the condition occurs most frequently in infants, adolescents, adults, or seniors. (Some body areas may have more than one circle and number.)

1. kyphosis

2. carpal tunnel syndrome

3. scoliosis

4. Osgood-Schlatter disease

5. ankylosing spondylitis

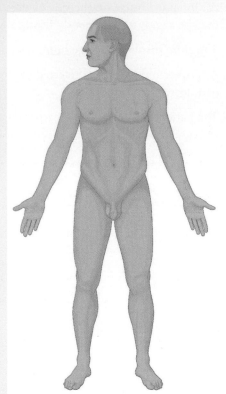

Diagnostic Tests and Examinations

Treating injuries of the musculoskeletal system often requires visualization of the inside of the body using one of the radiographic techniques described in Chapter 2. One of the most frequently used diagnostic imaging tools is **arthrography**, which involves injecting a radiopaque dye into a joint and taking an X-ray picture.

Certain blood tests assess how well the body is functioning and can help the practitioner make a diagnosis. An **erythrocyte sedimentation rate (ESR)**, also known as a *sed rate*, is a test by which the number of erythrocytes (red blood cells) that fall from the plasma are measured over time and that indirectly measures the amount of inflammation present in the body. The C-reactive protein (CRP) test is also used to measure the level of inflammation present in the body. This information can be helpful when diagnosing rheumatoid arthritis if other symptoms are present. Both ESR and CRP levels are used to assist in monitoring how well someone is responding to treatment for rheumatoid arthritis.

The **rheumatoid factor (RF) test** is a laboratory test looking for the presence of RF in the blood. RF is an antibody found in the serum of persons with rheumatoid arthritis.

Serum calcium (Ca) indicates whether the mineral calcium is being released into the blood, and is a measure of bony destruction. An elevated calcium level is called **hypercalcemia**.

Human leukocyte antigen (HLA) B-27 is a protein present on the white blood cells of persons with arthritic conditions such as ankylosing spondylitis. A blood test called **serum alkaline phosphatase** can determine the levels of HLA B-27 in the body. Although the chemical is necessary to build new bone, conditions such as osteomalacia and rheumatoid disease may cause an elevation in its levels.

Serum creatine phosphokinase (CPK) is an enzyme found in skeletal and cardiac muscle. An elevation of CPK in the serum may indicate muscular dystrophy, certain malignancies, and other illnesses.

Arthrocentesis is a procedure in which synovial fluid is removed and examined to diagnose a musculoskeletal disorder such as arthritis or gout.

Bone marrow aspiration and **biopsy** are procedures in which a long, thick needle is inserted through the skin and into the posterior iliac crest; a small amount of bone marrow is aspirated through the needle (see Figure 4.13). A biopsy involves examining a small piece of the core of the bone marrow to diagnose certain diseases, such as malignancies and infections.

An **electromyograph** is a test of muscle strength that measures a muscle's ability to contract via electrical stimulation. Bone density is measured by **photon absorptiometry**, which determines whether a person has osteoporosis. Table 4.8 lists some of the more common diagnostic procedures of the musculoskeletal system.

> **What's in a Word?**
>
> The term electromyography is made up the following word parts: *electro/o* meaning "electricity," *my/o* meaning "muscle," and *-graphy* meaning "process of recording."

FIGURE 4.13 Bone Marrow Aspiration

Bone marrow aspiration and biopsy are used to identify the cause of blood disorders and to determine if cancer or infection has spread to the bone marrow.

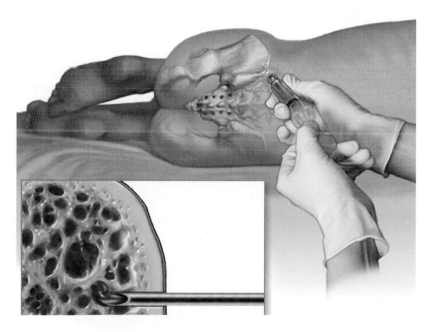

TABLE 4.8 | Musculoskeletal System Tests and Examinations

Term		Meaning
arthrography	[ar-**throg**-raf-ee]	X-ray during which radiopaque dye is injected to visualize a joint
arthroscopy	[ar-**thros**-kah-pee]	visual examination of the interior of a joint using an endoscope
calcium (serum)	[**kal**-see-um]	test that measures the amount of calcium in the blood
electromyography (EMG)	[ee-lek-trO-my-**og**-raf-ee]	method to measure muscle strength by testing the muscle's ability to contract using electrical stimulation
erythrocyte sedimentation rate (sed)	[er-**ith**-rO-sIt sed-ih-men-**tay**-shun rayt]	laboratory test by which the number of erythrocytes (red blood cells) that fall from the plasma are measured over time
human leukocyte antigen B-27	[**hyoo**-man **loo**-kO-sIt **an**-tih-jen]	designation of genetic makeup on chromosomes helpful in determining transplant matching and associated with certain diseases, in particular, arthritis
range of motion (ROM)		a passive measurement of a joint's ability to move along varying degrees of flexion and extension
response photon absorptiometry	[**fO**-ton ab-sorp-shee-**om**-ah-tree]	a test to measure bone density
rheumatoid factor (RF)	[**roo**-mah-toyd **fak**-tor]	antibody found in the serum of a person with rheumatoid arthritis
serum alkaline phosphatase	[**seer**-um **al**-kah-lIn **fos**-fah-tays]	laboratory test on the serum of the blood that measures whether there is an excess of new bone formation
serum creatine phosphokinase	[**seer**-um **kree**-ah-tin fos-fO-**kI**-nays]	laboratory test on the serum of the blood that may indicate certain illnesses and diseases; an enzyme found in skeletal and cardiac muscle
uric acid test	[**yoo**-rik **as**-id test]	test of the blood or urine to determine the amount of this chemical salt present

Checkpoint 4.4

Answer the following questions to identify any areas of the section that you may need to review.

1. What is the name of the procedure in which synovial fluid is removed and examined to diagnose conditions such as arthritis or gout?

   _____

2. What is the medical term for the condition of elevated calcium in the blood?

   _____

3. Which diagnostic imaging tool involves the injection of a radiopaque dye into a joint to take an X-ray picture?

   _____

Treatments

Healthcare practitioners use predetermined guidelines to direct patient care. These guidelines, known as clinical practice guidelines and evidence-based practices, have been developed by the specialty societies based on past clinical research. They represent the treatment pathways that have achieved the best outcomes. Treatment decisions generally fall into three categories: surgical, clinical, and pharmacological.

Surgical treatments are generally invasive as they involve a puncture or an incision into the skin. *Clinical treatments* are generally noninvasive and involve nonsurgical techniques (e.g., physical therapy). *Pharmacological treatments* involve the utilization of medicines (drugs) to treat specific illnesses or diseases. Medication therapies are regulated by the Food and Drug Administration (FDA). To be approved by the FDA for use in the United States, every medicine must be backed by research studies that have shown the medication to be effective in its treatment of a given disease and has a tolerable safety profile. The following sections provide an overview of treatments common to the musculoskeletal system.

Surgical Treatments

Fusing or connecting joint structures to make them immobile is called **fixation**. **Arthrodesis**, the surgical procedure for fixating joints, is performed in patients with severe arthritis or joint injuries to promote new bone formation.

Arthroplasty is the name for the procedure that involves placing a prosthesis consisting of the movable parts of the joint in the joint capsule; it is used in many areas of the body to replace damaged joints, such as a **resection** (excision, surgical removal) of bone to remove a malignant lesion, for instance. Then, a **bone graft** taken from another site in the person who is being operated on or from a cadaver may be inserted at the site to provide stability.

A **fracture**, or break in a bone, must be returned to normal alignment and then **immobilized** in a cast to promote correct new bone growth and healing. The method to realign the bone structures is called **reduction**. Several methods are used:

- A **closed reduction (CR)** is performed using either local or general anesthesia, since the procedure can be painful. The ends of the fractured bone are manually manipulated, externally, to position them into proper alignment.

- An **open reduction (OR)** is a surgical procedure performed in the operating room. An incision is made, and the injury is repaired directly. After the repair is made, the patient's wound is sutured.

- When there has been considerable damage to the bone, such as being crushed in an accident, it may be necessary to perform an **internal fixation (IF).** This invasive procedure involves the stabilization of broken bones into their correct position using screws, pins, and rods to hold the pieces together and promote healing (see Figure 4.14).

- Bones can be realigned by using **traction** to pull the fragments (each piece of a broken bone) into proper position (see Figure 4.15). A pulley and weight are used to pull the distal end of the bone into realignment with the proximal end. This noninvasive technique is commonly referred to as **external fixation (EF)**.

Table 4.9 lists additional surgical procedures and treatments related to the musculoskeletal system.

FIGURE 4.14	Internal Fixation

This procedure uses plates and screws outside the bone or rods inside the bone to stabilize a fracture.

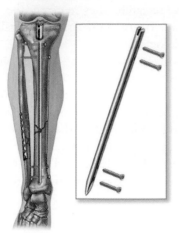

FIGURE 4.14	External Fixation

This procedure uses screws above and below the fracture, along with a device outside the skin to realign a bone.

TABLE 4.9 Surgical Treatments Associated with the Musculoskeletal System

Treatment		Description
amputation		procedure in which a body extremity is removed to control pain or the spread of disease
arthrocentesis	[ar-thrO-sen-**tee**-sis]	aspiration of fluid from a joint
arthrodesis	[ar-**throd**-eh-sis]	procedure in which a joint is fused or stabilized
arthroplasty	[**ar**-thrO-plas-tee]	procedure to create an artificial joint or to restore an injured joint
bunionectomy	[bun-yun-**eck**-tuh-mee]	removal of a bunion
debridement	[de-**breed**-mint]	removal of damaged, dead, or infected tissue to promote healing
myorrhaphy	[mye-**ore**-rah-fee]	suture of a muscle
osteoplasty	[**ahs**-tee-Oh-plas-tee]	repair of a bone
resection	[ree-**sek**-shun]	removal of all or part of an organ or body part
total hip replacement (THR)		removal of the ball and socket joint and replacement with an artificial prosthesis made of metal or ceramic
total knee replacement (TKR)		replacement of the entire knee joint
traction	[**trak**-shun]	bone realignment by pulling fragments into proper position

Pharmacological Treatments

The agents used in orthopedics often are aimed at relieving pain and decreasing inflammation (see Table 4.10). The most common analgesic agents are **nonsteroidal anti-inflammatory drugs** (**NSAIDs**), such as ibuprofen, and **salicylates**, such as aspirin. These drugs are prescribed for arthritis, bursitis, muscle aches, and pains and are often available over the counter. **Steroids** are sometimes injected directly into the affected joint for pain management. Many analgesics are currently being developed, and new ones frequently become available.

Severe rheumatoid arthritic conditions may be treated with **immunosuppressants**, since these conditions may have an immunological component. **Muscle relaxants** are used for muscle spasms and the associated muscle pain. Specific agents promote skeletal muscle relaxation.

Gout is treated with **uricosuric agents**, which lower the uric acid level in the blood, and NSAIDs; some are manufactured with an analgesic already combined.

TABLE 4.10 Pharmacological Agents for the Musculoskeletal System

Drug Class	Use	Generic Names	Brand Names
antigout preparations	decrease the uric acid in the blood	allopurinol, probenecid colchicine	Zyloprim, Col-Probenecid
anti-rheumatics	slow progression of rheumatoid arthritis	etanercept, infliximab	Enbrel, Remicade
immunosuppressants	reduce or suppress the strength of the immune system	gold sodium thiomalate, methotrexate	Aurolate, Rheumatrex
muscle relaxants	relax skeletal muscle and relieve pain	cyclobenzaprine	Flexeril
nonsteroidal anti-inflammatory agents (NSAIDs)	decrease pain and inflammation from conditions such as rheumatoid arthritis, sprains, strains, and sports injuries	ibuprofen, ketorolac tromethamine	Motrin, Advil, Toradol
salicylates (type of NSAID)	decrease pain and inflammation from conditions such as rheumatoid arthritis, sprains, strains, and sports injuries	aspirin	Anacin, Bufferin
steroids	decrease pain and inflammation from conditions such as rheumatoid arthritis, sprains, strains, and sports injuries	hydrocortisone injection	A-HydroCort

Checkpoint 4.5

Answer the following questions to identify any areas of the section that you may need to review.

1. What is the invasive procedure involving the stabilization of broken bones into their correct position using screws, pins, and rods to hold the pieces together and promote healing?

_____

2. What term best describes the visual examination of the interior of a joint using an endoscope?

_____

3. Name the pharmacological agents that are sometimes injected directly into the affected joint for pain management.

_____

Abbreviations

In the medical field, information is generally recorded in medical charts and in electronic medical records and provided to healthcare workers in medical shorthand. It is important that healthcare professionals become familiar with the abbreviations utilized on a daily basis to successfully perform the duties assigned in a typical workday. Table 4.11 provides a list of common abbreviations used in reference to conditions and treatments of the musculoskeletal system.

TABLE 4.11 Abbreviations Associated with the Musculoskeletal System

Abbreviation(s)	Meaning
AE/AEA	above-elbow amputation
AK/AKA	above-knee amputation
AP	anteroposterior
AROM	active range of motion
BE/BEA	below-elbow amputation
BK/BKA	below-knee amputation
C1, C2, etc.	cervical vertebrae (numbered according to area of the spine)
CDH	congenital dislocation of the hip
CR	closed reduction
DIP	joint distal interphalangeal joint
DJD	degenerative joint disease
EF	external fixation
EMG	electromyography
fx	fracture
HD	hip disarticulation
HNP	herniated nucleus pulposus (disk)
HP	hemipelvectomy
IF	internal fixation
IP joint	interphalangeal joint
IS	intracostal space
KD	knee disarticulation
L1, L2, etc.	lumbar vertebrae
MCP joint	metacarpophalangeal joint
OA	osteoarthritis
OR	open reduction
ortho	orthopedics
PIP joint	proximal interphalangeal joint
PROM	passive range of motion
RA	rheumatoid arthritis
ROJM	range of joint motion
S1, S2, etc.	sacral vertebrae
SD	shoulder disarticulation
T1, T2, etc.	thoracic vertebrae
TENS	transcutaneous electric nerve stimulation
THA	total hip arthroplasty
THR	total hip replacement
TKR	total knee replacement

Exercise 4.15   Word Building

Read each sentence, noting the partially completed medical term. Supply the missing part to complete the term.

1. A physio_____ is someone who studies the functions of the body.
2. Arthro_____ allows the physician to view the inside of the joint through a flexible, lighted instrument.
3. Myo_____ means "pathology or disease of a muscle."
4. _____itis means "inflammation of cartilage."
5. Vascul_____ means "pertaining to vessels."

Exercise 4.16   Comprehension Check

Read each sentence and write the meaning of each underlined word on the line below the sentence. Keep your answers brief. You may need to use a medical dictionary for this exercise.

1. Mr. Osborne is scheduled for an <u>electromyogram</u> this afternoon.

   _____

2. This patient is being referred to an <u>orthopedist</u>.

   _____

3. The <u>periosteum</u> was dissected away to reveal the <u>diaphysis</u>.

   _____

4. Microscopic examination of the material revealed several <u>osteocytes</u>.

   _____

5. <u>Endochondral ossification</u> has begun in the long bones.

   _____

Exercise 4.17   Matching

Match the list of procedures and treatments in column 2 with the diagnosis or condition in column 1. Write the letter of the diagnosis or problem in the space beside the name of the condition or diagnosis.

1. _____ fx
2. _____ scoliosis
3. _____ crushing fracture
4. _____ gout
5. _____ RA
6. _____ osteoporosis

a. photon absorptiometry
b. uricosuric agents
c. fracture reduction and casting
d. sed rate or ESR
e. open reduction/internal fixation
f. brace for torso

Exercise 4.18   Word Building

Find word parts in this chapter to construct medical terms for the definitions that follow. Write the term on the line beside the definition. Separate the parts with a slash (/).

1. study of bone _____

2. without blood supply _____

3. condition of death _____

4. within cartilage _____

5. inflammation of tendon _____

Exercise 4.19   Spelling Check

Indicate whether the underlined term is singular or plural by writing S or P on the line provided. For each plural term, provide the singular form; for each singular term, give the plural.

	S/P	Opposite Form
1. The <u>erythrocyte</u> count was abnormal.	_____	_____
2. Three surgeons participated in the <u>resection</u> of the diseased bone.	_____	_____
3. The structure of the <u>myofilaments</u> was examined.	_____	_____
4. There were a number of <u>grafts</u> performed from a single donor.	_____	_____
5. The patient had three separate <u>sprains</u>.	_____	_____

Exercise 4.20   Word Maps

Rearrange the following terms to create three flowcharts. For each chart, begin with a body part; then add a related disease or condition, and a test or procedure for that condition; finally, add a drug treatment for the disease.

feet	JRA	gout	immunosuppressants
arthrocentesis	allopurinol	ESR	osteoporosis
joints	calcium supplements	spine	photon absorptiometry

Chapter Review

After successfully completing this chapter, you should be able to correctly answer the following review questions. Answers are provided in the back of the text. Use this self-assessment opportunity to check your understanding of the content and determine whether you need to revisit any of the chapter's content.

Crossword Puzzle

Use the clues provided to fill in the puzzle with the correct terms. Enter one letter per square.

Across

3. extra fingers or toes
6. bone of the lower arm
8. inflammation of a bursa
10. bending at a joint
11. fingers and/or toes
14. pertaining to cartilage
15. physician specializing in the diagnosis and treatment of joint disorders
20. areas where bones of a newborn's skull meet
21. setting a broken bone
22. bones of the hand

Down

1. pertaining to the spine
2. heelbone
4. pertaining to both the lumbar and sacral areas of the spine
5. joint
7. physical, structural body
9. range of motion
12. bowleg
13. total hip replacement
16. bone at the back of the skull
17. inflammation of bone
18. first thoracic vertebra
19. pertaining to the skeleton

Matching

Match the following terms to their proper definitions.

1. _____ tendons
2. _____ periosteum
3. _____ sternocleidomastoid
4. _____ cardiac muscle
5. _____ lactic acid
6. _____ origin
7. _____ ossify
8. _____ kyphosis
9. _____ epicondylitis
10. _____ resection

a. to remove surgically

b. "humpback"

c. to become hardened bone

d. "tennis elbow"

e. muscle that turns the head from side to side

f. outer covering of bone

g. heavy cords that attach muscles to bone

h. involuntary muscles found only in the heart

i. a chemical substance released by muscle cells during increased activity

j. point of attachment for muscle at proximal end of bone

Identification

Correctly label the illustrations by writing the correct term on the lines provided.

1. _____   6. _____

2. _____   7. _____

3. _____   8. _____

4. _____   9. _____

5. _____   10. _____

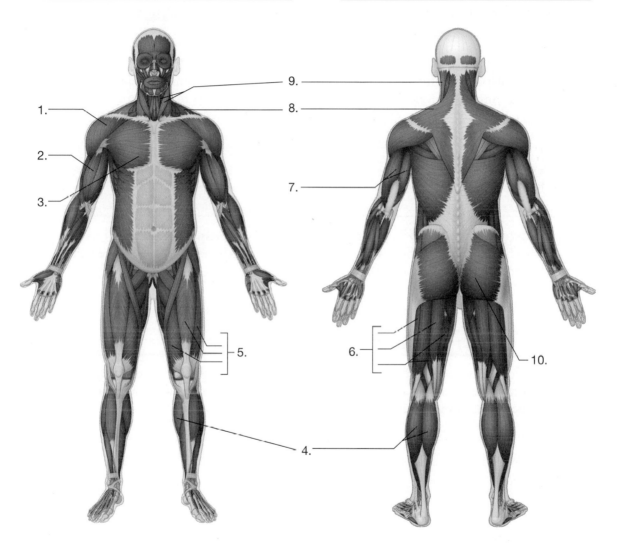

Abbreviations

Complete the following items by adding the appropriate abbreviations and the meaning of the abbreviations on the lines provided.

1. Mrs. Johnson is an 88-year-old retired schoolteacher who has been treated for osteoarthritis for the past six years. Pain and stiffness in her hip have recently prevented Mrs. Johnson from performing activities of daily living. She is an ideal candidate for what surgical procedure?

   _____

   _____

2. Advil, Motrin, and ibuprofen are all pharmacological agents that belong to this particular group of drugs. _____

   _____

3. This particular condition most commonly involves the chronic inflammation of the bones, joints, and connective tissues. What are the abbreviation and name for this particular condition?

   _____

   _____

4. An X-ray of Jason's ankle revealed a break in the continuity of bone. What are the abbreviation and medical term for his diagnosis? _____

   _____

5. Davis has spent the past few weeks experiencing muscle weakness, pain, and abnormal sensations. His physician has ordered the following diagnostic test, which measures muscle strength by testing muscular contractility using electrical stimulation. _____

   _____

Word-Building Challenge

Review the following list of terms. Apply your knowledge of musculoskeletal word parts to accurately identify the meaning of each new term. Write your answer on the line provided and then check your definition against the answer provided in the appendix.

1. chondromalacia _____

2. arthrotomy_____

3. syndesmoplasty _____

4. osteopenia _____

5. meniscectomy _____

Extension Activities

Complete the following activities as assigned by your instructor.

1. Figure 4.7 provides an overview of the major skeletal muscles. Using information found online, create a basic workout routine identifying one exercise for each muscle group outlined in the figure. Present the exercise plan as a PowerPoint presentation. Limit your presentation to 10–15 minutes.

2. Using the Internet, conduct a search locating a minimum of three of the pharmacological agents listed in Table 4.10. Post a brief summary in a classroom discussion forum or describe your findings in a class discussion. Be sure to give details regarding the various uses and contraindications provided for both the brand name and generic forms of the drugs.

3. With a small group of three to five classmates, review Figure 4.1 and create a game or activity that focuses on reviewing the bones specific to the arms and legs. Submit your game to the instructor or to the class.

Student eResources

The Course Navigator learning management system that accompanies this textbook offers multiple opportunities to master chapter content, including end-of-chapter exercises, a glossary of key terms with audio pronunciations, games, pronunciation coach, and additional activities such as engaging with the BioDigital® Human.

5 The Nervous System

> "The human brain has 100 billion neurons, each neuron connected to 10 thousand other neurons. Sitting on your shoulders is the most complicated object in the known universe."
>
> —**Michio Kaku,** theoretical physicist

Translation Challenge

Read this excerpt from a medical record and try to answer the questions that follow.

A 40 y/o female patient arrives at the emergency department complaining of a sinus headache, blurred vision, and slurred speech over the last 24 hours. She states that the symptoms had grown progressively worse, leading her to seek medical attention. Upon triage, she is immediately admitted to the hospital and diagnosed with ataxia, paresthesias, and progressive aphasia. She has a history of mild TIAs without loss of consciousness. The diagnosis is consistent with a cerebrovascular accident.

1. Was this patient experiencing symptoms from severe migraines, or did she have a stroke?

2. Is this patient having difficulty with speech and walking, or with sights and sounds?

3. Is a TIA a total internal arrest or a transient ischemic attack?

Learning Objectives

5.1 List and define word parts most commonly used to create terms related to the nervous system.

5.2 Label the organs of the nervous system and distinguish between the central nervous system and the peripheral nervous system.

5.3 Name and describe the function(s) of the major areas of the brain and spinal cord.

5.4 Describe the distribution and supply of nerve cells across the body.

5.5 Explain the role neurotransmitters play in communication between the brain and body.

5.6 List nervous system abnormalities and their effects.

5.7 Describe common conditions related to mental and behavioral health.

5.8 Name tests and treatments for major nervous system abnormalities.

5.9 State the meaning of abbreviations related to the nervous system.

5.10 Correctly use the terminology of the nervous system in written and oral communication.

5.11 Correctly spell and pronounce nervous system terminology.

5.12 Correctly spell and pronounce terms related to mental and behavioral health.

COURSE NAVIGATOR

Access Additional Chapter Resources

The nervous system serves as the body's electrical "wiring system" by sending the impulses and signals that drive all functions. Due to its complexity, this particular body system is often the most difficult to comprehend and the most challenging to diagnose and treat. The nervous system is responsible for directing all functions within the body, including skeletal movement, thought processes (e.g., memory), and the body's ability to maintain homeostasis (e.g., heart rate and breathing). The nervous system works alongside the endocrine system to process information collected from the senses and produce a response. If you've ever wondered how the body distinguishes pain from pleasure or how a person's reflexes react to a loud sound, this chapter has the answers.

The study of the nervous system is called **neurology**, and the physician who specializes in neurology is a **neurologist**. (Recall that the combining form *neur/o* means "nerve" and the suffix *-ology* means "study of," while the suffix *-ologist* means "one who specializes in.")

Nervous System Word Parts

As with the other body systems, a core of prefixes, combining forms, and suffixes serve as the source for most of the medical words associated with the nervous system. Table 5.1 lists common combining forms and their meanings. In addition to these combining forms, the following prefixes and suffixes appear often in words associated with the nervous system: prefixes: *hemi-* (half), *mono-* (one), *para-* (near, abnormal), *quadri-* (four);

and suffixes: *-cele* (herniation or protrusion), *-lepsy* (seizure), *-lysis* (breaking down/dissolving), *-oma* (pertaining to a tumor), *-paresis* (slight paralysis), and *-plegia* (paralysis).

TABLE 5.1 Combining Forms Associated with the Nervous System

Combining Form	Meaning	Example
astr/o	star-shaped	astrocytoma (a tumor originating from a star-shaped cell)
blast/o	young cells or tissue	neuroblastoma (a malignant tumor commonly seen in children younger than 10 years of age that originated from the autonomic nervous system)
cephal/o	head	diencephalon ("interbrain," region of the brain that houses the thalamus and hypothalamus)
cerebell/o	cerebellum	cerebellar (pertaining to the cerebellum)
cerebr/o	cerebrum	cerebral (pertaining to the brain)
chord/o, cord/o	cord	chordotomy (procedure to make an incision in the spinal cord)
crani/o	cranium	cranial (pertaining to the head)
cyt/o	cell	astrocyte (star-shaped cells within the central nervous system)
electr/o	electricity	electroencephalogram (record of the electrical activity of the brain)
encephal/o	related to the brain	encephalopathy (disorder or disease of the brain)
gangli/o	swelling, collection	ganglioneuroma (rare, benign tumors of the peripheral nervous system)
gli/o	gluey substance	neuroglia ("nerve glue," cells that physically hold neurons together)
kinesi/o	movement	dyskinesia (difficulty performing voluntary movements)
lob/o	lobe	lobectomy (removal of a lobe of the brain)
medull/o	medulla	medulloblastoma (a tumor commonly seen in children that originated from embryonic tissue)
mening/o	membrane covering brain and spinal column	meningitis (inflammation of the meninges, the protective membrane that covers the brain and spinal cord)
myel/o	spinal cord	myelocele (protrusion of the spinal cord)
neur/o	nerve	neuritis (inflammation of a peripheral nerve or nerves)
occipit/o	occiput (back of the head)	occipital lobe (lobe of the brain responsible for processing visual information)
onc/o	tumor	glioblastoma (a malignant tumor affecting the brain and spinal cord)
pariet/o	relationship to a wall	parietal lobe (lobe of the brain responsible for the integration of sensory information)
phas/o	speech	dysphasia (language disorder characterized by difficulty speaking)
psych/o	mental, the mind	psychiatrist (a physician who specializes in psychiatry)
radic/o	nerve root, spinal nerve root	radicotomy, (surgical procedure to destroy damaged nerve roots in the spinal cord to relieve pain)
rhiz/o	nerve root, spinal nerve root	rhizotomy (surgical procedure to destroy damaged nerve roots in the spinal cord to relieve pain)
somat/o	body	somatic nervous system (part of the nervous system that controls voluntary movements)
tempor/o	temporal	temporal lobe (lobe of the brain responsible for hearing, object recognition, language comprehension, and memories)

Anatomy and Physiology

The nervous system has two parts: the **central nervous system (CNS)**, consisting of the *brain* and *spinal cord*, and the **peripheral nervous system (PNS)**, which includes the 12 pairs of *cranial nerves* and the 31 pairs of *spinal nerves*. The CNS receives its messages from the PNS by way of sensory receptors. The information is then processed, initiating a command that is sent out to the muscles and glands. Figure 5.1 shows the organization of the nervous system, the flow of information into the body for processing via stimuli, and the body's route of output or response. Table 5.2 lists anatomy and physiology terms related to the nervous system.

FIGURE 5.1 Organization of the Nervous System (Flow of Information)

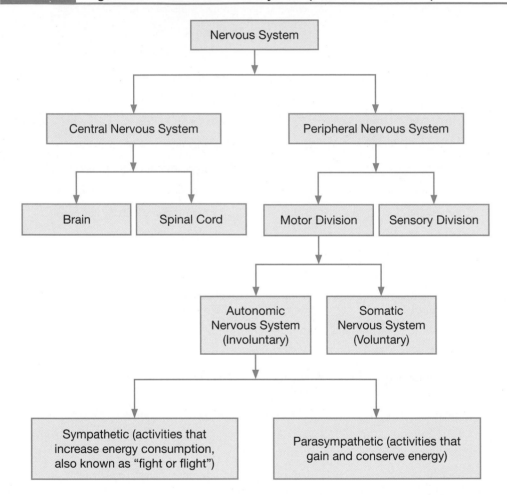

Term		Meaning	Word Analysis	
afferent neurons	[**af**-er-ent **noor**-ons]	nerves that collect sensory information through the five senses (sight, sound, touch, hearing, and taste)	*afferent* *neuron*	to bring to nerve
arachnoid	[ar-**ak**-noyd]	delicate, spiderweb-like membrane forming the middle of the three coverings of the CNS	*arachne* *-oid*	spider, cobweb appearance, resemblance
astrocyte	[**as**-trO-sIt]	large neuroglial cell of the nerve tissue	*astron* *-cyte*	star cell
autonomic nervous system	[aw-tO-**nom**-ik **ner**-vus **sis**-tem]	part of the nervous system that innervates smooth muscle, cardiac muscle, and gland cells (involuntary functions)	*auto-* *nomos*	self law
axon	[**ak**-son]	area of the nerve cell that conducts impulses away from the cell body	*axon*	axis
brain		organ housed within the cranium that is the center of the nervous system	*braegen*	brain
brainstem		portion of the brain	*braegen*	brain
catecholamine	[kat-eh-**kOl**-am-een]	hormones secreted in times of stress: epinephrine, norepinephrine, and dopamine	*catecholamine*	chemical name
cell body		body of a nerve from which dendrites and an axon arise		
central nervous system		composed of the brain and spinal cord		
cerebral cortex	[**ser**-eh-bral **kor**-teks]	area of the brain located in the outer portion of the cerebrum and responsible for voluntary motor functions	*cerebr/o* *cortic/o*	brain outer layer, cortex
cerebrospinal fluid	[**ser**-eh-brO-**spI**-nal **floo**-id]	fluid that surrounds the brain and spinal cord (provides cushion and protection)	*cerebr/o* *spin/o* *-al* *fluo*	brain spinal cord pertaining to flow
cerebrum	[se-**ree**-brum]	portion of the brain that includes the cerebral hemispheres	*cerebr/o*	brain
dendrite	[**den**-drIt]	treelike structure branching out of the nerve cell body, information enters the neuron via the dendrites after collection by sensory neurons	*dendrite*	tree
diencephalon	[dI-en-**sef**-ah-lon]	part of the brain that contains the hypothalamus and thalamus	*dia-* *en-* *cephal/o*	through inside head
dorsal root		sensory nerve cell located in the PNS	*dorsal*	pertaining to the back
dura mater	[**doo**-rah **may**-ter]	outer layer of the meninges	*dura* *mater*	hard mother
efferent neurons	[**ef**-er-ent **noo**-rons]	neurons that carry motor responses from the brain to the muscles and glands, motor neurons	*efferent* *neuron*	to bring out nerve
frontal lobe		area in the anterior portion of the brain	*frontal* *lobe*	front part, subdivision

Continues

Term		Meaning	Word Analysis	
ganglion	[**gang**-lee-on]	collection of nerve cell bodies in the PNS		
glia	[**glee**-ah]	supportive cells, also known as *neuroglia*, that hold and protect neurons	*glia*	glue
gyri	[**jI**-rI]	elevations that form the cerebral hemispheres	*gyros*	circle
hemisphere	[**hem**-is-feer]	a lateral half of the cerebrum or cerebellum	*hemi-spher/ o*	half globe
hypothalamus	[**hI**-pO-**thal**-ah-mus]	area of the brain that stimulates target organs to secrete hormones; located inferior to the thalamus	*hypo-thalam/o*	under thalamus
innervate (v)	[**in**-er-vayt]	to stimulate by nerve fibers	*in-nervus*	within nerve
interneurons	[in-ter-**noo**-rons]	groups of neurons between sensory and motor neurons	*inter-neuron*	between nerve
medulla oblongata	[med-**ul**-ah ob-long-**gah**-tah]	central structure of the brain	*medulla oblongata*	marrow long
meninges (pl)	[men-**in**-jeez]	membranes covering the brain and spinal cord	*mening/o*	membrane
microglia	[mI-**kro**-glee-ah]	phagocytic nerve cells	*micro-glia*	small glue
midbrain		area in the central portion of the brain	*mid-brain*	middle brain
myelin	[**mI**-el-lin]	fatty substance that covers components of the PNS	*myel/o*	the sheath of nerve fibers
neuroglia	[noo-**rog**-lee-ah]	cellular components of the CNS and PNS; nonneural tissue	*neur/o glia*	nerve glue
neurology	[noo-**rol**-ah-jee]	study of the nervous system and its components	*neur/o -logy*	nerve study of
neuron	[**noo**-ron]	cellular component of the nervous system; passes electrical messages from one part of the body to another	*neuron*	nerve
neurotransmitter	[noo-rO-**trans**-mit-er]	chemical released at synapses that passes the electrical impulse from one neuron to another	*neur/o transmission*	nerve to send across
node of Ranvier	[ron-vee-**ay**]	area between two segments of the axon of a nerve cell	*node Ranvier*	resembling a knot 19th-century French pathologist
occipital lobe	[ok-**sip**-ih-tal]	area of the brain located posteriorly	*occipit/o* *-al* *lobe*	the back of the head pertaining to part; subdivision
oligodendroglia	[ol-ig-O-den-**drog**-lee-ah]	type of glia cell that forms myelin in the CNS	*olig/o dendron glia*	a few, a little tree glue
parasympathetic nervous system	[**par**-ah-sim-pah-**thet**-ik]	part of the ANS located in the brain stem and sacral area of the spinal cord that slows the heartbeat and increases muscle movement of the digestive system	*para-* *sympathetic/o*	alongside, near; departure from normal relating to the sympathetic (autonomic) nervous system

Continues

Term		Meaning	Word Analysis	
parietal lobes	[pah-**rI**-eh-tal]	areas of the brain located on either side of the skull	*pariet/o*	denoting any relationship to a wall
			lobe	part; subdivision
peripheral nervous system	[pur-**if**-er-al]	system that includes the 12 pairs of cranial nerves, the 31 pairs of spinal nerves, and their branches	*peri-*	around, about
			phero	to carry
pia mater	[**pI**-ah **may**-ter]	innermost membrane of the meninges, covers the brain and spinal cord		
pons	[**ponz**]	portion of the brain located in the brainstem	*pons*	bridge
reflex arc	[**ree**-fleks ark]	transmission of nerve impulses and neurotransmitters that causes an involuntary movement in muscles	*reflex*	to bend back
			arc	bow
Schwann cells	[**shvahn**]	cells that make up the white, fatty myelin sheath that covers the axons outside of the CNS	*Schwann*	19th-century German histologist and physiologist
somatic nervous system	[sO-**mat**-ik]	system that involves skeletal (voluntary) muscle innervation	*somat/o*	body
sulci (pl)	[**sul**-sI]	grooves on the surface of the brain	*sulcus*	ditch
sympathetic nervous system	[sim-pah-**thet**-ik]	body's emergency system that sends a message to the adrenal medulla causing the release of stress hormones	*sympath/o*	refers to the sympathetic nervous system (part of the autonomic nervous system)
synapse	[**sin**-aps]	area of the nerve cells where neurotransmitters are released from one nerve cell to the next	*syn-*	together, with
			hapto	clasp
temporal lobe	[**tem**-por-al]	area of the brain located at the temples	*tempor/o*	temples (of the head)
			-al	pertaining to
			lobe	part, subdivision
thalamus	[**thal**-ah-mus]	area of the brain located in the center	*thalam/o*	thalamus
ventricle	[**ven**-trih-kul]	cavity of the brain	*ventricle*	belly

The Central Nervous System (CNS)

As previously mentioned, the CNS is divided into two parts: the brain and spinal cord. As information is collected by the PNS, this division is responsible for processing the information collected and triggering a direct response. The brain and spinal cord are protected by the bones that encase them (the skull and vertebrae). Both the brain and spinal cord are covered by fluid-containing membranes called **meninges**, which provide additional protection. Separated by spaces, three layers of meninges cover the CNS: the outer layer is called the **dura mater**, the middle layer is the **arachnoid mater**, and the inner layer is the **pia mater**.

In the brain, the thickest of these layers is the dura mater, as it is the most superficial and is responsible for holding the brain in place within the skull. The middle layer of meninges (arachnoid) is cushioned and nourished by a fluid called **cerebrospinal fluid** (CSF), which fills the subarachnoid space of the CNS. This protective fluid is also found in the **ventricles** (spaces) throughout the brain and in the central canal of the spinal cord. This fluid serves as a cushion to the brain from injury

Did You Know?

The central nervous system is often referred to as the command center for the human body.

when the head is jolted (e.g., during a motor vehicle accident or sports injury), but offers no protection in cases involving direct impact to the skull. CSF is also useful in the diagnosis of conditions affecting the nervous system. The pia mater is closest to the brain and contains the blood vessels responsible for providing nourishment to the brain. The pia mater is also tightly bound to the surface of the spinal cord, while the dura mater is superficial in relation to the body of each vertebra. Figure 5.2 shows the three layers of meninges as well as the location of CSF within the brain and spinal cord.

FIGURE 5.2 The Meninges of the Brain

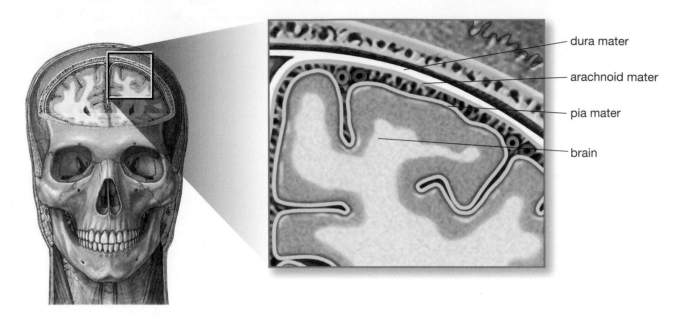

- dura mater
- arachnoid mater
- pia mater
- brain

In the Know: Epidurals

An epidural is a common method of pain relief used during childbirth. The medication is administered via a catheter inserted into the epidural space, between the dura mater and vertebra of the spinal cord (see the image at right). It is used as a temporary means to block the transmission of messages to nerves in or near the spinal cord, resulting in a loss of the sensation of pain.

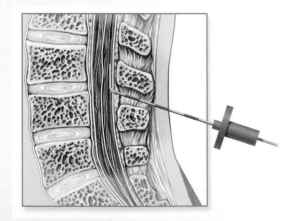

Brain

The **brain** is an organ made up of soft tissue and functions as the center of intellectual, sensation, and nervous activity. The brain, housed in the cranial cavity of the skull, is made up of four main parts: the cerebrum, cerebellum, diencephalon, and the brainstem. Figure 5.3 shows the locations of each main part of the brain.

FIGURE 5.3 The Brain's Four Main Parts

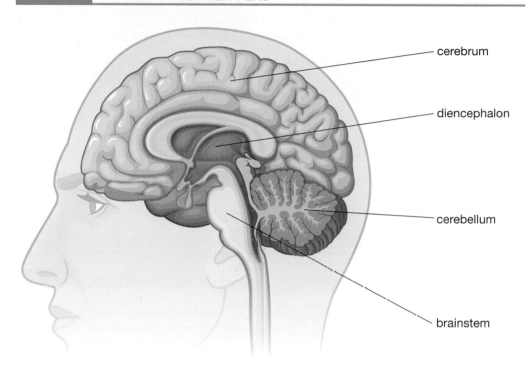

cerebrum

diencephalon

cerebellum

brainstem

The Cerebrum

The largest part of the brain is called the **cerebrum**, and its outer layer, the **cerebral cortex**, is composed of nerve cells called gray matter. This area controls functions such as thought, memory, reasoning, sensation, language, perception, and voluntary movement. Folds, or **gyri**, on the surface of the brain increase the amount of gray matter that can fit inside the skull. The cerebrum is divided into two **hemispheres**: the left hemisphere, which controls muscles on the right side of the body, reasoning, language, and skills necessary for math and science; and the right hemisphere, which controls the muscles on the left side of the body, imagination, insight, and artistic and musical abilities.

Each hemisphere is further divided into four lobes, also known as **cortical areas**. Deep grooves called **sulci** separate the lobes. Figure 5.4 shows the cerebral lobes and their specific functions. The **frontal lobe** is located in the front of the brain and is important in the control of voluntary motor functions, mood, and speech. It is critical in decision-making, thinking, and planning. The **temporal lobe** is located on the lateral aspect of the brain (behind the temples) and controls the olfactory (smell) and auditory (hearing) senses in addition to playing an integral part in comprehension of speech and memory. The **parietal lobe** is found on the top of the brain and is responsible for the instantaneous processing of sensory information such as touch, taste, temperature, pressure, and pain. The fourth and final division is the **occipital lobe**, located in the back of the brain. This lobe quickly processes visual information sent by the eyes.

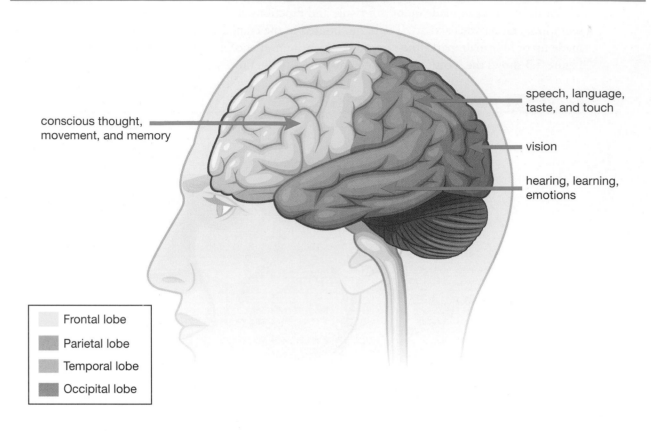

conscious thought, movement, and memory

speech, language, taste, and touch

vision

hearing, learning, emotions

	Frontal lobe
	Parietal lobe
	Temporal lobe
	Occipital lobe

The Cerebellum

The **cerebellum** is the posterior portion of the brain, just inferior to the occipital lobe of the cerebrum and has a unique shape. This particular area of the brain is responsible for the coordination of voluntary movements such as walking and writing. Damage to the cerebellum could result in the lack of one's ability to maintain balance and the loss of fine motor skills.

The Diencephalon

Inferior to the cerebrum and superior to the brain stem is the **diencephalon**, an area of the brain that contains the *thalamus* and the *hypothalamus* (see Figure 5.5). The **thalamus** enables the body to experience sensations such as touch, pain, and temperature by relaying impulses from the sense organs to the cerebral cortex. It is also responsible for emotions and feelings such as mood. The **hypothalamus** sits directly inferior to the thalamus, and despite the fact that it is small, it is one of the most important areas of the brain because it controls all the internal organs, including the heart and blood vessels, and serves as the main regulator or thermostat of body temperature. It is also involved in regulating sleep, water balance, and appetite. As described, the hypothalamus controls the involuntary functions

What's in a Word?

Recall that the term *inferior* means "lower" and *superior* means "upper."

of the autonomic nervous system. Impulses from the hypothalamus travel to the spinal cord and are sent to muscles throughout the body. Note that the pituitary gland (a major component of the endocrine system [discussed in Chapter 11]) is attached to the hypothalamus.

The Brainstem

The brainstem connects the spinal cord to the brain, and consists of the *midbrain*, the *pons*, and the *medulla oblongata*. The **brainstem** conducts impulses to and from the spinal cord, and is responsible for running many of the reflex centers of the body. Specifically the **midbrain**, which is the smallest portion of the brain stem, relays messages in response to auditory and visual stimuli. It is responsible for reflexes controlling movements of the eyes and head. The **pons** serves as a bridge between the cerebrum and the medulla oblongata and relays messages between them. The pons also plays a key role in dreaming, which takes place during REM sleep. The **medulla oblongata** is often considered the most important part of the brain as it is responsible for critical involuntary functions such as the regulation of heart rate, blood pressure, and breathing. Figure 5.5 shows a cross-section of the main parts of the brain from a sagittal viewpoint.

FIGURE 5.5 | Sagittal Section of the Brain

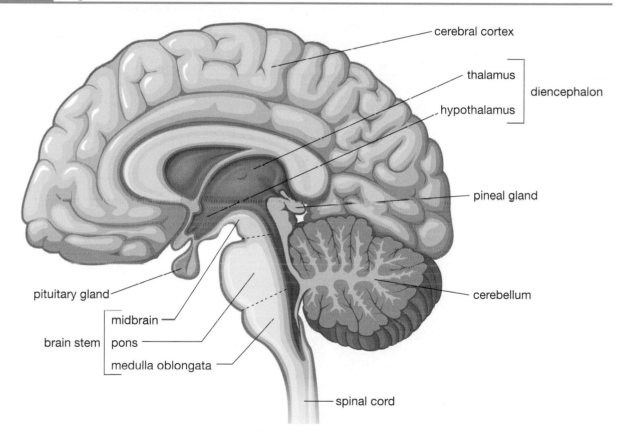

Spinal Cord

The brainstem is connected to the spinal cord. The **spinal cord** extends from the medulla oblongata down to the bottom of the first lumbar vertebra. It is surrounded and protected by the bones of the vertebral column and houses 31 pairs of spinal nerves. Depending on the individual's height, the spinal cord is about 17 to 18 inches long. It is composed of gray matter and white matter, or **myelinated nerve fibers** or spinal tracts. These tracts are actually pathways that conduct impulses to and from the brain. Ascending tracts that travel up to the brain transmit pain, touch, and temperature sensations. Motor impulses travel down the descending tracts from the brain. In other words, the spinal cord transmits sensory impulses *to* the brain and motor impulses *from* the brain.

What's in a Word?

Myel/o can mean bone marrow and spinal cord. An analysis of its context will help identify its intended meaning.

Peripheral Nervous System (PNS)

Like the CNS, the PNS plays an essential role in how the human body functions. Its overall job is to connect the central nervous system to the rest of the body to allow movement and behavior. The PNS is composed of the **cranial nerves** (12 pairs) and **spinal nerves** (31 pairs) and is divided into the **somatic nervous system (SNS)** and the **autonomic nervous system (ANS)**. The SNS's somatic nerve fibers **innervate** (send nerve impulses) to the skeletal muscles, which are under the voluntary control of the individual. The ANS's autonomic fibers innervate involuntary action, the actions not consciously controlled, such as those in smooth muscle, cardiac muscle, glandular tissue, and body parts involved in digestion. Table 5.3 lists the cranial nerves, the body area each controls, and the specific functions associated with each area. Figure 5.6 illustrates the various cranial and spinal nerves found in the PNS.

TABLE 5.3 The Cranial Nerves: Areas of Innervation and Functions

Cranial Nerve	Area of Innervation	Specific Brain Region Association	Function
olfactory (I)	nose	cerebrum	smell
optic (II)	eye	cerebrum	visual acuity and visual fields
oculomotor (III)	eye muscles	midbrain	eyeball movements; pupil size
trochlear (IV)	external eye muscles	midbrain	eye movements
trigeminal—ophthalmic branch (V)	skin and corneal reflex	pons	blinking
trigeminal—maxillary branch (V)	lower eyelid, upper lip, cheek, and nose	pons	sensations of face and eye
trigeminal—mandibular branch (V)	muscles of mastication (chewing)	pons	chewing
abducens (VI)	external eye muscles	pons	outward-turning eye movements
facial (VII)	taste; facial expressions	pons	movement of facial muscles and taste
vestibulocochlear—cochlear branch (VIII)	ear	pons	hearing
vestibulocochlear—vestibular branch (VIII)	ear	pons	balance
glossopharyngeal (IX)	throat muscles and salivary glands	medullaoblongata	movement of back of throat; taste
vagus (X)	throat, larynx, chest, and abdominal organs	medullaoblongata	gag reflex; swallowing; voice; heartbeat; and peristalsis
spinal accessory (XI)	muscles of lower neck and shoulders	medullaoblongata	head turning; shrugging; voice production
hypoglossal (XII)	muscles of tongue	medullaoblongata	movement of tongue and proper speech (enunciation)

FIGURE 5.6 The Cranial and Spinal Nerves of the PNS

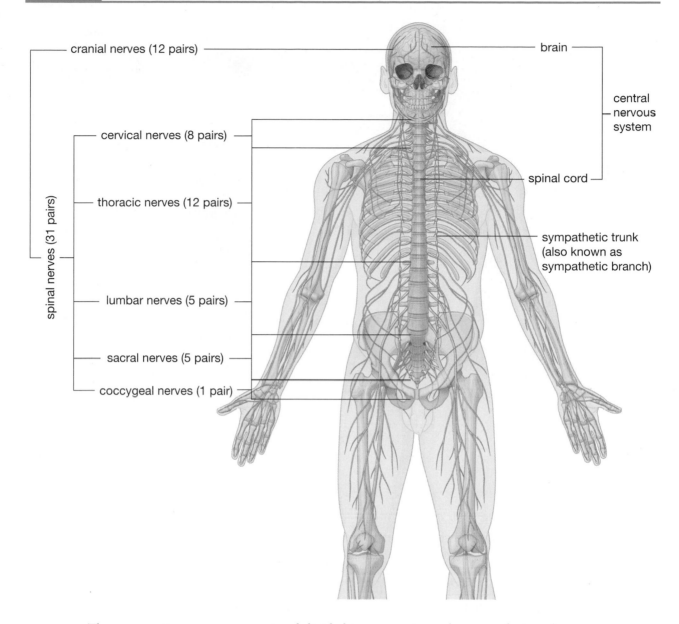

cranial nerves (12 pairs)

brain

central nervous system

cervical nerves (8 pairs)

spinal cord

thoracic nerves (12 pairs)

sympathetic trunk (also known as sympathetic branch)

lumbar nerves (5 pairs)

sacral nerves (5 pairs)

coccygeal nerves (1 pair)

spinal nerves (31 pairs)

The autonomic nervous system is subdivided in two sections: the *sympathetic* and *parasympathetic nervous systems*. The **sympathetic nervous system** is the body's emergency system that sends messages to the adrenal gland, causing the release of **catecholamines**, which are hormones released in response to stress (described in Chapter 11). The sympathetic nervous system is responsible for the initiation of the "fight or flight" response to a perceived threat. During this response, the individual's blood pressure, heart rate, respiration rate, and sweat production increase.

The **parasympathetic nervous system** functions as a control for the sympathetic system as it typically initiates the opposite response (e.g., slows the heart rate, lowers blood pressure, and returns the rate of respiration to normal). This response is often referred to as "rest and repose." This system has neurons located in the gray matter of the brainstem and the sacral area of the spinal cord. Figure 5.7 shows the pathways of the sympathetic and parasympathetic nervous systems as well as the body functions they involve.

FIGURE 5.7 Autonomic Nervous System

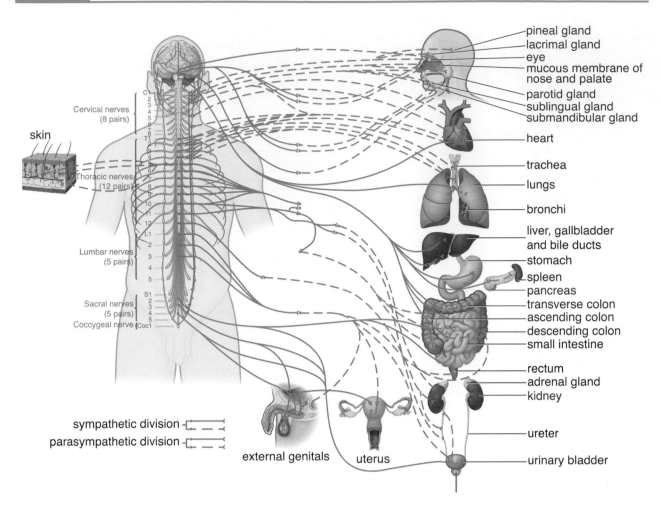

The cells of the nervous system are designed to pass information from one area to another. The **neuron** is the basic structural and functional unit of the nervous system. Figure 5.8 shows the structures of the neuron: the main portion is the **cell body**, with its nucleus; the **dendrites** receive information from other neurons or from sensory cells; and the **axon**, or long branch, sends information from the neuron to other neurons or to muscles or glands.

The axons outside of the CNS are surrounded by a white, fatty sheath called **myelin**, which is made up of **Schwann cells**. The **nodes of Ranvier** are the indentations between each adjoining Schwann cell. The Schwann cells of the PNS are covered by an outer cell layer called the **neurilemma**, which allows these axons to regenerate when injured. The axons within the CNS do not have this layer, so it is extremely difficult for these cells to self-repair when they are injured.

For neurons to transmit their signal, or impulse, they must be connected to one another. This connection takes place over a gap that exists between neurons called a **synapse**. The nerve impulse causes the release of **neurotransmitters**, chemicals that carry the signal across the synapse to the next neuron.

FIGURE 5.8 Neuron (Nerve Cell)

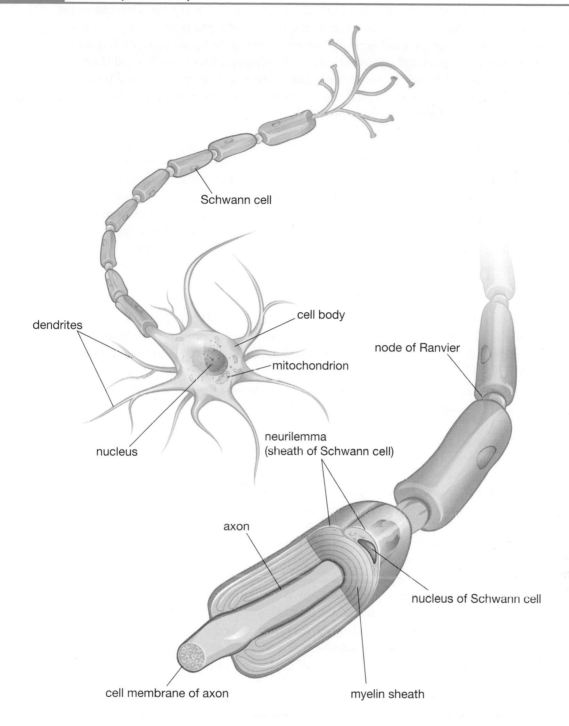

Schwann cell

dendrites

cell body

node of Ranvier

mitochondrion

nucleus

neurilemma
(sheath of Schwann cell)

axon

nucleus of Schwann cell

cell membrane of axon

myelin sheath

Neurotransmitters play an important role in the functions of both the central and peripheral nervous systems. **Acetylcholine** is the neurotransmitter responsible for muscle contraction in the brain as well as the secretion of various hormones. It is involved with attentiveness, wakefulness, thirst, sexuality, and aggression. Alzheimer's disease is associated with the lack of acetylcholine in certain regions of the brain. **Dopamine** is the neurotransmitter involved in controlling an individual's movement, posture, and overall mood. A decrease in dopamine levels in the brain has been associated with symptoms indicative of Parkinson's disease. **Serotonin** is the neurotransmitter known to regulate functions such as body temperature and sleep, mood, appetite, and pain. Depression has been linked to varying levels of serotonin in the body. **Endorphins** are the neurotransmitters responsible for responding to stimuli such as stress, fear, and pain. Endorphins are known to block pain and control emotions. Norepinephrine is another well-known neurotransmitter. Although it is commonly prescribed as a drug to raise blood pressure (by stimulating the contraction blood vessels), **norepinephrine** is important in preparing the body for the fight-or-flight response.

Types of Neurons

The three types of neurons are classified according to the direction in which they transmit their impulses. The **sensory neurons**, called **afferent neurons**, transmit impulses to the spinal cord and brain from all over the body through the five senses. The **motor neurons**, called **efferent neurons**, transmit impulses away from the brain and spinal cord to muscles and glandular tissue. Connecting neurons, called **interneurons**, conduct impulses from sensory neurons to motor neurons and lead to a response in a muscle, gland, or organ.

Special supportive cells called **glia**, or **neuroglia** ("nerve glue"), hold and protect the neurons. One type of glia, called **astrocytes** (meaning "star-shaped"), has threadlike protrusions from their surfaces that hold the neurons close to small blood vessels. Together, this compound structure forms the **blood-brain barrier**, which protects brain tissue from almost all harmful substances that may be carried in the blood. Small astrocytes, called **microglia**, are phagocytic cells that surround degenerating or inflamed brain cells and ingest them. **Oligodendroglia** are the glial cells that produce the myelin sheath and help to hold the neurons together.

Nerve Impulse Pathways

Nerves are constantly sending messages from one part of the body to another, from the outside in, and vice versa. Nerve impulses travel over billions of routes or pathways, called **reflex arcs**. The direction of the impulse is one-way and begins when a message is received through one of the five senses. The message then travels along the sensory reflex arc and is interpreted by the central nervous system. A message is then communicated via the motor reflex arc and a response occurs. One type of reflex arc is demonstrated when the doctor hits the patellar tendon below the knee with a small rubber hammer. This action elicits a reflex response that causes the knee to jerk, which moves the lower leg outward. The movement is caused by the stimulation of the stretch receptors in the muscle, whose signal travels along the length of the sensory neuron to the group of nerve cell bodies in the PNS, called **posterior** or **dorsal root ganglion**. The impulse continues along the dendrites, cell body, and axon of the motor neuron to the effector organ, in this case a muscle.

Reflexes

The **deep tendon reflexes (DTRs)** are assessed by hitting a rubber hammer against the various tendons: biceps, triceps, brachioradialis, quadriceps (knee jerk), and Achilles (ankle jerk). Nerve conduction from the muscle causes the connected muscle to react. Figure 5.9 shows the reflex arc.

Some reflexes are superficial because they have receptors in the skin rather than the muscles. Table 5.4 lists the types of superficial reflexes.

FIGURE 5.9 The Reflex Arc

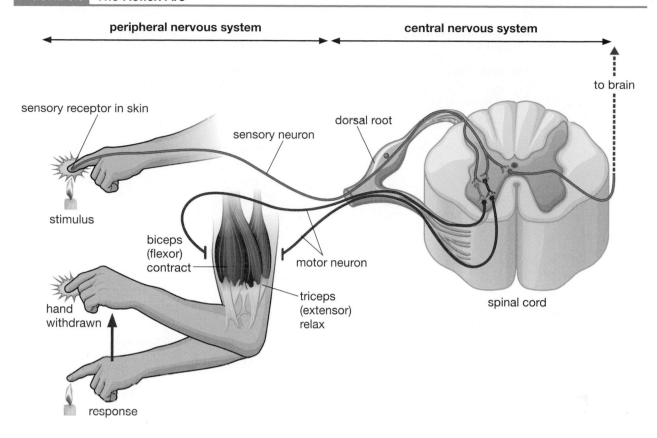

Certain reflexes are abnormal, indicating illness or an abnormal lesion within the brain or spinal cord. Because these reflexes are abnormal findings, the notation on the patient's chart indicates a positive finding. Table 5.5 describes these pathologic reflexes.

TABLE 5.4 Superficial Reflexes

Reflex	Description
abdominal reflex	back of hammer is moved from the side of the abdomen toward the midline; normal response is contraction of abdominal muscle on ipsilateral side and deviation of umbilicus toward the motion
cremasteric reflex	on the male, the inner aspect of the thigh is stroked and elevation of the ipsilateral testicle noted
plantar reflex	back of hammer is stroked up the lateral side of the sole of the foot and across the ball of the foot to elicit plantar flexion of the toe

TABLE 5.5 Abnormal Reflexes

Reflex		Description	Word Analysis	
Babinski	[bah-**bin**-skee]	stroking on the lateral aspect and across the ball of the foot causes extension of the great toe and fanning of the toes	Babinski	19th-century French neurologist
Brudzinski	[broo-**jin**-skee]	flexing chin to the chest elicits resistance and pain	Brudzinski	19th-century Polish physician
Kernig	[**ker**-nig]	when leg is raised straight, resistance and pain occur down the posterior thigh	Kernig	19th-century Russian physician

Checkpoint 5.1

Answer the following questions to identify any areas of the section that you may need to review.

1. The thalamus and hypothalamus are located in which area of the brain?

    _____

2. The brain and spinal cord are located in which division of the nervous system?

    _____

3. Which lobe of the brain processes visual information sent by the eyes?

    _____

4. How many pairs of spinal nerves attach to the spinal cord?

    _____

Exercise 5.1   Word Analysis

Identify the combining form for each definition in the first column, then use the combining form to create a medical term that matches the second definition.

Definition	Combining Form	Definition	Term
1. head	_____	pain in the head	_____
2. electricity	_____	record of electrical activity in the brain	_____
3. movement	_____	pertaining to movement	_____
4. spinal cord	_____	inflammation of the spinal cord	_____
5. nerve	_____	related to a nerve	_____

Exercise 5.2   Comprehension Check

Circle the correct term from the pair in each sentence.

1. Mr. Taber was referred to a neurologist/neuroma.

2. The patient's neurologist ordered an electrocardiogram/electroencephalogram.

3. Several patients in this hospital have been diagnosed with meningitis/meninges.

4. Ms. Murphy has a diagnosis of ganglioneuroma/ganglioplasty of the brachial nerve.

5. Astrocytes/Astrocytosis in the area were found to be abnormal.

Exercise 5.3   Spelling Check

Identify the correct term and its correct spelling for each definition provided. Read each choice very carefully and write the answer you select in the space beside the definition.

1. star cell
   astracyte/astracel/astronomical/astrocyte

   _____

2. cranial nerve involved in the sense of smell
   olpactory/offactory/olfactory/olfactorie

   _____

3. brain
   cerabral/cerebrul/cerebrum/cerebrospinal

   _____

4. specialist in the nervous system
   neonatologist/nephrologist/neuralogist/neurologist

   _____

5. portion of the brain located in the brainstem
   pawns/pons/pohns/ponns

   _____

Exercise 5.4   Word Building

Review the definitions below. Create a medical term using a combining form, a prefix, and a suffix that matches the definition. Write the correct medical term in the blank provided.

Combining forms		Prefixes		Suffixes	
neur/o	crani/o	hemi-	dys-	-itis	-al
cephal/o	mening/o	intra-	di-	-oma	-ic
kinesi/o	somat/o	pre-	para-	-cyte	-gram
astro	gangli/o	epi-	epi-	-plasty	-logy
myel/o	gli/o	en-	intra-	-otomy	-algia

Definition	Term
1. difficult movement	_____
2. star-shaped cell	_____
3. incision into a nerve	_____
4. within the head	_____
5. pertaining to the brain	_____

Exercise 5.5   Spelling Check

Find the misspelled words in the following sentences and write the correct spelling and definition on the blanks provided.

1. The myielin has been damaged, resulting in impaired function.

   _____

2. This patient's cerebelar area was damaged in a motor vehicle accident.

   _____

3. Dr. Houston performed a creniotomy in an effort to relieve the pressure.

   _____

4. The axions were unable to conduct nerve impulses.

   _____

5. A type of ancephalopethy causes the disturbances.

   _____

Exercise 5.6   Word Maps

Complete the concept map below showing the divisions of the nervous system.

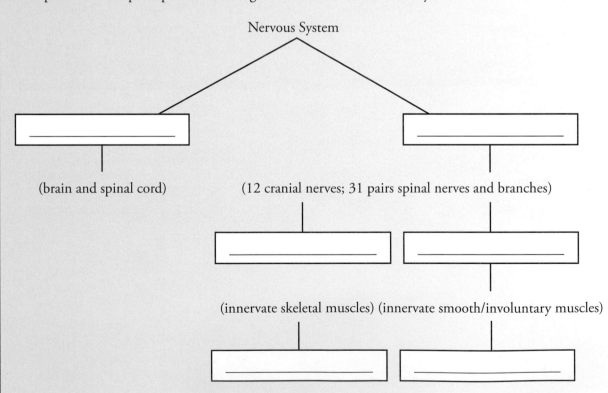

Conditions

Disorders of the nervous system, or neurological disorders, can present with a variety of symptoms. These symptoms include paralysis, numbness, twitching, weakness, headaches, seizures, and gait disturbances. Indications of possible neurological dysfunction include cognitive impairments such as forgetfulness and problems with word recognition, word retrieval, behavior, and ability to perform activities of daily living. A medical examiner may be able to determine the neurological source of an abnormality (e.g., the cerebrum, cerebellum, cranial nerves, or sensory-motor neurons) by the symptom displayed. Table 5.6 identifies some of the main terms related to conditions of the nervous system.

TABLE 5.6 Terms Associated with Nervous System Conditions

Term		Meaning	Word Analysis	
agnosia	[ag-**nO**-zsa]	impaired ability to recognize or comprehend the meaning of various sensory stimuli	a- gnosis -ia	without knowledge condition of
agraphia	[a-**graff**-ee-ah]	inability to write	a- graph/o -ia	no, not, without record condition
Alzheimer's disease	[**ahltz**-hI-merz]	neurologic disease involving the progressive loss of intellectual and cognitive functions	Alzheimer	19th-century German neurologist
amnesia	[am-**nee**-zsa]	loss of memory caused by brain damage, psychological trauma, disease, or the use of various sedating medications		
amyotrophia	[ay-**mI**-O-**trO**-fee-ah]	condition of progressively weakening muscles	a- my/o troph/o -ia	without muscle relating to nutrition; food condition
amyotrophic lateral sclerosis (ALS)	[ay-**mI**-O-**trO**-fik lat-er-al skler-**O**-sis]	progressive neuromuscular disorder of the lateral columns and anterior horns of the spinal cord characterized by atrophy, hyperreflexia, spasticity, and twitching; known as Lou Gehrig's disease	a my/o troph/o -ic scler/o -osis	without muscle relating to nutrition; food pertaining to hard condition
anencephaly	[an-en-**sef**-al-ee]	fatal disorder in which the newborn is without a brain	an- -en cephal/o -y	without within brain condition
aphasia	[ah-**fay**-zha]	impaired ability to speak or write due to a lesion in the brain	a- phas/o -ia	without speech condition of
apraxia	[ah-**prak**-see-ah]	impairment in the performance of skilled or purposeful movements	a- pratto -ia	without to do condition
ataxia	[ah-**taks**-ee-ah]	difficulty with motor coordination causing abnormal gait (walking)	a- taxis -ia	away order condition of
aura	[**aw**-rah]	symptoms that occur before a seizure	aura	breeze, odor, and light
Bell's palsy	[**pahl**-zee]	paralysis of the face (cranial nerve VII) brought on by a virus	Bell palsy	18th-century Scottish surgeon paralysis

Continues

Term		Meaning	Word Analysis	
cephalalgia	[seh-**fah**-lal-jah]	headaches	cephal/o	head
			-algia	pain
cerebral palsy	[**ser**-eh-bral **pahl**-zee]	paralytic neuromuscular disorder usually caused by an intrauterine event, birth trauma, or lack of oxygen at birth	cerebr/o	brain, cerebrum
			palsy	paralysis
cerebro-vascular accident	[ser-eh-brO-**vas**-kyoo-lar]	event that causes a decreased blood supply to the brain	cerebr/o	brain
			vascul/o	vessels (blood supply)
			accident	refers to an event
decerebrate	[dee-**ser**-eh-brayt]	implies being without a brain; an abnormal position or posture indicating brainstem dysfunction	de-	away, cessation
			cerebr/o	brain
			-ate	pertaining to
decorticate	[dee-**kor**-tih-kayt]	removal of the cortex; an abnormal posture indicating a lesion of the cerebral cortex	de-	away, cessation
			cortic/o	outer layer; cortex
			-ate	pertaining to
dementia	[dih-**men**-shee-ah]	progressive loss of cognitive and intellectual function	de-	away, cessation
			mens	mind
			-ia	condition of
dermatome	[**der**-mah-tOm]	sections of the skin innervated by the spinal nerves	derm/a	skin
			-tome	segment
dyslexia	[dis-**lek**-see-ah]	learning disorder characterized by difficulty reading and writing	dys-	difficult
			lex/o	word, speech
			-ia	condition of
dysphagia	[dis-**fay**-jee-ah]	difficulty swallowing	dys-	difficult, bad, painful
			phag/o	eat, swallow
			-ia	condition of
dysphasia	[dis-**fay**-zee-ah]	difficulty speaking	dys-	difficult, bad, painful
			phas/o	speech
			-ia	condition of
encephalitis	[en-seff-uh-**lI**-tis]	inflammation of the brain, most commonly caused by a viral infection	encephala/o	brain
			-itis	inflammation
epilepsy	[**ep**-ih-**lep**-see]	condition of recurrent seizures	epi-	above
			-lepsy	seizure
extrapyrami-dal tract	[eks-trah-pih-**ram**-ih-dal]	pathway that innervates the large muscles involved in walking, running, and so forth	extra-	other than, beyond, outside
			pyramidal	pyramid-shaped
hydrocephalus	[hI-drO-**sef**-ah-lus]	increased fluid in the brain	hydr/o	water
			cephal/o	brain
ictal	[**ik**-tal]	relating to a seizure; the actual period of time when the seizure occurs	ictus	stroke or seizure
			-al	pertaining to
infantile automatisms	[**in**-fan-tIl aw-**tom**-ah-tiz-ems]	reflexes that are normal for the newborn (automatisms are involuntary actions)	infans	not speaking
			auto-	referring to self
			matos	moving
intention tremor	[in-**ten**-shun **trem**-er]	fine-motor movement that occurs during precise actions	intentio	intention
			tremor	shaking
meningitis	[men-in-**jI**-tis]	inflammation of the meninges covering the brain and spinal cord (can be a result of viral or bacterial infections)	mening/o	meninges
			-itis	inflammation
meningomy-elocele	[men-**in**-gO-**mI**-el-O-seel]	protrusion of the spinal cord through the vertebrae	mening/o	refers to brain and/or meninges (spinal cord)
			myel/o	spinal cord
			-cele	swelling, hernia (protrusion)

Continues

Term		Meaning	Word Analysis	
microcephaly	[mI-krO-**sef**-ah-lee]	having a small head	micro- cephal/o -y	small, tiny head condition of
multiple sclerosis (MS)	[skler-**O**-sis]	disorder of the CNS in which the brain and spinal cord nerves are demyelinated, causing hard plaques	multi- scler/o -osis	many, much hard abnormal condition
muscular dystrophy	[**mus**-kyoo-lar **dis**-trah-fee]	hereditary, progressive, degenerative group of disorders affecting skeletal muscles	muscul/o -ar dys- troph/o -y	muscle pertaining to bad, difficult, painful nutrition condition
narcolepsy	[**nark**-uh-lep-see]	chronic brain disorder that involves the poor control of sleep-wake cycles	narc/o -lepsy	sleep seizure
neuritis	[noor-**eye**-tis]	inflammation of the nerves	neur/o -itis	nerve inflammation
opisthotonos	[O-pis-**thot**-ah-nus]	abnormal posture characterized by arching of the back, with head and heels bent backward	opisth/o tonos	backward, behind tone
paralysis	[par-**al**-ih-sis]	loss of voluntary movement	para- lys/o -is	near; abnormal; referring to both parts of a pair lysis, dissolution condition
paresis	[pah-**ree**-sis]	partial paralysis	paresis	letting go
paresthesia	[par-es-**thee**-zee-ah]	abnormal sensation	para- aesthesis	near; abnormal; referring to both parts of a pair sensation
Parkinson's disease		defect in extrapyramidal tract displaying various motor disturbances	Parkinson	18th-century British physician
poliomyelitis	[**pO**-lee-O-mI-el-**I**-tis]	inflammation of the gray matter of the spinal cord caused by infectious process	poli/o myel/o -itis	gray matter referring to marrow; spinal cord inflammation
radiculitis	[rad-ik-kyoo-**lI**-tis]	inflammation of the root of a spinal nerve	radicul/o -itis	nerve root inflammation
sciatica	[sI-**at**-ih-kah]	inflammation of the sciatic nerve that causes pain in lower extremities		
seizure	[**see**-zher]	sudden convulsion	seizure	grasp
spina bifida	[**spI**-nah **bif**-ih-dah]	congenital abnormality caused by a failure of one or more of the spinal arches to fuse	spin/o bifed	vertebral column separated into two parts
tetanus	[**tet**-nis]	commonly called "lockjaw," an infection characterized by muscle spasms, caused by *Clostridium* bacteria	tetanos	muscular spasms
Tourette syndrome	[too-**ret**]	syndrome characterized by facial and/or vocal tics caused by a defect in the basal ganglia resulting in excessive dopamine excretion	Tourette	19th-century French physician
transient ischemic attack	[**tran**-see-ent is-**kee**-mik ah-**tak**]	brief period in which blood supply to the brain is decreased	transient ischo -heme -ic	short-lived to keep back blood pertaining to

Assessing Neurological Disorders

As noted earlier, an examiner may be able to determine the source of the disorder based upon the symptoms. The assessment begins when the examiner observes the patient's speech, knowledge of current events, orientation to time and place, and ability to move parts of the body. The level of consciousness, affect (or mood), intellect, and memory are determined by reviewing the patient's history. This procedure is known as the mental status assessment. The neurologic examination proceeds in the following sequence: mental status, cranial nerves, motor function, sensory function, and reflexes.

The examiner next attempts to determine if the cranial nerves, which are part of the peripheral nervous system, are functioning properly. Twelve pairs of cranial nerves connect the brain to the sensory organs of the skin and the skeletal muscles in the head, neck, thorax, and abdominal cavity (see Figure 5.10).

FIGURE 5.10 Cranial Nerve Attachment

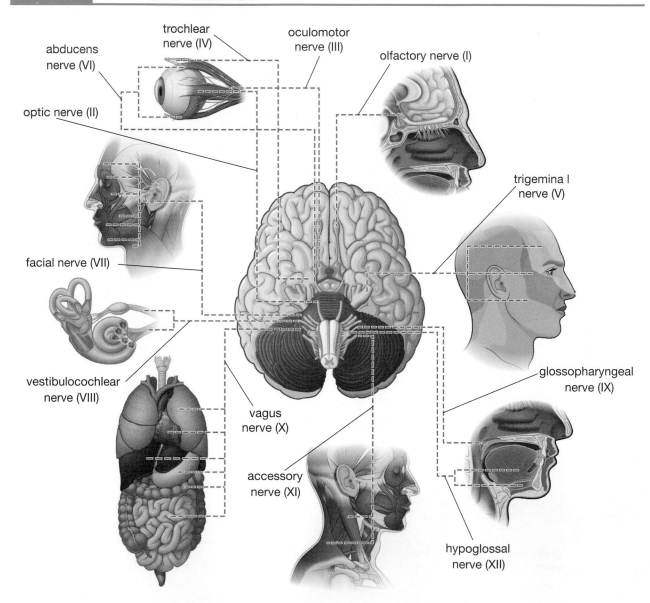

The 31 pairs of spinal nerves attach to the spinal cord in segments that correspond to the areas of the spine (see Figure 5.11), and emerge from the spinal cord to form the peripheral nerves of the trunk and limbs (areas not innervated by the cranial nerves). Different areas of the skin's surface, called **dermatomes**, are supplied by specific spinal nerves (see Figure 5.12). Spinal cord lesions can be identified and located by abnormalities in sensation on particular areas of the skin.

FIGURE 5.11 Spinal Nerves

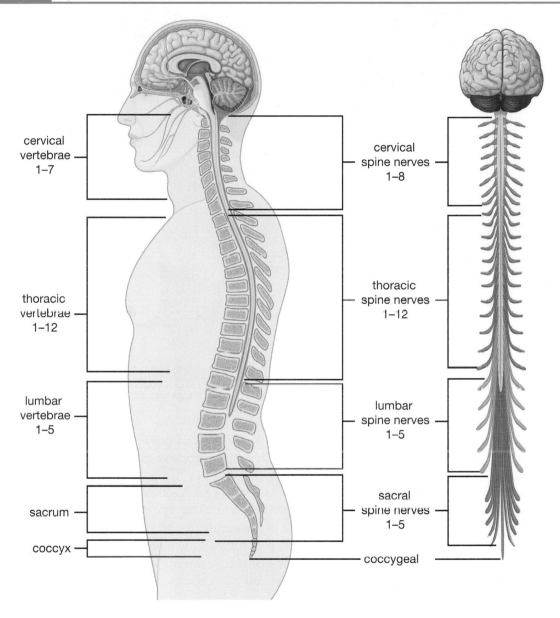

cervical
vertebrae
1–7

thoracic
vertebrae
1–12

lumbar
vertebrae
1–5

sacrum

coccyx

cervical
spine nerves
1–8

thoracic
spine nerves
1–12

lumbar
spine nerves
1–5

sacral
spine nerves
1–5

coccygeal

FIGURE 5.12 Dermatomes

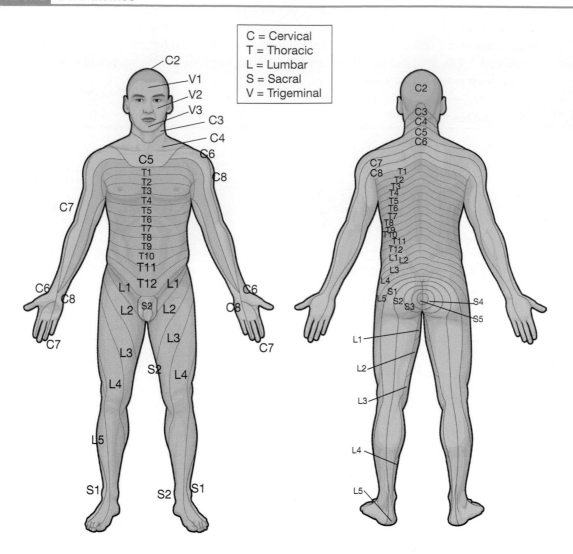

C = Cervical
T = Thoracic
L = Lumbar
S = Sacral
V = Trigeminal

Seizures can occur at any age and involve different muscles and areas of the body. Table 5.7 describes several types of seizures. An **aura**, or particular smell or feeling, often occurs before the seizure (the **preictal** phase) that can allow the individual to anticipate the actual seizure. The person may or may not lose consciousness, but loss of bowel and bladder control during the seizure is common. The period during the seizure is known as the **ictal** phase. This is the phase of the seizure in which others witness. The ictal phase can be convulsive (commonly called grand mal) including violent muscle contractions and loss of consciousness, or non-convulsive (known as petit mal) and consisting of a brief pause in activity. The **postictal** phase occurs after the seizure and is characterized by tiredness or sleep.

TABLE 5.7 Types of Seizures

Term		Meaning	Word Analysis	
grand mal	[grahn mahl]	sudden onset of generalized contraction of the muscles, causing the individual to fall (also called *tonic-clonic*)	*grand* *mal*	large illness
Jacksonian	[jak-**sO**-nee-an]	progressive spread of the seizure usually occurring on one side of the body	*Jackson*	19th-century English neurologist
myoclonic	[mI-O-**klon**-ik]	single or repetitive muscle jerks	*my/o* *klonos*	muscle tumult
petit mal	[**peh**-tee mahl]	brief pause in activity without loss of consciousness (also called *absence*)	*petit* *mal*	small illness
tonic-clonic	[**ton**-ik **klon**-ik]	sudden onset of generalized contraction of the muscles causing the individual to fall	*tonos* *klonos*	tone tumult

Abnormalities in muscle movement include **paresis** or **paralysis** of any body part (see Table 5.8). These aberrations refer to decreased and complete loss of motor ability, respectively, caused by a problem with either motor nerves or muscle fibers. Possible causes of paralysis include **poliomyelitis**, an infectious disease involving inflammation of the gray matter of the spinal cord; **Bell's palsy**, a type of unilateral paralysis of the face brought on by a virus; and malignant or nonmalignant lesions or tumors of the brain or spinal cord. Table 5.9 summarizes some common abnormal muscle movements. Several neuromuscular abnormalities involve the position of the body and are usually caused by lesions in the brain.

TABLE 5.8 Types of Paralyses

Term		Description	Word Analysis	
hemiplegia	[**hem**-ih-**plee**-jee-ah]	paralysis of one side of the body	*hemi-* *-plegia*	half paralysis
paraplegia	[par-ah-**plee**-jee-ah]	paralysis of the lower extremities	*para-* *-plegia*	denoting both parts of a pair paralysis
quadriplegia	[kwod-rih-**plee**-jee-ah]	paralysis of all four extremities	*quadri-* *-plegia*	four paralysis
spastic paraplegia	[**spas**-tik par-ah-**plee**-jee-ah]	type of paresis (partial paralysis) of the lower extremities in which there are spasms of muscle contractions	*spastic* *para-* *-plegia*	drawing in denoting both parts of a pair paralysis

TABLE 5.9 Types of Abnormal Muscle Movements

Term		Description	Word Analysis	
athetosis	[**ath**-eh-**tO**-sis]	constant, slow, involuntary movement of fingers and hands in all directions	*athetosis*	without position
chorea	[kO-**ree**-ah]	involuntary, irregular, spasmodic movement of limbs	*chorea*	dance
fasciculation	[fah-sik-yoo-**lay**-shun]	involuntary contraction of groups of muscle fibers	*fascis*	bundle
myoclonic (adj)	[mI-O-**klon**-ik]	involuntary, rapid contraction of a muscle group	*my/o* *klonos* *-ic*	muscle tumult pertaining to
tic	[tik]	habitual and usually voluntary contraction of certain muscles		
tremor	[**trem**-er]	involuntary repetitive, irregular contraction	*tremor*	shaking
twitch		very quick spasmodic contraction of a muscle group	*twiccian*	to pluck

Infants

The infant's neurological system is not completely developed at birth. The neurons are not yet myelinated (completed by about five years of age), motor activity is not coordinated, and movement is primarily under the control of primitive reflexes, called **infantile automatisms** (see Table 5.10). The cerebral cortex develops during the first year of life, causing these reflexes to disappear in a predictable timetable. Infantile automatism retention may be an indication of CNS disturbance.

Sensory and motor development gradually proceeds as the infant's neural tracts become myelinated, as myelin is needed to conduct most impulses. The infant will develop movement from head to toe and from trunk to extremities. Motor milestones are noted in the following order: lifts head, lifts head and shoulders, rolls over, moves whole arm, uses hands, walks. Milestones are measured as a means of assessing the infant through childhood.

Several congenital anomalies involve defects in the nervous system. The absence of the brain is known as **anencephaly**, a quickly fatal and relatively rare condition. **Microcephaly** refers to an abnormally small brain and head. **Hydrocephalus** relates to abnormally enlarged ventricles from the accumulation of CSF in the brain; this condition can be present at birth or occur at any time. **Meningomyelocele** is the condition caused by the protrusion of part of the spinal cord through a defect in the spinal column. Depending on the extent, the infant may be mildly to severely learning-disabled, have motor function disabilities, or be relatively unaffected. **Spina bifida** is also caused by a defect in the spinal canal's formation that allows the cord to protrude.

Cerebral palsy is a disorder that affects motor function. In infancy and childhood, it is generally caused by a perinatal event (e.g., birth trauma or lack of oxygen at birth). Affected infants may manifest mild to severe abnormalities ranging from ataxia and athetosis to seizures and paralysis.

TABLE 5.10 Infantile Automatisms

Reflex		Steps to Test the Reflex	Age at Appearance	Age at Disappearance
Babinski's sign	[bah-**bin**-skeez]	stroke infant's foot up the lateral edge and across the ball of the foot; note fanning of toes (positive Babinski's sign)	birth	by 24 months
Moro's reflex	[**mO**-rOz]	startle infant to note a symmetric abduction and extension of the arms and legs, fanning fingers, and curling of index finger and thumb to C position; then infant will bring arms and legs inward	birth	1–4 months
palmar grasp	[**pahl**-mer]	offer your finger to the infant from the ulnar side (away from the thumb); grasp should be tight	birth (strongest at 1–2 months)	3–4 months
placing reflex		hold infant upright under arms, near a table; touch top of foot to front of the table; note flexion of hip and knee to attempt to place foot on table	birth	4 days
plantar grasp	[**plan**-ter]	toes curl down tightly with firm touch at ball of foot	birth	8–10 months
rooting reflex		brush side of face near mouth and infant turns the head toward that side and opens mouth	birth	3–4 months
stepping reflex		hold infant upright under arms with feet on flat surface; note regular alternating steps	birth	9-12 months, walking
sucking reflex		touch lips and offer finger to suck (examiner notes strength of suck)	birth	10–12 months
tonic neck reflex	[**ton**-ik]	with infant supine and relaxed, turn head to one side; ipsilateral arm and leg should extend, and opposite arm and leg should flex; known as "fencing" position	2–3 months	4–6 months

Toddlers and School-Aged Children

Children's milestones, including play activities, reaction to parents, and cooperation, are observed and noted during the first 10 years. To determine motor activities, the examiner watches the child walk, get dressed, color, cut, ride a tricycle, and balance on one foot.

Muscular dystrophy refers to a group of disorders that are often hereditary which cause progressive muscle weakness and a loss of skeletal muscle mass. Symptoms commonly appear in this age group, primarily in boys. This disorder has no cure and many who are affected may eventually lose the ability to walk.

Attention-deficit/hyperactivity disorder (ADHD) is usually diagnosed in this age group. It is characterized by symptoms that can include such problems as underachievement in school, hyperactivity with a short attention span, obsessive-compulsive behaviors, and tics. Stimulant drugs are used to control the hyperactivity (see the section on pharmacological agents later in this chapter).

Tourette's syndrome is a disorder that begins in childhood and is characterized by repetitive, involuntary movements and vocalizations (called **tics**).

> **Did You Know?**
>
> A type of tic, called coprolalia [kop-**prO**-layl-yah] is the involuntary use of vulgar or obscene language (swearing).

Young Adults and Adults

Multiple sclerosis (MS) is a disorder characterized by the demyelinating of neurons in the CNS. The demyelinated areas within the affected neurons have been replaced by plaques in the brain and spinal cord. The cause of this disorder is unknown. Typical symptoms include muscle weakness (tremors), loss of balance and coordination, slurred speech, blurred vision, paresthesias, problems with memory and concentration, and mood changes. Remissions and exacerbations of the symptoms are common.

Seniors

The aging process causes loss of neurons, particularly in the brain and spinal cord, so the aging adult shows slower response. Motor response may also be slow, and the ability to taste and smell declines in this age group. While grip remains relatively strong, the muscles may appear atrophied. **Senile tremors** may be noted, including an **intention tremor** that occurs when the person attempts to move, particularly the head, hand, and tongue. Touch and pain sensation may be decreased because of the slowing of message transmission at the synapses and slowed responses at the deep tendon reflexes. **Parkinson's disease** is a chronic condition affecting the central nervous system. Symptoms of Parkinson's disease include tremors, slowed movement, stiffened limbs, and impaired balance and coordination. These symptoms tend to worsen over time. The average age at diagnosis of Parkinson's disease is 60.

The **cerebrovascular accident (CVA)**, commonly known as a **stroke**, is caused by mild to severe interruption of blood flow to the brain; a mild form is a **transient ischemic attack (TIA)**. TIAs are warning signs that a stroke may occur. A stroke or TIA can cause difficulties such as **aphasia** (inability or difficulty with speaking or writing); **dysphasia** (difficulty with language); **dysphagia** (difficulty swallowing); and **ataxia** (difficulty with motor coordination and muscle movement and gait).

> **To Note!**
>
> A *stroke* is also known as a cerebrovascular accident (CVA) or a transient ischemic attack (TIA).

Alzheimer's disease is a neurologic disease involving the progressive loss of intellectual and cognitive functions. It is the primary cause of senile dementia in persons over age 65. The risk of getting Alzheimer's disease doubles every five additional years. Researchers project that by the year 2050, more than 14 million Americans will have dementia. The disease results from structural changes in the brain and usually ends with total disability and ultimately death. Some of the criteria to diagnose Alzheimer's disease include acquired memory impairment, aphasia, **apraxia** (impairment in the performance of skilled or purposeful movements), **agnosia** (impairment in the ability to recognize or comprehend the meaning of various sensory stimuli), and a decline from prior baseline in functional abilities. The cause of Alzheimer's disease is still unknown, and extensive research is currently being conducted in this area. Recent research has indicated that low activity in the hippocampus area of the brain can be seen in Alzheimer's patients up to nine years before onset of symptoms.

Amyotrophic lateral sclerosis (ALS) is also known as *Lou Gehrig's disease* because of the famous baseball player who died of this disease. It is a chronic disease characterized by the progressive atrophy (weakness) of the muscles.

Cancers of the Nervous System

Neuro-oncology is a field of practice that involves oncologic diseases of the nervous system. Brain tumors are abnormal growths of brain tissue with or without involvement of the meninges. They may be malignant or benign, and may be classified as primary or secondary. Brain tumors are usually named for the tissue from which they arise. Symptoms of a brain tumor occur as a result of the expansion of the tumor into the brain tissue, which may cause many neurological dysfunctions such as headaches, dizziness, vomiting, ataxia, personality changes, and other symptoms depending upon the area of the brain that is affected.

> **What's in a Word?**
>
> In relation to cancer, the term *benign* means harmless or noncancerous. *Malignant* means harmful, invasive, and dangerous.

Lobectomy is a surgical removal of a portion of the brain to treat brain cancer or seizure disorders. Surgical removal and/or debulking of the tumor, important treatment modalities, are not always possible because of potential damage to the involved and surrounding tissues. Radiation and chemotherapy may also be used, although many chemotherapeutic agents are not effective because they do not cross the blood-brain barrier. Intracranial radiotherapy (radiation therapy that is given during the surgical excision) and chemotherapeutic implants (chemical-soaked wafers that slowly dissolve within the tumor or brain tissue) are among the newer treatments used to treat and try to control the growth of brain tumors. See Table 5.11 for a list of brain tumor types.

TABLE 5.11 Types of Brain Tumors

Name	Approximate Incidence	Characteristics
astrocytoma	6% of all brain tumors	slow-growing
brain stem gliomas	10% of all pediatric brain tumors	occurs most often in children
ependymomas	6% of all brain tumors	usually within 4th ventricle and extend into spinal cord
glioblastoma multiforme	23% of all brain tumors	arise in the cerebral hemisphere
oligodendrogliomas	5% of all brain tumors	occur usually in the frontal lobe
medulloblastoma	4% of all brain tumors	occurs most often in children
meningiomas	15% of all brain tumors	slow-growing, vascular tumors occurring in adults

Mental Health and Psychiatric Disorders

Mental health describes a person's psychological and emotional well-being. The term mental illness can be used in reference to a wide range of conditions affecting mental health. Disorders can affect one's mood, personality, development, thought processes, and behaviors. Mental health disorders include disruptive behavior disorders, eating disorders, affective disorders, anxiety disorders, neuroses, and psychoses. The field of mental health encompasses several types of practitioners. A physician who practices in the field of psychiatry, diagnosing and treating mental disorders, is called a **psychiatrist**. Another type of practitioner is a **psychologist**, a nonmedical person who may have a doctoral or a master's degree in methods of psychotherapy, analysis, and research. Social workers and counselors also care for persons with mental disorders.

TABLE 5.12 Mental Health and Psychiatric Terms

Term		Meaning	Word Analysis	
affect	[**a**-fect]	apparent mood or feelings		
anorexia nervosa	[ann-O-**rex**-ee-ah ner-**vO**-sah]	decreased eating, increased exercise and abuse of laxatives and diuretics	*anorexis* *nervosa*	without appetite nerves
bulimia nervosa	[bah-**lee**-me-ah ner-**vO**-sah]	binge eating followed by purging and abuse of laxatives and diuretics	*bous* *limos* *nervosa*	ox hunger nerves
catatonic schizophrenia	[cat-a-**tah**-nik skitz-O-**free**-nee-ah]	person does not speak, move, or relate to the outside world	*cat/a* *ton/o* *schizo-* *phren*	down, lower tone split mind
delusion		idea or belief with no basis in reality	*de* *ludo*	from play
disorganized schizophrenia	[skitz-O-**free**-nee ah]	ideas change from one to another with total disassociation; language may be incoherent	*dis* *organum* *schizo-* *phren*	not organ split mind
hallucinations		person hears voices or sees visions that do not exist	*alucinor*	for wander in mind
mania	[**may**-nee-ah]	increased activity and speech, and loss of good judgment	mania	frenzy
obsessive-compulsive disorder (OCD)		anxiety disorder in which excessive thoughts lead to repetitive behaviors that interfere with daily life, also known as *obsessive-compulsive neurosis*		
paranoid schizophrenia	[**pair**-a-noid skitz-O-**free**-nee-ah]	delusions of persecution and grandeur	*par/a* *-oid* *schizo-* *phren*	departure from normal resemblance to split mind

Disruptive Behavior Disorders

The most common disorder in the *DSM* (*Diagnostic and Statistical Manual of Mental Disorders*) classification is attention-deficit/hyperactivity disorder (ADHD), characterized by inattentiveness and impulsivity. It is usually diagnosed when a child first starts school. Children with ADHD are unable to concentrate and complete tasks. They may be disruptive and become a discipline problem in the classroom and at home. This disorder is ten times more common in boys, is usually familial, and may be helped by the administration of stimulant drugs. ADHD is thought to be caused by a neurological impairment. Tics may be associated with ADHD. Often the child will require psychological intervention to help gain control and mastery over actions and the feelings associated with them.

Autism spectrum disorder, also known as *autism*, refers to a group of disorders affecting brain development. These disorders are often characterized by difficulties in social interaction and communication, and repetitive behaviors. Signs are generally recognized in the first two years of life. **Asperger's syndrome** is a form of autism in which the individual has no intellectual disability, yet struggles in social interactions.

Affective Disorders

Affective disorders are disorders of the person's **affect**, a term for mood or emotions. They can range from abnormal and/or prolonged grief to mild or severe depression. Thinking of emotions as a continuum, it may be difficult to determine when a person is adapting to normal situations. However, prolonged affective disorders, or situations that prevent a person from functioning personally or in society, are abnormal. Any emotion that is suppressed may eventually become an affective disorder.

Depressive disorders may be considered depression that is outside the bounds of normal "feeling down" as a result of bereavement grief or other loss. Persons with depression lose interest in life or social contacts and may feel overwhelming hopelessness, helplessness, and suicidal ideation. **Manic-depressive disorders**, also called **bipolar disorders**, consist of episodes of depression and mania (excitement).

Anxiety Disorders and Neuroses

Certain disorders that affect the individual may be associated with moderate to severe levels of anxiety. A **neurosis** is a mental disorder characterized by anxiety that does not include any reality distortion.

Post-traumatic stress syndrome disorder (PTSD) is a fairly new diagnosis involving feelings of anxiety and stress following (even years later) a life stress or traumatic event. Combat veterans and victims of violent crime face a higher risk of this disorder than the general population.

Panic attacks are sudden episodes in which the person may feel like they are about to faint, have a heart attack, choke, go insane, or die. The attack passes, and the person may never experience another one. Panic disorder is characterized by recurrent panic attacks, and may be treated by psychotherapy and/or drugs.

Phobias (from the Greek *phobos*, meaning "fear") are actually panic disorders; the individual cannot cope with certain situations and has an intense fear of them. Specific phobias are listed in Table 5.13.

TABLE 5.13 Common Phobias

Phobia	Fear of	Word Analysis	
acrophobia	heights	*acr/o*	tip, peak
agoraphobia	being in a crowd or public place; leaving a familiar place	*agora*	marketplace
allodoxaphobia	others' opinions	*allo*	other
		doxa	concept, theory, opinion
astraphobia	lightning	*astro/a*	star
claustrophobia	being in a closed-in place	*claustrum*	enclosed space
entomophobia	insects	*entomo*	insects
hemophobia	blood	*hemo*	blood
hydrophobia	water	*hydro/a*	water
radiophobia	X-rays	*radio*	energy
social phobia (also called social anxiety disorder)	public scrutiny	*socius*	partner, companion
thermophobia	heat	*therm/o*	heat
xenophobia	foreigners	*xen/o*	strange, foreign

Obsessive-compulsive neurosis, also known as obsessive-compulsive disorder, is an anxiety disorder that presents with symptoms of recurring thoughts and repetitive acts that are performed ritualistically. Elimination of any step of the ritual causes severe anxiety.

Psychoses

A **psychosis** is differentiated from a neurosis in terms of the person's ability to cope with everyday living. Psychotic symptoms include hallucinations (seeing things that are not there), delusions (ideas for which there is no basis in reality), and bizarre behavior. **Schizophrenia** (there are a number of subtypes) is a type of disorder in which psychotic symptoms may be observed. The individual withdraws from reality and slips into a private world of the mind. Additional mental health and psychiatry terms are described in Table 5.12.

> **What's in a Word?**
>
> Schizophrenia literally means "split mind."

Eating Disorders

Anorexia nervosa and bulimia nervosa are disorders most common in teenage girls, and are associated with poor self-image and an obsession with weight and being "fat." Decreased eating, increased exercise, and the use of diuretics and laxatives characterize **anorexia nervosa**. **Bulimia nervosa** involves eating (often binging on food), followed by vomiting (called purging), and the use of diuretics and/or laxatives.

In the Know: Prevalence Rates of Mental Illness in the United States

Consider the following statistics identified by the National Alliance on Mental Illness (NAMI):[1]

- 1 in 4 adults—approximately 61.5 million Americans—are faced with a mental illness in a given year, compared to 1 in 5 youths ages 13 to 18.
- 1 in 17 adults—approximately 13.6 million—live with a serious mental illness (e.g., schizophrenia, depression, or bipolar disorder).
- Approximately 26 percent of homeless adults living in shelters live with serious mental illness.
- Approximately 20 percent of state prisoners have a recent history of mental illness.
- Serious mental illness costs the US $193.2 billion in lost earnings per year.
- Mood disorders such as depression are the third most common cause of hospitalization in the United States for both youth and adults.
- Although members of the military account for less than 1 percent of the US population, veterans represent 20 percent of suicides nationally.

[1] The National Alliance on Mental Illness (NAMI)—Mental Illness Facts and Numbers. Ken Duckworth, MD, March 2013.

Checkpoint 5.2

Answer the following questions to identify any areas of the section that you may need to review.

1. The death of a famous baseball player by the name of Lou Gehrig sparked worldwide attention to this chronic disease that leads to a progressive loss of muscle strength. What is this condition called?

   _____

2. This condition, which is often diagnosed in childhood, is characterized by facial and vocal tics (e.g., coprolalia) as well as the involuntary movement of both the arms and shoulders. What is this condition called?

   _____

3. Which condition generally presents itself shortly after birth and is a result of abnormally enlarged ventricles from the accumulation of CSF in the brain?

   _____

4. Which condition of the nervous system hinders one's ability to write?

   _____

Exercise 5.7   Word Analysis

Identify the root of each term by drawing a box around it. Then write the definition for the term on the line provided.

Term	Definition
1. neurological	_____
2. cephalocaudal	_____
3. meningomyelocele	_____
4. cerebrovascular	_____
5. demyelinating	_____

Exercise 5.8   Comprehension Check

Circle the correct term from the pair in each sentence.

1. The cranial nerve/nerves are intact.

2. The ventricles/ventricle are enlarged.

3. This patient's reflex/reflexes are abnormal.

4. This laboratory has studied the cerebral cortex/cortices of several species of mammals.

5. The muscular dystrophy/dystrophies constitute a group of neurological disorders that affect skeletal muscles.

Exercise 5.9 Matching

Identify and circle the correct spelling of the word in column 1, then write the letter of the definition on the line provided.

1. _____ preicical / preictal / parietal
2. _____ hydrocefalus / hydrocephalus
3. _____ neuril / neural / neutral
4. _____ ventricles / ventricular
5. _____ cortec / cortex / kortex
6. _____ cefalocaudal / cephalic / cephalocaudal
7. _____ quadraplegia / paraplegia
8. _____ transient ischemic attack / transiten ischimic attack
9. _____ siezure / seizure / seizural
10. _____ parisis / paresis / parasthesia

a. fluid-filled spaces within the brain
b. outer layer of the brain
c. pertaining to a neuron or neurons
d. "head-to-toe"
e. brief period of decreased blood supply to the brain
f. sudden convulsion
g. phase of a seizure preceding the actual convulsion
h. partial paralysis
i. paralysis of the lower extremities
j. literally meaning "water on the brain"

Exercise 5.10 Word Building

Use word parts or entire words to complete a term matching the definition. Write the part on the line provided.

1. different areas on the surface of the skin that are served by different nerves:
   _____tomes

2. one of the cranial nerves that serves the throat muscles and salivary glands:
   glosso_____

3. superficial reflex that involves plantar flexion of the toes when the lateral side of the sole of the foot and ball of the foot are stroked: _____ar reflex

4. primitive reflexes in the infant: infantile _____

5. infantile reflex in which baby grasps object placed in the hand: _____ grasp reflex

Exercise 5.11   Spelling Check

Circle the misspelled word or words in each sentence, then write the correct spelling of the word(s) on the line provided.

1. The child displayed signs of quadroplegia following the accident.

   _____

2. Larry developed Bell's palasy after a mild illness.

   _____

3. The patient displayed decorticuate posturing in the emergency room.

   _____

4. This 87-year-old female demonstrates atexia, aphiasia, and tremors.

   _____

5. The speech impairment is a result of an old cerebrevascluar accident.

   _____

Exercise 5.12   Word Maps

Complete the concept map below showing the stages of a seizure.

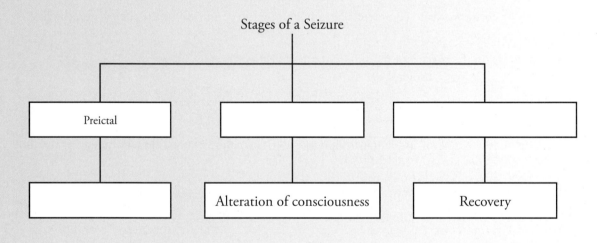

Exercise 5.13   Identification

On the line provided, write the name of the phobia described.

1. fear of heights   _____
2. fear of leaving a familiar place   _____
3. fear of being in a closed-in place   _____
4. fear of blood   _____
5. fear of others' opinions   _____

Exercise 5.14   Comprehension Check

Draw a circle around the correct term from each pair.

1. Joel, who is 10, is disruptive and unable to concentrate. He might have ADHD/DSM.
2. A person who is severely fearful of heights might be said to have acromania/acrophobia.
3. A general term for disorders of emotions is affective disorders/emotophobias.
4. Bipolar disorders consist of phobias/mania and depression.
5. A mental disorder characterized by anxiety without any reality distortion is a neurosis/nervosis.
6. Phobia/psychosis is from the Greek word meaning "fear."

Diagnostic Tests and Examinations

Most testing of nervous system function involves evaluation of the cranial nerves; muscle movement, strength and tone; and reflexes. Other tests can determine neuromuscular and neurosensory function and are performed during the physical examination.

Cerebellar function evaluation includes gait and balance tests. Observation of a person's walk can reveal abnormalities such as **ataxia** (uncoordinated or unsteady gait). The ability to walk a straight line and heel-to-toe walking are also assessed.

Tests for coordination involve the patient performing rapid alternating movements with the feet and fingers. The sensory system is assessed in several ways. Touch, vibration, temperature, discrimination, and position (kinesthesia) are elicited sensations.

A **lumbar puncture**, or **spinal tap**, is performed by inserting a small-gauge needle between the vertebrae at level L2-L3. The CSF is collected and tested to determine whether organisms or tumor cells are present. When intracranial pressure is increased, drainage of fluid may relieve some of the pressure. **Intrathecal** refers to the subarachnoid or subdural space. When medications are injected into the CSF, it is known as intrathecal administration.

Computerized axial tomography, called a CAT scan, is used to visualize the brain using X-ray images taken from many angles and then a single three-dimensional image is constructed from those images. Table 5.14 identifies tests and examinations associated with the nervous system (including psychological examinations).

Test or Exam	Description
brain scan	nuclear image with an injection of radioactive dye to scan and view the brain
computerized axial tomography (CAT) scan	scan used to visualize the brain using X-ray images that produce a three-dimensional image
electroencephalogram	measurement of the electrical activity of the brain
lumbar puncture	procedure performed by inserting a needle between the vertebrae at level L2–L3 to obtain CSF for examination, also known as *spinal tap*
magnetic resonance imaging (MRI)	method of scanning the brain using an electromagnetic field and radio waves to produce the image
nerve conduction velocity	test that measures travel speed of nerve impulse
positron emission tomography (PET)	thin X-ray beam is used to visualize a cross-section of the brain after injection of a radioactive isotope
Romberg test	neurological test used to determine cerebellar function; measures balance and is commonly used in field sobriety tests
single-photon emission computed tomography (SPECT)	scan using the injection of a radioactive sugar substance, metabolized by the brain; brain is then imaged
Rorschach [**roar**-shak]	a psychological evaluation that uses inkblots to examine a person's perception of the surrounding environment
Thematic Apperception Test (TAT)	a psychological evaluation in which patients are asked to make up stories from pictures provided by the examiner; widely used to reveal information about a patient's relationships, motives, concerns, conflicts, and needs
Wechsler Adult Intelligence Scale (WAIS)	test designed to measure intelligence

Soft Skills for Health Care: Time Management

The office opens at 9 a.m. Patients are waiting for the lobby doors to open at 8:45 a.m. By 9:05 a.m. the phone is ringing off the hook with patients looking to schedule, cancel, or confirm appointments. By midday you are juggling patients at check-in, in exam rooms, and handling billing concerns. The daily work life of a healthcare professional is filled with bumps and roadblocks impeding the quality of patient care. Your role is to learn the skills necessary to manage your time to ultimately respect the time of those you serve. These skills include the ability to identify and address the priorities of the day in the proper order, to set deadlines, to delegate tasks when appropriate, and to remain on task to allow yourself the time required to complete each task.

Checkpoint 5.3

Answer the following questions to identify any areas of the section that you may need to review.

1. A spinal tap is a procedure in which a small-gauge needle is inserted between the vertebrae at level L2-L3 in order to collect and test cerebrospinal fluid. What is another name for this procedure?

   _____

2. Which test is utilized to determine cerebellar function and measure balance?

   _____

3. What test requires a person to make up stories using ambiguous images?

   _____

Treatments

Healthcare practitioners use predetermined guidelines to direct patient care. These guidelines, known as clinical practice guidelines and evidence-based practices, have been developed by the specialty societies based on past clinical research. They represent the treatment pathways that have achieved the best outcomes. Treatment decisions generally fall into three categories: surgical, clinical, and pharmacological.

Surgical treatments are generally invasive as they involve a puncture or an incision into the skin. *Clinical treatments* are generally noninvasive and involve nonsurgical techniques (e.g., physical therapy). *Pharmacological treatments* involve the utilization of medicines (drugs) to treat specific illnesses or diseases. Medication therapies are regulated by the Food and Drug Administration (FDA). To be approved by the FDA for use in the United States, every medicine must be backed by research studies that have shown the medication to be effective in its treatment of a given disease and has a tolerable safety profile. The following sections provide an overview of treatments common to the nervous system.

Surgical Treatments

Any procedure involving a surgical opening into the skull is known as a craniotomy. A **lobectomy** is the excision of a lobe of the brain. A **ventriculotomy** is a surgical incision into a ventricle of the brain to relieve fluid pressure in patients with hydrocephalus or swelling from head trauma.

A **rhizotomy**, or **radicotomy**, is a surgical procedure to dissect nerve roots of the spine in order to relieve pain. A **chordotomy** is performed to interrupt the pain impulses to the brain by making an incision in the spinal cord. **Neuroplasty** is the surgical repair of a nerve. Table 5.15 identifies these and other common surgical procedures related to the nervous system.

TABLE 5.15   Surgical Treatment Associated with the Nervous System

Treatment		Description
chordotomy	[kore-**dah**-tuh-mee]	procedure performed by an incision in the spinal cord to stop pain, also spelled *cordotomy*
craniotomy	[kray-nee-**ah**-tuh-mee]	incision into the brain
lobectomy	[lO-**bek**-tuh-mee]	removal of a lobe of the brain
neuroplasty	[**noor**-O-plas-tee]	repair of a nerve
neurorrhaphy	[noo-**rOr**-ah-fee]	suturing together the ends of severed nerves
radicotomy	[rad-i-**kah**-tuh-mee]	procedure to dissect a nerve root of the spine
rhizotomy	[rI-**zah**-tuh-mee]	procedure to dissect a nerve root of the spine
ventriculotomy	[ven-trik-yoo-**lah**-tuh-mee]	incision into a ventricle of the brain

Clinical Treatments

The clinical methods of intervention for the nervous system generally involve the utilization of therapeutic counseling sessions targeting a specific behavior, thought process, or perception influencing the individual's mental state. Table 5.16 provides a list of therapeutic interventions commonly used to treat conditions of the nervous system.

TABLE 5.16   Clinical Treatments Associated with the Nervous System

Treatment	Description
behavioral therapy	patient is given a stimulus; an undesired behavior is replaced with a new response
cognitive therapy	assists the individual in altering unhealthy perceptions and patterns of thinking
hypnotherapy	used to form a new response, thought, attitude, feeling, or behavior in a subconcious patient
light therapy	light waves are used to treat depression caused by seasonal affective disorder (SAD)
psychoanalysis	utilizes the analysis of dream interpretations and defense mechanisms to treat dysfunctional behaviors attributed to the unconscious mind
transcutaneous electrical nerve stimulation (TENS)	controls pain via the application of electrical impulses to the skin

Pharmacological Treatments

Anticonvulsants are agents used to control seizures (see Table 5.17). The most common anticonvulsant agents include *hydantoins, benzodiazepines, carbamates*, and *barbiturates*. Many agents are used to help with hyperactivity, and ironically they are classified as CNS stimulant agents; the most common are **amphetamines** and **methylphenidates**. Although the mechanism of action is not fully understood, they may act by blocking the reuptake of dopaminergic neurons. They must be used with great caution.

Persons with Parkinson's disease often take several medications known as **anti-Parkinson** agents. The focus for treatment is the replacement of missing neurotransmitters; therefore, agents such as levodopa are used. Other drugs are often needed to control the debilitating symptoms of the disease.

Immunologic agents such as interferon and new biopharmaceuticals are being used for diseases that are thought to be autoimmune, such as multiple sclerosis.

Various muscle relaxants and nonsteroidal anti-inflammatory agents (NSAIDs) are used for neuromuscular aches and pains. They decrease inflammation and relax spasms often associated with pain, particularly in the spinal area of the back and neck.

TABLE 5.17 Pharmacologic Agents Relating to the Nervous System

Drug Class	Use	Generic Name(s)	Brand Name(s)
anesthetics	cause a loss of sensation	propofol lidocaine	Xylocaine Diprivan
anti-Alzheimer's (dementia)	inhibit acetylcholinesterase	donepezil galantamine tacrine	Aricept Reminyl Cognex
antianxiety	inhibits anxiety, also known as an *axiolytic*	venlafaxine	Effexor
anticonvulsants (e.g., barbiturates, benzodiazepines, carbamates, hydantoins)	interfere with the mechanisms that cause seizures	clonazepam clorazepate diazepam felbamate phenobarbital phenytoin sodium	Klonopin Tranxene Valium Felbatol Bellergal, Donnatal Dilantin
antidepressants	treat narcolepsy, ADHD, fatigue, and suppress the appetite	fluoxetine sertraline paroxetine phenelzine tranylcypromine bupropion methylphenidate venlafaxine	Prozac Zoloft Paxil Nardil Parnate Wellbutrin, Zyban Ritalin Effexor
antimania	mood stabilizer	lithium valproic acid carbamazepine	Lithobid Depakote Tegretol
anti-Parkinson agents	treat debilitating symptoms of Parkinson's disease	benztropine biperiden carbidopa-levodopa levodopa phenobarbital	Cogentin Akineton Sinemet Larodopa Bellergal, Donnatal
antipsychotics	control hallucinations and delusions	chlorpromazine mirtazapine haloperidol risperidone olanzapine	Thorazine Remeron Haldol Risperdal Zyprexa
hypnotics	promote sleep	temazepam/zolpidem	Restoril/Ambien
neuromuscular blockers	used in surgery to cause paralysis restricting patient movement	pancuronium	Pavulon
sedatives	inhibit the activity of neurons to calm and relax	alprazolam lorazepam	Xanax Ativan
stimulants (e.g., amphetamines)	stimulate the nervous system	dextroamphetamine methylphenidate	Dexedrine Ritalin

Checkpoint 5.4

Answer the following questions to identify any areas of the section that you may need to review.

1. What class of drug is used to control hallucinations and delusions?

_____

2. What specific condition of the nervous system is targeted by the use of light therapy?

_____

3. Which classification of drug is prescribed to interfere with mechanisms that can cause seizures?

_____

Abbreviations

Recall that in the medical field, information is generally recorded in medical charts and in the electronic medical record, and provided to patients in medical shorthand. It is important that healthcare professionals become familiar with the abbreviations utilized on a daily basis to successfully perform the duties assigned in a typical workday. Table 5.18 lists common abbreviations used in reference to the nervous system.

TABLE 5.18 Abbreviations Associated with the Nervous System

Abbreviations	Meaning
ADHD	attention-deficit/hyperactivity disorder
ADL	activities of daily living
ALS	amyotrophic lateral sclerosis
ANS	autonomic nervous system
BP	bipolar disorder
C1-C8	cervical nerves
CA	chronological age
CAT	computerized axial tomography
CNS	central nervous system
CP	cerebral palsy
CSF	cerebrospinal fluid
CT	computed tomography
CVA	cerebrovascular accident
DTR	deep tendon reflex
EchoEG	echoencephalography

Continues

Abbreviations	Meaning
EEG	electroencephalogram or electroencephalography
GAD	generalized anxiety disorder
GAF Scale	Global Assessment of Functioning, a subjective assessment tool used to rate ability to function on a scale of 1–100, where 1 = poor mental health and inability to function and 100 = good mental health and ability to function well
ICP	intracranial pressure
IQ	intelligence quotient (normal = 90–110)
L1-L5	lumbar nerves
LP	lumbar puncture
MA	mental age
MRI	magnetic resonance imaging
MS	multiple sclerosis
OCD	obsessive-compulsive disorder
PD	Parkinson's disease
PET	positron emission tomography
PNS	peripheral nervous system
PTSD	post-traumatic stress disorder
S1-S5	sacral nerves
SAD	seasonal affective disorder
SNS	somatic nervous system
SPECT	single-photon emission computed tomography
T1-T12	thoracic nerves
TBI	traumatic brain injury
TIA	transient ischemic attack
WAIS	Wechsler Adult Intelligence Scale
WISC	Wechsler Intelligence Scale for Children

Exercise 5.15   Word Analysis

Write the combining form for each term. Give the meaning of the combining form.

Term	Combining Form	Meaning
1. craniotomy	_____	_____
2. neuroplasty	_____	_____
3. rhizotomy	_____	_____
4. lobectomy	_____	_____

Exercise 5.16   Comprehension Check

Circle the correct term from the pair in each sentence. You may need to use a medical dictionary.

1. The doctor will order a CAT/MAT scan for this patient today.

2. During the neurological examination, the patient was unable to perform the Romberg/Romaine test without falling.

3. A lumbar puncture was performed; a sample of cerebrospinal/cerebral fluid was obtained and sent to the laboratory.

4. Please prepare Mrs. Martin for an EEG/GTT.

5. A brain scan/bran scan, performed after the accident, showed no abnormalities.

Exercise 5.17   Abbreviations

Provide a definition for each abbreviation.

1. ALS   _____

2. CNS   _____

3. DTR   _____

4. CSF   _____

5. MS   _____

Exercise 5.18   Word Building

Use the provided definition to accurately complete each term.

1. A _____vascul_____ accident is a mild stroke.

2. An electro _____ is a record of electrical activity in the brain.

3. _____ ar means pertaining to the nerves and muscles.

4. _____ y means pertaining to the nerves and senses.

5. A _____ refers to without coordination; unsteady or uncoordinated gait.

Exercise 5.19 Spelling Check

Read the terms that follow and then indicate whether the term is singular or plural by writing an S or a P after the term. Supply the other form (either singular or plural) of the term.

Term	P/S	Opposite Term
1. seizures	_____	_____
2. palsy	_____	_____
3. dermatome	_____	_____
4. neuroplasties	_____	_____
5. ventriculotomy	_____	_____

Exercise 5.20 Word Maps

Label the body illustrations to indicate the affected limbs and the degree of impairment in each classification. Place an X over the area(s) of the body that would be affected by each classification.

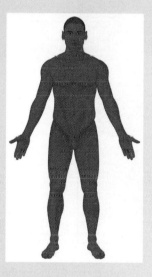

hemiplegia

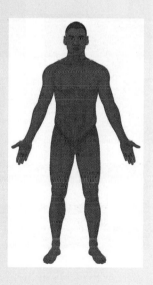

paraplegia

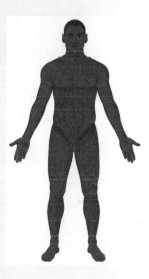

quadriplegia

After successfully completing this chapter, you should be able to correctly answer the following review questions. Answers are provided in the back of the text. This self-assessment opportunity allows you to check your understanding of the content and determine whether you need to revisit any of the chapter's content.

Crossword Puzzle

Use the clues provided to fill in the puzzle with the correct system terms. Enter one letter per square.

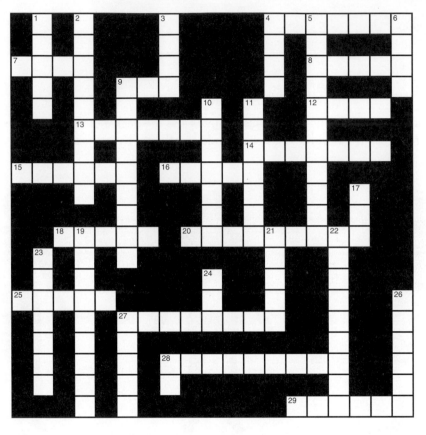

Across

4. inability to properly use language
7. special cells that protect neurons
8. combining form for speech
9. prefix meaning difficulty
12. folds on the surface of the brain
13. neurons that transmit nerve impulses to the spinal cord
14. impaired ability to recognize the meaning of various sensory stimuli
15. word root for cerebrum
16. part of the CNS in the cranium
18. cortical areas
20. special cells that hold and protect the neurons
25. _____ neck reflex
27. cranial nerve involved in hearing
28. cells that eat inflamed brain cells
29. sheath around axons outside the CNS; made up of Schwann cells

Down

1. French term meaning paralysis
2. composed of the pons, midbrain, and medulla oblongata
3. one of the structures that make up the brainstem
4. a particular smell or feeling that occurs before a seizure
5. nerve that controls muscles of the tongue
6. long branch from neuron to muscles
9. structures of a nerve cell; receive information from other neurons
10. neuron connections
11. toe flexion reflex

17. transient ischemic attack
19. lobe of the brain located at the back of the head
21. cranial nerve involved in

vision and visual fields
22. send nerve impulses
23. lobe in the front of the skull
24. central nervous system

26. basic structural cell
27. combining form for star-shaped
28. multiple sclerosis

Matching

Match the following terms to their proper definitions.

1. _____ acrophobia

2. _____ encephalitis

3. _____ hemophobia

4. _____ meningitis

5. _____ narcolepsy

a. fear of blood

b. fear of heights

c. any infection or inflammation of the membranes covering the brain and spinal cord

d. inflammation of the brain

e. disorder characterized by sudden attacks of sleep

Identification

Correctly label the illustration using the provided terms. Write the term's corresponding letter in the correct callout of the figure below.

1. _____ brainstem

2. _____ cerebellum

3. _____ cerebrum

4. _____ diencephalon

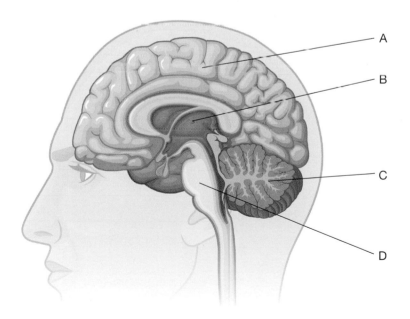

Abbreviations

Correctly identify the meaning of the abbreviations on the lines provided.

1. MS   _____
2. TIA   _____
3. PET   _____
4. CNS   _____
5. CAT   _____
6. CSF   _____

Word-Building Challenge

Select word parts from the lists to build a complete medical term for each definition given. Note that not all terms will have a root or combining form, prefix, and suffix. Some word parts may be used more than once. This exercise may require use of a medical dictionary.

Combining Forms	Prefixes	Suffixes
astr/o	a-	-al
blast/o	an-	-ary
cephal/o	bi-	-cele
cyt/o	de-	-esthesia
dur/o	dys-	-genesis
esthesi/o	en-	-ia
hemat/o	hydro-	-ic
hydro/o	hyper-	-lepsy
medull/o	hypo-	-logy
myel/o	per-	-lysis
narco/o	pre-	-oma
neur/o	sub-	-otomy
phag/o	quadri-	-ous
		-pathy
		-rrhaphy

1. tumor arising from immature nerve cells _____
2. pertaining to the medulla_____
3. breakdown of myelin _____
4. difficulty swallowing (eating) _____
5. blood tumor (collection of blood) below the dura _____
6. hernia of the spinal cord_____
7. seizure with numbness or drowsiness _____

8. pertaining to water in the brain _____

9. tumor arising from an astral cell_____

10. excess sensation _____

11. suture of a nerve_____

12. disease of the brain_____

Extension Activities

Complete the following activities as assigned by your instructor.

1. Use the Internet to research information on two different allied health career paths specializing in neuroscience (i.e., the study of brain function). Create an overview of the positions, including information on education and training requirements, salary, and job outlook. Present your findings in a classroom discussion forum.

2. Use the Internet to research and review a scholarly article on the brain's influence on learning styles. Identify your preferred style of learning. Submit a one-page informational essay to your instructor highlighting information specific to that particular part of the brain.

3. Photosensitivity has been identified as a trigger for seizures in individuals diagnosed with epilepsy. Research the relationship between seizures and flashing lights and post an overview of your findings in the discussion forum. Identify 2-3 examples of common exposures that may present a high risk to individuals with epilepsy.

Student eResources

The Course Navigator learning management system that accompanies this textbook offers multiple opportunities to master chapter content, including end-of-chapter exercises, a glossary of key terms with audio pronunciations, games, pronunciation coach, and additional activities such as engaging with the BioDigital® Human.

COURSE NAVIGATOR

The Special Senses

66Taste, touch and smell, hearing and seeing, are not merely a means to sensation, enjoyable or otherwise, but they are also a means to knowledge—and are, indeed, your only actual means to knowledge.99

—St. Thomas Aquinas

Translation Challenge

Read this excerpt from a physician's report of a patient encounter and try to answer the questions that follow.

SUBJECTIVE: A 23 y/o man complains of nausea, dizziness, and a loud ringing in his right ear.

OBJECTIVE: Upon examination, visual acuity at distance was 20/20 in both eyes. The intraocular pressure was 20 OU. There was good motility, and the pupils were normal. Patient has documented history of vertigo and hearing loss.

ASSESSMENT: Audiometric tests are conducted alongside balance assessments. Patient is referred for MRI and CT scans to r/o a possible brain tumor or MS.

PLAN: Patient will be treated for Ménière's disease pending results of MRI and CT scans.

1. What is the medical term for "ringing in the ear"?

2. What does OU stand for?

3. How is Ménière's disease treated?

Learning Objectives

6.1 List and define word parts most commonly used to create terms related to the senses.

6.2 Locate and identify structures of the eye and ear.

6.3 Describe the physiology of vision, hearing, smell, taste, and touch.

6.4 Describe common conditions related to the eye and ear.

6.5 Name tests and treatments used to diagnose and treat conditions related to the eye and ear.

6.6 State the meaning of abbreviations related to the special senses.

6.7 Use the language of the special senses correctly in oral and written communications.

6.8 Correctly spell and pronounce terminology related to each of the five special senses.

 **COURSE NAVIGATOR**
Access Additional Chapter Resources

The previous chapter explained the ways in which the brain processes information. Information is collected by a stimulus (receptor), carried by the nervous system to the brain, where the information is interpreted to generate a response. This chapter discusses the various sensory receptors used to collect that information.

The five special senses are vision (eyes), hearing (ears), smell (nose), taste (tongue), and touch (skin). Each of these senses serves as a connection to our environment. The senses can tell us when to be scared, when we are in danger, and when we are secure. We take our sensory organs for granted when they are working properly, but a malfunction of any of the senses can disrupt our body's ability to function appropriately.

> **To Note!**
>
> The five special senses are vision (eyes), hearing (ears), smell (nose), taste (tongue), and touch (skin).

Because the senses work together closely, this chapter addresses the anatomy, physiology, pathology, and vocabulary of all five senses. The primary focus is the terminology associated with the eyes and ears; the important relationships with smell, taste, and touch are highlighted in a final section, along with the essential associated terms. To fully grasp the concept of information collection, processing, and interpretation, you must first understand the relationship between the nervous system and special senses.

Word Parts Associated with Special Senses

> **What's in a Word?**
>
> The combining form *salping/o* means "tubes" and is used in reference to auditory tubes as well as uterine tubes (fallopian tubes).

As with the other body systems, a group of combining forms serves as the source for most of the medical words associated with vision. Table 6.1 lists common combining forms associated with the eyes and their meanings. The suffix *-opia* is important to note. You will see this suffix, which means "condition of vision," in a number of vision-related terms.

TABLE 6.1 | Combining Forms Associated with the Special Senses

Combining Form	Meaning	Example
Combining Forms Associated with the Eye		
ambly/o	dull	amblyopia (disorder in which vision in one of the eyes is reduced because the eye and brain are not properly working together, also known as "lazy eye")
aque/o	water	aqueous humor (a fluid found in the space between the cornea and iris, provides nourishment and gives the eye its shape)
blephar/o	eyelid	blepharitis (inflammation of the eyelids)
conjunctiv/o	conjunctiva	conjunctivitis (inflammation of the outer membrane of the eyeball, also known as "pink eye")
corne/o	cornea	corneal (pertaining to the cornea)
cor/o	cornea	corneal (pertaining to the cornea)
dacry/o	tear	dacryoadenitis (inflammation of a lacrimal gland)
dipl/o	double	diplopia (double vision)
emmetr/o	correct measure, well proportioned	emmetropia (normal refractive condition of the eye, perfect vision)
glauc/o	blue-gray	glaucoma (condition in which increased fluid pressure in the eye results in optic nerve damage)
irid/o	iris	iridectomy (surgical removal of part of the iris)
kerat/o	cornea	keratitis (inflammation of the cornea)
lacrim/o	tears	lacrimal (pertaining to tears)
mi/o	less	miotic (eyedrops that trigger the reduction, in size, of the pupils)
mydr/o	widen	mydriasis (dilation of the pupil)
nyctal/o	night	nyctalopia (night blindness)
ocul/o	eye	ocular (pertaining to the eye)
ophthalm/o	eye	ophthalmology (diagnosis and treatment of disorders and diseases of the eye)
opt/o	eye/vision	optometrist (a doctor of optometry [OD] who specializes in the prescription and personalized fit of lenses to improve vision)
palpebr/o	eyelid	palpebral (located on or near the eyelids)
phac/o	lens of the eye	phacolysis (surgical breakdown and removal of the lens of the eye)
phot/o	light	photophobia (abnormal sensitivity to light)
presby/o	old age	presbyopia (gradual loss of one's ability to focus on nearby objects, associated with aging)
pupill/o	pupil	pupillary (pertaining to the pupil, dark center of the iris)
retin/o	retina	retinitis (inflammation of the retina)
scler/o	sclera (outer membrane)	scleritis (inflammation of the sclerae)
scot/o	dark	scotoma (an area of decreased vision, also known as a "blind spot")
uve/o	uvea	uveitis (inflammation of the uvea)
vitre/o	glassy	vitreous humor (a clear gel that fills the space between the lens and the retina)
xer/o	dry	xerophthalmia (dry eye)
Combining Forms Associated with the Ear		
acous/o	hearing	acoustic (pertaining to sound/hearing)
audi/o	hearing, sound	audiology (the study of hearing)

Combining Form	Meaning	Example
aur/o	ear	aural forceps (scissor-like tool used to perform surgical procedures of the ear)
auricul/o	ear	auricular (pertaining to the ear)
labyrinth/o-	inner ear	labyrinthitis (inflammation of the nerves of the inner ear)
myring/o	tympanic membrane	myringotomy (incision of the eardrum)
ot/o	ear	otic (pertaining to the ear)
salping/o	tube	salpingeal (relating to the eustachian tube)
tympan/o	drum	tympanic membrane (eardrum)
Combining Forms Associated with Taste, Smell, and Touch		
cut/o, cutane/o	skin	subcutaneous (under/beneath the skin)
derm/o, dermat/o	skin	dermatology (the study of the hair, skin, and nails)
esthesi/o	feeling/sensation	paresthesia (feeling of prickling, burning, or numbness)
geus/o	taste	ageusia (loss of the sense of taste)
gloss/o	tongue	glossospasm (contraction of the muscles of the tongue)
lingu/o	tongue	lingual (pertaining to speech or language)
nas/o	nose	nasal (pertaining to the nose)
osm/o	sense of smell	anosmia (inability to smell odors)
rhin/o	nose	rhinoplasty (surgical repair of the nose)

Anatomy and Physiology of the Eye

The eye is the body's camera, scanning its surroundings and capturing complex visual data. Although this body organ is relatively small, it consists of numerous components, each of which plays an important role in achieving vision. Understanding the anatomy and physiology of the eye requires an understanding of both the internal and external structures of the eye. The following sections explain these structures in detail; Table 6.2 identifies common anatomy and physiology terms relating to the eyes.

TABLE 6.2 Anatomy and Physiology Terms Associated with the Eyes

Term		Meaning	Word Analysis	
accommodation	[ah-kom-ah-**day**-shun]	the ability to focus and see	*accommod/o*	to adapt
aqueous humor	[**ay**-kwee-us **hyoo**-mer]	watery fluid in front of the lens	*aqueous humor*	water-like clear liquid
canthus	[**kan**-thus]	angle formed where upper and lower eyelids meet	*kanthos*	corner
choroid	[**kO**-royd]	highly vascular membrane between retina and sclera	*chori/o*	membrane
conjunctiva	[kon-junk-**tI**-vah]	clear mucous membrane lining the inner eyelids and anterior of the eye	*conjunctus*	joining
cornea	[**kor**-nee-ah]	the outer portion of the eye through which light passes to the retina	*corneus*	horny membrane
epicanthic fold	[ep-ih-**kan**-thic]	extension of a skin fold over the inner angle or both angles of the eye	*epi-* *kanthos* *-ic*	upon corner pertaining to

Continues

Term		Meaning	Word Analysis	
fundus	[**fun**-dus]	part farthest away from the opening	*fundus*	bottom
intraocular	[in-trah-**ok**-yoo-ler]	within the eye	*intra-* *ocul/o* *-ar*	inside eye pertaining to
iris irides (pl)	[**I**-ris **ir**-ih-deez]	the colored portion of the eye	*irid/o*	iris
lacrimal	[**lak**-rih-mal]	pertaining to tears	*lacrim/o* *-al*	tears pertaining to
lacrimal caruncle	[**lak**-rih-mal **kar**-ung-kul]	small follicular area at the eye's medial angle	*lacrim/o* *-al* *caruncle*	tears pertaining to small, protruding mass of flesh
lacrimal punctum	[**lak**-rih-mal **punk**-tum]	point or opening within the upper and lower canthi to drain tears	*lacrim/o* *-al* *punctum*	tears pertaining to point
limbus	[**lim**-bus]	border of the cornea and sclera	*limbus*	edge, border
macula lutea maculae (pl)	[**mak**-yoo-lah **loo**-tee-ah **mak**-yoo-lee]	small yellowish spot on the retina	*macula* *luteus*	spot yellow
nasolacrimal	[nay-zO-**lak**-rih-mal]	pertaining to the nasal and lacrimal bones or ducts	*nas/o* *lacrim/o* *-al*	nose tears pertaining to
ophthalmologist	[off-thal-**mol**-ah-jist]	physician specializing in diseases of the eye	*ophthalm/o* *-logist*	eye one who studies
ophthalmology	[off-thal-**mol**-ah-jee]	the study of the eye	*ophthalm/o* *-logy*	eye study of
ophthalmoscope	[off-**thal**-mah-skOp]	instrument to view the eye	*ophthalm/o* *-scope*	eye instrument for visualizing an area
ophthalmus	[off-**thal**-mus]	eye	*ophthalm/o*	eye
optic	[**op**-tik]	pertaining to the eye or sight	*opt/o* *-ic*	vision relating to
optometrist	[op-**tom**-eh-trist]	professional who tests visual acuity and prescribes corrective lenses	*opt/o* *-metrist*	vision one who measures
palpebra	[pal-**pee**-brah]	eyelid	*pebra*	eyelid
pupil	[**pew**-pul]	central opening of the iris	*pupa*	doll
sclera	[**sklee**-rah]	outer, dense, fibrous, opaque white layer of the eye	*scler/o*	sclera
vitreous humor	**vit**-ree-us **hyoo**-mer	jelly-like fluid behind the lens	*vitre/o* *humor*	glassy clear liquid

External Eye Structures

The two eye sockets are located on the anterior surface of the skull, within the orbital cavity. Each socket is surrounded by the bones of the skull. Six muscles attach the eyeball to the orbit, allowing the eye to move in several directions. The outer structures of the eye serve to encase and protect the eyeball. See Figure 6.1.

The eyelids, or **palpebrae**, are composed of a thin protective layer of skin, muscle, and connective tissue. The eyelids shield the eyes from outside elements (e.g., dust and debris) and offer protection from extreme light and other potential causes of injury. The eyelids represent the thinnest layer of skin in the human body. The superior palpebra (upper eyelid) is divided into the **epicanthic fold** (skin fold of the upper eyelid) and the **canthus** (the corner of the eye). The superior and inferior palpebrae (lower eyelid) join on each side to form the internal (medial) and external (lateral) canthi. The **lacrimal gland**, located on the outer portion of each upper eyelid, is responsible for the production of tears, which lubricate and protect the eye. The tears empty into the **nasolacrimal sac**, through the nasolacrimal duct, and then into an opening within the nose. Figure 6.2 shows the flow of tears.

Within the rim of the upper and lower canthi are **meibomian glands**, which excrete an oily lubricating substance into the eye. This substance is produced to prevent the eyelids from sticking together. The upper and lower eyelid meet at the **palpebral fissure**, which is surrounded by eyelashes, which further protect the eye from environmental dangers.

The **conjunctiva**, the lining of the eye and eyelid is the area visualized when the physician looks at the eye. Its job is to provide a lining for the eye and eyelid.

FIGURE 6.1 External Eye Structure

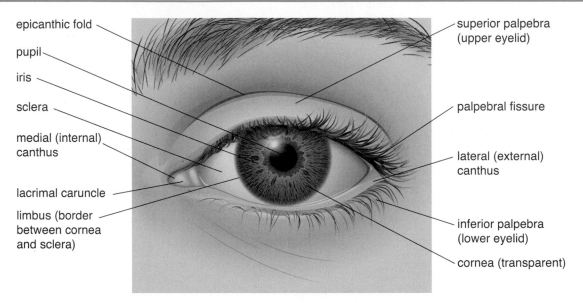

FIGURE 6.2 Flow of Tears

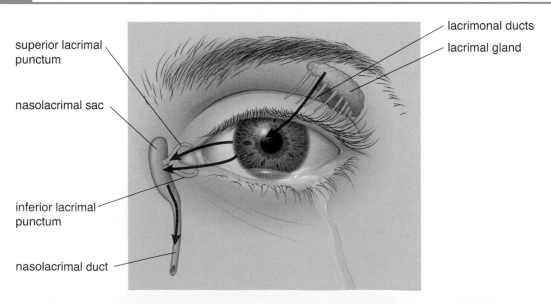

The **sclera** (the white of the eye) is the outer covering of the eyeball. It serves a protective function and contains sensory receptors. The sclera is covered by a clear, dome-shaped coating called the **cornea**. The cornea contains more nerve endings than any other structure in the body. It is here that light rays are refracted or "bent" as they enter the eye. It is also the location where a contact lens will rest. The cornea covers the **iris** (the colored portion of the eye) and **pupil** (the black center). The iris contains muscles that constrict and dilate the pupil to allow the appropriate amount of light onto the **retina**, the nerve tissue that sends messages to the brain.

Internal Eye Structures

The retina is composed of 10 layers containing two types of photoreceptors, about 120 million rods and 6 million cones, and neurons. **Rods** are extremely sensitive to light and are responsible for night vision, called **scotopic** vision. **Photopic** vision, or vision in bright light, and color vision are the function of the **cones**. They are the most sensitive to one of three different colors (red, blue, and green).

The **lens** is an elastic, highly movable disk located behind the pupil. It has a **ciliary body**, a muscle that causes the lens to bulge for focusing on near objects and to flatten for focusing on distant objects. This process is called **accommodation**. When the ciliary muscle is relaxed, the eye is considered to be in normal position, or **emmetropic**. Note that the combining form *emmetr/o* means "correct measure" or "well proportioned."

The process of vision occurs when light rays are refracted first through the lens system, consisting of the cornea and the crystalline lens, then to the retina (see Figure 6.3). The retina transforms this stimulus into nerve impulses that move through the optic nerve to the visual cortex of the brain. The image formed on the retina is upside down and reversed from the real image. As the image passes through the optic chiasm of the brain, it is transposed so that the right side of the brain sees the left side of the outside view and the left side of the brain sees the right side. Both eyes send pictures to the brain, which then merges the information into one image.

FIGURE 6.3 | **Internal Eye Structure: Sagittal View**

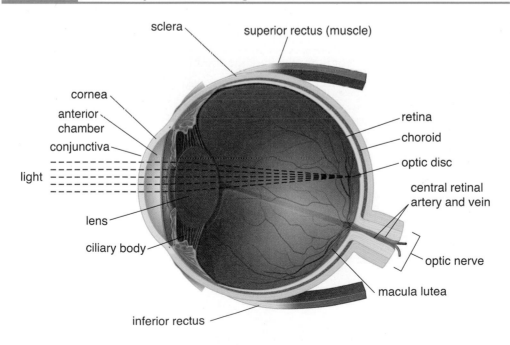

In the Know: The Vision System and Its Practitioners

Vision is the sense that permits us to view our surroundings and provides the brain with detailed information about what the eyes see. The study of the eye and its diseases is called **ophthalmology**. The professionals within this specialty include the **ophthalmologist**, a medical doctor (MD) who diagnoses and treats eye disorders; the **optometrist**, a doctor of optometry (OD) who specializes in the prescription and personalized fit of lenses to improve vision; and the **optician**, who takes the prescription from the MD or OD and cuts the glass or plastic to fill the prescription. During the past decade, subspecialties focusing on new eye surgeries have rapidly emerged. The increased life span of people has expanded the need for the correction and treatment of eye disorders, and researchers have responded with new products and procedures that make it possible to surgically correct abnormalities that previously were accepted as an inevitable product of growing older.

Checkpoint 6.1

Answer the following questions to identify any areas of the section that you may need to review.

1. Describe the visual acuity of one who is diagnosed as emmetropic.

   _____

2. What is the corresponding medical term for eyelid?

   _____

3. Which gland is responsible for the production of tears, which lubricate and protect the eye?

   _____

Exercise 6.1   Word Building

Supply a combining form for each definition; then use the combining form to create the term that matches the definition.

Definition	Combining Form	Term
1. study of the eye	_____	_____
2. inflammation of the eyelid	_____	_____
3. difficulty seeing at night	_____	_____
4. repair of the cornea	_____	_____
5. inflammation of the conjunctiva	_____	_____

Exercise 6.2 Comprehension Check

Using the context of the following sentences, circle the correct term from each pair.

1. The palpations/palpebrae protect the eye from bright lights and injury.
2. The nasolacrimal/nasopharyngeal duct drains tears from the eye.
3. Extraocular/Extraorbital muscles attach the eyeball to the orbit.
4. The retinue/retina is a structure essential for vision.
5. Light rays are refracted/retracted through the lens to the retina.

Exercise 6.3 Name the Term

Create the correct term for the definition given by providing the missing word parts.

1. _____ocular means beyond, or outside, the eye.
2. _____orbital means around the eye socket.
3. _____itis is an inflammation of the membrane that lines the lids and covers the front of the eye.
4. _____ocular means inside the eye.
5. _____l means pertaining to the transparent membrane that is part of the outer portion of the eye.

Exercise 6.4 Word Building

Use root words, combining forms, prefixes, and suffixes to construct a medical term to match each definition provided.

1. instrument used to examine the eye
2. field of medicine concerned with the eye   _____
3. pertaining to the cornea   _____
4. pertaining to the orbit   _____
5. pertaining to the pupil   _____

Exercise 6.5 Spelling Check

Find the misspelled words in the following sentences. Write the correct spelling on the blank provided.

1. Vishion is the sense that permits a person to view his or her surroundings.   _____
2. Many people wear disposable contact lenzes.   _____
3. Dr. Wharton is the clinic's opthalamologist.   _____
4. Lazer surgery can correct many eye problems.   _____
5. An opthician can fill a prescription for eyeglasses.   _____

Exercise 6.6   Identification

In the accompanying illustration of the eye, label the following structures.

1. palpebrae
2. medial canthus
3. cornea
4. palpebra (inferior)
5. sclera
6. iris
7. pupil
8. lateral canthus

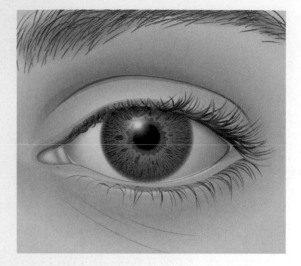

Anatomy and Physiology of the Ear

Ears are responsible for both hearing and maintaining balance. When both ears are working properly, we can hear the sounds around us and determine the direction of the source. When only one ear is working, it may be difficult to distinguish the direction of the source of sounds. Equilibrium is a complex mechanism that depends on normal fluid levels within the inner ear and on proper coordination of visual signals with the nervous system. Table 6.3 identifies common anatomy and physiology terms related to the ear.

TABLE 6.3   Anatomy and Physiology Terms Associated with the Ear

Term		Meaning	Word Analysis	
acoustic	[ah-**koos**-tik]	sound	*acoust/o* *-ic*	hearing pertaining to
amplitude	[**am**-plih-tood]	range or extent (of sound)	*ampli-* *-tude*	width quality or state
auditory	[**aw**-dih-tO-ree]	hearing	*audi/o* *-ory*	hearing pertaining to
aural	[**aw**-rel]	relating to the ear	*aur/o* *-al*	ear pertaining to
auricle	[**aw**-rih-kul]	external ear	*auricul/o*	ear
cerumen	[seh-**roo**-men]	earwax	*cera*	wax
cochlea	[**kOk**-lee-ah]	spiral-shaped structure within the ear	*cochlea*	snail
concha	[**kon**-kah]	the shell-shaped structure of the outer ear	*concha*	shell
endolymph	[**en**-dO-limf]	lymphatic fluid within the labyrinth	*endo-* *lymph*	within clear fluid

Term		Meaning	Word Analysis	
Eustachian tube	[yoo-**stay**-shun toob]	passageway leading from the middle ear to the nasopharynx		
fenestra ovalis	[feh-**nes**-trah O-**vay**-lis]	oval opening between the middle ear and the vestibule	*fenestra ovalis*	opening oval-shaped
fenestration	[fen-es-**tray**-shun]	formation of an opening into the labyrinth of the ear	*fenestra*	window-like opening
helix	[**hee**-liks]	folded edge of the external ear	*helix*	coil
incus	[**in**-kus]	anvil-shaped bone in the middle ear	*incus*	anvil
labyrinth	[**lab**-ir-inth]	structure of the inner ear	*labyrinth*	maze
malleus	[**mal**-lee-us]	bone of the middle ear	*malleus*	hammer
meatus	[mee-**ay**-tus]	opening	*meatus*	passage
organ of Corti	[**kor**-tee]	organ within the inner ear		
ossicle	[**os**-sih-kul]	bone of the middle ear	*os/i* *-icle*	bone small
periauricular	[pair-ee-aw-**rik**-yoo-ler]	surrounding the ear	*peri-* *auricul/o* *-ar*	around ear pertaining to
perilymph	[**pair**-ih-limf]	fluid surrounding the labyrinth	*peri-* *lymph*	around clear fluid
pinna	[**pin**-ah]	the external ear		
saccule	[**sak**-yool]	membranous sac within the vestibule	*sac* *-ule*	sac or bag small
semicircular canal	[sem-ih-**ser**-kyoo-ler kan-**al**]	fluid-filled loops in the labyrinth	*semi-* *circul/o* *canal*	half round passageway
stapes	[**stay**-peez]	small bone of the middle ear	*stapes*	stirrup
tragus tragi (pl)	[**tray**-gus]	small, goatee-shaped projection of cartilage on the outer ear		
tympanic membrane	[tim-**pan**-ik **mem**-brayn]	eardrum	*tympan/o* *-ic*	drum pertaining to
utricle	[**yoo**-trih-kul]	membranous pouch in the vestibule	*uter*	leather bag
vestibule	[**ves**-tih-byool]	the central cavity of the labyrinth	*vestibul/o*	space

In the Know: The Hearing System and Its Practitioners

The specialist in the diagnosis and treatment of ear diseases and hearing problems is the otorhinolaryngologist (*ot/o* means "ear;" *rhin/o* refers to "nose;" and *laryn/o* means "larynx"), also called an otolaryngologist or ENT (ear/nose/throat) specialist. These physicians also treat nose and throat problems. An audiologist is an allied health professional who tests a patient's hearing and recommends an appropriate type of hearing aid, if necessary.

Did You Know?

Earwax protects your ears by trapping dirt and dust and preventing it from entering the eardrum.

The ear is divided into three parts: the external ear, the middle ear, and the inner ear (see Figure 6.4). The visible portion of the external ear is called the **auricle**, or **pinna**. The auricle collects sound waves and passes them through the **external auditory meatus**, a canal leading to the eardrum. Glands within the auditory canal secrete **cerumen**, the brownish substance (earwax) that discourages microorganism growth and provides protection for the ear.

Middle Ear

The eardrum, or **tympanic membrane**, separates the external canal from the air-filled middle ear, a cavity that opens via the **Eustachian tube** into the nasopharynx (see Figure 6.4). The tube is usually closed, but it opens during swallowing, chewing, and yawning to equalize the air pressure on both sides of the membrane.

Beyond the tympanic membrane lies a series of three bones called the **ossicles** (auditory ossicles), consisting of the **malleus** (hammer), the **incus** (anvil), and the **stapes** (stirrup). Named for the objects they resemble, these tiny bones conduct sound vibrations to a membrane called the **oval window**, or **fenestra ovalis**, which amplifies the sound and transmits it into the inner ear.

FIGURE 6.4 | Ear: External, Middle, and Inner

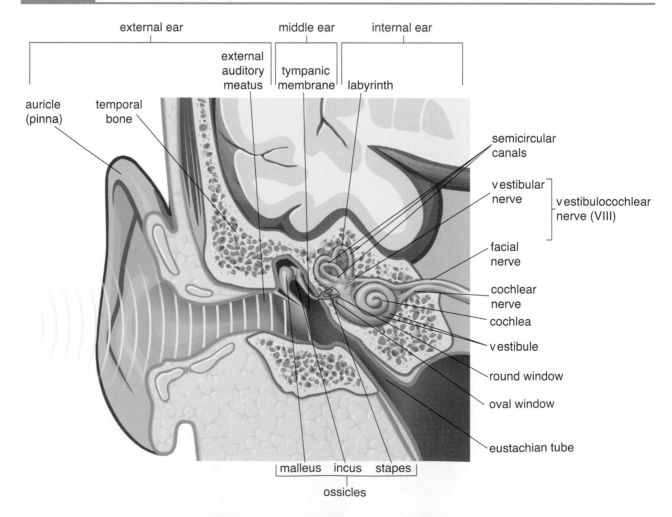

Internal (Inner) Ear

The inner ear is called the **labyrinth**, from the Greek word that means "maze," a term that describes the two types of channels that wind through the inner ear (see Figure 6.5). The labyrinth serves two functions as it is responsible for hearing as well as the body's equilibrium. One channel is the bony labyrinth, which is filled with fluid called **perilymph**. Also found within the bony labyrinth is the membranous labyrinth, a flexible tube filled with fluid called **endolymph**.

Special names exist for various sections of the bony labyrinth: vestibule, semicircular canals, cochlea, and the auditory and vestibular receptors of the eighth cranial nerve (vestibulocochlear nerve). The **cochlea** is considered the main organ of hearing. Moving fluid within the cochlea stimulates receptor hair cells, housed by the **organ of Corti**, to stimulate the auditory nerve to transmit the neural stimulation to the brain, where it is interpreted as sound.

The Process of Hearing

The outer, middle, and inner ear structures are all involved in the process of hearing (see Figure 6.6). The outer ear acts like a satellite dish antenna that "catches" sound waves and funnels them through the auditory canal until they strike against the tympanic membrane,

FIGURE 6.5 Inner Ear

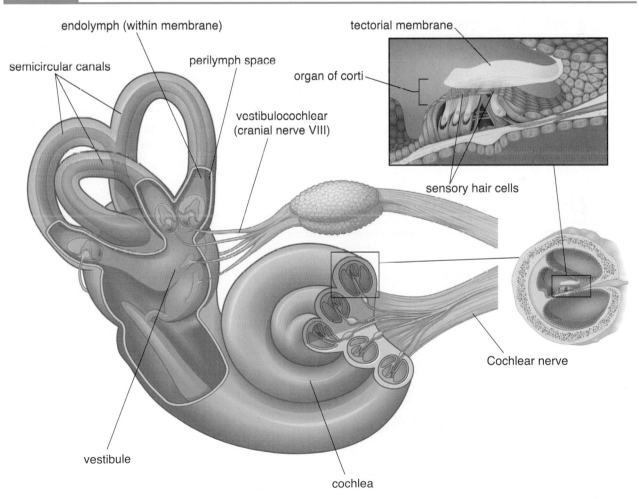

endolymph (within membrane)

tectorial membrane

semicircular canals

perilymph space

organ of corti

vestibulocochlear (cranial nerve VIII)

sensory hair cells

Cochlear nerve

vestibule

cochlea

FIGURE 6.6 Movement of Sound Waves

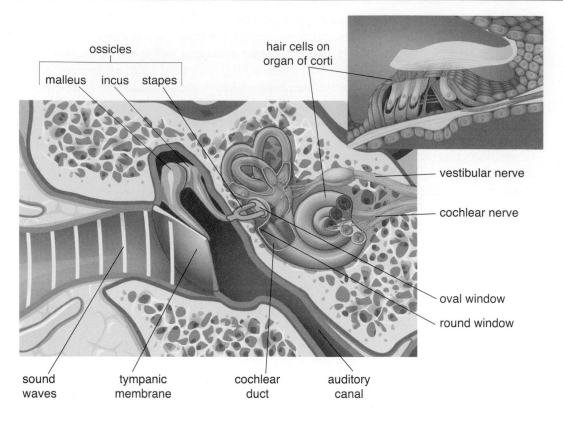

FIGURE 6.6 Movement of Sound Waves

ossicles

malleus incus stapes

hair cells on organ of corti

vestibular nerve

cochlear nerve

oval window

round window

sound waves

tympanic membrane

cochlear duct

auditory canal

causing vibrations. The middle ear structures pass the vibrations from one bone to another and on into the inner ear, where they are received and converted into nerve impulses by the cochlea. Finally, the nerve impulses travel through the auditory nerve to the brain, which translates them into sounds. The complicated process of hearing seems all the more remarkable when you consider that this chain of events occurs instantaneously.

Checkpoint 6.2

Answer the following questions to identify any areas of the section that you may need to review.

1. What structure of the ear is responsible for hearing and equilibrium?

   _____

2. What three tiny bones make up the auditory ossicles?

   _____

3. What structure, within the middle ear, provides a passageway to the throat?

   _____

Exercise 6.7   Word Analysis

Separate each term into its individual word parts using slashes. Identify each part by type using the following letters: P = prefix, S = suffix, and CF = combining form. Then provide a definition for the whole term. Remember that all word parts may not be found in any one term. Some terms will have only two word parts.

Word Analysis	**Definition**
1. tympanosclerosis	_____
	_____
2. periauricular	_____
	_____
3. otoscope	_____
	_____
4. biaural	_____
	_____
5. salpingeal	_____
	_____

Exercise 6.8   Matching

Match the terms in column 1 with the definitions in column 2. Write the letter of your selection on the line beside the term.

1. _____ pinna
2. _____ stapes
3. _____ meatus
4. _____ amplitude
5. _____ concha
6. _____ acoustic
7. _____ helix
8. _____ malleus
9. _____ incus
10. _____ limbus

a. border of the cornea and sclera
b. shell-shaped structure of the outer ear
c. anvil
d. opening
e. hammer
f. range or extent of sound
g. stirrup
h. folded edge of the outer ear
i. external ear
j. pertaining to sound

Exercise 6.9   Word Building

Use root words, combining forms, prefixes, and suffixes to construct a medical term to match each definition provided.

1. instrument used to examine the ear   _____

2. little sac (structure within the vestibule)   _____

3. pertaining to a drum (hearing)   _____

4. around the ear   _____

5. pertaining to the vestibule   _____

Exercise 6.10   Spelling Check

Find the misspelled words. Write the correct spelling on the lines provided.

1. Dr. Martino wrote the patient a prescrisption.

   _____

2. The membranous labaryrinth contains a fluid called entolymph.

   _____

3. The organ of Corti contains the autidiotory receptors.

   _____

4. The semicircular cannals are located behind the vestibular.

   _____

5. A cocchulea is a spiral-shaped structure.

   _____

6. Dr. Yates performed the miriengotomy on Jason yesterday.

   _____

Exercise 6.11   Word Maps

In the illustration of the ear, label the following structures.

1. auricle or pinna

2. external auditory meatus

3. tympanic membrane

4. eustachian tube

5. ossicular chain

6. cochlea

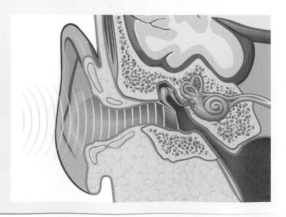

Anatomy and Physiology of Taste, Smell, and Touch

When we see food, we can smell it and even taste it without taking a bite. The senses of smell and taste are nearly inseparable. The sense of sight also is highly integrated with smell and taste. Working together, the three can stimulate the flow of saliva in the mouth. If one of these senses is not working correctly, such as during an upper respiratory infection, taste can be diminished.

The sense of touch is widely distributed, with high concentrations of receptors in a few critical areas, such as the pads of the fingertips. Because the nervous system is central to the sense of touch, problems are referred to a neurologist.

Taste

The sense of taste occurs on the tongue, which contains more than 10,000 taste buds located on the papillae of the tongue, roof of the mouth, and lining the walls of the throat. Each taste bud is made up of supporting cells that fill in space and hair cells known as the **gustatory receptors**.

The four basic tastes are sensed by different parts of the tongue: (1) sweet—tip of the tongue, (2) sourness—along the edges, (3) bitter—on the back, and (4) saltiness—on the anterior dorsum. Figure 6.7 shows the areas where the basic tastes are sensed. Exposure to spicy foods, once interpreted by the brain, activate pain receptors. Tastes cannot be translated until the chemicals present in the food or beverage are dissolved in saliva and interpreted.

FIGURE 6.7 Tongue Structure

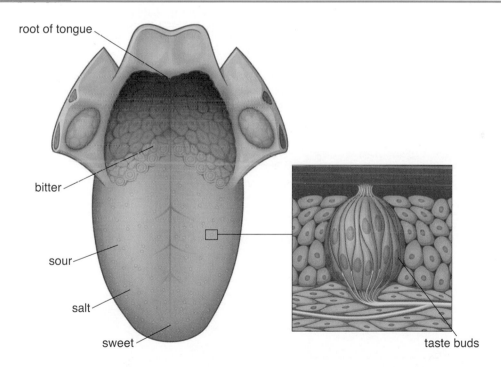

Smell

The sense of smell depends on hair cells within the nose that act as **olfactory** (smell-sensing) receptors. They lie at the roof of the nasal cavity and in the upper portion of the septum. These olfactory receptors merge into the olfactory nerve (cranial nerve I). From there, the information is sent across the olfactory bulbs and tract to be distributed for processing across various parts of the cerebrum. The information is then interpreted as a specific type of smell. Animals rely on their sense of smell for survival in various ways, including identifying food and danger sources. Humans can use the smell of noxious odors to protect them from harm, as well. Some odors may stimulate sexual arousal; others may trigger memory. The sense of smell also enhances the enjoyment and taste of foods, thereby improving health and nutrition.

Touch

Receptors all over the body can sense touch, although the receptors are most numerous in the skin of the fingers and lips and less abundant in the skin of the trunk. Touch includes the sensations of itch and tickle, light and deep pain, temperature changes, and **proprioception** (an awareness of the position of one's body parts in relation to the whole body).

In the Know: Proprioception

Proprioception is often referred to as one's sixth sense. Demonstrate your mastery of this particular sense by closing your eyes and extending your hand in any direction you choose. In your mind, identify the exact position of the outstretched hand and then open your eyes. Take note that you knew the exact location of your hand without seeing it move to its current location. Your brain was well aware of your hand's positioning thanks to the heightened sense of proprioception.

Sobriety tests conducted by law enforcement officers are yet another measurement of one's sense of proprioception. The tasks of "walking in a straight line" and "touching the finger to the nose" cannot be accomplished if the brain is unable to interpret complex processes because of an alcohol impairment.

Checkpoint 6.3

Answer the following questions to identify any areas of the section that you may need to review.

1. What are the four basic tastes?

_____

2. What sense do olfactory receptors support?

_____

3. What part of the body has fewer touch receptors?

_____

Exercise 6.12   Comprehension Check

Using the context of the following sentences, circle the correct term from each pair.

1. The lacrimal duct/olfactory bulb contains nerve cells that provide the sense of smell.

2. The gustatory/nasopharyngeal cells are part of the taste buds.

3. Dysgeusia/Hypogeusia is an abnormal sense of taste.

4. Osmesis/Osmosis is the act of smelling.

5. Papillae/Anosmia refers to an absence of the sense of smell.

Conditions of the Eye

Common conditions of the eye include nearsightedness and farsightedness. Many people wear corrective lenses to correct these conditions. Both are a result of the eyeball not being shaped perfectly. Nearsightedness, or **myopia**, results when the eyeball is too long, causing light rays to focus in front of the retina instead of on the retina (see Figure 6.8). Concave lenses, which are thicker at the sides than in the middle, are prescribed to focus the light correctly. Wearing these lenses allows the person to see far away objects clearly. Farsightedness, or **hyperopia**, results from a shorter-than-normal eyeball, causing light rays to focus behind the retina. This condition is corrected with convex lenses, which are thicker in the middle than at the sides. Wearing these lenses allows the person to see close objects clearly.

Diabetic retinopathy (damage to the retina due to diabetes) is a common complication of diabetes mellitus and the leading cause of blindness. The longer a person has diabetes, the greater the risk. **Conjunctivitis** is an inflammation of the conjunctiva and can be caused by bacterial, viral, fungal, or parasitic organisms. The bacterial and viral forms of pink eye are highly contagious. Symptoms of conjunctivitis include hyperemia

FIGURE 6.8 Eye and Vision Conditions

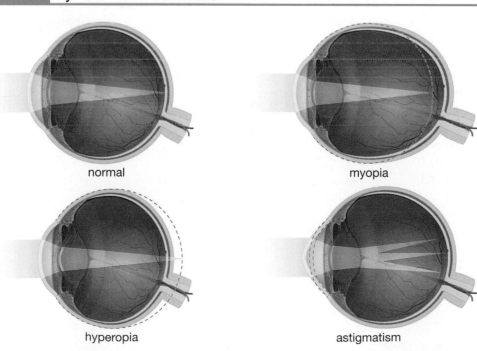

normal

myopia

hyperopia

astigmatism

(the red appearance gives it the nickname "pinkeye"), discharge (called "matter"), tearing, itching or burning, and a feeling of having a foreign body in the eye. Corneal abrasions occur from trauma, foreign bodies (including contact lenses), or any defect that impedes the flow of protective tears.

Keratitis is an infection of the cornea and can be caused by any organism that has entered the cornea through an abrasion. Because the eye allows infectious agents easy entry into the body, patients with severe infectious keratitis are hospitalized and placed on antibiotic therapy. Table 6.4 lists common conditions and diseases of the eye.

TABLE 6.4 Wellness and Illness Terms Associated with the Eye

Term		Meaning	Word Analysis	
amblyopia	[am-blee-**O**-pee-ah]	poor vision in one eye	*ambly/o*	dullness, dimness
			-opia	relating to vision
anisocoria	[an-I-sO-**kor**-ee-ah]	unequal pupils	*an-*	not
			is/o	equal
			cor/o	pupil
			-ia	condition
aphakia	[ah-**fay**-kee-ah]	absence of the lens of the eye	*a-*	absence of
			phak/o, phac/o	lens-shaped; lens
			-ia	condition of
astigmatism	[ah-**stig**-mah-tiz-em]	condition of unequal curvatures	*a-*	absence of
			stigma	identifying mark
			-ism	condition of; state of
blepharitis	[bleff-ah-**rI**-tis]	inflammation of the eyelid	*blephar/o*	eyelid
			-itis	inflammation
blepharoptosis	[bleff-ah-rop-**tO**-sis]	drooping of upper eyelid	*blephar/o*	eyelid
			-ptosis	drooping, sagging
cataract	[**cat**-ah-ract]	loss of transparancy of the lens of the eye, or its capsule		
chalazion	[ka-**lays**-ee-on]	inflammatory cyst or granuloma of the meibomian gland	*chalaza*	a sty
conjunctivitis	[kon-junk-ti-**vI**-tis]	inflammation of the lining of the eye	*conjunctus*	joining
			-itis	inflammation
corneal abrasion	[**kore**-nee-uhl a-**bray**-zhun]	scratch on the cornea		
dacryoma	[dak-**ree**-oma]	tumor-like swelling caused by obstruction of the tear duct	*dacry/o*	lacrimal gland (tear duct)
			-oma	tumor, mass
diplopia	[dih-**plO**-pee-ah]	double vision	*dipl/o*	double
			-opia	relating to vision
esophoria	[es-O-**fO**-ree-ah]	inward turning of the eye without double vision	*eso-*	inward; within
			phor/o	carrying; bearing
			-ia	condition of
esotropia	[es-O-**trO**-pee-ah]	inward turning of the eye with double vision	*eso-*	inward; within
			trope	turn
			-opia	relating to vision
exophoria	[eks-O-**fO**-ree-ah]	outward turning of the eye without double vision	*ex/o*	outward
			phor/o	carrying; bearing
			-ia	condition of

Continues

Term		Meaning	Word Analysis	
exotropia	[eks-O-**trO**-pee-ah]	outward turning of the eye with double vision	*ex/o*	outward
			trope	turn
			-opia	relating to vision
glaucoma	[glaw-**cO**-ma]	condition of increased intraocular pressure		
hyperopia	[hI-pur-**O**-pee-ah]	farsightedness	*hyper-*	above, beyond
			-opia	pertaining to vision
hypertropia	[hI-pur-**trO**-pee-ah]	condition in which one eye is higher than the other	*hyper-*	greater; above
			trope	turn
			-ia	condition of
keratitis	[ker-ah-**tI**-tis]	infection of the cornea	*kerat/o*	cornea
			-itis	inflammation
keratoconus	[ker-at-O-**kO**-nus]	progressive thinning of the cornea, causing a protrusion	*kerat/o*	cornea
			conus	conelike
leukocoria	[loo-kO-**kor**-ee-ah]	white reflection from a mass in the eye	*leuk/o*	white
			core/o	pupil
			-ia	condition of
macular degeneration		loss of visualization to fine details		
microphthal-mia	[mI-krof-**thal**-mee-ah]	abnormally small eye	*micro-*	small
			ophthalm/o	eye
			-ia	condition
myopia	[mI-**O**-pee-ah]	nearsightedness	*my/o*	muscle
			-opia	pertaining to vision
nyctalopia	[nik-tuh-**lO**-pee-ah]	difficulty seeing at night	*nyctal/o*	night
			-opia	pertaining to vision
presbyopia	[prez-bee-**O**-pee-ah]	farsightedness due to aging	*presby/o*	aging
			opia	pertaining to vision
retinoblas-toma	[ret-ih-nO-blas-**tO**-mah]	cancer of the retina	*retin/o*	retina
			blast	pertaining to budding of cells; immature cells
			-oma	pertaining to cancer
retinopathy	[ret-ih-**nop**-ah-thee]	disease of the retina	*retin/o*	retina
			-pathy	denoting disease
strabismus	[strah-**biz**-mus]	misalignment of the axis of the eyes because of weakness of the ocular muscles; crossed eyes		

In the Know: Eyelid Conditions

The eyelids play an important role in protecting the eyeball from injury and disease, and so it is important to seek medical attention whenever abnormalities of the eyelid become apparent. Irritation, inflammation, or infection of the eyelid, including **blepharitis**, an inflammation of the margins of the lid, or **chalazion**, a sterile granuloma (node or mass) from inflammation of the meibomian gland (lubricating glands), can be present. A sty (**hordeolum**) is an infection of the eyelid usually caused by *Staphylococcus aureus*.

Infants, Toddlers, and Adolescents

Within an hour of birth, the newborn is administered silver nitrate drops in the conjunctival sac of each eye to protect against gonococcal infection. Gonococcus is transmitted from an infected mother during the baby's passage through the birth canal. Immediate treatment has nearly eliminated the incidence rates in infants.

Infants have limited eye function. Although peripheral vision is present in the newborn, the **macula lutea** (central vision) is absent. It develops by about four months and matures by eight months. Eye movements are poorly coordinated until about three to four months. About 80 percent of infants are born farsighted, but this condition corrects itself after about eight months. Eyeball structure reaches adult size by about age eight.

Retinopathy of prematurity (ROP) is a type of blindness that occurs when an infant is born three or more months prematurely. In ROP, the retina is not fully developed in either eye. The fragile blood vessels become weak and eventually bleed, leading to scarring around the retina that detach it from the back of the eye, ultimately causing irreversible blindness.

Examination of the eye is difficult from infancy to young school age. Frequently, the physician must sedate the young patient to complete the examination. Inability to control the positions of the eyes should be diagnosed early in childhood. **Strabismus**, or lack of coordination between the eyes, is typically the result of a weakness in one of the muscles controlling eye movement. Diagnosis of this condition is usually made in childhood. **Diplopia** (double vision) is common and can lead to **amblyopia** (decreased vision), which is reversible if diagnosed before the age of about seven years. Other deviations of eye control include **esotropia** (inward turning of the eyes), **exotropia** (outward turning of the eyes), and **hypertropia** (upward squinting). Treatment options include drugs, eye exercises, special lenses, and surgery.

> ### What's in a Word?
>
> The nondecodable term *strabismus* means "squint." In the medical field, the word *squint* is often used in reference to strabismus.

FIGURE 6.9 Strabismus

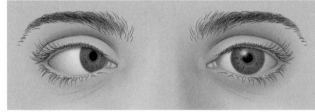

esotropia

hypertropia

exotropia

hypotropia

Retinoblastoma is a type of eye cancer most commonly seen in infants and toddlers. It is often diagnosed when **leukocoria** (white pupil) is first noted in the child's eye. Retinoblastoma can affect one or both eyes; when it is present in both eyes it is usually hereditary. Treatment includes **enucleation** (removal) of the entire affected eye and as much optic nerve as possible. When the condition affects both eyes, a number of other treatments are available to attempt to preserve vision in one eye.

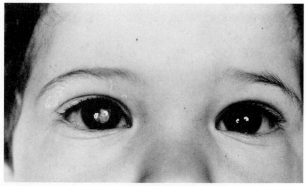
Evidence of retinoblastoma due to the patient's white pupil.

Keratoconus is a condition in which the collagen found in the cornea fails to perform its function of maintaining a dome-shaped cornea. It is generally present and diagnosed in the teen years and most often affects females. In keratoconus, vision is distorted, leading to astigmatism (blurred vision) and myopia (nearsightedness) that are difficult to correct even with eyeglasses or contact lenses. Surgery may be necessary to treat this condition.

Adults

Problems with accommodation, or shifting focus, begin to occur after the age of 40. The lens becomes increasingly hard, decreasing its ability to curve as needed. This inflexibility makes reading difficult, and is known as **presbyopia**, or farsightedness associated with aging.

According to the World Health Organization, glaucoma is the second leading cause of blindness (the inability to see images) in the world, although most cases can be prevented with early diagnosis and management. Most persons over the age of 35 are at risk. **Glaucoma** is a condition characterized by the buildup of fluid in the eye's drainage canals. The buildup is due to the canals being either clogged or blocked, and this leads to an increase in pressure inside the eye.

A **cataract** is a clouding of the normally clear lens of the eye. Cataracts are common in older people. Although usually associated with aging (by age 80, 50 percent of the population has had a cataract), cataracts can be caused by systemic diseases such as diabetes mellitus, as well as by radiation exposure and some medications. It can occur in one or both eyes and results in blurred and distorted vision.

Retinal detachment is a separation of the retina from the epithelial layer of its supportive tissue (see Figure 6.10). Loss of sight occurs because the detached rods and cones no longer receive nourishment. The most common type of detachment is **rhegmatogenous**, or tear-induced detachments, which occur in one of every 10,000 persons between 40 and 70 years of age. This specific type of retinal detachment is considered a medical emergency.

FIGURE 6.10 | Retinal Detachment

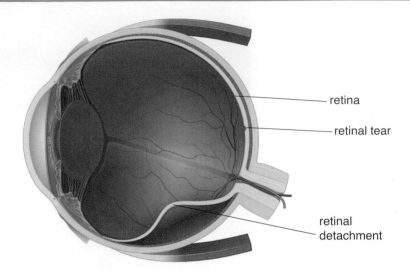

retina

retinal tear

retinal detachment

Seniors

As we age, the eye faces challenges that are directly related to the degeneration of its physical structure. The eyelids begin to droop, the retina fails to send accurate messages to the brain resulting in blurred vision, tear production is decreased, brown spots begin to develop on the sclerae, and the area of peripheral vision is reduced. **Macular degeneration** is the leading cause of severe visual impairment in people over 65 years of age. It is caused by damage to the photoreceptor cells in the macula, and it may be hereditary.

Checkpoint 6.4

Answer the following questions to identify any areas of the section that you may need to review.

1. What common complication of diabetes mellitus is the leading cause of blindness?

   _____

2. Hypertropia is the medical term used to describe upward squinting. Based on your knowledge of prefixes, what would be the medical term for downward squinting?

   _____

3. What is the medical term for the inward turning of the eyes?

   _____

Exercise 6.13 Word Analysis

Each of the following sentences contains an underlined medical term. Identify the root in the term by drawing a box around it and then supply the definition. Make a new, related term using the root or its combining form. Give a definition for the related term you have supplied.

Example: The diagnosis is bilateral `retino`blastoma, a cancer of the eye.

Root definition: pertaining to the retina

Related term and definition: retinopathy. Retinopathy means disease of the retina.

1. It will be necessary to perform an <u>iridectomy</u> because of damage to the left eye.

   Root definition: _____

   Related term and definition: _____

2. Curtis was referred by Dr. Pedigo for evaluation and possible radial <u>keratotomy</u>.

   Root definition: _____

   Related term and definition: _____

3. Elaine is an 86-year-old female, post CVA, whose vision is impaired due to severe <u>blepharoptosis</u>.

   Root definition: _____

   Related term and definition: _____

4. The instrument through which the inner eye is viewed is called the <u>ophthalmoscope</u>.

   Root definition: _____

   Related term and definition: _____

5. The patient is a 36-year-old male who recently experienced inflammation near his eye; more recently he has developed <u>dacryoadenitis</u> and is being treated for that condition.

   Root definition: _____

   Related term and definition: _____

Exercise 6.14 Comprehension Check

Select the correct medical term from the word bank to substitute for the underlined definition in each sentence. Some of the medical terms will not be used.

astigmatism	esotropia	presbyopia	strabismus
chalazion	ophthalmologists	retinoblastoma	glaucoma
esophoria	exophoria	hyperopia	sty

1. During routine screening to measure <u>increased intraocular pressure</u>, Gail was found to have an early stage of the disease. _____

2. Imp: <u>inflammatory growth of the meibomian gland</u>. _____

3. Procedures involving the eye are performed by <u>medical specialists in examination and treatment of the eye</u>. _____

4. The patient had surgery last week for a <u>tumor of the retina</u>. _____

5. The patient's eye condition was described as <u>deviating inward without double vision</u>. _____

Exercise 6.15 Matching

Match the terms in column 1 with the definitions in column 2. Write your choice on the line beside the definition.

1. _____ aphakia

2. _____ conjunctivitis

3. _____ hyperopia

4. _____ keratitis

5. _____ myopia

6. _____ retinopathy

a. inflammation of the lining of the eye

b. disease of the retina

c. absence of the lens of the eye

d. nearsightedness

e. infection of the cornea

f. farsightedness

Exercise 6.16 Word Building

Use prefixes, root words, combining vowels, and suffixes to create medical terms for the definitions given. Write the term in the space beside the definition. Separate the word parts with slashes.

1. surgical repair of the eyelids _____

2. drooping of the eyelid _____

3. pertaining to the eye _____

4. inflammation of the iris _____

5. surgical incision into the cornea _____

Exercise 6.17 Spelling Check

Find the misspelled medical term in each sentence, circle it, rewrite the term correctly, and add the definition.

1. The patient underwent a kerratoplasty several years ago.

_____

2. I will refer the patient to an opthalamologist in his geographic area.

_____

3. This four-year-old child has been diagnosed with miopya and requires vision correction.

_____

4. There is an outbreak of canjunctivittis at the local day-care center.

_____

5. Shrinkage of the vetrious caused traction on the retina and resulted in a posterior tear.

_____

Exercise 6.18 Word Maps

The image below shows a long eyeball. Correctly identify where light rays would fall after entering the cornea and then identify this condition on the provided line.

_____

Diagnostic Tests and Examinations of the Eye

When examining the eyes, the physician first observes the areas around them, looking for symmetry of the eyes, placement on the face, and the ability of the person to move the external eye muscles, eyebrows, and eyelids. This procedure screens for neuromuscular function.

The sclerae should appear white; the cornea should be clear and round. The pupils are checked for size, equal appearance, and reaction to light, an assessment that—if normal—appears in medical records as PERRLA (pupils equal, round, reactive to light and accommodation). In a darkened room and using an instrument called the ophthalmoscope, the physician looks straight into the eye and notes the light being reflected back; this is called a light reflex, and the reflected light is normally red. Also visible are the retinal blood vessels entering a point at the posterior area of the globe. This area is called the optic disk, which is also known as the *blind spot* because it has no visual receptors. Also visible is the yellowish spot of the macula lutea, which is responsible for central vision.

There are a variety of different examinations used to provide both preventive care and diagnostic testing for conditions of the eye. A thorough history precedes testing to identify the presence of symptoms or general health issues that could affect vision. Tests are given in visual acuity or clarity of vision, depth perception, color, pupil responsiveness, peripheral vision, eye muscle movements, focus, reflection, and overall health of the eye's structures and function. Table 6.5 provides an overview of the most frequently used tests, examinations, and pieces of equipment used to diagnose conditions and overall health of the eye.

TABLE 6.5 Vision Tests, Examinations, and Equipment

Procedure		Meaning
distance visual acuity		a measurement of one's ability to identify letters and objects from a specified distance (generally 20 feet) (e.g., Snellen eye chart)
fluorescein angiography	[flor-**ess**-ee-un an-jee-**ah**-gruh-fee]	procedure used to diagnose retinal disease via the injection of fluorescein dye
gonioscopy	[**gO**-nee-**os**-kah-pee]	procedure to visualize the anterior chamber angle to determine whether the angle is open or closed in glaucoma
slit lamp		use of a low-power microscope to examine various structures of the eye (e.g., eyelids, cornea, sclerae, iris)
perimetry	[pur-**im**-eh-tree]	test that measures the scope of the visual fields
phoropter	[fO-**rop**-ter]	testing device, also known as a *refractor*, used to determine one's prescription for eyeglasses
tonometry	[tO-**nom**-ah-tree]	test that measures for increased intraocular pressure (IOP), generally used to test for glaucoma
ophthalmic sonography	[off-**thalm**-mik sO-**nog**-ra-fee]	use of high-frequency sound waves to create an image of the structures within the eye, often used to detect a detached retina or presence of a foreign mass or object
ophthalmoscopy	[**off**-thalm-**mos**-kah-pee]	procedure to visualize the retina, retinal blood vessels, and the optic disk (the point where the optic nerve leaves the eye)

Checkpoint 6.5

Answer the following questions to identify any areas of the section that you may need to review.

1. What type of diagnostic exam is the Snellen eye chart?

   _____

2. Which diagnostic test measures intraocular pressure associated with glaucoma?

   _____

3. Which diagnostic instrument is also known as a refractor?

   _____

Treatments of the Eye

Treatment decisions generally fall into three categories: surgical, clinical, and pharmacological. *Surgical treatments* are generally invasive as they involve a puncture or an incision into the skin. *Clinical treatments* are generally noninvasive and involve nonsurgical techniques (e.g., corrective lenses). *Pharmacological treatments* involve the utilization of medicines (drugs) to treat specific illnesses or diseases. Medication therapies are regulated by the Food and Drug Administration (FDA). To be approved by the FDA for use in the United States, every medicine must be backed by research studies that have shown the medication to be effective in its treatment of a given disease and has a tolerable safety profile. The following sections provide an overview of treatments common to the eye.

A number of procedures to correct certain visual defects may now be done on an outpatient basis in the physician's office. These procedures typically require exacting measurement and delicate manipulation of the eye structures. The highly technical apparatus includes computerized sensing devices and high-magnification viewing devices.

Surgical Treatments

Surgical procedures to correct refractive problems by reshaping the cornea are called **keratotomy**. One eye procedure that has received a great deal of exposure because of marketing and publicity is LASIK (laser-assisted in situ keratomileusis), whereby the surface of the cornea is cut to form a flap. The underlying tissue is sculpted to the precise shape needed to correct the refractive error, and then the flap is replaced. Healing of the cut edge occurs quickly without sutures.

Severely diseased or damaged corneas can be replaced with full-thickness corneas and surrounding tissue taken from deceased donors. Using a circular blade called a trephine, the surgeon cuts out the damaged cornea and sutures a new cornea into place. Healing may be slow because of decreased number of blood vessels supplying the cornea. A transplant eye bank makes donated corneas available nationwide.

Lens replacement procedures to correct cataracts are now commonplace. The procedure may use ultrasound energy to dissolve and then extract the natural lens. Table 6.6 identifies various surgical procedures related to the eye.

TABLE 6.6 Surgical Treatments Associated with the Eye

Treatment		Description
blepharectomy	[**blef**-ah-rek-tO-mee]	excision of a lesion of the eyelid
blepharoplasty	[**blef**-ah-rO-plas-tee]	repair of an eyelid
cataract extraction	[**kat**-ur-akt]	removal of the lens to treat cataracts
cryoretinopexy	[crI-oh-ret-O-**pek**-see]	use of intense cold to seal a hole or tear in the retina
Dacryocystorhinostomy	[dak-ree-O-sis-tO-rI-**noss**-tuh-mee]	creation of an opening between the tear ducts and nose
enucleation	[eh-noo-klee-**ay**-shun]	excision of an eyeball
gonioplasty	[**gO**-nee-O-plas-tee]	contraction of the peripheral iris to eliminate contact with the trabecular meshwork
Iridotomy	[ear-rih-**dot**-ah-mee]	incision into the iris to allow drainage of the aqueous humor

Continues

Treatment		Description
Keratoplasty	[kair-**ret**-O-plas-tee]	corneal transplant
laser surgery	[**lay**-zer]	procedure used to correct vision, eliminating the need for use of corrective lenses, primary treatment of glaucoma and other eye disorders
peripheral iridectomy	[peh-**rif**-er-al ir-ih-**dek**-tah-mee]	procedure that creates a hole in the iris, allowing the aqueous humor to flow from the posterior chamber to the anterior chamber
phacoemulsification	[**fak**-O-ee-mul-sih-fih-**kay**-shun]	method of using ultrasonic waves to disintegrate a cataract, which is then aspirated and removed
sclerotomy	[skleh-**rot**-ah-mee]	formation of an opening in the sclera
sphincterotomy	[sfink-ter-**ot**-ah-mee]	procedure to make cuts in the iris sphincter muscle to allow pupillary enlargement
trabeculoplasty	[trah-**bek**-yoo-lO-**plas**-tee]	procedure to increase aqueous humor outflow to control IOP in open-angle glaucoma

Clinical Treatments

The most common clinical treatment related to the eyes are corrective lenses. Corrective lenses are designed to improve vision problems that may be caused by a structural abnormality to the eye, an injury to the eye, genetics, or advanced age. The most common type of vision problem in which corrective lenses are used to treat involves the eye's inability to effectively focus light on the retina (or back of the eye), also known as a *refractive error*. Lenses correct an individual's vision by bending the light rays into the direction of the retina, to the degree required, to produce a clear image. Corrective lenses can be worn as eyeglasses (in a frame) or contacts (directly on the eye). Eye exercises are another type of treatment that may be recommended for those suffering from eye strain. These activities require the eyes to focus on varying distances in the hopes the eyes become more effective on focusing.

Pharmacological Treatments

Ophthalmic agents may be divided into groups based on therapeutic use. Conjunctivitis is treated with topical antibiotics or corticosteroids. Miscellaneous agents include ocular lubricants, which act as artificial tears, and silver nitrate, which is administered to prevent gonococcal ophthalmic infections.

Miotic agents constrict the eye muscles during cataract surgery, keratoplasty, and iridectomy. Most commonly, miotic agents are used in the treatment of glaucoma to lower intraocular pressure.

Table 6.7 identifies common pharmacological treatments relating to the eyes.

TABLE 6.7 Pharmacological Treatments Associated with the Eyes

Drug Class	Description
antibiotics	treat bacterial infections, e.g., ciproflaxin
antihistamines	treat seasonal allergies (e.g., itchy, watery eyes), e.g., Benadryl
cycloplegics	paralyze the ciliary muscle to allow eye exam (generally used with children)
mydriatics	cause dilation of the pupil, generally used in refractive exams
miotics	cause pupil to constrict, generally used to treat glaucoma
ophthalmics	medication applied directly to the eye (i.e. solutions or ointments)

Checkpoint 6.6

Answer the following questions to identify any areas of the section that you may need to review.

1. Define keratoplasty.

   _____

2. Which group of medications is used to paralyze the ciliary muscle to perform an eye exam in children?

   _____

3. Which surgical procedure would result in the removal of a cloudy lens?

   _____

Exercise 6.19 Word Analysis

Draw a box around and define the combining form in each term. Then provide a definition for the entire term.

Term	Combining Form Definition	Term Definition
1. blepharoplasty	_____	_____
2. palpebral	_____	_____
3. retinitis	_____	_____
4. ophthalmoscope	_____	_____
5. lacrimal	_____	_____

Exercise 6.20 Comprehension Check

Read each sentence and select the term that best fits in the sentence. Place a circle around that term.

1. This patient is being referred to an otolaryngologist/ophthalmologist for an eye exam.
2. Examination of the retina/presbyopia revealed several aneurysms.
3. We will attempt a keratitis/keratoplasty.
4. During routine tonometry/palpebral screening, Ms. Freeman was found to have early-stage glaucoma.
5. The vitreous humor/inner canthus was removed as part of the retinoplasty.

Exercise 6.21   Matching

Match the treatment in column 1 with the condition in column 2. Write your choice on the line beside the definition.

1. _____ blepharectomy
2. _____ blepharoplasty
3. _____ corneal transplant
4. _____ corrective lenses
5. _____ laser surgery to reattach retina
6. _____ tonometry

a. eyelid injury
b. glaucoma
c. injury to the cornea
d. lesion on eyelid
e. myopia
f. retinal detachment

Exercise 6.22   Word Building

Write the term for each definition on the line provided. Separate the parts of the term with hyphens.

1. pertaining to the eye   _____
2. within the eye   _____
3. inflammation of the conjunctiva   _____
4. pertaining to the sclera   _____
5. around the orbit   _____

Exercise 6.23   Spelling Check

Provide the plural term for the terms listed.

1. cataract   _____
2. palpebra   _____
3. sclera   _____
4. sty   _____
5. retinopathy   _____

Exercise 6.24   Word Maps

Complete the diagram by providing medical terms or translations for each type of abnormality.

Abnormality:	nearsightedness	_____	farsightedness
Medical term:	_____	diplopia	_____
Abnormality:	turning inward of eye	turning outward of eye	poor vision in one eye
Medical term:	_____	_____	_____

Conditions of the Ear

There are a variety of conditions that may affect one's hearing and balance. These conditions can range from ear infections and tinnitus to Ménière's disease and vertigo. Often audiometric testing is used to test one's ability to hear and interpret sounds. Hearing impairment is the inability to hear as well as someone with normal hearing. Hearing impaired people can be hard of hearing (HOH) or deaf. Deafness is a condition in which a person cannot hear at all. There are many causes of hearing impairment, including congenital defects, complications from illness or infectious disease, drug use, exposure to excessive noise, and aging. Approximately half of all cases of deafness and hearing impairment could be prevented if the causes were identified and treated at the primary health care level. Table 6.8 lists the most frequently used terms describing conditions and diseases of the ear.

TABLE 6.8 Common Conditions and Diseases of the Ear

Condition		Meaning	Word Analysis	
anotia	[an-**O**-shyah]	absent ears	an/	without
			ot/o	ear
			-ia	condition
cerumen impaction	[sch-**roo**-min]	excessive buildup of wax in the ears	cerumin/o	cerumen/earwax
cholesteatoma	[kol-es-tee-at-**O**-mah]	tumor-like mass of scaly epithelial tissue and cholesterol in the middle ear	choleste/a	cholesterol
			-oma	tumor
labyrinthitis	[lab-ih-rin-**thI**-tis]	inflammation of the inner ear	labyrinth	maze
			-itis	inflammation
macrotia	[mak-**rO**-shee-ah]	large ears	macr/o	large
			ot/o	ear
			-ia	condition
mastoiditis	[**mass**-toy-**dI**-tis]	inflammation of the mastoid process, often seen as a result of untreated ear infections (otitis media)	mastoid/o	mastoid process
			-itis	inflammation
Ménière's disease	[main-**yairz**]	condition characterized by vertigo	Ménière	French physician

Continues

Condition		Meaning	Word Analysis	
microtia	[mI-**krO**-shee-ah]	small ears	*micr/o*	small
			ot/o	ear
			-ia	condition
myringitis	[mir-in-**jI**-tis]	inflammation of the tympanic membrane	*myring/o*	tympanic membrane
			-itis	inflammation
otalgia	[o-**tal**-jee-ah]	earache	*ot/o*	ear
			-algia	pain
otitis externa	[O-**tI**-tis eks-**ter**-nah]	inflammation of the external ear (swimmer's ear)	*ot/o*	ear
			-itis	inflammation
			externa	pertaining to the outside
otitis media	[O-**tI**-tis **mee**-dee-ah]	inflammation of the middle ear	*ot/o*	ear
			-itis	inflammation
			media	pertaining to the middle
otopyorrhea	[O-tO-**pI**-or-ree-ah]	pus in the ear	*ot/o*	ear
			py/o	pus
			-rrhea	discharge, flow
otorrhea	[O-tO-**ree**-ah]	drainage from the ear	*ot/o*	ear
			-rrhea	drainage, discharge
otosclerosis	[O-tO-sklah-**rO**-sis]	hardening of the bone surrounding the oval window	*ot/o*	ear
			scler/o	hard
			-sis	condition
polyotia	[pol-ee-**O**-shee-ah]	more than one ear on one side of the face	*poly-*	many
			ot/o	ear
			-ia	condition
presbycusis	[pres-bee-**kyoo**-sis]	the inability to hear sounds because of aging	*presby/o*	old age
			acusis	hearing
tinnitus	[tih-**nI**-tus/**tin**-ih-tus]	ringing in the ears	*tinnio*	jingling
			-tus	condition
tympanitis	[tim-peh-**nI**-tus]	inflammation of the eardrum	*tympan/o*	eardrum
			-itis	inflammation
tympanosclerosis	[tim-pah-nO-sklah-**rO**-sis]	hardening of the tympanic membrane	*tympan/o*	tympanic membrane
			scler/o	hardening
vertigo	[**ver**-tih-gO/ver-**tI**-gO]	sensation of spinning, dizziness	*verto*	turn

Infants and Children

Infants can be born with malformed ears, absent ears (**anotia**), or more than two ears (**polyotia**). Congenital disorders occur during development and include deformities of the pinna, large ears (**macrotia**), and small ears (**microtia**). Physicians screen for congenital deafness by clapping loudly next to the infant's ears during the first neonatal assessment. The noise should startle the child. Cochlear implant technology has revolutionized the rehabilitation of hearing-impaired children, enabling them to have marked gains in speech and understanding of spoken language.

One of the most common ear problems is **otitis media**, an inflammation of the middle ear. An upper respiratory infection can provide a trigger for this process. Children are plagued by otitis media because the Eustachian tube is shorter, narrower, and more curved than in an adult. Together, these factors allow bacteria from the nasopharynx to enter the middle ear easily, leading to inflammation and impaired drainage of fluid. Clinical signs of otitis media include redness (**infection**), bulging, retraction, perforation of the tympanic membrane, and the production of exudates. Ear pain, or **otalgia**, results from the increase in fluid and pressure. Pressure from the increased fluid can perforate the eardrum, or a deliberate perforation called a **myringotomy** may be performed. Perforation is accompanied by a bloody discharge, called **otorrhagia**. **Otopyorrhea**, a discharge of pus, may be present when the child has a serious ear infection.

Adults and Seniors

Certain ear illnesses are more common to adults than infants and children. **Labyrinthitis** is an inflammation of the inner ear resulting in vertigo, the sensation of spinning or dizziness. **Ménière's disease** is a disturbance of the labyrinth characterized by various manifestations, such as vertigo with or without tinnitus (ringing in the ears), hearing loss, nausea, and vomiting. Balance may also be affected. **Cholesteatomas** are a type of benign mass within the middle ear that appear in adults who have had chronic otitis media and rupture of the tympanic membrane.

Hearing loss is one of the most common conditions affecting older adults. It can result from changes in structure of the inner ear, changes in blood flow to the ear, injury to the nerves responsible for hearing, or damage to the tiny hairs in the ear responsible for transmitting sound to the brain. Age-related hearing loss is known as **presbycusis**. As the body ages, bone loses its calcium, becoming weak and porous, including the bone in and around the ear. **Otosclerosis** is the hardening of the spongy bone surrounding the oval window. Hardening of the tympanic membrane is called **tympanosclerosis**. Both of these processes result in hearing loss.

Checkpoint **6.7**

Answer the following questions to identify any areas of the section that you may need to review.

1. What is the clinical term for a middle ear infection?

   _____

2. A patient presents to the office with an extensive history of otalgia. What does this mean?

   _____

3. What is the clinical term for "ringing in the ears"?

   _____

Diagnostic Tests and Examinations of the Ear

Various tests and equipment are used to diagnose ear and hearing problems. Examples include visual examinations of the ear and the use of instruments to examine the inner ear or to evaluate the patient's hearing. Audiometry is the science of measuring hearing acuity. Many exams exist to test one's ability to hear sound and vibration as well as to ensure each ear is hearing sounds equally. Newborns are screened at birth for defects specific to hearing loss, while adults and children can be examined to determine their ability to locate the source of a sound. Table 6.9 identifies diagnostic tests and equipment related to the ear.

Soft Skills for Health Care: Active Listening

The Greek philosopher Diogenes once stated, "We have two ears and one mouth, so we should listen more and talk less." Patients who arrive in a healthcare facility are commonly dealing with pain, discomfort, and uncertainty about the prognosis of their health. It is imperative that healthcare providers do the best they can to understand the reason for the patient's visit and to assure the patient that he or she has the provider's undivided attention. This is done by an important skill called *active listening*. To be an active listener, keep eye contact, lean in slightly toward the patient, allow the patient to finish his or her thought before responding, listen intently, and be sure to repeat what you have heard back to the patient to ensure you have a strong understanding of the problem. Patients will appreciate your time, patience, and empathy toward their condition and generally be more receptive to treatment recommendations when they feel you truly engage in this manner.

TABLE 6.9 | Tests, Examinations, and Diagnostic Equipment Associated with the Ear

Term		Meaning
audiometer	[au-dee-**om**-eh-ter]	instrument for determining the intensity of sound a person can hear; various tests can be done to determine hearing threshold and hearing frequencies; evoked potential measures electrical stimulation from the cortex of the brain; localization measures a person's ability to locate the source of a sound
otoscope	[**O**-tO-skOp]	medical instrument used to visualize the external ear canal and the tympanic membrane; when a bulb tube is attached to the otoscope, air is pushed in by squeezing the bulb, making it possible to determine whether the membrane is moving in and out appropriately
otoscopy	[O-**tos**-kah-pee]	visual exam of the external auditory canal and tympanic membrane using the otoscope
Rinne's test	[**rin**-ez]	test that uses a tuning fork to compare the perception of air conduction with bone conduction in each ear; the person should hear air vibration longer than bone vibration
universal newborn hearing screening (UNHS) test		screening in newborns to test for birth defects such as hearing loss
Weber's test	[**web**-berz]	test that uses a tuning fork to determine whether sound is heard equally in both ears

Checkpoint 6.8

Answer the following questions to identify any areas of the section that you may need to review.

1. What is the name of the instrument used to conduct a visual examination of the external auditory canal and tympanic membrane?

2. What test do most states require on newborns before the child is discharged from the hospital?

3. What instrument is used to determine the intensity of sound a person can hear?

Treatments of the Ear

Healthcare practitioners use predetermined guidelines to direct patient care. Treatment decisions generally fall into three categories: surgical, clinical, and pharmacological. Recall that *surgical treatments* are generally invasive as they involve a puncture or an incision into the skin. *Clinical treatments* are generally noninvasive and involve nonsurgical techniques (e.g., physical therapy). *Pharmacological treatments* involve the utilization of medicines (drugs) to treat specific illnesses or diseases. Medication therapies are regulated by the Food and Drug Administration (FDA). To be approved by the FDA for use in the United States, every medicine must be backed by research studies that have shown the medication to be effective in its treatment of a given disease and has a tolerable safety profile. The following sections provide an overview of treatments common to the ear.

> **What's in a Word?**
>
> The combining forms *myringa/o* and *tympan/o* both mean "tympanic membrane."

Surgical Treatments

Performing procedures involving the ear is challenging as the interior of the ear is small and difficult to access. Nonetheless, the procedures are often performed in an outpatient surgical area, and the patient is released shortly after recovering from the anesthesia (see Table 6.10).

Clinical Treatments

Clinical treatments for the ear include hearing aids, which are devices designed to amplify sound for individuals with a hearing impairment. They do not have the ability to restore normal hearing but can improve sounds that an individual has trouble hearing. The type of hearing aid prescribed is dependent upon the type and severity of hearing loss, listening needs, and lifestyle. While hearing aids can vary in price, size, and special features, most hearing aids are digital and made up a microphone, amplifier, receiver, and batteries. Other clinical treatments include the removal of impacted ear wax (cerumen impaction removal) to help restore hearing and balance.

TABLE 6.10 Surgical Treatments Associated with the Ear

Procedure		Meaning
cochlear implant	[**kok**-lee-er]	hearing device implanted under the skin behind the ear; it sends electrical signals to electrodes implanted within the cochlea to stimulate nerves
labyrinthectomy	[lab-ih-rin-**thek**-tO-mee]	removal of the labyrinth
labyrinthotomy	[lab-ih-rin-**thot**-O-mee]	incision into the labyrinth
myringectomy	[mir-in-**jek**-tO-mee]	excision of the tympanic membrane
myringoplasty	[mir-**ing**-gO-plas-tee]	repair of the tympanic membrane
myringotomy	[mir-in-**got**-O-mee]	incision into the tympanic membrane, usually done to relieve fluid pressure; myringotomy or PE (pressure equalizer) tubes are placed through the incision to keep the fluid drained and pressure equalized, especially in children with chronic otitis media
otoplasty	[**O**-tuh-plass-tee]	plastic surgical repair of the ear
stapedectomy	[sta-pee-**dek**-tO-mee]	removal of the stapes in the middle ear, and insertion of a prosthesis
tympanectomy	[tim-pah-**nek**-tuh-mee]	excision of the tympanic membrane
tympanotomy	[tim-pah-**not**-uh-mee]	puncture of the tympanic membrane

Pharmacological Treatments

Pharmacological treatments of the ear typically belong to one of three categories: antibiotics, ceruminolytics, or otics. These particular medications are generally used to treat severe ear pain, infections of the inner ear (both bacterial and fungal), drainage, and wax build-up. Table 6.11 describes these treatments and provides some examples of each.

TABLE 6.11 Pharmacological Treatments Associated with the Ears

Drug Class	Description	Treatment Example
antibiotics	medications used to treat bacterial infections of the ear	amoxicillin
ceruminolytics	medications utilized to soften and break down earwax	Debrox
otics	medications applied directly to the external ear canal	Acetasol, Zinotic

Checkpoint **6.9**

Answer the following questions to identify any areas of the section that you may need to review.

1. What type of hearing device is generally implanted under the skin behind the ear and is designed to send electrical signals to stimulate nerves?

   _____

2. Name this procedure: In children with chronic ear infections, a surgical incision is made into the tympanic membrane and tubes are placed through the incision to keep the fluid drained and pressure equalized.

   _____

3. What type of antibiotic is generally used to treat bacterial infections of the ear?

   _____

Abbreviations

Recall that in the medical field, information is generally recorded in medical charts and the electronic medical record and provided to patients in medical shorthand. It is important that healthcare professionals become familiar with the abbreviations utilized on a daily basis to successfully perform the duties assigned in a typical workday. Table 6.12 provides a list of common abbreviations used in reference to the special senses.

> **To Note!**
>
> Some abbreviations are considered dangerous because they could be easily confused with other abbreviations.

TABLE 6.12 Abbreviations Associated with the Special Senses

Abbreviation	Meaning
Abbreviations Associated with the Ear	
ABR	auditory brainstem response
AC	air conduction
AD*	right ear (*auris dexter*)
AOM	acute otitis media
AS*	left ear (*auris sinister*)
ASL	American Sign Language
AU*	both ears (*auris uterque*)
BC	bone conduction
dB	decibel
EAC	external ear canal
EENT	eyes, ears, nose, and throat
ENT	ears, nose, and throat
OM	otitis media
Oto	otology
PE tubes	pressure-equalizing tubes
TM	tympanic membrane
UNHS	universal newborn hearing screening test
Abbreviations Associated with the Eye	
Acc	accommodation
D	diopter
DCR	dacryocystorhinostomy
ECCE	extracapsular cataract extraction
Em	emmetropia
EOM	extraocular movements
ERG	electroretinography
ICCE	intracapsular cataract extraction
IOL	intraocular lens
IOP	intraocular pressure
L&A	light and accommodation
LASIK	laser-assisted in situ keratomileusis
my	myopia
OD*	right eye (*oculus dexter*); doctor of optometry

Continues

Abbreviation	Meaning
OS*	left eye (*oculus sinister*)
OU*	both eyes (*oculus uterque*)
PAN	periodic alternating nystagmus
PERLA	pupils equal, reactive to light and accommodation
PERRLA	pupils equal, round, reactive to light and accommodation
PRK	photorefractive keratectomy
REM	rapid eye movement
ROP	retinopathy of prematurity
ST	esotropia
VA	visual acuity
VF	visual field
XT	xotropia

*Note that some abbreviations have been used for multiple terms and could cause confusion in a medical setting. Healthcare providers may consider these abbreviations too dangerous to use.

Exercise 6.25   Word Analysis

For each of the underlined medical terms sentences, identify the root by drawing a box around it. Supply the definition of the root. Then supply the definition of the whole term.

1. The patient is a six-month-old female, currently being treated with amoxicillin for bilateral <u>otitis media</u>.

   Root definition: _____

   Term definition: _____

2. Dr. Harmon will perform Timmy's <u>myringotomy</u> this afternoon.

   Root definition: _____

   Term definition: _____

3. Initial impression is abnormality of the <u>ossicular</u> chain, although further studies will be required to confirm this diagnosis.

   Root definition: _____

   Term definition: _____

4. Please schedule Mrs. Kelly for a <u>labyrinthectomy</u> at 10 a.m. tomorrow.

   Root definition: _____

   Term definition: _____

5. The persistence of fluid indicated the need for insertion of a <u>tympanostomy</u> tube in the left ear.

   Root definition: _____

   Term definition: _____

Exercise 6.26   Comprehension Check

Read each sentence, noting the pair of terms provided. Select the term that best fits the sentence and circle your choice.

1. Mr. Osborne is scheduled for a tympanectomy/amplitude this afternoon.
2. Sig: 3 gtt AD/ABR b.i.d.
3. A vestibular/stapedectomy tumor was located and excised.
4. Ossicular/Neuroplasty was performed in an attempt to partially restore the patient's hearing.
5. While he was hospitalized Mr. Myer reported tinnitus/polyotia.

Exercise 6.27   Name the Term

On the line provided, write the medical term that matches the underlined definition in each sentence.

1. The patient is a 60-year-old male who was diagnosed by Dr. Presley with a disturbance of the labyrinth characterized by vertigo, hearing loss, nausea, and vomiting.   _____

2. Suspect hearing loss due to a mass composed of cholesterol within the middle ear.   _____

3. Grace has come to the clinic today because of an increase in severity of her chronic ringing in the ears.   _____

4. Plan: hearing test to determine extent of hearing loss.   _____

5. Viewing with medical instrument used to examine the external ear canal and the tympanic membrane reveals heavy cerumen accumulation; unable to visualize TM.   _____

6. Plan: excision of the tympanic membrane.   _____

Exercise 6.28   Word Building

Use prefixes, root words, combining vowels, and suffixes to create medical terms for the definitions given. Write the term on the line provided. Separate the word parts with hyphens.

1. study of the ears   _____
2. without ears   _____
3. inflammation of the labyrinth   _____
4. surgical removal of the mastoid cells   _____
5. discharge or hemorrhage of the ear   _____

Exercise 6.29   Spelling Check

Correct the spelling of each term. Write your answer on the line provided.

1. auriclle   _____

2. cochalea   _____

3. endalymph   _____

4. meateaus   _____

5. ossiccle   _____

Exercise 6.30   Word Maps

Complete the diagram below to illustrate the process of hearing. Use the provided terms to complete the word map.

auditory nerve   ossicular chain
brain   oval window
external auditory meatus   tympanic membrane

Sound → Auricle → _____ → Auditory canal → _____

_____ → _____ → Inner ear → Auditory receptor cells

_____ → _____

After successfully completing this chapter, you should be able to correctly answer the following review questions. Answers are provided in the back of the text. Use this self-assessment opportunity to check your understanding of the content and determine whether you need to revisit any of the chapter's content.

Crossword Puzzle

Use the clues provided to fill in the puzzle with the correct terms. Enter one letter per square.

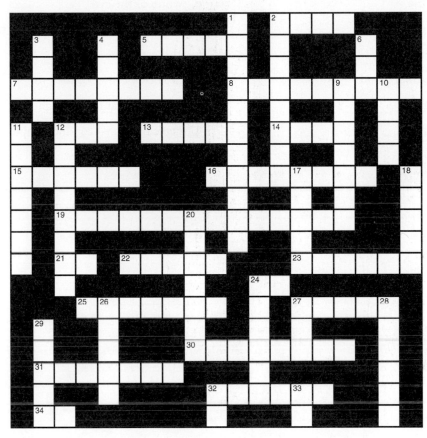

Across

2. disk behind the pupil
5. black center of the eye
7. little ears
8. visual field test
12. combining form meaning ear
13. point of greatest visual acuity
14. labyrinth
15. eye nerve tissue
16. double vision
19. inflammation of eye lining
21. abbreviation for left ear
22. combining form for nose
23. clear iris covering
24. abbreviation for right ear
25. otalgia
27. ear bone with anvil shape
30. night vision
31. absence of eye lens
32. ear bone with stirrup shape
34. doctor of optometry

Down

1. eyelid infection
2. pertaining to tears
3. colored portion of the eye
4. combining form meaning light
6. abbreviation for otolaryngologist
9. palpebrae
10. responsible for night vision
11. visible portion of the ear
12. fills glasses prescriptions
17. pertaining to the eye
18. Greek for angle
20. eyelid part
24. lacking ears
26. relating to the ear
27. symptom of glaucoma (abbreviation)
28. white eye covering
29. combining form meaning eye lens
32. abbreviation for esotropia
33. abbreviation for emmetropia

Matching

Match the parts of the eye to its corresponding description:

1. _____ palpebrae
2. _____ pupil
3. _____ iris
4. _____ cornea
5. _____ retina
6. _____ sclera
7. _____ canthus
8. _____ lacrimal gland
9. _____ lens
10. _____ cones

a. structure responsible for color vision
b. eyelids
c. colored portion of the eye
d. clear, transparent tissue at the front of the eye
e. white of the eye
f. responsible for the secretion of tears
g. corners of the eyes
h. the black center of the eye
i. structure that focuses light
j. nerve tissue that conducts impulses to the brain

Identification

Identify the parts of the following figure and write the name of each part on the lines provided.

auricle   Eustachian tube   labyrinth   stapes
cochlea   incus   malleus   tympanic membrane

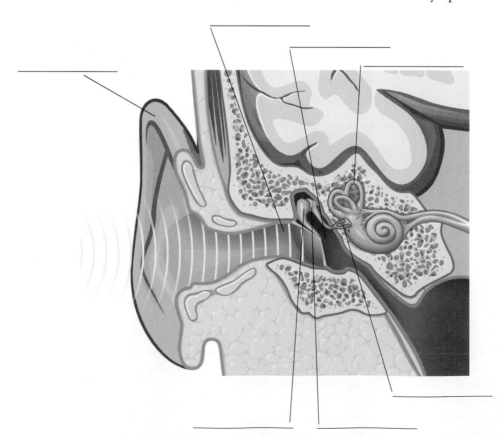

Identify the parts of the following figure and write the name of each part on the lines provided.

bitter   sour   root of tongue
sweet   salt

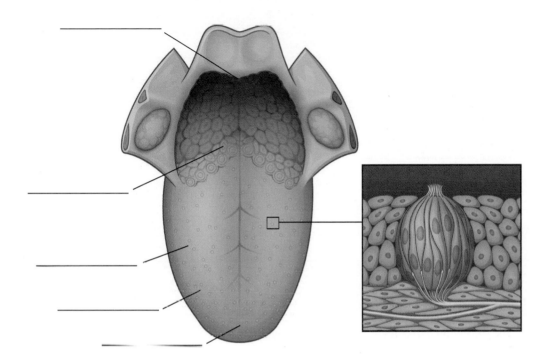

Abbreviations

Answer the following questions using your knowledge of abbreviations.

1. Jordan is an 18-month-old who has experienced reoccurring diagnoses of otitis media over the past year. Her primary care physician should refer her to what type of specialist to treat her condition?

   _____

2. Andre will turn 16 this summer and is eager to take his driving test to obtain his license. In addition to his successful completion of the driving portion of the exam, the Department of Motor Vehicles will also require a satisfactory score on an eye exam. What is this type of assessment called?

   _____

3. This particular condition often involves the turning outward of one or both eyes. What is the name and abbreviation for this particular condition?

   _____

4. An assessment of Kendall's visual field uncovered a mild concussion. The immediate test of his pupils followed the steps of PERRLA. What does this test check for?

   _____

Word-Building Challenge

Review the following list of terms. Apply what you have learned in this chapter by identifying the meaning of the word parts within the term and then writing the likely definition of the term on the line provided.

1. blepharoptosis _____

    _____

2. xerophthalmia _____

    _____

3. anisocoria _____

    _____

4. anacusis _____

    _____

5. stapedectomy _____

    _____

Extension Activities

Complete the following activities as assigned by your instructor.

1. The American Academy of Pediatrics has reported hearing loss as one of the most frequently occurring birth defects. When detected early, it can be treated and many potential developmental complications can be avoided. Utilizing the Internet, research the regulations and/or requirements for the universal newborn hearing screening (UNHS) test in your state of residence. Present your findings to your class and discuss your views on this type of testing in a classroom discussion forum.

2. Some researchers identify "proprioception" as the sixth sense of humans. Locate and review a scholarly article on this particular sense and submit a one-page informational essay to your instructor. Identify at least one condition that is attributed to the failure of this sense.

3. Cosmetic surgeons are constantly finding new ways to appeal to new clientele by providing new procedures. One such procedure is laser surgery that permanently changes one's eye color from brown to blue. Research the various vendors advertising this service and post an overview of the procedure in an informative essay or in your classroom online forum (if one exists). Identify pertinent factors such as cost, procedural steps, side effects, and the healthcare professionals qualified to perform the procedure.

Student eResources

The Course Navigator learning management system that accompanies this textbook offers multiple opportunities to master chapter content, including end-of-chapter exercises, a glossary of key terms with audio pronunciations, games, pronunciation coach, and additional activities such as engaging with the BioDigital® Human.

COURSE NAVIGATOR

The Respiratory System

"As people, no matter what we are doing, the whole body is living and breathing."

—Paul Dano, American actor

Translation Challenge

Read this excerpt from a transcribed physician's report and try to answer the questions that follow.

The patient was observed in orthopneic position having respirations at 30 per minute. The color was noted to be cyanotic. Edema was noted around the eyes and in the feet. There was obvious SOB with dyspnea upon lying down. During the examination, sputum was produced on several occasions.

Bilateral wheezes were noted in all lung fields.

1. This patient was lying flat in the bed. True or false?

2. The patient's color was normal. True or false?

3. What occurs when the patient lies down?

4. When lying down, the patient had difficulty with urine production. True or false?

Learning Objectives

7.1   List and define word parts most commonly used to create terms related to the respiratory system.

7.2   Name and label structures of the respiratory tract.

7.3   Describe functions of the mouth, nose, and lungs in respiration.

7.4   Explain the process of inhalation of oxygen and exhalation of carbon dioxide.

7.5   Explain the function of oxygen and carbon dioxide in the maintenance of homeostasis in the body.

7.6   List and describe various conditions of the respiratory system.

7.7   Name and describe tests, procedures, and pharmaceuticals specific to the respiratory system.

7.8   State the meaning of abbreviations related to the respiratory system.

7.9   Correctly use the respiratory system terminology in oral and written communication.

7.10   Correctly spell and pronounce respiratory system terminology.

COURSE NAVIGATOR

Access Additional Chapter Resources

The respiratory system is composed of the nose, mouth, pharynx, epiglottis, trachea, lungs, bronchi, bronchioles, and alveoli. These organs function with the circulatory system to facilitate the process of respiration, the transportation of oxygen to the body's cells and excretion of waste (carbon dioxide) from the body. The respiratory system is also responsible for the production of sound and speech.

Before birth, the fetus resides in the protective fluid of the amniotic sac, and all of its needs are passed from the mother through the placenta and umbilical cord. After the first gasp of air at birth, the infant must breathe to survive. With each inspiration (inward breath, also known as *inhalation*) through the nose or mouth, we inhale oxygen, use it, and convert it into carbon dioxide. Carbon dioxide, a waste product, is expelled with each expiration (outward breath, also known as *exhalation*). Humans cannot live for more than a few minutes without oxygen coming into the body and carbon dioxide going out of the body. The respiratory system is responsible for this process.

This chapter will provide an overview of the anatomical structures of the respiratory tract, a detailed description of the pathway taken to breathe air in and out, and an introduction to the various diagnostic tests, surgical procedures, and pharmaceutical agents used to treat conditions of the respiratory system.

Did You Know?

The average adult inhales and exhales approximately 12 to 20 times a minute.

In the Know: Specialties of the Respiratory System

The field of medicine concerned with the respiratory system is pulmonology, from the Latin term *pulmo* meaning "lung." A physician who specializes in the diagnosis and treatment of conditions affecting the lower respiratory tract is called a pulmonologist. A thoracic surgeon is a subspecialty focused on invasive procedures of the lungs and thoracic cavity. Allied health professionals that focus on the respiratory system include respiratory therapists and respiratory therapy technicians.

Respiratory therapists are healthcare practitioners with specialized training to treat patients with chronic breathing problems. A respiratory therapy technician is an allied health professional that assists clinicians with physical and diagnostic examinations, monitors patients with breathing problems, documents treatment progress, reports adverse reactions to clinicians, and is trained in the utilization of ventilators.

Respiratory System Word Parts

As with the other body systems, a core of combining forms serves as the source for most of the medical words associated with the respiratory system. There are also prefixes and suffixes that are commonly used to create respiratory terms, including *-ectasis* (dilation/expansion), *-pnea* (related to breath), and *-thorax* (chest/pleural cavity). Table 7.1 lists common word parts related to the respiratory system.

TABLE 7.1 Word Parts Associated With the Respiratory System

Prefix	Meaning	Example
a-	no, not, without, lack of	aphonia (loss of ability to produce sounds)
dys-	difficult, abnormal	dyspnea (difficulty breathing)
eu-	healthy, normal	eupnea (normal breathing)
ex-	out	exhale (to breathe out)
hyper-	excessive, above	hyperventilation (abnormal increase in breathing)
inter-	between	intercostal (between the ribs)
para-	near, beside, abnormal	paranasal (near the nose)

Combining Form	Meaning	Example
aer/o	air	aerobic (pertaining to air/oxygen)
adenoid/o	adenoid	adenoidectomy (surgical removal of the adenoids)
alveol/o	hollow sac	alveoli (tiny air sacs within the lungs, site of exchange for oxygen and carbon dioxide)
bronch/o	airway	bronchial (pertaining to the airway)
bronchiol/o	bronchiole	bronchiolitis (viral inflammation of the bronchioles, common in young children)
capn/o	carbon dioxide	hypercapnia (excessive carbon dioxide in the blood)
cost/o	rib	costal (pertaining to the ribs)
diaphragm/o (diaphragmat/o)	diaphragm	diaphragmatic breathing (deep breathing in which the abdomen expands as opposed to the chest)

Continues

hal/o	breathe	exhalation (to breathe out)
laryng/o	larynx	laryngoscope (instrument used to view the voicebox)
lob/o	lobe	RUL (right upper lobe of the lungs)
mediastin/o	mediastinum	mediastinum (the space between the lungs)
muc/o	mucus	mucous (pertaining to mucus)
nas/o	nose	nasopharynx (upper part of the throat, behind the nose)
or/o, (stomat/o)	mouth	oral (by mouth)
ox/o	oxygen molecule	oxygenation (process in which oxygen concentration increases within a tissue)
pariet/o	wall	parietal pleura (outer membrane that lines the chest wall)
pharyng/o	throat (pharynx)	pharyngeal (pertaining to the throat)
phon/o	sound	dysphonia (difficulty producing sounds, loss of voice)
phren/o (diaphragm/o)	diaphragm	phrenodynia (pain in the diaphragm)
pleur/o	rib area	pleural space (tiny area of space between the lungs and chest cavity that protects and cushions the lungs)
pne/o	breath	apnea (periods of interrupted breathing)
pneum/o	lung, air	pneumonitis (inflammation of the lungs)
pulmon/o	lung	pulmonary (pertaining to the lungs)
rhin/o	nose	rhinorrhea (runny nose)
sept/o	septum, wall	nasal septum (wall that divides the nasal cavity)
sinus/o, sin/o	sinus	sinusitis (inflammation of the sinuses often associated with a cold)
spir/o (hal/o)	breathing	spirometry (examination to measure breathing)
thorac/o (pector/o)	chest	thoracic (pertaining to the chest)
tonsil/o	tonsil	tonsillitis (inflammation of the tonsil)
trache/o	windpipe	tracheal (pertaining to the windpipe)
viscer/o	viscera, internal organs	visceral (pertaining to the viscera)
Suffix	**Meaning**	**Example**
-al	pertaining to	costal (pertaining to the ribs)
-ation	process of	respiration (process of breathing)
-dynia	pain	pleurodynia (pain in the chest)
-ectasis	dilation, expansion	atelectasis (a complete or partial collapse of a lung or the lobe of a lung)
-metry	process of measurement	pulse oximetry (test to measure the amount of oxygen in arterial blood)
-pnea	related to breath	bradypnea (abnormally slow breathing)
-ptysis	spitting	hemopytsis (coughing up/spitting up blood)
-rrhea	flow, discharge	rhinorrhea (runny nose)
-thorax	chest (pleural cavity)	pneumothorax (collapsed lung due to an abnormal collection of air or gas in the pleural space)

Anatomy and Physiology

The respiratory system is divided into the upper and lower respiratory tracts, as shown in Figure 7.1. The upper respiratory tract includes the nose, mouth, pharynx and larynx.

FIGURE 7.1 Organs of the Respiratory System

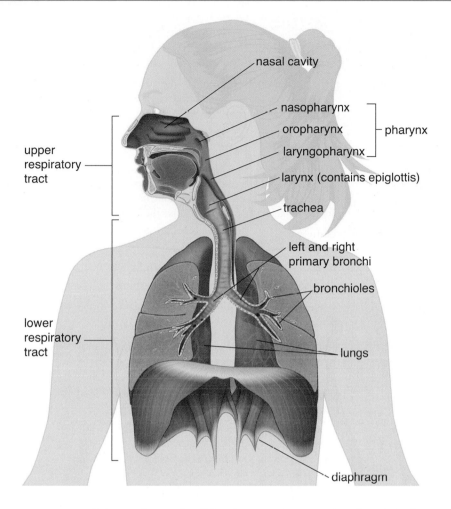

These structures are all located outside of the thoracic cavity in the chest. The lower respiratory tract consists of the structures within the **thorax**: the trachea, the entire bronchial tree, and the lungs. Table 7.2 lists the essential anatomy and physiology terms for the respiratory system.

The respiratory tract is lined with two protective features that work to prevent harmful substances such as dust, bacteria, viruses and allergens from entering the lungs. The first protective feature of the respiratory tract is the small hairs in the nose, called **cilia**. These serve a filtering function by limiting the passage of large particles into the nose. Cilia are also present along the air passages, where they maintain a clean route by moving in a sweeping motion. When cilia do not function properly, mucus builds up in the lungs and the risk rises for lower respiratory tract infections.

The second protective feature of the respiratory tract is called **mucus**. It is produced by cells in both the trachea and bronchial tubes. The role of mucus is to maintain moist air passages and assist cilia in preventing outside elements from entering the lungs. The respiratory tract secretes about one-half cup of mucus daily. Cilia move mucus from the lower respiratory tract up to the pharynx (throat), where it is then either coughed up or swallowed.

Did You Know?

Harmful substances like tobacco smoke, chemicals, and viruses, once inhaled, prevent cilia from functioning properly.

Term		Meaning	Word Analysis	
Adam's apple		projection on the anterior neck formed by the thyroid cartilage of the larynx		
alveolus	[al-**vee**-ah-lus]	small air sacs found at the end of the bronchiole branches; the site in which oxygen and carbon dioxide are exchanged	*alveol/o*	hollow sac
apex	[**ay**-peks]	top portion of the lung located beneath the upper ribs	*apex*	tip
bronchial tree	[**bron**-kee-el]	portion of the lower respiratory tract that looks like a tree, consisting of the two primary bronchi, like the trunk of the tree; the bronchioles, like the branches; and the alveoli, like the leaves	*bronch/o* *-al*	windpipe pertaining to
bronchiole	[**bron**-kee-Ol]	subdivision of the bronchi (less than 1 mm in diameter); part of the bronchial tree	*bronchiol/o*	bronchiole
bronchus	[**bron**-kus]	section of the respiratory tract formed from the trachea; it branches into right and left sections	*bronch/o*	windpipe
capillary	[**kap**-ih-lar-ee]	smallest unit of the vascular system; location of oxygen and carbon dioxide exchange	*capillaris*	relating to hair
carbon dioxide	[**kar**-bon dI-**ok**-sId]	gas molecule removed from the body by the process of respiration	*carbon dioxide*	charcoal two atoms of oxygen
cilia	[**sil**-ee-ah]	hair-like structures within the body that help to move substances; the cilia in the respiratory tract move foreign substances up and toward the outside world		
epiglottis	[ep-ih-**glot**-is]	elastic cartilage that acts as a valve over the glottis to prevent food from being sucked into the trachea during swallowing	*epi-* *glottis*	upon, following mouth of the windpipe
esophagus	[ee-**sof**-ah-gus]	structure between the pharynx and the stomach		
expiration	[eks-pih-**ray**-shun]	process of breathing out; exhalation	*exspirare*	breathing out
inspiration	[in-spih-**ray**-shun]	process of breathing in; inhalation	*inspirare*	breathing in
intercostal muscles	[in-ter-**kos**-tel]	muscles between the ribs	*inter-* *cost/o* *-al*	between rib pertaining to
laryngopharynx	[lah-**rin**-gO-**far**-enks]	area of the pharynx above the opening of the larynx	*laryng/o* *pharyng/o*	larynx pharynx
larynx	[**lair**-inks]	area of the respiratory tract between the pharynx and trachea; contains the vocal cords	*laryng/o*	larynx
lobes		sections of an organ or body part	*lobus*	lobe, part
lungs		organs within the chest cavity in which respiration and gas exchange take place	*lungen*	lung
mouth		oral cavity	*muth*	opening, orifice
mucosa	[myoo-**kO**-sah]	mucous tissue that lines many structures in the body	*muc/o*	mucus
naris	[**nay**-ris]	opening of the nose; nostril	*nasus*	nose
nasal septum	[**nay**-zel **sep**-tum]	separation of the nasal cavity	*nas/o* *-al* *septum*	nose pertaining to partition

Continues

Term		Meaning	Word Analysis	
nasopharynx	[nay-zO-**fair**-inks]	part of the pharynx located above the soft palate that opens into the nasal cavity and connects with the oropharynx	*nas/o* *pharyng/o*	nose pharynx
nose		opening of the body that provides air entry	*nosu*	nose
olfactory	[ol-**fak**-tah-ree]	relating to smell	*olfactorius*	smell
oropharynx	[**or**-O-**far**-inks]	area of the pharynx behind the mouth that joins the nasopharynx	*or/o* *pharyng/o*	mouth pharynx
oxygen	[**ok**-sih-jen]	gaseous element	*ox/o* *-gen*	oxygen producer
paranasal sinuses	[par-ah-**nay**-zel **sI**-nus-es]	cavities in the head that surround the nose; they lighten the weight of the skull	*para-* *nas/o* *-al* *sinus*	surrounding nose pertaining to cavity
pharynx	[**far**-inks]	area between the mouth and nasal cavities and the esophagus; the throat	*pharyng/o*	pharynx
pleura	[**ploor**-ah]	membrane surrounding the lungs	*pleur/o*	rib
pulmonology	[pool-mO-**nol**-ah-jee]	relating to the lungs; the area of medical practice that diagnoses and treats conditions affecting the lungs	*pulmon/o* *-logy*	lungs study of
respiration	[res-pih-**ray**-shun]	process of breathing	*re-* *spir/o* *-ation*	again breath process of
surfactant	[ser-**fak**-tent]	substance secreted into the alveoli to decrease surface tension		
trachea	[**tray**-kee-ah]	air tube that leads from the larynx into the chest, windpipe	*trache/o*	trachea

Pathway of Oxygen from Inhalation through Exhalation

The **nose** is the uppermost structure of the upper respiratory tract and the entry point for oxygen and other elements from the outside. Although air can enter the body through the mouth, it generally enters through the nares, or nostrils, and passes into the two nasal cavities, which are separated by the **nasal septum**. The air is warmed by the nasal hairs and mucus.

Beyond Words: Fun Facts About Your Sense of Smell

- Olfactory receptors are found in the nasal cavities; their nerve endings are responsible for the sense of smell.
- People can detect 10,000 different smells through more than 10 million scent receptors.
- Scent cells are renewed every 30 to 60 days.
- Most women have a better sense of smell than men.
- Dogs have nearly 44 times more scent cells than humans.

From the nasal cavity, air moves to the **pharynx**, or throat. The pharynx is a tube-like structure, about 5 inches long, extending from the nose into the upper chest. It consists of three sections, the **nasopharynx**, located behind the nose; the **oropharynx**, located behind the mouth; and the **laryngopharynx**, located at the lower end immediately above the larynx (see Figure 7.2). The pharynx continues to filter air as it passes into the body. Other functions of the pharynx include providing a passageway for food as it is swallowed and moved to the esophagus, and housing the tonsils and adenoids. (See Chapter 8 for a complete description of the tonsils and adenoids.)

FIGURE 7.2 The Pharynx

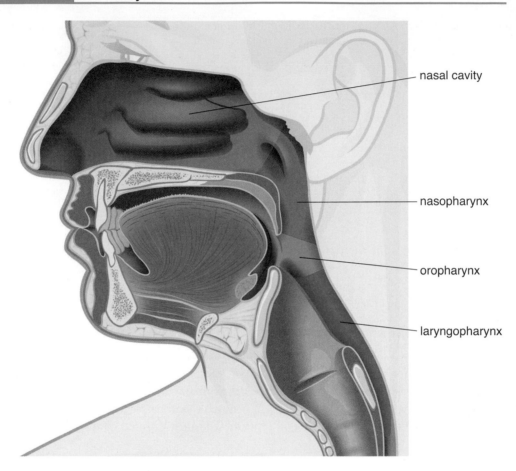

Below the laryngopharynx is the **larynx**, also known as the *voice box* (see Figure 7.3). The larynx is composed of areas made up of cartilage, the largest of which is the thyroid cartilage or **Adam's apple**. The vocal cords stretch across the larynx. The sound of the voice is produced by the larynx when air is passed between the two bands of the vocal cords. The **glottis** is the area between the vocal cords and resembles a "lid like" structure. The **epiglottis** covers the larynx during swallowing to prevent food from entering the trachea, or windpipe. If the epiglottis fails to close quickly during swallowing, food particles can enter the airway, blocking the flow of air into the lungs and causing choking.

In the Know: Paranasal Sinuses

Other structures of the upper respiratory tract include the four **paranasal sinuses**—frontal, maxillary, sphenoid, and ethmoid—named for the bones in which they lie. Sinuses are hollow spaces in the head that help produce mucus, lighten the weight of the skull, and amplify sound.

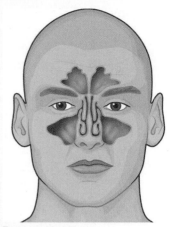

Paranasal sinuses

FIGURE 7.3 Trachea

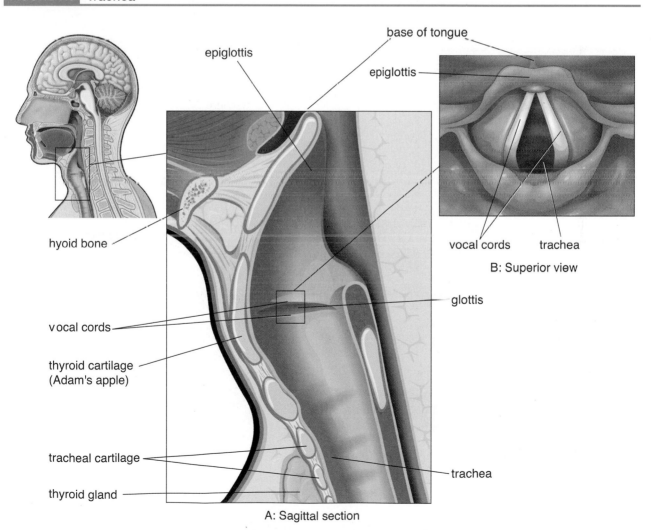

base of tongue

epiglottis

epiglottis

hyoid bone

vocal cords

trachea

B: Superior view

glottis

vocal cords

thyroid cartilage
(Adam's apple)

tracheal cartilage

trachea

thyroid gland

A: Sagittal section

Once inhaled air has traveled down the back of the throat (pharynx), it then enters the **trachea**, or windpipe. The trachea is a tube-like structure that extends about 4 to 5 inches into the lower respiratory tract. The trachea contains cilia to aid in removal of foreign substances and rings of cartilage to maintain an open passageway. Recall that cilia work continuously to capture and expel foreign matter toward the mouth, thus protecting the lungs. On its way to the lungs, the trachea divides into an air passage known as the **bronchial tree**, which is the next structure encountered on the journey within the respiratory system (see Figure 7.4).

The bronchial tree consists of right and left sections and resembles an upside down tree. The left main bronchus is approximately 1.5 to 2 inches long and leads into the left lung; the right bronchus is about 1 inch long and leads into the right lung. The bronchi divide further, until they reach the bronchioles (the branches of the tree). The bronchioles end in **alveoli** (the leaves), which are the areas where gas exchange takes place.

The **lungs** lie within the rib cage and consist of the right lung, which has three **lobes** or sections (superior, middle, and inferior), and the left lung, which has two lobes (superior and inferior). The superior, narrow portion, or **apex**, of each lung is found under the clavicle, or collarbone. The inferior portion, called the base, is wider and rests on the diaphragm. Covering the outer surfaces of the lungs and the inner surfaces of the ribs is the **pleura**, a thin, moist membrane that allows the lungs and ribs to move smoothly against each other during respiration.

> ### To Note!
>
> The bronchial tree looks a little like an upside-down tree within the body. The left and right bronchi form the trunks of the tree; the bronchioles form the branches; and the alveoli make up the tree's leaves.

FIGURE 7.4 Bronchial Tree

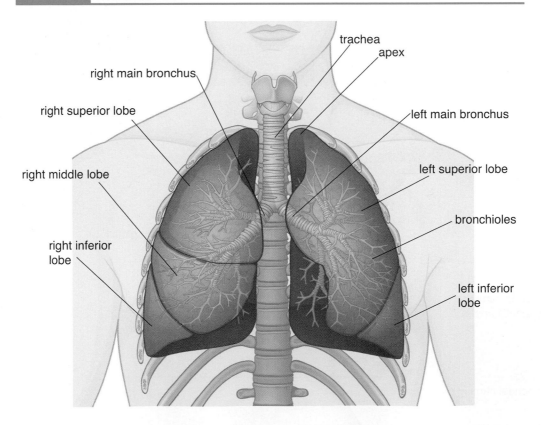

Respiration

Respiration consists of *inspiration*, in which oxygen is **inhaled**, through the nose or mouth, and *expiration*, in which carbon dioxide is **exhaled**. Recall that oxygen is required for life and carbon dioxide is the waste product of respiration. Key players in the respiration process are the **diaphragm**, a muscle located within the thoracic cavity, behind the ribs and under the lungs, and the **intercostal muscles**, which are attached to the ribs.

During inspiration, the chest cavity enlarges as the diaphragm contracts and the intercostal muscles cause the ribs to elevate. This movement enlarges the thoracic cavity and decreases pressure (creating a vacuum) within the cavity, which allows air to enter and the lungs to expand. During expiration the diaphragm relaxes, pushing on the lungs, increasing air pressure, and forcing the air out of the lungs. Figure 7.5 illustrates the mechanics of respiration.

FIGURE 7.5 Respiration

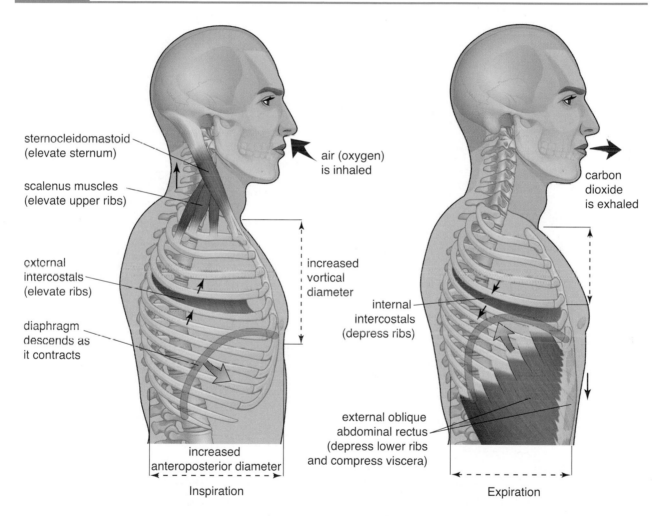

sternocleidomastoid (elevate sternum)

scalenus muscles (elevate upper ribs)

external intercostals (elevate ribs)

diaphragm descends as it contracts

increased anteroposterior diameter

Inspiration

air (oxygen) is inhaled

increased vertical diameter

carbon dioxide is exhaled

internal intercostals (depress ribs)

external oblique abdominal rectus (depress lower ribs and compress viscera)

Expiration

Gas Exchange

Gas exchange refers to the delivery of oxygen from the lungs into the body's bloodstream (inhalation) in exchange for the waste product of carbon dioxide from the bloodstream to the lungs (exhalation).

The process is handled jointly by the respiratory system and the circulatory system, which is the system that moves blood through the body via the blood vessels (veins and arteries). Respiration is a cooperative effort between the respiratory and circulatory systems as blood moves via the blood vessels to deliver oxygenated blood to the tissues and remove carbon dioxide. Blood is pumped from the heart into the artery leading to the lungs, filling the capillaries near the alveoli (see Figure 7.6). Both the alveoli and capillaries share a membrane in which oxygen and carbon dioxide gas can move freely between both body systems (i.e., respiratory and circulatory) through the process of **diffusion**.

Ultimately, oxygen molecules attach to red blood cells on their way to the heart to be distributed to all vital organs. Simultaneously, carbon dioxide molecules are removed from the body with each exhaled breath.

FIGURE 7.6 | **Exchange of Oxygen and Carbon Dioxide**

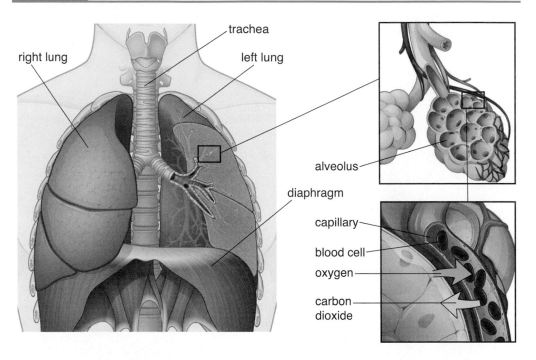

Checkpoint 7.1

Answer the following questions to identify any areas of the section that you may need to review.

1. What is the name of the small, hair-like structures found in the nose and the lining of the respiratory tract that filter inhaled air as protection from outside contaminants?

   _____

2. What is the name of the air tube that leads from the larynx into the chest (also referred to as the windpipe)?

   _____

3. What are the two main components of respiration?

   _____

Exercise 7.1 Word Analysis

Separate the following terms into their word parts, using slashes, then provide a definition for the term on the line provided.

	Word Parts	Definition
1.	pulmonary	_____
2.	aerophagia	_____
3.	pneumonitis	_____
4.	tracheostomy	_____
5.	pharyngeal	_____

Exercise 7.2 Comprehension Check

Circle the appropriate term from the pair in each sentence.

1. Upon examination of the patient's throat, it was noted that the epiglottis/epidermis was swollen and inflamed.
2. When the EMTs arrived, the patient was experiencing an episode of oxonea/apnea.
3. The workers developed osteitis/alveolitis after inhaling toxic fumes.
4. Carbon dioxide is inhaled/exhaled.
5. The upper portion of the lung is called the napex/apex.

Exercise 7.3 Identification

Supply the correct term for each definition. Write the term on the line provided.

1. process by which substances move from an area of higher concentration to an area of lower concentration

   _____

2. gas molecule removed from the body by the process of respiration

   _____

3. Latin for "tip"; the top portion of the lungs, located beneath the upper ribs

   _____

4. air tube that leads from the pharynx into the chest

   _____

5. separation of the nasal cavity

   _____

Exercise 7.4   Word Building

Use the provided definition and supply the missing word part to complete the sentence.

1. Hyper _____ ia means excess carbon dioxide.

2. Naso _____ means the area of the throat located behind the nose.

3. Para _____ sinuses are sinuses located around the nose: frontal, maxillary, sphenoidal, and ethnoidal sinuses.

4. _____ ial means pertaining to the airway.

5. _____ means breathing in, inspiration.

Exercise 7.5   Spelling Check

Circle the correctly spelled word from each pair in the following sentences.

1. The cilia/scilia line the respiratory/inspiratory tract.

2. The pharnyx/pharynx is a tube-like structure extending from the nose into the upper chest.

3. When the diaphragm/diaghram relaxes, it reduces the volume of the thoracic/theoretic cavity.

4. A substance called surfactent/surfactant covers the inside of the alveoli/alimentary canal.

5. The process of diffusion/difusion occurs when substances move from an area of higher concentration to an area of lower concentration.

Exercise 7.6   Word Map

Trace the path of air through the respiratory system during inhalation. Complete the diagram by labeling each area.

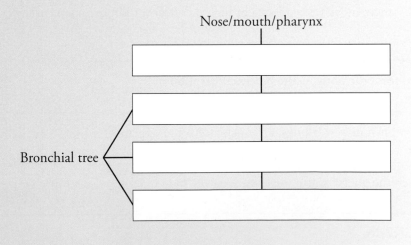

Exercise 7.7 Comprehension Check

Group the following terms into three categories:

alveoli, astrocyte, bronchioles, myelin sheath, nares, neurilemma, oropharynx, trachea

Upper Respiratory Tract   **Lower Respiratory Tract**   **Not in the Respiratory Tract**

_____   _____   _____

_____   _____   _____

_____   _____   _____

Conditions

Respiratory illnesses are often caused by the system's inability to protect the lungs from pollutants present in the outside environment. There are a number of diseases and disorders that directly affect the respiratory system. This section provides a brief overview of the most common conditions affecting this body system, including asthma, bronchiolitis, and chronic obstructive pulmonary disease.

Affecting more than 20 million people in the United States, **asthma** is a chronic inflammatory lung disease that causes the airways to tighten and narrow. Most often triggered by irritants in the air (such as tobacco smoke, pollen, animal dander, etc.), asthma "attacks" are caused by a contraction of the muscles along the respiratory tract. This results in a narrowing of the airway that prevents air from flowing adequately. Patients may experience wheezing and coughing which may lead to difficulty breathing and respiratory distress.

Often confused with bronchitis, **bronchiolitis** is an inflammation of the bronchioles. Recall that the bronchioles are the smallest branches of the bronchial tree. Bronchiolitis is usually caused by viruses prevalent in the winter months, including respiratory syncytial virus (RSV).

Chronic obstructive pulmonary disease (COPD) is a progressive lung disease that makes it hard to breathe. It is a term generally used to describe one of two different diseases affecting the lungs, emphysema and chronic bronchitis. **Emphysema** is the lungs' production of an excessive amount of mucus, which ultimately damages the alveoli. Often a result of long-term smoking, patients with emphysema experience difficulty breathing due to the inability to get enough oxygen into the blood. **Chronic bronchitis** is the inflammation of the bronchial tubes. This inflammation results in a mucus-producing cough, shortness of breath, and wheezing, and tightness in the chest.

The **common cold** is the most common respiratory infection. It is caused by more than 200 different viruses that produce inflammation in the upper respiratory tract. Symptoms may include a mild fever, cough, headache, runny nose, sneezing, and sore throat.

Hand washing, basic hygiene practices, the avoidance of exposure to smoke, and routine physicals are all ways to prevent the transmission of most respiratory illnesses. Table 7.3 lists other major wellness and illness terms relating to the respiratory system.

In the Know: Coughing

There are many different types and causes of coughs. A cough is a symptom of an illness, not an illness itself. Some of the more common causes are the common cold, asthma, sinusitis, seasonal allergies, croup, and pneumonia. Among the most serious causes of cough are tuberculosis (TB) and whooping cough (pertussis).

TABLE 7.3 Common Conditions Associated with the Respiratory System

Term		Meaning	Word Analysis	
acute respiratory failure (ARF)		disorder characterized by the sudden inability of the respiratory system to provide oxygen and/or remove carbon dioxide from the bloodstream		
asphyxia	[as-**fik**-see-ah]	body is unable to get sufficient oxygen to function, can cause unconsciousness or suffocation (death)		
asthma	[**as**-mah]	disorder in which airways are temporarily narrowed, resulting in difficulty in breathing, as well as coughing, gasping, and wheezing	*asthma*	difficulty breathing
atelectasis	[at-ah-**lek**-tah-sis]	absence of gases from the lungs because of the inability of the alveoli to expand; also known as a *collapsed lung*	*a-* *tel/o* *-ectasis*	not complete dilation or expansion
bronchiectasis	[bron-kee-**ek**-tah-sis]	dilation of the bronchi or bronchioles as a result of inflammatory disease or obstruction	*bronch/o* *ect/o* *-esis*	bronchus, windpipe outer condition
bronchiolitis	[bron-kee-O-**li**-tis]	inflammation of the bronchioles	*bronchiol/o* *-itis*	bronchiole inflammation
bronchogenic carcinoma	[**bron**-kO-jen-ik car-sin-**O**-ma]	lung cancer	*bronch/o* *-genic* *carcin/o* *-oma*	bronchus, windpipe beginning, production cancer tumor
bronchospasm	[bron-kO-**spaz**-um]	a sudden involuntary contraction of the bronchi (e.g., as a result of an asthma attack)	*bronchi/o* *spasm*	bronchus sudden, involuntary contraction
Cheyne-Stokes respiration	[**chayn stOks**]	deep, rapid breathing followed by a period of apnea		
chronic obstructive pulmonary disease (COPD)		chronic, progressive lung disease that makes it hard to breathe		
coryza	[kO-**rI**-zah]	common cold		
croup	[**kroop**]	laryngotracheobronchitis caused by a parainfluenza virus in infants and young children	*croup*	cry aloud

Continues

Term		Meaning	Word Analysis	
cyanosis	[sI-uh-nO-sis]	lack of oxygen in the blood leading to bluish discoloration of the skin	cyan/o -osis	blue abnormal condition
cystic fibrosis (CF)	[**sis**-tik fI-**brO**-sis]	hereditary disorder characterized by respiratory difficulties and frequent, mushy, foul-smelling stools because of missing pancreatic enzymes	cystic fibr/o -osis	refers to cysts fiber (fibrous) condition
deviated septum	[**dee**-vee-ay-tid **sep**-tum]	physical condition in which the nasal septum is off center, causing a possible obstruction of nasal passages	sept/o -um	wall structure
diphtheria	[dif-**theer**-ee-uh]	rare, bacterial infection characterized by a sore throat, fever, and headache		
dyspnea	[**disp**-nee-ah]	difficulty breathing, shortness of breath	dys- -pnea	difficult breathing
emphysema	[em-fih-**see**-mah]	chronic condition of increased air in the alveoli that cannot be exhaled	emphysema	bellows
epiglottitis	[ep-ih-glot-**I**-tis]	usually an acute illness caused by the *Haemophilus influenzae* type B organism; may cause respiratory obstruction	epi- glottis -itis	over, on mouth of the windpipe inflammation
flail chest		life-threatening medical condition in which a portion of the rib cage becomes separated from the chest wall, usually due to severe trauma		
hemoptysis	[he-**mop**-tih-sis]	coughing up blood	hem/o -ptysis	blood spitting
hemothorax	[hee-mO-**thor**-aks]	blood in the chest cavity	hem/o -thorax	blood chest
hyperventilation		shortness of breath due to anxiety		
influenza	[in-floo-**en**-zah]	acute condition of the respiratory tract, also known as the *flu*		
laryngitis	[lair-in-**jI**-tis]	inflammation of the voice box	laryng/o -itis	larynx/voicebox inflammation
mesothelioma	[mez O thee lee **O**-ma]	type of lung cancer of the pleura	meso- thel/o -oma	middle a nipple-like structure; a cellular layer tumor
non-small cell lung cancer (NSCLC)		most common type of lung cancer		
obstructive sleep apnea (OSA)	[**ap**-nee-ah]	common sleep disorder in which there are repetitive pauses in breathing during sleep	a- -pnea	not, without breathing
pertussis	[pur-**tuss**-is]	bacterial infection of the respiratory tract commonly referred to as *whooping cough*		
pharyngitis	[fair-in-**jI**-tis]	inflammation or infection of the throat, generally leading to symptoms of sore throat	pharyng/o -itis	pharynx, throat inflammation
pleural effusion	[**ploor**-el ef-**yoo**-zhun]	condition in which fluid from the body accumulates in the pleural cavity	pleur/o -al effusion	lungs pertaining to pouring out

Continues

Term		Meaning	Word Analysis	
pleurodynia	[**ploor**-O-**din**-ee-ah]	pain in the chest caused by inflammation in the muscles of the ribcage	pleur/o pleura -dynia	rib
pleurisy	[**ploo**-rih-see]	inflammation of the pleura (membrane around the lungs)	pleur/o -y	rib condition
pneumoconiosis	[noo-mO-kO-nee-**O**-sis]	condition in which there is an abnormal accumulation of dust in the lungs (e.g., asbestos or black lung disease)	pneum/o coni/o -osis	lung dust abnormal condition
pneumonia	[noo-**mO**-nee-ah]	inflammation of the lung tissue	pneum/o -ia	lungs, air, gas condition
pneumothorax	[noo-mO-**thO**-raks]	condition in which air is present in the pleural cavity, resulting in a collapsed lung	pneum/o thorac/o	lungs, air, gas chest
pulmonary abscess	[**pul**-mun-nair-ee **ab**-ses]	accumulation of pus in the lungs	pulmon/o -ary	lung pertaining to
pulmonary edema	[**pul**-mun-nair-ee eh-**dee**-mah]	accumulation of fluid in the lungs	pulmon/o -ary	lung pertaining to
pyothorax	[pI-O-**thor**-aks]	pus in the chest cavity	py/o -thorax	pus chest
respiratory syncytial virus (RSV)	[sin-**sish**-uhl]	highly contagious respiratory virus common in young children and older adults with symptoms that mimic a severe cold but often result in hospitalization		
rhinitis	[rI-**nI**-tis]	inflammation of the mucous membranes of the nose	rhin/o -itis	nose inflammation
rhinomycosis	[rI-nO-mI-**kO**-sis]	abnormal condition of fungus in the nose	rhin/o myc/o -osis	nose fungus abnormal condition
severe acute respiratory syndrome (SARS)		viral respiratory condition caused by the coronavirus		
small cell lung cancer (SCLC)		second most common type of lung cancer (associated with smoking)		
sinusitis	[sI-nah-**sI**-tis]	inflammation of one of the paranasal sinuses	sinus -itis	cavity inflammation
sputum	[**spyoo**-tum]	mucus coughed up from the lungs and expelled through the mouth		
tachypnea	[tak-ip-**nee**-ah]	rapid breathing	tachy- -pnea	fast breathing (rapid breathing)
tracheostenosis	[tray-kee-O-sten-**O**-sis]	narrowing of the windpipe	trache/o -stenosis	windpipe narrowing
tuberculosis	[too-ber-kyoo-**lO**-sis]	disease caused by the organism *Mycobacterium tuberculosis*; forms infectious tubercles	tubercul/o -osis	tubercle condition
upper respiratory infection (URI)		inflammation or infection of the upper respiratory tract		

Lung cancer, also known as **bronchogenic carcinoma**, is the leading cause of cancer deaths in men and women (see Figure 7.7). This is a group of malignant tumors usually associated with cigarette smoking. Lung cancer is divided into two categories: non-small cell lung cancer (NSCLC) and small cell lung cancer (SCLC). In early-stage disease, NSCLC is treated with surgery. In more advanced disease, surgery and/or radiation therapy, with or without chemotherapy, may be used. Small cell lung cancer is highly malignant and is usually in an advanced stage at time of diagnosis. It is treated with surgery, chemotherapy, and radiation therapy, although treatment is considered palliative (comfort care).

Mesothelioma is a rare malignant tumor arising from the lining of the pleural surface of the lungs. It is associated with exposure to asbestos (a substance that was commonly used in building materials until it was found to be harmful when inhaled).

| FIGURE 7.7 | Lung Cancer |

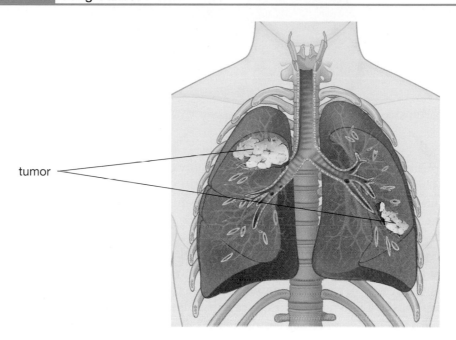

tumor

Fetuses, Infants, and Children

Lung tissue develops during the first five weeks of fetal life. By 16 weeks the pathways for respiration are the same as in the adult. In utero, the respiratory system is the only nonfunctional system. Surfactant appears by about 32 weeks to help the newborn breathe once it is outside the mother's womb. The first breath is taken at birth. When the umbilical cord is cut, the placental blood supply is cut off, and the newborn begins to use his or her own respiratory and circulatory systems to sustain life.

Meconium aspiration is the condition that occurs when a newborn inhales (aspirates) a mixture of meconium (baby's first feces, ordinarily passed after birth) and amniotic fluid during labor and delivery. The inhaled meconium generally causes a partial or complete blockage of the baby's airways and must be removed immediately.

Premature infants who are born before surfactant has been produced are at risk for **infant respiratory distress syndrome (IRDS)**, a life-threatening condition and major cause of death of premature infants. The inability of the alveoli to inflate completely causes them to collapse, a condition known as **atelectasis** (see Figure 7.8). A synthetic drug, called surfactant replacement therapy, is now available for preterm infants to replace the missing surfactant. Chapter 14 will take a closer look at the diagnostic tests and treatments

FIGURE 7.8 Atelectasis

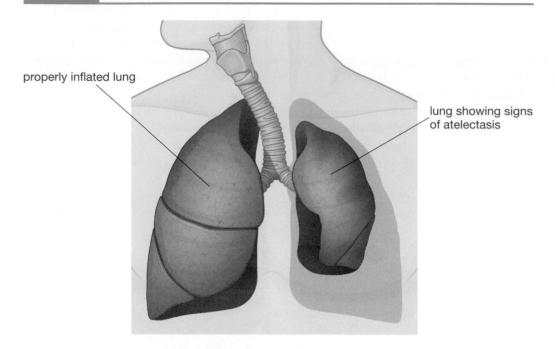

properly inflated lung

lung showing signs of atelectasis

given to premature infants at risk for critical respiratory conditions upon birth due to underdeveloped lungs.

The infant breathes through the nose rather than the mouth until about three months of age. The chest is rounded, and there is little thoracic expansion. Normally, the newborn takes thirty to forty breaths per minute. Infants and young children are especially vulnerable to **respiratory syncytial virus (RSV),** a type of virus that causes cells to mesh rather than remain singular. In adults, the virus produces only cold-like symptoms, but children can become extremely ill with **pneumonia,** an inflammation of lung tissue.

Cystic fibrosis (CF) is an inherited disease that causes an excess build up of mucus in the bronchial tree leading to airway obstruction. CF is usually diagnosed in infancy. An inherited disease, it causes airway obstruction and pancreatic insufficiency. **Pancreatic insufficiency** is the inability to properly digest food and results in gas, diarrhea, weight loss, and stomach pain. Children with CF must take pancreatic enzymes to replace those missing so that their systems can absorb food properly. The patient has frequent episodes of pneumonia. Careful **pulmonary hygiene** (formerly referred to as pulmonary toilet), or deep breathing and percussion, is necessary to loosen the thick, sticky secretions associated with this disease.

Young children tend to suffer from frequent **upper respiratory infections (URIs).** Several factors cause this phenomenon. First, as described in Chapter 6, the Eustachian tubes are shorter and more curved in children than they are in adults; these characteristics provide an easy entryway in children for bacteria. Second, each time a child is exposed to an outside organism, he or she becomes sick with the associated disease; many of these organisms cause URIs. On the positive side, however, the child then develops immunity against these organisms.

Croup is a common respiratory problem caused by certain viruses and occurs most frequently in infants and young children. Croup produces difficult and noisy respiration and a bark-like cough. **Bronchiolitis** is caused by a viral pathogen and is characterized by difficulty breathing, respiratory distress, and pneumonia.

Did You Know?

Vaccination for respiratory diseases such as pertussis, measles and diphtheria has improved the mortality rate for children.

Acute epiglottitis is a life-threatening condition in which the epiglottis swells and blocks airflow to the lungs. This condition is rare but is dangerous, especially for young children. It is frequently caused by the *Haemophilus influenzae* type B organism, but may also be a result of burns to the throat from hot liquids.

Recall that *asthma* is a chronic lung disease characterized by narrow airways due to inflammation caused by allergic reactions to the environment, foods, or other substances. Patients typically experience recurring episodes of wheezing, coughing, and shortness of breath. Asthma is often first diagnosed in childhood.

Young Adults

Active young adults may be exposed to the potential for injury, including trauma to the respiratory system, from motor vehicle collisions, occupational injuries, and sports or household mishaps. One of the more serious conditions is pneumothorax (sometimes called "collapsed lung"), which is air collecting in the pleural space (where the lung tissue is normally "inflated"). The air (blood or pus can also collect there) in that space prevents the lung tissue from fully expanding, which inhibits gas exchange. If it is severe enough, pneumothorax can lead to a disruption of both pulmonary and cardiac function and even death. Hemothorax is the collection of blood within the pleural cavity. Like pneumothorax, this condition limits the lungs' ability to expand. Hemothorax is commonly caused by blunt force or trauma to the chest.

Seniors

Through the aging process, the costal cartilages become calcified, and chest expansion may be decreased. This decreased expansion prevents good air entry and makes the older person especially susceptible to respiratory diseases. The most common is emphysema, in which loss of alveolar elasticity prevents movement of air from the air sacs. Chronic **bronchitis**, a continual inflammation of the bronchi, is associated with emphysema.

Recall that COPD is a chronic, progressive lung disease that makes it hard to breathe. It is also known as **chronic obstructive lung disease (COLD)**. In the late stages of COPD/COLD, the affected person becomes extremely weak and requires a continuous delivery of oxygen via an external source.

Tuberculosis is a contagious, infectious disease, caused by the organism *Mycobacterium tuberculosis*. The disease is commonly found in areas where people live very close together, have poor nutrition and lowered immune systems, and are therefore at higher risk of transmission. The spread of tuberculosis was decreasing in the United States until the outbreak of HIV/AIDS; this type of infection is commonly seen in patients who have compromised immune systems. The incidence of tuberculosis has also increased as a result of multi-drug resistant strands of the disease. Drug resistance is a direct result of the failure to complete the full course of antibiotic treatments.

Pneumonia is an inflammatory condition that affects lung tissue. It is usually caused by infectious organisms (bacterial or viral), but may also result from inhaling or aspirating chemicals. The examiner may hear chest sounds similar to rattling fremitus (vibration) or dullness on percussion (signaling fluid in the lungs, see Figure 7.9).

> **To Note!**
>
> Although conditions such as bronchitis, pneumonia, and tuberculosis are not restricted to the elderly, seniors are especially suseptible to respiratory diseases.

FIGURE 7.9 Fluid in the Lungs (Alveoli)

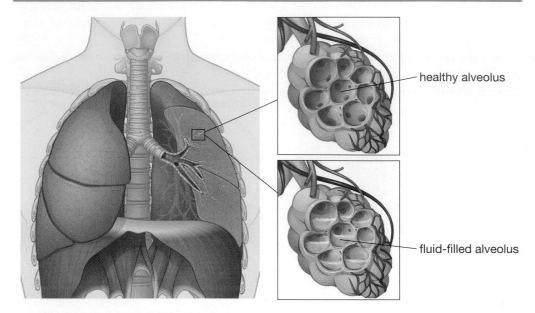

healthy alveolus

fluid-filled alveolus

Checkpoint 7.2

Answer the following questions to identify any areas of the section that you may need to review.

1. What is the medical term for the narrowing of the windpipe?

   _____

2. What medical condition is an inherited disease, usually diagnosed in infancy, known to cause airway obstruction and pancreatic insufficiency?

   _____

3. Shorter, more curved Eustachian tubes and increased exposure to outside organisms put children at higher risk to develop what respiratory condition?

   _____

Exercise 7.8   Word Analysis

Draw a box around the root in each term. Write the definition for the root word and then write the definition for the entire term on the lines provided.

Term	Root Word Definition	Whole Term Definition
1. pyrothorax	_____	_____
2. cyanosis	_____	_____
3. pulmonary	_____	_____
4. epiglottitis	_____	_____
5. bronchiolitis	_____	_____

Exercise 7.9 Comprehension Check

Circle the appropriate term from each pair in the following sentences.

1. Cystic fibrosis/fibrositis is usually diagnosed in infancy.

2. Infants and young children are especially vulnerable to RSV/RSVP.

3. UIR/URI is a common diagnosis in children.

4. Atolitis/Atelectasis is a Greek term meaning "incomplete expansion."

5. Pleurisy/Purist is an inflammation of the membrane around the lungs.

Exercise 7.10 Word Building

Use prefixes, root words, combining forms, and suffixes to create medical terms for the definitions given. Write the term on the line provided.

1. inflammation of the nose _____

2. surgical incision into the trachea _____

3. surgical repair of the thorax _____

4. blood in the chest cavity _____

5. removal of a lung _____

Exercise 7.11 Spelling Check

Identify each term as singular or plural by writing a P or S beside the term; then give the opposite form (either plural or singular) on the line provided.

1. bronchi _____ _____

2. alveoli _____ _____

3. lung _____ _____

4. cilia _____ _____

5. capillary _____ _____

Exercise 7.12   Word Building

The following list has seven terms that describe respiration, all using the same suffix. Complete the terms to match the definitions.

Definition	Term
1. difficult breathing	_____/pnea
2. easy or normal breathing	_____/pnea
3. rapid breathing	_____/pnea
4. slow breathing	_____/pnea
5. shortness of breath when lying flat	_____/pnea
6. shallow and/or rapid breathing	_____/pnea

Exercise 7.13   Word Maps

Categorize the following wellness and illness terms according to the life stage in which they usually appear.

cystic fibrosis	emphysema	IRDS
respiratory syncytial virus	croup	chronic obstructive lung disease
bronchogenic carcinoma	acute epiglottitis	bronchitis

Fetus/Infant/Child

_____

_____

_____

_____

_____

_____

Adult/Senior

_____

_____

_____

_____

_____

_____

Diagnostic Tests and Examinations

To Note!

The utilization of a stethoscope involves listening (as opposed to visually observing a condition).

Many patients are familiar with the traditional tests conducted during a physical examination. After obtaining a patient's vital signs (temperature, blood pressure, heart rate, and rate of respiration), physicians generally progress to tests specific to the respiratory system. This includes listening to the patient's chest by way of **auscultation and percussion (A&P)**. Auscultation is performed using a stethoscope; percussion, also known as *tapping*, is done with the hands. The objective of auscultation and percussion is to identify areas of abnormal breath sounds and changes in lung density.

The physician's assessment of the respiratory system continues by looking at the nose, observing for a deviated septum or other abnormalities that might decrease the amount of air entering the body. The chest is inspected for size, shape, and symmetry. Respirations are counted as movements of the chest during inspiration and expiration. Posture, contour, and movement are important elements in proper air exchange. Infants and children normally breathe with the diaphragm muscle, while most adults use the chest muscles.

Palpation of the back includes feeling for **fremitus**, the vibrations caused by breathing. A resonant sound should be produced when **percussing**, or tapping, on the chest over the area of the lungs. The ribs and sternum produce a dull sound. On **auscultation** with the stethoscope, the examiner listens for breath sounds on inspiration and expiration.

Abnormal, or **adventitious**, sounds on auscultation indicate the type of abnormality present. These sounds are usually described as discontinuous, discrete sounds, called **crackles** or **rales**; or continuous, coarse, or musical sounds, which include **wheezes** and **rhonchi**. Table 7.4 lists the sounds heard during auscultation of the chest. Table 7.5 lists terms describing abnormalities in the physical examination of the respiratory system.

> **What's in a Word?**
>
> The combining form *tympan/o* means "drum." The term *tympany* describes a drum-like sound heard during an examination (when the chest is filled with an abnormal amount of air).

TABLE 7.4 Sounds Heard during Auscultation of the Chest

Term		Description
bronchophony	[bron-**kaw**-fah-nee]	abnormal sounds heard from the lungs and bronchi while patient is speaking
egophony	[eh-**gof**-fun-nee]	nasal quality heard through stethoscope
hiccup		involuntary contractions of the diaphragm
pleural rub	[**ploo**-rahl]	sounds loudest at the end of inspiration; caused by the lung wall scraping against the pleura
rales		heard during forced respiration usually at the end of inspiration; caused by air rushing through mucus; often heard in patients with a respiratory disease, (e.g. pneumonia, congestive heart failure, or pulmonary edema)
rhonchi	[**rahn**-kI]	continuous sounds, usually more prominent during expiration and cleared with coughing; loud gurgling noises transmitted from secretions in the pharynx
stridor	[**strI**-dor]	high-pitched, like wind blowing, indicating obstruction of the larynx or trachea
tympany	[**tim**-fun-nee]	drum-like sound heard during an examination when chest is filled with an abnormal collection of air or gas
wheeze	[**weez**]	whistling, squeaking, musical sound made by air passing through narrowed airways

Soft Skills for Health Care: Adaptability

When you work in a healthcare profession, you will be required not only to learn on the job but also to keep up to date on changes that take place in medical care. This type of adjustment, called adaptability, is essential for healthcare professionals.

As the healthcare industry transitions from a paper-based system to electronic health records (EHR), healthcare professionals must be willing and able to adapt and embrace change. Technological advancements in the last decade have changed healthcare and raised the expectation of those on both ends of the spectrum. Patients are seeking more advanced tools of communication when accessing health information (i.e. patient portals, text messages, health information apps, telemedicine, and social media). Likewise, the current generation of tech savvy health professionals will expect the industry to parallel technology present in other fields. In order to be proficient at your job, you must invest the time necessary to obtain the technical skills required to keep up with the times and efficiently utilize the new applications that are implemented in your facility. In addition, you must have the ability to communicate the advantages of these changes to the seasoned professionals on your team and patients that may be resistant to change.

TABLE 7.5 | Abnormalities in the Physical Examination of the Respiratory System

Term		Meaning
aphonia	[ah-**fO**-nee-ah]	loss of ability to produce sounds from the vocal cords
apnea	[**ap**-nee-ah]	periods in which breathing is temporarily slowed or interrupted
bradypnea	[braid-**ee**-nee-ah]	abnormally slow breathing
clubbing		abnormal enlargement of the fingertips often seen in patients with lung disease
cyanosis	[sI-ah-**nO**-sis]	bluish color associated with decreased oxygen
dyspnea	[**disp**-nee-ah]	difficulty breathing, shortness of breath (SOB)
epistaxis	[**ep**-ih-stak-sis]	nosebleed
eupnea	[yoop-**knee**-ah]	normal breathing
fremitus	[**frem**-ih-tus]	vibration transmitted to the hand lying on the chest
hypercapnia	[hI-pur-**kap**-nee-ah]	having too much carbon dioxide
hyperpnea	[hI-pur-**nee**-ah]	abnormally deep or rapid breathing
hyperventilation	[hI-pur-ven-tih-**lay**-shun]	breathing that is deeper and more rapid than normal; may cause dizziness and light-headedness
hypoxia	[hI-**pok**-see-ah]	having too little oxygen
orthopnea	[or-thop-**nee**-ah]	difficulty breathing when lying down
orthopnea position		position in which a person sits up and leans forward in order to breathe
rhinorrhea	[rI-nO-**ree**-ah]	runny nose
stridor	[**strI**-der]	high-pitched, noisy breath indicating a tracheal obstruction
tachypnea	[tak-ip-**nee**-ah]	rapid breathing
thoracodynia	[thor-uh-kO-**din**-ee-ah]	chest pain

One of the most common procedures performed to assess the respiratory system is the chest X-ray. This procedure can help the examiner determine the presence of an abnormality such as infection, masses, collapsed lungs, or increased fluid. When further complications are suspected, or if further detail of the respiratory structures is required to obtain an accurate diagnosis, the physician orders a computed tomography (CT) or magnetic resonance imaging (MRI) scan of the chest. PET scans are used to show how well the lungs and their surrounding tissues are functioning.

A **bronchogram**, or lung scan, is an X-ray procedure that uses a contrast dye to view the bronchial tree. Bronchoscopy is an examination of the bronchi using a flexible instrument called an endoscope, which is inserted through the mouth. **Endoscopy** and **laryngoscopy** use the same instrument to view the larynx, trachea, and esophagus. Table 7.6 lists diagnostic procedures for the respiratory system.

TABLE 7.6   Diagnostic Procedures for the Respiratory System

Term		Meaning
arterial blood gas		test that measures the amount of oxygen and carbon dioxide present in the blood
bronchoscopy	[bron-**kos**-kO-pee]	examination of the bronchi
chest X-ray (CXR)		most common imaging test for respiratory system; can be conducted with or without contrast dye
computed tomography (CT)		imaging technique that can capture cross sections of the respiratory system for diagnostic purposes
endoscopy	[en-**dos**-kO-pee]	examination of interior structures of the body with an endoscope
laryngoscopy	[lar-in-**gos**-kah-pee]	procedure to view the larynx using an endoscope
lung perfusion scan		test used to detect pulmonary embolism; captures an image of blood flow to the lungs
lung ventilation scan		test that measures the lungs' ability to take in air
magnetic resonance imaging (MRI)		computerized imaging test that is used to detect chest trauma, tumors in the lungs, and pulmonary embolisms
Mantoux skin test	[mon-**too**]	intradermal injection of PPD (tuberculin); used to detect the presence of tuberculosis (TB) antibodies
oximeter		instrument that measures the amount of O_2 in the bloodstream
pulmonary function tests	[**pul**-mah-nair-ee]	tests using a special instrument called a spirometer to measure the function of the lungs
pulse oximetry	[ok-**sim**-uh-tree]	test used to measure oxygen in arterial blood via a device that is generally clipped to the patient's fingertip
spirometry	[spI-**rom**-ah-tree]	pulmonary function test; used to measure the air capacity of the lungs
stethoscope	[**steth**-uh-skOp]	an instrument used to listen to sounds within the chest and other parts of the body
thoracoscopy	[thor-ah-**koss**-kuh-pee]	test that provides visual exam of the chest
throat culture		test used to identify a bacterial, viral, or fungal infection present in the throat
tuberculin skin test (TB test)		test used to detect the presence of a bacterium that causes tuberculosis

Pulmonary function tests help in diagnosing chronic obstructive pulmonary disease (COPD) and other lung disorders. These breathing tests include the measurement of lung volume and the distribution of gases as they are diffused within the respiratory system.

A **spirometer** measures the amount of air exchanged during each breath. The normal person can take in about 500 ml (about a pint) of air during inspiration and expel it entirely during expiration. The **tidal volume (TV)**, named for the flow of the tides, measures the air inhaled and exhaled, while the **vital capacity (VC)** measures the largest amount of air breathed out in one expiration after a maximal inhalation. Other measurements include the **expiratory reserve volume (ERV)**, the largest amount of air that can be forced out after expiring the tidal volume; **inspiratory reserve volume (IRV)** represents the maximal amount of air that can be inhaled. The **residual volume (RV)** is the air that remains in the lungs after forceful expiration. Table 7.7 lists pulmonary function test abbreviations.

TABLE 7.7 Pulmonary Function Test Abbreviations

Abbreviation	Meaning
ERV	expiratory reserve volume
FEF	forced expiratory flow
FEF$_{25-75}$	forced mid-expiratory flow during the middle half of the FVC
FEV	forced expiratory volume
FEV1	forced expiratory volume in 1 second
FEV3	forced expiratory volume in 3 seconds
FVC	forced vital capacity
FVL	flow volume loop
IRV	inspiratory reserve volume
PEF	peak expiratory flow
RV	residual volume
TV	tidal volume
VC	vital capacity

Checkpoint 7.3

Answer the following questions to identify any areas of the section that you may need to review.

1. What is the medical term used to describe the process of listening to chest sounds during a physical examination?

_____

2. Pulmonary function tests are used to diagnose conditions of the respiratory system. Specifically, what instrument is used to measure the amount of air exchanged in each breath?

_____

3. Traditionally, the suffix -scope is used to describe an instrument to view a particular body system during the diagnostic process. How does the meaning of this suffix differ when used in the medical term stethoscope?

_____

Treatments

Recall that *surgical treatments* are generally invasive as they involve a puncture or an incision into the skin. *Clinical treatments* are generally noninvasive and involve nonsurgical techniques (e.g., physical therapy). *Pharmacological treatments* involve the utilization of medicines (drugs) to treat specific illnesses or diseases. Medication therapies are regulated by the Food and Drug Administration (FDA). To be approved by the FDA for use in the United States, every medicine must be backed by research studies that have shown the medication to be effective in its treatment of a given disease and has a tolerable safety profile. The following text will provide an overview of treatments common to the respiratory system.

Surgical Treatments

Most surgical procedures involving the respiratory system are conducted to repair or remove a malfunctioning part or correct an existing defect. **Adenoidectomies** are surgical procedures common in young children with repeated episodes of infections to the ears and tonsils. The pharyngeal tonsils are removed to reduce the recurrence of infection.

A **pneumonectomy** is a procedure in which an entire lung is removed. It is generally performed when cancer has affected the whole lung and a **lobectomy** (the removal of the section of the lobe containing cancerous cells) will not provide effective treatment.

Septoplasty is a surgical procedure to correct a deviated nasal septum, a displacement of the bone and cartilage dividing the two nostrils. Septoplasty is most commonly performed to improve one's ability to breathe through the nose. The surgical procedure to correct defects in the nose is known as **rhinoplasty** (sometimes called a "nose job"); it can be performed for functional or cosmetic reasons. Table 7.8 identifies surgical procedures that are common to the respiratory system.

> **What's in a Word?**
>
> Recall that the suffixes *-ectomy*, *-plasty*, and *-tomy*, mean "surgical removal," "surgical repair," and "incision" respectively.

TABLE 7.8 | Surgical Treatments Associated with the Respiratory System

Treatment		Description
adenoidectomy	[ad-noyd-**ek**-tuh-mee]	removal of the pharyngeal tonsils/adenoids
bronchoplasty	[**bron**-kO-plas-tee]	surgical repair or reconstruction of the bronchus, generally to restore integrity
laryngectomy	[lar-in-**jek**-tah-mee]	removal of the voice box
laryngotomy	[lar-in-**got**-ah-mee]	incision of the larynx
lobectomy	[lO-**bek**-tah-mee]	excision of an entire lobe of a lung
pneumonectomy	[noo-mO-**nek**-tuh-mee]	removal of an entire lung
rhinoplasty	[**rI**-nO-plas-tee]	procedure to correct the nose for medical or cosmetic reasons
septoplasty	[**sep**-tO-plas-tee]	corrective procedure to straighten the nasal septum
sinusotomy	[sI-nuh-**sot**-ah-mee]	incision of a sinus
thoracentesis	[thor-ah-sen-**tee**-sis]	procedure to place a hole in the pleural space to remove fluid
tonsillectomy	[ton-sih-**lek**-tuh-mee]	removal of the palatine tonsils

Clinical Treatments

The clinical treatments specific to the respiratory system are generally utilized to maintain open airways in patients who are experiencing emergency situations. Endotracheal **intubation** is the insertion of a tube into the nose or mouth to provide for artificial breathing. When the patient cannot maintain a patent (open and unblocked) airway on their own. Endotracheal intubation occurs prior to placing the patient on life support or mechanical ventilation. A **tracheostomy** is performed in patients with a large object blocking the airway or an inability to breathe on their own. This clinical procedure involves the creation of an opening into the throat and the insertion of a tube to provide a temporary breathing apparatus. Tracheostomies are performed when the patient will need long term assistance with secretion removal or breathing. A **tracheotomy** is used in emergency situations to gain immediate access to a patient's airway.

Conditions involving difficult breathing (such as sleep apnea) can be treated using continuous positive airway pressure (CPAP) and bilevel positive airway pressure (BiPAP). BiPAP and CPAP machines allow patients the ability breathe uninterrupted. These units deliver air pressure through a mask to prevent the muscles of the throat from collapsing and becoming obstructed, as the air pressure acts as a splint. BiPAP and CPAP units are generally used overnight in the patient's home. Table 7.9 identifies clinical treatments that are common to the respiratory system.

TABLE 7.9 Clinical Treatments Associated with the Respiratory System

Treatment		Description
BiPAP (bilevel positive airway pressure)		the use of mild air pressure to keep the airways, delivers a single pressure open, delivers an inhale pressure and an exhale pressure, also known as BPAP
CPAP (continuous positive airway pressure)		the use of mild air pressure to keep the airways open
endotracheal intubation	[en-**dO**-tray-kee-ul in-too-**bay**-shun]	insertion of a tube into the nose or mouth to provide for artificial breathing
laryngotomy/bronchotomy	[lair-in-**got**-ah-mee]/[bron-**kot**-O-mee]	medical procedure to maintain an open airway
thoracotomy	[thor-ah-**kot**-ah-mee]	incision into the chest wall as a preparation for surgery
tracheostomy	[tray-kee-**os**-tuh-mee]	procedure to make an opening into the throat to insert a tube temporarily
tracheotomy	[tray-kee-**ah**-tuh-mee]	(emergency) incision into the trachea to gain access to the airway

Pharmacological Treatments

Many of the agents used to correct problems in the respiratory system are antibiotics, which are important in fighting infections. Cough and cold preparations can be purchased over the counter or with a prescription. Allergy medications are given to suppress the symptoms of allergies and colds. Table 7.10 lists pharmacologic agents pertinent to the respiratory system.

TABLE 7.10 Pharmacologic Agents Associated with the Respiratory System

Drug Class	Use	Generic Name	Brand Names
antibiotics, antibacterials, antimicrobials	treat bacterial infections	gentamicin tobramycin cefaclor cefazolin ceftazidime clarithromycin amoxicillin vancomycin	Garamycin Tobrex Ceclor Ancef Fortaz Biaxin Amoxil Vancocin
antifungals	treat fungal infections	amphotericin B fluconazole nystatin	Fungizone Diflucan Mycostatin
antihistamines	decrease the symptoms of allergies (see Chapter 8 for further discussion)	loratadine	Claritin Benadryl Allegra

Continues

Drug Class	Use	Generic Name	Brand Names
antimycobacterial (antituberculosis)	treat *Mycobacterium* infections	ethambutol isoniazid rifampin	Myambutol Nydrazid Rifadin
antitussives	suppress cough	benzonatate codeine guaifenesin dextromethorphan	Tessalon Delsym various brands Robitussin-DM
antivirals	treat viral disease	acyclovir zidovudine	Zovirax Retrovir
bronchodilators	open the respiratory airways and prevent further constriction	albuterol sulfate theophylline beclomethasone dipropionate ipratropium bromide	Proventil, Ventolin Theochron Beconase Atrovent
decongestants	decrease the stuffy nose and congested sinus cavities associated with URI	pseudoephedrine sulfate	Sudafed
expectorants	medications that promote the excretion of mucus from the respiratory tract	guaifenesin	Mucinex
inhaled corticosteroids	medications that reduce airway inflammation to improve breathing (nasal or oral)	fluticasone mometasone furoate	Flonase Nasonex
mucolytic	breaks up or liquifies mucus	acetylcysteine	Mucomyst

Checkpoint 7.4

Answer the following questions to identify any areas of the section that you may need to review.

1. Your patient requires assistance with breathing and a tube was just inserted into his or her mouth and connected to a ventilator. What is this process called?

   _____

2. What is the procedure that involves the creation of an opening into the throat and the insertion of a tube to provide a temporary breathing apparatus?

   _____

3. Which type of medication is prescribed to open the respiratory airways and prevent further constriction?

   _____

Abbreviations

Recall that in the medical field, information is generally recorded in medical charts and provided to patients in medical shorthand. It is important that healthcare professionals become familiar with the abbreviations utilized on a daily basis to successfully perform the duties assigned in a typical workday. Table 7.11 provides a list of common abbreviations used in reference to the respiratory system.

TABLE 7.11   Abbreviations Associated with the Respiratory System

Abbreviation	Meaning
ABG	arterial blood gas
A&P	auscultation and percussion
AFB	acid-fast bacilli
AP	anterior posterior (used with X-ray views)
ARDS	acute respiratory distress syndrome
ARF	acute respiratory failure
BiPAP	bilevel positive airway pressure
CF	cystic fibrosis
CO_2	carbon dioxide
COLD	chronic obstructive lung disease
COPD	chronic obstructive pulmonary disease
CPAP	continuous positive airway pressure
CPR	cardiopulmonary resuscitation
CT	computed tomography
CTA	clear to auscultation
CWP	coal worker's pneumoconiosis
CXR	chest X-ray
DOE	dyspnea on exertion
DNR	do not resuscitate
ENT	ears, nose, and throat
HHN	handheld nebulizer
IRDS	infant respiratory distress syndrome
IPPB	intermittent positive pressure breathing
IS	incentive spirometry
LLL	left lower lobe of lung
LUL	left upper lobe of lung
MDI	metered-dose inhaler
MDRTB	multidrug-resistant tuberculosis
O_2	oxygen
OSA	obstructive sleep apnea
PA	posterior anterior (used with X-ray views)
PAP	positive airway pressure
PFT	pulmonary function test
RAD	reactive airway disease
RDS	respiratory distress syndrome
RLL	right lower lobe of lung
RML	right middle lobe of lung
RSV	respiratory syncytial virus
RUL	right upper lobe of lung
SARS	severe acute respiratory syndrome

Continues

Abbreviation	Meaning
SOB	shortness of breath
T&A	tonsillectomy and adenoidectomy
TB	tuberculosis
TLC	total lung capacity
URI	upper respiratory infection
VC	vital capacity

Exercise 7.14   Word Analysis

Divide each term into its individual word parts. Then write a definition of the term. Use hyphens to separate the word parts.

1. laryngoscope _____

2. nasal _____

3. pulmonologist _____

4. spirometry _____

5. rhinitis _____

Exercise 7.15   Comprehension Check

Circle the correct term from the pair in each sentence.

1. Mr. Tyson has an order for home O$_2$ for his <u>COPD/DOD</u>.

2. The doctor prescribed codeine as an <u>antitussive/antiemetic</u> for Tara's cough.

3. The patient's temperature was 102° F; the physician ordered ASA as an <u>antipyretic/antitussive</u>.

4. <u>Intubation/Mediation</u> was achieved without difficulty, and inhalation anesthesia was started at 8:05 A.M.

5. The patient was on assisted <u>ventilation/application</u> for three weeks following the accident.

Exercise 7.16   Matching

Match the term to the definition.

1. _____ stridor

2. _____ hypoxia

3. _____ hypercapnia

4. _____ dyspnea

5. _____ bronchiolitis

a. difficulty breathing

b. noisy breathing indicating a tracheal obstruction

c. inflammation of the bronchioles

d. having too much carbon dioxide

e. having too little oxygen

Exercise 7.17   Word Building

Supply the word parts to complete each term, according to the definition provided.

1. Laryngo_____ means "inflammation of the larynx, trachea, and bronchi."

2. Dys_____ refers to difficulty breathing.

3. _____y means "pertaining to respiration or breathing."

4. A lob_____ is a removal of a lobe of the lung.

5. _____eal intubation is the insertion of a tube into the nose or mouth for assisted ventilation.

Exercise 7.18   Spelling Check

If each of the following terms are spelled correctly, write "correct" in the blank. If spelled incorrectly, please write the correct spelling on the line provided.

1. organusm _____

2. X-ray   _____

3. virusses   _____

4. imhalation _____

5. infection   _____

Exercise 7.19   Word Maps

The terms listed below are names of respiratory-related diagnostic tests and examinations and treatments. Place each term under the correct heading.

endoscopy	laryngoscopy	pulmonary function tests
intubation	laryngotomy	pulse oximetry
laryngectomy	lobectomy	

Diagnostic Tests and Examinations   **Treatments**

_____   _____

_____   _____

_____   _____

_____   _____

_____   _____

Chapter Review

After successfully completing this chapter, you should be able to correctly answer the following review questions. Answers are provided in the back of the text. Use this self-assessment opportunity to check your understanding of the content and determine whether you need to revisit any of the chapter's content.

Crossword Puzzle

Use the clues provided to fill in the puzzle with the correct terms. Enter one letter per square.

Across

2. separates the nasal cavity
5. membrane surrounding the lungs
9. tiny hollow sacs containing air
11. area of pharynx behind the mouth
13. muscles between and attached to the ribs, used in respiration
17. pertaining to the lungs
18. suffix meaning incision
19. pertaining to the nose
20. substance in the alveoli; decreases surface tension
22. name for type of membrane that lines respiratory system
24. Latin for tube
27. waste gas exhaled by humans
28. nostrils

Down

1. physician specializing in the respiratory system
3. a combining form meaning air
4. elastic cartilage that acts as valve on top of larynx
6. sections of the lungs
7. windpipe
8. root meaning blue
10. instrument used to examine the larynx
12. a combining form meaning nose
14. breathing out
15. hairlike structures that propel mucus and invading matter toward the mouth
16. prefix meaning difficult or painful
21. suffix meaning breath
23. Latin for cavity
25. abbreviation for infection of the upper respiratory tract
26. prefix meaning within

Matching

Match the following terms to their corresponding definitions.

1. _____ thoracotomy
2. _____ thoracentesis
3. _____ pharyngitis
4. _____ lobectomy
5. _____ rhinorrhea
6. _____ hyperpnea
7. _____ cyanotic
8. _____ bronchoscopy

a. discharge from the nose (runny nose)

b. condition of blueness (blue color of skin and mucous membranes)

c. visual examination of the bronchi with a lighted instrument

d. incision into the chest

e. abnormally deep breathing

f. puncture of the chest to remove fluid

g. inflammation of the pharynx

h. removal of a lobe (of the lung)

Identification

Label the illustration below with the correct terms from the word bank list.

bronchioles
diaphragm
larynx
lungs
nasal cavity
pharynx
trachea
respiratory tract

1. _____
2. _____
3. _____
4. _____
5. _____
6. _____
7. _____
8. _____

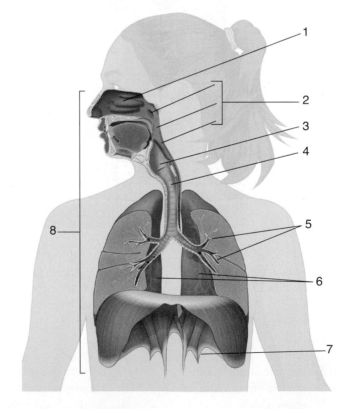

Abbreviations

Read the following sentences and spell out the abbreviation(s) on the line provided.

1. The doctor requested a CXR to confirm the diagnosis of TB.

   _____

2. The patient displayed COPD-related symptoms upon admission to the emergency department (DOE and a chronic cough).

   _____

3. The patient's noncompliance with the recommended treatment regimen led to a diagnosis of MDRTB.

   _____

4. After working over 25 years in the mines, the patient has recently been diagnosed with CWP.

   _____

Word-Building Challenge

Review the following list of new terms. Apply your knowledge of respiratory word parts to accurately identify the meaning of each new term. Write your answer on the line provided and then check your definition against the answer provided in the appendix.

Term	Definition
1. bronchiectasis	_____
2. tracheomalacia	_____
3. sinusotomy	_____
4. tachypnea	_____
5. hypopnea	_____

Extension Activities

Complete the following activities as assigned by your instructor.

1. Research multidrug-resistant tuberculosis (MDR-TB) and the importance of compliance with treatment protocols outlined to treat this condition. Write a brief informative essay that identifies the following:
   - Why is adherence to treatment protocols so important?
   - What role does the local health department play in compliance?
   - Are there any disciplinary actions as a result of patient noncompliance?

2. Imagine that as part of your responsibilities in your office, you have been asked to create a smoking cessation program for patients at-risk for lung disease. Create a short presentation (using PowerPoint or your own visuals) that addresses the following: background/prevalence of lung cancer, risks associated with smoking, and various recommendations for smoking cessation. Be prepared to present your work.

3. Historically, secondhand smoke has resulted in more illness in non-smoking individuals than that of smokers. Identify an example of recent legislation to prohibit smoking in public places. Provide a one-page summary of the legislation and the outcome, then write a one-page persuasive essay that identifies if you agree with the legislation. Support your views with logical reasoning.

Student eResources

The Course Navigator learning management system that accompanies this textbook offers multiple opportunities to master chapter content, including end-of-chapter exercises, a glossary of key terms with audio pronunciations, games, pronunciation coach, and additional activities such as engaging with the BioDigital® Human.

The Cardiovascular System

" The reason we have cancer and heart disease is the same reason you can't get rid of the wear and tear on your tires on your car: as soon as you use them, you are wearing them away. You can't make eternal tires, and it's the same with the human body. **"**

—S. Jay Olshansky, scientist

Translation Challenge

Read the following excerpt from a physician's report and try to answer the questions that follow it.

The patient was taken to the CCU after cardiac catheterization with balloon angioplasty. Following the procedure, there was no evidence of ischemia, and the patient was released to the post-CCU without incident.

1. What is cardiac catheterization?

2. In what part of the patient's body was the balloon placed?

3. Define ischemia and what effects it can have on the heart.

Learning Objectives

8.1 Identify and define word parts most commonly used to create terms related to the cardiovascular system.

8.2 Identify structures of the heart.

8.3 Explain the pathway of blood flow through the body.

8.4 Trace the sequence of the cardiac cycle.

8.5 Describe functions of the heart and major vessels.

8.6 Identify common conditions of the cardiovascular system.

8.7 Name tests and treatments for major cardiovascular abnormalities.

8.8 State the meaning of abbreviations related to the cardiovascular system.

8.9 Use terminology associated with the cardiovascular system correctly in written and oral communication.

8.10 Correctly spell and pronounce terms of the cardiovascular system.

✳ COURSE NAVIGATOR
Access Additional Chapter Resources

The cardiovascular system is responsible for the delivery of blood throughout the body. This system, also known as the *circulatory system*, is composed of the **heart** and **blood vessels** (arteries, veins, and capillaries).

By practical measures, the heart ranks as one of the hardest-working organs. It pumps approximately 1.5 gallons of blood per minute, and works 24 hours each day of our lives. Many consider the heart to be the most important organ of the body. As the engine of the cardiovascular system, the heart pumps blood, nutrients, lymph, chemical gases, electrolytes, and other components from one area of the body to another through the blood vessels, the "roadway" of the system. The cardiovascular system is further divided into two separate systems of circulation, pulmonary and systemic. **Pulmonary circulation** carries blood between the heart and lungs, while **systemic circulation** is the movement of blood between the heart and all other parts of the body. These systems of circulation will be discussed in greater detail in this chapter.

In the Know: Cardiovascular System Specialties

The medical specialty that focuses on the cardiovascular system is known as **cardiology** (*cardi* is from the Greek *kardia*, meaning "heart"). The physicians who treat problems of this system include cardiologists and surgeons. *Interventional cardiologists* specialize in procedures involving the placement of catheters to treat arterial blockages. *Thoracic surgeons* treat coronary blockages with surgery and also treat heart valves with repair or replacement, heart tumors, and congenital defects. *Vascular* (or *cardiovascular*) *surgeons* treat arterial disease of the blood vessels. Cardiovascular technologists and technicians assist physicians in diagnosing and treating conditions affecting the heart and blood vessels. Technicians who specialize in electrocardiograms (EKGs or ECGs), stress testing, and Holter monitors are known as cardiographic or EKG technicians.

Cardiovascular System Word Parts

As with other body systems, a core of word parts serves as the source for most of the medical words associated with the cardiovascular system. Table 8.1 lists word parts used in reference to the cardiovascular system.

TABLE 8.1 Word Parts Associated with the Cardiovascular System

Prefix	Meaning	Example
a-	without	arrhythmia (abnormal heart rhythm)
brady-	slow	bradycardia (slow heartbeat)
con-	together	contraction (process of pulling together)
e-	out	ejection (process of forcing or throwing out)
endo-	within	endocardium (tissue that lines the chambers and valves of the heart)
hyper-	excessive	hypertension (elevated blood pressure)
hypo-	deficient	hypotension (below normal blood pressure)
per-	through	percutaneous (through the skin)
pre-	before	precordium (area of the chest wall that lies anterior to the heart)
tachy-	fast	tachycardia (fast heartbeat)
trans-	through	transmyocardial (through the myocardium)

Combining Form	Meaning	Example
angi/o	vessel	angiogram (an X-ray image of the heart's blood vessels)
aort/o	aorta	aortic (pertaining to the aorta)
apic/o (apex/o)	apex	apical (pertaining to the apex)
arteri/o	artery	arterial (pertaining to the arteries)
arteriol/o	artery	arteriole (small artery)
ather/o	deposit of pasty material	atherosclerosis (presence of hardened fat/plaque in the arteries)
atri/o	atrium	atrioventricular (pertaining to the atria and the ventricles)
capn/o	carbon dioxide	capnograph (an instrument to monitor the concentration of exhaled carbon dioxide)
cardi/o	heart	cardiodynamics (the action of the heart in pumping blood)
coron/o	crown or circle	coronary bypass (surgery to reroute bloodflow)
cyan/o	blue	cyanosis (lack of oxygen in the blood)
endocardi/o	endocardium	endocardium (tissue that lines the chambers and valves of the heart)
isch/o	hold back	ischemia (restriction in blood supply to the heart)
lumin/o	lumen	luminal (pertaining to the lumen)
myocardi/o	myocardium	myocardium (the muscular wall of the heart)
pariet/o	wall	parietal pericardium (outermost layer of the membrane surrounding the heart)
pericardi/o	pericardium	pericardium (a double-layered sac that encloses the heart)
phleb/o	vein	thrombophlebitis (a blood clot that is blocking one or more of the veins)
pulmon/o	lung	pulmonary (pertaining to the lungs)
rhythm/o	rhythm	rhythmic (pertaining to rhythm)

Continues

Combining Form	Meaning	Example
scler/o	hardening	sclerosis (abnormal condition of hardening or stiffening of a structure)
sept/o	wall/partition	septum (a structure that divides)
sin/o	sinus	a cavity within a bone or other tissue
sphygm/o	relating to the pulse	sphygmomanometer (an instrument used to measure blood pressure)
sten/o	narrowing, constriction	stenosis (an abnormal narrowing in the blood vessels)
steth/o	chest	stethoscope (a medical instrument used to listen to the internal sounds of the human body)
thromb/o	blood clot	thrombosis (the formation of a blood clot)
valvuv/o	valve	valvular (pertaining to the valves)
varic/o	twisted, swollen vein	varicosity (an enlarged vein)
vas/o	vessel	vasoconstriction (the narrowing of the blood vessels as a result of the contraction of the muscular walls of the vessels)
vascul/o	vessel	vascularity (highly visible, prominent veins)
ven/o	vein	venule (small vein)
ventricul/o	ventricle	ventricular (pertaining to the ventricles)

Suffix	Meaning	Example
-cardia	heart condition	bradycardia (slow heartbeat)
-ia	condition	arrhythmia (abnormal heart rhythm)
-megaly	enlargement	cardiomegaly (enlargement of the heart)
-osis	condition	cyanosis (lack of oxygen in the blood)
-pathy	disease	cardiomyopathy (disease of the heart muscle)
-plasty	surgical repair	valvuloplasty (surgical repair of a heart valve)
-sclerosis	abnormal condition of hardening	arteriosclerosis (condition of hardened arterial walls)
-tension	process of stretching/pressure	hypotension (condition in which blood pressure is below normal)

Anatomy and Physiology

The **heart** is the critical organ within the cardiovascular system and is located in the center of the thoracic cavity, between the lungs (see Figure 8.1). It is protected by the sternum in front and the spinal column in back (anterior and posterior protection). Two-thirds of the heart is located on the left side of the chest, with the pointed portion, the **apex**, facing downward and to the right, and the base facing upward on the left side.

This fist-sized organ has a wall made up of three layers (see Figure 8.2):

- The **pericardium** is the outermost layer; it is responsible for protecting the heart.

- The **myocardium** is the middle layer; it is made up of thick muscle tissue (cardiac muscle) that contracts to pump blood out of the heart and sustains blood flow throughout the entire body.

- The **endocardium** is the innermost layer; it is made up of thin tissue that lines the four chambers of the heart and heart valves.

FIGURE 8.1 | Location of the Heart

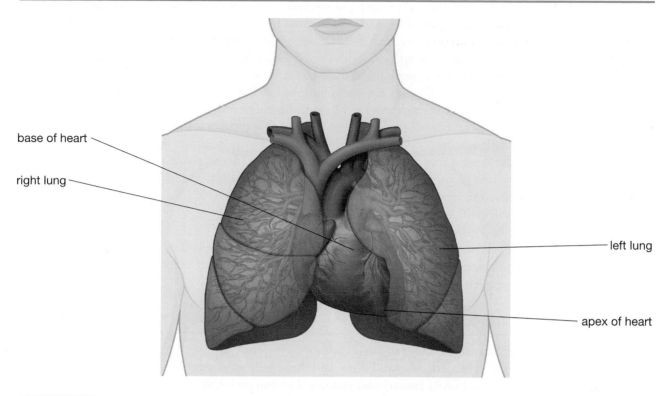

base of heart

right lung

left lung

apex of heart

FIGURE 8.2 | Layers of the Heart

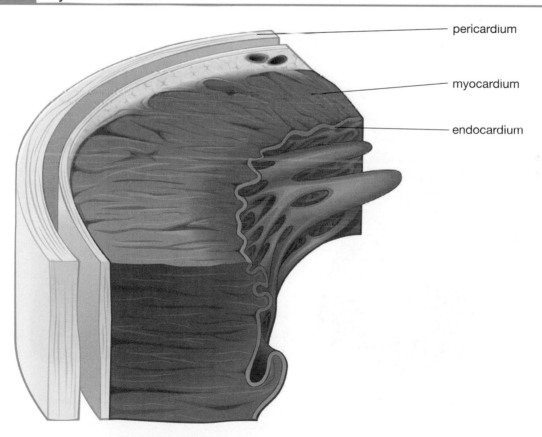

pericardium

myocardium

endocardium

The pericardium is further divided into two layers of connective tissue known as the **parietal (outer)** and **visceral (inner)** pericardium. The pericardium is often referred to as the **epicardium** because it sits on top of the heart's surface. Fluid between these two layers provides lubrication and prevents friction when the heart beats. This fluid is found in the pericardial sac or cavity and is known as **pericardial fluid**. A small amount of pericardial fluid is normal. Certain illnesses cause a buildup of fluid which can prevent the heart from pumping normally and can become life threatening.

The heart is a hollow organ consisting of four distinct chambers named for their specific location within the heart (see Figure 8.3). The upper portion of the heart is made up of the **right and left atria** (the receiving chambers for incoming blood) and the lower chambers house the right and left ventricles, which pump blood to all vessels leaving the heart. The heart is divided into right and left sections by a wall commonly referred to as the **septum**.

The atrium is divided by a wall called the **interatrial septum**, while the ventricles are separated by a wall known as the **interventricular septum**. The right half of the heart pumps oxygen-depleted blood to the lungs, where it is resupplied with oxygen. The left half pumps oxygen-rich blood to the body's tissues.

Heart Valves

Heart valves assist with blood throughout the heart. The four valves are the atrioventricular valves, the bicuspid valve, tricuspid valve, and the semilunar valves. Valves connect the **upper (atria)** and lower **(ventricles)** chambers within each half of the heart. These valves, known as **atrioventricular (AV) valves**, open and close to regulate blood flow.

FIGURE 8.3 **External and Internal Views of the Heart**

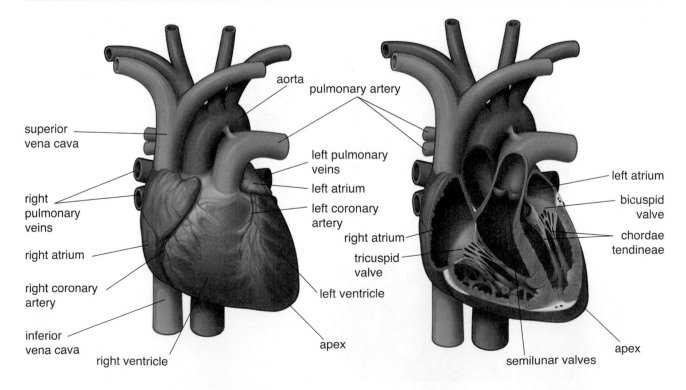

The **mitral valve**, also known as the **bicuspid valve**, separates the left atrium from the left ventricle. The **tricuspid valve** separates the right atrium from the right ventricle. The AV valves open and close together and work to prevent blood from flowing back into the atria. The valves are attached to the heart wall by string-like structures called **chordae tendineae**. The ventricular chambers contain additional valves known as **semilunar valves**. Most commonly referred to as the pulmonary and aortic valves, they lead into the large vessels of the body that carry blood to and from the heart. The **pulmonary semilunar valve** is located at the opening of the pulmonary artery, and the **aortic semilunar valve** is located at the opening of the aorta. The semilunar valves also open and close simultaneously. The semilunar valves are closed when the AV valves are open and open when the AV valves are closed. Table 8.2 lists additional anatomy and physiology terms for the cardiovascular system.

TABLE 8.2 Anatomy and Physiology Terms Associated with the Cardiovascular System

Term		Meaning	Word Analysis	
aorta	[ay-**or**-tah]	main artery in the body	aort/ aorta –a	noun ending suffix
apex apices (pl)	[**ay**-peks] [**ap**-ih-seez]	lowest part of the heart, the tip	apic/o	apex
arteriole	[ar-**teer**-ee-Ol]	small vessels in the body responsible for blood pressure; they lead into the capillaries	arteri/o -ole	artery small
artery	[**ar**-ter-ee]	blood vessel that carries oxygenated blood away from the heart	arteri/o	artery
atrioventricular node (AV)	[**ay**-tree-O-ven-**trik**-yoo-ler]	area of the heart responsible for the conduction of electrical impulses	atri/o ventricul/o	atrium ventricle
atrioventricular valve (AV)	[a-tree-O-ven-**trik**-yoo-ler]	prevents backflow of blood into atria during contraction of ventricles	atri/o ventricul/o -ar	atrium ventricles pertaining to
atrium	[**ay**-tree-um]	upper chambers of the heart	atri/o -um	atrium (of the heart) tissue or structure
bicuspid valve	[bI-**cus**-pid valv]	allows blood to flow from the left atrium into the left ventricle (has two flaps); also known as the *mitral valve*	bi- cuspis	two point
brachial artery	[**bray**-kee-ul]	vessel that supplies blood to the arm and hand, used to measure blood pressure in the arm	brachi/o -al	arm pertaining to
bundle of His	[hiss]	group of nerve fibers that conduct electrical impulses from the AV node to the ventricles	His	19th-century German physician
capillary	[**kap**-ih-lar-ee]	smallest of the body's blood vessels; where oxygen and carbon dioxide are exchanged		
carotid artery		vessel that supplies blood to the brain, pulse can be felt on each side of the neck		
chordae tendineae	[**kor**-dee ten-**dih**-nee-ee]	string-like structures that connect the AV valves to the wall of the heart	chord tendineae	tendinous structure tendons
coronary arteries	[**kor**-uh-nare-ee **ar**-ter-eez]	structures responsible for supplying the heart with blood	coron/o– ary arteri/o	heart, crown pertaining to artery
diastole	[dI-**as**-tO-lee]	relaxation of the heart muscle; part of the cardiac cycle in which the heart refills with blood	diastole	dilation
diastolic pressure	[dI-as-**tol**-**ik** **preh**-sher]	represents the minimum arterial pressure (recorded as the bottom number in a blood pressure reading)	diastole -ic	dilation pertaining to

Continues

Term		Meaning	Word Analysis	
endocardium	[en-dO-**kar**-dee-um]	thin layer of tissue that lines the chambers and valves of the heart	*endocardi/o* *-um*	endocardium tissue or structure
epicardium	[ep-ih-**kar**-dee-um]	membrane that forms the inner layer of the pericardium; covers the myocardium	*epi-* *cardi/o* *-um*	cover heart tissue or structure
femoral artery	[**fem**-or-ul]	vessel that supplies blood to the leg	*femor/o* *-al*	femur, thigh bone pertaining to
high-density lipoprotein (HDL)	[lip-O-**prO**-teen/ lI-pO-**prO**-teen]	fatty substance (type of lipid) found in the blood that decreases the risk of heart attack (good cholesterol)	*lip/o* *prote/o*	fatty protein
inferior vena cava	[**vee**-nuh **kay**-vuh]	carries deoxygenated blood from the lower half of the body into the right atrium	*ven/o* *cava*	vein plural of cavus (cavity)
low-density lipoprotein (LDL)	[lip-O-**prO**-teen/ lI-pO-**prO**-teen]	fatty substance (type of lipid) found in the blood that increases the risk of heart disease (bad cholesterol)	*lip/o* *prote/o*	fatty protein
lumen	[**loo**-men]	cavity of a blood vessel	*lumen*	Latin for "an opening"
mitral valve	[**mI**-trel valv]	allows blood to flow from the left atrium into the left ventricle (has two flaps); also known as the *bicuspid valve*		
myocardium	[mI-O-**kar**-dee-um]	cardiac muscle surrounding each chamber of the heart	*my/o* *cardi/o* *-um*	muscle heart tissue or structure
normal sinus rhythm (NSR)		presence of normal electrical activity in the heart or heart rate		
pericardium	[per-ih-**kar**-dee-um]	membrane that surrounds the heart	*peri-* *cardi/o* *-um*	around; surround heart tissue or structure
pulmonary artery	[**pul**-muh-nair-ree **ar**-ter-ee]	carries deoxygenated blood from the heart to the lungs	*pulmon/o* *-ary*	lung pertaining to
pulmonary vein	[**pul**-muh-nair-ree **vayn**]	carries oxygenated blood from the lungs to the heart	*pulmon/o* *-ary*	lung pertaining to
pulse		dilation of an artery from the contraction of the heart causing blood to be sent into the vessel		
Purkinje fibers	[poor-**kin**-zheh **fI**-bers]	specialized cells located in the walls of the ventricles that are part of the heart's conduction system; relay impulses from the AV node to the ventricles, causing them to contract; essential for maintaining a consistent heart rhythm	*Purkinje*	19th-century Bohemian anatomist
radial artery	[**ray**-dee-ul]	vessel that supplies blood to the hand	*radi/o* *-al*	wrist bone pertaining to
semilunar valves	[sem-ih-**loo**-ner valvs]	valves responsible for carrying blood away from the heart	*pulmon/o* *-ary*	lung pertaining to
septum		wall separating the right and left chambers of the heart	*sept/o* *-um*	wall/partition tissue or structure
sinoatrial node (SA)	[sin-O-**ay**-tree-ul]	area of the heart responsible for the timing of each heartbeat; also known as the *primary pacemaker*	*sin/o* *atri/o* *-al*	sinus atrium pertaining to

Continues

Term		Meaning	Word Analysis	
superior vena cava	[**vee**-nuh **kay**-vuh]	carries deoxygenated blood from the upper half of the body into the right atrium	*ven/o* *cava*	vein plural of cavus (cavity)
systole	[**sis**-tO-lee]	contraction of the heart muscle; part of the cardiac cycle in which blood is pumped out of the heart	*systole*	to contract
systolic pressure	[sis-**tol**-ik]	represents the maximum arterial pressure (recorded as the top number in a blood pressure reading)	*systole* *-ic*	to contract pertaining to
tricuspid valve	[trI-**kus**-pid valv]	prevents backflow of blood into the right atrium; located between the right atrium and right ventricle; also known as the *right atrioventricular valve*	*tricuspis* *-oid*	three point like or resembling
triglycerides	[trI-**glis**-er-Ids]	fatty substances within the blood	*tri-* *glycer/o* *-ide*	three chemical substance compound
vein	[vayn]	vessel that carries unoxygenated blood toward the heart	*ven/o*	vein
vena cava	[**vee**-nah **kay**-vuh]	largest vein in the body	*ven/o* *cava*	vein plural of cavus (cavity)
ventricles	[**ven**-trih-kuls]	two chambers of the heart responsible for pumping blood	*ventricul/o*	ventricle
venules	[**vee**-nyools]	small vessels that collect blood from the capillaries and join to form veins	*ven/o* *-ule*	vein small

Blood Flow through the Heart

While various methods are used to describe the concept of blood flow through the heart, one very effective method is to use the analogy of a sponge. Put a dry sponge into a sink filled with water. The sponge absorbs part of the water. When you take the sponge out of the water and squeeze it, it releases the water.

The flow of deoxygenated blood into the heart's chambers represents the sponge filling with water in preparation to perform its primary function. Once the lungs replenish blood with oxygen and nutrients, the pumping of oxygenated blood out of the heart represents the squeezing of water out of the sponge. This is a continuous cycle of filling and emptying.

The pumping of blood through the heart begins with a process called **atrial systole** (see Figure 8.4). Blood enters the right atrium through the large vessels known as the **superior** and **inferior venae cavae**. This blood arrives from all over the body. It is depleted of oxygen and high in carbon dioxide. The superior vena cava collects unoxygenated blood from the upper portion of the body while the inferior vena cava collects unoxygenated blood from the lower portion of the body.

From the right atrium, the blood flows into the right ventricle through the tricuspid valve. When the heart contracts (squeezes), the blood is forced from the right ventricle through the pulmonary semilunar valve into the pulmonary artery, beginning the process of pulmonary circulation. The contraction of the heart forcing blood out of the ventricles is known as **ventricular systole** (see Figure 8.5). From the pulmonary artery, the blood flows to the lungs, where the carbon dioxide is extracted and expelled (exhaled) and the

What's in a Word?

The process of blood moving through the heart is also known as *cardiac* or *coronary circulation*.

To Note!

Recall that *pulmonary circulation* is the flow of blood between the heart and the lungs.

FIGURE 8.4 | Blood Flow through the Heart: Atrial Systole

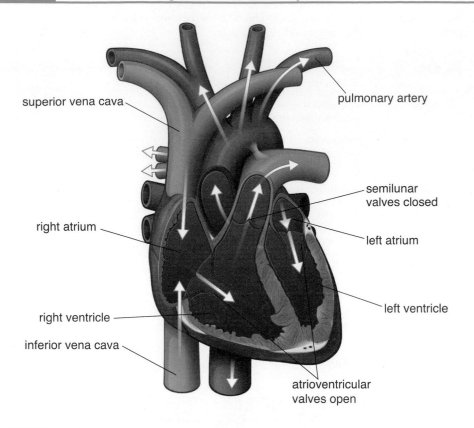

superior vena cava

pulmonary artery

semilunar valves closed

right atrium

left atrium

left ventricle

right ventricle

inferior vena cava

atrioventricular valves open

FIGURE 8.5 | Blood Flow through the Heart: Ventricular Systole

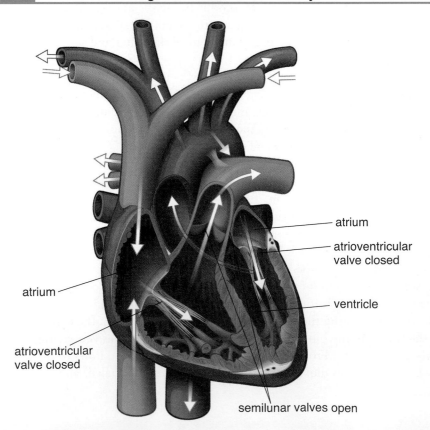

atrium

atrioventricular valve closed

atrium

ventricle

atrioventricular valve closed

semilunar valves open

blood is replenished with oxygen. This portion of pulmonary circulation is known as the process of gas exchange. Figure 8.6 depicts the process of gas exchange during pulmonary circulation.

The reoxygenated blood now enters the left side of the heart via the pulmonary veins. Once it enters the left atrium, the blood passes through the mitral valve into the left ventricle, where it completes the cycle by being reoxygenated and pumped back into the blood vessel network for circulation throughout the body. Oxygenated blood flows from the liver to the inferior vena cava and from the head and upper extremities to the superior vena cava, feeding the body's cells crucial oxygen. Recall that this process is known as *systemic circulation*. As the supply of oxygen is depleted, the blood is recirculated into the right atrium, flowing through the tricuspid valve into the right ventricle. It then passes through the pulmonary semilunar valve into the pulmonary artery on its way to the lungs, and the cycle is repeated.

FIGURE 8.6 Gas Exchange during Pulmonary Circulation

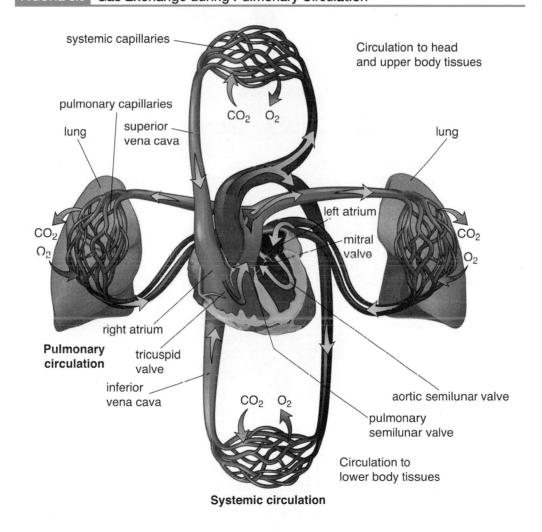

The Cardiac Cycle

The system that causes the heart's pumping action is an electrical circuit. This conduction system, often referred to as the **cardiac cycle**, is initiated in an area called the **sinoatrial (SA) node**, which determines the rhythm of the heartbeat. (The autonomic nervous system is responsible for the heart rate.) The SA node is also known as the body's *primary pacemaker*. The electrical impulse travels from the SA node (1) to the **atrioventricular (AV) node** (2), to the **AV bundle** (or **bundle of His**) (3), to the **Purkinje fibers** (4), initiating the contraction of the heart and circulation of blood (see Figure 8.7). A single heartbeat is equivalent to a completed cardiac cycle. Specialists for the electrical system are called electrophysiologists or EP cardiologists.

FIGURE 8.7 Conduction System of the Heart

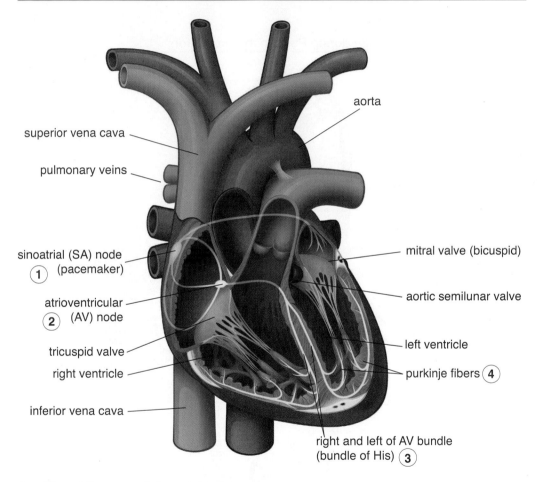

In the Know: Heart Rate

Heart rate is the number of times the heart beats in a minute, while a regular heart rhythm, known as sinus rhythm, is the pattern of the normal heartbeat. Rhythms can be regular or irregular or irregularly irregular. The latter is the definition of atrial fibrillation. The normal sinus rhythm for an adult is generally regular with a heart rate between 60 and 100 beats per minute. A slow heart rate (bradycardia) is less than 60 beats per minute and a fast heart rate (tachycardia) is more than 100 beats per minute.

Circulation of Blood: The Blood Vessels

Blood is carried throughout the body by a series of blood vessels. Figure 8.8 shows the major arteries and Figure 8.9 shows the major veins. In addition to moving blood from the heart to the capillaries for nutrient and gas exchange, each type of blood vessel has its own function.

The **arteries** carry oxygenated blood away from the heart through the largest artery, the **aorta**, toward vessels that become progressively smaller, **arterioles**, and finally ending in the smallest vessels, **capillaries**, where nutrients and gases are exchanged. The arteries and arterioles help to maintain the body's blood pressure. They constrict and dilate to keep the

FIGURE 8.8 Major Arteries of the Body

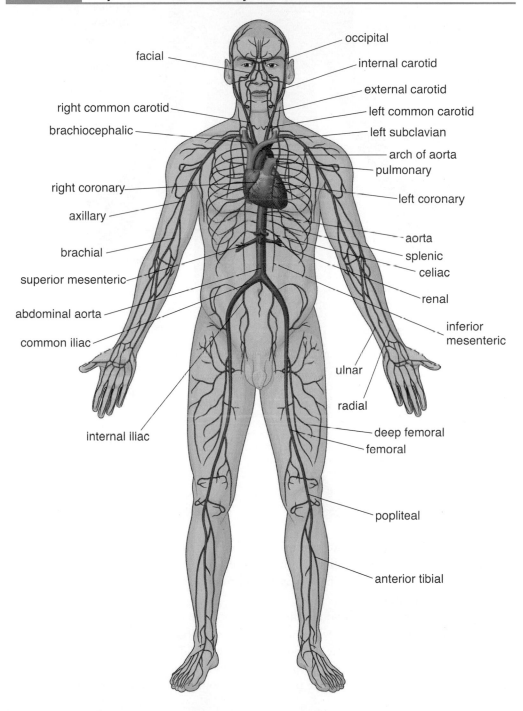

FIGURE 8.9 Major Veins of the Body

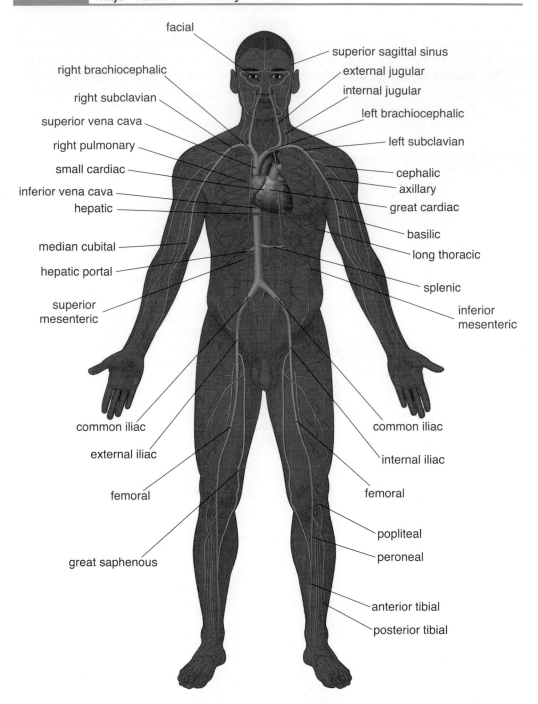

facial
superior sagittal sinus
right brachiocephalic
external jugular
right subclavian
internal jugular
superior vena cava
left brachiocephalic
right pulmonary
left subclavian
small cardiac
cephalic
inferior vena cava
axillary
hepatic
great cardiac
median cubital
basilic
hepatic portal
long thoracic
superior mesenteric
splenic
inferior mesenteric
common iliac
common iliac
external iliac
internal iliac
femoral
femoral
popliteal
peroneal
great saphenous
anterior tibial
posterior tibial

blood flow within the vessels and throughout the body at an even pressure gradient. This gradient ensures that the blood flows from the largest vessels to the smallest. Arteries have thick muscular walls that allow the expansion and contraction necessary to maintain blood flow and blood pressure.

Veins carry deoxygenated blood to the heart. Blood then enters the venous system, going into tiny **venules**, which eventually lead into the larger **veins**, the largest being the superior and inferior venae cavae. Blood from the head and arms flows into the superior vena cava and blood from the lower body parts flows into the inferior vena cava. Veins have one-way valves that prevent the backflow of blood. Arteries and veins are similar in structure as they are both composed of three layers, including a thin outer layer of connective tissue, a middle layer of smooth muscle, and an inner layer of connective tissue. The inner layer of each surrounds the passage through which blood flows, known as the **lumen**. The middle layer is the thickest in arteries while the inner layer is the thickest in veins.

The heart has its own circulatory system, referred to as **coronary circulation**, which supplies it with nutrients and oxygen. The **right** and **left coronary arteries** deliver the blood directly into the heart muscle. When one or both of these important vessels become clogged, a heart attack results.

The **pulse**, which can be felt in different parts of the body, is actually an artery expanding and contracting as blood surges through it. A pulse may be palpated in any place that allows an artery to be compressed against a bone. The most commonly used pulse point is over the radial artery at the wrist. Figure 8.10 shows the areas of the body where pulses can be felt. The rate, rhythm, and strength of the pulse provide insight into the function of the heart and vessels.

What's in a Word?

The term *coronary* is derived from the root *coron*, which means "circle" or "crown." The Latin word *coronas* means "crown."

FIGURE 8.10 **Pulse Points**

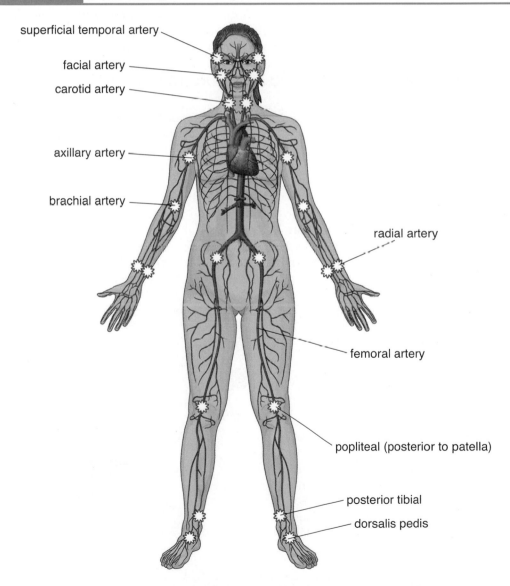

- superficial temporal artery
- facial artery
- carotid artery
- axillary artery
- brachial artery
- radial artery
- femoral artery
- popliteal (posterior to patella)
- posterior tibial
- dorsalis pedis

Blood flows through the body via the arteries and veins. The systemic circulation is the blood flow from the left ventricle through the body as a whole. The pulmonary circulation is the flow of blood from the right ventricle to the lungs via the pulmonary artery (for exchange of gases) and then back to the left atrium through the four **pulmonary veins**.

Blood Pressure

Blood pressure is a measurement of the force or pressure exerted by blood on the walls of an artery when the heart contracts pumping blood into the body (**systole**), and when the contraction relaxes and the heart refills with blood (**diastole**).

High blood pressure, or **hypertension**, means that resistance within the vessels is increasing which could prevent adequate blood flow to the body's tissues. One danger of high blood pressure is the risk that a vessel could rupture, causing a type of stroke known as a hemorrhagic stroke or ischemic stroke. Long term complications of high blood pressure include damage to the heart, kidneys, brain, and eyes. When this damage is present, it is referred to as "end organ damage." Low blood pressure, or **hypotension**, could mean that too little blood is flowing to the organs of the body, such as the brain, heart, liver, and kidneys. This lack of oxygenation (resulting from decreased circulation) could cause serious damage to the organs and the body as a whole and perhaps result in permanent damage to the organs or death.

In the Know: How Is Blood Pressure Measured?

Healthcare professionals measure blood pressure with an instrument called a sphygmomanometer (sfig-mO-muh-**nah**-muh-ter). The cuff of the sphygmomanometer is wrapped around the patient's upper arm and inflated with air to create pressure, while a stethoscope is placed over the brachial artery of the same arm. Once the cuff is inflated, the brachial artery will be compressed, briefly stopping blood flow. Blood pressure is measured as air is gradually released from the cuff, allowing blood to flow through the artery again. The healthcare professional uses the stethoscope to listen to this flow. The first pulse as the blood flows through is a measure of the **systolic pressure**, the pressure at the peak of each heartbeat, also known as *ventricular systole*. This is often described as a tapping or knocking sound. The **diastolic pressure** is noted when the sounds disappear. Diastolic pressure represents the pressure when the heart is resting between beats. Blood pressure is written as a fraction; for example, a person could have a blood pressure of 120/80 (spoken as 120 over 80). The gauge of the sphygmomanometer is used to obtain the numerical reading. Hypertension is defined as a systolic pressure greater than 140 or diastolic pressure over 90. Hypotension is defined as a systolic pressure less than 90 or a diastolic pressure under 60.

Note that healthcare professionals categorize hypertension as one of three types. Essential (primary) hypertension describes high blood pressure with no known secondary cause. Secondary hypertension describes high blood pressure caused by another medical condition. And malignant hypertension is extremely high blood pressure that occurs suddenly and results in organ damage.

Checkpoint **8.1**

Answer the following questions to identify any areas of the section that you may
need to review.

1. What is the pathway of electrical impulses in the cardiac cycle?

   _____

2. What is another name for the bicuspid valve?

   _____

3. What two chambers make up the upper portion of the heart?

   _____

   _____

Exercise 8.1   Identification

Correctly label the illustration by writing the letter of the corresponding callout on the line provided next
to each term.

1. _____ aorta

2. _____ apex

3. _____ pulmonary arteries

4. _____ pulmonary veins

5. _____ right atrium

6. _____ right ventricle

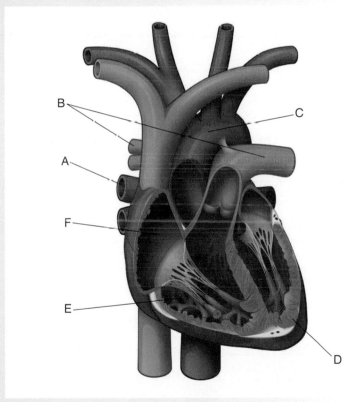

Exercise 8.2   Comprehension Check

Read each sentence and determine which word best fits the sentence. Circle your choice.

1. The medical specialty that diagnoses and treats disorders of the heart is cardiology/hartology.

2. The heart is located in the abdominal/thoracic cavity.

3. The innermost layer of the membrane surrounding the heart is the vascular/visceral pericardium.

4. The two halves of the heart are separated by the speculum/septum.

5. Contractions of the heart are called systole/diastole.

Exercise 8.3   Matching

Match the terms from column 1 with the definitions in column 2. Write the letter of the definition on the line provided.

1. _____ hypotension

2. _____ atria

3. _____ arteries

4. _____ veins

5. _____ AV node

6. _____ arterioles

a. upper chambers of the heart

b. tiny arteries

c. vessels that carry blood toward the heart

d. part of the heart's conduction system responsible for moving impulses through the heart

e. low blood pressure

f. vessels that carry blood away from the heart

Exercise 8.4   Word Building

Select a word part from the list to create the correct term for the definition provided. Note that not all word parts in the list will be used.

atrioventricul/o	*cardiopulmon/o*	*peri-*
cardi/o	*endocard*	*thromb/o*
cardiomy/o	*myocardi/o*	*ven/o*

1. _____osis means "condition of a blood clot."

2. _____itis is an inflammation of the heart muscle.

3. _____pathy means "disease of the heart muscle."

4. _____ar "means pertaining to the atrium and the ventricle."

5. _____cardium means "surrounding the heart."

Exercise 8.5 Spelling Check

Identify each term as singular or plural by writing a S or P on the short line provided; then give the opposite form (e.g., either plural or singular) on the second, longer line provided.

Term	S/P	Opposite Form
1. The <u>apices</u> of all of the hearts in the study were measured.	_____	_____
2. All of the <u>valves</u> in his heart were damaged by the toxin.	_____	_____
3. These vessels are known as the inferior and superior <u>venae cavae</u>.	_____	_____
4. The atrial and ventricular <u>septa</u> were intact.	_____	_____
5. The <u>lumina</u> of the vessels were patent.	_____	_____

Exercise 8.6 Word Maps

The concept map on the left illustrates the flow of blood past the major valves of the heart. Complete the map by placing labels in the proper order.

tricuspid valve
pulmonary valve
mitral or bicuspid valve
aortic valve

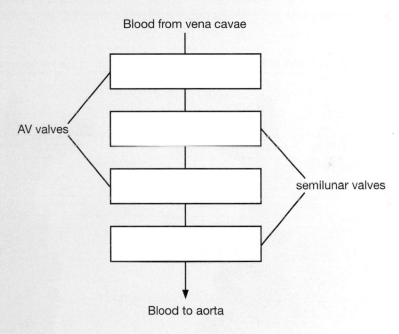

Conditions

A wide range of conditions affect the heart. As described earlier in this chapter, the heart is made up of a variety of different components, each with its own specific responsibility. Collectively, each component works together to create a functioning system. Dysfunction in any one area can create a systemic condition or a malfunction within the heart. This section identifies some effects of dysfunctioning parts.

Bradycardia is a term used to describe a slow heart rate in relation to the individual's age. This condition need not be significant, although it may decrease oxygenated blood to all parts of the body. Aging, medications used to treat high blood pressure, and damage to the heart's electrical system can lead to bradycardia. Some athletes, particularly runners, commonly have slow heart rates. **Tachycardia** describes a rapid heart rate. Tachycardia is the body's response to sending (perfusing) an adequate supply of oxygenated blood throughout the body in order to maintain homeostasis. Poor blood supply to the heart, high blood pressure, heart failure, cardiomyopathy, tumors, and infections can lead to tachycardia.

Cardiomegaly is an enlargement of the heart that can occur for a variety of reasons. Chronic hypertension, a viral infection, environmental toxins, genetics, and unknown factors can cause cardiomegaly. This condition can also occur when the muscular walls of the heart become too thick. When the heart enlarges there is often a decline in its ability to pump effectively. Figure 8.11 shows a specific type of cardiomegaly, that affecting the left ventricular, also known as *hypertrophy*.

Table 8.3 lists additional wellness and illness terms pertaining to the cardiovascular system, and Table 8.4 summarizes abnormalities in the vasculature (the arrangement of blood vessels).

FIGURE 8.11   A Normal Heart and a Heart with Ventricular Hypertrophy

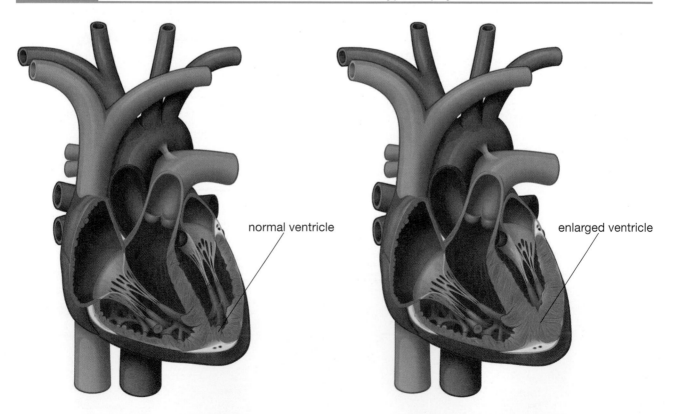

normal ventricle

enlarged ventricle

Term		Meaning	Word Analysis	
angina pectoris	[**an**-jI-nah (an-**jI**-nah) pek-**tor**-is]	pain in the chest (and often other areas such as arm, jaw, and back) caused by decreased blood flow (insufficient oxygen) to the heart	*angi/o*	blood vessel
aortic stenosis	[a-**Or**-tik sten-**O**-sis]	narrowing of the aortic valve, the main artery carrying blood from the heart to the rest of the body	*aort/o* *-ic* *stenosis*	aorta pertaining to narrowing
arrhythmia	[ah-**rith**-mee-ah]	irregular heart rhythm=	*a-* *rhythm* *-ia*	abnormal beat condition of
atrial fibrillation (a-fib)	[**ay**-tree-uhl fih-brill-**lay**-shun]	rapid, irregular (quivering) heart rate that causes poor blood flow, most common type of arrhythmia	*atri/o* *-al*	atrium pertaining to
bradycardia	[bray-dee-**kar**-dee-ah]	slow heartbeat	*brady-* *cardi/o* *-ia*	slow heart condition of
cardiac arrest		sudden, unexpected loss of heart function, breathing, and consciuosness	*cardi/o* *-ac*	heart pertaining to
cardiodynia	[kar-dee-**O**-**din**-ee-uh]	pain in the heart region	*cardi/o* *-dynia*	heart pain
cardiomegaly	[**kar**-dee-O-**meg**-ah-lee]	enlargement of the heart	*cardi/o* *megal/o* *-y*	heart enlarged condition of
cardiomy-opathy	[kar-dee-O-mI-**ah**-puh-thee]	disease of the heart muscle affecting the ability of the heart to pump blood to the rest of the body	*cardi/o* *my/o* *-pathy*	heart muscle disease
clubbing		club-shaped digits resulting from decreased blood flow and oxygenation		
congestive heart failure (CHF)	[kon-**jes**-tiv]	condition in which the heart and vessels have difficulty pumping blood throughout the body		
coronary artery disease (CAD)	[**kore**-uh-nair-ree]	buildup of fat deposits (plaque) in the coronary artery resulting in restricted blood flow	*coron/o* *-ary*	heart pertaining to
corpulmonale	[kor-pool-mah-**nahl**-ec]	enlargement of the right ventricle of the heart resulting from diseases in the lungs and pulmonary arteries	*cor* *pulmon/o*	heart lung
cyanosis	[sI-uh-**nO**-sis]	lack of oxygen in the blood (bluish skin and nail beds)	*cyan/o* *-osis*	blue abnormal condition
diaphoresis	[dI-uh-fO-**ree**-sis]	excessive sweating		
ectopia	[ek-**tO**-pee-ah]	heartbeat outside the regular rate and rhythm; originates outside the normal SA node regulation	*ecto-* *-ic*	outer, external pertaining to
endocarditis	[**en**-dO-kar-**dI**-tis]	inflammation of the endocardium	*endo-* *cardi/o* *-itis*	within, inner heart inflammation
fibrillation	[fih-bril-**ay**-shun]	extremely rapid heartbeats in which the heart muscle fibers are beating at different times, quivering, and are asynchronous		

Continues

Term		Meaning	Word Analysis	
heart block		partial or complete block of the electrical impulses from the SA node		
infarct	[**in**-farkt]	death of a part of the heart because of decreased blood supply		
ischemia	[is-**kee**-mee-ah]	decreased blood flow	*isch/o*	deficiency, suppression
			-emia	condition of blood
mammary soufflé	[**mam**-er-ee **soo**-flay]	soft blowing sound heard on auscultation of a pregnant female's heart because of increased vascularity in breasts	*mamm/o*	breast
			-ary	pertaining to
			souffler	to blow
myocardial infarction	[mI-O-**kar**-dee-al in-**fark**-shun]	decreased blood flow to the heart leading to tissue death of the heart muscle itself, also known as a *heart attack*	*my/o*	muscle
			cardi/o	heart
			-al	pertaining to
myocarditis	[mI-O-kar-**dI**-tis]	inflammation of the heart muscle	*my/o*	muscle
			cardi/o	heart
			-itis	inflammation
palpitation	[pal-pih-**tay**-shun]	feeling of the heartbeat within the chest	*palpitation*	throb
paroxysmal tachycardia	[par-oks-**iz**-mel tak-ee-**kar**-dee-ah]	sudden onset of rapid heartbeats	*paroxysmal*	sharp irritation
			tachy-	rapid
			cardi/o	heart
			-ia	condition of
pericarditis	[per-ih-kar-**dI**-tis]	inflammation of the fluid-filled sac that surrounds the heart	*peri-*	surrounding
			cardi/o	heart
			-itis	inflammation
pulmonary edema	[**pul**-muh-nair-ree eh-**dee**-muh]	excess fluid in the lungs	*pulmon/o*	lung
			-ary	pertaining to
tachycardia	[tak-ee-**kar**-dee-ah]	rapid heartbeat	*tachy-*	rapid
			cardi/o	heart
			-ia	condition of
ventricular fibrillation (v-fib)	[ven-**trik**-yoo-lur fih-brill-**lay**-shun]	rapid, irregular heart rate that is life-threatening, common in cardiac arrest patients	*ventricul/o*	ventricle
			-ar	pertaining to

TABLE 8.4 Abnormalities in the Vasculature

Term		Meaning	Word Analysis	
aneurysm	[**an**-yoo-riz-em]	balloon-like swelling of an artery	*aneurysm*	dilation
arteriosclerosis	[ar-**teer**-ee-O-skler-**O**-sis]	condition in which the walls of the small arteries are hardened	*arteri/o*	artery
			scler/o	hardening, thickening
			-osis	condition
arteriostenosis	[ar-**teer**-ee-O-sten-**O**-sis]	narrowing of the arteries	*arteri/o*	artery
			sten/o	narrowing
			-osis	condition

Continues

Term		Meaning	Word Analysis	
arteritis	[ar-ter-**I**-tis]	inflammation of an artery	*arteri/o*	artery
			-itis	inflammation
atherosclerosis	[**ath**-er-O-skler-**O**-sis]	blockage caused by lipid (fat substances) deposits in the arteries	*ather/o*	pasty material
			scler/o	hardening
			-osis	condition
embolism	[**em**-bO-liz-em]	obstruction of a vessel	*embol-*	something within
			-ism	condition of
hemorrhoid	[**hem**-uh-royd]	painfully inflamed varicose veins around the anus or lower rectum, also known as *piles*		
hyperlipemia	[**hI**-per-lip-**ee**-mee-ah]	increased fatty substances (lipids) in the blood	*hyper-*	increased
			lip/o	fatty
			-emia	condition of blood
hypertension	[hI-per-**ten**-shun]	high blood pressure	*hyper-*	increased
			tensio	to stretch
hypotension	[hI-pO-**ten**-shun]	low blood pressure	*hypo-*	decreased
			tensio	to stretch
peripheral vascular disease (PVD)	[puh-**rif**-uh-rul **vas**-kyoo-lur]	any disorder or condition that affects blood vessels outside of the heart and brain		
phlebitis	[fleh-**bI**-tis]	inflammation of a vein	*phleb/o*	vein
			-itis	inflammation
Raynaud's disease (phenomenon, syndrome)	[ray-**nOz**]	cyanosis of the fingers due to arterial contraction; usually caused by cold	*Raynaud*	19th-century French physician
superior vena cava syndrome	[soo-**peer**-ee-or **vee**-nah **kay**-vuh **sin**-drOm]	obstruction of the superior vena cava causing swelling of the vessels of the neck, coughing, and difficulty breathing	*superior*	above
			vena	vein
			cava	plural of cavus (cavity)
thrombophlebitis	[throm-bO-fleh-**bI**-tis]	inflammation in a vein caused by the formation of a blood clot	*thromb/o*	blood clot
			phleb/o	vein
			-itis	inflammation
thrombosis	[throm-**bO**-sis]	clot formation in the blood vessels	*thromb/o*	blood clot
			-osis	condition
thrombus	[**throm**-bus]	blood clot	*thromb/o*	blood clot
varicose vein	[**var**-ih-kOs vayn]	dilated and twisted vein usually found in the legs, may be superficial or deep	*varic/o*	twisted, swollen
			-ose	vein
				pertaining to
vasoconstriction	[vas-O-kon-**strik**-shun/vay-zO-kon-**strik**-shun]	narrowing of a vessel	*vas/o*	vein
			con-	with
			strictus	to draw together
vasodilation	[vas-O-dI-**lay**-shun/vay-zO-dI-**lay**-shun]	dilation of a vessel	*vas/o*	vein
			dilation	to spread out
vasospasm	[**vas**-O-spaz-em]	involuntary contraction in a vein	*vas/o*	vein

Fetuses and Newborns

The fetal heart begins to beat at approximately the third week of pregnancy. A major difference in the cardiovascular systems of a fetus and a newborn is the presence of the **ductus arteriosus (DA)**, a blood vessel that connects the aorta and pulmonary artery. While in the mother's womb, a fetus does not use the lungs because oxygen is delivered from the mother's placenta. The ductus arteriosus is responsible for carrying blood away from the heart and sending it directly to the body, bypassing the fetal lungs. The ductus arteriosus is no longer needed after birth when the newborn begins using her or his own lungs to supply oxygen to the body. Generally, the DA closes 10–15 hours after birth. Sometimes this blood vessel fails to close, resulting in a condition called **patent (open) ductus arteriosus**, which produces an excessive flow of blood into the lungs that increases the blood pressure in the pulmonary arteries.

Another type of shunt unique to the fetal heart is the **foramen ovale**. This structure develops around the fourth week of gestation and allows oxygenated blood to flow from the left to the right atrium. At birth the baby's lungs inflate and independent breathing begins. Within about an hour of birth, the foramen ovale closes. The failure of this hole to close naturally results in a condition called **patent foramen ovale (PFO)**, which occurs in 25 percent of all births.

A **murmur**, a type of irregular heart sound, may be heard for several days following birth until the fetal shunts are closed entirely. A persistent murmur may indicate the incomplete closure of a fetal shunt. A newborn's heart rate may range from 100 to 180 beats per minute and then will decrease to about 120–140 per minute when awake and about 70–90 per minute when asleep.

Skin color is critical in assessing cardiac status, particularly in the newborn. Congenital heart defects may impair cardiac function. For example, the aorta and pulmonary artery may be transposed, positioned in the opposite locations from where they should be (i.e., the aorta is located within the right ventricle, and the pulmonary artery is located within the left ventricle). This defect is called **transposition of the great vessels**. Figure 8.12 A–G and Table 8.5 provide descriptions and illustrations of other defects.

TABLE 8.5 | Congenital Heart Defects

Defect	Description	
atrial septal defect (ASD)	abnormal opening in the wall that separates the top two chambers of the heart (atrial septum), resulting in excessive pulmonary blood flow	**FIGURE 8.12A** Atrial Septal Defect (ASD)

Continues

Defect	Description	
coarctation of the aorta	narrowing of the aorta; the heart must pump harder to force blood through; often occurs with other heart defects	**FIGURE 8.12B** Coarctation of the Aorta 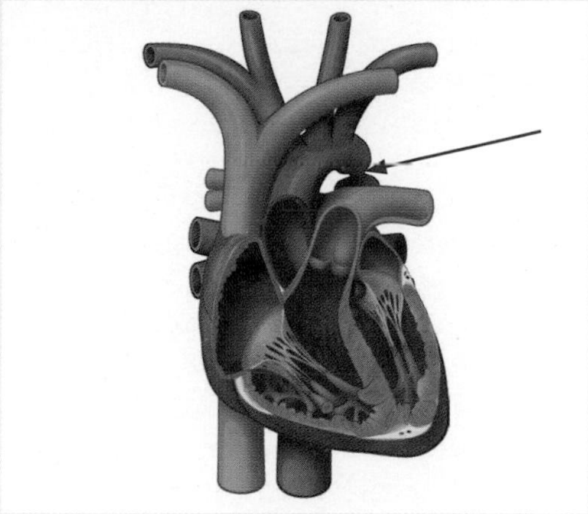
patent foramen ovale	condition in which the foramen ovale remains open following birth	**FIGURE 8.12C** Patent Foramen Ovale 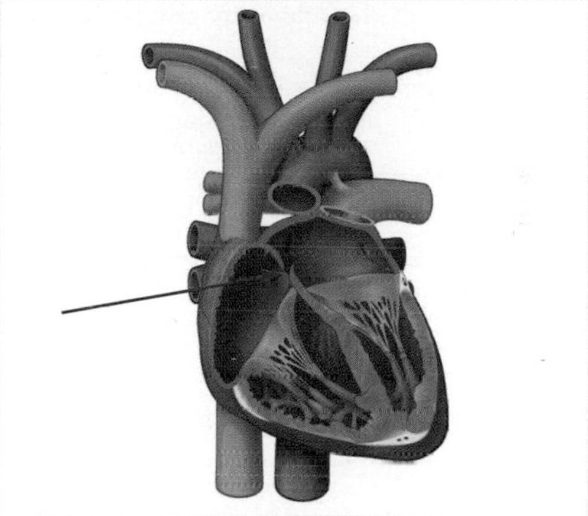
patent ductus arteriosus (PDA)	condition in which the ductus arteriosus remains open following birth	**FIGURE 8.12D** Patent Ductus Arteriosus (PDA) 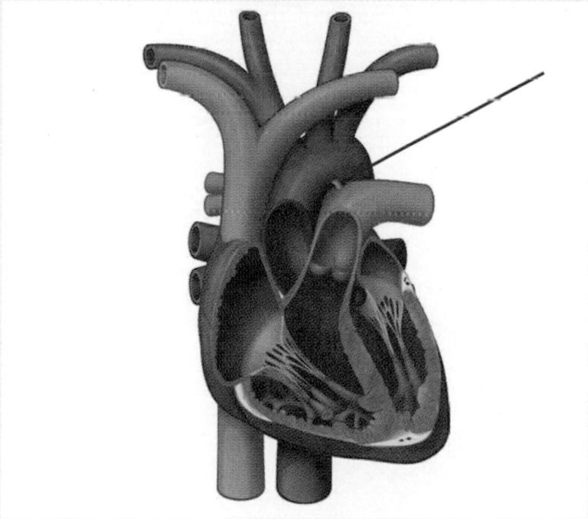

Continues

Defect	Description	
pulmonic stenosis	improper development of the pulmonary valve in the first 8 weeks of pregnancy	**FIGURE 8.12E** Pulmonic Stenosis 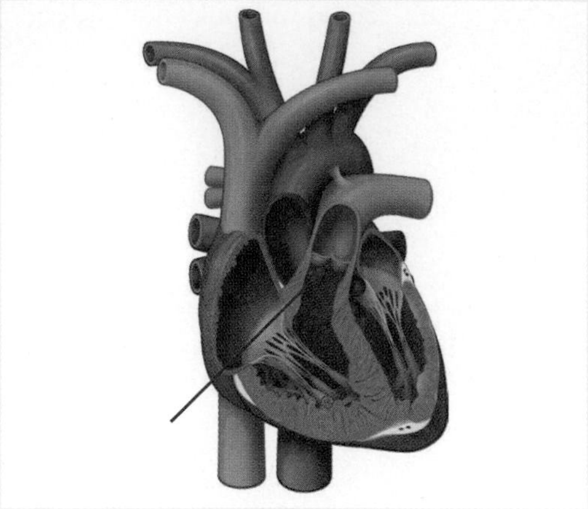
tetralogy of Fallot	abnormality consisting of four defects: (1) pulmonary artery stenosis (narrowing of the pulmonary valve); (2) ventricular septal defect; (3) right ventricular hypertrophy (muscle of the right ventricle is enlarged); and (4) overriding of the aorta (aorta is located between the left and right ventricles; this defect is the most common cause of blue baby syndrome, a condition that is due to excessive oxygen-poor blood circulating to the body)	**FIGURE 8.12F** Tetralogy of Fallot 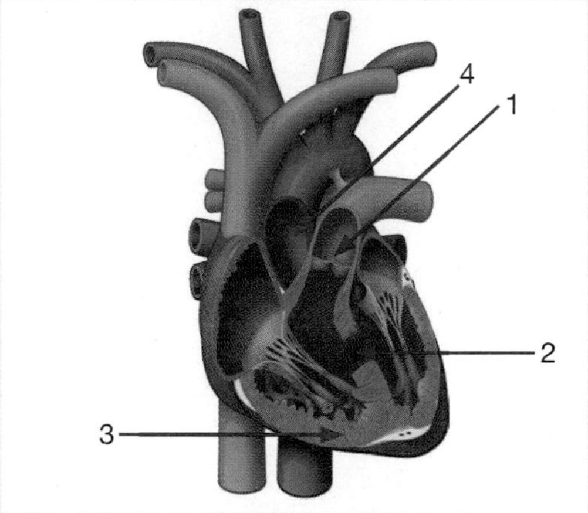
ventricular septal defect (VSD)	abnormal opening or hole in the septum between ventricles (allows blood from both sides of the heart to mix)	**FIGURE 8.12G** Ventricular Septal Defect (VSD) 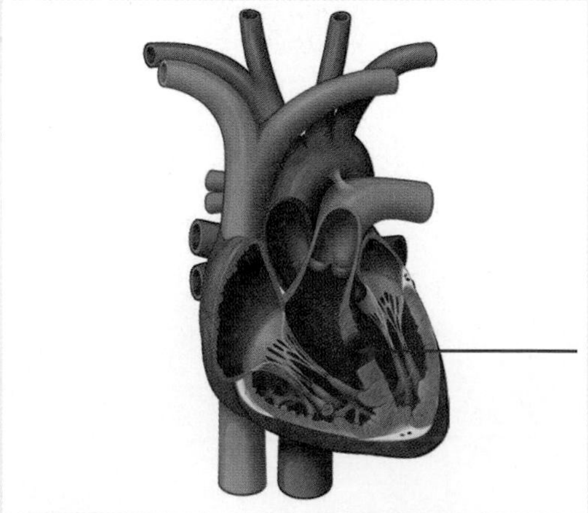

Children

The assessment of cardiovascular problems in children includes growth and development, activity level, school performance, skin color, and **clubbing** of fingers and toes (softened nail beds, short and bulging digits). A child who is not growing appropriately or has decreased energy may have inadequate circulation or poorly oxygenated blood. **Innocent** or **functional** murmurs in childhood are not uncommon. These murmurs have no significance, but the child is usually referred to a pediatric cardiologist for further testing to make that determination.

Pregnant Women

During pregnancy, the blood volume increases by about 40 percent, causing changes within the cardiovascular system. To compensate for the increased blood volume, pulse rate increases and blood pressure changes. Toward the end of pregnancy and in lactating mothers, a murmur termed **mammary soufflé** may be heard because of the increased blood flow through the vessels leading to the mammary artery in the breasts.

Adults and Seniors

As a person matures, the factors of lifestyle, habits, and general health figure significantly into the aging of the cardiovascular system. Tobacco, alcohol, diet, weight, cholesterol, diabetes, exercise, and stress can all influence cardiac risk. It is important to control these factors as there are aspects—age and genetics—that we cannot control.

Certain changes occur normally as a person ages. The blood pressure increases by about 25 percent from ages 20 to 80 years because of the normal calcification (narrowing) of the large arteries. The left ventricular wall thickens by about 25 percent to accommodate the stiffening of the vessels. **Arrhythmias**, irregular heartbeats, may be found in the aging adult. **Ectopic** heartbeats, those outside the normal conduction pathway from the SA to the AV nodes, also may occur. This condition can be used to describe the presence of extra heartbeats or skipped heartbeats.

Coronary artery disease (CAD) is a common illness as we age. Plaque, cholesterol, and other compounds build up on the inside of the arteries. This buildup reduces the diameter of an artery (narrowing) and leads to a reduction in blood flow. CAD is commonly known as the "hardening" of the arteries. Hardened arteries result in blockages that lead to an inadequate supply of oxygenated blood to the heart, a condition known as **ischemia**. Angina is the chest pain that develops as a result of ischemia. Treatment consists of medicines, balloons and stents, and bypass surgery.

If the blockages cause an extended disruption in blood flow, this can result in the permanent loss of heart muscle in the affected area and may lead to systolic heart failure. Symptoms include shortness of breath, difficulty breathing while lying flat, and increased fatigue.

Congestive heart failure develops when the heart is weakened and does not pump blood efficiently. This condition could be the result of narrowed arteries in the heart or high blood pressure. Symptoms include the buildup of fluid in the arms, legs, ankles, feet, lungs, and around the heart (which can become life-threatening).

Although valve defects may be present at birth, some defects result from calcification of the valve. Calcium buildup can occur as an individual ages. The murmurs associated with valve defects are listed in Table 8.6. Table 8.7 describes abnormal heart sounds.

Did You Know?

Heart failure occurs without congestion. Heart failure can be classified as systolic or diastolic heart failure and acute, chronic, or acute on chronic heart failure.

TABLE 8.6 Valve Defects

Type of Defect or Murmur	Description
aortic regurgitation	blood flows in two directions as blood leaks back in the aorta each time the ventricle relaxes (during diastole)
aortic stenosis	aortic valve narrows, obstructing blood flow into the aorta; heart is forced to work harder to pump blood, eventually weakening heart muscle
mitral regurgitation	mitral valve fails to close tightly, leading to backflow; blood moves inefficiently through the heart
mitral stenosis	a disorder in which mitral valve does not open properly, restricting blood flow through the heart
mitral valve prolapse (MVP)	condition in which the two valves between the left atrium and left ventricle do not close properly; common cause of a heart murmur
pulmonic regurgitation	pulmonic valve fails to close tightly, leading to backflow from the pulmonary artery to the right ventricle
tricuspid regurgitation	blood flows in two directions as blood leaks back through the tricuspid valve into the right atrium
tricuspid stenosis	tricuspid valve is narrowed and does not open properly, decreasing the flow of blood from the right atrium into the right ventricle during diastole

TABLE 8.7 Abnormal Heart Sounds

Term	Description
bruit	high-pitched blowing or swishing sound, pronounced **broo**-ee
click	clicking caused by mitral valve prolapse (click murmur syndrome, Jod Baslow disease, or floppy valve syndrome)
flutter	extremely rapid, irregular heart beat
gallop	very rapid heartbeat that sounds like a horse's gallop
murmur	gentle blowing, fluttering, humming sound
rub	friction heard as a grating (scratching) sound from inflamed pericardial surface rubbing during heart's contraction
rumble	low-pitched murmur
thrill	type of heart sound that can be felt as a vibration by placing the hand over the heart

Checkpoint 8.2

Answer the following questions to identify any areas of the section that you may need to review.

1. What is the name of the blood vessel that closes soon after birth and is responsible for connecting the aorta and pulmonary artery in a fetus?

   _____

2. Which abnormal heart sound resonates as a high-pitched blowing or swishing sound?

   _____

3. What medical condition develops when the heart muscle is weakened and does not pump efficiently?

   _____

Exercise 8.7   Word Analysis

On the line in the Word Analysis column, write each term divided into its word parts by hyphens. Identify the parts by type, using a letter for each part (P = prefix, CF = combining form, or S = suffix). Then define the term.

Term	Word Analysis	Definition
1. pericarditis	_____	_____
2. pulmonic	_____	_____
3. stenosis	_____	_____
4. myocardial	_____	_____
5. endocarditis	_____	_____

Exercise 8.8   Comprehension Check

Circle the appropriate term from each pair in the following sentences.

1. Mr. Donnelley has been experiencing palpations/palpitations for the past week.

2. The ECG revealed several exotic/ectopic beats.

3. The patient's existing respiratory problems were exacerbated by her conclusive/congestive heart failure.

4. Marked clubbing/clutting was noted in the phalanges of both hands.

5. An ECG was ordered to evaluate the patient's arrhythmias/arrithymia.

Exercise 8.9   Matching

Match the terms in column 1 with the definitions in column 2. Write the letter of the definition in the space beside the term.

1. _____ thrombus
2. _____ valvular
3. _____ hypotension
4. _____ arterial stenosis
5. _____ systole

a. condition of narrowing of an artery
b. blood clot
c. low blood pressure
d. pertaining to a valve
e. contraction of the heart

Exercise 8.10 Word Building

Create a term to match the definition given. Suffixes have been provided.

1. condition of narrowing or constriction   _____-osis

2. condition of hardening   _____-osis

3. x-ray of a blood vessel   _____-gram

4. around the heart   _____-al

5. structure within the heart   _____-ium

Exercise 8.11 Spelling Check

In the sentences that follow, incorrect prefixes or suffixes are used in the medical terms. Provide the correct prefix or suffix for each term by writing the corrected term on the blank line provided.

1. The patient's bacterial endocardioma was treated with antibiotics.

   _____

2. An embolotomy is an obstruction of a vessel.

   _____

3. Mr. Bowers was brought to the emergency room with a hypercardial infarction.

   _____

4. Cardiotrophy is an enlargement of the heart.

   _____

5. The patient's prelipemia was diagnosed with laboratory tests.

   _____

Exercise 8.12   Word Maps

1. List the four major heart valves.

   _____   _____

   _____   _____

2. Provide the terms that match the definitions/descriptions.

   _____ restriction of blood flow due to narrowing

   _____ backflow of blood due to incomplete closure of valve

3. Using the information from questions 1 and 2, create a concept map showing eight major types of valvular defects; describe each briefly. (Hint: start with the four valve names.)

Diagnostic Tests and Examinations

Heart disease is the leading cause of death for both men and women in the United States. Public health efforts now target prevention programs in smoking cessation, lowering cholesterol and high blood pressure, the maintenance of healthy weight, and active lifestyles/exercise to reduce the risk of heart disease. Public access defibrillator (PAD) programs have also been implemented across the country placing AEDs (automated external defibrillators) in public places in order to reduce emergency response times for those experiencing sudden cardiac arrest.

Chest pain has been reported as the main reason over 6 million people are rushed to the emergency room each year in the United States; chest pain accounts for 25 percent of all hospital admissions. Healthcare facilities have protocols in place when caring for patients who present with symptoms of heart-related illness. Many heart-related illnesses present quickly, but others can be diagnosed during routine physical exams.

The physical examination involves inspection of the patient's temperature, as well as inspecting the color and texture of the patient's skin. Cyanosis, or bluish color, of the skin or nail beds may indicate insufficient oxygenated blood flow throughout the body. Paleness may suggest decreased blood flow. All pulses are palpated. A strong, regular pulse should be felt at all pulse points (see Figure 8.9). A weak pulse could indicate decreased circulation or a blockage leading to that pulse area.

The **stethoscope** is an instrument used to **auscultate**, or listen to, the heart. The normal heart sound is a steady *lub-dub*. The *lub*, documented as S1, is the first sound heard and represents the closing of the AV valves as the ventricles contract (systole). It is a longer and lower-pitched sound than the *dub*, S2, which is the sound of the semilunar valves closing in relaxation (diastole). The examiner listens to the heart on several specific areas of the chest to hear each of the possible sounds of the valves in systole and diastole.

In the Know: The Emergency Medical Treatment and Labor Act

Congress has a standard in place ensuring public access to emergency services regardless of ability to pay; this is known as the Emergency Medical Treatment and Active Labor Act (EMTALA), passed in 1986. Facilities can lose federal Medicare and Medicaid funding if they fail to screen, stabilize, and transfer patients who arrive with medical emergencies (including patients in labor). Facilities can be fined for turning away patients or for not providing appropriate care.

Many of the problems that occur within the cardiovascular system develop gradually, and patients often do not display signs and symptoms until the situation has become advanced. For instance, coronary artery disease is a slow process of plaque buildup in the blood vessels. Chest pain might provide a warning, but usually the individual does not realize that the heart muscle has been damaged until a heart attack occurs.

Some health providers feel that every five years, adults over the age of 20 should undergo a routine screening blood test often referred to as a **lipid profile**. This test measures the serum **cholesterol (total)**, the **high-density (HDL)** and **low-density lipoproteins (LDL)**, and the **triglycerides** levels in the blood. Cholesterol levels represent one of the risk factors for developing arteriosclerosis. A high blood concentration of cholesterol (total), low-density lipoproteins (LDL), and triglycerides increases the risk for arteriosclerosis. Individuals with heart disease or abnormal lipid levels should be screened every one to two years.

A common screening method to evaluate cardiac status is the **electrocardiogram (ECG** or **EKG)**. This test determines the electrical activity generated through the heart's conduction system. Each time electrical currents spread through the tissues on the surface of the body, the heart pumps. The ECG is a graphic record that traces these signals (see Figure 8.13). When the heart muscle is damaged or abnormalities occur in the cardiac cycle, the ECG can detect these changes in the form of premature beats, irregular beats, or life threatening arrhythmias. The **echocardiogram** is an ultrasound of the heart that provides a view of the four heart valves, the pumping strength of the heart, and can evaluate congenital defects. This is a noninvasive procedure, which means that no incision is made. A **multigated acquisition (MUGA)** scan is used to evaluate the functions of the heart's ventricles using an intravenously administered radioactive tracer that makes the movement of blood show more clearly on the scan. This scan can give a specific evaluation of the pumping strength of the heart.

Table 8.8 identifies common diagnostic tests and examinations used to discover cardiovascular system conditions.

Did You Know?

A MUGA scan is also known as *nuclear blood scan*, *cardiac blood pooling imaging*, *nuclear ventriculography*, and *radionuclide ventriculograph*.

FIGURE 8.13 | Heart Rhythms in ECG Tests

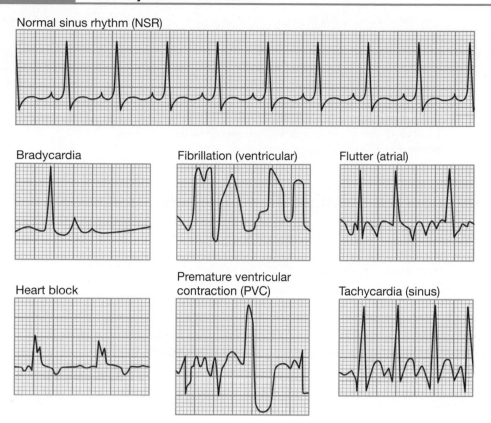

Normal sinus rhythm (NSR)

Bradycardia

Fibrillation (ventricular)

Flutter (atrial)

Heart block

Premature ventricular contraction (PVC)

Tachycardia (sinus)

TABLE 8.8 | Diagnostic Tests and Examinations Associated with the Cardiovascular System

Term		Meaning
angiography	[an-jee-**og**-raf-ee]	procedure to determine the flow of blood through the heart and main vessels; a catheter is inserted into a main vessel and threaded into the coronary artery; dye is injected through the catheter and the heart is visualized on a on a monitor; also known as a *cardiac catherization*
auscultation and percussion	[oss-kull-**tay**-shun] [pur-**kuh**-shun]	process of listening (auscultating) to internal body sounds, generally by using a stethoscope or tapping (percussing)
blood pressure (BP)		measurement of systolic over diastolic pressure; measured using a sphygmomanometer
cardiac enzymes test		test that detects the amount of cardiac enzymes present in the blood; assesses whether a patient is currently experiencing or recently had a heart attack
echocardiogram	[ek-O-**kar**-dee-O-gram]	ultrasound that records the function of the valves and flow of blood through the heart
electrocardiography (ECG/EKG)	[ee-lek-trO-kar-dee-**ah**-graf-ee]	recording of electrical impulses of the heart
Holter monitor	[**hOl**-tur]	portable electrocardiograph worn to record the heart's functioning during a patient's normal daily activities
magnetic resonance imaging (MRI)		imaging tool used to detect areas of myocardial infarction, narrowing, and obstructed blood flow
positron emission tomography scan (PET)	[**poz**-ih-tron ee-**mih**-shun tO-mah-graf-ee]	imaging test that uses a radioactive substance called a tracer to identify disease or obstructed blood flow in the heart

Continues

Term		Meaning
serum cholesterol	[**seer**-em kO-**les**-ter-ol]	blood test to determine the level of the lipid cholesterol in the blood
thallium stress test	[**thal**-ee-um]	the radioactive substance thallium is injected into the patient to enable visualization of the heart's functioning during activity (walking on a treadmill) and then resting after the exercise, used to identify the presence or absence of CAD; also known as *myocardial perfusion imaging (MPI)*
transesophageal echocardiography (TEE)	[trans-eh-sof-ah-**jee**-al **ek**-O-kar-dee-**og**-raf-ee]	test in which a probe is passed down the throat and into the esophagus to produce a detailed ultrasound image of the heart

Soft Skills for Medical Professionals: Professional Appearance

You may encounter a variety of workplace environments that dictate what you can and cannot wear to the office. Whether you are looking for work or have been employed at the same job for decades, maintaining a professional appearance is essential. Those who deal directly with patients in a healthcare facility may be required to wear scrubs that are neat and clean, keep their nails short and unpolished, and avoid perfumes, cigarette smoke, and any odors that could offend patients with odor sensitivities. Many of these rules are enforced to keep the facility clean and assist in providing high-quality care to patients. In addition to following the dress code, healthcare professionals practice good hygiene and represent themselves and their employer in the best possible manner.

Checkpoint 8.3

Answer the following questions to identify any areas of the section that you may need to review.

1. What is the name of the serum test that measures the levels of total cholesterol, HDL, LDL, and triglycerides in the blood?

   _____

2. What common screening method is used to determine cardiac status?

   _____

3. What radioactive substance is injected into a patient to enable visualization of heart function during activity (walking on a treadmill) and then resting after the exercise?

   _____

Treatments

Healthcare practitioners use predetermined guidelines to direct patient care. These guidelines, known as clinical practice guidelines and evidence-based practices, have been developed by the specialty societies based on past clinical research. They represent the treatment pathways that have achieved the best outcomes. Treatment decisions generally fall into three categories: surgical, clinical, and pharmacological.

Surgical treatments are generally invasive as they involve a puncture or an incision into the skin. *Clinical treatments* are generally noninvasive and involve nonsurgical techniques (e.g., physical therapy). *Pharmacological treatments* involve the utilization of medicines (drugs) to treat specific illnesses or diseases. Medication therapies are regulated by the Food and Drug Administration (FDA). To be approved by the FDA for use in the United States, every medicine must be backed by research studies that have shown the medication to be effective in its treatment of a given disease and has a tolerable safety profile. The following sections provide an overview of treatments common to the cardiovascular system.

Surgical Treatments

Cardiac surgery has evolved from bypassing obstructed vessels and the repair or replacement of valves to transplants that involve the replacement of the entire heart. **Coronary artery bypass grafts (CABG)** are used to bypass blocked sections of obstructed heart vessels with grafts taken from other parts of the body to restore blood flow to the heart muscle.

Interventional cardiology is a specialty that has evolved over the past 30 years and continues to grow as new procedures are developed. In **cardiac catheterization**, also known as an **angiogram**, a doctor threads a flexible tube (catheter) into the heart through one of the large vessels, usually starting in the femoral artery in the groin or the radial artery. A dye is injected into the catheter, and through fluoroscopy, the heart and surrounding blood vessels, including areas of blockage and restriction, can be seen on a monitor. Repair can often be achieved during angiography through a **balloon angioplasty procedure**, or **percutaneous transluminal coronary angioplasty (PTCA)**. In the balloon angioplasty, or PTCA, a catheter with a balloon tip is inserted into the obstructed vessel; the balloon is then inflated to open the vessel and allow the free flow of blood. Stents are also used to treat coronary artery disease. These tube-like devices are placed within the coronary arteries to keep the arteries open and maintain blood flow (see Figure 8.14). Stents can be bare-metal or drug-eluding. Bare-metal stents can become blocked when the body's immune

---

FIGURE 8.14 Percutaneous Transluminal Coronary Angioplasty (PTCA)

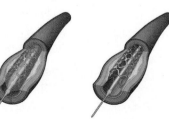

obstructed artery

a tiny balloon is temporarily inserted

the balloon is inflated to widen the clogged artery

stent placed to help prop the artery open

balloon and catheter removed, stent is a permanent fixture

response initiates the growth of scar tissue over the stent. Drug-eluding stents reduce the incidence of re-occlusion by releasing drugs that prevent the body from rejecting the stent. Other procedures remove plaque from the blood vessels. An **endarterectomy** is a procedure to remove the lining of an artery that contains plaque (see Figure 8.15). Table 8.9 identifies common surgical procedures related to the cardiovascular system.

FIGURE 8.15 Endarterectomy

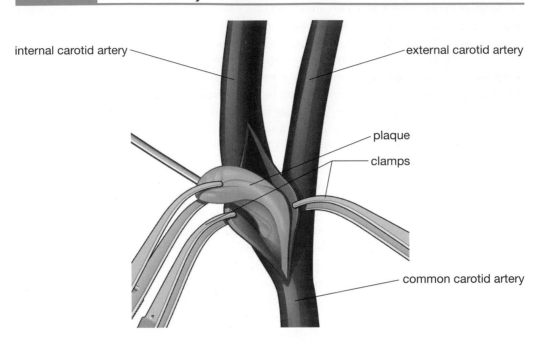

internal carotid artery — external carotid artery — plaque — clamps — common carotid artery

TABLE 8.9 Surgical Treatments Associated with the Cardiovascular System

Treatment		Description
angiectomy	[an-jee-**ek**-tuh-mee]	removal of a blood vessel
angioplasty	[**an**-jee-O-**plas**-tee]	procedure to repair a vessel, usually a main vessel of the heart
atherectomy	[ath-uh-**rek**-tuh-mee]	removal of plaque from the coronary artery through a catheter
balloon angioplasty	[**an**-jee-O-**plas**-tee]	procedure in which a balloon-tipped catheter is inserted into the coronary artery and then inflated to push plaque against the vessel walls and free an obstruction
cardiac pacemaker		small device placed in the chest or abdomen to help control abnormal heart rhythms
coronary artery bypass graft (CABG)	[**kor**-ah-nar-ee]	procedure that surgically places a healthy artery or vein on each side of an obstructed vessel, allowing blood to go around (bypass) the blockage
coronary stent		tube-like device placed within the coronary arteries to keep the arteries open and maintain blood flow
defibrillator	[dee-**fib**-ruh-lay-tur]	external or implantable medical device that transmits an electric shock to the heart to restore a normal rhythm
heart transplant		procedure to remove a damaged or diseased heart and replace it with a healthy heart
percutaneous transluminal coronary angioplasty (PTCA)	[per-kyoo-**tay**-nee-us trans-**loo**-min-al **an**-jee-O-**plas**-tee]	procedure in which a balloon-tipped catheter (a stent) is inserted into the coronary artery and then inflated to push plaque against the vessel walls and free an obstruction
phlebectomy	[fleh-**bek**-tuh-mee]	removal of a vein

Continues

Treatment		Description
thrombophlebectomy	[throm-bO-fluh-**bek**-tuh-mee]	removal of a thrombus (clot) from a vein
sclerotherapy	[skleh-rO-**thair**-uh-pee]	cosmetic procedure in which a solution is injected to fade varicose/spider veins
valvuloplasty	[**val**-vyoo-lO-plas-tee]	repair of a constricted heart valve through the use of a balloon-tipped catheter

Pharmacological Treatments

Agents used in cardiology involve those that improve the function and rhythm of the heart muscle (for example, beta-blockers, angiotensin convertase enzyme inhibitors, and antiarrhythmics); eliminate excess fluid (diuretics); or ensure the flow of blood through the vessels (such as anticoagulants). Note that although calcium channel blockers (CCBs) are used to treat hypertension, angina, and some arrythmias; CCBs are to be avoided in patients in heart failure. Other agents include antihypertensives to decrease blood pressure and hypolipidemics to decrease serum cholesterol levels. Many patients take multiple drugs to achieve therapeutic results or to avoid the undesirable side effects of other drugs. Table 8.10 describes the drugs that are most commonly used to treat problems with the cardiovascular system.

TABLE 8.10 Pharmacologic Agents Associated with the Cardiovascular System

Drug Class	Use	Generic Name	Brand Name
angiotensin-converting enzyme (ACE) inhibitors	relax blood vessels, prevent vasoconstriction; commonly used to prevent hypertension and heart failure	captopril enalapril lisinopril quinapril ramipril	Capoten Vasotec Prinivil Accupril Altace
antianginals (nitrates)	relax and widen blood vessels, relieve the pain of acute angina; also used to prevent hypertension and heart failure	nitroglycerin (Nitro)	Isordil (isosorbide dinitrate) Nitrolingual (spray) Nitrostat (sublingual) Minitran (patch)
antiarrhythmics	improve/restore abnormal rhythms	amiodarone flecainide	Cordarone, Pacerone Tambocor
anticoagulants	keep blood flowing without thromboses; prevent the formation of blood clots	aspirin heparin warfarin	Bufferin, Ecotrin Hep-Lock Coumadin
beta-blockers	block receptors in the heart to decrease the heart rate and the force of contraction, lowering blood pressure	atenolol propranolol metoprolol	Tenormin Inderal Lopressor, Toprol
calcium channel blockers	inhibit the flow of calcium into the heart and blood vessels, leading to muscle relaxation	amlodipine nifedipine verapamil diltiazem	Norvasc Adalat, Procardia Calan, Verelan Cardizem, Dilacor
diuretics	decrease fluid retention by promoting increased urinary output (diuresis)	furosemide hydrochlorothiazide	Lasix Hydrodiuril
hypolipidemics	decrease cholesterol level in the blood	lovastatin simvastatin	Mevacor Zocor
thrombolytics "clot-busters"	dissolve blood clots	tissue plasminogen activator (tPA), streptokinase, tenecteplase	TNKase

In the Know: Future Directions of the Cardiovascular System

Technology advances every day and continues to advance in the medical field. Numerous mobile applications have been created to assist health care providers in the care of their patients. For implantable cardiac devices, such as pacemakers, mobile applications have the ability to monitor and report real-time diagnostic information. This type of information is essential for clinical care and will allow physicians to access cardiac device diagnostic information and patient data directly from their mobile devices, allowing them to review a patient's last transmission, compare this information to the patient's clinical history, triage, and take action as needed.

Checkpoint 8.4

Answer the following questions to identify any areas of the section that you may need to review.

1. What is the name of the procedure that attempts to improve blood flow in an obstructed vessel by inserting a balloon?

   _____

2. What external or implantable medical device transmits an electric shock to the heart to restore a normal rhythm?

   _____

3. Which class of drug is used to relax blood vessels and relieve the pain of acute angina?

   _____

Abbreviations

In the medical field, information is generally recorded in medical charts and provided to healthcare workers in medical shorthand. It is important that healthcare professionals become familiar with the abbreviations used on a daily basis to successfully perform the duties assigned in a typical workday. Table 8.11 provides a list of common abbreviations used in reference to conditions and treatments of the cardiovascular system.

TABLE 8.11 Abbreviations Associated with the Cardiovascular System

Abbreviation	Meaning
AF	atrial fibrillation
AMI	acute myocardial infarction
AS	aortic stenosis
ASD	atrial septal defect
ASHD	arteriosclerotic heart disease
AV	atrioventricular; also abbreviated as A-V
BBB	bundle-branch block

Continues

Abbreviation	Meaning
BP	blood pressure
CAD	coronary artery disease
CCU	coronary care unit
CHF	congestive heart failure
CO	cardiac output
CO_2	carbon dioxide
CPR	cardiopulmonary resuscitation
CV	cardiovascular
CX	circumflex (artery)
DOE	dyspnea on exertion
DVT	deep vein thrombosis
ECG or EKG	electrocardiogram
ECHO	echocardiogram
HDL	high density lipoprotein
HF	heart failure
HTN	hypertension
ICA	internal carotid artery
IMA	internal mammary artery
IV	intravenous
LA	left atrium
LAD	left anterior descending coronary artery
LCA	left coronary artery
LDL	low-density lipoprotein
LIMA	left internal mammary artery
LMCA	left main coronary artery
LPA	left pulmonary artery
LV	left ventricle
MI	myocardial infarction
MPA	main pulmonary artery
MR	mitral regurgitation
MS	mitral stenosis
MVP	mitral valve prolapse
O_2	oxygen
PA	pulmonary artery
PAC	premature atrial contraction
PAT	paroxysmal atrial tachycardia
PDA	posterior descending artery; patent ductus arteriosus
PMI	point of maximal impulse
PND	paroxysmal nocturnia dyspnea
PTCA	percutaneous transluminal coronary angioplasty
PV	pulmonary vein
PVC	premature ventricular contraction
PVD	peripheral vascular disease
RA	right atrium
RCA	right coronary artery

Continues

Abbreviation	Meaning
RIMA	right internal mammary artery
RPA	right pulmonary artery
RV	right ventricle
SA	sinoatrial node
SCA	sudden cardiac arrest
SOB	shortness of breath
SSS	sick sinus syndrome
TS	tricuspid stenosis
TV	tricuspid valve
VF	ventricular fibrillation
VSD	ventricular septal defect
VT	ventricular tachycardia

Exercise 8.13   Word Analysis

On the line in the Word Analysis column, write each term divided into its word parts by slashes. Identify the parts by type, using a letter for each part (P = prefix, CF = combining form, and S = suffix). Then define the term.

	Term	Word Analysis	Definition
1.	cardiology	_____	_____
2.	vascular	_____	_____
3.	thrombosis	_____	_____
4.	septal	_____	_____
5.	ventricular	_____	_____

Exercise 8.14   Spelling Check

Read each sentence and determine whether the boldface terms are spelled correctly. If the spelling is correct, write the word "correct" on the blank line. If the spelling is incorrect, rewrite the word accurately on the blank line.

1. The gunshot injury included damage to the patient's **inferior venous cannae**.   _____

2. Each of Dr. Benton's patients has a yearly **lipstick** risk panel.   _____

3. Dr. Thompson's patient is scheduled for a **PCAT** tomorrow.   _____

4. Mr. Blaise will have the **CABAGE** procedure this morning.   _____

5. **Cardiac inzymes** were also elevated.   _____

Exercise 8.15   Matching

Match each procedure or treatment in column 2 with the description of the procedure or treatment in column 1.

1. _____ visualize heart action during exercise and recovery

2. _____ assess the electrical conduction system of the heart to determine cardiac status

3. _____ remove a damaged blood vessel

4. _____ visualize the heart and vasculature by fluoroscopy

5. _____ assess the risk of heart disease related to a fatty substance found in the blood

a. electrocardiogram

b. lipid risk panel

c. thallium stress test

d. angiography

e. angiectomy

Exercise 8.16   Word Building

Identify word parts in this chapter to construct medical terms for the definitions that follow. Note that part of each term has been provided. Complete the term by writing the missing word part on the blank provided.

1. study of the heart _____ology

2. record of the electrical activity of the heart electro_____

3. pertaining to the atrium _____al

4. agent against clotting (coagulation) anti _____

5. agent against cardiac pain (angina) _____al

Exercise 8.17   Spelling Check

Identify each term as singular or plural by writing a P or an S beside the term; then write the opposite form (i.e., either singular or plural) on the line provided.

Term	P/S	Opposite Form
1. ventricle	_____	_____
2. atrium	_____	_____
3. vena cava	_____	_____
4. angioplasty	_____	_____
5. diuretic	_____	_____

Exercise 8.18   Identification

Review the image below and 1) identify the procedure and 2) describe the procedure in your own words.

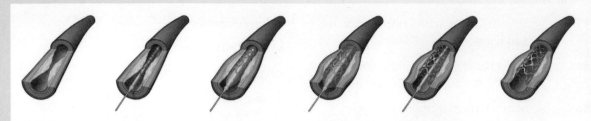

1. Procedure: _____

2. Description: _____

_____

_____

_____

_____

_____

_____

_____

_____

_____

Chapter Review

After successfully completing this chapter, you should be able to correctly answer the following review questions. Answers are provided in the back of the text. Use this self-assessment opportunity to check your understanding of the content and determine whether you need to revisit any of the chapter's content.

Crossword Puzzle

Use the clues provided to fill in the puzzle with the correct terms. Enter one letter per square.

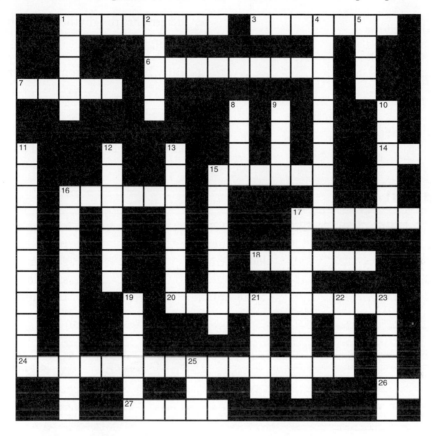

Across
1. dilation of an artery
3. death of a part of the heart
6. inflammation of a vein
7. lip/o
14. sinoatrial node
15. chest pain of cardiac origin
16. abnormal heart sound produced by turbulent blood flow in the heart
17. tiny vein
18. my/o
20. instrument for listening
24. hardening of an artery

26. abbreviation for mitral stenosis
27. word part meaning narrowing

Down
1. largest artery in the body
2. tachy
4. listen to sounds produced in the body
5. thrombus
8. phleb/o; vas/o
9. word part meaning surrounding
10. angi/o
11. rapid heart rate
12. pertaining to the heart

13. heart inflammation
15. vessels that carry blood away from the heart
16. inflammation of the heart muscle
17. involuntary contraction of a vein
19. fatty substances
21. cardio
22. word part meaning condition
23. word part meaning surgical removal
25. prefix meaning with

Matching

Match the following terms to their proper definitions.

1. _____ arteries
2. _____ mitral valve
3. _____ capillaries
4. _____ cardiomegaly
5. _____ cyanosis
6. _____ endocardium
7. _____ myocardium
8. _____ pericardium
9. _____ sinoatrial (SA) node
10. _____ tachycardia

a. outermost layer of the heart
b. middle layer of the heart
c. innermost layer of the heart
d. separates the left atrium from the left ventricle
e. determines the rhythm of the heartbeat
f. smallest vessels
g. carry blood away from the heart
h. rapid heart rate
i. enlargement of the heart
j. lack of oxygen in the blood

Identification

Using the provided terms, label the illustration by writing the correct term on its corresponding line.

aorta	left atrium	right ventricle
apex	left ventricle	semilunar valves
chordae tendinae	mitral valve	superior vena cava
inferior vena cava	right atrium	tricuspid valve

1. _____
2. _____
3. _____
4. _____
5. _____
6. _____
7. _____
8. _____
9. _____
10. _____
11. _____
12. _____

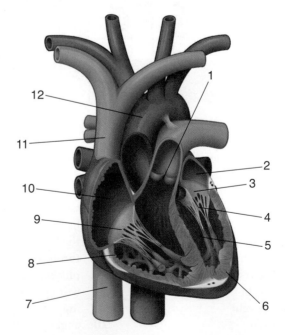

Abbreviations

Identify the correct complete name of the abbreviations in the sentences provided.

1. The image taken of the patient's LAD was sent to the specialist. _____

2. The doctor ordered a MUGA. _____

3. The patient suffered from CAD. _____

4. She was sent to the CCU to meet with her next patient. _____

5. The patient suffered from SOB and a physical exam was ordered. _____

Word-Building Challenge

Review the following list of terms. Apply what you have learned in this chapter by identifying the meaning of each term. Write your answer on the line provided.

1. thrombophlebitis _____

   _____

2. cardiodynia _____

   _____

3. dysrhythmia _____

   _____

4. hypotension _____

   _____

5. pericardiocentesis _____

   _____

6. angiogenesis _____

   _____

Extension Activities

Complete the following activities as assigned by your instructor.

1. Search the Internet for local medical practitioners who perform procedures related to the treatment of scleroderma (varicose veins). What type of medical specialists perform these procedures? Is the procedure viewed as cosmetic or as a medical necessity? Create a post in the discussion forum to share your findings with the class.

2. This chapter briefly mentioned the congressional statute enacted in 1986 titled EMTALA. This legislation was implemented to prevent healthcare facilities from restricting access to emergency care to those who have the means to pay for the services rendered. Conduct an Internet search to obtain specific information regarding this legislation. Who are "participating providers" and how can they be affected by noncompliance? How does the legislation define an "emergency medical condition"? When can a patient be transferred to another facility? Go one step further and find an example in which this legislation has been successful in identifying and disciplining a facility for noncompliance. Share your findings with the class as directed by your instructor.

3. Access to AEDs (automated external defibrillators) by non-healthcare professionals has become common in the United States owing to the presence of PAD (public access defibrillation) programs. Create a presentation on the benefits of PAD programs in the United States. What types of facilities have implemented them? What are the requirements for implementing a program? What protection is provided to those who use an AED on members of the general public? Present your findings in a PowerPoint presentation with 5–10 slides.

Student eResources

The Course Navigator learning management system that accompanies this textbook offers multiple opportunities to master chapter content, including end-of-chapter exercises, a glossary of key terms with audio pronunciations, games, pronunciation coach, and additional activities such as engaging with the BioDigital® Human.

9

Hematology

> "If you're a blood donor, you're a hero to someone, somewhere, who received your gracious gift of life."
>
> —**Blood Bank Slogan**

Translation Challenge

Read the following excerpt from a physician's report and try to answer the questions that follow it.

> The female patient complained of extreme shortness of breath and having no energy. A CBC was ordered that revealed a hemoglobin of 6.2 and a hematocrit of 26. The patient was placed on oxygen and given 2 units of PRBCs. Iron supplements were prescribed for the patient at discharge. The final diagnosis was hypoxia due to severe anemia.

1. What caused the patient's shortness of breath?
2. What is a CBC and what information does it provide the physician?
3. Define hypoxia.
4. What element is necessary for the production of hemoglobin?

Learning Objectives

9.1 List and define word parts most commonly used to create terms related to hematology.

9.2 Recognize word forms that are commonly used to characterize blood and its components.

9.3 Describe the structure and function of blood cells.

9.4 Explain the process of hematopoiesis and the growth and maturation of blood cells.

9.5 Name and describe tests and treatments related to hematology.

9.6 State the meaning of abbreviations related to hematology.

9.7 Use the language of hematology correctly in written and oral communication.

9.8 Correctly spell and pronounce hematology terminology.

COURSE NAVIGATOR

Access Additional Chapter Resources

The study of blood and its components is known as **hematology**. Blood is the specialized body fluid that transports nutrients, gases, hormones, and cells throughout the body. Because blood plays a critical role in the function of all body systems, references to blood-related words, tests, and procedures appear throughout all types of medical communication. The physician who specializes in the field of hematology is a **hematologist**. A physician who is trained in hematology is usually trained in oncology as well (*onc/o*, pertaining to cancer), so the practice is often called hematology-oncology or "hem-onc." This chapter addresses hematology, including the anatomy and physiology, common conditions, diagnostic tests, and treatment options.

In the Know: Occupations in Hematology

A hematologist is a physician who specializes in the field of hematology. Medical assistants work with hematology testing in physicians' offices and with blood testing in laboratories. Other allied health occupations related to hematology include laboratory technicians, perfusionists, and blood bank technologists.

What's in a Word?

Note that the combining form *myel/o* means both "bone marrow" and "spinal cord." Context should be considered when you encounter this combining form.

Hematology Word Parts

As with other body systems, a core of combining forms, prefixes, and suffixes serves as the source for most of the medical words associated with hematology. The combining forms *hem/o* and *hemat/o* are used to create many of the terms related to blood and blood components. The Greek root "haima" is also used to describe blood or blood parts. It is not uncommon to see this medical specialty referred to as Haematology. Table 9.1 lists common word parts, their meanings, and an example.

TABLE 9.1 Word Parts Associated with Hematology

Prefix	Meaning	Example
a-/an-	no, not, without	agranulocyte (WBC that does not contain granules in its cytoplasm)
ad-	to	administer (to give)
anti-	against	antithrombin (medication to prevent blood clots)
cata-	down	catalyst (substance that increases the rate of reaction)
hypo-	under, less	hypochromic (low-colored cells—pale)
mega-	large	megakaryocyte (a large cell present in the bone marrow)
micro-	small, tiny	microcyte (small cell)
mono-	one	monocyte (large WBC with a single well-defined nucleus)
pan-	all	pancytopenia (a shortage of all types of blood cells)
poly-	many	polymorphonuclear (many-shaped nucleus)
pro-	before, forward	ProTime (blood test to determine clotting time)
trans-	through, across	transfusion (transferring blood from one person to another)

Combining Form	Meaning	Example
anis/o	unequal	anisocytosis (different-sized cells)
blast/o	immature cell	blastogenesis (production of new cell)
chrom/o	color	chromocyte (any colored or pigmented cell)
cyt/o	cell	cytoplasm (the gel substance within a cell)
erythr/o	red	erythrocyte (red blood cell)
granul/o	granular, granules	granulocyte (white blood cell that contains granules in the cytoplasm)
hemat/o	blood	hematologist (physician who studies blood and blood-forming tissues)
hem/o	blood	hemolysis (breakdown of red blood cells)
hepat/o	liver	hepatomegaly (enlarged liver)
kary/o	nucleus	megakaryocyte (a large cell present in the bone marrow)
leuk/o	white	leukocyte (white blood cell)
lymph/o	lymph	lymphadenopathy (enlargement of a lymph node)
morph/o	shape	morphology (shape and structure of a cell)
myel/o	bone marrow, spinal cord	myelofibrosis (disease of the bone marrow)
neutr/o	neutral	neutrophil (granulocyte, white blood cell)
nucle/o	nucleus	nuclei (multiple nucleus)
organ/o	organ	organomegaly (enlargement of organs)
phag/o	eating	phagocytosis (condition in which phagocytes ingest/eat solid particles)
plasm/o	formed; plasma	plasmapheresis (removal, treatment, and return of blood to circulation)
poikil/o	irregular	poikilocytosis (condition caused by irregularly shaped red blood cells)
reticul/o	reticulum (a fine network of cells)	reticulocyte (immature red blood cell)
ser/o	serum (fluid part of blood)	serous (benign fluid found in some body cavities)
spher/o	sphere-shaped	spherocyte (a ball-shaped cell)
splen/o	pertaining to the spleen	splenectomy (removal of the spleen)
thromb/o	blood clot	thrombosis (formation of a blood clot)

Continues

Suffix	Meaning	Example
-blast	immature cell	blast (immature blood cell in the bone marrow)
-cyte	cell	lymphocyte (agranulocyte, white blood T cell)
-emia	blood condition	hypovolemia (decreased blood volume due to the loss of blood or body fluids)
-globin	protein molecule	hemoglobin (protein molecule in RBCs that carries oxygen)
-ia	condition	anemia (condition of decreased red blood cells)
-lysis, -lyze	to break up	hemolyze (break down red blood cells)
-oma	tumor, mass	multiple myeloma (blood cancer that forms in plasma cells found within the bones)
-penia	shortage, deficiency	leukopenia (abnormal deficiency in WBCs)
-phil	attraction	hemophilia (condition in which blood fails to clot [gather by coagulation] normally)
-poiesis	formation, production	hematopoiesis (the formation of blood)
-thrombin	clotting substance	prothrombin (clotting factor, a component necessary for the normal clotting of blood)

Anatomy and Physiology

Blood is a fluid that contains so many millions of floating cells that it is almost impossible to imagine the total number of blood cells in the human body. Blood has many different functions. It is responsible for the:

- transportation of oxygen, nutrients, and antibodies throughout the body
- formation of clots to prevent excessive blood loss
- delivery of waste products to the kidneys and liver (which filter and clean the blood)
- regulation of body temperature

A **complete blood count** is a standard blood analysis, usually referred to by its initials, CBC. The normal CBC has approximately 5,000,000 red blood cells, 300,000 platelets, and nearly 10,000 white blood cells in one drop of blood!

Blood is composed of a fluid portion called **plasma** and a cellular portion called **formed elements** (see Figure 9.1). Blood is a mixture of approximately 55% plasma and 45% blood cells (formed elements). Plasma holds the cellular portion and also carries nutrients, electrolytes (salts), hormones, and waste products. Important plasma proteins include blood clotting factors: **albumin**, which thickens the blood; and **globulins**, which provide protective antibodies against foreign invaders. **Antibodies** are specialized cells in the blood that are produced in response to an antigen, which are substances that signal the body to produce a protective, immune response.

Did You Know?

Blood accounts for 7 to 8 percent of a person's total body weight.

Table 9.2 lists anatomy and physiology terms related to hematology. The sections that follow this table will explain the concepts of blood cell formation (hematopoiesis), red blood cells, blood types, white blood cells, platelets, and clotting.

TABLE 9.2 Anatomy and Physiology Terms Associated with Hematology

Term		Meaning	Word Analysis	
agglutinate	[ah-**gloo**-tih-nayt]	to adhere and form clumps	*a-* *gluten*	to glue
agglutinin	[ah-**gloo**-tih-nin]	substances that cause particles to coagulate or clump together	*a-* *gluten*	to glue
agranulocyte	[**a-gran**-yoo-lO-sIt]	WBC that does not contain granules in its cytoplasm	*a-* *granul/o* *-cyte*	without granular cell
antibody	[**an**-tih-bod-ee]	specialized cell (immunoglobulin) in the blood that is produced in response to an antigen; a protective protein produced by the body	*anti-* *body*	against body
antigen	[**an**-tih-jen]	substance that signals the body to produce an immune response (antibody)	*anti-* *-gen*	against to produce
basophil	[**bay**-sO-fil]	WBC that contains histamine and heparin; prevents blood clotting; assists the body in allergic reactions	*bas/o* *-phil*	base attraction
catalyst	[**kat**-ah-list]	substance that accelerates a chemical reaction	*cata-* *-lyze*	down to break up
coagulation	[kO-ag-yoo-**lay**-shun]	process in which a liquid (e.g., blood) changes to a solid; clotting		
differentiate	[dif-er-**en**-shee-ayt]	to produce more than one characteristic; having more than one characteristic		
eosinophil	[e-O-sin-O-fil]	WBC that defends against parasites and allergens	*eosin* *phil/o*	a dye attraction
erythrocyte	[er-**ih**-thrO-sIt]	blood cell that carries oxygen and carbon dioxide	*erythr/o* *cyte*	red cell
erythropoiesis	[er-ih-thrO-poy-**ee**-sis]	process of producing RBCs (erythrocytes)	*erythr/o* *-poiesis*	red formation, production
erythropoietin	[er-ih-thrO-**poy**-et-in]	hormone that simulates RBC production	*erythr/o* *-poiesis*	red formation, production
fibrin	[**fI**-brin]	elastic protein that is part of the clotting mechanism	*fibr/o*	fiber
fibrinogen	[fI-**brin**-O-jen]	globulin in the blood that helps to produce a clot	*fibr/o* *-gen*	fiber to make
glycoprotein	[**glI**-kO-**prO**-teen]	substance made up of carbohydrate and protein	*glyc/o* *protos*	pertaining to sugar first
granulocyte	[**gran**-yoo-lO-sIt]	WBC that contains granules in its cytoplasm	*granul/o* *-cyte*	granular cell
hematopoiesis	[**hem**-ah-tO-poy-**ee**-sis]	formation and maturation of blood cells	*hemat/o* *-poiesis*	blood formation, production
hemoglobin	[**hee**-mO-**glO**-bin]	protein in the RBC that carries oxygen	*hem/o* *-globin*	blood globule
hemostasis	[**hee**-mO-stay-sis]	the stopping of blood flow from an injured blood vessel		
hormone	[**hor**-mOn]	chemical substance secreted by specific organs and/or glands and carried into the bloodstream to stimulate another organ		

Continues

Term		Meaning	Word Analysis	
hypochromic	[hI-pO-**krO**-mik]	RBC that has decreased hemoglobin, resulting in pale color	*hyp/o* *-chrom* *-ic*	under, less color pertaining to
isohemagglu-tinin	[I-sO-he-mah-**gloo**-tih-nin]	antibodies responsible for reactions to blood transfusions	*is/o* *hem/o* *agglutinin*	equal blood substances that cause particles to coagulate or clump together
leukocyte	[**loo**-kO-sIt]	WBC that defends the body against foreign substances	*leuk/o* *-cyte*	white cell
lymphocyte	[**lim**-fO-sIt]	WBC involved in immunity	*lymph/o* *-cyte*	pertaining to lymph cell
macrocyte	[**mak**-rO-sIt]	large RBC	*macro-* *-cyte*	large cell
megakaryo-cyte	[meg-ah-**kair**-ee-O-sIt]	a large cell present in the bone marrow responsible for the production of platelets	*mega-* *kary/o* *-cyte*	large nucleus cell
microcyte	[**mI**-krO-sIt]	small RBC	*micro-* *-cyte*	small cell
monocyte	[**mon**-O-sIt]	one of the WBCs found in lymph nodes, the spleen, and bone marrow; a phagocytic cell that engulfs and kills bacteria and plays a role in killing tumor cells	*mono-* *-cyte*	one cell
neutrophil	[**noo**-trO-fil]	WBC that seeks, ingests, and kills bacteria	*neutron* *-phil*	neutral (dye) attraction
oxyhemoglo-bin	[oks-ee-hee-mO-**glO**-bin]	combination of oxygen and hemoglobin; oxygenated blood of the arteries	*oxy-* *hem/o* *globin*	oxygen blood globule
plasma	[**plaz**-mah]	the liquid component of blood, responsible for the transportation of blood cells throughout the body		
platelet	[**playt**-let]	blood cell that helps form the plug that stops bleeding at the site of an injury		
polymorpho-nuclear	[**pol**-ee-mor-fO-**noo**-klee-ar]	variety of cells that have various forms of nuclei	*poly-* *morph/o* *nucle/o* *-ar*	many shape nucleus pertaining to
prothrombin	[prO-**throm**-bin]	protein necessary for clot formation	*pro-* *thromb/o*	before blood clot
Rh factor		an inherited protein present on the surface of RBCs, could be harmful during pregnancy		
thrombin	[**throm**-bin]	enzyme that is the final step in the formation of a clot	*thromb/o*	blood clot
thrombocyte (platelet)	[**throm**-bO-sIt]	blood cell that helps form the plug that stops bleeding at the site of an injury	*thrombo* *cyte*	clot cell
thrombopoi-esis	[throm-bO-poy-**ee**-sis]	process of platelet formation	*thromb/o* *-poietin*	blood clot formation, production
thrombopoi-etin	[throm-bO-**poy**-eh-tin]	hormone that stimulates platelet cell formation	*thromb/o* *-poiesis*	blood clot formation, production
transfusion	[trans-**fyoo**-zhun]	process of moving a blood product from one person's body to another	*trans-* *fusion*	across, transfer to connect

FIGURE 9.1 Formed Elements of Blood

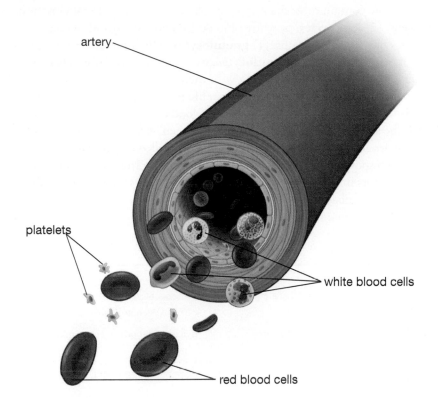

The human body contains between 4 to 6 liters of blood, accounting for about 8 percent of a person's weight. The plasma portion of the blood is approximately half the volume of the whole blood and about 4–5 percent of body weight. **Serum** is plasma without the **fibrinogen**, a globulin that helps to produce clotting. Serum is used to provide antibodies to patients whose own bodies are not producing enough of a specific type of antibody. To obtain serum, whole blood is allowed to stand in a tube or container until it clots and settles to the bottom of the container. The fluid that remains on top is the serum.

The volume of blood and its cellular components change over an individual's life span. As a person grows and more tissue mass develops, the proportion of blood decreases. Table 9.3 depicts these changes and translates the amounts into household measurements.

TABLE 9.3 Blood Volume by Age

Age	Weight (kg)	Total Blood Volume (mL/kg)	Measurement (cup[s])
Premature infant	2.4	90–105	0.95
Newborns	3.3	78–86	1.1
1-year-old	9.6	73–78	3
5-year-old	18.0	80–86	6.15
Adult (male)	70.0	68–88	22

Hematopoiesis

Blood and bone marrow contain three main types of blood cells: (1) **erythrocytes**, also called red blood cells; (2) **leukocytes**, or white blood cells; and (3) **thrombocytes**, or platelets. Leukocytes have two subgroups: (1) **granulocytes**, which include **neutrophils**, **eosinophils**, and **basophils**; and (2) **agranulocytes**, which include **lymphocytes** and **monocytes**. Table 9.4 lists the cell groups along with their normal values (number or percentage in a given amount of blood fluid), functions, life spans, and associated illnesses.

Hematopoiesis (sometimes spelled *hemopoiesis*), or blood cell formation, begins in the bone marrow with the stem cell, which is called "uncommitted" because it can become any type of cell as it matures and differentiates. Special hormones called **colony-stimulating factors** are released in response to the body's needs for blood cells. The process is not well understood, but the factors influence the number and rate at which specific blood cells are produced. The factors are probably released in response to a feedback mechanism to ensure that the body has an appropriate supply of the various blood cells.

TABLE 9.4 The Blood Cells

Blood Cell	Normal Values	Function
erythrocytes (red blood cells, or RBCs)	4.0–5.5/mm³	carry oxygen and carbon dioxide
leukocytes (white blood cells, or WBCs)	5,000–10,000/mm³	defend the body against foreign substances
Subgroup granulocytes		
neutrophils	50%–70%	seek, ingest, and kill bacteria
eosinophils	1%–4%	defend against parasites and allergens
basophils	0.4%	secretes histamine and heparin, but role is uncertain
Subgroup agranulocytes		
lymphocytes (lymphs)	20%–40%	play key role in immunity by producing antibodies
monocytes	2%–8%	phagocytic cells that engulf and kill bacteria and play a role in killing tumor cells
thrombocytes (platelets)	140,000–450,000/mm³	promote hemostasis by forming a plug (clot) at the site of an injury to a blood vessel

Erythrocytes (Red Blood Cells)

The production of red blood cells (RBCs) is called **erythropoiesis**, and it is controlled by the hormone **erythropoietin**. When the body requires more RBCs—for example, in conditions such as **hypoxia** (decreased oxygen level) and **anemia** (decreased number of RBCs)—cells in the kidney secrete erythropoietin. During the process of **differentiation**, a stem cell becomes a particular type of blood cell. RBCs begin as immature cells in the bone marrow. They mature over a period of seven days prior to being released into the bloodstream. RBCs live only 120 days so a continual need for manufacturing and maturing of RBCs through erythropoiesis is constant. Unlike other cells, RBCs do not have a nucleus. Not having a nucleus allows RBCs to change shape and move through blood vessels in the body.

The RBC is biconcave in shape, meaning it resembles a caved-in disk. Some sources refer to its shape as that of a donut. RBCs are thick around the

Did You Know?

The hemoglobin and hematocrit are part of the CBC. However, if the physician is only interested in these two measurements he or she might order an "H and H."

rim, thin in the middle, soft, and pliable. A special protein in RBCs called **hemoglobin** is responsible for the transportation of oxygen and carbon dioxide. Hemoglobin carries oxygen from the lungs to the body's cells and their waste product, carbon dioxide, back to the lungs where it is exhaled. **Oxyhemoglobin** is the molecule formed when oxygen and hemoglobin meet. RBCs get their color from hemoglobin. The portion of blood made up of RBCs is called **hematocrit**, which is commonly used as a measure of RBC levels.

Blood Types

Each person has a particular blood type (A, B, AB, or O), depending on genetic makeup and the kind of antigens present on the surface of their RBCs (see Figure 9.2). The body recognizes antigens that belong in the host body, as well as antigens invading from the outside. To protect itself from foreign antigens, the body produces substances called antibodies, which reside in blood plasma. When antibodies react with RBC antigens, called agglutinogens, they may **agglutinate**, or clump together. These RBC antibodies are called **agglutinins**.

FIGURE 9.2 Blood Types

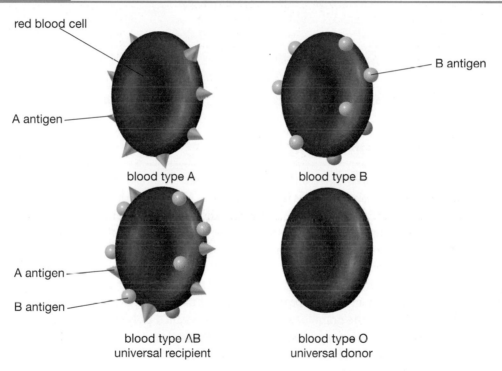

red blood cell

A antigen

blood type A

B antigen

blood type B

A antigen

B antigen

blood type AB
universal recipient

blood type O
universal donor

Blood type letters represent the antigens on the surface of the RBCs. Persons with blood type A carry the A antigen and antibodies against B (anti-B); persons with blood type B carry the B antigen and antibodies against A (anti-A); persons with type O blood have no antigens and carry both the anti-A and anti-B antibodies; persons with type AB blood carry both the A and the B antigens and no antibodies. Antigens are inherited, but may be produced by exposure to the RBCs of another person, either through a transfusion or during pregnancy. Table 9.5 lists blood types and compatibilities.

To summarize, the antibodies present determine the type of blood an individual can safely "receive" through a transfusion. Individuals with Type A blood carry antibodies to Type B blood. If Type B blood is received, the body would perceive it as foreign and reject it. Individuals with Type O blood are referred to as **universal donors**. The absence of antigens from the surface of their blood permits these individuals the ability to safely donate to all other blood types. Those with Type AB blood are referred to as **universal recipients**. The absence of antibodies affords these individuals the opportunity to receive blood from all other blood types. Blood is also classified by another antigen, the Rh factor, which will be discussed in Chapter 16.

The exchange of donated blood from one recipient to another intravenously (through an IV) is known as the **transfusion** of blood. Before blood is transfused from one person to another, the donor's blood is typed and crossmatched with that of the recipient. A sample of each is mixed together to determine whether the blood types are compatible. If they are not, the mixture will clump, or agglutinate. The RBC antibodies responsible for reactions following blood transfusions are called **isohemagglutinins**. Although rare, reactions to blood transfusions can affect the function an individual's kidneys and lungs. Symptoms include back pain, chills, blood present in the urine, dizziness, or fever that occur immediately following or days after the transfusion.

TABLE 9.5 Blood Types and Compatibilities

If a Person's Blood Type is	Antibodies in Plasma	Frequency of Occurrence	Can Be Safely Transfused with (receive)
type A	anti-B	40%	types A, O
type B	anti-A	10%	types B, O
type AB	none	4%	types A, B, AB, O (universal recipient)
type O	anti-A, anti-B	45%	type O (universal donor)

Leukocytes (White Blood Cells)

The leukocytes (white blood cells, or WBCs) are the body's soldiers, ready and able to attack and destroy bacteria and other foreign invaders. Named for their nearly white appearance under the microscope, WBCs cannot be viewed unless a stain is first applied to the slide. Normally there are 5,000–10,000 WBCs per microliter of blood, much fewer than RBCs and accounting for approximately 1% of blood in the body.

The WBCs are divided into two primary groups: **granulocytes** (so named because of a grainy appearance when properly stained and seen under a microscope); and **agranulocytes** (without a grainy appearance). Each of these groups has subgroups, as shown in Figure 9.3. The granulocytes are sometimes called **polymorphonuclear leukocytes**, PMNs, polys, or segs. The three types of granulocytes are neutrophils, eosinophils, and basophils, and each has a particular defensive function (see Table 9.2).

Neutrophils are the most common type of leukocyte as they account for approximately 55-70% of all WBCs. Neutrophils provide an immediate response to invaders. As phagocytes, neutrophils seek, ingest, and kill bacteria that do not belong in the body. These particular WBCs are produced constantly, as they live less than a day.

Eosinophils are a type of WBC responsible for the body's defense against parasites and allergens.

Basophils are a type of WBC instrumental in the healing process of damaged tissue. They contain histamine and heparin which work together to thin the blood, ultimately slowing the clotting process in order to draw blood to the affected area.

The agranulocytes include lymphocytes, responsible for immunity, and monocytes, tasked with the job of fighting severe infections and the destruction of tumor cells.

FIGURE 9.3 | Components of Blood

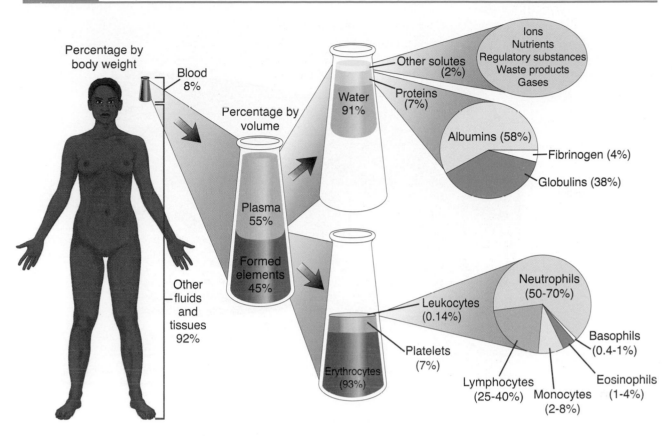

Percentage by body weight

Blood 8%

Other fluids and tissues 92%

Percentage by volume

Plasma 55%

Formed elements 45%

Water 91%

Other solutes (2%)

Proteins (7%)

Ions
Nutrients
Regulatory substances
Waste products
Gases

Albumins (58%)

Fibrinogen (4%)

Globulins (38%)

Leukocytes (0.14%)

Platelets (7%)

Erythrocytes (93%)

Neutrophils (50-70%)

Basophils (0.4-1%)

Eosinophils (1-4%)

Monocytes (2-8%)

Lymphocytes (25-40%)

Platelets

Platelets, also called **thrombocytes**, are small fragments of cells that help blood clot or coagulate. Platelets form in the bone marrow from **megakaryocytes**, or large cells. Each microliter of circulating blood contains about 300,000 platelets, which live about seven days. Platelets rush to the site of an injury and adhere to the blood vessel wall, helping the body form a clot, which covers the wound and prevents blood from leaking out. The hormone that regulates platelet production is **thrombopoietin**. (Immunoglobulins and lymphocytes are discussed in more detail in Chapter 10.)

> **Did You Know?**
>
> Too many platelets can cause unnecessary clotting (which can lead to a stroke or heart attack), while low counts can lead to extensive bleeding.

Clotting

As part of the body's work to maintain normal functioning of the blood (hemostasis), the body immediately reacts to stop the bleeding when a blood vessel is damaged. It does so by launching three processes: (1) vasoconstriction (of small blood vessels) to decrease blood flow; (2) platelet plug formation; and (3) local blood coagulation, leading to the formation of a fibrin thrombus (blood clot).

The clotting process begins when the damaged tissue exposes collagen to the circulating blood. This collagen exposure causes certain clotting factors and platelets to come to the site of the injury. As the platelets arrive, they become sticky and form a temporary plug. This process forms a stable clot in less than fifteen minutes in a person with normal clotting capabilities. See Figure 9.4.

FIGURE 9.4 | Blood Clot Formation

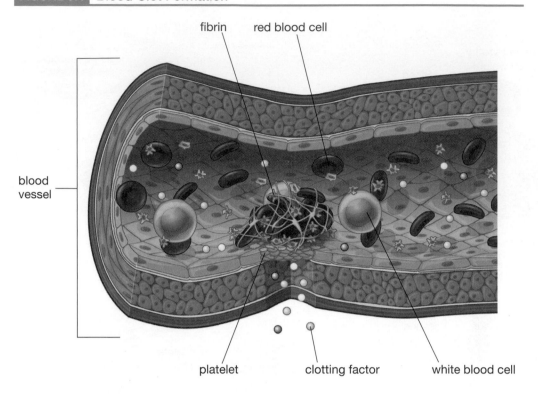

fibrin   red blood cell

blood vessel

platelet   clotting factor   white blood cell

Checkpoint 9.1

Answer the following questions to identify any areas of the section that you may need to review.

1. Which type of blood cell is the most numerous?

   _____

2. What cell rushes to the site of an injury to help blood to clot?

   _____

3. Describe the functions of a neutrophil.

   _____

   _____

   _____

   _____

   _____

Exercise 9.1   Word Analysis

Separate the terms into their word parts and give a definition for each whole term. Use a slash to separate the word parts and label each part (P = prefix, CF = combining form, and S = suffix).

	CF	**S**	
Example:	granul/o /	-cyte,	filled with granules

Term	**Word Analysis**	**Definition**
1. anemia	_____	_____
2. microcytic	_____	_____
3. hypochromic	_____	_____
4. splenectomy	_____	_____
5. hepatomegaly	_____	_____

Exercise 9.2   Comprehension Check

Read each sentence and circle the term that is most appropriate.

1. Hypermegaly/Organomegaly means "enlarged organ."
2. Hypoxia/Hyperoxia means "decreased oxygen."
3. Microcytic/Macrocytic means "pertaining to large cells."
4. Leukocytes/Melanocytes/Erythrocytes are white blood cells.
5. Phrenology/Hematology/Oncology is the study of the blood.

Exercise 9.3   Matching

Match the term in column 1 with the correct definition in column 2. Write the letter of the definition on the line beside the term.

1. _____ antibodies
2. _____ antigens
3. _____ oxyhemoglobin
4. _____ hemoglobin
5. _____ catalyze

a. combination of oxygen and hemoglobin

b. to speed up

c. substances that signal the body to produce an immune response

d. protect the body from foreign antigens

e. oxygen-carrying pigment in red blood cells

Exercise 9.4   Word Building

Supply roots, combining forms, or word parts to create a term that completes each sentence.

1. Blasto_____ means "immature cell."

2. A _____cyte is a white blood cell.

3. Phago_____sis means "cell eating."

4. _____ous means "pertaining to serum."

5. Baso_____ is a type of white blood cell.

Exercise 9.5   Spelling Check

Circle the correctly spelled word from each pair in the following sentences.

1. To obtain serum/serium, the cellular components of blood are allowed to clot, leaving only the fluid.

2. Plasma/Pilazma is the fluid portion of the blood.

3. Albumin/Albuminum and globulins/gobulines are plasma proteins.

4. Oxyhemoglobin/Oxihemaglobin is the molecule formed when oxygen and hemoglobin join.

5. Large RBCs are called macrocytes/macrocysts; small RBCs are called microcytes/microcysts.

Exercise 9.6   Word Maps

Arrange the following list of terms in a graphic organizer that illustrates the components of blood, starting with whole blood. Hint: Think in terms of groups and subgroups.

cellular components   fibrinogen   WBCs
plasma   serum   whole blood
RBCs   thrombocytes

```
┌─────────────┐
│ whole blood │
└─────────────┘

┌──────────┐        ┌──────────┐
│          │        │          │
└──────────┘        └──────────┘

┌────────┐ ┌────────┐ ┌────────┐ ┌────────┐ ┌────────┐
│        │ │        │ │        │ │        │ │        │
└────────┘ └────────┘ └────────┘ └────────┘ └────────┘
```

Conditions

Conditions associated with hematology often directly affect red blood cells, white blood cells, platelets, blood vessels, bone marrow, lymph nodes, the spleen, and/or the proteins responsible for the clotting of blood. **Pernicious anemia** is a condition in which the body is unable to absorb enough Vitamin B12 into the gastrointestinal tract, resulting in a decreased number of red blood cells. This condition can lead to **megaloblastic anemia**, a blood disorder in which the number of red blood cells is lower than normal and the body's organs and tissues do not have an adequate supply of oxygen to function.

When blood leaks outside a blood vessel, either from a traumatic injury or from spontaneous causes, an **ecchymosis** (plural: ecchymoses) is formed. Commonly called a bruise, an ecchymosis will change color from the immediate reddish-purple spot, fade to brown, and then disappear, as the collected blood under the skin is cleared away by the body's own mechanisms. A severe injury may result in a hematoma (a large, firm collection of blood) that may require surgical intervention if it does not resolve on its own.

The disorder **immune thrombocytopenic purpura (ITP)** can occur at any age; the acute form is seen most often in children, while the chronic form, defined as lasting at least one year, is more common in adults. ITP occurs when platelets are destroyed in the spleen, resulting in a low platelet count. The body's decreased clotting ability places the patient at risk for life-threatening bleeding. Treatment consists of drugs that fool the immune system into slowing the destruction of platelets, but if treatment does not maintain a safe platelet count the patient may need to undergo a **splenectomy**, the surgical removal of the spleen.

Aplastic anemia is a condition leading to decreased bone marrow function and the reduced production of red blood cells. Aplastic anemia is often **idiopathic** (having an unknown cause), but may be the result of ionizing radiation, chemotherapeutic agents, benzene, or other agents. An autoimmune disorder is one that occurs when the body forms antibodies against itself. **Autoimmune hemolytic anemia** is the body's destruction of its own red blood cells via antibodies, which leads to anemia.

Thrombosis is a condition of increased clotting that occurs within the blood vessels. The clot is called a **thrombus**, and when a thrombus forms in a vital organ, such as the brain or heart, its effects can be life threatening. A stroke may be caused by a thrombus. If the thrombus dislodges and reaches a blood vessel that is too small to let it pass through in the bloodstream, it is called an **embolus**. This particular type of stroke would be treated with blood thinners to dissolve the clot. Table 9.6 lists conditions related to hematology.

TABLE 9.6 Conditions Associated with Hematology

Term		Meaning	Word Analysis	
anemia	[ah-**nee**-mee-ah]	condition of decreased hemoglobin level	an- -emia	without blood
aplasia	[ah-**play**-zha]	defective development of a blood cell line	a- -plasia	without formation
autoimmune	[aw-tO-ih-**myoon**]	process in which the person's immune system turns against itself (relating to antibodies that attack the cells of the body producing them)	auto- immun/o	self immune
ecchymosis	[ek-ih-**mO**-sis]	black-and-blue mark caused by leakage of blood from the vessel	ecchyme chyme -osis	out of, away from juice condition

Continues

Term		Meaning	Word Analysis	
embolus	[**em**-bO-lus]	clot that has broken loose within the circulatory system	*embolus*	a plug
epistaxis	[ep-ih-**staks**-is]	nosebleed		
erythroblastosis fetalis	[er-**ih**-thrO-blas-**tO**-sis fee-**tay**-lis]	life-threatening disorder caused by an incompatibility between mother and fetal blood	*erythr/o* *blast/o* *-osis* *fetalis*	red immature cell condition of the fetus
extramedullary	[eks-trah-**med**-yoo-lair-ee]	outside the bone marrow cavity	*extra-* *medull/o* *-ary*	beyond medulla, marrow pertaining to
hematoma	[**hee**-ma-**tO**-mah]	an area of blood that has extravasated from the vessel and is confined in a space	*hemat/o* *-oma*	blood tumor
hemoglobinopathy	[hee-mO-glO-bin-**op**-ah-thee]	disease caused by a problem with the hemoglobin	*hem/o* *globin* *-pathy*	blood globule disease
hemolysis	[hee-**mol**-ih-sis]	destruction of the RBC	*hem/o* *-lysis*	blood destruction
hemorrhage	[**hem**-ah-rej]	uncontrolled bleeding	*hem/o* *-rrhage*	blood to burst forth
hemosiderosis	[hee-mO-sid-er-**O**-sis]	excessive accumulation of a greenish-yellow substance (known as *hemosiderin*) in the liver and spleen caused by iron in the blood	*hem/o* *sider/o* *-osis*	blood iron condition
hepatomegaly	[**hep**-ah-tO-**meg**-ah-lee]	enlarged liver	*hepat/o* *-megaly*	pertaining to the liver large
hypovolemia	[hI-pO-vah-**lee**-me-ah]	decreased blood volume due to loss of blood or body fluids	*hypo-* *vol/o* *-emia*	deficient volume blood condition
hypoxia	[hI-poks-ee-ah]	having too little oxygen	*hyp/o* *-oxy* *-ia*	under, less oxygen condition of
immune thrombocytopenic purpura	[ih-**myoon** throm-bO-sI-tO-**pee**-nik **pur**-pyoo-rah]	autoimmune disorder that produces platelet antibodies and results in the destruction of the body's own platelets	*immune* *thromb/o* *cyt/o* *-penic* *purpura*	free from catching a specific infectious disease blood clot cell pertaining to deficiency purple
iron-deficiency anemia		common condition in which the body lacks a sufficient supply of iron, which is necessary to produce hemoglobin used to carry oxygen to the body's cells		
megaloblastic anemia	[**meg**-ah-lO-**blas**-tik ah-**nee**-mee-ah]	condition of enlarged erythrocytes	*megal/o* *blast/o* *-ic* *an-* *-emia*	large immature cell pertaining to without blood
menorrhagia	[men-or-**ray**-jee-ah]	increased or excessive menstrual flow	*men/o* *-rrhagia*	menstruation to burst forth
morphology	[morf-**ol**-ah-jee]	study of shape	*morph/o* *-ology*	shape the study of

Continues

Term		Meaning	Word Analysis	
myelodysplasia	[**mI**-el-O-dis-**play**-see-ah]	abnormality of the bone marrow	*myel/o* *dys-* *-plasia*	bone marrow separation formation
myelofibrosis	[mI-el-O-fI-**brO**-sis]	formation of excessive scar tissue in the bone marrow	*myel/o* *fibr/o* *-osis*	bone marrow fibrous condition
occult	[ok-**kult**]	hidden	*-cultus*	to cover
pallor	[**pal**-or]	pale appearance	*pallor*	pale
pancytopenia	[pan-sI-tO-**pee**-nee-ah]	severe reduction of all blood cell lines	*pan-* *cyt/o* *-penia*	all, entire cell deficiency
polycythemia vera	[pol-ee-sI-**thee**-mee-ah **vee**-rah]	condition of increased RBCs	*poly-* *cyt/o* *hem/o* *-ia* *vera*	many cell blood condition true
splenomegaly	[**splee**-nO-**meg**-ah-lee]	increased size of the spleen	*splen/o* *-megaly*	spleen large
septicemia	[sep-tuh-**see**-me-ah]	bacteria in the blood as a result of a severe, life-threatening infection, also known as *sepsis*		
thrombocyto-penia	[throm-bO-sI-tO-**pee**-nee-ah]	decreased platelets	*thromb/o* *cyt/o* *-penia*	platelet, clot cell deficiency
thrombosis	[throm-**bO**-sis]	clot formation in the blood vessels	*thromb/o* *-osis*	platelet, clot condition

Many abnormalities of the blood are defined by the number, color, size and shape, or morphology of the blood cells. Tables 9.7 through 9.11 list the terms for these abnormalities.

TABLE 9.7 Abnormalities in the Number of Blood Cells

Type and Subtype	Too Few	Too Many
agranulocytes		
lymphocytes	lymphocytopenia	lymphocytosis
monocytes		monocytosis
erythrocytes (red blood cells)	erythrocytopenia	erythrocytosis
		polycythemia
reticulocytes		reticulocytosis
granulocytes	granulocytopenia	granulocytosis
neutrophils	neutropenia	neutrophilia
eosinophils		eosinophilia
basophils		basophilia
leukocytes (white blood cells)	leukocytopenia, also called leukopenia	leukocytosis
thrombocytes (platelets)	thrombocytopenia	thrombocytosis

TABLE 9.8 Abnormalities in the Color of Blood Cells*

Term		Meaning	Word Analysis	
hypochromia	[hI-pO-**krO**-mee-ah]	too little hemoglobin	hypo-	less than
			chrom/o	color
			-ia	condition of
polychromasia	[pol-ee-krO-**may**-zee-ah]	purple-tinged when stained; young red blood cell that is seen with increased red blood cell production, as in pernicious anemia or any hemolytic anemia or in response to any blood loss	poly-	many
			chrom/o	color
			-ia	condition of

*Refers to the amount of hemoglobin in the red blood cells

TABLE 9.9 Abnormalities in the Size of Blood Cells

Term		Meaning	Word Analysis	
microcyte	[**mI**-krO-sIt]	small RBC	micro-	small
microcytic	[mI-krO-**sit**-ik]		-cyte	cell
macrocyte	[**mak**-rO-sIt]	large RBC	macro-	large
macrocytic	[mak-rO-**sit**-ik]		-cyte	cell

TABLE 9.10 Abnormalities in the Morphology of Red Blood Cells

Term		Meaning	Word Analysis	
anisocytosis	[an-is-O-sI-**tO**-sis]	variation in the size of cells	anis/o	unequal
			cyt/o	cell
			-osis	condition
poikilocytosis	[poy-kil-O-sI-**tO**-sis]	irregularly shaped cells	poikil/o	irregular
			-cyt/o	cell
			-osis	condition
rouleaux	[roo-**lO**]	a stack of RBCs	rouleaux	to roll
sickle cell		sickle-shaped cell	sickle	shape
spherocyte	[**sfee**-rO-sIt]	sphere-shaped cell	spher/o	globe
			-cyte	cell

TABLE 9.11 Abnormalities in the Morphology of White Blood Cells

Term		Meaning	Word Analysis	
leukocytosis	[loo-kO-sI-**tO**-sis]	an abnormal increase in the number of white blood cells	leuk/o	white blood cell
			cyt/o	cell
			-osis	abnormal condition
leukopenia	[loo-kO-**pee**-knee-ah]	an abnormal decrease in the number of white blood cells	leuk/o	white blood cells
			-penia	shortage, deficiency
neutropenia	[new-trO-**pee**-knee-ah]	an abnormal decrease in the number of neutrophils due to disease destruction or damage	neutr/o	neutral
			-penia	shortage, deficiency

Fetuses, Infants, and Children

Specific kinds of blood cells can be recognized in the fetus by the third week of gestation. As blood vessels develop, stem cells migrate to the future sites of blood production. The liver is the main site of blood cell production from the second to the sixth month of gestation, at which time blood formation starts in the bone marrow. During fetal life, the spleen, lymph nodes, and thymus are also sites of hematopoiesis (see Figure 9.5).

Jaundice is a condition in newborns with an excessive amount of bilirubin present in the blood, also known as hyperbilirubinemia. Bilirubin is a substance that is made when the body breaks down old red blood cells. The skin and the white part of the eyes look yellow in a newborn with jaundice.

At birth, the body's bone marrow is the chief factory for blood production. The liver ceases to produce blood cells two weeks after birth. In infants, blood cells are actively produced in the medullary cavities of all of the bones (red marrow). During childhood, active marrow in the long bones is replaced by fatty tissue (yellow marrow), so that by the time a person reaches his or her 20th birthday, active blood production takes place only in the flat bones, such as the skull, vertebrae, sternum, ribs, clavicles, scapulae, and pelvis. However, in disease states such as **sickle cell anemia** (abnormally low levels of hemoglobin produced by sickle-shaped RBCs) or **myelofibrosis** (the forming of fibrous tissue in the bone marrow), the yellow marrow and fetal hematopoietic organs can resume active hematopoiesis. When fetal hematopoietic organs resume making blood cells, it is called **extramedullary hematopoiesis**.

FIGURE 9.5 Hematopoiesis Tree

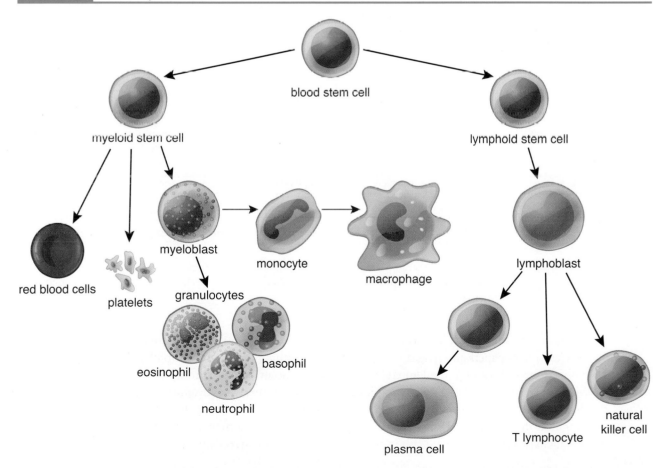

As mentioned earlier, a person's blood group and Rh type are inherited from the parents. This inheritance becomes significant when an Rh-negative mother is carrying an Rh-positive fetus (a condition known as **erythroblastosis fetalis**; this condition is covered in greater detail in Chapter 16. The most common hematologic disorder in infancy and childhood is dietary **iron deficiency**, since the human diet during the first year contains very few foods rich in iron. The infant's rapid growth during the first year of life depletes iron stores, leaving the baby dependent on iron from foods. Dietary iron deficiency is common from about nine to twenty-four months of age.

The possibility of **occult blood loss** must be considered in every child with iron deficiency anemia. Gastrointestinal bleeding can be caused by a peptic ulcer, Meckel's diverticulum (a pouch or sac in the intestine remaining from a stage of embryonic development), or polyps (see Chapter 11). In infants, gastrointestinal bleeding may result from intolerance to cow's milk.

Many childhood diseases associated with the blood system are of genetic origin, meaning that they are passed from the parent to the child through the genes. Table 9.12 lists the major hereditary blood diseases.

TABLE 9.12 Hereditary Hematologic Disorders

Term	Meaning	Word Analysis	
disseminated intravascular coagulation (DIC)	condition affecting an individual's ability to form blood clots to stop bleeding		
glucose-6-phosphate dehydrogenase deficiency (G-6-PD)	disorder of an RBC enzyme causing hemolysis	*glucose-6-phosphate dehydrogenase*	an enzyme
hemophilia	hemophilia A, factor VIII deficiency	*hem/o* *-philia*	blood fondness
hereditary elliptocytosis (or ovalocytosis)	inherited disorder in which 50-90% of RBCs are rod-shaped (oval)	*elliptl/o* *cyt/o* *-osis*	oval-shaped cell condition
hereditary spherocytosis	inherited disorder in which RBCs are sphere-shaped	*spher/o* *cyt/o* *-osis*	spherical cell condition
sickle cell anemia	inherited disorder in which RBCs are shaped like sickles	*sickle* *an-* *-emia*	curved without blood
thalassemia	inherited disorder in which the body fails to produce normal amounts of RBCs	*-emia*	blood
von Willebrand's disease	an inherited disorder in which the body fails to produce a sufficient amount of the clotting protein von Willebrand factor (VWF) which can lead to extensive or excessive bleeding	*von Willebrand*	Finnish physician

Sickle cell anemia is a hereditary disorder that has been well publicized through medical articles in newspapers and magazines. It is the most common **hemoglobinopathy** (hemoglobin-related disease) in the United States, but it also occurs widely throughout Africa, the Mediterranean, and the Middle East. Sickle cell anemia is caused by abnormal hemoglobin that makes the RBCs assume a sickle shape. These sickle-shaped cells are less pliable and get caught in the blood vessels, causing painful crises (episodes) that may lead to inadequate blood circulation and tissue death in the affected body part (**infarction**). Typical sites of vessel-blocking crises include (1) the bones of the hand and foot, resulting in hand-foot syndrome, which commonly occurs in infants during the first year of life; (2) other bones throughout the body; (3) the central nervous system, producing **cerebral thrombosis** (stroke) and **hemorrhage** (uncontrolled bleeding); (4) the abdomen; (5) the chest, sometimes resulting in **acute chest syndrome**, a severe, life-threatening infarction of the lung; and (6) the penis, where **priapism** (prolonged penile erection) can occur. **Hand-foot syndrome** is redness, swelling, and pain on the palms of the hands and soles of the feet, often a side effect of certain types of chemotherapy. Figure 9.6 illustrates the path of normal blood cells and of sickle cells. Note that sickle cells may lead to blood vessel blockage.

The enzyme **glucose-6-phosphate dehydrogenase** (**G-6-PD**) is found in all cells. A deficiency of this enzyme in the red blood cells results in **hemolytic anemia**, or **G-6-PD deficiency**, in which the red blood cells are rapidly destroyed, or **hemolyzed**. Glucose-6-phosphate dehydrogenase deficiency is a hereditary disorder that can be triggered by exposure to certain foods, infections, and medications.

What's in a Word?

Infarction is a term that describes tissue death caused by the obstruction of blood flow to an organ or region of tissue.

FIGURE 9.6 | Normal Blood Flow and Sickle Cell Crisis

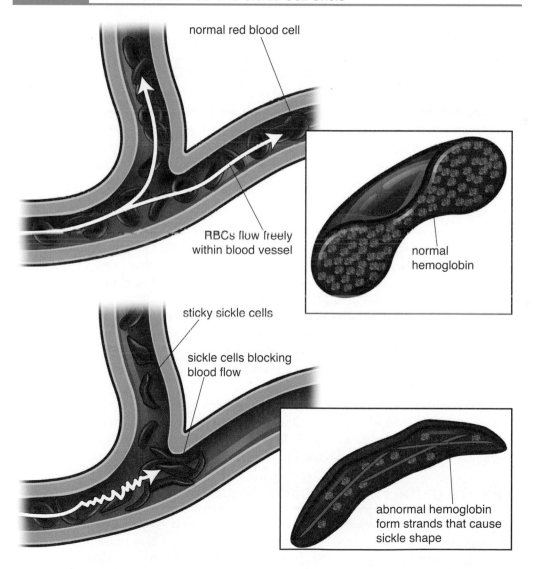

normal red blood cell

RBCs flow freely within blood vessel

normal hemoglobin

sticky sickle cells

sickle cells blocking blood flow

abnormal hemoglobin form strands that cause sickle shape

Hereditary spherocytosis occurs in one of every five thousand individuals. **Hereditary spherocytosis** is a disorder of the RBC membrane that causes the cell to assume the shape of a sphere (hence the name *spherocyte*). Spherocytes become isolated in the spleen, resulting in hemolysis, anemia, and splenomegaly.

Thalassemia (ineffective RBC production) becomes evident clinically in the second half of the first year of life when the infant loses his or her fetal hemoglobin. Pallor, splenomegaly, and decreased appetite are the typical presenting signs. Thalassemia is caused by an unequal production of alpha and other globin chains. Extramedullary hematopoiesis produces progressive enlargement of the spleen and liver. Treatment involves administering RBC transfusions to maintain a fairly normal hemoglobin level. Iron overload, or hemosiderosis, from repeated blood transfusions is a side effect that involves every organ in the body. Death from cardiac hemosiderosis usually occurs during the second or third decade of life.

Another hereditary disorder, **von Willebrand's disease**, is caused by abnormal platelet function and a decreased level of von Willebrand factor. The disorder is characterized by easy bruising, **epistaxis** (nosebleed), bleeding from gums, oozing from cuts, **menorrhagia** (abnormally heavy menstrual bleeding), and severe bleeding after trauma or surgery.

Hemophilia is a genetic disorder that often first becomes apparent when an infant boy bleeds excessively after circumcision. It is caused by a decreased or dysfunctional factor VIII that is carried by the female and transmitted to the male. Hemophilia is linked to the X chromosome. A female carrier has a 50-50 chance that each son will have hemophilia and a 50-50 chance that each daughter will be a carrier. A hemophilic male cannot transmit the disease to his sons, but all of his daughters will be carriers.

Fanconi's anemia is a hereditary condition associated with congenital anomalies, including **microcephaly** (abnormally small head), **microphthalmia** (abnormally small eyes), absence of radii and thumbs, abnormalities of heart and kidney, short stature, and hyperpigmentation of the skin. The average age at onset is six to eight years; bruising due to **thrombocytopenia** (decreased platelet production) may be the first symptom. In about 5 to 10 percent of cases, acute myelogenous leukemia will develop.

Adults and Seniors

Iron deficiency as a result of gastrointestinal bleeding occurs most frequently in the adult. There may be an underlying problem such as an ulcer, gastrointestinal cancer, polyps, or other GI disorders (discussed in Chapter 11). Iron deficiency anemia is a common condition in adults who take aspirin or NSAIDS, as well.

Myelodysplasia, or **myelodysplastic syndrome**, occurs most frequently in adults. These patients are prone to ineffective hematopoiesis, producing fewer circulating blood cells. The cells the body can produce may be abnormal in shape and appearance in patients with myelodysplastic syndrome. This condition is progressive and usually transforms into a form of leukemia.

Polycythemia vera is a disorder associated with a high hemoglobin level that arises from an increase in total RBC volume. Often a sign of a preleukemic state, this disorder is potentially dangerous because it causes an increase in blood **viscosity**, or thickness, and the heightened risk of thrombosis. This condition tends to affect only those people over age 60.

Cancers of the Hematopoietic System

The physician who treats cancers of the hematopoietic system is a **hematologist-oncologist**. These types of cancer usually arise in the bone marrow, the body's blood-making organ. **Leukemia** is the most common malignancy of the hematopoietic system. There are different types of leukemia, depending on the blood cell line that develops the malignant abnormality. Leukemia is manifested by the proliferation (multiplication) of abnormal blood cells within the bone marrow. For instance, acute lymphoblastic leukemia is manifested by an abnormal population of lymphoblasts in the bone marrow. Eventually, the bone marrow space becomes overpopulated by malignant cells, and the cells are pushed out of the bone marrow, where they can be seen in the blood during laboratory testing.

The patient with leukemia may present with pallor, ecchymoses, petechiae, fatigue, history of recurrent illness, pain, and fever. All of the signs and symptoms occur because the normal blood cells are being crowded out of production by the very fast growing leukemia cells. Table 9.13 describes the types of leukemia, the cell lines from which they arise, and the typical age at diagnosis.

Many of the leukemias, especially those diagnosed in childhood, are treatable and potentially curable with **chemotherapy** (*chemo*, meaning "chemical"; *therapy*, meaning "treatment") and/or biotherapy.

TABLE 9.13 Types of Leukemia

Type of Leukemia	Cell Line	Most Common Age at Presentation
acute lymphoblastic leukemia	lymphoid	childhood
acute myelogenous leukemia	myeloid	late teens–adulthood
acute monocytic leukemia	monocyte	adulthood
acute promyelocytic leukemia	promyelocyte	young adulthood
chronic myelogenous leukemia	myeloid	late teens–adulthood
chronic lymphocytic leukemia	lymphoid	older age

Lymphomas are a type of malignancy that affect the tissues of the lymphatic system, and are often classified as hematologic malignancies. There are two major categories of lymphoma: **Hodgkin's**, named for the British physician who first identified it; and **non-Hodgkin** lymphoma, often classified by the specific cell type of origin. Hodgkin lymphoma is a rare cancer of the lymphatic (immune) system. This condition compromises an individual's ability to fight infection. Non-Hodgkin lymphoma is one of the most common types of cancer in the United States. **Multiple myeloma** is a malignancy affecting plasma cells.

Checkpoint 9.2

Answer the following questions to identify any areas of the section that you may need to review.

1. What condition produces affected males and carrier females?

   _____

2. Gastrointestinal bleeding can cause what condition in adults?

   _____

3. A red blood cell that takes on the shape of a ball is known as a what?

   _____

Exercise 9.7   Word Analysis

Identify the root or combining form in each of the following underlined terms by drawing a box around it, and then supply the definition of the root and the definition of the entire term.

1. Splenomegaly can indicate that blood cells are trapped in the spleen.

   _____

2. Hemoglobinopathy is detected by laboratory tests.

   _____

3. The red blood cells are destroyed in the process of hemolysis.

   _____

4. Erythrocytopenia, a disorder of red blood cell production, can lead to anemia.

   _____

5. Bruising due to thrombocytopenia may be an early manifestation of a hereditary anemia.

   _____

Exercise 9.8   Comprehension Check

Select the correct medical term from the list to substitute for the underlined definition in each sentence.

anemia   menorrhagia
embolus   occult
epistaxes   splenomegaly

1. The patient is a 60-year-old male who was diagnosed   _____
   with a condition of decreased hemoglobin.

2. The child was brought to the office with severe,   _____
   recurrent nosebleeds.

3. Katherine has come to the clinic today because of   _____
   pronounced increased menstrual flow.

4. There is no evidence of increased size of the spleen. _____

5. Plan: stool specimen for hidden blood.   _____

Exercise 9.9   Matching

Match the term or abbreviation in column 1 with the correct definition in column 2. Write the letter of the definition on the line beside the term.

1. _____ hemoglobinopathy   a. study of shape
2. _____ hemosiderin   b. hidden
3. _____ morphology   c. nosebleed
4. _____ occult   d. iron in the blood
5. _____ epistaxis   e. disease caused by problem with hemoglobin

Exercise 9.10   Word Building

Supply roots, combining forms, or word parts to create a term that completes each sentence.

1. _____venous means "within a vein."
2. Hemo_____ means "pertaining to flow of blood."
3. Thrombo_____ refers to the presence of a blood clot.
4. An_____ means "without blood" (deficiency of iron in the blood).
5. Morpho_____ is the study of shape or form.

Exercise 9.11   Spelling Check

Find the misspelled medical terms in each sentence. Then rewrite the terms correctly and define them on the blanks provided.

1. Mr. Knowles was admitted with a diagnosis of hemesiderosus. _____

   _____

2. Microscopic studies revealed widespread hemmolysis. _____

   _____

3. Acute chest syndrome is an acute life-threatening infearction of the lung. _____

   _____

4. Sickle cell anemia is the most common hemogloboniopathy in the United States. _____

   _____

5. The infant has been diagnosed with a hereditary hemotalogic disorder. _____

   _____

Exercise 9.12 Word Maps

Place the appropriate term or group of terms in each of the boxes that follow. Fill in the symptom boxes first; then add the diagnostic terms and disease or effects terms that relate to each symptom.

anemia
splenomegaly
enlarged liver
hemolysis, congestive heart failure, extramedullary hematopoiesis
hepatomegaly
pale lips, nail beds, and inside of mouth
enlarged spleen
pale appearance
isolated blood cells, extramedullary hematopoiesis, hemolysis

Symptom			
Diagnostic term for symptom			
Disease or effects			

Diagnostic Tests and Examinations

The status of a patient's blood system is best evaluated by laboratory tests. However, certain aspects of patient history and physical examination can provide insight into the hematologic system. For example, the examiner queries the patient about activities: "Do you get out of breath when walking up stairs?" If the answer is yes, it may mean that the patient is out of shape or that the patient may be anemic. The examiner also observes the coloring of the patient, including the lips, the inside of the mouth, the mucous membranes of the lower inner eyelid, and the nail beds. These areas should be pink. If any are pale, the condition is noted as **pallor**, which may indicate anemia.

The physician pays particular attention to the liver and spleen. An enlarged liver or spleen may indicate blood conditions, such as hemolysis or extramedullary hematopoiesis, and should be addressed.

The hematopoietic system is evaluated by three major laboratory tests: (1) **complete blood count (CBC)**, (2) **white blood cell count with differential**, and (3) **peripheral blood smear**. Several additional procedures evaluating blood cell production and clotting properties are used to diagnose a variety of abnormalities.

Complete Blood Count (CBC)

The CBC includes various tests. In addition to the count of the RBCs and the WBCs, there are also measurements of a patient's RBC size and hemoglobin content (called the RBC indices), which serve as indicators of health or illness. Cell size is represented as **mean corpuscular volume (MCV)**. The amount of hemoglobin carried in the RBC is called the **mean corpuscular hemoglobin (MCH)**. The **MCH concentration (MCHC)** represents the concentration of hemoglobin within the average RBC. There may also be a platelet count included. Production of RBCs is assessed by the **reticulocyte** (young RBC) count. If the hemoglobin value is decreased, a high reticulocyte count would suggest that young RBCs are being produced.

The count of the WBC line is called the differential. The number of these cells changes normally from newborn through adolescence, when the values reach the adult range.

Peripheral Blood Smear

The smear is a specimen of blood placed on the slide and viewed under the microscope. This is a test of the size and appearance of blood cells, as well as the presence of abnormally shaped cells. Any abnormal value in the CBC or abnormal morphology seen on the peripheral smear is a possible indication of illness or disease. Change can also be the result of abnormal production or increased destruction of normal blood cells.

Additional Blood Tests and Procedures

Table 9.14 lists common tests and procedures related to the blood. A patient's production of neutrophils, platelets, and RBCs may be assessed using a **bone marrow aspiration**, a test performed by inserting a special needle through the skin into the bone marrow cavity and aspirating some fluid (bone marrow) into the syringe (see Figure 9.7). A **bone marrow biopsy** involves taking a small specimen, or core, of the bone marrow. Each of these tests is usually performed on the posterior superior iliac crest. The specimen is viewed under the microscope to determine numbers of blood cells.

TABLE 9.14 Tests and Examinations Associated with Hematology

Term	Description
activated partial thromboplastin time (APTT)	test to determine clotting rate
blood smear	test that utilizes a drop of blood spread thinly on a glass slide; the slide is bathed in a stain and viewed under the microscope when it dries; each cell absorbs the stain
blood typing	test to identify an individual's blood type
bone marrow aspiration and biopsy	test that requires a sample of the fluid portion of the bone marrow obtained using a special needle (Jamshidi or Illinois) that is inserted through the skin into the bone marrow space of the bone (posterior superior iliac crest in most cases; anterior iliac crest and sternum less commonly)
complete blood count and differential (CBC with Diff)	test performed on blood to determine the value of each of the blood cells, usually analyzed by computerized equipment (e.g., a Coulter counter)
Coombs' test	test to detect antibodies in the serum that react with antigens on the patient's RBCs; used to determine whether the patient has an autoimmune hemolytic anemia (Note: Coombs was an English immunologist.)
hematocrit (HCT)	test used to determine the number of red blood cells in the blood
hemoglobin (Hgb, Hb, HGB)	test to measure the level of protein substance present to carry oxygen to the tissues
platelet count	test to measure the amount of platelets present in the blood to assist with clotting
prothrombin time (PT)	test to determine clotting rate; prothrombin is a glycoprotein necessary for clotting; also known as *internatational normalized ratio (INR)*
reticulocyte count	test to determine the number of young cells that will become RBCs

FIGURE 9.7 Bone Marrow Biopsy and Aspiration

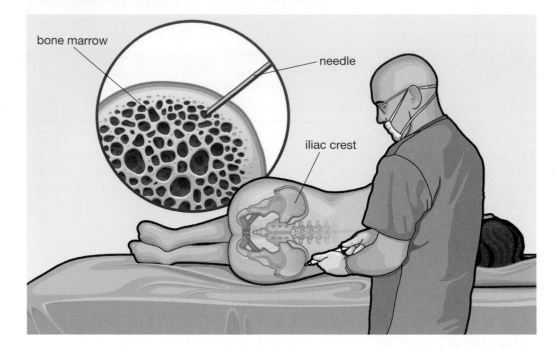

Blood clotting can also be evaluated with specific tests. A bleeding time is used to measure the time it takes for clotting to occur after a small wound is made on the skin. The **prothrombin time (PT)/INR (international normalized ratio)** and the **activated partial thromboplastin time (APTT)** are additional tests used to assess clotting.

Coombs' test detects antibodies in the serum that react with antigens on the patient's RBCs. The test can determine whether the patient has an autoimmune hemolytic anemia, or if the patient is experiencing a reaction to a transfusion.

Checkpoint 9.3

Answer the following questions to identify any areas of the section that you may need to review.

1. The measurements of a patient's RBC size and hemoglobin content are called what?

   _____

2. What procedure involves the use of a needle to obtain a sample of fluid from bone marrow for diagnostic testing?

   _____

3. Which test detects antibodies in the serum that react with antigens on the patient's RBCs?

   _____

Treatments

Healthcare practitioners use predetermined guidelines to direct patient care. These guidelines, known as clinical practice guidelines and evidence-based practices, have been developed by the specialty societies based on past clinical research. They represent the treatment pathways that have achieved the best outcomes. Treatment decisions generally fall into three categories: surgical, clinical, and pharmacological.

Surgical treatments are generally invasive as they involve a puncture or an incision into the skin. *Clinical treatments* are generally noninvasive and involve nonsurgical techniques (e.g., physical therapy). *Pharmacological treatments* involve the utilization of medicines (drugs) to treat specific illnesses or diseases. Medication therapies are regulated by the Food and Drug Administration (FDA). To be approved by the FDA for use in the United States, every medicine must be backed by research studies that have shown the medication to be effective in its treatment of a given disease and has a tolerable safety profile. The following sections provide an overview of treatments common to the hematologic system.

Surgical Treatments

Pheresis is a procedure that involves removing some blood into a special centrifuge that separates the cells by removing harmful substances from the blood and returning the filtered blood to the body. Excess WBCs are removed as a treatment in leukemia patients. Harmful red blood cells are removed in patients with sickle cell disease (**apheresis**). **Plasmapheresis** is used to treat multiple sclerosis and as a form of plasma donation. Blood components that can be separated by pheresis are the WBCs (**leukapheresis**), the plasma (plasmapheresis), and the platelets (**plateletpheresis**).

Blood and blood-product transfusions are also available for hematologic conditions. Blood and blood-product transfusions can be used for patients who suffer from hematologic disorders (such as hemophilia) and who require transfusions to keep the disorder under control.

Some anemic patients need a transfusion of blood to maintain normal hemoglobin levels. Patients who lose blood during surgery or after an accident may also require additional blood. In most cases, patients are given packed red blood cells (PRBC) rather than whole blood.

Another common treatment is a bone marrow transplant using stem cells. A stem cell is a specialized cell that develops into a healthy blood cell. The **bone marrow transplant**, also known as a bone marrow transfusion, is a procedure that harvests healthy bone marrow from a donor and then transfuses the harvested marrow into a patient who is unable to produce healthy blood cells (because of chemotherapy or a condition such as aplastic anemia). Chemotherapy destroys the bone marrow, making it unable to produce healthy blood cells. Bone marrow may be collected and frozen for future use. Patients who have undergone intensive chemotherapy for hematologic cancers benefit from these types of transfusions. Like blood donations, bone marrow donations must be compatible between the patient and the donor. Bone marrow donors can be from the patient (collected during remission), family members, or an unrelated donor. Donors are matched to recipients through human leukocyte antigen (HLA) tissue typing. Table 9.15 lists surgical treatments associated with hematology.

Did You Know?

Platelets can be given separately from whole blood to patients with bleeding disorders.

Did You Know?

National bone marrow donation registries help to match patients to potential donors.

TABLE 9.15 Surgical Treatments Associated with Hematology

Treatment	Description
blood transfusion	the process of receiving blood or blood components through an intravenous (IV) line
bone marrow transplant	procedure that replaces lost or destroyed bone marrow with healthy bone marrow provided by a donor (self or compatible match)
pheresis	procedure that uses as centrifuge to filter and separate blood components
apheresis	removal of harmful red blood cells from the body
leukapheresis	removal of harmful white blood cells from the body
plasmapheresis	removal of plasma from the body for the purpose of donation
plateletpheresis	removal of platelets from the body for the purpose of donation, also known as *thrombapheresis*
splenectomy	removal of the spleen

In the Know: Blood Donation

To obtain the material necessary for these transfusions, blood and blood products are collected from people who choose to donate blood through the American Red Cross or other blood donation organizations. One unit of collected blood can help save as many as three lives.

A blood donation contains about one pint of blood plus several small tubes of blood for testing. Once the donation is collected, it is labeled and sent for processing. The blood is centrifuged and the components (red blood cells, platelets, and plasma) and the small tubes are sent for testing. While the blood is being processed, the small tubes are tested at one of the Red Cross's three national testing centers. The blood undergoes 12 tests, including blood type and checking for infections. If a unit is found to be positive for infection or disease, it is immediately discarded and the donor is notified. Once the blood is cleared for transfusion, it can be stored at 43 degrees Fahrenheit for up to 42 days.

Blood components are separated by a process known as pheresis. The pheresis procedure is completed by placing a needle in the donor's large vein and drawing blood that is placed in a large centrifuge. The centrifuge separates the blood components that can be drawn out of the donor's blood. The remaining blood is then returned to the donor's circulation system.

Pharmacological Treatments

Several classifications of pharmacologic agents are used in hematology (see Table 9.16). **Thrombolytic** agents break down clots that have formed. **Antithrombotic** agents, also called **anticoagulants**, prevent clots from forming; agents that promote clotting are called **coagulants**. Pharmacological agents derived from blood products are used to treat hemophilia. Antifibrinolytic agents prevent excessive bleeding.

Growth factors are agents used to stimulate the growth of specific cells in the bone marrow. Growth factors include granulocyte colony-stimulating factor (G-CSF), granulocyte-macrophage colony-stimulating factor (GM-CSF), and erythropoietin (EPO). Much research is under way to find other growth factors to stimulate hematopoietic cells within the bone marrow.

TABLE 9.16 Pharmacologic Agents Associated with the Blood

Drug Class	Use
antianemics	increase the number of red blood cells or the amount of hemoglobin in the blood
anticoagulant (antithrombotic)	prevents blood from clotting
antihemophilic factors	promote clotting
biological response modifier: interferon	stimulates the body's own immune system
colony-stimulating factor	stimulates RBC production
granulocyte colony-stimulating factor	stimulates the formation of neutrophils
granulocyte-macrophage colony-stimulating factor	stimulates the formation of myeloid cells in the bone marrow
hemostatic/antifibrinolytic	prevents the breakdown of a clot
hemostatic/synthetic ADH	promotes clotting
thrombolytic	breaks down clots

Soft Skills for Medical Professionals: Teamwork & Motivation

Just as treatment for patients with hematology-oncology conditions involves multiple modalities, the healthcare team involved in providing treatment is also diverse. The physician is the team leader overseeing patient care, but it takes many different healthcare professionals to administer and monitor these complex treatments. When a patient visits the office or hospital, he or she is greeted by an administrative professional. Once paperwork is completed, the patient is assessed by the nursing and allied health staff. Lab work and X-rays are completed by personnel in those departments. The physician sees the patient and directs the treatment plan that is carried out by the healthcare team. It takes all these professionals to provide the care necessary for the patient. As a medical professional, your ability to work with this wide variety of health providers and participants has a direct impact on the care your patients receive. It is in everyone's best interests to work together, communicate effectively and clearly, and seek the best possible outcome and care for each patient. This common goal will help motivate all members of the care team.

Checkpoint 9.4

Answer the following questions to identify any areas of the section that you may need to review.

1. What does the acronym CBC stand for?

   _____

2. Where on the body is the most common site for a bone marrow biopsy?

   _____

3. What class of drugs breaks down blood clots?

   _____

Abbreviations

In the medical field, information is generally recorded in medical charts and in electronic medical records and provided to healthcare workers in medical shorthand. It is important that healthcare professionals become familiar with the abbreviations used to successfully perform the duties assigned in a typical workday. Table 9.17 provides a list of common abbreviations used in reference to conditions and treatments of the blood.

TABLE 9.17 Abbreviations Associated with Hematology

Abbreviation	Meaning
AHF	antihemophilic factor VIII
AHG	antihemophilic globulin factor VIII
ALL	acute lymphoblastic leukemia
AML	acute myeloblastic leukemia (also known as *acute myelogenous leukemia*)
ANC	absolute neutrophil count
APML	acute promyelocytic leukemia
baso	basophil
BMT	bone marrow transplant
CBC	complete blood count
CLL	chronic lymphocytic leukemia
CML	chronic myelogenous leukemia
diff	differential
eosin/eos	eosinophil
ESR	erythrocyte sedimentation rate
HCT/Hct	hematocrit
HGB/Hgb	hemoglobin
HLA	human leukocyte antigen
ITP	immune thrombocytopenic purpura
IV	intravenous
lymphs	lymphocytes
MCH	mean corpuscular hemoglobin
MCHC	mean corpuscular hemoglobin concentration
MCV	mean corpuscular volume
mono	monocyte
PA	pernicious anemia
plts/PLT	platelets
PMN	polymorphonuclear neutrophil
polys	polymorphonuclear neutrophils
PT	prothrombin time
PTT	partial thromboplastin time
RBC	red blood cell
sed rate	sedimentation rate
segs	segmented neutrophils
WBC	white blood cell

Exercise 9.13   Word Analysis

Give the definition of the following combining forms. Then build a term with each and use the term in a sentence.

Combining Form	Definition	Term
1. *erythr/o*	_____	_____
	_____	
2. *splen/o*	_____	_____
	_____	
3. *hem/o*	_____	_____
	_____	
4. *thromb/o*	_____	_____
	_____	
5. *cyt/o*	_____	_____
	_____	

Exercise 9.14   Comprehension Check

Circle the term that best completes each sentence.

1. Plasmapheresis/electrophresis was used to supply plasma for the patient.

2. Janice is being referred to a hematologist/hematosiologist.

3. Hattie's prothrombin/thrombopoietin time was evaluated yesterday.

4. Dan's Coombs' test detected the antibodies/hormones.

5. A bone marrow aspiration and biopsy will be done to assess Timmy's bone marrow/white blood cells.

Exercise 9.15   Matching

Match the abbreviations in column 1 with the definitions in column 2. Write the letter of the definition in the space beside the abbreviation.

1. _____ PTT	**a.** platelets
2. _____ CBC	**b.** sedimentation rate
3. _____ sed rate	**c.** partial thromboplastin time
4. _____ AHF	**d.** complete blood count
5. _____ plts	**e.** antihemophilic factor VIII

Exercise 9.16 Word Building

Supply roots, combining forms, or word parts to create a term that completes each sentence.

1. Pro_____in time is a test of blood clotting.

2. Mono_____ means "one cell" (type of white blood cell).

3. _____lysis is a breakdown of red blood cells.

4. Hemato_____ is the formation of blood.

5. Poly_____nuclear refers to cells that have different shaped nuclei.

6. _____coagulant means "against clotting."

Exercise 9.17 Comprehension Check

Write the correct definition for each abbreviation on the blank provided.

1. Hct   _____

2. Hgb   _____

3. MCH   _____

4. mono   _____

5. polys   _____

Exercise 9.18 Word Maps

Complete the following table of medications using terms from the list that follows.

antihemophilic factors
granulocyte colony-stimulating factor
prevents blood from clotting

stimulates the body's own immune system
stimulates RBC production

Drug Class	Use
anticoagulant (antithrombotic)	_____
_____	promote clotting
biological response modifier: interferon	_____
colony-stimulating factor	_____
_____	stimulates the formation of neutrophils

Chapter Review

After successfully completing this chapter, you should be able to correctly answer the following review questions. Answers are provided in the back of the text. Use this self-assessment opportunity to check your understanding of the content and determine whether you need to revisit any of the chapter's content.

Crossword Puzzle

Use the clues provided to fill in the puzzle with the correct terms. Enter one letter per square.

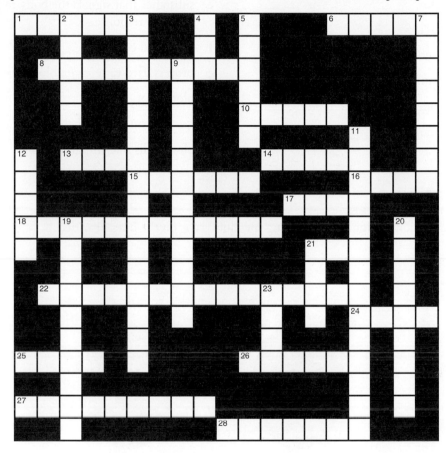

Across

1. hidden
6. stomat/o
8. uncontrolled bleeding
10. white
13. combining form for blood
14. echin/o
15. test to detect autoimmune hemolytic anemia
16. blood condition
17. elliptical
18. chemical treatment
21. erythr/o

22. "defenders of the body"
24. many
25. embolus
26. fluid portion of the blood that contains the cellular components
27. nosebleed
28. defective development of a blood cell line

Down

2. schist/o
3. decreased platelets
4. thalassa

5. Jamshidi
7. "tumor of blood"
9. enlargement of the liver
11. abnormality of the bone marrow
12. chyme
19. black-and-blue mark caused by leakage of blood from a vessel (bruising)
20. destruction of red blood cells
21. rouleaux
23. cyte

Matching

Match the following terms to their proper definitions.

1. _____ pheresis
2. _____ erythrocyte
3. _____ antibody
4. _____ thrombosis
5. _____ pallor
6. _____ platelets
7. _____ sphereocytosis
8. _____ anemia
9. _____ antigen
10. _____ hemorrhage

a. a protective protein produced by the body
b. paleness; may indicate anemia
c. low iron level in the blood
d. life-threatening bleeding
e. substance that signals the body to produce an immune response
f. red blood cell
g. process used to separate blood components
h. blood clot
i. a condition of ball-shaped cells
j. blood cells that initiate clotting

Identification

Correctly label the illustrations by identifying the blood type on the lines provided.

1. _____   3. _____

2. _____   4. _____

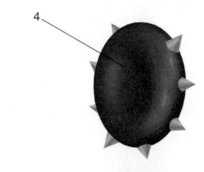
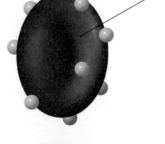

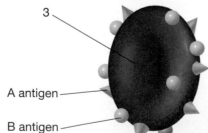

A antigen

B antigen

Abbreviations

Rewrite the following paragraph and replace all of the abbreviations with the correct definitions.

The patient presented at the physician's office with complaints of shortness of breath and loss of energy. She appears pale. A *CBC* with *diff* is ordered. Results show a decreased *HGB* and *HCT*. Changes in the *MCH*, *MCV*, and *MCHC* show a nutritional anemia. *PT* and *PTT* were within normal limits. The patient was crossmatched and prepared for a blood transfusion. The patient was given a prescription for iron supplements and was to return to the office in six weeks.

Word-Building Challenge

Review the following list of terms. Apply what you have learned in this chapter by identifying the meaning of the word parts within the term and then writing the likely definition of the term on the line provided.

1. lymphocytosis _____
   _____
   _____

2. erythrocytosis _____
   _____
   _____

3. phagocytosis _____
   _____
   _____

4. granulocyte _____
   _____
   _____

5. hypoxemia _____
   _____
   _____

Extension Activities

Complete the following activities as assigned by your instructor.

1. Search the Internet for plasma donation centers in your local geographic area. Gather the following information and create an informative PowerPoint presentation to present to your class. What are the basic requirements for donors (e.g., age, weight, medical screening parameters)? What process is used for plasmapheresis? What can donors expect (Does it hurt? How long will the process take?)? How often can plasma be donated? What will the donated plasma be used for? How does the facility compensate donors?

2. Hematology is a specialized field of medicine with a wide variety of career paths for allied health professionals. Choose a specific career path in allied health within a hematology setting and search the Internet to answer the following questions: What is the average salary for this particular health professional? What types of facilities would employ this type of health professional? What type of specialized training is required to work in this field? Find a minimum of two job postings in your area and share your findings with the class.

3. Cord blood banking is the process of collecting and storing a newborn's umbilical cord blood stem cells for potential medical use. How is the industry currently marketing this practice? What is the process used to collect and store a newborn's cord blood? What is the difference between donating a baby's cord to a public blood bank versus storing it at a private blood bank for use? What is the cost of cord banking? What research is currently being conducted in regard to cord banking? What are the most noted successes and failures in this research? What risk factors have been identified in reputable scientific research findings? What are some diseases that cord blood stem cells could possibly be used to treat? Is this trend expected to continue? Create a one- to two-page essay and present your findings to your class. Be sure to cite all of your sources.

Student eResources

The Course Navigator learning management system that accompanies this textbook offers multiple opportunities to master chapter content, including end-of-chapter exercises, a glossary of key terms with audio pronunciations, games, pronunciation coach, and additional activities such as engaging with the BioDigital® Human.

The Lymphatic System

" There are receptors to these molecules in your immune system, in your gut and in your heart. So when you say, 'I have a gut feeling' or 'my heart is sad' or 'I am bursting with joy,' you're not speaking metaphorically. You're speaking literally. "

—**Deepak Chopra,** author

Translation Challenge

Read the following physician report excerpt and try to answer the questions that follow it.

> Since his previous examination, the patient has continued to have active medical problems. With regard to his HIV infection, he continues to have a decreasing CD4 count. He continues his AZT therapy. His physical examination revealed palpable lymph nodes in the cervical, axillary, and inguinal areas.

1. What does the abbreviation HIV mean?

2. Is AZT a type of exercise or a type of medication?

3. In which parts of the body are the above mentioned lymph nodes located?

Learning Objectives

10.1 List and define word parts most commonly used to create terms related to the lymphatic system.

10.2 Identify organs of the lymphatic system.

10.3 Describe the role of lymphocytes in the body's defense mechanism.

10.4 Explain the elements of immunity.

10.5 Delineate the function of immunization in protecting the body.

10.6 Recognize and describe common conditions of the lymphatic system.

10.7 Name tests and treatments for major lymphatic system abnormalities.

10.8 State the meaning of abbreviations related to the immune system.

10.9 Correctly utilize lymphatic system terminology in written and oral communication.

10.10 Correctly spell and pronounce terms of the lymphatic system.

COURSE NAVIGATOR
Access Additional Chapter Resources

Tiny, microscopic enemies lurk everywhere in our environment. Harmful toxins, bacteria, fungi, viruses, parasites, and even cells within the body can attack and cause a host of problems ranging from sneezing and rashes to life-threatening illnesses. Fortunately, the body's **immune system** can successfully protect against many of these dangers. Individuals with intact immune systems are generally able to fight off most infections. Note that the combining form *immun/o* means "safety" or "protection."

The **lymphatic system** is responsible for filtering and destroying pathogens removed from the tissues. When blood travels through the body, blood vessels leak fluid into body tissues. This fluid provides nutrients to the cells and washes body tissue, collecting waste products such as bacteria and damaged or cancerous cells. This fluid then drains into the lymph vessels. Like the veins and arteries of the cardiovascular system (but much smaller), lymph vessels branch out throughout the body, connecting various lymphatic organs and aiding the body's immune system. The main organs of the lymphatic system are the tonsils, spleen, and thymus. Alongside lymph nodes, each organ is responsible for the filtering and removal of microorganisms found throughout the body.

In the Know: Specialists of the Lymphatic System

Immunology is the study of the functioning of the immune system and the interrelationships between this system and the rest of the body. **Immunologists** treat patients with acute and chronic disorders that attack the body's defense system. The emergence of acquired immunodeficiency syndrome (AIDS) in the 1980s prompted extensive research that generated an expanded understanding of the immune system. **Allergists** are physicians trained in the diagnosis and treatment of asthma and allergies. Allied health professionals involved in the care and treatment of lymphatic system conditions include certified medical assistants, phlebotomists, and allergy technicians.

Lymphatic System Word Parts

As with other body systems, a core of word parts serves as the source for most of the medical words associated with the lymphatic system. Table 10.1 lists common word parts and their meanings.

TABLE 10.1 Word Parts Associated with the Lymphatic System

Prefix	Meaning	Example
a-	absence	anemia (condition in which there is a deficiency in red blood cells in the body; leads to overall weakness)
ana-	back, away	anaphylaxis (severe response to an allergen)
anti-	against	antigen (foreign substance that triggers an immune response and/or production of antibodies)
auto-	self	autoimmune disease (condition in which the body's immune system attacks healthy tissues by mistake)
hyper-	excessive	hypersplenism (overactive spleen, filters damaged cells from the bloodstream too early and too quickly)
in-	within	involution (the shrinkage of an organ or tissue from enlarged to its normal size)
mono-	one	monocyte (largest type of white blood cell)
syn-	joined together	syndrome (a group of symptoms that occur together; relating to a specific disease)

Combining Form	Meaning	Example
aden/o	gland	adenoids (lymph glands located in the back of the throat)
auto-	self	autologous (transplant in which cells or tissues are obtained from the same individual)
axill/o	armpit	axillary (pertaining to the armpits)
bacteri/o	bacteria	bacteriology (the study of bacteria)
cyt/o	cell	leukocytes (white blood cells)
immun/o	immune	immunity (an organism's resistance to an infection or disease)
inguin/o	groin	inguinal (pertaining to the inguinal region, groin)
lymph/o (lymphat/o)	lymph	lymphatic (relating to lymph or its secretion)
lymphaden/o	lymph gland	lymphadenopathy (disease of the lymph nodes)
lymphangi/o	lymph vessel	lymphangitis (inflammation of the lymph vessels)
macro-	large	macrophage (white blood cells that ingest foreign particles/invaders; fight infection)
neutr/o	neutral	neutrophils (the most abundant type of white blood cell; fight off infection; purplish in color)
path/o	disease	pathology (the study of disease)
phag/o	to eat, swallow	phagocytose (to engulf and destroy bacteria and other foreign particles)
splen/o	spleen	splenectomy (removal of the spleen)
thrombocyt/o	clotting cell	thrombocyte (clotting cells)
thym/o	thymus	thymocyte (a cell that develops in the thymus; a precursor to T cells)
tonsill/o	tonsils	tonsillitis (inflammation of the tonsils)
tox/o	poison	toxic (caused by a toxin or poison)

Suffix	Meaning	Example
-cyte	cell	lymphocyte (lymph cells; responsible for the identification of foreign substances in the body)
-edema	inflammation, swelling	lymphedema (type of swelling in which lymph builds up in tissues)
-gen	producing	agglutinogens (antigens that cause the blood to clump together)
-itis	inflammation	lymphadenitis (inflammation of a lymph node)

Continues

Suffix	Meaning	Example
-oid	resembling	adenoid (lymph glands located in the back of the throat)
-osis	condition	lymphocytosis (abnormal increase in lymphocytes)
-penia	abnormal reduction	leukopenia (decrease in the number of white blood cells)

Anatomy and Physiology

The lymphatic system is composed of specialized organs, ducts, and cells located throughout the body. The organs of this system include the thymus, tonsils, lymph nodes, and spleen, as shown in Figure 10.1. The lymphatic system is responsible for protecting and defending the body from the outside world and from internal mechanisms that cause the body to turn against itself. Common anatomy and physiology terms related to the lymphatic system are listed in Table 10.2.

FIGURE 10.1 Components of the Lymphatic System

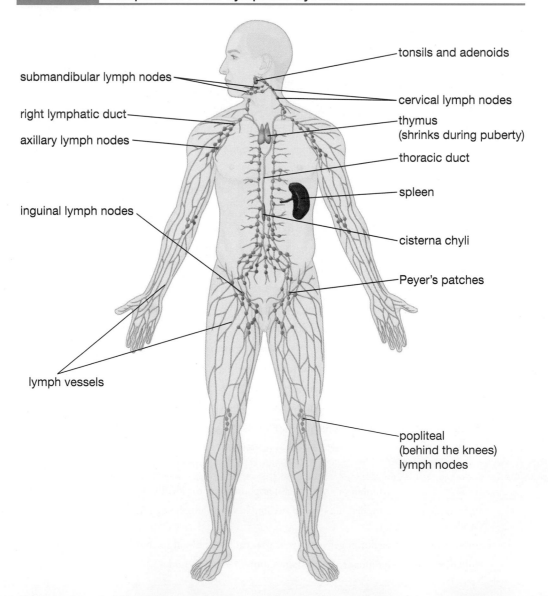

submandibular lymph nodes

right lymphatic duct

axillary lymph nodes

inguinal lymph nodes

lymph vessels

tonsils and adenoids

cervical lymph nodes

thymus (shrinks during puberty)

thoracic duct

spleen

cisterna chyli

Peyer's patches

popliteal (behind the knees) lymph nodes

Term		Meaning	Word Analysis	
adenoid	[**ad**-ah-noyd]	lymph organs (glands) located in the back of the throat	*aden/o*	gland
			-oid	resembling
afferent	[**af**-er-ent]	toward; flowing in; to bring to		
antibody	[**an**-tih-bod-ee]	substance in the blood that is produced in response to an antigen; a protective protein produced by the body	*anti-*	against
antigen	[**an**-tih-jen]	substance that produces an immune response (i.e., triggers the production of antibodies)	*anti-*	against
			-gen	producing
axillary lymph nodes	[**ak**-sil-air-ee **limf**]	lymph nodes that may swell due to an injury or infection in the breast, chest, abdomen, and upper limbs	*axill/o*	armpit
			-ary	pertaining to
			lymph/o	lymph
cisterna chyli	[sis-**ter**-nah kI-li]	sac responsible for collecting lymph from the digestive tract, drainage point, also known as the *cysterna chyli*		
complement	[**kom**-pleh-ment]	substance present in the body that can destroy dangerous cells by triggering inflammation, drawing white blood cells to the affected area	*complement*	complete
efferent	[**ef**-er-ent]	outward; flowing away from; to bring out		
humor	[**hyoo**-mer]	watery fluid in the body		
immunity	[im-**myoon**-ih-tee]	not susceptible	*immun/o*	immune; free
immuno-globulin (Ig)	[im-myoo-nO-**glob**-yoo-lin]	protein in the body that helps to destroy antigens; also known as *antibodies*	*immun/o*	immune
immunology	[im-myoo-**nol**-ah-jee]	practice and study of the immune system	*immun/o*	immune
			-logy	study of
inflamma-tory response	[in-**flam**-ah-tor-ee]	bodily response produced when an injury occurs; the affected area generally exhibits the following signs: swelling, redness, warmth, and pain	*in-*	in, into
			flamma	flame, fire
			-ory	condition
inguinal lymph nodes	[in-**gwin**-null **limf**]	lymph nodes that may swell due to injury or infection in the foot, leg, groin, or genitals	*inguin/o*	groin
			lymph/o	lymph
interferon	[**in**-ter-**feer**-on]	protective proteins that help the body fight viruses by "interfering" with the virus's ability to multiply or replicate		
involution	[in-vO-**loo**-shun]	return of an organ or tissue from enlarged to normal size	*in-*	within
			volution	to roll up
lingual tonsils	[**lin**-gwul **ton**-silz]	tonsils found on each side of the tongue	*lingu/o*	tongue
			al	pertaining to
lymph	[**limf**]	fluid that circulates throughout the lymphatic system		
lymph node	[limf]	organ of the lymphatic system responsible for the collection and filtration of foreign particles; located in the lymph vessels; becomes enlarged or inflamed to signal infection	*lymph/o*	lymph
			node	knot
lymphatic vessels	[lim-**fat**-ik]	thin structures that filter and carry fluid away from tissues before returning fluid to the blood	*lymphangi/o*	lymph vessel
macrophage	[**mak**-rO-fayj]	white blood cells that ingest foreign particles/invaders; fight infection; phagocytic cell in the tissues	*macro-*	large
			-phage	to eat

Continues

Term		Meaning	Word Analysis	
monocyte	[**mon**-O-sIt]	largest type of white blood cell; found in lymph nodes, the spleen, and bone marrow; a phagocytic cell that engulfs and kills bacteria and plays a role in the destruction of tumor cells	*mono-* *-cyte*	one cell
neutrophil	[**noo**-trO-fil]	the most abundant type of white blood cell; purplish in color; fights off infection by seeking, ingesting, and killing bacteria	*neutro-* *-phil*	neutral attraction
palatine tonsils	[**pal**-ah-tIn **ton**-silz]	tonsils found on the left and right sides of the pharynx (throat)	*palat/o*	palate
phagocytosis	[fag-O-sI-**tO**-sis]	process of ingesting cells or foreign substances	*phag/o* *cyt/o* *-osis*	eat cell condition
phagocyte	[**fag**-O-sIt]	a cell that engulfs and destroys bacteria and other foreign particles	*phag/o* *-cyte*	eat cell
pharyngeal tonsils	[far-**in**-jee-al **ton**-silz]	commonly referred to as the adenoids; tonsils found at the back of the throat in the nasal cavity; part of the body's defense system; block foreign substances from entering the body	*pharyng/o* *-al*	pharynx pertaining to
right lymphatic duct	[lim-**fat**-ik]	lymph vessel that drains fluid from the right upper limb, right side of the chest cavity, and right halves of the head and neck	*lymph/o*	lymph
spleen		organ located on the left-hand side of the body, underneath the rib cage and behind the stomach; houses macrophages to eliminate old/damaged cells, lymphocytes to fight infection, and platelets to aid in clotting	*thorac/o* *-ic* *duct(us)*	chest pertaining to duct (vessel)
thoracic duct	[thO-**ras**-ik dukt]	largest lymph vessel in the body; drains most of the body		
thymosin	[**thI**-mO-sin]	hormone of the thymus gland that stimulates the thymus to release its hormones	*thym/o*	thymus
thymus	[**thI**-mus]	organ located in the mediastinum (breastbone); vital to the development of the immune system until puberty	*thym/o*	thymus
tonsil	[**ton**-sil]	lymph tissue located at the back of the mouth and nose, above the throat; houses a large number of cells that help protect the body against infection		

Organs of the Immune System

The **thymus** is an organ found in the middle section of the chest cavity known as the **mediastinum**. It lies anterior to (in front of) the heart and posterior to (behind) the sternum. Its major function is to produce **lymphocytes**, also known as **T cells**, the cells responsible for protecting the body from pathogens (disease). The thymus does not function during adulthood as all growth and development occur before birth and throughout childhood. The thymus reaches its maximum size during the adolescent years, when it weighs between 35 and 40g (just over an ounce). All of the T cells used by the immune system are produced by the thymus before the body reaches puberty. Following puberty, the thymus begins to shrink, a process called **involution**, and eventually becomes fatty tissue.

Located in the upper left quadrant of the abdomen, behind the stomach, the **spleen** is the largest structure within the lymphatic system. Bacteria and foreign substances present in the blood passing through the spleen are filtered by lymphocytes and then ingested and destroyed by macrophages, a process also known as **phagocytosis**. Additionally, the spleen removes or filters old and damaged red blood cells (RBCs). The spleen is also responsible for the storage of platelets, which aid in blood clotting. The spleen can contain more than 1 pint of blood at any given time, which is roughly 10 percent of the total amount of blood in an adult's body. Therefore, any injury to the spleen can cause serious blood loss, and removal of the spleen may be necessary to stop the bleeding.

The **tonsils** are structures made up of lymph tissue. They are found at the back of the mouth and nose, above the throat. Tonsils form a protective ring in the mouth and back of the throat, where they filter foreign particles from the nose and mouth. Because they are the first line of defense against the outside environment, it's not uncommon for the tonsils to become infected. When they are doing their job fighting infections, a sore throat develops. The three sets of tonsils are (1) the **palatine tonsils**, located on each side of the throat; (2) the **pharyngeal tonsils**, or **adenoids**, located in the posterior opening of the nasopharynx (the area connecting the nose and throat); and (3) the **lingual tonsils**, located on both sides of the base of the tongue (see Figure 10.2).

FIGURE 10.2 Tonsils

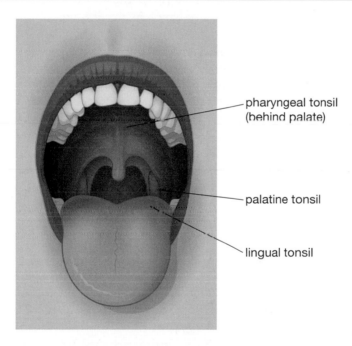

pharyngeal tonsil (behind palate)

palatine tonsil

lingual tonsil

In the Know: Tonsillectomy and Adenoidectomy (T&A)

Tonsils are the tissues at the back of the throat responsible for filtering out bacteria and viruses. The tonsils are prone to infection and are often removed when a patient has frequent infections that remain despite the use of antibiotics or when a patient experiences problems with breathing and swallowing due to inflammation, ultimately affecting sleep. This procedure is called a **tonsillectomy and adenoidectomy (T&A)**. Statistically, 20 percent of T&As are performed due to infection and 80 percent to treat sleep apnea. A tonsillectomy is one of the most common surgical procedures for children in the United States.

Lymph nodes are found in clusters throughout the body, as shown in Figure 10.1. Lymph nodes range in size from a pinhead to a lima bean. The lymph nodes found in the head, arms, and legs are located close to the surface. Those found in the neck are located both at the surface level and deeper inside the body. The lymph nodes found in the trunk and internal organs are located very deep within the body. Overall, lymph nodes serve as the filtration system of **lymph**, a specialized fluid containing lymphocytes, which flows from specific areas of the body to trap foreign organisms. Swollen (enlarged) lymph nodes signal infection and will generally return to their usual size once the body's immune system eliminates the infection.

Lymph Vessels

The lymph nodes are drained by a system of lymph vessels separate from the vessels of the circulatory system (the system that carries blood throughout the body). Lymph fluid flows into two vessels, the **right lymphatic duct** and the **thoracic duct**, which eventually empty their lymph into the veins of the neck. The largest lymphatic vessel is the thoracic duct, which drains about three-fourths of the body. The right lymphatic duct drains lymph from the right upper extremity (i.e., shoulder, arm, forearm, wrist, and hand) and the right side of the head, neck, and upper torso (see Figure 10.1). The vessels of the lymphatic system have one-way valves to maintain the flow of lymph in one direction.

Lymph Node Filtering System

The filtering process begins when lymph enters the node through the **afferent** (toward) lymph vessels to be filtered of bacteria and other harmful substances. (Note that afferent vessels carry fluid or messages toward an organ or part. The term *afferent* is Latin for "to carry." Recall that afferent nerve fibers carry information collected from the sensory receptors to the central nervous system for processing.) After these harmful organisms are removed, the lymph then exits through the **efferent** (away) lymph vessel, similar to the activity of efferent nerves carrying messages away from the central nervous system by way of motor responses. The one-way flow mechanism prevents bacteria from flowing through the entire body. The entry and exit of lymph through the nodes are important to the clinical care of a patient. For instance, if a patient has an infection in the left ear, the drainage of the bacteria would cause the lymph nodes of the left side of the neck to swell, because they are filled with dead bacterial cells, signaling infection. Once treated, the lymph nodes would return to normal size as all harmful substances would be filtered out.

Cells of the Lymphatic System

Physical barriers, such as the skin and mucous membranes, serve as the first line of defense against infection (nonspecific immunity). If an organism manages to overcome the physical barrier (e.g., through a cut in the skin or even chapped hands such as eczema), the cells of the lymphatic system are then summoned to join the fight (specific immunity). These cells include monocytes, neutrophils, B cells, and T cells, also known as *B* and *T lymphocytes*.

Neutrophils and **monocytes** circulate in the blood and move into the tissues, when needed, to fight infection. Once inside the tissues, the monocytes mature into phagocytic cells called **macrophages**. These specialized cells are responsible for the destruction of invading cells. Generally, these cells have the ability to attack a small number of foreign substances. When necessary, they can also send out signals to command the production of larger immune cells, such as lymphocytes, in the affected area.

B Cells

B lymphocytes, or **B cells**, are found in large numbers throughout the body. They are produced in the bone marrow, but live in lymph nodes and other lymphatic tissues (e.g., the spleen). When an antigen, or substance that the body perceives as foreign, is detected, the B cells change into plasma cells that produce proteins called **immunoglobulins** (also known as *antibodies*). These immunoglobulins trap the antigens by attaching themselves to the surface of the organism, alerting the body to destroy them. Because the immuno-globulins are released into the body's blood and lymph fluids (referred to as humors), the process is known as **humoral immunity**. These cells can replicate quickly and produce a large amount of antibodies. Once the infection has been destroyed, most B cells and plasma cells die. A few remain in the bone marrow and lymph nodes and are available to produce antibodies if needed to protect against future infection. These cells are commonly known as **memory B cells**.

T Cells

The **T lymphocytes**, also called **T cells**, are responsible for attacking and destroying foreign substances (such as viruses and cancer cells). Like B cells, T cells are produced in the bone marrow, but unlike B cells, T cells develop in the thymus under the stimulation of **thymosin**, the hormone secreted by the thymus. As they mature, T cells migrate to the lymph nodes and lymph organs. When a virus invades the body, T cells respond by multi-plying rapidly. The antigen then binds to the protein on the surface of the T cell, making it a sensitized T cell (see Figure 10.3). These sensitized cells kill invading cells by releasing substances that are deadly to the invaders. As a final step, macrophages move to the area and phagocytose (eat/ingest) the invading cells.

FIGURE 10.3 T Cell Function

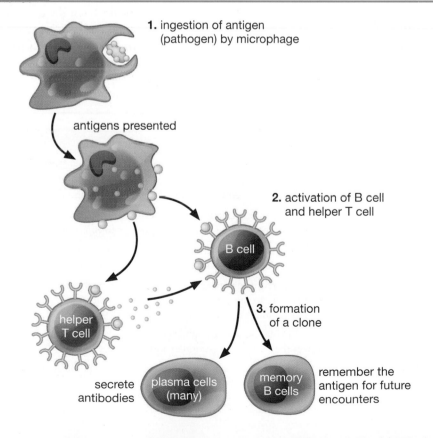

1. ingestion of antigen (pathogen) by microphage

antigens presented

2. activation of B cell and helper T cell

B cell

3. formation of a clone

helper T cell

secrete antibodies

plasma cells (many)

memory B cells

remember the antigen for future encounters

T lymphocytes are responsible for the activation of B cells, attacking infected or malignant cells throughout the body, as well as triggering the production of antibodies, which is discussed later in this chapter. Unfortunately, T cells are also responsible for the rejection of foreign tissues used to repair and restore function (e.g., skin grafts and transplanted organs). Additionally, T cells produce small proteins called **interferons**. These proteins *interfere* with the virus's ability to replicate itself once it invades the body. Pharmaceutical interferon is used to treat certain cancers, some types of hepatitis, and some other conditions.

Types of Immunity

The lymphatic system provides the body with two types of defense mechanisms: nonspecific immunity and specific immunity. **Nonspecific immunity** is innate, as it is the defense system you were born with. In contrast, **specific immunity** is developed by the body in response to exposure to a virus or other foreign substance (such as bacteria). The skin and mucous membranes provide nonspecific immunity by preventing outside organisms from entering the body. Tears and mucus provide another example of nonspecific immunity. Tears wash foreign invaders out of the eyes, and mucus traps foreign substances before they can enter the respiratory system. Specific immunity is acquired as the body recognizes (remembers) substances to which it was previously exposed. A virus entering the body may make the person sick, but the second time it appears, the body recognizes the organism and destroys it, leaving the individual with no symptoms. The person is then said to be immune to that particular organism.

The **inflammatory response**, another example of nonspecific immunity, occurs when the body is damaged or when foreign organisms enter it (see Figure 10.4). Tissue damaged by heat, trauma, bacteria, or other mechanisms trigger the release of **mediators**, substances that activate immune cells. First to arrive at the scene are the white blood cells (WBCs). The accumulation of WBCs causes the external signs of inflammation: heat and redness resulting from increased blood flow, and swelling and pain from the damaged tissue. The WBCs enter the tissue and immediately initiate **phagocytosis**, a process in which bacteria and damaged cells are destroyed, thus increasing blood flow and promoting tissue repair. Table 10.3 summarizes the subgroups of specific immunity.

TABLE 10.3 Types of Specific Immunity

Type	Description
acquired immunity	immunity that involves the presence of antibodies (may be either natural or artificial)
• active acquired artificial immunity	a vaccine is administered to stimulate the production of antibodies/memory cells so that when disease enters the body it is recognized and destroyed
• active acquired natural immunity	person contracts a specific disease; body then produces antibodies and memory cells to fight off the disease (also known as *humoral immunity*)
• passive acquired artificial immunity	antibodies are injected into a person following a possible exposure to the pathogen; provides immediate protection (e.g., tetanus and rabies gamma globulins)
• passive acquired natural immunity	immunity received when a mother passes her antibodies to the fetus through the placenta and to the newborn through her breast milk; the baby is immune to specific diseases for a few months until it is able to develop its own antibodies
active immunity	immunity developed through exposure to a disease; antibodies are produced that protect the body upon second exposure
natural (genetic) immunity	immunity that is programmed into an individual's DNA at birth; does not involve the presence of antibodies
• species immunity	genetic immunity to animal diseases

FIGURE 10.4 Inflammatory Response

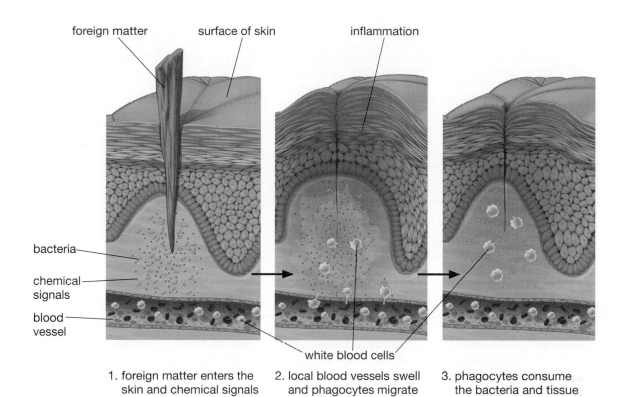

foreign matter   surface of skin   inflammation

bacteria

chemical signals

blood vessel

white blood cells

1. foreign matter enters the skin and chemical signals are released

2. local blood vessels swell and phagocytes migrate to the area

3. phagocytes consume the bacteria and tissue begins to heal

In the Know: Vaccines and Herd Immunity

Vaccines are used to develop specific immunity by imitating an infection in the body. While the imitated infection does not cause an actual illness, it does initiate the body's production of T cells and antibodies. These produced T cells and antibodies are then prepared for future exposure to that particular illness.

Community immunity, also known as *herd immunity*, is the indirect protection from a particular illness that occurs when a large percentage of a population has been immunized. When a large percentage of the population has been immunized a measure of protection is provided for those who have not been vaccinated. This method of immunity has been used to control a variety of contagious diseases, (e.g., influenza, measles, mumps, rotavirus, and pneumoccocus).

Checkpoint **10.1**

Answer the following questions to identify any areas of the section that you may need to review.

1. Which type of immunity is received when a mother passes her antibodies to the fetus through the placenta or to the newborn through her breast milk?

   _____

2. What organ is responsible for housing macrophages to eliminate damaged cells, lymphocytes to fight infection, and platelets to aid in clotting?

   _____

3. What substances of the lymphatic system are responsible for the activation of immune cells following tissue damage?

   _____

Exercise **10.1**   Identification

Write the number of the five anatomical structures on the appropriate location on the accompanying figure. Then write the combining form on the first line under each structure name.

1. axillary lymph nodes

   _____

2. tonsils

   _____

3. inguinal lymph nodes

   _____

4. spleen

   _____

5. lymphatic vessels

   _____

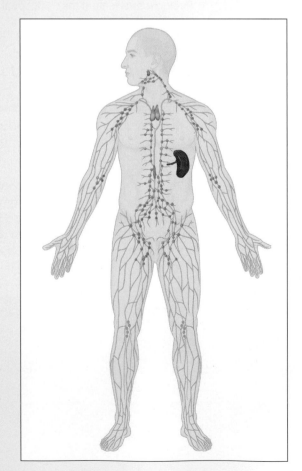

Exercise 10.2 Spelling Check

Read each sentence and correct the spelling of the underlined word or words; then supply a definition.

1. The <u>mediastunim</u> was opened and the thymus gland located. _____

   _____

2. The <u>pharyngeltonsins</u> were found to be enlarged. _____

   _____

3. The <u>palatintonsuls</u> were covered with thick exudate. _____

   _____

4. There were many <u>macrofages</u> in the tissue surrounding the wound. _____

   _____

5. The patient was told that a repeat exposure to this <u>antegen</u> could prove fatal. _____

   _____

Exercise 10.3 Word Building

Provide the missing word parts to create the correct term for the definition provided.

1. _____osis means "condition of cell eating."
2. _____itis refers to inflammation of cells.
3. _____pathy refers to disease of the lymph gland.
4. _____logous means "referring to the self."
5. _____cyte means "thymus cell."

Exercise 10.4 Matching

Select a term from column 1 to match each definition in column 2. Write your choice on the line beside the term.

1. _____ thymus
2. _____ immunology
3. _____ macrophage
4. _____ artificial immunity
5. _____ nonspecific immunity

a. type of large white blood cell that devours invading cells and debris

b. gland of the immune system located in the mediastinum above the heart

c. study of the immune system

d. type of immunity acquired through deliberate exposure (immunization)

e. type of immunity an individual is born with

Exercise 10.5 Word Building

Use roots, combining forms, prefixes, and suffixes to construct a medical term to match each definition provided.

Definition	Term
1. study of the immune system	_____
2. protein that helps destroy antigens	_____
3. pertaining to the spleen	_____
4. one cell (type of WBC)	_____
5. pertaining to watery fluid in the body (humor)	_____

Exercise 10.6 Word Maps

Organize the following methods of immunity by writing them in the proper column.

Methods of Acquiring Immunity
antibodies passed from mother to fetus
inflammatory response
mechanical barriers (e.g., skin, tears, and mucus membranes)
previous exposure to a disease
vaccinations

Nonspecific Immunity	**Specific Immunity**

Conditions

The immune system undergoes many changes throughout an individual's lifetime. Lymphoid tissue is the only tissue in the body that reaches adult growth during childhood, usually by age six. It continues to develop rapidly, surpassing adult size by puberty, then slowly begins to decrease. This phenomenon is believed to occur because children must produce antibodies and fight a variety of foreign substances from the surrounding environment.

A healthcare provider assesses the immune system by obtaining a complete history, performing a physical examination, and ordering laboratory tests. Frequent illness may suggest that the patient has an incompetent compromised immune system. To assess the immune system's functioning, the examiner palpates all areas containing superficial lymph nodes (refer to Figure 10.1). Enlarged lymph nodes, or swollen glands, can sometimes indicate infection. Nodes that have responded to infection feel spongy or like hard pellets (**shotty**). These **reactive nodes** are freely movable under the examiner's touch. Firm, fixed lymph nodes may signal an infection, a serious disorder, or a cancerous node. An enlarged liver or spleen, which can be identified by percussion or palpation, suggests an abnormality.

Table 10.4 describes common conditions associated with the lymphatic system.

TABLE 10.4 Conditions Associated with Immunity

Term		Meaning	Word Analysis	
acquired immuno-deficiency syndrome (AIDS)	[ah-**kwIrd** im-myoo-nO-deh-**fish**-en-see **sin**-drOm]	group of illnesses that occur as a result of infection with the HIV-1 virus	*immun/o* *deficiency*	immune to fail
anaphylaxis	[an-ah-fih-**lak**-sis]	severe reaction caused by increased sensitivity to a substance	*ana-* *phylaxis*	back; away protection
asthma	[**as**-mah]	disorder in which airways are temporarily narrowed, resulting in breathing difficulty, coughing, gasping, and wheezing; may be triggered by an overactive immune system		
ataxia telangiectasia	[ah-**tak**-see-ah tel-an-jee-ek-**tay**-see-ah]	progressive, hereditary immunodeficiency disorder involving the nervous and lymphatic systems; results in weakened immune system	*a-* *taxia* *tel/o* *angi/o* *ect/o* *-ia*	absence order distance, end blood vessels outside condition
autoimmune	[aw-tO-ih-**myoon**]	condition in which the person's immune system turns against itself (relating to antibodies that attack the cells of the body producing them)	*auto-* *immun/o*	one; oneself immune
diabetes (type 1)	[dI-ah-**bee**-teez]	metabolic disease caused by decreased production of insulin (normally produced in the pancreas); considered to be autoimmune in nature		
glomerulonephritis	[glom-**er**-yoo-lO-neh-**frI**-tis]	autoimmune condition of the thyroid whereby the body's immune system mistakenly attacks and destroys healthy thyroid cells	*glomerul/o* *nephr/o* *-itis*	glomerulus kidney inflammation
Graves' disease		autoimmune condition of the thyroid; a form of hyperthyroidism		
Hashimoto's thyroiditis	[hah-shee-**mO**-tOz rhI-roy-**dI**-ris]	autoimmune condition of the thyroid whereby it is infiltrated with lymphocytes	Hashimoto *thyroid/o* *-itis*	Japanese surgeon thyroid inflammation
hemolytic anemia	[**hee**-mO-**lit**-ik ah-**nee**-mee-ah]	autoimmune disorder caused by antibodies directed to destroy RBCs, leading to anemia	*hem/o* *-lytic* *an-* *-emia*	blood destruction, dissolution without blood
immunodeficiency	[im-myoo-nO-deh-**fish**-en-see]	state in which an individual has decreased immune function	*immun/o* *deficiency*	immune to fail
lymphoma	[lim-**fO**-mah]	type of cancer that originates in the cells of the immune system	*lymph/o* *-oma*	lymph tumor
mononucleosis	[mah-nO-noo-klee-**O**-sis]	an infection transmitted through saliva and caused by the Epstein-Barr virus, also called "mono" or "the kissing disease"	*mono-* *nucle/o* *-osis*	one nucleus abnormal condition

Continues

Term		Meaning	Word Analysis	
myasthenia gravis	[mI-as-**thee**-nee-ah **gra**-vis]	autoimmune disorder leading to weakness of voluntary (skeletal) muscle	*my/o* *a-* *-sthenia*	muscle without condition of strength
pernicious anemia	[pur-**nish**-us ah-**nee**-mee-ah]	vitamin B_{12} deficiency caused by an immunological condition preventing absorption	*an-* *-emia*	without blood condition
retrovirus	[**ret**-rO-vI-rus]	type of virus; a retrovirus causes HIV	*retro-* *vir/o* *-us*	backward virus structure
rheumatoid arthritis	[**roo**-mah-toyd ar-**thrI**-tis]	autoimmune condition, causes pain and inflammation of the joints, usually begins after age 40, more common in women	*rheumat/o* *-oid* *arthr/o* *-itis*	watery flow full of joint inflammation
sarcoidosis	[sahr-koy-dO-sis]	an inflammatory disease that affects the lungs and lymph glands, associated with increased activity of the immune system	*sarc/o* *-osis*	flesh abnormal condition
scleroderma	[skler-O-**der**-mah]	immunological disorder characterized by thickening of the skin; can be systemic	*scler/o* *derm/a*	hardness skin
severe combined immunodeficiency syndrome (SCIDS)		inherited disorders that cause severe abnormalities in immune system functions		
shotty	[**shot**-ee]	hard, round pellets, freely movable, normal-feeling lymph node		
systemic lupus erythematosus (SLE)	[sis-**tem**-ik **loo**-pus er-ih-them-ah-**tO**-sus]	autoimmune disorder in which the body mistakenly attacks healthy tissue	*systemic* *erythem/a* *-osus (-osis)*	affecting many parts of the body (skin, joints, kidneys, brain) redness condition
thrombocytopenia	[throm-bO-sI-tO-**pee**-nee-ah]	hereditary disorder characterized by abnormal immune system function (immunodeficiency) and the reduced ability to form blood clots	*thromb/o* *cyt/o* *-penia*	clot, clotting cell deficiency
Wiskott-Aldrich syndrome	[**vis**-kot-**awl**-drich **sin**-drOm]	hereditary immunodeficiency disorder characterized by the reduced ability to form blood clots	*syn-* *-drome*	joined; together to run, running

Infants and Children

An infant is born with the mother's immunity, which provides protection for several months. The newborn can acquire further immunity from the bacterial and viral antibodies present in breast milk. As the immune system develops, the child begins to produce antibodies in response to antigens. The lymph nodes are large in childhood and respond to invading organisms by enlarging further.

In the early months, children receive immunization against many organisms. Immunizations are usually given over time and in several doses to stimulate the formation of antibodies and memory within the T cells. Stringent worldwide immunization practices have eradicated many diseases that once killed an incalculable number of people across the world. Some of the deadly diseases that are now almost entirely preventable include hepatitis B, diphtheria, tetanus, pertussis, pneumonia and meningitis caused by *Haemophilus influenzae* type b (Hib), polio, measles, mumps, rubella, and varicella (chickenpox).

In the Know: Childhood Immunizations

There is an ongoing debate among parents, health officials, and pediatricians regarding the safety of vaccines administered to infants and young children. These include vaccines for diphtheria, tetanus, and pertussis (DTaP); IPV (inactive polio virus); and measles, mumps, and rubella (MMR). Vaccines may have mild side effects, such as a fever or soreness; however, some parents believe that immunizations have the potential for causing severe side effects. Many parents also feel that immunizations are unwarranted given that many of the diseases for which an infant is being immunized are uncommon today. On the other side of the argument are those who believe that the illnesses can cause a real threat to the particular child, as well as to society at large if the general population were not immunized. More information can be found at the following website: http://MedTerm.ParadigmCollege.net/VaccineSafety.

Common Childhood Infections

The tonsils are a frequent site of infection in youngsters who have upper respiratory infections (URIs) and viral illnesses. Sometimes abdominal pain is associated with lymph drainage of the abdominal (mesenteric) lymph nodes.

Although young children may experience many upper respiratory illnesses, they usually do not develop serious bacterial infections unless they have an underlying condition, such as **immunodeficiency**. Children whose current weight or rate of weight gain is significantly lower than that of children of similar age and gender (a syndrome called failure to thrive [FTT]), should also be tested for immunodeficiency. Primary immunodeficiency is inherited and may affect any part of the immune system. (Secondary immunodeficiency occurs as a result of an infection or virus, such as HIV, which is discussed later in this chapter.)

Hereditary Immune System Diseases

While they exist, inherited immune system disorders are considered rare. **Severe combined immunodeficiency (SCID)** is a group of inherited disorders that cause severe abnormalities in the lymphatic system. Children with SCID cannot make antibodies and have incompetent lymphoid tissues. A bone marrow transplant from a matched donor is the only available cure.

Ataxia telangiectasia is another hereditary disease affecting the nervous and lymphatic systems. Children with this disease are often stricken with weakened immune systems. A weakened immune system leads to frequent infections. **Wiskott-Aldrich syndrome** is a hereditary immunodeficiency disorder characterized by a reduced ability to form blood clots.

Adults and Seniors

As we age, the immune system seems to function less efficiently. Certain illnesses tend to appear in people over age 60, including autoimmune disorders. These disorders are diagnosed when autoantibodies are present, cells that target and destroy themselves.

Lupus is an autoimmune condition in which an individual's immune system attacks its own healthy cells, via the production of autoantibodies (antibodies that attack the body's normal cells). No evidence exists connecting lupus to a specific trigger or infection. There are three main types of lupus: systemic lupus erythematosus (SLE), skin lupus, and drug-induced lupus. SLE is the most common and the most serious. SLE can affect the skin, joints, brain, heart, lungs, and kidneys. Skin lupus does not affect the body's organs, but can cause a rash (and possibly scarring) on the face, neck, scalp, and ears. Drug-induced lupus is similar to SLE and is caused by a reaction to certain medications. Once an individual stops taking the medication, the symptoms often cease. Table 10.5 lists the most common autoimmune disorders and the body's response.

TABLE 10.5 Autoimmune Disorders and Typical Age at Onset

Disorder	Typical Age at Onset	Body's Response
celiac disease	any age	When food containing gluten (a protein found in wheat, rye, and barley) is ingested, the body has an immune response that attacks the small intestine.
diabetes (type 1)	childhood	Cells that produce insulin in the pancreas are destroyed.
glomerulonephritis (Goodpasture's syndrome)	any age; common in children aged 3–10	Immune systems overreact to an infection and antibodies attack the kidneys and lungs.
Graves' disease (thyrotoxicosis/hyperthyroidism)	young adults	The immune system creates antibodies that cause the thyroid to grow, thus overproducing thyroid hormone.
Hashimoto's thyroiditis	age 30–50	The immune system attacks the thyroid gland, thus resulting in hypothyroidism.
hemolytic anemia	over age 50	Antibodies are created that attack and destroy red blood cells.
immune thrombocytopenic purpura	any age; common in children under 10	Antibodies are created that attack and destroy platelets necessary for the process of blood clotting.
multiple sclerosis (MS)	young adults	The immune system attacks the central nervous system (CNS), damaging myelin (the fatty material that surrounds and protects nerve fibers).
myasthenia gravis	age 20–30 in women, over 50 in men	Antibodies attack and destroy the acetylcholine receptors needed for muscle contraction.
pernicious anemia	over age 60	The immune system attacks and destroys the mucus-secreting cells of the stomach, thus inhibiting the production of intrinsic factor (IF) and the absorption of vitamin B_{12} by the body; ultimately the body fails to make enough RBCs.
rheumatoid arthritis (RA)	over age 40	The immune system attacks the lining of the bones and joints.
scleroderma	age 35–50	The immune system triggers the overproduction of collagen in the body, resulting in the buildup of scar tissue on the skin and internal organs (fibrosis).
systemic lupus erythematosus (SLE)	young adults; more common in females	The immune system creates antibodies that attack its own tissues (e.g., skin, joints, kidneys, brain, and other organs).
vitiligo	age 10–30	The immune system attacks its melanocytes (pigment-producing cells), resulting in white patches of skin on different parts of the body.

Allergies

Allergies are among the most common reasons people visit a doctor or pharmacy. Hay fever, certain types of asthma, and hives are the major types of allergic reactions. As a group, allergies produce a range of responses—from the minor annoyances of a runny nose and itchy eyes to potentially fatal, life-threatening reactions. In the Unites States between 1991 and 2001, there were 2,281 incidents of allergic reactions to vaccines reported out of the 1.9 billion vaccinations administered. The estimated incidence of allergic reactions to food in the pediatric population is approximately 6 to 8 percent, compared to the incidence of allergic reaction to an antibiotic in the same population reported at 7.3 percent.

The most common allergy is **hay fever**, named by Charles Harrison Blackley in England in 1869. Blackley was the first to show a connection between pollen and hay fever by performing a skin test. Pollen was applied through a small break in the skin in order to trigger a positive reaction. Thus, the name *hay fever* was coined for the symptoms produced by the illness.

Allergic reactions occur because of the antibody immunoglobulin E (IgE) and are believed to be genetic. The first time an allergy-prone person comes in contact with a substance to which he or she is allergic (an allergen), the body produces large amounts of IgE. The IgE molecules attach to the surface of the mast cells and basophils, a type of white blood cell in the circulating blood that migrates to the tissues. Mast cells are found in large quantities in the lungs, skin, tongue, and linings of the nose and intestinal tract.

The second encounter with an allergen produces a type I allergic reaction. Immunoglobulin E signals the mast cells or basophils to release chemicals, including histamine, heparin, and other substances. These substances cause the telltale allergy symptoms: runny nose and eyes, itching, sneezing, and so forth. If an allergic reaction is severe, it may result in **anaphylactic shock**, a severe, potentially life-threatening reaction that includes swelling of the tissues, including the throat, and a rapid drop in blood pressure. Anaphylactic shock requires immediate treatment. Common causes include insect bites and stings, exposure to certain foods (e.g., nuts, seafood, citrus), and medications. **Asthma** is actually a local anaphylactic reaction resulting from swelling within the respiratory tract. Type I reactions can be induced by certain foods, air contaminants, cosmetics, cleaning products, animals, flowers, trees, grasses, insects, drugs, and other things.

Figure 10.5 depicts the chain reaction resulting from a bee sting in a susceptible person. This type I response can cause a local or severe allergic reaction, including anaphylaxis.

FIGURE 10.5 **Reaction from a Bee Sting**

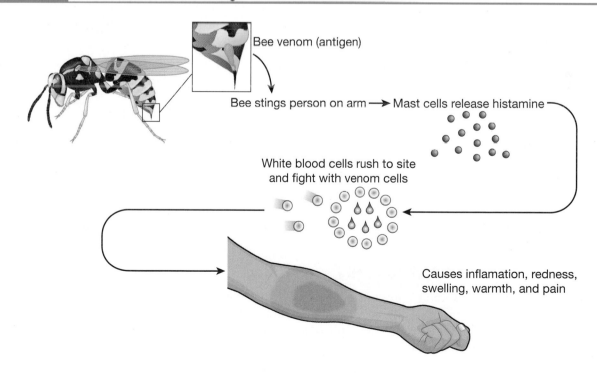

Bee venom (antigen)

Bee stings person on arm → Mast cells release histamine

White blood cells rush to site and fight with venom cells

Causes inflamation, redness, swelling, warmth, and pain

Human Immunodeficiency Virus

Human immunodeficiency virus (HIV) is the virus that causes **acquired immunodeficiency syndrome (AIDS)**. HIV is commonly transmitted through unprotected sexual contact, direct blood transfusions, intravenous drug use, and from an infected mother to the fetus. HIV is a **retrovirus**, meaning it has the ability to insert a copy of its own genetic material into the cell of its host. Once the virus enters the body, it attaches itself to a T cell and works its way inside that cell. Once inside, it convinces the T cell to replicate (copy) itself. The copies go on to invade other T cells, multiply, and inhibit the T cells from properly fighting off infections, a condition that also is known as immunodeficiency. The illnesses that attack once the immune system is compromised are known as opportunistic infections. The body is also at greater risk for certain cancers when the number of T cells is reduced, as the immune system is unable to destroy and clear away cancer cells. Note that an increased incidence rate of two rarely diagnosed conditions (e.g., pneumocystis and Kaposi's sarcoma) led physicians to identify a relationship between HIV and the body's immune system.

CD4 are the specialized types of T cells that the HIV virus kills. The normal range of CD4 cells in healthy adults is between 600–1500. As HIV infection progresses, the number of CD4 cells declines. When an individual's CD4 count falls below 200, he or she is diagnosed with AIDS. Death in individuals with HIV/AIDS is caused by an opportunistic infection associated with a compromised immune system, not the virus itself. Table 10.6 lists some of the illnesses associated with AIDS.

TABLE 10.6 Malignancies and Opportunistic Diseases Associated with AIDS

Disease	Description
Malignancies	
Kaposi's sarcoma	a cancer that develops from the cells that line lymph or blood vessels; most commonly found in older men but now seen in persons with AIDS
lymphoma	a group of blood cell tumors that develop from lymphatic cells; can be localized or systemic
Infections	
candidiasis	fungal infection that affects the mouth and throat (thrush); often present in an immunocompromised host
cytomegalovirus (CMV)	herpesvirus that severely affects those infected with HIV
Mycobacterium avium–intracellulare (MAI) complex	mycobacterial infection that is often seen in the later stages of AIDS
Pneumocystis carinii pneumonia (PCP)	most common opportunistic infection found in AIDS patients
tuberculosis (TB)	*Mycobacterium* that causes infection, usually in the lungs but sometimes disseminated, particularly in the immunocompromised host

Preventing the Spread of HIV

The spread of HIV can be prevented by avoiding contact with other people's bodily fluids. Using a condom when having sexual relations and not sharing needles are the major preventive measures. Although select pharmaceutical agents can slow the progress of the disease (see the later section on pharmaceuticals), HIV and the illnesses it brings are life threatening.

Soft Skills for Health Care: Ethics

Ethics is a system of moral principles that govern an individual's behavior. There are two types of ethics: one based on personal moral standards and another that is based on society, class, or culture. As a healthcare professional in charge of patient care and information, your actions and behavior must withstand the highest scrutiny. Healthcare professionals who work with patients must abide by HIPPA laws and their organization's own code of conduct. Go to http://MedTerm.ParadigmCollege.net/Privacy for more information on health information privacy. For additional information on ethics, read the Soft Skills Solutions series text *Lead with Integrity! Leadership & Ethics* published by JIST Publishing.

Checkpoint 10.2

Answer the following questions to identify any areas of the section that you may need to review.

1. What condition is commonly characterized by the following symptoms: swelling of the tissues, including the throat, and a rapid drop in blood pressure?

   _____

2. What condition leads to an individual's immune system turning against itself (i.e., antibodies attack the cells of the body producing them)?

   _____

3. What metabolic disease is caused by the decreased production of insulin, and is considered to be autoimmune in nature?

   _____

Exercise 10.7   Word Analysis

For each term listed, identify the root word by drawing a box around it. In the space provided, write a definition for the root word and a definition for the entire term.

Example: [arthro]graphy   joint   record of a joint

Term	Root Definition	Term Definition
1. immunology	_____	_____
2. hypersplenism	_____	_____
3. hemolytic	_____	_____
4. leukocytes	_____	_____
5. immunodeficiency	_____	_____

Exercise 10.8 Comprehension Check

Read each sentence and determine which word best fits the sentence. Circle your choice.

1. The examiner palpates/palpitations the lymph nodes.

2. As the immune/autoimmune system develops, the child begins to produce antibodies.

3. Lymphoid/Lymphosis tissue reaches adult size by about age six.

4. Pernicious/Precious anemia is an autoimmune disorder found in older persons.

5. Lymphosis/Lymphoma is a malignancy of lymph tissue.

Exercise 10.9 Matching

Match each of the following terms in column 1 with a definition in column 2. Write the corresponding letter of the definition in column 2 on the line beside the term in column 1.

1. _____ scleroderma

2. _____ retrovirus

3. _____ hemolytic anemia

4. _____ pernicious anemia

5. _____ autoimmunity

a. condition in which the immune system attacks its own body

b. type of virus that causes HIV

c. vitamin B_{12} deficiency caused by immunological condition

d. immunological disorder characterized by thickening of the skin

e. autoimmune disorder that results in destruction of RBCs

Exercise 10.10 Word Building

Use prefixes, root words, combining vowels, and suffixes to create medical terms for the definitions given. Write the term in the space beside the definition.

Definition	Term
1. pertaining to the system	_____
2. pertaining to lymph	_____
3. pertaining to the liver	_____
4. like or resembling lymph	_____
5. surgical removal of a lymph node	_____

Exercise 10.11   Spelling Check

In the sentences that follow, incorrect prefixes or suffixes are used in the medical terms. Provide the correct prefix or suffix for each term by writing the corrected term on the line below the sentence.

1. Several immunitists have attempted to diagnose the problem.

_____

2. Macrophils were observed ingesting bacteria in the tissue sample.

_____

3. Avolution of the organ resulted in a smaller size.

_____

4. A progen can cause an individual to produce antibodies.

_____

5. The thoracosis duct is a vessel of the lymphatic system.

_____

Diagnostic Tests and Examinations

Laboratory tests are vitally important in diagnosing lymphatic disorders. One common test is the measurement of immunoglobulins (antibodies) present in the blood, while other tests can determine T cell counts and their level of functioning. Antibodies from diseases such as polio and cytomegalovirus (CMV) can be detected in a blood test that measures B cell function. CMV is a viral infection in the herpes family of viruses that rarely leads to symptomatic illness. The presence of HIV is assessed with an antibody detection test: the **enzyme-linked immunosorbent assay (ELISA)** or the **Western blot**. The ELISA is generally the first blood test used to screen for HIV antibodies. If positive, the Western blot is used to confirm HIV infection.

ELISA tests are used to test blood for HIV.

Allergy testing is a common practice. Scratch tests (described in Chapter 3) can identify specific allergies. **Lymphangiography** is the viewing of lymphoid tissue following the injection of a radiopaque substance. It is not performed often today, since it is possible to visualize the lymphoid tissue with an imaging process called a gallium scan. In a **gallium scan**, a substance called gallium is injected into the patient; a scan is then performed to evaluate whether any lymph nodes are enlarged or affected. Table 10.7 lists tests used to diagnose conditions related to the lymphatic system.

TABLE 10.7 Tests Associated with the Immune System

Test	Description
allergy test	patch, scratch, or intradermal injection of an allergen is used to trigger hypersensitivity
antibody detection test	detects the presence of specific antibodies
biopsy of lymph vessels	removal of a section of a lymph node or vessel to diagnosis
blood culture	detects the presence of bacteria or disease-causing pathogens (i.e., viruses, fungi, and parasites)
complete blood cell count (CBC)	evaluates overall health and detects specific disorders (measures the concentration of WBCs and RBCs)
ELISA	highly sensitive blood tests used to detect the presence of antibodies to HIV
hematocrit (Hct)	measures the percentage of RBCs in the blood
gallium scan	gallium is injected to enhance the visibility of lymphoid tissue
lymphangiography	injection of a radiopaque substance to enhance the visibility of lymphoid tissue; also referred to as lymphography
monospot test	detects the presence of mononucleosis
RAST test	blood test measuring the amount of allergy-causing antibodies in the bloodstream
Western blot	test used to confirm HIV infection, generally follows a positive ELISA test result
white blood cell (WBC) count	measures the percentage of leukocytes in the blood (an increase in the number of leukocytes can indicate the presence of infection)

Checkpoint 10.3

Answer the following questions to identify any areas of the section that you may need to review.

1. Which blood tests are used to detect the presence of antibodies to HIV?

   _____

2. What substance is injected into a patient during a gallium scan?

   _____

3. What diagnostic test measures the percentage of RBCs in the blood?

   _____

Treatments

Healthcare practitioners use predetermined guidelines to direct patient care. These guidelines, known as clinical practice guidelines and evidence-based practices, have been developed by the specialty societies based on past clinical research. They represent the treatment pathways that have achieved the best outcomes. Treatment decisions generally fall into three categories: surgical, clinical, and pharmacological.

Surgical treatments are generally invasive as they involve a puncture or an incision into the skin. *Clinical treatments* are generally noninvasive and involve nonsurgical techniques (e.g., physical therapy). *Pharmacological treatments* involve the utilization of medicines (drugs) to treat specific illnesses or diseases. Medication therapies are regulated by the Food and Drug Administration (FDA). To be approved by the FDA for use in the United States, every medicine must be backed by research studies that have shown the medication to be effective in its treatment of a given disease and has a tolerable safety profile. The following sections provide an overview of treatments common to the lymphatic system.

Surgical Treatments

One procedure that is not being performed as commonly as it was a generation ago is **tonsillectomy and adenoidectomy (T&A)**. The operation is most often performed in children or adolescents who experience recurrent infections of the tonsils that cause frequent illness associated with fevers, recurrent documented bacterial infections (e.g., otitis media), sinusitis as a result of these infections, and loss of school days. A specialist called an otolaryngologist, or an ear, nose, and throat (ENT) physician, usually performs this relatively short surgical procedure. Table 10.8 lists surgical procedures used to treat conditions related to the lymphatic system.

> **What's in a Word?**
>
> The suffix -*ectomy* means "surgical removal." Note how often this word part is used in Table 10.8.

TABLE 10.8 Surgical Treatments Associated with the Lymphatic System

Treatment		Description
adenoidectomy	[ad-eh-noyd-**ek**-tuh-mee]	removal of adenoids
lymphadenectomy	[lim-fa-duh-**nek**-tuh-mee]	removal of a lymph node
splenectomy	[spleh-**nek**-tuh-mee]	removal of the spleen
thymectomy	[thI-**mek**-tuh-mee]	removal of thymus gland
tonsillectomy	[tawn-sul-**ek**-tuh-mee]	removal of tonsils

Pharmacological Treatments

Antibiotics are commonly used in the treatment or prevention of bacterial infections. The first antibiotics were produced from natural substances such as mold and fungi. Antibiotics are used to kill or inhibit the growth of bacteria present in the body. Specific antibiotics are prescribed according to the infectious organism in which the antibiotic is designed to treat. Note that the word *antibiotic* comes from *anti-*, meaning "against," and *bi/o*, meaning "life."

Many pharmacologic agents have been developed to treat the progression of HIV. Designed to interfere with the replication of the virus, these **antiretroviral** agents include azidothymidine (AZT), or zidovudine; dideoxyinosine, or didanosine (DDI); and lamivudine (3TC). **Protease inhibitors** such as saquinavir are also used to prevent the virus from copying itself (replicating). The goal of protease inhibitors is to reduce the amount of HIV and hepatitis C virus (viral load) in the body.

Herpes viruses can be treated with acyclovir, an **antiviral** agent.

Patients who have an immunodeficiency disorder may require **intravenous immunoglobulin** infusions at least monthly. This medication therapy works to boost antibody levels that may be decreased or lacking in the patient's body.

Numerous **antihistamines** are prescribed for allergies. These agents block the release of histamine, which causes the allergic symptoms. Table 10.9 lists pharmacological medications used to treat lymphatic system-related conditions.

TABLE 10.9 Pharmacologic Agents Associated with the Lymphatic System

Drug Class	Use	Generic Name	Brand Names
antibiotic (penicillin)	treat bacterial infections	penicillin, amoxicillin	Veetids Amoxil
antibiotic (sulfonamide)	treat bacterial infections	sulfamethoxazole and trimethoprim	Bactrim, Septra, Sulfatrim
antihistamines	block histamine receptors to manage allergy symptoms	clemastine, diphenhydramine, loratadine, fexofenadine	Tavist, Benadryl, Claritin, Allegra
antiviral agents	interfere with (inhibit) viral replication	acyclovir, didanosine (DDI), zidovudine (AZT), foscarnet (PFA)	Zovirax, Videx, Retrovir, Foscavir
corticosteroids	suppress the immune system and reduce inflammation	hydrocortisone prednisone	Cortizone Deltasone
immunosuppressants	reduce the body's immune response (generally used to lower the body's ability to reject a transplanted organ)	azathioprine cyclosporine	Imuran Sandimmune
protease inhibitors	inhibit the growth of HIV	indinavir sulfate	Crixivan
vaccines (immunizations)	administered to provide immunity to a disease	MMR (measles, mumps, rubella) and varicella (chickenpox)	

Checkpoint 10.4

Answer the following questions to identify any areas of the section that you may need to review.

1. What procedure is performed in children or adolescents who experience recurrent infections of the tonsils?

   _____

2. What surgical treatment results in the removal of a section of a lymph node or vessel to diagnosis or treat a condition?

   _____

3. What class of drug is used to treat bacterial infections?

   _____

Abbreviations

In the medical field, information is generally recorded in medical charts and in electronic medical records and provided to healthcare workers in medical shorthand. It is important that healthcare professionals become familiar with the abbreviations used on a daily basis to successfully perform the duties assigned in a typical workday. Table 10.10 lists common abbreviations used to refer to conditions and treatments of the lymphatic system.

TABLE 10.10 Abbreviations Associated with the Lymphatic System

Abbreviation	Meaning
AIDS	acquired immunodeficiency syndrome
AZT	azidothymidine
bx	biopsy
CBC	complete blood cell count
ELISA	enzyme-linked immunosorbent assay
Hct	hematocrit
HIV	human immunodeficiency virus
Ig	immunoglobulin
Neut	neutrophils
PCP	*Pneumocystis carinii* pneumonia
RBC	red blood cells
SLE	systemic lupus erythematosus
T&A	tonsillectomy and adenoidectomy
TB	tuberculosis
WBC	white blood cells

Exercise 10.12 Word Building

Use the root word or combining form given and add other word parts to build a term that matches the definition. Write the term on the line provided.

	Combining Form	Definition	Term
1.	*splen/o*	removal of the spleen	_____
2.	*angi/o*	repair of a vessel	_____
3.	*mono*	single cell	_____
4.	*phag/o*	condition of cell eating	_____
5.	*thym*	pertaining to the thymus gland	_____

Exercise 10.13 Comprehension Check

Read each sentence and determine which word best fits the sentence. Circle your choice.

1. Connie will have a tonsiloma/tonsillectomy this morning.

2. Microscopy revealed several lymphocytes/lymphocytedema.

3. The afferent/efferent vessel carries the fluid away from the node.

4. Mrs. Wilson is an antilogous/autologous donor.

5. Mediaphages/Macrophages are phagocytic cells found in diseased or injured tissues.

Exercise 10.14   Matching

Match the list of tests and treatments in column 2 with the diagnosis or condition in column 1. Write the letter of the test or treatment in the space beside the name of the the diagnosis or condition.

1. _____ suspicion of HIV   a. T&A

2. _____ allergic reaction   b. scratch test

3. _____ enlarged lymph nodes   c. ELISA

4. _____ recurrent infections of the tonsils d. gallium scan

5. _____ specific allergies   e. Benadryl

Exercise 10.15   Word Building

Find word parts in your text to construct medical terms for the definitions that follow. Write the term on the blank beside the definition.

Definition	Term
1. blood condition of decreased RBCs	_____
2. pertaining to a node	_____
3. against (bacterial) life	_____
4. like or resembling lymph	_____
5. against a virus	_____

Exercise 10.16   Spelling Check

Read each term and determine whether it is spelled correctly. If the word is spelled incorrectly, write the correct spelling on the line provided.

1. monucyte   _____

2. tonsiles   _____

3. adenaid   _____

4. aneamia   _____

5. imunnodificencies _____

Exercise 10.17　Word Maps

The following concept map lists some common drug classifications with their actions and uses. Complete the map by filling in the blank spaces.

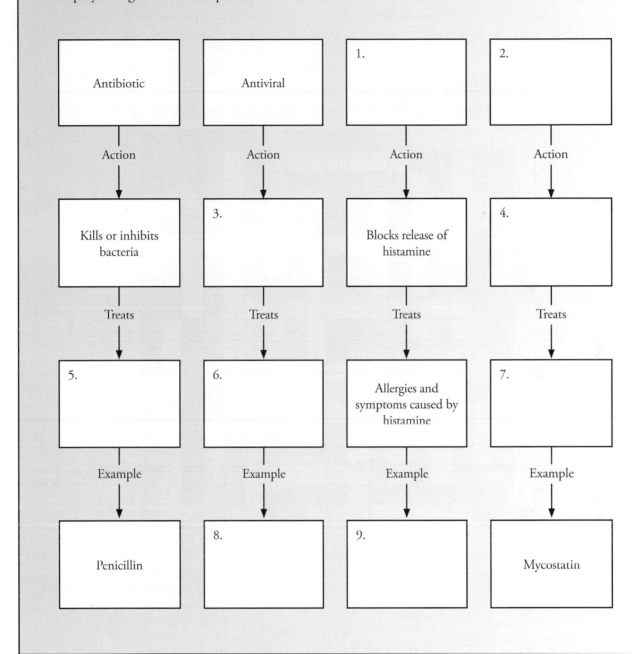

Chapter Review

After successfully completing this chapter, you should be able to correctly answer the following review questions. Answers are provided in the back of the text. This self-assessment opportunity allows you to check your understanding of the content and determine whether you need to revisit any of the chapter's content.

Crossword Puzzle

Use the clues provided to fill in the puzzle with the correct terms. Enter one letter per square.

Across

1. local anaphylactic reaction in the respiratory system
4. diabetes antigen
7. suffix meaning "study of"
9. enzyme linked screening test
10. red blood cell
12. lymphoid tissue located on either side of the pharynx
16. specialist in the immune system
19. part of the lymphatic system, also called adenoid
21. glycoprotein that helps the body fight viruses
25. not susceptible
27. hormone of the thymus gland
28. number of sets of tonsils

Down

1. combining form for gland
2. watery fluid
3. causes the body to produce antibodies against it
5. "condition of cell eating"
6. "lymph tumor"
8. largest lymphoid structure, located in upper left quadrant of abdomen
11. cyt/o
13. organ or tissue returns to normal size
14. gallium _____
15. collection and filtration capsules of the lymphatic system
16. intravenous
17. immunoglobulin
18. "large eating cell"
20. means "like or resembling a gland"
21. abbreviation for Immunoglobulin E
22. combining form for poison
23. assay that detects IgE-bound allergens
24. taxia
26. abbreviation for otolaryngologist

Matching

Match the following terms to their proper definitions.

1. _____ anaphylaxis
2. _____ bacteriology
3. _____ candidiasis
4. _____ Graves' disease
5. _____ immunodeficiency
6. _____ interferons
7. _____ Kaposi's sarcoma
8. _____ *Mycobacterium tuberculosis*
9. _____ nasopharynx
10. _____ palatine tonsils

a. lacking in one or more components of the immune system

b. located on either side of the throat

c. area connecting the nose and throat

d. small proteins produced by T cells

e. study of bacteria

f. autoimmune disorder of the thyroid causing hyperthyroidism

g. severe allergic reaction

h. fungal infection that affects the mouth and throat (thrush) often present in an immuno-compromised host

i. a cancer that develops from the cells that line lymph or blood vessels, most commonly found in older men but now seen in persons with AIDS

j. organism that causes tuberculosis

Identification

Label the illustration by writing the correct term on the corresponding lines provided.

axillary lymph nodes   popliteal lymph nodes   thoracic duct
cervical lymph nodes   right lymphatic duct   tonsils
cisterna chyli   spleen
inguinal lymph nodes   submandibular lymph nodes

1. _____   6. _____

2. _____   7. _____

3. _____   8. _____

4. _____   9. _____

5. _____   10. _____

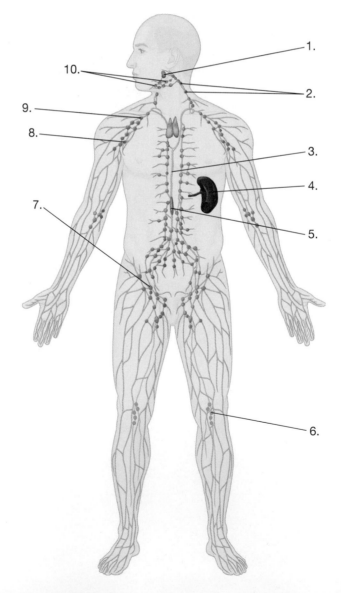

Abbreviations

Identifying the abbreviation of each term.

1. biopsy _____

2. enzyme-linked immunosorbent assay _____

3. hematocrit _____

4. immunoglobulin _____

5. systemic lupus erythematosus _____

Word-Building Challenge

Review the following list of terms. Apply what you have learned in this chapter by identifying the meaning of each term. Write your answer on the lines provided.

1. thymic _____

_____

2. lymphoid _____

_____

3. antiviral _____

_____

4. bacterial _____

_____

5. adenoidectomy _____

_____

Extension Activities

Complete the following activities as assigned by your instructor.

1. Concerns over the use and misuse of prescription medications to treat bacteria that enter the body have been discussed for decades. Search the Internet for scholarly articles addressing the question: Do antibiotics weaken the immune system? Create a post in your class discussion forum, or in whatever format assigned by your instructor, to share your findings with the class.

2. Go to http://MedTerm.ParadigmCollege.net/TimothyRayBrown to read the article, "Doctor Who Cured 'Berlin Patient' of HIV." After reading the article, write a one-page summary of your thoughts related to this sensitive subject. Support your work with logical reasoning and examples from the article.

3. Create a presentation on the prevalence rates of lupus among African American women. Why are African American women three times more likely to develop lupus than people of other races and genders? What risk factors have been identified in scientific research and statistical findings? Present your findings in a 5–10 slide PowerPoint presentation.

Student eResources

The Course Navigator learning management system that accompanies this textbook offers multiple opportunities to master chapter content, including end-of-chapter exercises, a glossary of key terms with audio pronunciations, games, pronunciation coach, and additional activities such as engaging with the BioDigital® Human.

The Digestive System

> **"**The road to health is paved with good intestines.**"**
>
> —**Sherry A. Rogers,** author and physician

Translation Challenge

Read the following excerpt from a medical record and try to answer the questions that follow.

> The patient is a 34 y/o man being seen today upon referral by his primary care physician to a gastroenterologist. The patient presents with a history of severe epigastric abdominal pain of 5-6 months duration. Patient complains of a constant, sharp, burning pain throughout the day that does not vary in severity. Attempts to resolve his symptoms included a change in his diet as well as over-the-counter and prescription antacids. The pain has not changed or worsened following treatment efforts. GERD is suspected and additional testing, including esophageal manometry and EGD, is recommended.

1. What is a gastroenterologist?

2. What is GERD and what causes it?

3. What is an EGD and what is its purpose?

Learning Objectives

11.1 List and define word parts most commonly used to create terms related to the digestive system.

11.2 Identify anatomical structures of the digestive system (gastrointestinal tract).

11.3 Explain the flow of food through the digestive system.

11.4 Explain the role of digestive enzymes.

11.5 List and describe conditions and abnormalities common to the digestive system.

11.6 Name tests and treatments for major conditions of the digestive system.

11.7 State the meaning of abbreviations related to the digestive system.

11.8 Use the terminology of the digestive system in written and oral communication.

11.9 Correctly spell and pronounce terminology associated with the digestive system.

COURSE NAVIGATOR
Access Additional Chapter Resources

Did You Know?

According to the Centers for Disease Control and Prevention, there is an average of 51 million patient visits to outpatient medical facilities annually owing to conditions of the digestive system.

To carry out all of its vital functions, the body requires a constant supply of nutrients. We usually obtain these nutrients by eating food. The function of the digestive system, also known as the **gastrointestinal (GI) system**, is to convert food into the nutrients necessary for the body's survival. Nutrients are used as an energy source for growth, cell repair, and the elimination of waste products from the body. The study of the gastrointestinal system is called **gastroenterology**, which includes the processes ingestion, digestion, absorption, and elimination of the food we consume daily.

This chapter will discuss anatomical structures within the digestive system and their role in the digestive process, as well as tests, procedures, and pharmaceutical agents unique to conditions associated with the digestive system. During your career as a healthcare professional, you will likely encounter many patients who present signs and symptoms directly related to a condition of the digestive system. Become familiar with highlighted terms throughout this chapter so you can successfully recognize these conditions in your role as a healthcare professional.

Digestive System Word Parts

To better understand the concepts presented in this chapter, it is important to have a basic knowledge of the word parts associated with the digestive system. While you may recognize many of the prefixes and suffixes from earlier chapters (e.g., *a-*, *dys-*, *sub-*, *-ectomy*, *-rrhea*, and *-scopy*), many combining forms are unique to this particular body system. Table 11.1 lists prefixes, suffixes, and combining forms related to the digestive (GI) system.

TABLE 11.1 Word Parts Associated with the Digestive System

Prefix	Meaning	Example
a-	without	achalasia (condition in which the muscle of the esophagus fails to contract, resulting in difficulty swallowing)
dys-	abnormal, bad	dysphagia (difficulty swallowing)
endo-	within	endoscopy (process of viewing structures within the body)
exo-	outside	exodontist (one who specializes in the extraction/removal of teeth)
micro-	small, tiny	microvilli (tiny projections in the small intestine that assist in the absorption of nutrients)
neo-	new	neonatal (relating to birth, new birth)
par-	near	paracentesis (surgical puncture near a body cavity to withdraw excess fluid)
peri-	surrounding, around	periodontal (surrounding a tooth)
re-	again	regurgitation (the return of swallowed food to the mouth)
sub-	under, below	sublingual (under the tongue)
supra-	above	suprapubic (above the pubic bones)

Combining Form	Meaning	Example
amyl/o	starch	amylase (an enzyme produced by the pancreas that assists with the digestion of carbohydrates)
an/o	anus	anal (relating to the anus)
ankl/o	bent, fixed, stiffening	ankyloglossia (tongue-tied; the tongue is not freely movable)
append/o, appendic/o	appendix	appendicitis (inflammation of the appendix)
bol/o	bolus	bolus (a mass of chewed food ready to be swallowed)
cec/o	cecum	cecitis (inflammation of the cecum)
celi/o	abdomen	celiac (pertaining to the abdomen)
cheil/o (chil/o)	lips	cheilitis, chilitis (inflammation of the lips)
chol/o (chol/e)	bile	cholangitis (inflammation of the bile vessels)
cholecyst/o	gallbladder	cholecystitis (inflammation of the gallbladder)
choledoch/o	common bile duct	choledochitis (inflammation of the common bile duct)
col/o (colon/o)	colon	colonoscopy (process of viewing structures inside the colon, large intestine, with an instrument)
cyst/o	bladder, pouch	cystadenoma (benign tumors commonly found in the pancreas)
dent/o	teeth	dentition (the type, number, and arrangement of normal teeth within the mouth)
diverticul/o	diverticulum, pouch	diverticulum (pouch or sac that develops on the outside of the wall of the colon)
duoden/o	duodenum	duodenal (pertaining to the small intestine)
enter/o	intestines	enteritis (inflammation of the intestine, often resulting in diarrhea)
esophagi/o	esophagus	esophageal (pertaining to the esophagus)
gastr/o	stomach	gastroenteritis (inflammation of the stomach and small intestine)
gingiv/o	gums	gingivitis (gum disease characterized by redness, swelling, and bleeding)
gloss/o	tongue	glossopharyngeal (pertaining to the tongue and pharynx)
glyc/o	sugar	glycosuria (sugar in the urine)
hepat/o	liver	hepatomegaly (abnormal condition of an enlarged liver)
herni/o	rupture, hernia	herniorrhaphy (surgical repair of a hernia)
ile/o	ileum	ileostomy (an opening created during surgery used to move waste out of the body when the colon or rectum is not functioning properly)

Continues

Combining Form	Meaning	Example
jejun/o	jejunum	jejunectomy (excision of all or part of the jejunum)
kin/e	motion, movement	kinetic (pertaining to motion)
lapar/o	abdomen	laparoscopy (diagnostic procedure used to view the internal organs of the abdomen and female reproductive system)
lip/o	fat, lipid	liposuction (cosmetic procedure used to slim and reshape specific areas of the body by removing excess deposits of fat)
lith/o	stone (calcification)	cholelithiasis (gallstones)
mandibul/o	jaw	mandibular (pertaining to the jaw)
nat/o	related to birth	prenatal (before birth)
necr/o	death	necrosis (death of body tissue)
odont/o	tooth	orthodontia (branch of dentistry that treats misalignments and occlusions of the teeth and jaw)
or/o	mouth	oral (pertaining to the mouth)
pancreat/o	pancreas	pancreatic (related to the pancreas)
pharyng/o	pharynx (throat)	pharyngeal (pertaining to the throat)
proct/o	rectum, anus	proctology (field of medicine specializing in disorders of the rectum, anus, and colon)
prote/o	protein	proteins (building blocks of body tissue that serve as a food source)
pylor/o	pylorus (gatekeeper)	pyloroplasty (surgical repair to widen the opening in the lower part of the stomach [pylorus] so that stomach contents can empty into the small intestine [duodenum])
rect/o	rectum	rectal (pertaining to the rectum)
sial/o	saliva	sialolith (most common disease of the salivary glands; formation of stones [calculi] that result in pain and swelling under the tongue)
sigmoid/o	sigmoid colon	sigmoidoscopy (diagnostic procedure to view the inside of the sigmoid colon and rectum)
splen/o	spleen	splenectomy (surgical removal of the spleen)
stom/a	mouth	stomatitis (inflammation of the mucous membrane of the mouth)
typhl/o	cecum	typhlitis (inflammation of the cecum, a pouch that marks the beginning of the large intestine)
viscer/o	internal organs	visceral (pertaining to the organs)

Suffix	Meaning	Example
-algia	pain	gastralgia (pain in the stomach)
-ary, -al, -ac, -ic	pertaining to	maxillary (pertaining to the upper jaw)
-ase	enzyme	protease (an enzyme that assists in the breakdown of protein)
-cele	herniation, protrusion	gastrocele (herniation of part of the stomach, gastric pouch)
-chezia	condition of stools	hematochezia (passage of bloody stools)
-dynia	pain	gastrodynia (pain in the stomach)
-ectomy	surgical removal	polypectomy (removal of a polyp)
-emesis	vomit	hematemesis (vomiting of blood)
-flux	flow	reflux (flowing back)
-ia	condition of	aglossia (congenital defect in which a baby is born with no tongue)
-iasis	presence of disease	cholelithiasis (presence of stones in the gallbladder)
-itis	inflammation	ulcerative colitis (chronic inflammation of the colon and rectum resulting in diarrhea)
-megaly	enlargement	hepatomegaly (abnormal enlargement of the liver)
-osis	condition	cirrhosis (chronic liver disease)
-pepsia	digestive condition	dyspepsia (indigestion)

Continues

Suffix	Meaning	Example
-pexy	surgical fixation	gastropexy (attachment of the stomach to the abdominal wall or diaphragm)
-phagia	eating, swallowing	aphagia (the inability or refusal to swallow)
-plasty	surgical repair	stomatoplasty (surgical repair of the mouth)
-rrhea	discharge, flow	diarrhea (abnormal discharge of watery stools)
-scopy	process of viewing	fluoroscopy (X-ray procedure that shows internal structures in real time on a monitor)
-stalsis	contraction	peristalsis (contractions of the intestines used to move food toward the stomach)
-stomy	surgical opening	colostomy (an artificial opening created to redirect the flow of bowels)
-tresia	condition of an opening	esophageal atresia (congenital defect in which the esophagus lacks a normal opening)

Anatomy and Physiology

Visualize the digestive or gastrointestinal (GI) tract as a long tube (in adults, approximately 29 feet long) with openings on both ends. For the body to survive, this tube must take in and absorb nutrients and eliminate wastes. Also known as the **alimentary canal**, the GI tract includes the mouth, pharynx, esophagus, stomach, small and large intestines, the rectum and the anus, and accessory organs (the liver, gallbladder, and pancreas) (see Figure 11.1). Table 11.2 lists anatomy and physiology terms for the digestive system.

FIGURE 11.1   Organs of the Digestive System

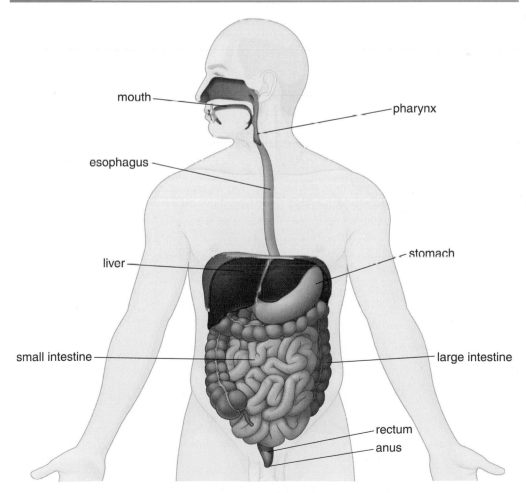

Term		Meaning	Word Analysis	
alimentary canal	[al-ah-**men**-ter-ee kah-**nal**]	gastrointestinal tract	*alimentum* *-ary*	nourishment pertaining to
amino acid	[ah-**mee**-nO **as**-id]	compound that serves as an essential building block for proteins; also referred to as *amines*		
amylase	[**am**-ah-lays]	type of chemical substance (enzyme) secreted by the pancreas; reacts to starches	*amyl/o* *-ase*	starch relating to an enzyme
anal canal	[**ay**-nel kah-**nal**]	passageway through which fecal material is passed	*an/o* *-al*	anus pertaining to
anus	[**ay**-nus]	exit site of the digestive canal from which feces are excreted	*an/o* *-us*	anus structure, thing
bile	[**bIl**]	dark green to yellowish-brown substance secreted by the liver and passed into the duodenum; aids with the breakdown of fats for digestion		
carbohydrate	[kahr-bO-**hI**-drayt]	compound containing carbon atoms composed of small molecules such as sugars and other starches	*carbo-* *hydr/o* *-ate*	carbon water state of
cardiac sphincter	[**kahr**-dee-ak **sfink**-ter]	muscle ring between the distal end of the esophagus and opening into the stomach that prevents food from going back up the esophagus; also called the *lower esophageal sphincter*	*cardi/o* *-ac* *sphincter*	heart pertaining to band of muscles
cecum	[**see**-kum]	sac that lies below the ileum and is the beginning of the large intestine	*cec/o*	cecum
cholecystokinin	[kO-lee-sis-tO-**kI**-nin]	hormone that stimulates digestion of fat and protein	*chol/e* *cyst/o* *kin/e*	bile bladder, pouch movement, motion
chyme	[**kIm**]	semi-digested food passed from the stomach to the duodenum		
colorectal	[kO-lO-**rek**-tul]	pertaining to the colon and the rectum	*col/o* *rect/o* *-al*	colon rectum pertaining to
common bile duct		outlet for bile to be passed into the duodenum (small intestine); formed by the joining of the common hepatic and cystic ducts (of the liver and gallbladder)		
deciduous	[dee-**sid**-yoo-us]	primary teeth (also called baby teeth) that fall out and are replaced by permanent teeth	*deciduous*	falling off, shedding
duodenum	[doo-O-**dee**-num/ doo-**od**-en-um]	first portion of the small intestine	*duoden/o* *-um*	duodenum structure, thing
diverticulum	[dI-ver-**tik**-yoo-lum]	an abnormal pocket or sac found in a weakened area of the GI tract		
emulsify	[ee-**mul**-sih-fye]	combining two liquids that generally do not mix (e.g., oil and water)		
enteric	[en-**ter**-ik]	pertaining to the small intestine	*enter/o* *-ic*	small intestine pertaining to
enzyme	[**en**-zIm]	protein that makes other substances change; enzyme names usually end in *–ase* (e.g., lipase reacts to fats/lipids)		

Continues

Term		Meaning	Word Analysis	
esophagus	[ee-**sof**-ah-gus]	structure between the pharynx and stomach	*esophag/o*	esophagus
feces	[**fee**-seez]	substance excreted (defecated) from the body; composed of undigested material, waste from food, and other materials		
frenulum	[**fren**-yoo-lum]	fold of skin beneath the tongue that anchors it to the floor of the mouth		
fundus	[**fun**-dus]	part farthest away from the opening	*fundus*	base of an organ
gastric juice	[**gas**-trik joos]	secretion from the stomach	*gastr/o* *-ic*	stomach pertaining to
gastroenter-ology	[**gas**-trO-en-ter-**ol**-ah-jee]	study of the digestive system	*gastr/o* *enter/o* *-logy*	stomach intestine study of
glucose	[**gloo**-kOs]	a type of sugar	*gluc/o* *-ose*	sugar, glucose pertaining to
hepatic	[heh-**pat**-ik]	pertaining to the liver	*hepat/o* *-ic*	liver pertaining to
ileum	[**il**-ee-um]	portion of the small intestine from the jejunum to the ileocecal opening	*ile/o* *-um*	ileum structure, thing
jejunum	[jeh-**joo**-num]	portion of the small intestine between the duodenum and ileum	*jejun/o* *-um*	jejunum structure, thing
large intestine	[in-**tes**-tin]	section of the digestive tract below the small intestine	*intestin/o*	intestine
liver	[**liv**-er]	largest gland in the body; secretes bile and filters out toxic, harmful substances		
mastication	[mas-tih-**kay**-shun]	process of chewing	*masticate*	to chew
mesentery	[**mez**-en-ter-ee]	fold of tissue that spans from the peritoneum covering most of the small intestine		
microvilli	[mI-krO-**vil**-I]	tiny projections in the small intestine that assist in the absorption of nutrients	*micro-* *vill/o*	small *villus*
omentum	[O **men** tum]	a fold of fatty tissue that connects the stomach with other abdominal organs, a membrane that encloses the bowels	*omentum*	Latin for apron
pancreas	[**pan**-kree-as]	gland responsible for the digestion of proteins, carbohydrates, and fats		
parietal	[pah-**rI**-eh-tel]	wall of a cavity	*pariet/o* *-al*	wall pertaining to
parotid	[pah-**rot**-id]	salivary gland located near the ear		
peristalsis	[pair-ih-**stal**-sis]	action of the intestine characterized by alternating contraction and relaxation to propel food substances forward	*peri-* *-stalsis*	surrounding contraction
peritoneum	[pair-ih-tO-**nee**-um]	tissue that lines the abdominal cavity		
plicae	[**plI**-see]	circular folds of the intestines covered with villi		
protein	[**prO**-teen]	a chain of amino acids, also known as the building blocks of life		
pyloric sphincter	[pI-**lor**-ik **sfink**-ter]	muscular band that holds food in the stomach while it is being digested	*pylor/o* *-ic* *sphincter*	*pylorus* pertaining to band of muscles
pylorus	[pI-**lO**-rus]	bottom part of the stomach		

Continues

Term		Meaning	Word Analysis	
rectum	[**rek**-tum]	final portion of the digestive tract	*rect/o*	rectum
rugae	[**roo**-gee]	the lining of the stomach is tucked into rugae, or folds, that expand when filled to allow better absorption of contents	*ruga*	fold, ridge, wrinkle
saliva	[sah-**ll**-vah]	secretion from the salivary glands in the mouth that begins the process of digestion	*sial/o*	saliva
small intestine	[in-**tes**-tin]	portion of the digestive tract between the stomach and large intestine		
stomach	[**stum**-ek]	sac between the esophagus and the small intestine		
sublingual	[sub-**ling**-gwal]	under the tongue	*sub-* *lingu/u* *-al*	under tongue pertaining to
submandibular	[sub-man-**dib**-yoo-ler]	below the mandible (jaw)	*sub-* *mandibul/o* *-ar*	under jaw pertaining to
suprapubic	[soo-prah-**pyoo**-bik]	area of the abdomen above the pubic bones	*supra-* *publ/o* *-ic*	above pubis, pubic pertaining to
tooth		anatomical structure within the mouth formed of calcium; responsible for the breakdown of food through mastication (chewing)		
umbilicus	[um-**bil**-ih-kus (also um-bil-**I**-kus)]	the navel (belly button)		
uvula	[**yoo**-vyoo-lah]	fleshy structure hanging in the back of the throat that prevents food from entering the nasopharynx		
vermiform appendix	[**ver**-mih-form ah-**pen**-diks]	structure known as the appendix; tube attached to the cecum that lies close to the wall of the rectum		
villi	[**vil**-I]	hair-like projections within the intestine	*villus*	tiny hairs
visceral	[**vis**-er-al]	internal organs	*viscer/o* *-al*	internal organs pertaining to

Identifying the Specialty: The System and Its Practitioners

Specialists who care for diseases of the digestive system include gastroenterologists, who specialize in the GI tract and liver, and surgeons who specialize in surgical procedures of the system's organs. Various other specialties share responsibility for treating disorders of the teeth and gums (e.g., dentists, periodontists, and exodontists) and lower GI tract (e.g., proctologists). Allied health professionals play an important supporting role in the diagnosis and treatment of conditions affecting the digestive system. Medical sonographers are instrumental in collecting the information necessary to identify systemic abnormalities, and dietitians assist in the planning and preparation of meals for those with special nutritional needs.

The Digestive Process

Ingestion is the physical consumption of food or fluids through the mouth, by eating or drinking. Chewed food, or bolus, is then broken down in the gastrointestinal tract as it undergoes digestion. During this process, large food molecules are reduced to smaller molecules that can be dissolved in water. Enzymes are responsible for breaking down molecules so nutrients can be extracted. These molecules are then absorbed through the small intestine into the bloodstream through the action of small finger-like projections known as villi. The last step in the digestive process is the elimination of the unused portion of food products as waste (feces). The following sections offer a more detailed look at the specific anatomical structures responsible for each step of the digestive process.

The Mouth

Ingestion begins when food enters the mouth. Like all other parts of the GI tract, the mouth has a mucous membrane lining that lubricates the passing food and protects the mouth from the body's digestive juices. The mouth (see Figure 11.2) is composed of the roof, which has a hard and soft palate, and a structure at the back called the **uvula**, which—with the soft palate—prevents food from entering the nasal cavity. On the floor of the mouth is the **tongue**, which is a muscle. A thin membrane called the **frenulum** attaches the tongue to the floor of the mouth. The tongue contains the sensory receptors for taste, as described in Chapter 6. The tongue's job is to guide chewed food to the back of the throat to be swallowed and transported to the esophagus.

FIGURE 11.2 | Mouth Cavity

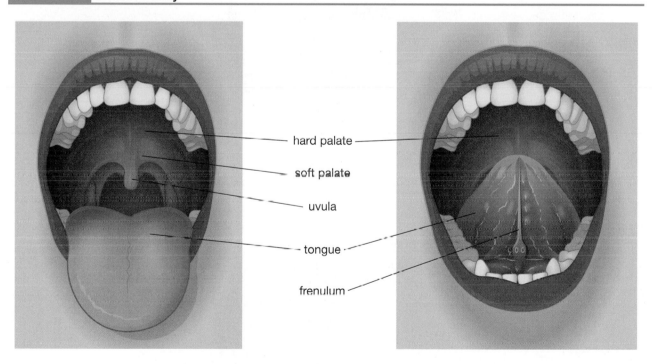

hard palate

soft palate

uvula

tongue

frenulum

During the digestive process, the **teeth** are the organs of **mastication**, or chewing. Teeth break, tear, and crush food into smaller pieces and help mix it with mucus and enzymes. Humans are born without teeth, but by about six to eight months of age, the **deciduous** (baby) teeth break through the gum line. Physically, a tooth is quite similar to a tree. A portion of it is visible and the roots are found beneath the surface. Each tooth consists of the crown, which is the visible portion in the mouth; the root, which is found below the gum line in a bony socket, called the **alveolus**; and the neck, which is between the crown and the root. The solid portion of a tooth consists of **dentin** and **enamel**, covering the exposed portion of the crown. Enamel is the hard layer of tissue that forms on the tooth prior to its eruption into the mouth. Enamel protects the crown from the stress of chewing, grinding, and biting. Beneath the enamel is a layer called dentin. It is much softer and is responsible for giving the tooth its color. Although coffee, tea, tobacco, and poor hygiene practices are often to blame for stains to the enamel, most tooth discoloration is a result of overexposures to external elements (e.g., fluoride) and conditions related to dentin. A thin layer of connective tissue called **cementum** surrounds the dentin and helps anchor each tooth to the bones of the jaw. Figures 11.3 and 11.4 show shows the deciduous and adult teeth and the average age of eruption for each.

FIGURE 11.3 | Deciduous (Baby) Teeth

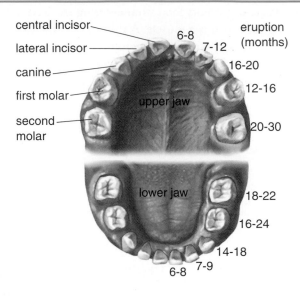

FIGURE 11.4 | Adult Teeth

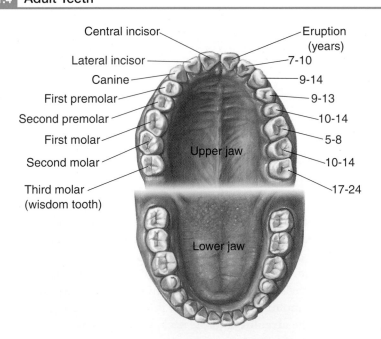

The Pharynx and Esophagus

During mastication (chewing), a digestive enzyme called salivary amylase is working to chemically break down all carbohydrates (starches and sugars). This particular enzyme is found in saliva, a substance composed mainly of mucus that is secreted to moisten food along its journey. There are three pairs of **salivary glands (parotids, submandibulars**, and **sublinguals)**, which collectively secrete about 1 liter of saliva per day (Figure 11.5). These glands are connected to the GI tract by ducts into which they secrete their saliva. Once food has been chewed and swallowed, it passes from the mouth to the **pharynx (throat)**. Although the pharynx is also part of the respiratory system, food must pass through it to reach the **esophagus**, referred to as the food pipe. The esophagus is about 10 inches long uses a wave-like, muscular contraction (peristalsis) to move the food bolus through the esophagus and toward the stomach (see Figure 11.6). A ring of muscle tissue called the **cardiac sphincter** lies at the end of the esophagus. It can contract to close the esophagus off from the stomach to prevent food and stomach acid from going back up the esophagus.

FIGURE 11.5 Salivary Glands

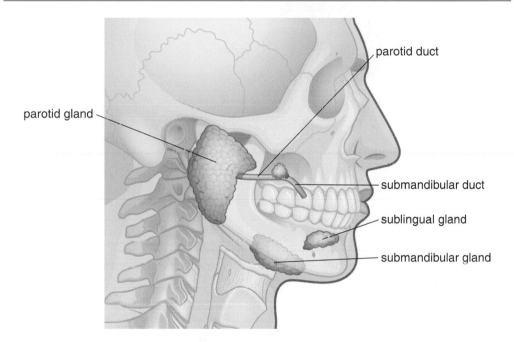

The Stomach

The stomach is an expandable pouch that lies within the abdominal cavity under the diaphragm (see Figure 11.1). One of the strongest organs of the body, the stomach is composed of three layers of smooth muscle that run in different directions. It is divided into three sections: the **fundus**, which is the upper portion; the **body** in the center; and the **pylorus** at the bottom. A **pyloric sphincter** holds food in the stomach while it is being digested.

The stomach is lined with mucous membranes containing thousands of gastric glands that secrete **gastric juice** and **hydrochloric acid**. When the stomach is empty, the lining is tucked into **rugae**, or folds. When food reaches the stomach, the muscle walls contract to expose the food to enzymes, called pepsins, which break down the protein molecules present in food particles into

> **Did You Know?**
>
> The stomach of the average adult holds 1.5 liters (6 cups) of food, but can expand to hold up to 4 liters (one gallon) of food.

FIGURE 11.6 Stomach

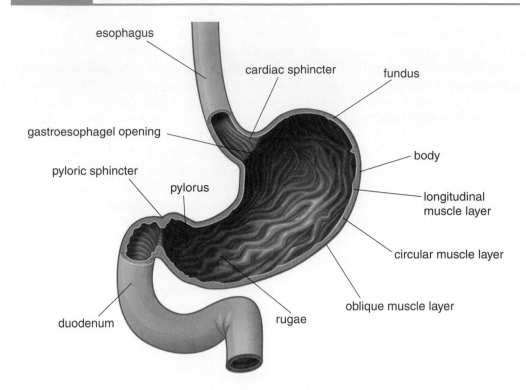

esophagus

cardiac sphincter

fundus

gastroesophagel opening

body

pyloric sphincter

longitudinal
muscle layer

pylorus

circular muscle layer

oblique muscle layer

duodenum

rugae

amino acids. Pepsin generally does not damage the stomach, which is lined with a protective covering called mucus. The final mixture is a semi-solid substance called **chyme**. At the end of the digestive process, strong wave-like muscle contractions **(peristalsis)** propel the chyme farther down into the digestive tract.

The Small Intestine

The next structure in the digestive tract is the **small intestine**, the main organ of digestion in the human body. The small intestine is named for its diameter rather than its length (estimated to be 20–25 feet). As the longest part of the digestive system, the small intestine lies between the stomach and large intestine. As shown in Figure 11.7, it is divided into three main sections—the duodenum, the jejunum, and the ileum—all of which are protected by a mucous lining. This long tube houses thousands of glands that secrete digestive juices and also contains plicae, circular folds covered with tiny projections called villi. Smaller structures called microvilli cover each villus to provide a large contact area to promote the absorption of nutrients. Each villus contains blood capillaries and lymph vessels called lacteals, which are responsible for the absorption of lipid (fatty) materials from chyme. Chemical digestion takes place in the duodenum as the pyloric sphincter relaxes to allow stomach contents to enter. Ducts located in the middle of the duodenum empty digestive juices from the pancreas (lipase enzymes) and bile from the liver. During chemical digestion in the small intestine, carbohydrates are changed to simple sugars, such as **glucose**. Fats remain undigested until they are broken down by bile into fatty acids and glycerol. This process also occurs in the small intestine. The next stage of digestion is the absorption of the molecules—amino acids, glucose, fatty acids, and glycerol. They are transported through the lining of the small intestine and into the blood and lymph to provide the body with the nutrients essential for the body to function.

FIGURE 11.7 Small Intestine

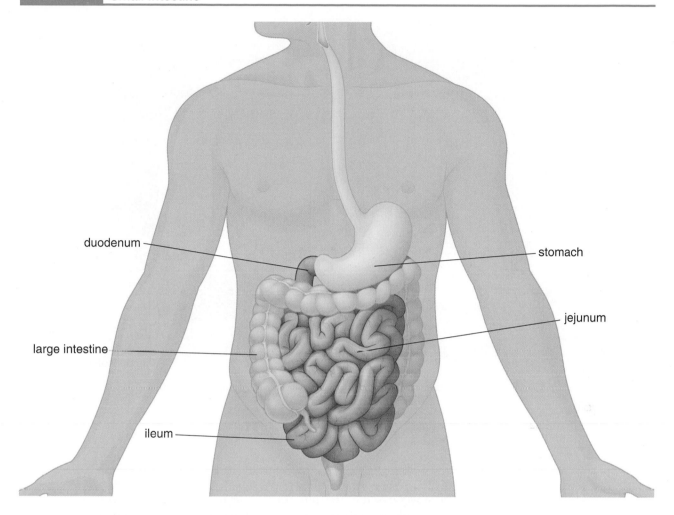

duodenum

stomach

jejunum

large intestine

ileum

The Large Intestine

The final stage of digestion occurs in the large intestine. The primary function of the large intestine, often referred to as the colon, is to eliminate waste products from the body. Water and other substances found in the chyme, collected in the small intestine, are reabsorbed through the walls of the small intestine. This process causes the chyme to change to the consistency of feces, the formed, sticky substance that is eventually eliminated from the body. The sphincter at the end of the small intestine, called the **ileocecal valve**, holds the undigested material until it passes into the **large intestine**, which is only about 5 feet in total length but wider in diameter (approximately 2.5 inches) than the small intestine.

The large intestine (see Figure 11.8) has seven main sections:

- cecum
- ascending colon
- transverse colon
- descending colon
- sigmoid colon
- rectum
- anal canal

FIGURE 11.8 Divisions of the Large Intestine

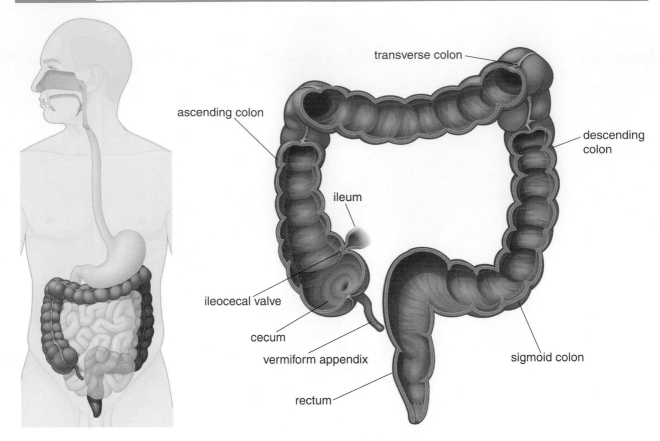

transverse colon

ascending colon

descending colon

ileum

ileocecal valve

cecum

vermiform appendix

sigmoid colon

rectum

Because the large intestine contains no villi, it has less surface area for absorption, and material passes through the large intestine slowly, taking from one to five days. Chyme, referred to as feces when it moves into the large intestine, enters the large intestine at the cecum, passes to the ascending colon, travels across the transverse colon, through the descending and sigmoid colons, and is held at the end of the anal canal until it is passed out of the **anus**, the external opening of the rectum. The process of discharging feces from the body is called **defecation**. Collectively, the small and large intestines are referred to as the **bowels**, extending from the pyloric sphincter of the stomach to the anus.

> **Did You Know?**
>
> It takes between 24 to 72 hours to fully digest food.

Accessory Organs

Several organs aid in digestion but are not considered part of the digestive tract. They are often referred to as accessory organs for the role they play in digestion. The accessory organs of the digestive system are the pancreas, liver, and gallbladder. The pancreas lies behind the stomach. Because it secretes pancreatic juice into ducts that lead outside the body and it secretes hormones directly into the bloodstream, it is considered both an exocrine and an endocrine gland. Pancreatic juice, which is made up of enzymes that can digest the three types of food molecules—proteins, fats, and carbohydrates—is extremely important to digestion. It also contains a substance called bicarbonate, which neutralizes excess stomach acid. The pancreas is also responsible for the production of insulin, the hormone used by the body to convert sugar into energy.

The **liver** is the largest organ within the abdomen and the largest gland in the body. The liver is vital to life. It is responsible for the production of bile, the storage of vitamins and minerals, the destruction of old red blood cells, and the detoxification of blood of harmful substances (e.g. alcohol and drugs). The liver is divided into right and left lobes and is considered an exocrine gland because it secretes bile into **hepatic** (from the Greek *hepar* for "liver") ducts. The secretion of bile process begins with the presence of fat in the chyme that passes into the small intestine. The fat stimulates the secretion of the hormone **cholecystokinin** by the duodenum. This hormone stimulates the **gallbladder** to contract and move **bile** (the substance that breaks down, or **emulsifies** fats) into the duodenum through the **common bile duct**, which is formed by the joining of the common hepatic duct with the cystic duct (see Figure 11.9). The gallbladder is located just below and attached to the liver in the abdominal cavity. While the gallbladder's main function is the storage of bile, as described above, the body can function without it. If the gallbladder is removed, bile flows directly from the liver into the intestine.

FIGURE 11.9 Liver, Pancreas, Gallbladder, and Bile Ducts

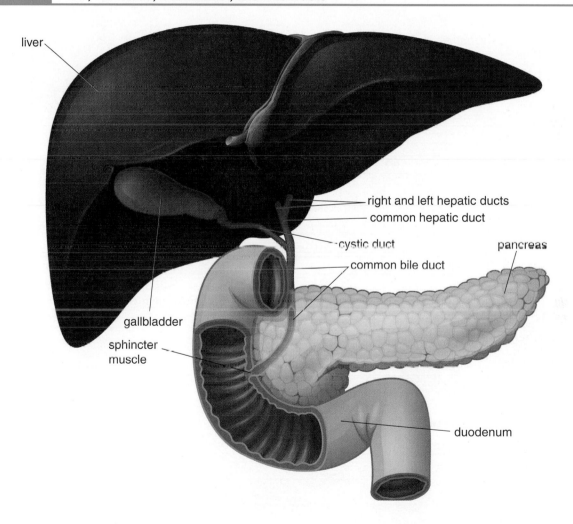

Additional Digestive Structures

Not all structures in the abdominal cavity are directly involved with the process of digestion. Specifically, the **vermiform appendix**, known simply as the *appendix*, and the peritoneum play no role in the digestive process. The appendix is attached to the cecum of the large intestine, and lies close to the wall of the rectum. Although the appendix is primarily composed of lymphatic tissue, it plays only a minor role in the immune system.

The **peritoneum** is a membrane that lines the abdominal cavity. This membrane includes a **parietal** layer, which covers the cavity walls, and a **visceral** layer, which covers each organ. Peritoneal fluid keeps the two layers from rubbing against each other. The two extensions to the peritoneum are the **mesentery**, which lies between the parietal and visceral layers like a pleated fan covering most of the small intestine, and the greater **omentum**, which hangs down over the intestines like an apron.

Checkpoint 11.1

Answer the following questions to identify any areas of the section that you may need to review.

1. What is chyme called once it enters the large intestine?

   _____

2. What are the four main stages of the digestive process?

   _____

   _____

3. What is the name of the substance that breaks down or emulsifies fats in the small intestine?

   _____

Exercise 11.1   Word Analysis

Using slashes, separate the terms into their individual word parts. Identify each word part by writing a "P" for prefix, "S" for suffix, or "CF" for combining forms under the word part. Then, supply a definition of the entire term.

Example: sub|lingu|al   under the tongue
                 P | CF | S

Term	Word Analysis	Definition
1. colitis	_____	_____
2. gastroscopy	_____	_____
3. hepatomegaly	_____	_____
4. pancreatic	_____	_____
5. pyloroplasty	_____	_____
6. proctologist	_____	_____

Exercise 11.2   Comprehension Check

Use context clues to identify and circle the correct term in each sentence.

1. The patient's cardiac sphincter/cardiac cycle is incompetent and allows stomach contents to pass into the esophagus.

2. The stomach produces hydrochloric/hypochloric acid.

3. The terminal portion of the small intestine is the ileum/jejunum.

4. Laparoscopy/Peristalsis propels the chyme farther down the digestive tract.

5. The hepatic/hepatitic ducts were completely obstructed.

6. Masticayse/Amylase is an important enzyme.

Exercise 11.3   Matching

Match the terms in column 1 with the definitions in column 2. Write the letter of the definition on the line provided.

1. _____ frenulum

2. _____ carbohydrates

3. _____ pyloric sphincter

4. _____ mastication

5. _____ peristalsis

6. _____ bile

a. chewing

b. ring of muscle between the stomach and esophagus that holds food in the stomach while it is digested

c. muscle contractions that propel chyme farther down the digestive tract

d. thin membrane that attaches the tongue to the floor of the mouth

e. chemical compounds of starches and sugars

f. substance secreted by the liver and stored in the gallbladder

Exercise 11.4   Word Building

In the examples that follow, the correct combining form is used, but the prefix or suffix does not match the definition. Rewrite the word, using the correct word part.

1. duodenectomy: pertaining to the duodenum   _____

2. gastritis: removal of the stomach   _____

3. pregastric: below the stomach   _____

4. hepatoscopy: pertaining to the liver   _____

5. sigmoidotomy: examination of the   _____
   sigmoid colon through an instrument

Exercise 11.5   Spelling Check

For each sentence, write the correct spelling of each misspelled word on the line provided.

1. The study of the gasterintestinal system is called gastroenrterology.

   _____

2. The GI tract is also known as the elementary canal.

   _____

3. There are three pairs of salaviary glands.

   _____

4. The desiduous teeth are also called baby teeth.

   _____

5. The lining of an empty stomack is folded into rugby.

   _____

Exercise 11.6   Word Maps

The diagram below traces the route nutrients follow through the digestive tract. Fill in the missing information.

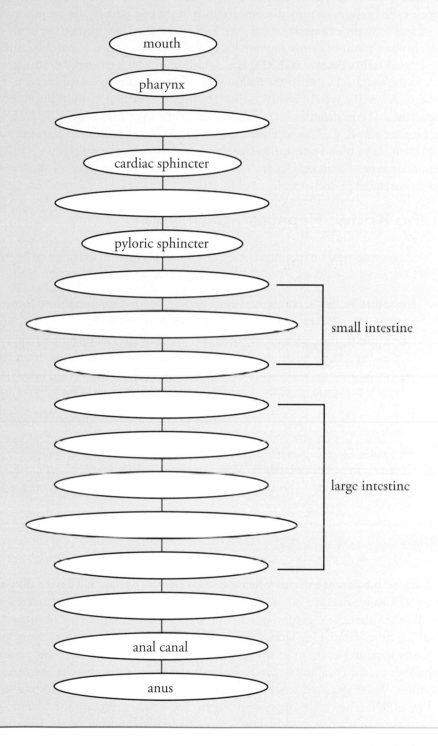

mouth

pharynx

cardiac sphincter

pyloric sphincter

small intestine

large intestine

anal canal

anus

Conditions

Heartburn is a common ailment of the digestive system. **Heartburn** is caused by the irritation of the esophagus from excess stomach acid. Food reenters the esophagus by a process called **reflux**, causing discomfort, burping, a bad taste in the mouth, pain in the chest, and sometimes **emesis** (vomiting). Reflux can signal the formation of an ulcer; it may also be a result of eating too quickly or indicate other digestive problems. **Gastroesophageal reflux disease (GERD)** is a condition in which contents in the stomach flow back to the esophagus due to the inability of the lower esophageal sphincter to function properly. A specific type of reflux, GERD, results in a burning pain in the esophagus. **Hepatitis** is a term meaning an inflammation of the liver. Hepatitis A, B, C, D, and E are. Hepatitis A, B, C, D, and E are caused by viral pathogens found in some foods, such as shellfish, or in blood transmitted through transfusions, intravenous (IV) drug use, and occupational needle sticks. Hepatitis can also be caused by excessive alcohol consumption over an extended period of time.

In the Know: Hepatitis Transmission

There are five types of hepatitis (A, B, C, D, and E), but not all types of hepatitis are transmitted in the same manner. The list below describes how each hepatitis type is transmitted.

Hepatitis A: highly contagious virus transmitted through exposure to contaminated blood or other potentially infectious body fluids and/or the fecal-oral route of transmission

Hepatitis B: virus transmitted through exposure to contaminated blood or other potentially infectious body fluids (especially via sexual contact), preventable via vaccination

Hepatitis C: virus transmitted through exposure to contaminated blood or other potentially infectious body fluids, known to be asymptomatic, resulting in cirrhosis of the liver

Hepatitis D: virus transmitted through through exposure to contaminated blood or other potentially infectious body fluids, can only exist with hepatitis B

Hepatitis E: virus transmitted through contaminated drinking water, typically encountered during international travel

Note that hepatitis B and C are a major threat to healthcare providers due to accidental exposures in the workplace.

Lactose intolerance occurs when the sugar lactose cannot be digested properly in the GI tract. This intolerance can occur at any age and is characterized by gassiness and, often, diarrhea after the ingestion of dairy products. Individuals can avoid these symptoms by taking drugs containing lactase, an enzyme which breaks down the lactose in foods.

Constipation can occur at any age. This problem develops when food passes too slowly through the GI tract and water in the chyme or feces is absorbed by the small and large intestines. Water loss produces hardened fecal material that is difficult to pass through the anal canal. **Diarrhea** is the opposite problem. Food passes through the system too quickly and not enough water is absorbed, which results in loose, watery stools. **Ileus** is a condition in which there is an absence of peristalsis, the muscle contractions that cause movement in the intestine. This may result in a blockage (obstruction) as stools are not moved through the bowels. Paralytic ileus is a condition in which the intestine fails to contract normally in order to move waste out of the body. It generally occurs as a complication following abdominal surgery.

The most prevalent types of cancers occurring in the digestive system are generally carcinomas that begin in the skin and epithelial tissues that line organs. These include cancers of the head and neck, colon, pancreas, and stomach. Hepatoma, or hepatocellular carcinoma, is the most common type of liver cancer, and it accounts for 80% of all cancer diagnoses originating from the liver. Of all cancers that affect both men and women in the United States, **colorectal cancer** is the second leading cause of death. The two main factors affecting the occurrence of colorectal cancer are age and diet. Risk increases with age and decreases in those who eat a high-fiber vegetarian diet. Health conditions that increase the risk of colorectal cancer include **inflammatory bowel disease (IBD)**, **chronic ulcerative colitis**, **Crohn's disease**, and a family history of colon cancer. Surgery is performed on localized tumors (those that have not spread to other parts of the body). Radiation and chemotherapy are used as alternative treatments.

Figure 11.11 displays the common diseases of the digestive tract and their locations. Table 11.3 defines wellness and illness terms related to the GI system.

FIGURE 11.11 Diseases Common to the Digestive Tract

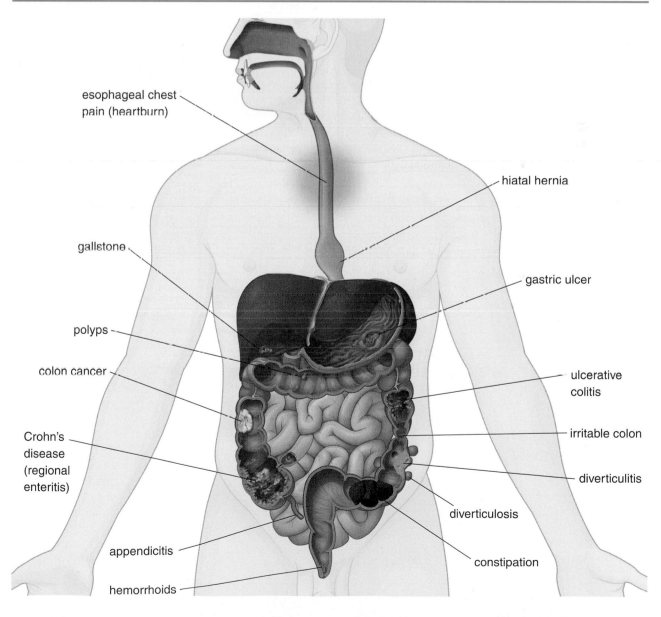

TABLE 11.3 Conditions Associated with the Digestive System

Term		Meaning	Word Analysis	
General Conditions				
appendicitis	[ah-pen-dih-**sI**-tis]	inflammation of the appendix (actual name is vermiform appendix)	_appendic/o_ _-itis_	appendix inflammation
bowel (abdominal) distension	[**bou**-uhl dih-**sten**-shun]	the accumulation of air (gas) or fluid in the abdomen, causing it to expand or swell beyond its normal size; a symptom of an illness	_abdomin/o_ _-al_	abdomen pertaining to
celiac disease	[**see**-lee-ak]	condition in which a sensitivity to gluten (a protein found in wheat) results in the inability to digest food	_celi/o_ _-ac_	abdomen pertaining to
constipation	[kon-stih-**pay**-shun]	condition in which food passes too slowly through the GI tract, and water is absorbed from the small and large intestines, causing fecal material to become hard and difficult to pass through the anal canal		
Crohn's disease	[**krOnz**]	chronic type of irritable bowel disease (IBD) affecting the digestive tract; results in abdominal pain, diarrhea, fever, and weight loss; the body's immune system attacks the GI tract	_Crohn_	20th-century American gastroenterologist
cystic fibrosis	[**sis**-tik fI-**brO**-sis]	hereditary disorder characterized by difficulty breathing and frequent, mushy, foul-smelling stools because of the insufficient production of enzymes by the pancreas to absorb food properly excessive production of mucus along the GI tract and respiratory tract		
diarrhea/ dysentery	[dI-ah-**ree**-ah]	frequent, loose, watery stools from improper absorption of water in the colon	_dia-_ _-rrhea_	through discharge, flow
dumping syndrome		a condition in which food is dumped too quickly from the stomach into the small intestine after meals, common after gastric surgery		
emesis	[**em**-eh-sis]	vomit; vomiting	_-emesis_	vomit (note: also used as a suffix)
eructation	[ee-ruk-**tay**-shun]	the release of air from the stomach through the mouth; burping, belching		
fistula	[**fis**-chew-lah]	an abnormal connection between an organ, vessel, or intestine		
flatus	[**flay**-tus]	gas generated in the stomach or intestines and passed through the anus		
gastroenteritis	[gas-trO-en-teh-**rI**-tis]	inflammation of the stomach and small intestine, stomach flu, often due to food poisoning, resulting in nausea, abdominal pain, and diarrhea	_gastr/o_ _enter/o_ _-itis_	stomach intestine inflammation
gastroesophageal reflux disease (GERD)	[gas-trO-ee-soff-uh-**jee**-uhl **ree**-fluks]	condition in which contents in the stomach flow back to the esophagus due to the inability of the lower esophageal sphincter to function properly, resulting in a burning pain in the esophagus	_gastr/o_ _esophag/o_ _-eal_ _re-_ _-flux_	stomach esophagus pertaining to back flow
hematemesis	[hee-mah-**tim**-uh-sis]	vomiting of blood	_hemat/o_ _-emesis_	blood vomit
hiccup	[**hik**-up]	involuntary contraction of the diaphragm followed by the sudden closure of the glottis (an opening at the upper part of the larynx)		

Continues

Term		Meaning	Word Analysis	
irritable bowel syndrome (IBS)		a condition in which the digestive system appears normal but does not function as it should; also known as *spastic colon* or *spastic bowel*		
lactose intolerance	[**lak**-tOs in-**tol**-er-ens]	a condition in which lactose, a sugar, cannot be digested properly by the GI tract; characterized by gassiness and often diarrhea after ingestion of dairy products	*lactose*	sugar
melena	[mah-**lee**-nah]	condition in which bleeding in the upper GI tract causes black, tarry stools		
mucositis	[myoo-**kO**-sI-tis]	inflammation of the mucous membranes; often present in the GI tract as a result of chemotherapy	*mucos/o* *-itis*	mucus inflammation
nausea	[**nah**-see-ah]	having the urge to vomit; does not always result in vomiting		
peritonitis	[pair-uh-tuh-**nI**-tis]	inflammation of the inner wall lining of the abdomen (peritoneum); often resulting from a ruptured appendix	*periton/o* *-itis*	perotineum inflammation
reflux	[**ree**-fluks]	backward flow of stomach contents (as in heartburn)	*re-* *-flux*	back flow
regurgitation	[ree-gur-jih-**tay**-shun]	the backward flow of food within the body (i.e., vomiting)		
ulcer	[**ul**-ser]	a hole in the protective lining of a membrane (e.g., peptic ulcers occur in the lining of the stomach or small intestine)		
volvulus	[**vahl**-vyoo-lus]	an obstruction caused by twisting of the stomach or intestine		

Conditions Associated with the Mouth

Term		Meaning	Word Analysis	
aglossia	[ah-**glos**-ee-ah]	birth defect in which an infant is born with no tongue	*a-* *gloss/o* *-ia*	without tongue, language condition of
ankyloglossia	[an-kıl-O-**glos**-ee-ah]	tongue-tied; the tongue is not freely movable (generally the result of a short, thick frenulum)	*ankyl/o* *gloss/o* *-ia*	bent, fixed tongue; language condition of
aphthous stomatitis	[**aff**-thus stO-mah-**tI**-tis]	common condition in which lesions recur on the mucous membranes of the mouth; also known as *mouth ulcers* or *canker sores*	*aphth/o* *-ous* *stomat/o* *itis*	ulceration pertaining to mouth inflammation
cheilitis/ cheilosis	[kI-**lI**-tis]/ [kI-**lO**-sis]	painful inflammation and cracking of the corners of the lips and mouth	*cheil/o* *-itis* *-osis*	lips inflammation abnormal condition
cleft palate	[kleft **pal**-et]	birth defect in which a baby's lip and mouth fail to form properly during pregnancy, resulting in an opening at the roof of the mouth, often accompanied by cleft lip		
dental caries	[**care**-eez]	the development of cavities due to the interaction between food and bacteria in the mouth	*dent/i* *-al*	teeth pertaining to
gingivitis	[jin-ji-**vI**-tis]	inflammation of the tissues that surround and support the teeth (gums), resulting in redness, swelling, and bleeding; gum disease	*gingiv/o* *-itis*	gums inflammation
halitosis	[hal-i-**tO**-sis]	bad, offensive-smelling breath	*halit/o* *-osis*	breath abnormal condition

Continues

Term		Meaning	Word Analysis	
herpetic stomatitis	[her-**peh**-tik stO-mah-**tI**-tis]	viral infection of the mouth resulting in the presence of sores and ulcers (fever blisters/cold sores)	*stomat/o* *-itis*	mouth inflammation
malocclusion	[mal-O-**kloo**-zhun]	condition in which the teeth do not align perfectly when the jaw is closed, abnormal bite	*mal-* *-occlusion*	bad condition of closure
periodontal disease/pyorrhea/ (gum disease)	[pair-ee-O-**don**-tul]/ [pI-or-**ree**-uh]	condition in which the gums pull away from the teeth, forming pockets of inflammation that become infected; can lead to the loss of teeth; often a result of untreated gingivitis	*peri-* *odont/o* *-al* *py/o* *-rrhea*	surrounding tooth pertaining to pus flow, discharge
plaque	[**plak**]	a sticky deposit of film that forms on the teeth, resulting in tartar buildup and tooth decay if not removed daily		
stomatitis	[stO-mah-**tI**-tis]	condition that causes painful swelling and sores in the mouth	*stomat/o* *-itis*	mouth inflammation

Conditions Associated with the Pharynx and Esophagus

Term		Meaning	Word Analysis	
achalasia	[ak-uh-**lay**-zsa]	condition in which the esophagus loses the ability to efficiently move food down into the stomach; the absence of esophageal peristalsis	*a-* *-chalasia*	without condition of relaxation
Barrett's esophagus		damage to the lower portion of the esophagus, often a result of chronic reflux disease		
dysphagia	[dis-**fay**-jah]	difficulty swallowing	*dys-* *-phagia*	abnormal, bad eating, swallowing
esophageal atresia	[ee-soff-uh-**jee**-uhl ah-**tree**-zsa]	a birth defect in which the esophagus of a newborn does not connect to the stomach, resulting in difficulty swallowing	*esophag/o* *a-* *-tresia*	esophagus not, without condition of an opening
esophagitis	[ee-sof-ah-**jI**-tis]	inflammation of the espohagus	*esophag/o* *-itis*	esophagus inflammation
pyrosis	[pI-**rO**-sis]	heartburn; painful, burning sensation in the esophagus; often a result of indigestion	*pyr/o* *-osis*	fire abnormal condition
tracheoesopha-geal fistula	[**tray**-kee-O-ee-soff-uh-jee-el **fis**-chew-lah]	birth defect in which a newborn has an abnormal connection (fistula) between the trachea and the esophagus, resulting in food entering the trachea and causing choking	*trache/o* *esophag/o* *-eal* *fistula*	trachea esophagus pertaining to an abnormal connection

Conditions Associated with the Stomach

Term		Meaning	Word Analysis	
dyspepsia	[dis-**pep**-see-ah]	condition in which feelings of nausea, fullness, and heartburn occur shortly after meals; indigestion	*dys-* *-pepsia*	abnormal, bad digestive condition
gastralgia	[gas-**tral**-zsa]	stomach pain, gastrodynia	*gastr/o* *-algia*	stomach pain
gastritis	[gas-**trI**-tis]	inflammation of the lining of the stomach, dyspepsia	*gastr/o* *-itis*	stomach inflammation
hiatal (hiatus) hernia	[hI-**ay**-tel (hI-**ay**-tus) **her**-nee-ah]	a condition in which a portion of the stomach bulges out near the esophagus and diaphragm	*hiat/o* *-al* *hernia*	opening pertaining to rupture
pyloric stenosis	[pI-**lor**-ik steh-**nO**-sis]	condition in which an infant suffers from an enlarged pylorus (the opening between the stomach and small intestine that allows food to pass through); causes projectile vomiting soon after feeding	*pylor/o* *-ic* *sten/o* *-osis*	pylorus pertaining to constriction condition

Continues

Term		Meaning	Word Analysis	
Conditions Associated with the Small and Large Intestines				
colitis	[kO-**lI**-tis]	inflammation of the colon (large intestine)	*col/o* *-itis*	colon inflammation
diverticulitis	[dI-ver-tik-yoo-**lI**-tis]	inflammation of the diverticula (pouches) occurring in the walls of the colon as a result of diverticulosis	*diverticul/o* *-itis*	diverticulum inflammation
diverticulosis	[dI-ver-tik-yoo-**lO**-sis]	condition in which diverticula (pouches) develop in the lining of the colon	*diverticul/o* *-osis*	diverticulum abnormal condition
diverticulum	[dI-ver-tik-**yoo**-lum]	pouch or sac that develops on the outside of the wall of the colon; herniation of the lining of the intestine	*diverticul/o* *-um*	diverticulum structure, thing
hematochezia	[hee-mat-O-**kee**-zee-ah]	condition in which bright red blood is present in feces; generally indicates bleeding in the large intestine	*hemat/o* *-chezia*	blood condition of stools
Hirschsprung disease	[**hersh**-sprung]	birth defect in which a newborn's nerve cells do not develop normally within the wall of the intestine, resulting in poor muscle movement and the inability to pass a bowel movement	*Hirschsprung*	19th-century Danish physician
ileus	[**il**-ee-us]	condition in which there is an absence of peristalsis (muscle contractions that cause movement) in the intestine, causing a blockage (obstruction)	*ileus*	Greek for "to roll up tightly"
inflammatory bowel disease (IBD)		chronic conditions that cause inflammation in parts of the intestines, leading to serious digestive problems		
inguinal hernia	[**in**-gwin-el **her**-nee-ah]	a condition in which a portion of the intestine bulges out into the inguinal canal	*inguin/o* *-al* *hernia*	groin pertaining to rupture
intussusception	[**in**-tus-sus-**sep**-shun]	condition in which one part of the intestine folds into another portion, causing a blockage		
irreducible (incarcerated) hernia		condition in which intestine or abdominal tissue fills the hernia sac and cannot be pushed back		
malabsorption syndrome		inability of small intestines to absorb nutrients leading to malnutrition	*mal-*	bad
neonatal necrotizing enterocolitis (NEC)	[nee-O-**nay**-tel **nek**-rO-**tIz**-ing **en**-ter-O-kO-**lI**-tis]	most common, serious intestinal disease present among premature infants, resulting in intestinal tissue death; cause is unknown but may be due to bacteria and decreased blood supply to the intestines	*neo-* *-nat/o* *-al* *necr/o* *enter/o* *col/o* *-itis*	new birth pertaining to death intestine colon inflammation
polyp	[**pah**-lip]	mass of tissue or projection from the surface of the intestine; may or may not have the potential to become malignant		
reducible hernia		protrusion of an organ or intestine that can be pushed back into the opening		
strangulation	[stran-gyoo-**lay**-shun]	condition in which a portion of the intestine is trapped in the pouch of a hernia, resulting in a decreased supply of blood to the remaining portion of the intestine		

Continues

Term		Meaning	Word Analysis	
umbilical hernia	[um-**bil**-ih-kul **her**-nee-ah]	a condition in which a portion of the intestine bulges out through a weakness in the abdominal wall around the umbilicus (navel); can be seen at the belly button	*umbilic/o* *-al* *hernia*	umbilicus pertaining to rupture

Conditions Associated with the Liver, Pancreas, and Gallbladder

Term		Meaning	Word Analysis	
cholangitis	[kO-lan-**jI**-tis]	bacterial infection caused by the obstruction/blockage of a bile duct; results in inflammation (usually caused by a gallstone or tumor)	*cholangi/o* *-itis*	bile vessel inflammation
cholecystitis	[kO-leh-sis-**tI**-tis]	inflammation of the gallbladder, commonly resulting from a blockage of the cystic duct	*chol/e* *cyst/o* *-itis*	gall, bile bladder, sac, pouch inflammation
cholelithiasis	[kO-leh-lith-**I**-ah-sis]	gallstone formation in the gallbladder or bile ducts	*chol/e* *lith/o* *-iasis*	gall, bile stones presence of disease
cirrhosis	[**suh**-rO-sis]	chronic liver damage that results in scarring and liver failure; most commonly associated with long-term alcohol abuse or viral hepatitis	*cirrh/o* *-osis*	orange-yellow in color abnormal condition
cystadenoma	[sist-aden-**O**-mah]	benign tumor of the pancreas	*cyst/o* *aden/o* *-oma*	bladder, cyst gland tumor
hepatitis (viral)	[hep-ah-**tI**-tis]	disease that causes inflammation of the liver; caused by viral pathogens found in food or blood	*hepat/o* *-itis*	liver inflammation
hepatoma (hepatocellular carcinoma)	[heh-puh-**tO**-mah]	most common type of liver cancer	*hepat/o* *-oma*	liver tumor
jaundice	[**jawn**-dis]	yellowish color of the skin and whites of the eyes due to the increased level of bile pigment (bilirubin) in the blood; also known as *icterus*	*jaune*	French word for "yellow"
pancreatitis	[pan-kree-uh-**tI**-tis]	inflammation of the pancreas	*pancreat/o* *-itis*	pancreas inflammation

Conditions Associated with the Rectum and Anus

Term		Meaning	Word Analysis	
anal (anorectal) abscess	[an-O-**rek**-tal **ab**-ses]	an area near the rectum or anus that is inflamed due to the collection of pus, a symptom of infection		
anal fissure	[**a**-nul **fish**-ur]	condition in which a cut or tear occurs in the anus, generally resulting from the passing of large or hard stools	*an/o* *-al*	anus pertaining to
hemorrhoid	[**hem**-or-oyd]	the presence of swollen and inflamed veins in the lower rectum and anus, pockets of tissue filled with blood vessels (commonly called *piles*)		
imperforate anus	[im-**pur**-fer-ayt **ay**-nus]	birth defect in which a newborn has no anal opening		
proctitis	[prok-**tI**-tis]	inflammation of the rectum and anus, also known as *rectitis*	*proct/o* *-itis*	rectum and anus inflammation
pruritus ani	[proo-**rI**-tis **ah**-nI]	common condition in which there is an irritation around the anus, resulting in intense itching		
ulcerative colitis	[**ul**-ser-ah-tiv kO-**lI**-tis]	chronic form of IBD characterized by inflammation and the presence of ulcers in the lining of the colon and rectum, resulting in abdominal pain, rectal bleeding, and severe cases of diarrhea	*col/o* *-itis*	colon inflammation

Soft Skills for Health Care: Teamwork

During your career you will be expected to work as part of a team. In the workplace, some tasks require more than one person to complete them. As a healthcare professional, you may need to work with patients to solve an issue related to their care. Working as part of a team can make your tasks easier or more difficult to complete, depending on how well individuals in the group work together. Good teammates demonstrate reliability and flexibility, work respectfully and constructively, and contribute to the team to the best of their ability. This skill is essential in showing your employer, colleagues, and patients the value you bring to the organization.

Infants

The premature infant is at great risk for a disorder called **neonatal necrotizing enterocolitis (NEC)**, which is characterized by death of the tissues of the ileum and colon. The cause is unknown but may be due to bacteria and decreased blood supply to the intestines. NEC is the most common, serious intestinal disease present among premature infants.

The newborn has a protruding belly button due to the attachment of the umbilical cord in utero (while in the uterus). The abdominal muscles of a newborn are not completely developed, making the abdominal wall fairly thin and an infant's abdominal organs easy to palpate, especially the liver, which is large in the newborn. The abdomen is bulging, and it may be possible to see an **umbilical** or **inguinal hernia**, if one is present, especially when the infant cries. A hernia occurs when a portion of the intestine is pushed out through a weakened area of the tissue that would normally contain it. Thus an umbilical hernia can be seen at the belly button and an inguinal hernia in the inguinal area, or groin.

During the first examination of the newborn, the physician checks for an anal opening so that elimination (bowel movements) may occur. **Imperforate anus** describes a condition in which an infant has no anal opening. Congenital disorders such as **aglossia** (absence of the tongue), **ankyloglossia** (tongue-tied), and **cleft palate** (an incomplete closure at the roof of the mouth) are noted and corrected as soon as possible so that the infant can receive good oral nutrition. The first stool of the newborn, called **meconium**, is greenish-black and sticky and occurs within 24 hours of birth. When the infant eats after birth, the stools change color and texture and become fecal smelling.

A **tracheoesophageal fistula (T-E fistula)** is a birth defect in which a newborn has an abnormal connection (fistula) between the trachea and the esophagus, resulting in food entering the trachea and causing choking. **Pyloric stenosis** is a condition in which an infant suffers from an enlarged pylorus (the opening between the stomach and small intestine that allows food to pass through). It causes projectile vomiting soon after feeding. This condition most commonly appears in male infants at around six weeks of age and may require treatment such as dilation or surgical intervention to repair the condition.

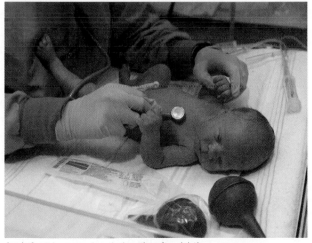

An infant is examined shortly after birth.

Children

The genetic disorder **cystic fibrosis (CF)** is diagnosed in infancy or early childhood. It is an inherited disease that causes airway obstruction and pancreatic insufficiency (the inability to properly digest food due to a lack of digestive enzymes produced by the pancreas and excessive production of mucus). Patients must take pancreatic enzymes so that food can be absorbed properly. The child's stool is sticky and foul smelling as a result of the missing pancreatic enzymes. The buildup of mucus in the lungs results in obstructed airways and bacterial infections. Respiratory problems associated with the disease are discussed in Chapter 7.

An intussusception can occur at any time but most commonly presents in childhood and most often in males. **Intussusception** is the enfolding (telescoping) of one part of the intestine into another, causing a blockage. **Crohn's disease** is characterized by diarrhea, cramps, abdominal pain, weight loss, and sometimes fever. It is a chronic inflammatory disorder of the terminal ileum that involves ulcers, fibrosis of the bowel, and fistulas. In Crohn's frequent surgeries occur to remove severely affected portions of the bowel. This can result in "short bowel syndrome" where the length of the small intestine is no longer sufficient to properly absorb adequate amounts of water, vitamins, and nutrients from food. **Ulcerative colitis** is a chronic condition that causes anemia, pain, rectal bleeding, increased colon cancer risk, and electrolyte imbalance. Symptoms include ulceration of the colon and rectum, with inflammatory changes in the bowel.

Volvulus is an obstruction caused by twisting of the stomach or intestine. It causes a blockage that may cut off blood flow, damaging part of the intestine. It is often the result of a birth defect called intestinal malrotation, which most often occurs in the first year of life.

Adults and Seniors

One of the most common GI disorders affecting adults is the **ulcer**, or hole in the protective lining of a membrane (mucosa) of the GI tract. Gastric ulcers occur in the stomach area, and duodenal ulcers are found in the duodenum (small intestine), where there is a high concentration of hydrochloric acid from the stomach. Researchers have discovered that a bacterium called *Helicobacter pylori* is largely responsible for ulcers. While stress is a factor in the formation of ulcers, treatment is now directed toward antibiotics that destroy and inhibit the growth of the bacteria.

Hemorrhoids are painful pockets of tissue filled with blood vessels. They frequently occur in pregnant women but are a common problem among adults of both sexes. During pregnancy, pressure from the growing uterus and an increased blood flow to the pelvic area can cause the veins in the rectal wall to swell. This disorder, often called **piles**, is characterized by the presence of swollen and inflamed veins in the lower rectum and anus.

> **Did You Know?**
>
> Patients with conditions related to stomach ulcers often have an imbalance between the production of hydrochloric acid and pepsin in the stomach.

Diverticula are pouches that develop in the lining of the colon, causing bleeding and inflammation. Diverticulosis is the presence of these pouches commonly found in the intestines of middle-aged persons. Further complication involves inflammation of a diverticulum and is known as diverticulitis. **Polyps**, masses of tissue or projections from the surface of the intestine that vary in shape, are also found in the GI tract. Although usually benign, polyps can become cancerous. Another disorder found in older persons is the **hiatal hernia**, sometimes called *hiatus hernia*. A hernia of the stomach, it pushes out near the esophagus and diaphragm, causing indigestion, pain, and discomfort, especially when the person lies down.

Checkpoint 11.2

Answer the following questions to identify any areas of the section that you may need to review.

1. What is the name of the condition in which the esophagus loses the ability to efficiently move food down into the stomach?

   _____

2. What type of hernia can be pushed back into the opening from which it has protruded?

   _____

3. What term describes the first elimination of feces (stool) by a newborn following birth?

   _____

Exercise 11.7   Word Analysis

List a definition for the combining form in each term. Then supply a definition for the entire term.

Term	Combining Form	Definition	Term Definition
1. aglossia	_____	_____	_____
2. stenosis	_____	_____	_____
3. cholelithiasis	_____	_____	_____
4. hepatitis	_____	_____	_____
5. stomatitis	_____	_____	_____

Exercise 11.8   Comprehension Check

Circle the correct term from each pair in the following sentences.

1. The hypergastric/hypogastric area is below the stomach.

2. Cystic fibrosis/Crohn's fibrosis is a genetic disease.

3. Both T-E fistula/ET fishtula and hypochloric stenosis/pyloric stenosis are congenital disorders.

4. Cholecystitis/Cholelithiasis describes the formation of gallstones.

5. The doctor was able to diagnose intubation/intussusception based on the results of the exam.

Exercise 11.9 Matching

Match the terms in column 1 with the definitions in column 2. Write the letter of the definition on the line provided.

1. _____ ulcer
2. _____ emesis
3. _____ reflux
4. _____ jaundice
5. _____ hemorrhoid

a. painful outpouching of veins in the anal area
b. yellowish color of skin due to increased bile pigments in the blood
c. vomiting
d. backward flow of stomach contents
e. hole in the mucosa

Exercise 11.10 Word Building

Use root words, combining forms, prefixes, and suffixes to construct a medical term to match each definition. Separate the parts of the term with a hyphen (-).

1. above the stomach   _____

2. inflammation of the liver   _____

3. inflammation of the colon   _____

4. flow through   _____

5. without tongue   _____

Exercise 11.11 Spelling Check

Using contextual clues to determine meaning and then circle the correct plural or singular form in each word pair.

1. The examination located several diverticula/diverticulum in the sigmoid colon.

2. The abdomen was marked and divided into four quadrant/quadrants.

3. Several proteins/protein have been identified as allergens.

4. The hepatic duct/ducts were removed.

5. The villi/villus in the intestines demonstrated morphological abnormalities.

Exercise 11.12 Word Maps

Group the following illness terms under the GI tract area where they occur.

constipation   heartburn   inguinal hernia
diverticulitis   hemorrhoids   intussusception
gastric ulcer   hiatal hernia   umbilical hernia

Stomach   **Intestines**   **Rectum/Anus**

_____   _____   _____

_____   _____   _____

_____   _____   _____

_____   _____   _____

Diagnostic Tests and Examinations

During an assessment of the digestive system, the examiner first observes the patient's general appearance, since nutritional status can be indicated by general size, height, and weight. The examiner also takes a complete history to evaluate the overall general health of the patient. Questions concerning nutrition (what is eaten, when, and over how long a period?), digestion (is there is any pain during or after eating, abdominal swelling, bloating, burping, or gassiness?), and elimination (what are the color, texture, and pattern of bowel movements?) are the focus of a patient's most recent medical history.

The physical examination begins with the mouth and teeth as proper oral hygiene is important to good digestion. The examination continues with the abdomen to determine size, shape, and other pertinent characteristics. The examiner uses the stethoscope to listen to the abdomen for bowel sounds, followed by percussion (tapping), which indicates the sizes and shapes of the organs. Lastly, the abdomen is palpated using light touch and then deep touch under the rib area and along the entire abdomen down to the pelvis. When symptoms warrant it, the healthcare provider may examine the rectum and anus using a gloved finger. This allows the palpatation of the prostate gland which can help determine if the patient has an enlarged prostate, prostate nodules, etc. A small sample of stool may also be collected and tested for the presence of blood.

As discussed in Chapter 2, the abdomen is divided into four quadrants—right and left upper and lower quadrants—and sometimes into regions—the epigastric, the area between the lower margins of the ribs; the umbilical, the area surrounding the umbilicus (belly button); and the hypogastric or suprapubic, the area above the pubic bone. Figure 11.10 provides a visual illustration of these areas and lists the organs located within each one. When performing a physical examination of the abdomen, it is important to know which anatomical structure lies in each quadrant in order to effectively identify the source of all signs and symptoms presented and arrive at an accurate diagnosis.

A variety of different examinations are used to provide both diagnostic testing for conditions of the digestive (GI) system and preventative care. A patient's history always precedes tests and examinations as it serves as a way to determine if an individual is currently experiencing any symptoms or if the presence of general health problems could possibly affect digestive function.

What's in a Word?

A common suffix used to describe examination terminology is -*scopy*, which means "process of viewing."

FIGURE 11.10 Divisions of the Abdomen

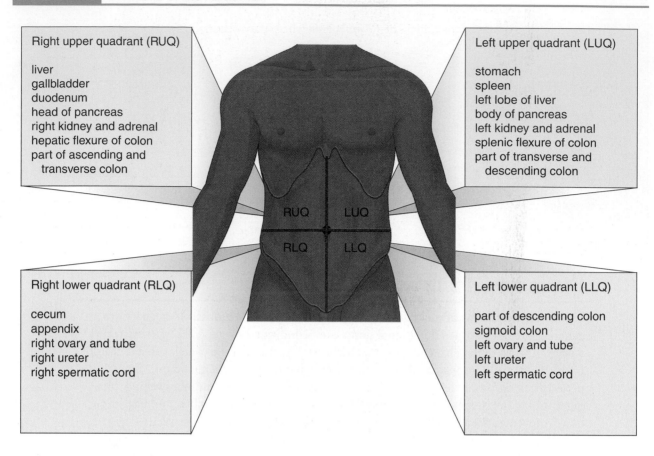

Right upper quadrant (RUQ)

liver
gallbladder
duodenum
head of pancreas
right kidney and adrenal
hepatic flexure of colon
part of ascending and
  transverse colon

Left upper quadrant (LUQ)

stomach
spleen
left lobe of liver
body of pancreas
left kidney and adrenal
splenic flexure of colon
part of transverse and
  descending colon

Right lower quadrant (RLQ)

cecum
appendix
right ovary and tube
right ureter
right spermatic cord

Left lower quadrant (LLQ)

part of descending colon
sigmoid colon
left ovary and tube
left ureter
left spermatic cord

Several laboratory blood tests can assess the functioning of organs within the GI tract. **Amylase** and **lipase** can be measured in blood serum to detect levels of pancreatic enzymes. Specific blood tests can detect the presence of the antigens that cause viral hepatitis.

X-ray procedures are particularly important for diagnosing diseases and conditions in the GI tract. A "**GI series**" refers to a set of X-rays, including the barium swallow, which visualizes the upper GI system, and the barium enema, which visualizes the lower GI system. **Cholangiography** is a radiologic study performed to view the gallbladder and its ducts for diagnostic purposes. Many GI diagnostic procedures use an **endoscope** and other instruments. The endoscope is a flexible tube with fiberoptic imaging to allow the physician to look inside the esophagus, stomach, and other areas. Some of the common studies (note the suffix *-scopy*) include **gastroscopy** (stomach), **colonoscopy** (colon), **sigmoidoscopy** (sigmoid colon), and **proctoscopy** (rectum and anal area).

Table 11.4 provides an overview of the most frequently used tests, examinations, and equipment used to diagnose conditions and overall health of the digestive system.

TABLE 11.4 — Diagnostic Tests and Examinations for the Digestive System

Term		Meaning
abdominal ultrasound		diagnostic tool that provides a picture of the upper abdominal organs (liver, pancreas, kidneys, gallbladder, spleen, and certain abdominal blood vessels)
amylase	[**am**-ah-lays]	blood test to measure the amount of amylase, an enzyme secreted by the pancreas
barium enema	[**bair**-ee-um **ih**-nuh-mah]	an X-ray of the colon (large intestine) using a contrast dye (barium) to diagnose conditions affecting the lower GI tract
barium swallow	[**bair**-ee-um]	an X-ray of the esophagus, stomach, and small intestine using a contrast dye (barium) that is swallowed to diagnose conditions affecting the upper GI tract
biopsy	[**bI**-opp-see]	a diagnostic examination in which a sample of cells or tissues is collected and tested to determine the presence of a specific disease (e.g., liver biopsy)
cholangiography	[kO-lan-jee-**ahg**-rah-fee]	X-ray of the gallbladder and its ducts
cholecystography	[kO-lee-sis-**tahg**-rah-fee]	an diagnostic procedure used to assess the function of the gallbladder following the ingestion of iodine
colonoscopy	[kO-lon-**os**-kah-pee]	visual examination of the colon using a scope to diagnose conditions related to abdominal pain, rectal bleeding, constipation, cancer, and other intestinal problems
endoscopy	[en-**dos**-kO-pee]	examination of interior structures of the body with an endoscope
esophageal manometry	[mah-**nah**-mah-tree]	diagnostic test to assess the function of the muscles of esophagus upon swallowing food, useful in patients diagnosed with GERD and conditions related to reflux
esophagogastroduodenoscopy (EGD)		diagnostic procedure in which a scope is swallowed in order to view the back of the throat, esophagus, and stomach.
fluoroscopy	[floo-**rah**-skuh-pee]	an X-ray technique used as a diagnostic tool to obtain visual images of moving structures in real-time
gallbladder ultrasound		diagnostic tool that provides a picture of the gallbladder, pancreas, and common bile duct
gamma-glutamyl transferase (GGT)	[**gam**-uh gloo-**tah**-mil]	diagnostic test used to detect the level of GGT (liver) enzymes present in the blood, effective tool in assessing liver damage
gastroscopy	[gas-**tros**-kah-pee]	visualization of the stomach with an endoscope
GI series		X-ray procedures such as the barium swallow and barium enema in which a contrast medium (barium) is given either orally or rectally; an X-ray is taken to visualize the flow of the barium through the GI tract
Hemoccult test	[**hee** mO kult]	diagnostic test used to detect blood in stool, which may indicate bleeding along the GI tract
laparotomy	[lap-uh-**rah**-tuh-mee]	surgical procedure in which a large incision is made through the abdominal wall in order to investigate abdominal pain; also known as *celiotomy*
lipase	[**lIp**-ays]	diagnostic test used to measure the amount of lipase in the blood, a pancreatic enzyme responsible for the absorption of fat
liver function tests		tests to determine the functioning of the liver
proctoscopy	[prok-**tos**-kah-pee]	visual inspection of the rectum and anal canal using a proctoscope, generally performed prior to rectal surgery
sigmoidoscopy	[sig-moy-**dos**-kah-pee]	visualization of the sigmoidal region of the colon
stool culture		diagnostic exam used to test for the presence of microorganisms in a sample of feces that can attribute to gastrointestinal conditions (i.e. bacteria, fungi, viruses, parasites)
total bilirubin	[**bil**-lee-ru-bin]	diagnostic exam used to detect the presence of jaundice (liver function)

Checkpoint 11.3

Answer the following questions to identify any areas of the section that you may need to review.

1. Which radiographic procedure uses barium contrast dye to diagnose conditions affecting the lower GI tract?

   _____

2. Which diagnostic procedure uses iodine to assess the function of the gallbladder?

   _____

3. Which procedure is a visual examination of the colon using a scope?

   _____

Treatments

Healthcare practitioners use predetermined guidelines to direct patient care. These guidelines, known as clinical practice guidelines and evidence-based practices, have been developed by the specialty societies based on past clinical research. They represent the treatment pathways that have achieved the best outcomes. Treatment decisions generally fall into three categories: surgical, clinical, and pharmacological.

Surgical treatments are generally invasive as they involve a puncture or an incision into the skin. *Clinical treatments* are generally noninvasive and involve nonsurgical techniques (e.g., physical therapy). *Pharmacological treatments* involve the utilization of medicines (drugs) to treat specific illnesses or diseases. Medication therapies are regulated by the Food and Drug Administration (FDA). To be approved by the FDA for use in the United States, every medicine must be backed by research studies that have shown the medication to be effective in its treatment of a given disease and has a tolerable safety profile. The following sections provide an overview of treatments common to the digestive system.

Surgical Treatments

Surgical procedures of the GI tract, signaled by the suffix *-ectomy*, include the **gastrectomy**, removal of the stomach or part of the stomach; **appendectomy**, removal of the appendix; **cholecystectomy**, removal of the gallbladder; and **colostomy** and **ileostomy**, in which an artificial opening is made in the abdominal wall and the end of the colon is attached to the opening. The colostomy and ileostomy are necessary when portions of the large or small intestine are removed because of cancer or other destructive diseases. Ostomies may be temporary or permanent. If temporary, the bowel can be anastamosed (reconnected) and stool may again be eliminated thru the anal canal and anus. An appendectomy is generally performed as an emergency procedure and involves the surgical removal of the appendix. The appendix (see Figure 11.11) becomes inflamed and fills with pus, leading to severe abdominal pain. Table 11.5 provides an overview of the most common procedures used to treat conditions of the digestive system.

FIGURE 11.11 Normal Anatomy with Appendix

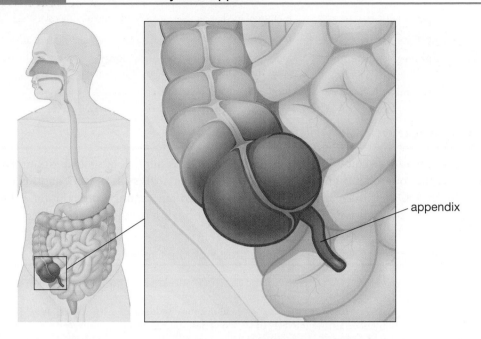

appendix

TABLE 11.5 Surgical Treatments Associated with the Digestive System

Treatment		Description
anastomosis	[ah-nas-tih-**mO**-sis]	procedure in which two structures are connected (e.g., two sections of the intestines)
appendectomy	[ap-en-**dek**-tah-mee]	removal of the appendix
bariatric surgery	[bair-ee-**at**-rik]	procedures used to achieve weight loss by reducing the size of the stomach (e.g., gastric bypass, sleeve, and bands)
cholecystectomy	[kO-leh-sis-**tek**-tah-mee]	removal of the gallbladder
colostomy	[kO-**los**-tah-mee]	procedure to remove part of the colon and make an artificial opening in the abdominal wall for the excretion of feces
enema	[**in**-ah-mah]	procedure in which liquid or gas is injected into the rectum, typically to promote the elimination of waste (feces), also used for cleansing, to treat severe constipation, or in preparation for diagnostic imaging
feeding tube (gastric gavage)	[gah-**vazhh**]	medical device used to provide nutrition to patients who cannot obtain nutrition by typical methods (by mouth), are unable to swallow safely, or need nutritional supplements
gastrectomy	[gas-**trek**-tah-mee]	removal of the stomach or part of the stomach
hemorrhoidectomy	[hem-roy-**dek**-tuh-mee]	excision or removal of hemorrhoids
herniorrhaphy	[her-nee-**or**-raf-ee]	repair of a hernia, suture of the abdominal wall
hernioplasty	[her-nee-**O**-plah-stee]	surgical repair of a hernia
hyperalimentation	[hI-pur-a-lih-men-**tay**-shun]	the artificial supply of nutrients, typically done intravenously (by IV)
ileostomy	[il-ee-**os**-tah-mee]	procedure to remove a portion of the ileum and attach the remaining end to an opening made in the abdominal wall
laparoscopic surgery	[lap-rO-**scO**-pik]	minimally invasive surgery in which incisions are made through the abdominal wall and a scope is used to perform the procedure
nasogastric intubation	[nay-sO-**gas**-trik in-too-**bay**-shun]	medical procedure in which a plastic tube (NG tube) is inserted through the nose, throat, and down into the stomach to deliver food and medicine directly to the stomach or remove substances from it

Continues

Treatment		Description
paracentesis	[pair-ah-sin-**tee**-sis]	procedure used to remove excess fluid from a body cavity (e.g., abdominal cavity)
polypectomy	[pah-lee-**pek**-tuh-mee]	removal of a polyp
pyloromyotomy	[pI-lor-O-mI-**ah**-tuh-mee]	incision into the muscles of the pylorus in order to assist the stomach in emptying contents into the small intestine
stomatoplasty	[**stO**-mat-tO-plas-tee]	surgical repair of the mouth

Pharmacological Treatments

Many agents address conditions of the digestive system. A number of such agents are available over the counter, including vitamin supplements, antacids such as Tums and Rolaids, and laxatives. Others, such as Prilosec, Nexium, and Zofran, require a prescription. Table 11.6 describes the common pharmacologic agents utilized in treating GI tract illnesses.

TABLE 11.6 Pharmacological Treatments Associated with the Digestive System

Drug Class	Use	Generic Name	Brand Name
antacid and antiflatulents	decrease acidity and gas by neutralizing the level of hydrochloric acid in the stomach	aluminum hydroxide with magnesium hydroxide	Maalox
		aluminum hydroxide, magnesium hydroxide, and simethicone	Mylanta
		calcium carbonate	Tums, Rolaids
antidiarrheals	stop diarrhea	loperamide	Imodium A-D
		bismuth subsalicylate	Pepto-Bismol
		diphenoxylate and atropine	Lomotil
antiemetics	stop or prevent nausea or vomiting	prochlorperazine	Compazine
		promethazine	Phenergan
		metoclopramide	Reglan
		scopolamine	Hyoscine, Transderm Scop
		ondansetron	Zofran
antispasmodics and anticholinergics	decrease GI spasms	dicyclomine	Bentyl
		hyoscyamine, atropine, scopolamine, and phenobarbital	Donnatal
appetite suppressants (anorexiants)	decrease appetite	phentermine	Adipex-P
		dextroamphetamine	Dexedrine
digestive enzymes	replace pancreatic enzymes	pancrelipase (amylase, lipase, and protease)	Pancrease, Ultrase, Viokase
		lactase	Lactaid
duodenal ulcer adherent	coats the stomach lining	sucralfate	Carafate
gallstone dissolution agents	dissolve gallstones	ursodiol	Actigall
		metoclopramide	Reglan
histamine (H_2) receptor antagonists	treat ulcers	famotidine	Pepcid
		cimetidine	Tagamet
		ranitidine	Zantac

Continues

Drug Class	Use	Generic Name	Brand Name
laxatives	stimulate the GI tract to produce stool	psyllium	Metamucil
		docusate	Colace
		senna	Senokot
		sodium phosphate enema	Fleet Enema
		bisacodyl	Dulcolax
nutritional supplements	supplement diet	none	Ensure, Osmolite
proton pump inhibitors	inhibit gastric acid secretion	omeprazole	Prilosec
		esomeprazole	Nexium
		lansoprazole	Prevacid
vaccines	prevent hepatitis B, prevent hepatitis A	hepatitis B vaccine	BayHep B
		hepatitis A vaccine	Havrix
vitamin supplements	supplement dietary intake	multivitamins	Vicon Forte, Poly-Vi-Flor, Tri-Vi-Flor

In the Know: Medications and Their Effect on Digestive Health

At times, it is necessary for physicians to prescribe medications that are known to cause irritation to the digestive system. As physicians prescribe medications and recommend treatment options to address various conditions, they consider a variety of factors. Contraindications of combined medications, side effects, allergic reactions, and cost all play an integral role in deciding what medications to recommend. Medications may contain fillers and additives that can be detrimental to the health of individuals with food allergies (e.g., gluten intolerance). Certain antibiotics can cause diarrhea, while other medications are known to lead to constipation. NSAIDs (nonsteroidal anti-inflammatory drugs), such as ibuprofen, are the most common cause of irritation to the lining of the stomach. Some medications (including oral contraceptives and antibiotics) are known to interfere with the esophageal sphincter, ultimately leading to reflux disorders. Individuals who experience difficulty swallowing tablets and capsules must also be made aware of the impact crushing certain medications can have on the digestive tract. Many over-the-counter medications can relieve or ease these side effects.

Checkpoint 11.4

Answer the following questions to identify any areas of the section that you may need to review.

1. What surgical procedure is used to remove a portion of the ileum and attach the remaining end to an opening made in the abdominal wall?

   _____

2. What government entity regulates and approves medications created by individual manufacturers?

   _____

3. What is the medical term for the artificial supply of nutrients, typically done intravenously (by IV)?

   _____

Abbreviations

In the medical field, information is generally recorded in medical charts and in electronic medical records and provided to healthcare workers in medical shorthand. It is important that healthcare professionals become familiar with the abbreviations used on a daily basis to successfully perform the duties assigned in a typical workday. Table 11.7 provides a list of common abbreviations used in reference to conditions and treatments of the digestive system.

TABLE 11.7 Abbreviations Associated with the Digestive System

Abbreviation	Meaning
a.c.	before meals
BaE or BE	barium enema
BM	bowel movement
BS	bowel sounds
CF	cystic fibrosis
COL	colonoscopy
CT scan	computed tomography
EGD	esophagogastroduodenoscopy
GB	gallbladder
GERD	gastroesophageal reflux disease
GGT	gamma-glutamyl transpeptidase
GI	gastrointestinal
HAL	hyperalimentation
HAV	hepatitis A virus
HBV	hepatitis B virus
HCV	hepatitis C virus
HCl	hydrochloric acid
HDV	Hepatitis D virus
HEV	Hepatitis E virus
IBD	inflammatory bowel disease
IBS	irritable bowel syndrome
IH	inguinal hernia
IO	intestinal obstruction
IVC	intravenous cholangiography
Lap	laparoscopy
LES	lower esophageal sphincter
LFT	liver function test
LLQ	left lower quadrant

Continues

Abbreviation	Meaning
LUQ	left upper quadrant
NEC	neonatal necrotizing enterocolitis
N&V	nausea and vomiting
n.p.o.	nothing by mouth
opim	other potentially infectious body fluids
p.c.	after meals
PEG	percutaneous endoscopic gastrostomy
p.p.	postprandial (after eating)
PPI	proton pump inhibitors
PUD	peptic ulcer disease
RLQ	right lower quadrant
RUQ	right upper quadrant
TPN	total parenteral nutrition (hyperalimentation)
UC	ulcerative colitis
UGI	upper gastrointestinal

Exercise 11.13   Word Analysis

Identify the combining form or forms in each term and write the definition of the combining form in the first blank. Then write the definition of the entire term in the second blank.

Term	Combining Form Definition	Term Definition
1. cholecystectomy	_____	_____
2. dental	_____	_____
3. sigmoidoscopy	_____	_____
4. proctitis	_____	_____
5. enteral	_____	_____

Exercise 11.14   Comprehension Check

This exercise provides practice in determining word meaning according to context. Circle the correct word from the two choices in each sentence.

1. Amylase and lipase can be measured to ascertain the functioning of the pancreas/esophagus.

2. The patient had a barium swallow/barium enema performed to determine the cause of symptoms affecting her upper GI tract.

3. Dr. Malone ordered a GI series/GERD series for the patient he saw this morning.

4. Dr. Baker will assist Dr. Malone with the emesis/endoscopy.

5. This patient has been receiving hyperalimentation/appendicitis for the past three months.

Exercise 11.15   Matching

Match the abbreviations in column 1 with the definitions in column 2. Write the letter of the definition on the line provided.

1. _____ a.c.
2. _____ GI
3. _____ IVC
4. _____ LUQ
5. _____ LFT

a. gastrointestinal
b. left upper quadrant
c. liver function test
d. intravenous cholangiography
e. before meals

Exercise 11.16   Abbreviations

Spell out the following abbreviations on the provided lines.

1. p.c. _____

2. HCl _____

3. LES _____

4. N&V _____

5. BE _____

Exercise 11.17   Word Maps

Endoscopic procedures to examine different areas of the gastrointestinal tract have different names, all indicating that an instrument is used to visualize the area. Provide the correct term for the scope examination of each area indicated. In the second column of lines, write the name of a disease associated with the area.

Location	Procedure	Disease
1. esophagus	_____	_____
2. stomach	_____	_____
3. small intestine	_____	_____
4. large intestine (colon)	_____	_____
5. sigmoid colon	_____	_____
6. rectum	_____	_____

Chapter Review

After successfully completing this chapter, you should be able to correctly answer the following review questions. Answers are provided in the back of the text. Use this self-assessment opportunity to check your understanding of the content and determine whether you need to revisit any of the chapter's content.

Crossword Puzzle

Use the clues provided to fill in the puzzle with the correct terms. Enter one letter per square.

Across

1. inflammation of the appendix
4. word part meaning stomach
5. absence of the tongue
7. abbreviation for after meals
9. below the stomach
11. umbilicus
12. hole in the mucosa
13. jaune
15. flexible, lighted instrument used to view the inside of structures in the body
16. chewing
17. enzyme secreted by the pancreas
18. secreted by the liver and stored in the gallbladder
21. vomiting
23. relating to birth
24. fleshy structure at the back of the throat, prevents food from entering nasopharynx
25. lip/o
26. inflammation of the liver
27. first elimination of the newborn

Down

1. proct/o
2. having any feet
3. necr/o
4. removal of the stomach
6. lactose
8. col/o
10. removal of the gallbladder
14. type of laxative
19. absence of peristalsis, causing obstruction in the intestine
20. example of a nutritional supplement
22. secretion of the salivary glands
26. abbreviation for hyperalimentation

Matching

Match the following terms to their proper definitions.

1. _____ umbilicus
2. _____ polyp
3. _____ suprapubic
4. _____ appendicitis
5. _____ fistula
6. _____ hiatal hernia
7. _____ rectum
8. _____ duodenum
9. _____ gastroenterology
10. _____ cholecystectomy

a. an abnormal connection between an organ, vessel, or intestine

b. surgical removal of the gallbladder

c. study of the digestive system

d. hernia of the stomach

e. inflammation of the appendix

f. the navel

g. first part of the small intestine

h. mass of tissue or projection from the surface of the intestine

i. area of the abdomen above the pubic bones

j. final portion of the digestive tract

Identification

Correctly label the illustrations by writing the correct term on the lines provided.

ascending colon
cecum
descending colon
rectum
sigmoid colon
transverse colon
vermiform appendix

1. _____
2. _____
3. _____
4. _____
5. _____
6. _____
7. _____

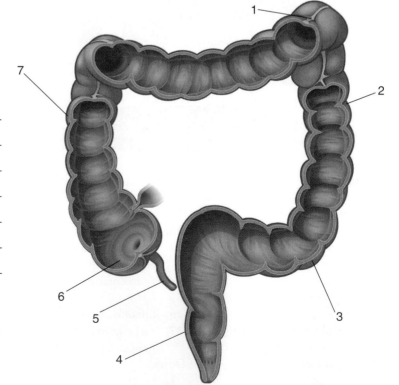

Abbreviations

Answer the following questions using your knowledge of digestive system abbreviations.

1. Braylon is a 12-day-old baby who has experienced trouble digesting food properly following a premature birth. Her primary care physician should refer her for testing to detect the presence of what condition?

   _____

2. What type of diagnostic test or examination is most likely to be conducted for suspected conditions of the lower GI tract (large intestine)?

   _____

3. This particular condition is often a concern in the food preparation areas of restaurants as it is transmitted through contaminated food and drinking water. What is the name and abbreviation for this particular condition?

   _____

4. A physical assessment of Jeremy's skin, nail beds, and mucous membranes revealed the presence of jaundice. His medical records show a history of chronic alcohol abuse. What laboratory test should his physician request to assess liver damage?

   _____

Word-Building Challenge

Supply the word parts to complete each term, according to the definition provided.

1. _____ ectomy means surgical removal of the gallbladder.

2. _____ itis is an inflammation of the gallbladder.

3. _____ graphy is diagnostic procedure used to assess the function of the gallbladder following the ingestion of iodine.

4. _____ scopy refers to examination of the colon using an instrument.

5. _____ stomy is the surgical creation of an artificial opening from the colon to the outside of the body.

6. _____ ectomy means removal of the stomach.

7. _____ scopy is an examination of the stomach using an instrument.

8. _____ scopy is an examination of the rectum using an instrument.

9. _____ stomy refers to the surgical creation of an artificial opening from the ileum to the outside of the body.

10. An _____scope is an instrument with a flexible tube used to view the interior of the body.

11. _____tomy refers to an incision into the stomach to investigate abdominal pain.

12. _____ectomy means removal of the appendix.

Extension Activities

Complete the following activities as assigned by your instructor.

1. Hiccups are a condition that many of us have experienced over the course of our existence. It is also one that has historically created a great deal of confusion in regard to causes and cures (home remedies). Conduct an Internet search on hiccups to obtain some fun facts to share with your classmates. For example, will holding your breath and counting to 10 make them disappear? How about drinking a glass of water? Can someone literally "scare" them out of you? Be sure to use scholarly sources when conducting your research. Post your findings in the classroom discussion forum.

2. Have you ever wondered why your stomach rumbles or growls at random times throughout the day? Is it because you are hungry? Use the Internet to research the medical term for stomach rumbling, *borborygmi*. Compose a one-page essay to share your findings with your instructor.

3. Historically, insurance coverage for procedures related to weight loss has been viewed as cosmetic in the eyes of health insurance companies. What are some common requirements for eligibility for bariatric surgery? Do you believe a higher health insurance premium should be charged to individuals deemed obese per established guidelines, much like that applied to smokers? Why or why not? Create a PowerPoint presentation of 10–12 slides to share with the class.

Student eResources

The Course Navigator learning management system that accompanies this textbook offers multiple opportunities to master chapter content, including end-of-chapter exercises, a glossary of key terms with audio pronunciations, games, pronunciation coach, and additional activities such as engaging with the BioDigital® Human.

12

The Urinary System

Translation Challenge

Read this excerpt from a physician's progress report, and try to answer the questions that follow.

> This 56 y/o male is seen in follow-up for recent pyelonephritis and microscopic hematuria. He has been referred to urology because of occasional mild dysuria. He denies any flank or abdominal pain, nausea, or vomiting. There is mild CVA tenderness on examination.

1. Define pyelonephritis.
2. "Microscopic hematuria" refers to what clinical condition?
3. The patient is experiencing dysuria. What symptoms is the patient presenting?
4. Define the term CVA as it relates to this patient's condition.

Learning Objectives

12.1 List and define word parts most commonly used to create urinary system terms.

12.2 Locate and label structures of the urinary tract.

12.3 Describe the process of urine formation.

12.4 List and describe conditions and abnormalities common to the urinary system.

12.5 Name tests and treatments for major urinary system abnormalities.

12.6 State the meaning of abbreviations related to the urinary system.

12.7 Use terminology of the urinary system in written and oral communication correctly.

12.8 Correctly spell and pronounce urinary system terminology.

COURSE NAVIGATOR

Access Additional Chapter Resources

The **urinary system**, also known as the *renal system*, is responsible for the filtering of waste and excess fluid from the bloodstream by the formation, storage, and elimination of **urine** (fluid waste) from the body. Additionally, the urinary system maintains the levels of electrolytes in the body and produces hormones responsible for the regulation of blood pressure. All components of the urinary tract must work together for the urinary system to function effectively. This system consists of the kidneys, ureters, urinary bladder, and urethra. This chapter will provide an overview of the function of each organ, the process of urine formation and excretion, and conditions and treatments associated with the urinary system.

In the Know: Specialists of the Urinary System

Urology is the branch of medicine that focuses on the diagnosis and treatment of conditions related to the male and female urinary tracts and the male reproductive organs. **Nephrology** is the medical specialty focusing on the diagnosis and treatment of conditions related to kidney function. Specialists include urologists and nephrologists. Allied health professionals involved in the care and treatment of urinary conditions include certified medical assistants, phlebotomists, sonographers, and radiation technicians.

Urinary System Word Parts

As with other body systems, a collection of word parts serve as the source for most of the medical words associated with the urinary system. Medical professionals use several terms for urine excretion: *micturition*, *urination*, and *voiding*. The combining forms, prefixes, and suffixes for these and other essential urinary system terms are listed in Table 12.1.

TABLE 12.1 Word Parts Associated with the Urinary System

Prefix	Meaning	Example
a-, an-	no, not, without	anuria (inability to produce urine)
di-	through, complete	diuretic (any substance that promotes the production of urine)
dia-	through	diaphoresis (excessive sweating)
dys-	difficult, painful	dysuria (painful urination)
en-	in	enuresis (involuntary urination, especially at night; also known as "bed-wetting")
poly-	many, frequent	polyuria (excessive urination)

Combining Form	Meaning	Example
cyst/o	bladder	cystoscope (instrument used to visually examine the inside of the urinary bladder and urethra)
electr/o	electric	electrolytes (minerals that help keep the body's fluid levels in balance)
glomerul/o	glomerulus	glomeruli (tiny blood vessels at the entrance of each kidney; help filter blood and remove excess fluid, which forms urine)
glycos/o	sugar, glucose	glycosuria (sugar in the urine)
hydr/o	water	hydration (the process of maintaining the proper balance of water and electrolytes in the body)
lith/o	stone, calcification	nephrolithiasis (condition in which calculi are present in the kidneys; also known as a *kidney stone*)
meat/o	passageway or opening	urinary meatus (the opening of the urethra where urine exits the body)
nephr/o	kidney	nephrology (branch of medical science that diagnoses and treats conditions of the kidneys)
olig/o	scanty, few	oliguria (the production of abnormally small amounts of urine)
peritone/o	peritoneum	retroperitoneal space (located behind the abdominal cavity in the peritoneum; houses the kidneys)
pyel/o	renal pelvis	pyelonephritis (inflammation of the kidney due to a bacterial infection; also known as a *kidney infection*)
py/o	pus	pyuria (pus in the urine)
ren/o	kidney	renal (pertaining to the kidney)
tub/o, tub/u	tube (little tube)	tubular (pertaining to a little tube)
ur/e	urea	urea (waste produced by the body after proteins are broken down and removed through urine)
ureter/o	ureter	ureters (ducts used to move urine from the kidneys to the bladder)
urethr/o	urethra	urethral (pertaining to the urethra, the structure connecting the urinary bladder to the urinary meatus; responsible for removing urine from the body)
urin/o	urine	urinary (relating to urine or the urinary system)
ur/o	urine	urogenital (pertaining to the urinary and genital organs)
vesic/o	bladder	vesicotomy (a surgical opening in the bladder to the outside of the body)

Suffix	Meaning	Example
-cele	herniation, protrusion	cystocele (herniation of the bladder into the vagina)
-dipsia	condition of thirst	polydipsia (excessive thirst)
-esis	state, condition of	diuresis (increased or excessive production of urine)
-iasis	condition, presence of	urolithiasis (stones found in the urinary bladder or urinary tract; also known as *urinary calculi*)
-itis	inflammation	cystitis (inflammation of the urinary bladder)

Continues

Suffix	Meaning	Example
-lith	stone, calcification	cystolith (urinary calculus, kidney stone)
-lysis	destruction, to break up, dissolve	urethrolysis (removal of scar tissue from the urinary bladder, the result of a prior surgical procedure)
-osis	condition	hydronephrosis (swelling of a kidney due to the buildup of urine)
-pexy	repair, fixation	nephropexy (surgical fixation of a floating kidney to the retroperitoneum)
-ptosis	drooping, prolapse	nephroptosis (condition in which the kidney drops into the pelvis when standing; also known as *floating kidney*)
-sis	process, action	dialysis (process of removing waste and excess water from the blood when the kidneys are not functioning properly)
-tripsy	crushing	lithotripsy (process of crushing stones that may be obstructing the kidneys, bladder, or ureters)
-ule	little, small	tubule (small tube)
-uria	urine	nocturia (excessive urination at night)

Anatomy and Physiology

The urinary system, shown in Figure 12.1, is made up of two kidneys, two ureters, the urinary bladder, and urethra.

FIGURE 12.1 Urinary System

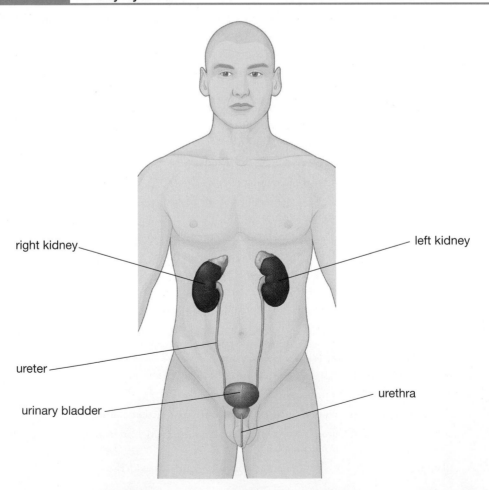

The **kidneys** are bean-shaped organs about the size of a fist that filter waste from the bloodstream and produce urine to excrete from the body. The outer portion of the kidney is called the **cortex**, and the inner portion is the **medulla**. The renal pelvis and calyces extend from the medulla of the kidneys and connect to the ureters, which drain urine into the bladder. The kidneys are located in the area just above the waist in the **retroperitoneal area**, that is, behind the peritoneum. The right kidney sits a little lower than the left. Each kidney is completely covered by a thick layer of fat that protects it from injury.

Kidney filtration occurs through millions of microscopic units within the renal cortex called **nephrons**. Failure to perform either of these vital functions would quickly result in the buildup of toxins in the body. The term *renal* means "pertaining to the kidney." Figure 12.2 shows the structures inside a kidney.

The **ureters** are thin, muscular tubes responsible for moving urine from the kidneys to the bladder. There is a ureter on each side of the bladder branching from each kidney. Urine drains from the renal pelvis, down the ureters, into the urinary bladder.

The **urinary bladder** stores urine until it is ready to be excreted from the body. It is connected to the **urethra**, which is the passageway of urine to the outside of the body. The external opening at the end of the urethra is called the **urinary meatus**.

Table 12.2 lists important anatomical and physiological terms derived from the combining forms introduced in Table 12.1 or taken directly from their original form in other languages.

FIGURE 12.2 **Kidney Structure**

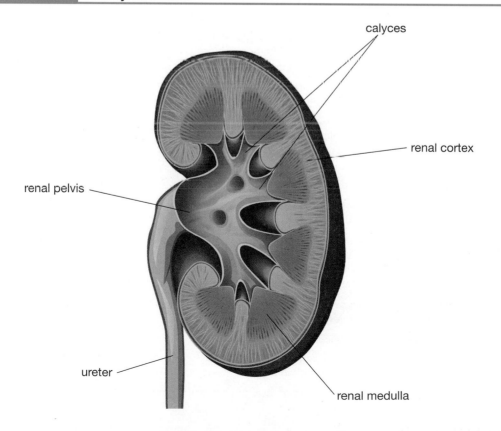

calyces

renal cortex

renal pelvis

renal medulla

ureter

Term		Meaning	Word Analysis	
afferent renal arteries		branch from the renal artery that supplies blood to the kidneys; helps to regulate blood pressure	ren/o al- arteri/o	kidney pertaining to artery
bladder	[**blad**-er]	an expandable organ in the lower abdomen that collects and stores urine until it is removed from the body		
Bowman's capsule	[**bO**-menz **kap**-sul]	a thin sac-like structure of the renal corpuscle that surrounds the glomerulus		
calyx	[**cal**-ics]	one of the branches of the renal pelvis, chambers that collect urine (plural, calyces)		
cortex	[**kor**-teks]	outer portion of an organ, such as the kidney		
costoverte-bral angle	[kos-tO-**ver**-tah-brel]	area on the back over the 12th rib; may indicate kidney disease if a thump to the area, with a fist, causes pain during a physical examination	cost/o vertebr/o -al	ribs vertebra pertaining to
distal convo-luted tubule	[**dis**-tel **kon**-vO-loot-ed **too**-byool]	one of four sections of the renal tubule; farthest from the renal corpuscle	distal con- tub/o -ule	away from with, together tube little
efferent renal arteries		carry blood away from the glomerulus following filtration	ren/o al- arteri/o	kidney pertaining to artery
electrolyte	[ee-**lek**-trO-lIt]	minerals that help keep the body's fluid levels in balance	electr/o -lysis	electric to dissolve, break up
external urethral sphincter	[eks-ter-nel yoo-**ree**-threl **sfink**-ter]	voluntary muscle that controls the retention and release of urine from the bladder	urethr/o	urethra
filtration	[fil-**tray**-shun]	process of passing a substance through a filter; in the urinary system filtration of blood occurs in the glomeruli to form urine		
glomeruli	[glO-**mer**-yoo-lI]	tiny blood vessels at the entrance of each kidney; help filter blood and remove excess fluid, which forms urine (singular-glomerulus)		
hilum	[**hI**-lum]	a fissure in the kidneys where the renal arteries enter and the renal veins and ureters exit		
internal urethral sphincter	[in-**ter**-nel yoo-**ree**-threl **sfink**-ter]	involuntary muscle that controls the release of urine from the bladder	urethr/o	urethra
kidneys	[**kid**-neez]	paired organs that produce and remove urine from the body		
loop of Henle	[**hen**-lee]	one of four sections of the renal tubule; connects the proximal and distal convoluted tubules; named after the German anatomist, Friedrich Gustav Jakob Henle	Henle	German anatomist
medulla	[meh-**dul**-ah]	inner portion of the kidney; contains the renal pyramids	medull/o	medulla
micturition	[mik-tyoo-**rish**-un]	elimination of urine from the bladder		
nephron	[**nef**-ron]	microscopic unit that makes up the functional structure of the kidneys	nephr/o	kidney
parenchymal tissue	[pair-**en**-kuh-mul]	specialized tissue of the urinary system responsible for kidney function		

Continues

Term		Meaning	Word Analysis	
peritubular capillaries	[pair-eh-**too**-byeh-lar]	tiny blood vessels that provide the blood supply for much of the nephron	*peri-* *tub/u* *-lar*	around tube pertaining to
proximal convoluted tubule	[**proks**-ih-mel **kon**-vO-loot-ed **too**-byool]	first segment of the renal tubule; nearest to the renal corpuscle	*proxim/o* *con-* *tub/u* *-ule*	proximal; nearest with, together tube little
reabsorption	[ree-ab-**sorp**-shun]	process of retaining fluid and electrolytes from the kidney back into the blood	*re-*	again
renal corpuscle	[**ree**-nel **kor**-pus-ul]	area of the nephron located in the cortex; contains the glomeruli and Bowman's capsule	*ren/o*	kidney
renal pelvis	[**ree**-nel **pel**-vis]	area at the upper end of the ureter; acts as a funnel for urine flowing to the ureters	*ren/o*	kidney
renal tubule	[**ree**-nel **too**-byool]	part of the nephron composed of the proximal and distal convoluted tubules, the loop of Henle, and the collecting ducts	*ren/o* *-al* *tub/o*	kidney pertaining to tube
retroperitoneal space	[**ret**-rO-pair-ih-tO-**nee**-el]	located behind the abdominal cavity in the peritoneum, houses the kidneys	*retro-* *peritone/o* *-al*	behind, backward peritoneum pertaining to
trigon	[**trI**-gone]	triangular region of the bladder, typically where bladder infections occur		
tubule	[**too**-byool]	small tube	*tub/o* *-ule*	tube little
ureter	[yoo-**ree**-ter]	ducts used to move urine from the kidneys to the bladder	*ureter/o*	ureter
urethra	[yoo-**ree**-thrah]	structure connecting the urinary bladder to the urinary meatus; responsible for removing urine from the body	*urethr/o*	urethra
urinary meatus	[**yoo**-rin-air-ee mee-**ay**-tus]	the opening of the urethra where urine exits the body)	*urin/o* *meat/o*	urine passageway
urinary secretion	[**yoo**-rin-air-ee seh-**kree**-shun]	movement of substances from the peritubular capillaries into the urine via the distal convoluted and collecting tubules		
urinate	[**yoo**-rin-ayt]	to eliminate urine	*urin/o*	urine
urination	[yoo-rin-**ay**-shun]	process of eliminating urine	*urin/a* *-tion*	urine process of
urine	[**yoo**-rin]	fluid (waste) that is voided from the body; filtered from the blood in the kidney	*urin/o*	urine
void		to eliminate urine		

Beyond Words: Facts about Kidneys

- If one kidney is removed, within two months the remaining kidney will increase in size by 50 percent to handle the task of filtration for the entire body.
- All blood in the body is filtered 400 times daily through the kidneys.
- A single kidney can filter more than 1 million gallons of blood over a person's lifetime (enough to fill a small lake).

Nephrons

Nephrons are the functional units in the kidney that produce urine by filtering waste and excess fluid from the bloodstream. There are approximately 1 million nephrons in each kidney. Each nephron consists of the renal corpuscle and the renal tubule. Figure 12.3 shows a nephron's structure. The **renal corpuscle** is the area of the nephron that contains a twisted structure called the **glomerulus** (which serves as the capillary system of the kidney) and **Bowman's capsule** (which surrounds the glomeruli). Filtration takes place in the glomeruli.

The **renal tubule** is a part of the nephron and is composed of four parts: the **proximal convoluted tubule**, the **loop of Henle** extending from the proximal tubule, the **distal convoluted tubule**, and the **collecting ducts**. Collectively, all parts of the renal tubule work together to transport urine from the glomeruli to the renal pelvis while allowing water and salts to be reabsorbed into the blood for use.

FIGURE 12.3 Nephron

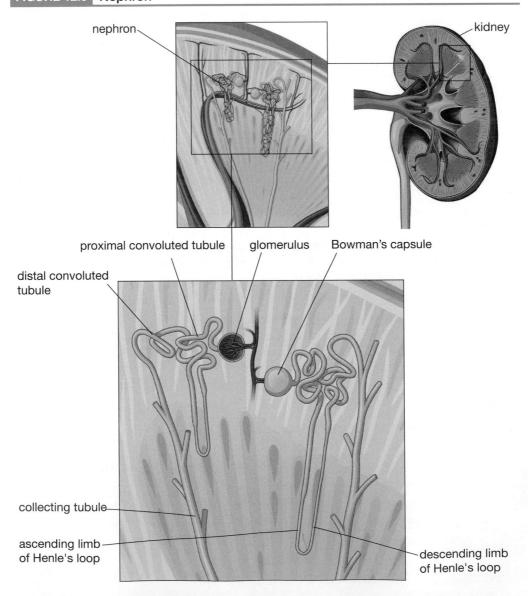

Urine Formation

The main function of the kidneys is to produce urine (see Figure 12.4), but kidneys must also perform important tasks such as filtering fluid, electrolytes, and metabolic waste materials from the blood. The kidneys help maintain blood pressure and the delicate balance of fluid and **electrolytes**, the chemical substances in the blood.

Urine formation begins with the **filtration** of blood in the glomeruli. When the glomerular blood pressure becomes high enough, water and dissolved materials are driven out into Bowman's capsule. This is a feedback loop because when the pressure falls below a certain level, filtration and urine production cease. Approximately 125 mL of fluid are filtered through the glomeruli each minute.

What's in a Word?

The term *glomeruli* is the plural form of *glomerulus*.

FIGURE 12.4 | Urine Formation

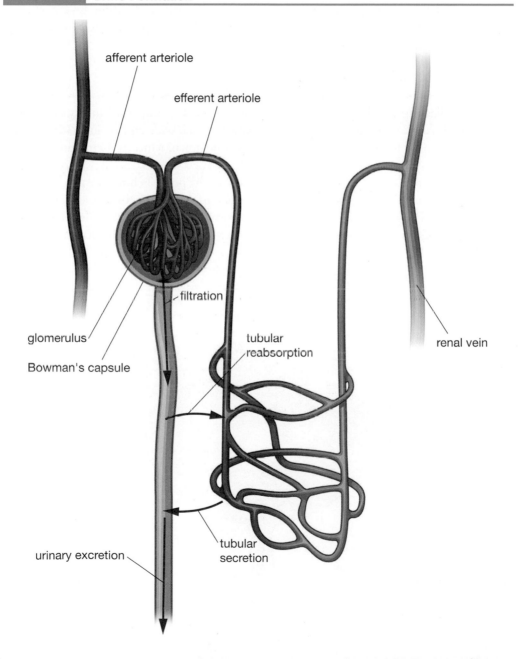

afferent arteriole

efferent arteriole

filtration

glomerulus

Bowman's capsule

tubular reabsorption

renal vein

urinary excretion

tubular secretion

The next phase is **reabsorption**, when substances are moved out of the renal tubules into the surrounding **peritubular capillaries** by diffusion, osmosis, and active transport. Reabsorption begins in the proximal convoluted tubules, proceeds through the loop of Henle to the distal convoluted tubules, and ends in the collecting tubules. Approximately 180 liters of water are reabsorbed from the proximal tubules each day.

The final step of urine formation is **secretion**, during which substances move from the surrounding capillaries into the urine within the distal and collecting tubules. Reabsorption and secretion are almost opposite: reabsorption moves substances out of the urine into the blood; secretion moves substances out of the blood into the urine. These substances include hydrogen and potassium ions, creatinine, ammonia, and some drugs.

The final product of urine is removed from the body via the urethra during a process called **urination**. Urination is also known as *voiding* and *micturition*. Medical professionals may also refer to this process as **excretion**. Aside from urine formation, the kidneys are also responsible for the balance of electrolytes in the blood. For example, if the level of sodium (Na) is low in the blood, the kidneys will reabsorb more sodium and secrete urine that is sodium poor. High levels of sodium in the blood will result in the secretion of sodium rich urine.

The Urinary Bladder

From the collecting tubules, urine drains into the renal pelvis, down the ureter, and into the urinary bladder. The ureters are narrow (about 1/4 inch wide and 12 inches long) and made of thick muscle that contracts to move the urine down. Mucous membranes line the inside.

The urinary bladder (see Figure 12.5) is located in the pelvis behind the pelvic bones. The elastic fibers and involuntary muscles that make up the urinary bladder allow it to stretch and hold large amounts of urine. When empty, the bladder is wrinkled and folded into **rugae** (ridges), except for one area on the posterior surface. This area, called the **tri-**

FIGURE 12.5 Bladder Structure

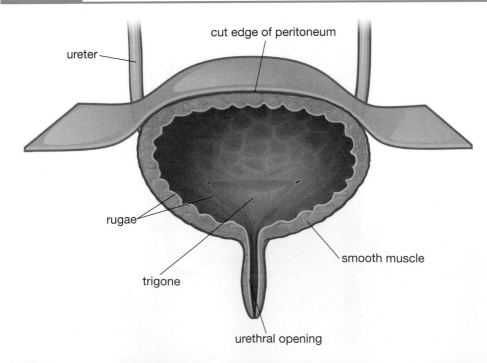

gone, is always smooth. The urinary bladder expands to provide room for the urine and contracts to excrete it.

The bladder is connected to the urethra and contains the same mucous membrane lining as the ureters. The urethra is only about 1.5 inches long in women and about 8 inches long in men. Recall that the urinary meatus at the end of the urethra is the external opening for the voiding of urine. While we do not have the ability to control kidney function, we can control when the bladder is emptied (urination). Two sphincters (rings of muscle) lead from the bladder. The **internal urethral sphincter** is located at the exit of the bladder and assists in keeping urine in the bladder. The **external urethral sphincter**, also known as the *muscles of the pelvic floor*, surround and support the urethra. These sphincters seal off the bladder so urine can accumulate. During urination, brain signals send a message to the muscular walls of the bladder to tighten and the sphincter muscles to relax. Urine is then squeezed out of the bladder through the urethra. The internal sphincter is under involuntary nerve control, and the external sphincter is under voluntary control.

The bladder can hold approximately 300 to 400 mL of urine (slightly less than 2 cups). The signal to initiate urination is sent to the brain when the volume of urine reaches about 350 mL, although adults become aware of the accumulation of urine at about 150 mL.

To Note!

Urination is also known as "voiding" and "micturition." The term *voiding* is often used in the medical office and in charts.

Beyond Words: Facts about Urine

- Urine is 95% water, 2.5% urea, and 2.5% minerals/salts and enzymes.
- It's a myth that healthy urine is clear in color. Although dark-yellow urine is a sign of dehydration, clear urine is a sign of overhydration (excess water in the body).
- Urine is *not* the best remedy for jellyfish stings. Seawater is a safer, more effective treatment for jellyfish stings.
- In a healthy urinary system, urine can remain in the bladder for up to 5 hours before excretion.

Checkpoint 12.1

Answer the following questions to identify any areas of the section that you may need to review.

1. List the main organs of the urinary system.

   _____

   _____

2. What is the main function of the kidneys?

   _____

3. What is another word for urination?

   _____

Exercise 12.1   Word Analysis

For each term in the left column, write the combining form in the next column, the combining form's definition in the third column and the original term's definition in the fourth column.

Term	Combining Form	Definition	Term Definition
1. cystectomy	_____	_____	_____
2. renal	_____	_____	_____
3. ureterectomy	_____	_____	_____
4. urethritis	_____	_____	_____
5. nephrectomy	_____	_____	_____

Exercise 12.2   Comprehension Check

Circle the correct term in each sentence.

1. The ureter/urethra carries urine from the bladder to the outside of the body.
2. Glomerulus/Glucose is an important part of the nephron.
3. The nephritis/nephron is the functional unit of the kidney.
4. Proximal and distal tubules/tubercles are structures in the renal system.
5. Nephritis/Nephronosis is a disease that can cause scarring in the kidneys.

Exercise 12.3   Matching

Match the term in column 1 with the correct definition in column 2. Write the letter of the definition on the line provided.

1. _____ urology
2. _____ nephrologist
3. _____ urinary meatus
4. _____ retroperitoneal
5. _____ cortex

a. outermost portion of the kidney
b. specialist in the study of the kidneys
c. "behind the peritoneum"
d. study of the urinary system
e. external opening at the end of the urethra

Exercise 12.4   Word Building

Use suffixes from the list and the provided combining forms to create a term to match each definition.

-al	-ia	-plasty
-analysis	-itis	-stomy
-ectomy	-logy	-tomy
-gram	-osis	-uria
-graphy	-pathy	

	Combining Form	New Term Definition	New Term
1.	pyel/o	inflammation of the renal pelvis	_____
2.	nephr/o	surgical removal of the kidney	_____
3.	ren/o	pertaining to the kidneys	_____
4.	urin/o	pertaining to urine	_____
5.	cyst/o	inflammation of the bladder	_____

Exercise 12.5   Spelling Check

Identify the misspelled terms in the sentences below. Write the correct spelling and the definition of the term on the line following each sentence.

1. The tissue surrounding the patient's kidney was abnormal, failing to protect the renal medula.

   _____

2. The renul pelivs was dilated. _____

   _____

3. Cysotoscopy was performed three days ago. _____

   _____

4. This patient had an intrevenous pyleogram last week. _____

   _____

5. Bouman's capasule was easily identified in the microscopic sample. _____

   _____

Exercise 12.6 Identification

Label the illustration by placing the corresponding letter (A–H) on the line provided beside each anatomical label.

1. _____ afferent arterioles

2. _____ bowman's capsule

3. _____ efferent arterioles

4. _____ excretion

5. _____ filtration

6. _____ glomerulus

7. _____ renal vein

8. _____ tubular secretion

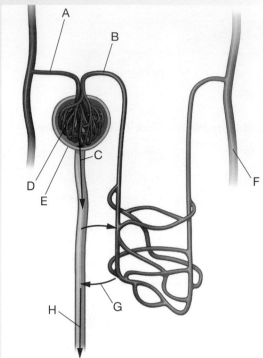

Conditions

The term **renal function** is typically used to describe the health status of an individual's kidneys. Two fully functioning kidneys equate to 100 percent renal function, while the presence of a single fully functioning kidney equates to 50 percent renal function. Serious health problems develop once renal function falls below 20 percent. Levels below 15 percent generally require dialysis or possibly a kidney transplant. Increased age, injury, illness, and exposure to certain drugs can affect the functionality of the kidneys and urinary system.

Frequency and *urgency* are terms for the feeling that urine must be passed but actually very little urine is produced; **nocturia** means the need to urinate during the night. **Incontinence** (loss of bladder control) and **overactive bladder** (the sudden urge to urinate) are two of the most common urinary conditions among women.

Anuria means that no urine is produced, and this is considered a medical emergency because the inability to eliminate wastes through urination will cause poisons to build up in the body to fatal levels. Decreased urine production, called **oliguria**, is serious and must be investigated further. **Polyuria** is frequent urination and can indicate diabetes mellitus (see Chapter 13) or other disorders. The examiner also asks about characteristics of the urine: color, odor, the appearance of unusual substances or particles within the urine such as blood, a condition called **hematuria**. Diabetes, a condition covered in Chapter 13, can cause various symptoms affecting the urinary system (e.g., polydipsia and glycosuria).

A **urinary tract infection (UTI)** can potentially cause an infection anywhere within the system, and the urine's warmth and moisture make the bladder a particularly vulnerable organ. A UTI is characterized by dysuria, fever, frequency, urgency, and occasionally pyuria. **Pyelonephritis** is an inflammation of the internal structures of the kidney, usually resulting from a bacterial urinary tract infection. It is commonly referred to as a kidney infection and is often the result of an untreated UTI.

Table 12.3 lists common conditions of the urinary system.

TABLE 12.3 Conditions Associated with the Urinary System

Term		Meaning	Word Analysis	
acute renal failure (ARF)		the sudden reversible loss of kidney function; occurs within a few hours to a few days, can be fatal	*ren/o* *-a*	kidney pertaining to
chronic kidney disease (CKD)		the gradual loss of kidney function, also known as *irreversible chronic kidney failure*; leads to renal failure		
cystitis		usually caused by bacterial infection	*cyst/o* *-itis*	bladder inflammation
cystocele	[**sis**-tO-seel]	condition involving a hernia of the bladder that pushes into the vagina; the wall between the bladder and vagina is usually weakened, stretched, and torn during childbirth	*cyst/o* *-cele*	bladder herniation
end-stage renal disease (ESRD)		condition in which the kidneys are no longer able to function; survival requires the use of dialysis or a kidney transplant; often a result of diabetes or high blood pressure		
glomerulone-phritis (GN)	[glom-**er**-yoo-lO-neh-**frI**-tis]	acute inflammation of the filtering cells in the kidneys (glomeruli); usually a response to an infection	*glomerull/o* *nephr/o* *-itis*	glomerulus kidney inflammation
horseshoe kidney		birth defect in which kidneys fuse together to form a horseshoe shape during fetal development; also known as *renal fusion*		
hydronephrosis	[hI-drO-neh-**frO**-sis]	condition in which the kidney swells in response to the buildup of urine and inability for urine to drain	*hydr/o* *nephr/o* *-osis*	water kidney condition
hypospadias	[hI-pO-**spay**-dee-uhs]	urethral opening is not at the usual location on the head of the penis, second most common birth defect in males		
incontinence	[in-**kon**-tih-nense]	involuntary loss of control		
lupus nephritis	[**loo**-pis neh-**frI**-tis]	condition in which lupus causes inflammation in the kidneys, resulting in the inability to adequately remove waste from the body; can lead to end-stage renal disease	*nephr/o* *-itis*	kidney inflammation
nephritis	[neh-**frI**-tis]	inflammation of the kidneys	*nephr/o* *-itis*	kidney inflammation
nephrolith	[neh-**frO**-lith]	kidney stone usually made from calcium	*nephr/o* *-lith*	kidney stone (calcification)
nephrolithiasis	[neh-**frO**-lih-**thI**-uh-sis]	condition of having kidney stones	*nephr/o* *-lith* *-iasis*	kidney stone (calcification) condition
nephropathy	[neh-**frah**-pah-thee]	kidney disease	*nephr/o* *-pathy*	kidney disease
nephroptosis	[neh-frop-**tO**-sis]	abnormal condition in which the kidney drops into the pelvis upon standing; also known as a *floating kidney*	*nephr/o* *-ptosis*	kidney drooping, prolapse

Continues

Term		Meaning	Word Analysis	
nephrotic syndrome	[neh-**frah**-tik]	kidney disease characterized by protein in the urine; also known as *nephrosis* [neh-**frO**-sis]	*nephr/o* *-sis*	kidney condition
polycystic kidney disease	[pah-lee-**sis**-tik]	genetic condition in which fluid-filled cysts form and grow in the kidneys	*poly-* *cyst/o* *-tic*	frequent, many bladder, sac pertaining to
pyelonephritis	[pI-el-O-nef-**rI**-tis]	inflammation of the internal structures of the kidney; usually from bacterial infection	*pyel/o* *nephr/o* *-itis*	relating to the renal pelvis kidney inflammation
renal adenoma	[**ree**-nul ad-ih-**nO**-mah]	most common form of benign kidney tumors; small and slow growing	*ren/o* *-al* *aden/o* *-oma*	kidney pertaining to gland tumor
renal cell carcinoma	[**ree**-nul kar-sih-**nO**-mah]	most common type of kidney cancer; also known as *renal cell cancer*	*ren/o* *-al* *carcin/o* *-oma*	kidney pertaining to cancer tumor
renal colic	[**ree**-nul **kah**-lik]	pain in the abdomen and back as a result of a kidney stone	*ren/o* *-a*	kidney pertaining to
renal failure		a condition in which the kidneys lose the ability to filter waste from the blood and balance fluids	*ren/o* *-a*	kidney pertaining to
renal hypertension		high blood pressure as a result of kidney disease; also known as *renovascular hypertension*	*ren/o* *vascul/o* *-ar*	kidney vessel pertaining to
renal oncocytoma	[**ree**-nul on-kO-sI-**tO**-mah]	benign kidney tumors that can grow quite large		
renal sclerosis	[**ree**-nul sklah-**rO**-sis]	hardening of the arteries of the kidneys; also known as *nephrosclerosis*	*ren/o* *-al* *-sclerosis*	kidney pertaining to hardening
transitional cell carcinoma of the bladder (TCC)		cancer occurring in the cells that line the inside of the bladder; most common form of bladder cancer	*carcin/o* *-oma*	cancer tumor
uremia	[yoo-**ree**-mee-ah]	excessive accumulation of urea (a waste product normally removed by the kidneys) in the blood	*ur/e* *-emia*	urine blood
ureteritis	[yoo-ree-ter-**I**-tis]	inflammation of the ureter(s)	*ureter/o* *-itis*	ureter inflammation
ureterocele	[yoo-**ree**-tur-O-seel]	birth defect in which the presence of two ureters on a single kidney (known as a duplicated collecting system) results in inflammation that blocks the flow of urine out of the ureter	*ureter/o* *-cele*	ureter herniation
urethral stenosis	[yoo-**ree**-thruhl stah-**nO**-sis]	narrowing of the urethra; caused by injury, trauma, previous surgery, or infection; also known as *urethral stricture*	*urethr/o* *-al* *-stenosis*	urethra pertaining to narrowing
urethritis	[yoo-reh-**thrI**-tis]	inflammation of the urethra	*urethr/o* *-itis*	urethra inflammation
urinary retention		inability to release urine		
urinary tract infection		infection anywhere within the urinary tract	*ur/i* *-ary*	urine relating to

Continues

Term		Meaning	Word Analysis	
urolithiasis	[yoo-roh-lih-**thI**-uh-sis]	the formation of stones in the kidney, bladder, and urethra; also known as *urinary calculi*	*ur/o* *lith/o* *-iasis*	urine stone, calcification condition
urosepsis	[yoo-rO-**sep**-sis]	severe illness that develops as the result of a bacterial infection that has spread from the urinary tract to the bloodstream; life-threatening if left untreated	*ur/o* *-sepsis*	urine infection
vesicoureteral reflux	[**ves**-ih-kO-yoo-**ree**-ter-el **ree**-fluks]	condition in which urine flows backward from the bladder into the ureter	*vesic/o* *ureter/o* *re-* *-flux*	urinary bladder ureter again, back flow
Wilms' tumor		most common type of cancer in children that starts in the kidneys; most cases affect one kidney; also known as *nephroblastoma*	Wilms	German surgeon

Infants and Children

One anomaly that may be present in the kidneys of the newborn is **horseshoe kidney**, which is caused by improper prenatal formation of the kidneys. Infants born with this condition have a band of tissue attaching the kidneys to each other, thus forming one horseshoe-shaped kidney.

Urinary tract infections in childhood are more common in girls than in boys because the female urethra is shorter, and outside organisms have more accessibility to enter the urinary tract by migrating up through the urinary meatus. When a young girl has more than one urinary tract infection, testing is recommended to determine if there are any abnormalities or deformities within the urinary system. For boys, the first UTI warrants evaluation.

Enuresis, or bed-wetting, is not uncommon in school-aged children. If a child who has never been a bed wetter begins enuresis, several issues should be considered. First, laboratory examination of the urine and a physical examination should rule out the possibility of a UTI. If there is no infection or other abnormality, then it may be necessary to look for a psychosocial cause, such as "schoolitis," problems with peers, or family problems, to name a few. The child should also be tested for type 1 diabetes.

Wilms' tumor is a malignancy of the kidney usually diagnosed in infancy; it is also known as *nephroblastoma*. It is most commonly found in one kidney but may be found in both. Treatment consists of surgical removal of the tumor and the affected kidney, chemotherapy, and radiation therapy, depending upon the extent of disease at diagnosis.

Adolescents

Systemic lupus erythematosus (SLE), often referred to as **lupus**, is most commonly diagnosed in teenage girls. The first manifestations of the disorder may be nephritis, characterized by hematuria and proteinuria with normal renal function in less severe cases. In severe cases, there may be decreased renal function or nephrotic syndrome. Lupus is an autoimmune disorder (see Chapter 10) in which certain antibodies attack cells in various organs, including the heart, lungs, central nervous system, and kidneys.

Adults and Seniors

A **calculus**, or stone in the kidney (kidney stone), is called a **nephrolith**. **Nephrolithiasis** (kidney stones) is an extremely painful condition that afflicts adults more often than children. This condition is characterized by **renal colic**, or pain in the abdomen, and severe pain in the flank (kidney area of the back). Kidney stones cause pain by stretching a structure. A stone in the ureter that is larger than the diameter of the ureter causes extreme pain. Once the stone moves to the bladder, no pain is present as it is now smaller than the size of the bladder. Once passed into the urethra, pain returns as the stone is much larger than its passageway. If a stone is too large to pass, it may have to be removed with surgical procedures.

Renal cell carcinoma, a malignancy that affects the kidney, is usually found in adults.

Problems in the senior age-group are often the result of decreased competence of the muscles within the urinary tract. **Incontinence**, the inability to hold urine, can be caused by the loss of muscle control of the urinary sphincters. A condition called **cystocele** is a hernia of the bladder that pushes down into the vagina. **Vesicoureteral reflux** occurs when there is incompetence of one of the urinary sphincters, allowing urine to flow backward—up from the bladder to the ureters. Table 12.4 lists terms relating to urine production.

TABLE 12.4 Terms Associated with Urine Production

Term		Meaning	Word Analysis	
albuminuria	[al-byoo-mih-**noor**-ee-ah]	protein in the urine	*albumin/o* *–uria*	protein urine
anuria	[an-**yoo**-ree-ah]	inability to produce urine	*an-* *-uria*	without urine
azotemia (uremia)	[a-zO-**tee**-mee-ah]	condition of excessive uria in the blood, an indication of non-functioning kidneys		
bacteriuria	[bak-tur-ee-**yoo**-ree-ah]	presence of bacteria in the urine	*bacteri/o* *-uria*	bacteria urine
diuresis	[dI-**yoo**-ree-sis]	increased or excessive production of urine		
dysuria	[dis-**yoo**-ree-ah]	pain or difficulty with urination	*dys-* *-uria*	painful, difficult urine
enuresis	[en-**yoo**-ree-sis]	bed-wetting		
frequency (of urination)		urination that occurs often with little actual production of urine		
glycosuria	[glI-kohs-**yoor**-ee-ah]	presence of excessive sugar in the urine, typically associated with diabetes	*glycos/o* *-uria*	glucose, sugar urine
hematuria	[hee-mah-**too**-ree-ah/ hem-ah-**too**-ree-ah]	blood in the urine	*hemat/o* *-uria*	blood urine
hesitancy	[**hez**-ih-ten-see]	inability to start the urine stream, or the involuntary interruption of the stream		
hypercalciuria	[**hI**-pur-kal-sih-**yoo**-ree-ah]	increased calcium in the urine; most common cause of kidney stones	*hyper-* *calc/o* *-uria*	increased calcium urine
incontinence (of urine)	[in-**kon**-tih-nens]	inability to hold urine	*in-*	not, in, within
ketonuria	[ket-O-**noor**-ee-ah]	abnormal accumulation of ketones (an alternative energy source) in the urine, seen in individuals with diabetes		
nocturia	[nok-**too**-ree-ah]	urination at night	*noct/i* *-uria*	night urine

Continues

Term		Meaning	Word Analysis	
oliguria	[ol-ih-**gyoo**-ree-ah]	production of very little urine	*olig/o*	scanty, few
			-uria	urine
polyuria	[pol-ee-**yoo**-ree-ah]	production of an increased amount of urine	*poly-*	frequent, many
			-uria	urine
proteinuria	[prO-teen-**ur**-ee-ah]	abnormal accumulation of protein in the urine, indication of kidney damage		
pyuria	[pI-**yoor**-ee-ah]	presence of pus in the urine		
urgency	[**er**-jen-see]	feeling of having to pass urine immediately, but with little actual urine production		
urinary retention		inability to void (release) urine; also known as *ichuria*		

Checkpoint 12.2

Answer the following questions to identify any areas of the section that you may need to review.

1. UTIs are more common for females than males because of what anatomical variation (or difference)?

   _____

2. What is another name for calculus, or nephrolith?

   _____

3. An incompetence of one of the urinary sphincters, allowing urine to flow backward (up from the bladder to the ureters), is known as what condition?

   _____

Exercise 12.7   Word Building

First, write a definition of the combining form on the line provided. Then use the combining form to create a term that matches the definition given, and write the term on the second line.

1. **Combining form:** *ur/o*   Definition: _____

   Definition: pus in the urine   Term: _____

2. **Combining form:** *lith/o*   Definition: _____

   Definition: condition of kidney stones   Term: _____

3. **Combining form:** *nephr/o*   Definition: _____

   Definition: study of the kidneys   Term: _____

4. **Combining form:** *cyst/o*   Definition: _____

   Definition: inflammation of the bladder   Term: _____

5. **Combining form:** *urethr/o*   Definition: _____

   Definition: inflammation of the urethra   Term: _____

Exercise 12.8 Spelling Check

Study each sentence and note whether the singular or plural form of the term should be used. Write S if the form should be singular, or P if it should be plural. Then write the corrected form of the term, if necessary.

	S or P	Corrected Form
1. There are many <u>nephron</u> in a kidney.	_____	_____
2. The <u>glomeruli</u> are malformed.	_____	_____
3. The <u>tubule</u> collect the urine.	_____	_____
4. Albumin is a <u>proteins</u> that appears in the urine in certain abnormalities.	_____	_____
5. The <u>urethras</u> was severely inflamed.	_____	_____

Exercise 12.9 Matching

Select a term from column 1 to match each definition in column 2. Write the number of your selection in the blank beside the term.

1. _____ cortex
2. _____ medulla
3. _____ nephrons
4. _____ glomeruli
5. _____ ureter

a. tubelike structure that carries urine from the kidneys to the bladder

b. marrow-like inner portion of the kidney

c. capillary loops within Bowman's capsule

d. microscopic units within the kidney that filter substances

e. outermost portion of the kidney

Exercise 12.10 Word Building

Use prefixes, root words, combining vowels, and suffixes to create medical terms for the definitions given. Write the term on the line provided.

1. inflammation of the ureters _____

2. pus in the urine _____

3. inflammation of the urethra _____

4. inflammation of the internal structures of the kidney, usually from bacterial infection _____

5. inflammation of the kidneys _____

Exercise 12.11   Spelling Check

Underline each misspelled term or terms in the following sentences. Then write the term's correct spelling and its definition on the line provided.

1. When laboratory tests revealed piurea, the physician ordered additional diagnostic tests._____

   _____

2. Nephritis is often characterized by hemeturia and proetinuria._____

   _____

3. Systemic lupis eryethematosis is most commonly diagnosed in teenage girls. _____

   _____

4. Eneuresis is not uncommon in the school-aged child. _____

   _____

5. The cappillary wall of the glomeurulus became increasingly permeable. _____

   _____

Exercise 12.12   Matching

Select a condition from column 1 to match each definition in column 2. Write the number of your selection in the blank beside the term.

1. _____ anuria   a. bed-wetting

2. _____ bacteriuria   b. blood in the urine

3. _____ diuresis   c. inability to hold urine

4. _____ enuresis   d. inability to produce urine

5. _____ hematuria   e. increased production of urine

6. _____ incontinence   f. presence of bacteria in the urine

7. _____ oliguria   g. production of very little urine

8. _____ pyuria   h. pus in the urine

Diagnostic Tests and Examinations

During the physical examination of a patient with a urinary tract complaint, the physician palpates the kidney area (an area known as the **costovertebral angle**) and bladder, evaluates the urine through tests, and questions the patient about any difficulty with urination. Can the patient pass urine? Is there any pain (dysuria) involved? Is there any difficulty in starting the urine stream (hesitancy)? Is there an inability to hold the urine (incontinence)? The examiner also asks about the amount of urine produced, its color, odor, and appearance.

The most common screening test for urinary tract problems is **urinalysis (UA)**, the analysis of urine via the collection of a freshly voided sample of urine in a specimen cup. The microscopic urinalysis is the study of the urine sample under a microscope. This particular examination evaluates the sample for the presence or absence of pus and/or bacteria. Another type of urinalysis is performed using a urine dipstick, a plastic test strip used to identify specific abnormalities in the urine sample (e.g., chemical reactions related to acidity, glucose, protein, blood, bacteria, ketones, and liver and kidney functioning). If a urinary tract infection is suspected, a clean-catch or catheterized specimen is obtained. **Clean-catch** is a method of collecting an uncontaminated urine sample for analysis by cleansing the external genitalia prior to collection. This method was developed to prevent bacteria normally present on the skin from contaminating the sample. A **catheterized urine sample** is collected by inserting a tube, called a catheter, through the urethra and directly to the bladder.

The urinalysis can detect blood, glucose, and/or **creatinine** (a substance that is elevated with kidney dysfunction). The blood test called **blood urea nitrogen (BUN)** can determine the level of urea in the blood, which indicates normal or abnormal kidney function. The **creatinine clearance** measures how well blood is being filtered through the kidneys. The glomerular filtration rate is a diagnostic tool used to assess how well the kidneys are functioning by estimating the amount of blood passing through the glomeruli (filters) per minute.

Several X-ray and scanning techniques are used to view the structures within the urinary tract. A simple screening X-ray is known as a **KUB (kidneys, ureters, bladder) X-ray**. A **renal scan** is an X-ray using a radioactive substance to view the kidneys. The **cystogram** is an X-ray of the bladder; **cystoscopy** is the procedure in which the cystoscope, a type of endoscope, is inserted through the external urinary meatus to view the

FIGURE 12.6 Cystoscopy

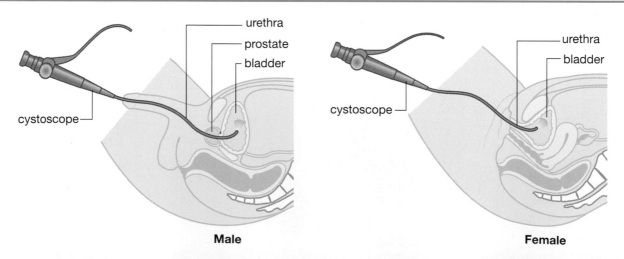

Male   Female

urethra and bladder (see Figure 12.6). An **intravenous pyelogram (IVP)** is an X-ray taken to view the kidneys and other structures after a dye is injected.

An MRI of the kidney area, including abdomen and pelvis, can identify any structural abnormalities or tumor growths. **Nephroscopy** is the visual examination of the inside of the kidney for the purpose of diagnosis and treatment. The nephroscope is the instrument used to locate, destroy, and suction kidney stones utilizing high-frequency sound waves. Table 12.5 lists these and other urinary tests, examinations, and equipment.

TABLE 12.5 Urinary Tests, Examinations, and Equipment

Test or Tool	Description
biopsy	diagnostic test that involves collecting small pieces of tissue, usually through a needle, for examination under a microscope (i.e., kidneys, bladder, ureters, urethra)
blood urea nitrogen (BUN)	blood test to measure the urea; an indication of kidney function
catheter	instrument inserted into the bladder through the urethra; generally used as a temporary surgical procedure to allow urine to drain freely for the purpose of collection, testing, and diagnosis
clean-catch urine sample	method of collecting a urine sample for analysis; it requires cleansing the external genitalia prior to collecting a urine sample to prevent bacteria normally present on the skin from contaminating the sample
creatinine clearance	test that measures how well blood is being filtered through the kidney
cystogram	X-ray examination of the bladder using a cystoscope (type of endoscope) inserted through the urethra to visualize the bladder, pronounced "**sis**-tO-gram"
cystourethroscopy	diagnostic tool used to view the inside of the lower urinary tract (i.e., urethra, prostate, or bladder); also known as *cystoscopy*
glomerular filtration rate	diagnostic test used to assess how well the kidneys are functioning by estimating the amount of blood passing through the glomeruli (filters) per minute
intravenous pyelogram (IVP)	X-ray using contrast medium injected into the vein to view the kidneys, ureters, and urinary bladder
kidneys, ureters, bladder imaging (KUB)	an imaging tool typically used to diagnose GI conditions such as bowel obstruction, constipation, gallstones, and kidney stones; the X-ray beam is placed over the abdomen
nephrotomography	sectional X-ray examination of the kidneys
renal scan	diagnostic X-ray procedure in which nuclear medicine is used to examine the functioning of the kidneys
retrograde pyelogram	diagnostic procedure in which a contrast dye is injected into the ureter in order to evaluate the flow of urine from the bladder to the kidney, opposite its normal path of flow
specific gravity	diagnostic test used to evaluate the body's water balance and urine concentration
urinalysis	laboratory study of the urine used to diagnose conditions of the urinary tract, kidneys, and diabetes
voiding cystourethrography (VCUG)	imaging tool that uses X-rays to create "real time" or moving images of the lower urinary tract

Soft Skills for Medical Professionals: Workplace Relationships

Considering that you spend roughly half your waking hours at work, it is only natural that you would build and maintain relationships with your colleagues. Workplace relationships can be beneficial to the work environment, but care should be taken that they remain professional. Consider the following tips for maintaining successful workplace relationships:

- Set professional boundaries.
- Put your work responsibilities first.
- Build trust before sharing personal information.
- Treat everyone equally.

For more information on how to navigate workplace relationships, hierarchies, and conflicts, refer to *Play Nice & Stay Employed: Workplace Relationships & Conflict Negotiations* from the *Soft Skills Solutions* series by JIST Publishing.

Checkpoint 12.3

Answer the following questions to identify any areas of the section that you may need to review.

1. The study of a freshly voided sample of urine under the microscope is known as what test?

   _____

2. What urine sample collection method requires cleansing the external genitalia prior to collection?

   _____

3. What type of X-ray uses a radioactive substance to view the kidneys?

   _____

Treatments

Healthcare practitioners use predetermined guidelines to direct patient care. These guidelines, known as clinical practice guidelines and evidence-based practices, have been developed by the specialty societies based on past clinical research. They represent the treatment pathways that have achieved the best outcomes. Treatment decisions generally fall into three categories: surgical, clinical, and pharmacological.

Surgical treatments are generally invasive as they involve a puncture or an incision into the skin. *Clinical treatments* are generally noninvasive and involve nonsurgical techniques (e.g., physical therapy). *Pharmacological treatments* involve the utilization of medicines (drugs) to treat specific illnesses or diseases. Medication therapies are regulated by the Food and Drug Administration (FDA). To be approved by the FDA for use in the United States, every medicine must be backed by research studies that have shown the medication to be effective in its treatment of a given disease and has a tolerable safety profile. The following sections provide an overview of treatments common to the urinary system.

As noted previously, kidney failure that results in an inability to process or produce urine is a medical emergency, and dialysis may have to be performed to sustain life. **Dialysis** is a procedure used to treat kidney failure by cleansing the blood of waste products through artificial means (a dialysis machine). The machine contains a membrane and a fluid bath. A special tube, called a shunt, is inserted into the patient's vein to circulate blood through the dialysis machine. The machine filters the blood, separating the large particles (such as blood cells) from small ones (such as urea and other waste products). The waste products remain in the dialyzing solution while the electrolytes and other essential products are returned intravenously to the patient. In hemodialysis, a dialysis machine and a special filter called an artificial kidney, or a dialyzer, are used to clean the blood. A special tube is attached, usually to the arm, and blood is filtered through the machine. A patient with kidney failure may need two to three hemodialysis procedures per week. Hemodialysis is administered in a dialysis center and usually takes place three days per week. Each treatment takes approximately four hours.

Another dialysis, **peritoneal dialysis (PD)**, can be administered in the patient's home. During PD, a fluid is introduced directly into the peritoneal cavity through a special opening created in the abdominal wall. The membranes of the peritoneal cavity are used as a filter for the blood and the transfer of waste products and electrolytes. The fluid remains in the peritoneal cavity for several hours before it is drained back into the container.

Surgical Treatments

A **nephrectomy** is the total removal of a kidney; a **cystectomy** is the removal of all or part of the bladder. If a cystocele is present, a **cystopexy** may be performed to attach the bladder to a supporting structure to prevent it from herniating. A **nephrostomy** may be performed to create an opening from the kidney to the outside of the body so that urine can drain.

Table 12.6 lists common surgical treatments relating to the urinary system.

> **To Note!**
>
> Combining forms and the common procedural suffixes (such as -*plasty*, -*stomy*, -*ectomy*, -*pexy*, and -*tomy*) make up urinary system surgical terms.

TABLE 12.6 Surgical Treatments Associated with the Urinary System

Treatment		Description
cystectomy	[sis-**tek**-tah-mee]	removal of the bladder
cystopexy	[**sis**-tO-peks-ee]	repair of the bladder by anchoring it to a supporting structure
hemodialysis	[**hee**-moh-dI-**al**-ah-sis]	most common treatment for advanced kidney failure; removal of waste products from the blood with a machine used for filtering; conducted at an outpatient clinic
nephrectomy	[neh-**frek**-tah-mee]	removal of all or part of the kidney
nephrolithotomy	[neh-frO-lith-**ah**-tO-mee]	incision of the kidney made to remove a kidney stone
nephropexy	[**neh**-frO-pek-see]	fixation of a floating kidney to the abdominal wall
nephrostomy	[neh-**fros**-tuh-mee]	procedure to create an opening from the kidney to the outside to drain urine by the use of a catheter
nephrotomy	[neh-**frah**-tuh-mee]	incision into the kidney
peritoneal dialysis	[pair-ih-tO-**nee**-al dI-**al**-ah-sis]	home treatment for kidney failure in which the peritoneal membranes are used as a filter for the transfer of wastes out of the body and electrolytes into the body
renal dialysis	[**ree**-nel dI-**al**-ah-sis]	life-sustaining treatment used to filter waste and excess from the blood when the kidneys are unable to function adequately

Continues

Treatment		Description
renal transplant		procedure to transfer a donated kidney into a person whose kidneys are no longer functioning properly (e.g., someone with end-stage renal disease)
urethrolysis	[yoo-ree-**thrawl**-ih-sis]	procedure in which scar tissue is removed from the urethra; may be a result of previous surgery
vesicotomy	[ves-sih-**kah**-tuh-mee]	incision of the urinary bladder
vesicourethral suspension		surgery to stabilize the position of the urinary bladder

Clinical Treatments

Extracorporeal shock wave lithotripsy (ESWL), commonly called lithotripsy, is a clinical procedure that uses ultrasonic, high-energy waves to "shock" the kidney stone and break it up into dust or sand-sized pieces. In some patients, the procedure may eliminate the need for surgery since the crushed stones may be passed through the urethra more easily. The machine that generates the ultrasonic waves is called a lithotripter.

TABLE 12.7 Clinical Treatments Associated with the Urinary System

Treatment	Description
catheterization	procedure used to collect and/or drain urine by inserting a tube, called a catheter, through the urethra and directly into the bladder
extracorporeal shock wave lithotripsy (ESWL)	procedure that uses ultrasonic, high-energy waves to "shock" the kidney stone and break it up into dust or sand-sized pieces, also known as *lithotripsy*

Pharmacological Treatments

Recall that antibiotics are commonly used in the treatment or prevention of bacterial infections. Note that the word *antibiotic* comes from *anti-*, meaning "against," and *bi/o*, meaning "life." Bactrim and Cipro are examples of antibiotics commonly used to treat urinary tract infections.

Many pharmacologic agents have been developed to treat a variety of different conditions. Diuretics, or water pills, are used to treat kidney disease, high blood pressure, heart disease, and edema. The goal of diuretics is to promote the production of urine by increasing the excretion of salt and water from the kidneys.

Contrarily, antidiuretics are often used to suppress the formation of urine. They are used in the treatment of diabetes and enuresis, also known as *bed-wetting*. Patients who experience urinary incontinence are generally treated with anticholinergic medications such as Ditropan and Detrol.

Table 12.8 describes some of the common pharmacologic agents used to treat problems of the urinary tract.

TABLE 12.8 Pharmacologic Agents Associated with the Urinary System

Drug Class	Use	Generic Name	Brand Name
analgesics	relieve urinary pain or burning	phenazopyridine	Pyridium
antibiotics	treat infection	ciproflaxin fosfomycin levoflaxin nitrofurantoin sulfamethoxazole with trimethoprim	Cipro Monurol Levaquin Macrobid, Macrodantin, Furadantin Bactrim, Septra
antidiuretics	treat diabetes insipidus and bed-wetting; suppress the formation of urine	vasopressin (also known as *ADH* or *antidiuretic hormone*) desmopressin	Pitressin DDAVP, Stimate
antigout agents, uric acid lowering agents	prevent attacks of gouty arthritis and uric acid kidney stones	allopurinol	Zyloprim
anticholinergics	treat urinary incontinence	tolterodine oxybutynin	Detrol Ditropan/Oxytrol
diuretics	promote urination; also commonly used to treat high blood pressure and congestive heart failure	urosemide spironolactone hydrochlorothiazide	Lasix Aldactone Hydrodiuril
urinary alkalinizers	increase the pH of urine, assist in treating acidosis or drug overdoses	potassium citrate, sodium citrate, and citric acid solutions	Cytra-3, Polycitra
urinary antispasmodics	treat overactive bladder and urinary incontinence	oxybutynin	Ditropan
urinary acidifiers	decrease the pH of urine, assist in preventing kidney stones, most often used in animals	ammonium chloride, methionine	

Checkpoint 12.4

Answer the following questions to identify any areas of the section that you may need to review.

1. What is the name of the procedure that clears the blood of waste products using artificial means?

   _____

2. Complete removal of a kidney is known by what term?

   _____

3. What procedure uses shock waves to break up kidney stones?

   _____

Abbreviations

In the medical field, information is generally recorded in medical charts and in electronic medical records and provided to healthcare workers in medical shorthand. It is important that healthcare professionals become familiar with the abbreviations used on a daily basis to successfully perform the duties assigned in a typical workday. Table 12.9 lists common abbreviations used in reference to conditions and treatments of the urinary system.

TABLE 12.9 Abbreviations Associated with the Urinary System

Abbreviation	Meaning
AGN	acute glomerulonephritis
ATN	acute tubular necrosis
ARF	acute renal failure
BUN	blood urea nitrogen
C&S	culture and sensitivity test
cath	catheterization
CC	clean-catch urine specimen
CKD	chronic kidney disease
CRF	chronic renal failure
CVA	costovertebral angle
cysto	cystoscopy
ESRD	end-stage renal disease
ESWL	extracorporeal shock wave lithotripsy
GFR	glomerular filtration rate
GN	glomerulonephritis
GU	genitourinary
HD	hemodialysis
I&O	intake and output
IPD	intermittent peritoneal dialysis
IVP	intravenous pyelogram
IVU	intravenous urography
KUB	kidneys, ureters, bladder (X-ray)
PD	peritoneal dialysis
PKD	polycystic kidney disease
RP	retrograde pyelogram
TCC	transitional cell carcinoma
UA, U/A	urinalysis
UC	urine culture
UTI	urinary tract infection
VCUG	voiding cystourethrography

Exercise 12.13 Word Building

Write the definition of each combining form in the Definition column. Then write a term using that combining form in the Term column.

Combining Form   **Definition**   **Term**

1. *nephr/o* _____ _____

2. *ur/o* _____ _____

3. *ren/o* _____ _____

4. *glomerul/o* _____ _____

5. *py/o* _____ _____

Exercise 12.14 Word Analysis

Draw a box around the combining form in each term. Provide a definition for the combining form, and then define the whole term.

    Term   **Definition of Combining Form**   **Definition of Term**

1. nephrologist _____ _____

2. urinal _____ _____

3. renal _____ _____

4. glomerular _____ _____

5. cystitis _____ _____

Exercise 12.15 Comprehension Check

Write the medical term for the underlined phrase in each sentence.

1. Dr. Harrison performed a <u>kidney removal</u> this morning. _____

2. Harriet underwent a <u>procedure to remove part of her bladder</u> after she was diagnosed with a tumor in her bladder. _____

3. <u>Removing wastes from the blood using fluids instilled into and then removed from the patient's abdomen</u> is a procedure that can be performed in the patient's home. _____

4. <u>Filtering blood by routing it through a special machine</u> will be required if the kidneys fail. _____

5. The <u>special endoscope for viewing the interior of the bladder</u> was inserted through the external urinary meatus. _____

Exercise 12.16 Abbreviations

Provide a definition for each abbreviation.

1. KUB _____

2. CKD _____

3. BUN _____

4. GFR _____

5. IVP _____

Exercise 12.17 Word Building

Supply the word parts to complete each term, according to the definition provided.

1. _____ plasty = surgical repair of the ureter

2. cyst _____ = surgical removal of the bladder

3. nephr _____ = surgical removal of the kidney

4. cysto _____ = herniation of the bladder into the vagina

5. litho _____ = crushing of stones

6. uretero _____ = surgical creation of an opening between the ureter and the outside of the body

Exercise 12.18 Spelling Check

Indicate whether each term is singular or plural by writing an S or a P after the term. Then supply the opposite form (singular or plural) of the term.

Term	S or P	Opposite Form
1. cystectomies	_____	_____
2. glomeruli	_____	_____
3. catheterizations	_____	_____
4. urinalysis	_____	_____
5. analgesic	_____	_____

Exercise 12.19   Matching

Select a surgical treatment term from column 1 to match each definition in column 2. Write the number of your selection in the blank beside the term.

1. _____ nephrectomy

2. _____ nephrolithotomy

3. _____ nephropexy

4. _____ nephrostomy

5. _____ nephrotomy

a. fixation of a floating kidney to the abdominal wall

b. incision into the kidney

c. incision of the kidney made to remove a kidney stone

d. procedure to create an opening from the kidney to the outside to drain urine by the use of a catheter

e. removal of all or part of the kidney

Chapter Review

After successfully completing this chapter, you should be able to correctly answer the following review questions. Answers are provided in the back of the text. Use this self-assessment opportunity to check your understanding of the content and determine whether you need to revisit any of the chapter's content.

Crossword Puzzle

Use the clues provided to fill in the puzzle with the correct terms. Enter one letter per square.

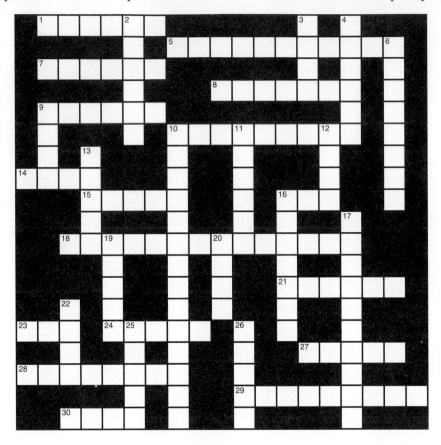

Across

1. opening
5. substance that conducts electricity in a fluid
7. nephr/o, ren/o
8. the body's container for urine
9. outer portion of an organ
10. blood in the urine
14. corpus
15. glyc/o
16. prefix meaning painful
18. structure that surrounds the glomerulus
21. -pexy
23. pyo

24. prefix meaning behind
27. hem/o
28. inflammation of the bladder
29. inflammation of the kidney
30. root for urine

Down

2. tube-like structure that carries urine from the kidney to the bladder
3. to excrete urine
4. pus in the urine
6. bed-wetting
9. pertaining to the colon

10. condition in which the kidney swells in response to the buildup of urine and inability for urine to drain
11. inability to produce urine
12. suffix meaning inflammation
13. root for bladder
16. painful urination
17. pain in the abdomen and back as a result of kidney stone
19. hydro/o
20. word part meaning cavity
22. word part meaning condition
25. prefix meaning outside
26. -lith

Matching

Match the following terms to their proper definitions.

1. _____ bladder
2. _____ calyx
3. _____ cystectomy
4. _____ electrolytes
5. _____ filtration
6. _____ glomeruli
7. _____ renal pelvis
8. _____ retroperitoneal
9. _____ urethra
10. _____ voiding

a. chemical substances in the blood

b. branch of the renal pelvis

c. passing a substance through a filter to separate out particulate matter

d. tiny blood vessels within Bowman's capsule that help filter blood and remove excess fluid

e. tube that carries urine from the bladder to the outside of the body

f. area at the upper end of the ureter

g. "behind the peritoneum"

h. body's container for urine; distends when filled

i. excreting urine

j. removal of all or part of the bladder

Identification

Correctly label the illustration using the provided terms. Write the term on the corresponding line provided.

calyces
renal cortex
renal medulla
renal pelvis
ureter

1. _____

2. _____

3. _____

4. _____

5. _____

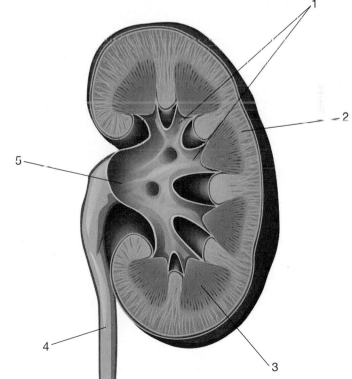

Abbreviations

Provide the full meanings for the following abbreviations.

1. AGN _____
2. ARF _____
3. cysto _____
4. GN _____
5. HD _____
6. ESWL _____
7. UA _____
8. UTI _____
9. I&O _____
10. PD _____

Word-Building Challenge

Review the following list of new terms. Apply your knowledge of urinary word parts to accurately identify the meaning of each new term. Write your answer on the line provided and then check your definition against the answer provided in the appendix.

1. transurethral _____

_____

2. nephrosis _____

_____

3. vesicoureteral _____

_____

4. uremia _____

_____

5. hypoalbuminemia _____

_____

Extension Activities

Complete the following activities as assigned by your instructor.

1. Search the Internet for medical practices surrounding the use of urine therapy in the treatment of various medical conditions. What types of treatment practices exist in China and Germany in relation to urine therapy? What types of conditions are treated with these methods? Are they accepted practices in the United States? Why or why not? Create a post in the discussion forum to share your findings with the class.

2. Urine output can be used to assess the overall health status of an individual. Changes in color, odor, or frequency of urination can be indicators of a variety of health conditions. Search the Internet to obtain 3–5 examples of conditions/symptoms specifically associated with variables of urine output. Create a PowerPoint presentation of 5–10 slides outlining your findings.

3. End-stage renal disease is the leading indicator for kidney failure in the United States requiring a transplant. What are the guidelines of eligibility to be added to the waiting list for a kidney transplant? What is the average time taken to receive a kidney as a recipient on the donor list? How many people are currently awaiting a kidney on the transplant list? Is this a state or a national effort? Share your findings with the class as directed by your instructor.

Student eResources

The Course Navigator learning management system that accompanies this textbook offers multiple opportunities to master chapter content, including end-of-chapter exercises, a glossary of key terms with audio pronunciations, games, pronunciation coach, and additional activities such as engaging with the BioDigital® Human.

13

The Endocrine System

> "If you skew the endocrine system, you lose the pathways to self. When endocrine patterns change, it alters the way you think and feel. One shift in the pattern tends to trip another."

> —**Hilary Mantel,** writer

Translation Challenge

Read this excerpt from a history and physical report and try to answer the questions that follow.

> HPI: Mrs. Smith presented with complaints of polydipsia, polyuria, and polyphagia. She reported a recent 5-pound weight loss.

> PE: On physical examination, she appeared tired and listless, with poor skin turgor. Mucous membranes appeared dry. Respiration deep and rapid. Temperature 100.8°F.

> Laboratory Data: Blood glucose level 350.

> Plan: FBS in the morning.

1. What behaviors would a patient with polydipsia demonstrate?

2. Does polyphagia mean that the patient's symptoms have had many phases or is Mrs. Smith very hungry?

3. What is a FBS test and why is it given in the morning?

Learning Objectives

13.1 Identify and define word parts most commonly used to describe the endocrine system.

13.2 Identify major endocrine glands.

13.3 Name major hormones secreted by endocrine glands and their associated function(s).

13.4 Describe the role of negative feedback in maintaining homeostasis.

13.5 Describe the body's physiological response to various hormonal abnormalities.

13.6 Recognize and describe common conditions of the endocrine system.

13.7 Name diagnostic tests and treatments associated with hormonal abnormalities.

13.8 Define abbreviations related to the endocrine system.

13.9 Use endocrine system vocabulary correctly in written and oral contexts.

13.10 Correctly spell and pronounce terminology related to the endocrine system.

COURSE NAVIGATOR

Access Additional Chapter Resources

The endocrine system is collectively made up of glands that produce and store hormones responsible for the overall balance of many important life functions (homeostasis). This system is responsible for the regulation of metabolism, growth and development, reproduction, sleep, and mood.

The endocrine system utilizes ductless glands to secrete **hormones**, also called chemical messengers, directly into the bloodstream as needed by the body. Some hormones directly affect one specific target organ. Other hormones, known as **tropic hormones**, stimulate a target organ to secrete its own hormones. Endocrine glands transport hormones that are used within the body, and exocrine glands are responsible for the production of substances that are carried outside the body through ducts, such as sweat. This chapter will provide an overview of the specific hormones associated with each endocrine gland, common hormonal abnormalities, diagnostic tests and examinations unique to conditions of the endocrine system, and recommended treatment methods.

In the Know: Specialists of the Endocrine System

The area of medicine concerned with the endocrine system is called **endocrinology**, and the physician who specializes in this field is an **endocrinologist**. Endocrinologists often work in concert with other specialists, depending on the system and the hormones involved. Dietitians and nutritionists are often involved in the treatment of individuals diagnosed with conditions of the endocrine system. These allied health professionals specialize in educating individuals on the impact food has on overall health and well-being.

Endocrine System Word Parts

As with other body systems, a core of word parts serves as the source for most of the medical words associated with the endocrine system. The word *endocrine* is derived from the prefix *endo-*, meaning "within," and the combining form *crin/o*, meaning "to secrete." The suffix *-crine*, used throughout this chapter, also means "to secrete." Table 13.1 lists common prefixes, combining forms, and suffixes used in reference to the endocrine system.

TABLE 13.1 Word Parts Associated with the Endocrine System

Prefix	Meaning	Example
a-	without	aplasia (birth defect in which an organ or tissue fails to develop or function normally)
ad-	to, toward	adrenal (near or on the kidney)
anti-	against	antidiabetics (drug used to treat diabetes by lowering glucose levels in the blood)
endo-	within	endocrine (to secrete within the body)
exo-	outside	exophthalmus (outward protrusion of one or both eyeballs)
hyper-	excessive, above	hypercalcemia (condition in which there is excessive calcium in the blood)
hypo-	deficient, below	hypoglycemia (condition in which there is deficient sugar in the blood)
para-	alongside, near	parathyroid (near, adjacent to the thyroid gland)
poly-	many, excessive	polydipsia (excessive thirst)
supra-	above	suprarenal (above the kidneys, also known as *adrenal glands*)

Combining Form	Meaning	Example
aden/o	glands	adenocarcinoma (type of cancer that forms within glands throughout the body)
andr/o	masculine	androgen (hormone responsible for the development of male characteristics, male sex organs)
adren/o	adrenals	adrenal (endocrine glands located on top of each kidney; responsible for the excretion of steroid hormones and adrenaline)
calc/o	calcium	hypocalcemia (condition in which there is a deficiency of calcium in the blood)
crin/o	secrete	endocrine (to secrete within)
estr/o	female	estrogen (hormone responsible for female reproductive system development)
gluc/o, gly/c	glucose (sugar)	glucosuria (presence of glucose in the urine)
gonad/o	sex organs	gonadotropin (hormones secreted by the pituitary gland; affect the function of male and female gonads)
ket/o	ketone	ketoacidosis (excessive amount of acids [ketones] in the blood)
pancreat/o	pancreas	pancrelipase (combination of enzymes used to assist in the digestion of food)
somat/o	relationship to the body	somatotropin (hormone produced by the anterior pituitary gland; responsible for stimulating growth and cell reproduction; also known as *growth hormone*)
thyr/o	thyroid	thyroxin (the major hormone secreted into the bloodstream by the thyroid gland)
trop/o	turning toward, changing	thyrotropin (a hormone that stimulates the thyroid to release two other hormones; also known as *thyroid-stimulating hormone*)

Suffix	Meaning	Example
-crine	to secrete	exocrine (to secrete outwardly through a duct)
-ectomy	surgical removal	thyroidectomy (removal of the thyroid gland)
-ia	state of, condition	polyphagia (excessive hunger)
-ism	state of, condition	hypothyroidism (deficient production of thyroid hormone)
-uria	urinary condition	polyuria (excessive production, passing of urine)

Anatomy and Physiology

The endocrine glands are located throughout the body, as shown in Figure 13.1. Endocrine glands include the pineal body, hypothalamus, pituitary, thyroid, parathyroid, thymus, adrenal, pancreatic, and reproductive glands. Recall from Chapter 3 that **exocrine glands** secrete substances outside the body. **Endocrine glands** are ductless and secrete their hormones directly into the bloodstream, which carries the hormones to specific organs. Think of the endocrine system as the body's communication center, or postal service. There are three different points of interest when mailing a package: the sender, method of delivery, and the receiver. In this particular example, the endocrine gland that produces and stores the hormone acts as the sender emitting the hormone "message" into the bloodstream. The bloodstream acts as the delivery mechanism, transporting the hormone to the target organ, the final destination, or receiver. Once the target organ receives the hormone, it opens the "message" and follows the instructions provided. Table 13.2 identifies common anatomy and physiology terms related to the endocrine system.

FIGURE 13.1 Endocrine Glands

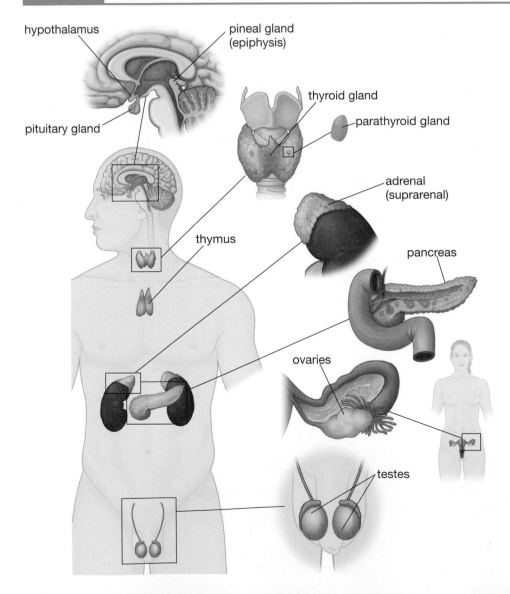

Term		Meaning	Word Analysis	
adrenal cortex	[ah-**dree**-nal **kor**-teks]	outer portion of the adrenal glands; secrete hormones called steroids	*adren/o* *-al*	adrenals pertaining to
adrenal gland (suprarenal)	[ah-**dree**-nal]	small endocrine gland located at the top of each kidney	*adren/o* *supra-* *ren/o* *-al*	adrenals above kidney pertaining to
adrenal medulla	[ah-**dree**-nal med-**ul**-ah]	inner portion of the adrenal glands; secrete hormones responsible for the "fight or flight" stress response	*adren/o* *-al*	adrenals pertaining to
androgen	[**an**-drO-jen]	steroid hormone (testosterone) stimulates, controls the development of male sex characteristics	*andr/o* *-gen*	male to produce
antagonist	[an-**tag**-ah-nist]	one process or agent that works against another		
calcitonin	[kal-sih-**tO**-nin]	hormone that increases calcium in bone and lowers the calcium in blood		
catecholamine	[**kat**-eh-**kOl**-am-een]	hormones secreted in times of stress: epinephrine, norepinephrine, and dopamine		
colloid	[**kol**-oyd]	yellowish, translucent substance resembling glue that stores thyroid hormones until needed by the body		
corticosteroid	[kor-tuh-kO-**ster**-oid]	anti-inflammatory hormone produced by the adrenal cortex		
endocrine gland	[**en**-dO-krin]	type of gland that secretes hormones directly into the bloodstream	*endo-* *-crine*	within secrete
estrogen	[**es**-trO-jen]	hormone that stimulates female sex characteristics; controls the menstrual cycle		
exocrine gland	[**eks**-O-krin]	type of gland that secretes substances out of the body through ducts	*exo-* *-crine*	outside, outward secrete
glucagon	[**gloo**-kah-gon]	hormone secreted by the islet cells of the pancreas; increases the level of glucose in the blood	*gluc/o*	glucose (sugar)
glucocorticoid	[**gloo**-kO-**kor**-tih-koyd]	steroid hormones	*gluc/o* *corticoid*	glucose (sugar) hormone of the adrenal cortex
gonads	[**gO**-nads]	an organ that produces male and female reproductive cells (testes and ovaries)	*gonad/o*	gonads
homeostasis	[hO-mee-O-**stay**-sis]	state of having all body functions in balance	*home/o* *-stasis*	same stop, standing, controlling
hormone	[**hor**-mOn]	chemical substance secreted by specific organs and/or glands and carried into the bloodstream to stimulate the function of another organ; the body's chemical messengers		
hyperglycemia	[**hI**-per-glI-**see**-mee-ah]	condition in which there are excessive levels of glucose present in the blood	*hyper-* *glyc/o* *-emia*	increased, excessive sugar, glucose blood condition
hypoglycemia	[**hI**-pO-glI-**see**-mee-ah]	condition in which there is a deficient level of glucose present in the blood	*hypo-* *glyc/o* *-emia*	decreased, low sugar, glucose blood condition
hypothalamus	[hI-pO-**thal**-ah-mus]	area of the brain that stimulates specific hormones to be released or restrained; located inferior to the thalamus	*hypo-* *thalam/o*	below, under thalamus

Continues

Term		Meaning	Word Analysis	
insulin	[**in**-suh-lin]	hormone secreted by the islet cells of the pancreas; decreases the level of glucose in the bloodstream		
islets of Lang-erhans (islet cells)	[**I**-lets of **Lang**-er-hahns]	little masses of cells resembling islands in the pan-creas, responsible for the production and secretion of endocrine hormones (glucagon and insulin)	*islet* *Langerhans*	small island 19th-century German anatomist
isthmus	[**is**-mus]	narrow area that connects two larger parts		
melatonin	[mel-ah-**tO**-nin]	hormone secreted by the pineal gland, respon-sible for the body's sleep/wake cycle, which is also known as *circadian rhythm* (the body's mechanism to differentiate day and night)		
metabolism	[meh-**tab**-ah-liz-em]	process that causes chemical change in the body by converting food into energy	*meta-* *-ism*	change state, condition, process
mineralocorti-coid	[**min**-er-al-O-**kor**-tih-koyd]	steroid hormone secreted by the adrenal cortex; responsible for the balance of salt (sodium) and water throughout the body	*corticoid*	hormone secreted by the adrenal cortex
negative feedback		process that controls hormone production in response to the hormone level in the blood		
norepinephrine	[nOr-ep-uh-**nef**-rin]	hormone produced by the adrenal medulla, responsible for the flight of flight response, also called noradrenalin		
ovary	[**O**-vah-ree]	female reproductive gland (found in pairs)	*ovari/o*	ovary
pancreas	[**pan**-kree-as]	organ located posterior to the stomach; has both endocrine (stimulates the release of glucagon and insulin) and exocrine functions (stimulates the release of digestive enzymes)		
parathyroid gland	[par-ah-**thI**-royd]	gland adjacent to the thyroid that secretes para-thormone, the hormone that regulates calcium level in the blood	*para-* *thyroid* *(thyr/o)*	alongside, near thyroid gland
pineal body	[**pin**-ee-al]	gland located in the center of the brain; respon-sible for the secretion of melatonin		
pituitary gland (hypophysis)	[pih-**too**-ih-tare-ee] [hI-**poff**-ih-sis]	tiny gland located behind the optic nerve in the brain; often referred to as the master gland; con-trols growth and development in addition to the functions of other endocrine glands	*hypophys/o* *pituitary/o*	pituitary gland pituitary gland
placenta	[plah-**sen**-tah]	organ that provides transfer of substances between the fetus and the mother		
positive feedback		process in which a body's response to a stimulus is enhanced or promoted by hormone production		
progesterone	[prO-**jes**-ter-On]	steroid hormone secreted by the ovary and placenta; important for the regulation of ovulation and men-struation; maintains the uterus during pregnancy; available synthetically for use in hormone therapy		
prototype	[**prO**-tO-tIp]	the first form or type from which others are copied		
somatostatin	[sO-mah-tO-**stat**-in]	hormone secreted by the hypothalamus that inhibits growth hormone release	*somat/o* *-stasis* *-in*	body stop, standing, not in, within
somatotropin	[sO-mah-tO-**trO**-pin]	growth hormone produced by the pituitary gland, responsible for controlling the rate of growth, also known as *growth hormone*		

Continues

Term		Meaning	Word Analysis	
testes	[**tes**-teez]	male reproductive glands located within the scrotum; male gonads; testicles; testis (singular)	*test/os*	testicle
testosterone	[tes-**tos**-ter-On]	hormone secreted by the testes; responsible for the development of male sex characteristics	*test/o*	testicle
thymosin	[**thI**-mO-sin]	hormone (of the thymus gland) that stimulates the thymus to release its hormones; responsible for the development of T cells that fight disease	*thym/o*	thymus
thymus	[**thI**-mus]	organ located behind the mediastinum; responsible for the development of the immune system until puberty	*thym/o*	thymus
thyroid gland	[**thI**-royd]	gland located in the anterior portion of the neck; secretes the thyroxine (T_4) and triiodothyronine (T_3) hormones that regulate the body's metabolism	*thyr/o*	thyroid
thyroxine (T_4)	[thI-**rok**-sin]	hormone secreted by the thyroid gland; helps to regulate the body's metabolism	*thyr/o*	thyroid
triiodothyro-nine (T_3)	[trI-I-O-dO-**thI**-rO-neen]	hormone secreted by the thyroid gland; helps to regulate the body's metabolism	*tri-* *iodo-* *thyronine*	three iodine amino acid related to thyroxine
tropic hormones	[**trO**-pik]	pituitary hormones that affect growth or function of other endocrine glands	*trop/o*	turning

Types of Endocrine System Hormones: Steroid and Nonsteroid Hormones

The endocrine system produces two types of hormones: steroid hormones and nonsteroid hormones. **Steroid hormones** are messengers that pass directly into the cells of the target organ and to the nucleus of the cell where they bind to receptor proteins. This process requires several hours. Cortisol is one example of a steroid hormone. The release of cortisol is controlled by the hypothalamus. It is produced by the adrenal gland and released in response to stress and a low concentration of glucose in the blood. Cortisol triggers an antistress and anti-inflammatory response in the body.

Nonsteroid hormones are often referred to as "secondary messengers" because they do not have the ability to penetrate cell membranes. Instead, nonsteroid hormones travel from an endocrine gland to the target organ and then trigger the production and activation of another hormone. This process takes place outside the cell membrane and occurs in a matter of seconds or minutes. Adrenaline, also known as *epinephrine*, is one example of a nonsteroid hormone. When adrenaline is released in response to an immediate stressor (e.g., the anticipation of a possible danger), it produces the **fight-or-flight response**, the body's physical preparation either to escape or do battle when faced with a dangerous or challenging situation. Adrenaline builds up quickly in the body, producing increased heart rate, sweating, shallow breathing, and heightened senses.

While some hormones are designed to provide an immediate response triggered by an event outside the body, others are responsible for assisting the body in maintaining homeostasis. We first learned about homeostasis in Chapter 2, where we illustrated the concept by comparing the cooling of the body through sweating to the function of a thermostat in keeping a home at a comfortable temperature.

To Note!

The endocrine system works in collaboration with the nervous system by releasing hormones that stimulate physical reactions. Endocrine hormones provide the brain with feedback to be processed and used to instruct the body.

Hormones are used to maintain balance for various processes inside the body. The production and release (secretion) of hormones are controlled by glands of the endocrine system. The body secretes hormones at a rate that keeps their level in the blood almost constant. The body can do this because it receives continuous feedback from its systems.

Negative feedback occurs when the hormone level in the blood elevates or falls beyond a desired range. Production of that particular hormone is then stopped. The goal of the negative feedback loop is to return the body to its original state. For example, if you have your home's thermostat set at 75 degrees Fahrenheit, the receptors within your air-conditioning unit will detect any rise in the temperature above 75 degrees and signal the system to run until the temperature inside the home returns to the desired setting. Once it reaches the desired temperature, the system stops running. Another example of negative feedback is the release of insulin into the bloodstream. After a person eats a meal, the level of glucose (blood sugar) present in the blood increases.

In response, the pancreas releases the hormone insulin, which converts the products of food into usable energy and lowers the amount of glucose in the blood. Once the blood sugar level reaches the normal range, the pancreas stops releasing insulin.

When the concentration of the hormone in the blood decreases below a specified range, more of the hormone is produced. This process works to keep hormones at the right level in the blood. Figure 13.2 illustrates the negative feedback loop involving insulin.

Positive feedback is the opposite of negative feedback in that the stimulus is now enhanced (promoted) by the release of a hormone. An example of positive feedback is the role the hormone oxytocin plays in childbirth (see Figure 13.3). Oxytocin is released by the pituitary gland during childbirth to enhance the speed and strength of uterine contractions. Once the baby has been delivered, the release of oxytocin is stopped.

> ### To Note!
>
> Negative feedback is used to stop the forward progress of the initial stimulus, while positive feedback enhances the action of the stimulus.

FIGURE 13.2 | Negative Feedback Loop

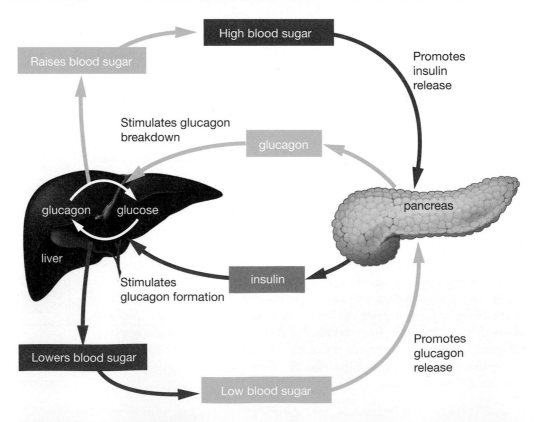

FIGURE 13.3 Positive Feedback

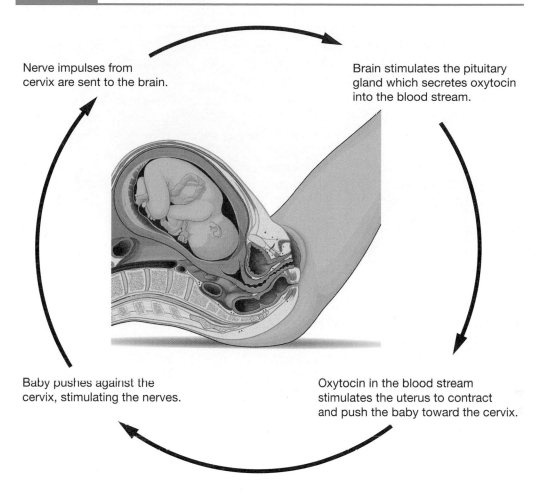

Nerve impulses from cervix are sent to the brain.

Brain stimulates the pituitary gland which secretes oxytocin into the blood stream.

Baby pushes against the cervix, stimulating the nerves.

Oxytocin in the blood stream stimulates the uterus to contract and push the baby toward the cervix.

The Endocrine Glands and Their Functions

The endocrine system plays a role in every cell, organ, and function within the human body. Recall that the endocrine system is composed of hormones and glands. Glands are groups of cells in which information is transferred. Glands are responsible for the production and secretion (release) of hormones throughout the body. As discussed, endocrine glands release hormones directly into the bloodstream, and exocrine glands release secretions directly into the skin or mouth (e.g., sweat and saliva).

In cephalocaudal (top to bottom) order, the endocrine glands include the *pineal body*, the *hypothalamus*, and the *pituitary*, all of which are located in the brain (see Figure 13.4). In the neck and upper-chest area are the *thyroid*, the *parathyroid*, and *thymus glands*. The adrenal glands are located on top of the kidneys in the area of the back just above the waist. The *pancreas* is located in the upper abdomen, and completing this system are the *reproductive organs* in the lower abdomen. Refer back to Figure 13.1 to see the location of the endocrine glands within the body.

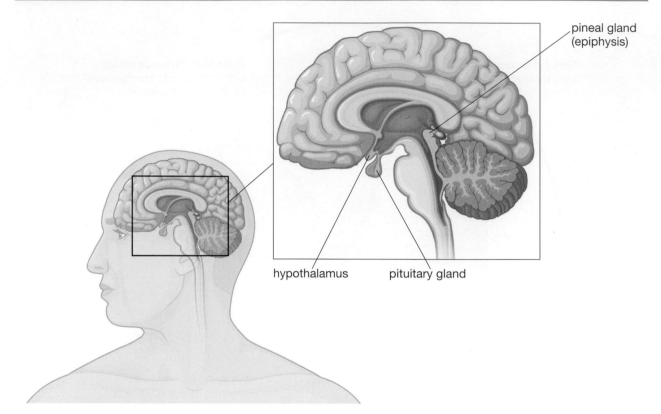

pineal gland (epiphysis)

hypothalamus   pituitary gland

Pineal Body

The **pineal body** is believed to control the body's internal clock. Although the complete role and all functions of the pineal gland are not fully understood, scientists do know that the pineal gland secretes the hormone melatonin. **Melatonin** is the substance that turns on the biological clock at puberty and also regulates circadian rhythms (day and night sleep patterns). Darkness stimulates the production of melatonin; light inhibits its release.

Hypothalamus

The **hypothalamus** connects the endocrine system to the nervous system through the pituitary gland, also known as the *hypophysis*. **Releasing factors (RF)** are used to carry signals to the pituitary gland to stimulate or inhibit production and release of hormones throughout the body. Table 13.3 shows the hormones specific to the hypothalamus and their functions. Each of these hormones are released into the bloodstream and travel immediately to the anterior lobe of the pituitary, where they exert their effects. Each hormone is released in periodic intervals. In fact, replacement hormone therapy with these particular hormones does not work unless the replacements are also given in periodic intervals.

Pituitary Gland

The pituitary gland is connected to the hypothalamus. Although it is small (the size of the tip of the little finger), the **pituitary gland** is the "master gland" that controls the release of most hormones in the body. It is vital to an individual's overall well-being. The pituitary gland is divided into the **adenohypophysis** (anterior) and **neurohypophysis**

TABLE 13.3 Hypothalamus Hormones and Their Functions

Hormone	Action
corticotropin-releasing hormone (CRH)	stimulates the release of adrenocorticotropic hormone (ACTH)
dopamine (neurotransmitter)	inhibits the release of norepinephrine and insulin
gonadotropin-releasing hormone (GnRH)	stimulates the release of follicle-stimulating hormone (FSH) and luteinizing hormone (LH)
growth hormone-releasing hormone (GHRH)	stimulates the release of growth hormone (GH)
prolactin-inhibiting hormone	inhibits the release of prolactin
prolactin-releasing hormone	stimulates the release of prolactin
somatostatin	inhibits the release of glucagon and insulin
thyrotropin-releasing hormone (TRH)	stimulates the release of thyroid-stimulating hormone (TSH) and prolactin

(posterior) lobes; each lobe secretes different hormones. The anterior pituitary controls the production and release of seven hormones, and the posterior pituitary releases two hormones. The anterior pituitary gland controls seven hormones, including **growth hormone (GH)**, commonly known as puberty hormones; **thyroid-stimulating hormone (TSH)**, which regulates metabolism; prolactin, the hormone responsible for the production of breastmilk; and **adrenocorticotrophic hormone (ACTH)**, the hormone responsible for the stress response (see Table 13.4 for a comprehensive list).

TABLE 13.4 Pituitary Hormones

Anterior Pituitary Hormones	Action
Tropic hormones	
adrenocorticotropic hormone (ACTH)	stimulates the release of steroid hormones, which reduce stress and maintain healthy blood pressure (e.g., cortisol)
follicle-stimulating hormone (FSH)	in females, stimulates the ovaries to release eggs; in males, stimulates the testes to produce sperm
luteinizing hormone (LH)	in females, stimulates ovulation by the regulation of estrogen; in males, stimulates testosterone to be secreted by the testes
thyroid-stimulating hormone (TSH)	stimulates the thyroid gland to release its hormones, ultimately resulting in the body's regulation of metabolism
Nontropic hormones	
growth hormone (somatotropin) (GH)	increases protein production in many tissues to promote growth and development in childhood and promotes healthy bone and muscle mass in adults; converts proteins to glucose
melanocyte-stimulating hormone (MSH)	stimulates production and release of the melanin pigment in skin (see Chapter 3); not technically an anterior pituitary hormone as it can be extracted from all parts of the pituitary
prolactin	stimulates milk production in the breast
Posterior Pituitary Hormones (both are nontropic)	**Action**
antidiuretic hormone (ADH)	decreases the amount of water lost through the kidneys
oxytocin	causes uterine contractions during childbirth and promotes the release of breast milk

The posterior pituitary releases both **antidiuretic hormone (ADH**, also known as **vasopressin)**, which assists the kidneys in balancing water throughout the body, and **oxytocin**, which stimulates the flow of milk in nursing mothers. As discussed earlier in this chapter, oxytocin also increases the strength of uterine contractions during childbirth. It is often administered to women who experience **dystocia**—decreased contractions—during labor and delivery. Oxytocin is one of the few hormones released through a positive feedback mechanism; that is, the stronger the contractions, the more oxytocin is released into the bloodstream.

The pituitary gland also produces tropic hormones that stimulate other endocrine glands to produce and secrete their own hormones. Figure 13.5 depicts the pituitary gland and the hormones it produces.

FIGURE 13.5 Pituitary Hormones

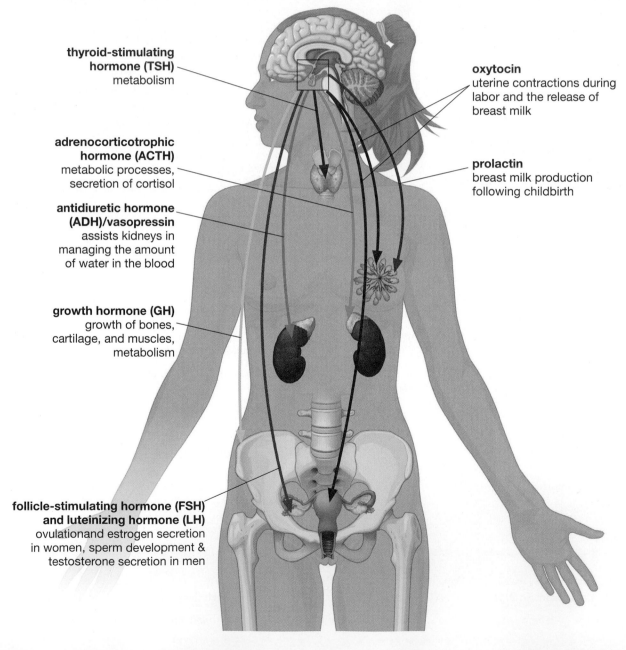

thyroid-stimulating hormone (TSH)
metabolism

adrenocorticotrophic hormone (ACTH)
metabolic processes, secretion of cortisol

antidiuretic hormone (ADH)/vasopressin
assists kidneys in managing the amount of water in the blood

growth hormone (GH)
growth of bones, cartilage, and muscles, metabolism

follicle-stimulating hormone (FSH) and luteinizing hormone (LH)
ovulationand estrogen secretion in women, sperm development & testosterone secretion in men

oxytocin
uterine contractions during labor and the release of breast milk

prolactin
breast milk production following childbirth

Thyroid and Parathyroid Glands

The **thyroid gland** is located in the lower portion of the neck, below the larynx (see Figure 13.6). It is a butterfly-shaped gland that has two lobes connected by a small, thin **isthmus** (a narrow connection between organs). The thyroid gland stores two hormones, **triiodothyronine (T_3)** and **thyroxine (T_4)**. T_3 and T_4 are stored as a **colloid**, a glue-like substance, until needed by the body. The thyroid gland's release of T_3 and T_4 is triggered by the pituitary gland's release of thyroid-stimulating hormone (TSH).

The names T_3 and T_4 indicate the number of atoms of iodine contained in each molecule, and iodine must be present in the diet to ensure adequate production of these two hormones. The thyroid hormones influence every cell in the body: they direct **metabolism** (the use of cellular energy), cellular replication, and brain development.

The thyroid gland also secretes **calcitonin**, or **thyrocalcitonin**, which is released in response to high levels of calcium in the blood. When blood calcium levels are high, the excess calcium is deposited into bone. Normally, osteoclasts would then be responsible for breaking down bone and filtering the calcium into the bloodstream. Instead, the calcitonin hormone is secreted to inhibit the work of osteoclasts. This balancing process is another example of homeostasis and a negative feedback loop as it returns calcium levels to a normal range.

The **parathyroid glands** are located alongside the thyroid glands in the neck (see Figure 13.6). While the number of parathyroid glands can vary from person to person, most have a total of four glands. It is unknown why the number of glands varies from one person to the next. The parathyroid glands secrete **parathyroid hormone**, or **parathormone (PTH)**, which is also responsible for regulating calcium levels in the blood. When the blood calcium levels decrease, PTH promotes the work of osteoclasts, thus breaking down bone and freeing calcium, which then moves into

> ### To Note!
>
> Recall that *osteoblasts* are cells that produce bone and *osteoclasts* are cells that resorb bone to help shape new bone.

FIGURE 13.6 Thyroid and Parathyroid Glands

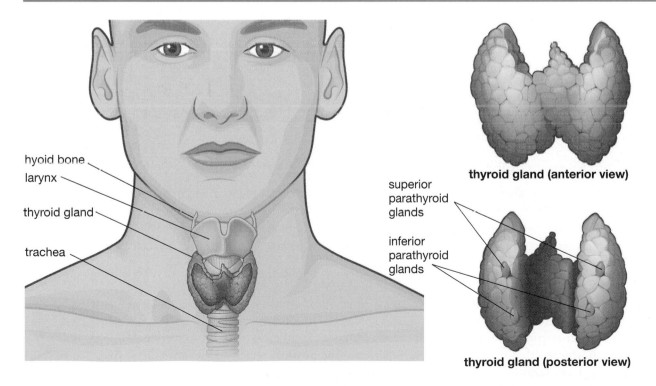

hyoid bone
larynx
thyroid gland
trachea

thyroid gland (anterior view)

superior parathyroid glands

inferior parathyroid glands

thyroid gland (posterior view)

the bloodstream. This process, in turn, increases the blood calcium level. High levels of calcium in the blood will result in the inhibition of PTH production and release.

PTH works in conjunction with calcitonin to ensure the correct amount of calcium in the blood; however, these two hormones perform opposite functions, creating what is called an **antagonistic feedback effect**. When the calcium concentration in the blood increases, calcitonin is secreted; when the calcium level decreases, PTH is secreted. Figure 13.7 illustrates this antagonistic process.

FIGURE 13.7 | Antagonistic Feedback Effect

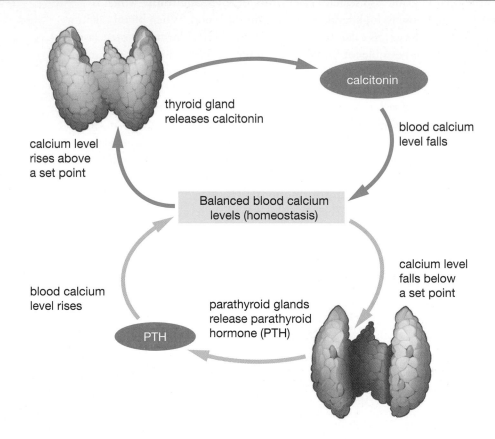

Thymus Gland

The **thymus gland**, located in the mediastinum in the chest of infants and pre-adolescents, secretes the hormone **thymosin** and plays an important role in immune function. The thymus gland atrophies and no longer exists by adolescence. (Refer to Chapter 10 for a further discussion of the thymus and its immune function.)

Adrenal Glands

The **adrenal glands** are triangular-shaped glands located on the top of each kidney (see Figure 13.1). Each adrenal gland consists of an outer portion, the **cortex**, and an inner portion, the **medulla**. The cortex and the medulla synthesize and secrete different hormones that perform different functions. The medulla secretes hormones known as **catecholamines**. The cortex secretes three types of corticosteroid hormones.

The three types of hormones produced by the adrenal cortex are **glucocorticoids**, **mineralocorticoids**, and sex hormones. As a group, corticosteroids produced by the adrenal cortex regulate blood pressure by maintaining the body's electrolytes, salt, and water levels, help to regulate metabolism, stimulate the production of glucose, assist in the stress response, and play a role in the development of secondary sex characteristics. Sex hormones are responsible for sexual maturity (puberty) and reproduction. The adrenal medulla functions as part of the autonomic nervous system, which was described in Chapter 5. The adrenal medulla secretes the catecholamines epinephrine and norepinephrine. **Epinephrine**, or **adrenaline**, is the primary hormone secreted and it accounts for about 80 percent of the adrenal medulla's secretion. Epinephrine causes the "fight or flight" response. This reaction is also known as the *stress response*. **Norepinephrine** works alongside epinephrine as it prepares the brain and body for action by increasing heart rate and blood pressure.

In the Know: Fight or Flight

Consider the physical changes that take place in your body when you are frightened:

- Blood flow decreases to the tissues that need it least, such as the gastrointestinal tract and the kidneys.

- Blood flow increases to the areas that need to perform in an emergency situation, including the heart, the lungs, skeletal muscles, and brain.

- The adrenal medulla secretes catecholamines, which increase metabolism and elevate the level of blood glucose (to provide increased energy).

Pancreatic Glands

The **pancreas**, an organ located in the upper abdomen, contains clumps of cells scattered throughout its structure. These cells are called **pancreatic islets**, or **islets of Langerhans**, and are actually microscopic hormone-secreting endocrine glands. The pancreas has both exocrine function, in the form of digestive enzymes (discussed in Chapter 11), and endocrine function. The pancreas's major function is to control sugar levels and the metabolism of sugar within the body.

Within the pancreatic islets there are three types of cells: alpha cells, beta cells, and delta cells. Each cell type produces a different hormone.

1. **Alpha cells** secrete **glucagon**, which raises the blood glucose concentration by converting glycogen in the liver to glucose. When the blood glucose level falls, alpha cells release glucagon to increase it.

2. **Beta cells** secrete insulin, perhaps the best-known hormone, which is essential for proper body functioning. **Insulin**, which is regulated by the level of glucose in the blood, decreases blood glucose levels by storing glucose as fat in adipose tissue. Therefore, insulin is an antagonist to glucagon.

3. **Delta cells** secrete the hormone somatostatin. **Somatostatin** interferes with the release of growth hormone and glucagons, which decreases the blood glucose level. This is referred to as a **hypoglycemic** effect. Release of growth hormone and glucagons causes the opposite effect, **hyperglycemia**, or elevated blood glucose concentration.

> **To Note!**
>
> The endocrine system works in collaboration with the digestive system by releasing hormones that regulate glucose levels throughout the body for energy consumption.

Beyond Words: Hunger Pains or Pangs?

There are hormones present in the human body that are not produced or secreted by the endocrine system. Ghrelin is a hormone secreted by an empty stomach in response to hunger. This particular hormone is responsible for alerting the body that it is time to eat and ultimately causing your stomach to "growl."

The phrase "hunger pains" is a common one, but the correct phrase is actually "hunger pangs." *Pang* is a word that means "a sudden, sharp pain or painful emotion." Hunger pangs usually begin between 12 and 24 hours after the last meal.

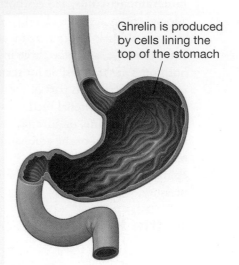

Ghrelin is produced by cells lining the top of the stomach

Reproductive Organs

The organs of reproduction are also endocrine glands. **Ovaries** in the female secrete **estrogen**, which promotes the development of female sex characteristics. They also secrete **progesterone**, which, after egg fertilization, works to prevent miscarriage and prepares the mammary glands for milk production. The **placenta** is also an endocrine structure, secreting human chorionic gonadotropin (hCG), estrogen, and progesterone. A placenta forms and functions only temporarily, during gestation. In the male, the **testes** secrete **testosterone**, the hormone that promotes male sex characteristics. The structure and function of these glands and hormones (both male and female) are discussed further in Chapters 14 and 15.

Checkpoint 13.1

Answer the following questions to identify any areas of the section that you may need to review.

1. The pituitary gland is controlled by which part of the brain?

_____

2. Which hormones stimulate specific target organs to produce their own hormones?

_____

3. By what other name is the anterior lobe of the pituitary gland known?

_____

Exercise 13.1 Word Analysis

Separate the terms into their word parts using slashes (/) and give a definition for each term.

1. adrenal _____

2. pancreatitis _____

3. glucosuria _____

4. hyperglycemic _____

5. endocrine _____

Exercise 13.2 Comprehension Check

Circle the correct word from each pair to fit the following sentences.

1. A portion of the placenta/placebo was retained.

2. Adrenal humors/hormones affect the nervous system.

3. The patient was found to be deficient in calcitonin/calcaneus.

4. The hypoglycemia/hypothalamic area of the brain was affected.

5. Testes/ovaries produce male sex hormones.

Exercise 13.3 Matching

Match the term or abbreviation in column 1 with the correct definition in column 2. Write the letter of the definition on the line provided.

1. _____ endocrine glands

2. _____ negative feedback

3. _____ hormones

4. _____ hypothalamus

5. _____ thymus

6. _____ pituitary gland

a. gland that secretes thymosin and plays a role in immune function

b. substances secreted by the ductless glands of the endocrine system

c. connected to the hypothalamus

d. ductless glands that secrete their products directly into the bloodstream

e. process by which secretion of almost all hormones in the body is controlled

f. area of the brain that provides a connection between the nervous system and the endocrine system

Exercise 13.4   Word Building

In the sentences that follow, the correct combining form is used in each underlined term, but the prefix or suffix does not match the definition. Rewrite the word, supplying the correct word part.

1. The <u>postdiuretic hormone</u> is a hormone of the pituitary that exerts its influence on the kidneys.

   _____

2. The <u>hyperthalamus</u> provides a connection between the nervous system and the endocrine system.

   _____

3. The <u>hyporenal gland</u> is located atop each kidney and has a cortex and a medulla that secrete different hormones.

   _____

4. <u>Subcalcemia</u> means elevated calcium level.

   _____

5. <u>Peribolism</u> is a process that causes chemical change in the body; cellular energy.

   _____

Exercise 13.5   Spelling Check

Correct the misspelled words in each sentence by writing the correct spelling on the blank provided.

1. Progusterone is one of the stoeroid hormones. _____

2. The ovarys are part of the female reprdouctive system. _____

3. The minerialcorticoids influence sodium metaboluism. _____

4. Melatoninun is secreted by the pinal gland. _____

5. The ilsets of Langerhands are found in the pancreaus. _____

Exercise 13.6   Concept Map

The accompanying concept map depicts the endocrine functions of the pancreas. Fill in the missing information.

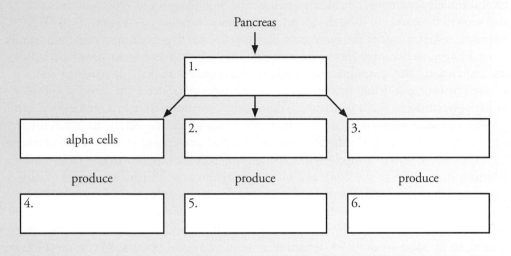

Conditions

Malfunctions that occur in the endocrine glands and the hormones they secrete can cause problems throughout the body. Hormonal abnormalities occur because of too little or too much secretion. These abnormalities are named with the prefixes *hypo-* (too little) and *hyper-* (too much) plus the particular organ or hormone name. Table 13.5 lists hormonal abnormalities and the manifestations associated with them.

TABLE 13.5   Hormonal Abnormalities

Gland	Hormone	Hyper- (excessive production/secretion)	Hypo- (deficient production/secretion)
adrenal	glucocorticoid	Cushing disease	Addison disease
hypothalamus	antidiuretic hormone	syndrome of inappropriate antidiuretic hormone (SIADH), hyponatremia	diabetes insipidus, polyuria, polydipsia
ovaries	estrogen	precocious puberty	Turner's syndrome
pancreas	insulin	hyperinsulinism (hypoglycemia)	diabetes mellitus (types 1 & 2)
parathyroid	parathormone	hypercalcemia, tetany, hypertension, kidney stones	hypocalcemia
pineal	melatonin	seasonal affective disorder	anxiety, mood disorders
pituitary	somatotropin (growth hormone)	acromegaly, gigantism	dwarfism
testes	testosterone	precocious puberty	hypogonadism (eunuchism)
thyroid	thyroid hormone	Graves' disease, exophthalmia	cretinism, myxedema

Hypoglycemia (low blood sugar) can occur during any stage of life, from birth to old age. Individuals with type 1 diabetes are at a higher risk, and may experience hypoglycemia or "insulin reaction" if they do not eat a well-balanced diet, exercise, and take insulin as needed. The term literally means "decreased glucose in the blood." A low blood sugar level stimulates hormones, including epinephrine, norepinephrine, glucagon, cortisol, and growth hormone, to raise the blood glucose concentration (see Figure 13.2). This hormone response causes the symptoms that appear with hypoglycemia: sweating, palpitations, hunger, tachycardia, tremors, confusion, headache, difficulties in speech, irritability, and anxiety. The symptoms are usually irregular (except in diabetic patients) and are relieved by eating or drinking a substance containing sugar. Severe and lengthy episodes of hypoglycemia can result in seizures, stupor (unresponsiveness), coma, and even death.

Pheochromocytoma is a rare tumor, usually benign, that is generally found in the adrenal medulla. It results in the secretion of increased amounts of epinephrine and norepinephrine, which lead to symptoms of hypertension, palpitations, headaches, facial flushing (warmth and redness of the skin), and increased perspiration. Treatment consists of surgical removal of the tumor and treatment with antihypertensives to control symptoms.

Thyroid carcinoma is a malignant (cancerous) tumor of the thyroid gland. The most common types of thyroid carcinomas are papillary (PTC) and follicular (FTC). Together they make up approximately 95 percent of all cases of thyroid cancers. PTC is most likely a result of exposure to radiation. Both are treated by thyroidectomy, radiofrequency ablation, and sometimes chemotherapy. **Radiofrequency ablation** is a technique in which high-frequency energy, in the form of heat, is used to destroy cancer cells. Chemotherapy, also known as *chemo*, is treatment that uses a combination of chemical substances (anti-cancer drugs) in a particular regimen to destroy cancer cells. Thyroid suppression therapy with thyroid hormone can prevent the recurrence of tumors. Adrenocortical carcinoma, pituitary adenoma, and islet cell carcinoma (pancreatic) are other endocrine cancers.

Other illnesses associated with the endocrine system are listed in Table 13.6.

TABLE 13.6 Conditions Associated with the Endocrine System

Term		Meaning	Word Analysis	
acromegaly	[ak-rO-**meh**-guh-lee]	condition in which the pituitary gland produces too much growth hormone in adulthood, resulting in enlarged hands, feet, jaw, lips, nose, and forehead	*acro-*	extremities
			-megaly	enlargement
Addison's disease	[**add**-ih-suns]	rare condition in which the adrenal glands fail to produce enough hormones, resulting in abdominal pain, low blood pressure, fatigue, and dehydration, commonly auto-immune-related, also known as *hypocortisolism*		
adrenocortical carcinoma	[**ah**-dree-nO-kor-tih-cul kar-sih-**nO**-mah]	rare type of endocrine cancer in which malignant cells form in the outer layer of the adrenal gland	*adren/o* *cortic/o*	adrenal gland cortex, outer portion
			-al	pertaining to
			carcin/o	cancer
			—oma	tumor
ambiguous genitalia		condition when a newborn's genitals are neither clearly female nor clearly male		
aplasia		absence or defective development of the thymus and parathyroid glands, associated with a weakened immune system; also known as *DiGeorge syndrome*		

Continues

Term		Meaning	Word Analysis	
cretinism	[**kreet**-in-iz-um]	condition caused by hypothyroidism in children, symptoms include short stature (stunted growth), obesity, and learning disabilities		
Cushing's disease	[**cush**-ing]	rare condition in which the adrenal glands produce excessive amounts of hormone over time, resulting in a full, round face ("moon-face"), added fat on the back of the neck ("buffalo hump"), excessive weight gain (mostly in abdominal area, with thin legs/arms), excessive hair growth on face, neck, and chest, hypertension, mood disorders, and muscle wasting, also called *hypercortisolism*		
diabetes insipidus	[dI-ah-**bee**-teez in-**sip**-ih-dus]	condition in which the hypothalamus fails to produce a sufficient supply of antidiuretic hormone, resulting in polydipsia and polyuria		
diabetes mellitus	[dI-ah-**bee**-teez **mel**-ih-tus]	group of conditions that lead to excessive amounts of sugar in the blood (high blood glucose), resulting in polyuria, polydipsia, and polyphagia		
diabetic keto-acidosis (DKA)	[dI-ah-**bee**-teez kee-tO-as-ih-**dO**-sis]	condition in which there is a buildup of acids in the blood	*ket/o* *acid/o* *-osis*	ketone acid abnormal condition
dwarfism	[**dworf**-iz-um]	condition in which the pituitary gland produces deficient amounts of growth hormone, resulting in short stature		
gestational diabetes	[jes-**tay**-shun-ul dI-ah-**bee**-teez]	a form of high blood sugar during pregnancy, usually resolves following birth		
gigantism	[jI-**gan**-tiz-um]	condition in which the pituitary gland produces too much growth hormone during childhood, resulting in enlarged hands, feet, jaw, lips, nose, and forehead		
goiter	[**goy**-ter]	chronic enlargement of the thyroid gland, most commonly caused by iodine deficiency		
Graves' disease		immune system disorder caused by the excessive production of thyroid hormone; causes anxiety, weight loss, and irregular heartbeats, most common form of hyperthyroidism		
hermaphrodit-ism	[her-**maf**-rO-dIt-iz-um]	abnormal arrangement of chromosomes or the presence of primary sex characteristics for both genders while in utero		
hyperinsulinism	[hI-pur-**in**-suh-lin-iz-um]	condition in which there is an excessive level of insulin in the blood	*hyper-* *insulin/o* *–ism*	excessive insulin condition
hyperthyroid-ism	[hI-pur-**thI**-royd-iz-um]	excessive thyroid hormone production, resulting in weight loss, a rapid or irregular heartbeat, sweating, and irritability, also called *overactive thyroid* or *thyrotoxicosis*	*hyper-* *thyroid/o* *–ism*	excessive thyroid gland condition
hyperparathy-roidism	[hI-pur-pair-uh-**thi**-royd-iz-um]	excessive parathyroid hormone production, resulting in high levels of calcium in the blood and urine and deficient supplies of calcium in the blood, weakened bones, and kidney stones	hyper-parathyroid/o –ism	excessive parathyroid gland condition
hypogonadism	[hI-pO-**gO**-nad-iz-um]	condition in which the gonads fail to function properly, testes in men and ovaries in women	*hypo-* *gonad/o* *–ism*	deficient sex organ condition

Continues

Term		Meaning	Word Analysis	
hypoparathy-roidism	[hI-pO-pair-uh-**thI**-royd-iz-um]	condition in which the production of parathyroid hormone is deficient, resulting in low levels of calcium in the blood, weakened bones, muscle cramps, and spasms (tetany)	*hypo-* *parathyroid/o* *—ism*	deficient parathyroid gland condition
hypothyroidism	[hI-pO-**thI**-royd-iz-um]	condition in which the production of thyroid hormone is deficient, resulting in fatigue, weight gain, mood swings, and lethargy, also called *underactive thyroid*	*hypo-* *thyroid/o* *—ism*	deficient thyroid gland condition
islet cell carcinoma (pancreatic)	[**eye**-lit cell kar-sih-**nO**-mah]	pancreatic cancer, fourth leading cause of cancer death in the United States		
myxedema	[miks-ah-**dee**-mah]	condition resulting from an underactive thyroid in adults, causes weight gain, hair loss, and lethargy; a form of hypothydroidism		
panhypopitu-itarism	[pan-hI-pO-pih-**too**-ih-tair-iz-um]	rare condition in which there is an undersecretion of pituitary hormones, resulting in extreme and progressive weight loss, premature aging, hair loss, and weakness, also known as *Simmond's disease* or *pituitary cachexia*	*pan-* *hypo-* *pituitary/o* *—ism*	all deficient pituitary condition
pheochromo-cytoma	[fee-O-krO-mah-sI-**tO**-mah]	benign tumor that causes the secretion of increased amounts of epinephrine and norepinephrine, usually found in the adrenal medulla		
pituitary adenoma	[pih-**too**-ih-tair-ree a-den-O-mah]	benign, slow-growing tumors in the pituitary gland		
prolactinoma	[prO-lak-tih-**nO**-mah]	most common type of benign pituitary tumor, results in the hypersecretion of prolactin hormone		
precocious puberty	[prah-kO-**shus**]	condition in which a child's body begins changing into that of an adult too soon		
prediabetes	[pree-dI-ah-**bee**-teez]	condition in which levels of blood glucose levels are higher than normal, yet not high enough for a diagnosis of type 2 diabetes, also called impaired glucose tolerance		
syndrome of inappropriate antidiuretic hormone (SIADH)		hypersecretion of antidiuretic hormone from the hypothalamus, causes the body to retain water and become depleted of electrolytes (e.g. sodium)		
thyroid carcinoma	[thI-**royd** kar-sih-**nO**-mah]	malignant tumor of the thyroid	*thyroid* *carcin/o* *—oma*	thyroid cancer tumor
type 1 diabetes		chronic condition resulting from the body's inability to produce adequate insulin, usually diagnosed in children and young adults, also known as *juvenile diabetes* or *insulin-dependent diabetes mellitus (IDDM)*		
type 2 diabetes		condition resulting from the body's inability to produce adequate insulin, also known as *adult-onset* or *non-insulin dependent diabetes mellitus (NIDDM)*		
Turner's syndrome		chromosomal disorder in which a female is born with only one X chromosome, resulting in delayed puberty, infertility, heart defects, and certain learning disabilities, also known as *gonadal dysgenesis*		

Fetuses, Newborns, and Infants

The endocrine system evolves early in fetal development. The abnormal development of organs, abnormal secretion of tropic hormones, or abnormal arrangement of chromosomes can cause birth defects in the fetus.

Congenital **hypothyroidism** occurs in about 1 in 4,000 infants worldwide. In 90 percent of these infants, the thyroid is missing. Severe hypothyroidism results in a condition called **cretinism**, in which the child may be short and obese, and have learning disabilities. Because the symptoms of hypothyroidism are so serious, even life threatening, all infants are screened for it at birth. Early identification and intervention with thyroid hormone replacement therapy can reverse some of the effects.

The abnormal arrangement of chromosomes or the presence of primary sex characteristics for both genders while in utero can cause **hermaphroditism**. **Ambiguous genitalia** result when the newborn's genitals are neither clearly female nor clearly male. Determining the baby's gender requires tests to identify the actual chromosomal makeup and an ultrasound to determine whether a uterus and ovaries are present. In some cases, surgery is performed to construct female genitalia or testosterone is injected to stimulate penile growth.

Assessment of the infant at birth can identify potential endocrine abnormalities. Hormonal dysfunction may be present if the relationship between a baby's weight and length differ from the normal ranges on a growth chart; if the limbs' overall size, shape, and relationship to the body are abnormal; or if the size and shape of the sex organs is abnormal. Growth charts can be found on the Centers for Disease Control and Prevention (CDC) website: http://MedTerm.ParadigmCollege.net/growthchart.

Aplasia (absence or defective development) of the thymus and parathyroid glands is known as DiGeorge syndrome, a rare genetic disease diagnosed at birth that is often associated with a weakened immune system, distinct physical features, developmental delays, and heart defects. Some infants with this condition may have **tetany** (severe and prolonged muscle spasms), which requires emergency management. Other infants may not display signs and symptoms until days or weeks after birth.

There is a risk that infants of diabetic mothers will be unusually large, with an abnormally large body (**macrosomia**). Hypoglycemia develops in about 75 percent of these infants. If the mother's diabetes was diagnosed and controlled during gestation, the infant may not develop symptoms of hypoglycemia for hours or days after birth. Within the first three days of life, an infant experiencing hypoglycemia may become irritable and lethargic (sluggish) and suck poorly during feedings. These infants do have a greater-than-normal risk of developing diabetes later in life.

Children and Adolescents

Type 1 diabetes, a condition also known as *juvenile diabetes*, is a chronic condition usually diagnosed in children and young adults. Affecting less than 5 percent of the US population, type 1 diabetes is an autoimmune illness in which the body attacks the cells producing insulin, resulting in the body's inability to produce adequate insulin (the hormone responsible for converting glucose to usable energy). Type 1 diabetes is the most common endocrine disorder of childhood and adolescence. Individuals with type 1 diabetes depend on an external supply of insulin to maintain homeostasis, generally via daily insulin injections or an insulin pump. This type of diabetes is also known as *insulin-dependent diabetes mellitus (IDDM)*.

The insulin deficiency of type 1 diabetes creates an increased blood glucose concentration that is known as **hyperglycemia**. A high blood sugar level results in **glucosuria**, or increased glucose in the urine. Glucosuria, in turn, causes the kidneys to produce more urine, a condition called **polyuria**. Frequent bed-wetting is often an early sign of diabetes in a child with no history of such behavior. The increased frequency of urination, diuresis, results in a loss of electrolytes, and dehydration soon follows. Dehydration then stimulates the body's thirst (polydipsia). The loss of glucose and electrolytes from the urine causes a daily loss of about 1,000 calories, approximately half of the calories needed by a child. Therefore, weight loss follows, in spite of the increased appetite that occurs to compensate for the lost calories.

Did You Know?

In medical school students are often taught the "3 Ps of diabetes." They include *polydipsia* (thirst), *polyuria* (frequent urination) and *polyphagia* (hunger).

Diabetic ketoacidosis (DKA) is a condition in which there is a buildup of acids in the blood. DKA can be life-threatening and is a direct result of the body's lack of an adequate supply of insulin used by the cells to convert sugar into usable energy. Instead, the body is forced to use fat as an energy source, ultimately producing acids called ketones that build up in the blood. In contrast, the immediate effects of type 2 diabetes is much more subtle. The hyperglycemia is frequently discovered through routine testing during a physical exam. The long-term effects of uncontrolled or poorly controlled hyperglycemia are frightening. Damage to delicate nerves and blood vessels can lead to a much higher incidence of heart disease, blindness (retinopathy), kidney failure (nephropathy), and limb amputations (peripheral vascular disease) due to poor circulation.

Adults and Seniors

Individuals with **type 2 diabetes mellitus**, formerly known as adult-onset diabetes, may require the use of oral medications (including insulin), to maintain homeostasis. The classic symptoms of diabetes are polyuria (frequent urination), polydipsia (extreme thirst), polyphagia (increased appetite), and weight loss. According to the CDC, type 2 diabetes, usually diagnosed in adults aged 40 years or older, is now becoming more common among children and adolescents, particularly in individuals of Latin, African, or Native-American descent. Increases in childhood obesity, physical inactivity, and prenatal exposure to diabetes in the mother have become widespread, and may contribute to the increased development of type 2 diabetes during childhood and adolescence. The CDC projects that by the year 2050, one in three Americans will have type 2 diabetes.

A common condition among women under 40 is **hyperthyroidism** (also known as *thyrotoxicosis*), which is the excessive production of thyroid hormone. Hyperthyroidism can result in an immune system disorder known as **Graves' disease**. Common symptoms include anxiety, hand tremors, weight loss, enlargement of the thyroid glands (goiters), sensitivity to heat (excessive sweating), irregular heartbeats, and exophthalmos (protruding eyeballs resulting from the presence of swollen tissue behind the eye socket).

Myxedema is a form of hypothyroidism that occurs in older adults as a result of an underactive thyroid. The severely low levels of thyroid hormone lead to waxy skin that may appear swollen, weight gain, hair loss, lethargy (sluggishness), and sensitivity to cold. These symptoms can be reversed by the administration of thyroid replacement therapy.

In the Know: Osteoporosis

According to the Centers for Disease Control and Prevention, nearly 1 in 10 older adults in the United States has osteoporosis. Osteoporosis is a disease that affects bones and joints and is most often diagnosed in the aging population. Although osteoporosis (previously discussed in Chapter 4) is usually considered a bone disorder, it often falls under the treatment scope of endocrinologists because of its underlying causes. Many postmenopausal women develop this disease as a result of low levels of estrogen hormone. Estrogen helps to maintain bone mass. Without estrogen, bones become less dense and are more prone to fractures. Postmenopausal patients with osteoporosis are generally treated with hormone replacement therapies. Other patients may develop osteoporosis as a result of an overactive thyroid (e.g., hyperthyroidism), which is classified as secondary osteoporosis.

Checkpoint 13.2

Answer the following questions to identify any areas of the section that you may need to review.

1. Decreased levels of glucose (sugar) in the blood results in what condition?

   _____

2. What condition occurs in older adults as a result of thyroid atrophy?

   _____

3. Name the medical term for increased appetite.

   _____

4. Extreme hypothyroidism is known as what medical term?

   _____

5. What is the medical term for severe and prolonged muscle spasms?

   _____

Exercise 13.7   Word Maps: Hyperglycemia

Each term in the list is part of the type 1 diabetes process. Number the terms (1 to 6) in the order in which they occur in the process.

_____ polyuria

_____ hyperglycemia

_____ dehydration

_____ weight loss

_____ glucosuria

_____ polydipsia

Exercise 13.8   Comprehension Check

Supply a term to match the definition provided.

1. _____ means manifested by gigantism and/or acromegaly

2. _____ means excessive thirst

3. _____ means excessive eating

4. _____ means absent or defective development

5. _____ means buildup of acids in the blood

Exercise 13.9   Comprehension Check

Select the correct medical term from the word bank to substitute for the underlined definition in each sentence.

axillary	diuresis	hermaphroditism
bradypnea	dysfunction	hyperglycemia
chromosomal	edematous	ketoacidosis
dehydrated	glycosuria	tachycardia

1. <u>Pertaining to chromosomes</u> derangements can produce various abnormalities in the fetus.

   _____

2. The problem is a result of thyroid <u>difficult, abnormal, or faulty function</u>.

   _____

3. Urinalysis revealed a marked <u>condition of sugar in the urine</u>.

   _____

4. Upon arrival in the emergency room, the patient was severely <u>in a condition without water</u>.

   _____

5. The patient had <u>a rapid heart rate</u>.

   _____

Exercise 13.10   Matching

Match the term in column 1 with the definition in column 2. Write the letter of the definition in the space beside the term.

1. _____ endocrinologist
2. _____ polydipsia
3. _____ polyphagia
4. _____ adrenal
5. _____ ADH
6. _____ pituitary gland
7. _____ neurohypophysis
8. _____ TSH
9. _____ calcitonin
10. _____ insulin

a. literally, "on the kidneys (renal)"
b. antidiuretic hormone
c. has two lobes
d. posterior lobe of the pituitary gland
e. specialist in the endocrine system
f. hormone secreted by the thyroid gland
g. excessive thirst
h. hormone secreted by the pancreas
i. thyroid-stimulating hormone
j. excessive hunger

Exercise 13.11   Word Building

Supply word parts to complete the terms that follow, using the context of the sentences as a guide.

1. Thyro_____ is a condition of thyroid poisoning (destructive excess of thyroid hormone).

2. _____-al glands are located at the top of each kidney.

3. _____cyte is a thymus cell.

4. _____oma means tumor of the thymus.

5. Endo_____ glands secrete hormones directly into the bloodstream.

Exercise 13.12   Spelling Check

Write the correct spelling of each term on the blank provided.

1. glucagun   _____
2. metabloic   _____
3. parthromone   _____
4. glucocrotorticoid   _____
5. medula   _____

Exercise 13.13 Word Maps

Complete the concept map by filling in the missing labels.

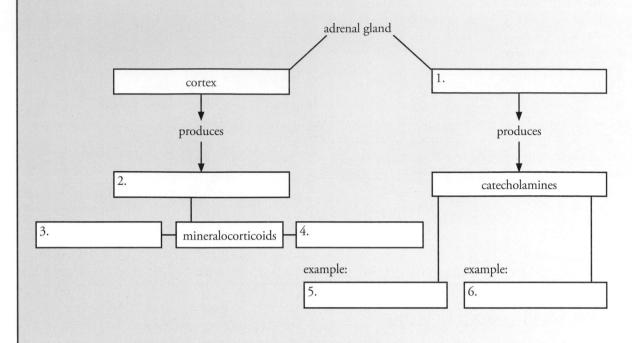

Diagnostic Tests and Examinations

Any malfunction in the endocrine glands and the hormones they secrete can cause problems in almost every body system. Observation of the patient's physical size, body shape, and physical and developmental milestones can provide important clues in diagnosing abnormal hormone secretion. Visual signs of possible endocrine imbalance include abnormal hair distribution, patchy hair loss, spotty skin pigmentation, and tremors.

A patient's medical history (past and current) can also reveal information about endocrine health and potential problems. For example, a patient with a family history of endocrine diseases such as diabetes or thyroid disease may be at higher risk of certain disorders. The family history may contain information about diabetes symptoms: **polyuria** (excessive urination), **polydipsia** (increased thirst), and **polyphagia** (increased appetite). The history may also contain information about other symptoms of endocrine disorders, such as changes in skin pigmentation or texture, intolerance to heat or cold, excessive sweating, and an abnormal relationship between appetite and weight. Beyond the physical examination and a complete history, the most important assessment of hormonal function comes from laboratory testing.

Most endocrine testing measures hormone levels in the blood; however, some testing checks the tropic hormones to determine their proper functioning. For example, Thyroid testing can be performed by measuring the serum T_3 and T_4 levels.

The parathyroid hormone level is measured directly in the blood. A persistent hypercalcemic state may indicate a defect in parathormone function. Measurements of catecholamines are used to assess adrenal function by determining norepinephrine and epinephrine concentrations in the blood. Also, a **urinalysis (UA)** can be conducted to examine the visual, chemical, and microscopic components of urine. Test strips are used to absorb small amounts of urine to be assessed within minutes (for the presence of glucose, ketones, and blood in urine).

Pancreatic islet functioning can be checked with a **fasting blood sugar (FBS)** test, in which the patient's blood glucose level is tested after a 12-hour fast. Another test, the **glucose tolerance test (GTT)**, is performed in the morning, after a 12-hour fast. After the patient is given a portion of glucose orally, blood tests are performed over several hours to determine the blood glucose levels over time. The **postprandial (PP) test** measures blood glucose concentration after a meal. Table 13.6 lists examples of tests used to diagnose conditions of the endocrine system.

TABLE 13.6	**Tests Associated with the Endocrine System**
Test	**Description**
A1c	average measurement of blood glucose levels over a 3-month period; generally used to monitor efficacy of diabetes treatment, also referred to as *HbA1c*
fasting blood sugar (FBS)	blood test performed following a 12-hour fast; measurements are taken of the current concentrations of glucose in the blood
glucometer	instrument used to measure the levels of blood sugar present in the blood
hormone tests	measures the levels of specific hormones present in the blood (ADH, growth hormone, cortisol, TSH, parathyroid)
oral glucose tolerance test (GTT)	blood test performed following a 12-hour fast; highly concentrated glucose drink is consumed and the body's response is monitored
radiographic tests	used to help diagnose some conditions, for example growth hormone deficiency with early closure of growth plates
radioimmunoassay (RIA)	measures hormones
thyroid echography	ultrasound exam of the thyroid
thyroid function tests (TFTs)	blood tests used to assess the normal functioning of the thyroid (specifically the levels of T_3, T_4, and calcitonin)
thyroid scan	utilizes radioactive iodine to determine the overall health of the thyroid
thyroxine test	diagnostic test for hyperthyroidism

In The Know: An Ancient Diagnostic Test

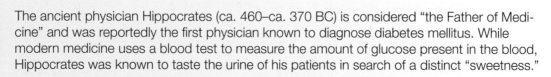

The ancient physician Hippocrates (ca. 460–ca. 370 BC) is considered "the Father of Medicine" and was reportedly the first physician known to diagnose diabetes mellitus. While modern medicine uses a blood test to measure the amount of glucose present in the blood, Hippocrates was known to taste the urine of his patients in search of a distinct "sweetness."

Checkpoint 13.3

Answer the following questions to identify any areas of the section that you may need to review.

1. What instrument is used to measure the levels of blood sugar present in the blood?

   _____

2. What laboratory test utilizes radioactive iodine to determine the overall health of the thyroid?

   _____

3. Which diagnostic test is used to measure average levels of blood glucose over a 3-month period?

   _____

Treatments

Healthcare practitioners use predetermined guidelines to direct patient care. These guidelines, known as clinical practice guidelines and evidence-based practices, have been developed by the specialty societies based on past clinical research. They represent the treatment pathways that have achieved the best outcomes. Treatment decisions generally fall into three categories: surgical, clinical, and pharmacological.

Surgical treatments are generally invasive as they involve a puncture or an incision into the skin. *Clinical treatments* are generally noninvasive and involve nonsurgical techniques (e.g., physical therapy). *Pharmacological treatments* involve the utilization of medicines (drugs) to treat specific illnesses or diseases. Medication therapies are regulated by the Food and Drug Administration (FDA). To be approved by the FDA for use in the United States, every medicine must be backed by research studies that have shown the medication to be effective in its treatment of a given disease and has a tolerable safety profile. The following sections provide an overview of treatments common to the endocrine system.

Surgical Treatments

Treating dysfunctional or diseased endocrine glands often involves surgery to remove part of or the entire gland. If a gland is removed or partially removed, hormone replacement therapy will be needed. Table 13.7 lists some of the common procedures involving the endocrine system. The suffix *-ectomy* is used in each of the terms in Table 13.7. Recall that *-ectomy* means "surgical removal."

TABLE 13.7 Surgical Treatments Associated with the Endocrine System

Treatment	Description
adrenalectomy	removal of the adrenal gland
hypophysectomy	removal of the pituitary gland; hormone replacement is necessary
lobectomy	removal of lobe of an organ or gland (e.g., lobe of the pituitary)
pancreatectomy	excision of all or part of the pancreas to remove a tumor or treat inflammation
parathyroidectomy	removal of the parathyroid gland(s)
pinealectomy	removal of the pineal gland
thymectomy	removal of thymus gland
thyroidectomy	removal of the thyroid gland

Pharmacological Treatments

Physicians prescribe various pharmaceutical agents to augment decreased or absent function of a particular hormone or to suppress hormone secretion. The exception is the use of adrenal corticosteroids, such as prednisone and hydrocortisone, which are used for many disorders and conditions. Their anti-inflammatory and antiallergic properties make them particularly valuable. Table 13.8 lists common pharmacological agents used to treat endocrine system conditions.

TABLE 13.8 Pharmacological Agents Associated with the Endocrine System

Drug Class	Used to Treat	Generic Name	Brand Name
antidiabetics	type 1 diabetes	insulin therapy, injections, pumps	Novolog, Humulin N, Lantus
	type 2 diabetes	metformin	Glumetza, Glucophage, Fortamet, Riomet
antithyroid	hyperthyroidism	methimazol	Tapazole
corticosteroid	underfunctioning adrenal cortices (e.g., in Addison's disease)	prednisone	Deltasone
growth hormone	growth inhibitions	somatotropin	Genotropin
posterior pituitary hormone	diabetes insipidus	vasopressin, desmopressin acetate	Pitressin, Vasostrict
thyroid hormone	hypothyroidism	levothyroxine	Synthroid

Soft Skills for Medical Professionals: Leadership

Working with others gives you the opportunity to demonstrate leadership. In addition to the basic soft skills that every employee should display, such as professionalism, communication, teamwork, and self-management, a leader has the ability to guide his or her teammates through difficult or exhausting workplace situations. Although many managers and supervisors received those titles by displaying leadership, you do not need an official title to display leadership skills. These skills include being responsive to the needs of others, flexible when faced with change, appreciative of the efforts made by others, and able to lead by example. Practicing these skills and applying them on the job will assist in creating a culture in which other healthcare professionals see a value in leadership.

Checkpoint 13.4

Answer the following questions to identify any areas of the section that you may need to review.

1. Insulin therapy is generally used to treat which type of diabetes?

_____

2. What type of hormone replacement therapy treats underfunctioning adrenal cortices?

_____

3. Synthroid is a pharmaceutical agent used to treat what type of thyroid dysfunction?

_____

Abbreviations

In the medical field, information is generally recorded in medical charts and in electronic medical records and provided to healthcare workers in medical shorthand. It is important that healthcare professionals become familiar with the abbreviations utilized on a daily basis to successfully perform the duties assigned in a typical workday. Table 13.9 provides common abbreviations used in reference to the endocrine system.

TABLE 13.9 Abbreviations Associated with the Endocrine System

Abbreviation	Meaning
ACTH	adrenocorticotropic hormone
ADH	antidiuretic hormone (vasopressin)
A1c	average glucose level
BG	blood glucose
BMR	basal metabolic rate
Ca	calcium
CHT	congenital hypothyroidism
DI	diabetes insipidus
DKA	diabetic ketoacidosis
DM	diabetes mellitus
DR, DRP	diabetic retinopathy
FBS	fasting blood sugar
FSH	follicle-stimulating hormone
GD	Graves disease
GH	growth hormone
GHRH	growth hormone-releasing hormone

Continues

Abbreviation	Meaning
GTT	glucose tolerance test
HG	hypoglycemia
HGH	human growth hormone
HVA	homovanillic acid
IDDM	insulin-dependent diabetes mellitus
K	potassium
LH	luteinizing hormone
MSH	melanocyte-stimulating hormone
Na	sodium
NIDDM	non-insulin dependent diabetes mellitus
OT	oxytocin
PIH	prolactin-inhibiting hormone
PP	postprandial
PRH	prolactin-releasing hormone
PRL	prolactin
PTH	parathyroid hormone (parathormone)
RIA	radioimmunoassay
SIADH	syndrome of inappropriate antidiuretic hormone
T_3	triiodothyronine
T_4	thyroxine
TFT	thyroid function test
TRH	thyrotropin-releasing hormone
TSH	thyroid-stimulating hormone
UA	urinalysis
VMA	vanillylmandelic acid

Exercise 13.14   Word Building

Write the definition of each combining form in the Definition column. Then create a term using that combining form in the Term column.

Combining Form	Definition	Term
1. *adren/o*	_____	_____
2. *aden/o*	_____	_____
3. *thyr/o*	_____	_____
4. *crin/o*	_____	_____
5. *ket/o*	_____	_____

Exercise 13.15 Word Analysis

Write the meaning of the underlined term on the line below the sentence. You may need to use a medical dictionary for this exercise. Keep your answers brief.

1. <u>Endemic goiter</u> can result from an inadequate diet.

   _____

2. <u>Hyponatremia</u> is frequently a result of over activity of the adrenal cortex.

   _____

3. The patient was admitted to the hospital with an <u>electrolyte</u> imbalance.

   _____

4. We will identify the <u>sella turcica</u> and locate the pituitary gland.

   _____

5. <u>Gastrin</u> is necessary for proper digestive function.

   _____

Exercise 13.16 Word Building

Supply the word parts to complete each term, according to the definition provided.

1. endocrino_____ means disorder of an endocrine gland
2. melano_____ means black cell
3. _____lysis means breakdown of fats
4. _____calcem_____ means condition of excessive calcium in the blood
5. _____thyroid means around or near the thyroid

Exercise 13.17 Check for Accuracy

Supply the correct definition for each abbreviation by writing the definition on the line beside the abbreviation.

1. T_3 _____
2. T_4 _____
3. LH _____
4. FBS _____
5. GTT _____

Exercise 13.18   Word Maps

The concept map below shows the sequence of events in the development and treatment of hyperglycemia (diabetes mellitus) and hypoglycemia. Label the blank areas of the map to complete the information.

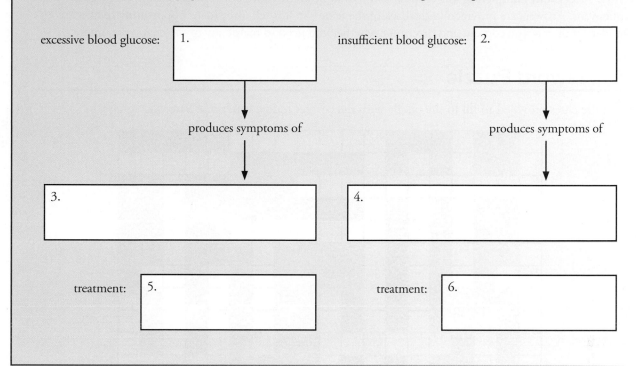

excessive blood glucose: | 1.

produces symptoms of

insufficient blood glucose: | 2.

produces symptoms of

3.

4.

treatment: | 5.

treatment: | 6.

After successfully completing this chapter, you should be able to correctly answer the following review questions. Answers are provided in the back of the text. Use this self-assessment opportunity to check your understanding of the content and determine whether you need to revisit any of the chapter's content.

Crossword Puzzle

Use the clues provided to fill in the puzzle with the correct terms. Enter one letter per square.

Across

3. narrow portion that connects two larger parts
5. endocrine gland that is part of the female reproductive system
7. responsible for the body's "internal clock"
8. literally meaning "like or resembling a shield"
10. abbreviation for sodium
12. abbreviation for oxytocin
16. severe and prolonged muscle spasms
17. combining form that means female
19. hormone secreted by alpha cells in the pancreas

21. promotes development of secondary sex characteristics in the female
22. gland whose name means "below the thalamus"
24. yellowish, translucent substance resembling glue
25. inflammation of a gland
26. endocrine gland located in the upper abdomen, behind the stomach

Down

1. causes abnormally small testes and penis
2. tumor of a gland
3. hormone-secreting endocrine glands in the pancreas

4. instrument for measuring glucose (sugar) in the blood
6. process or agent that works against another
9. _____ of Langerhans
11. organ that provides transfer of substances between fetus and mother
13. endocrine gland located in the mediastinum
14. suffix meaning surgical removal
15. first form or type from which others are copied
18. any disease or condition of a gland
20. combining form meaning sugar
23. scinti _____; process that measures radioactive uptake

Matching

Match the following glands to the hormone that they produce.

1. _____ adrenals
2. _____ hypothalamus
3. _____ ovaries
4. _____ pancreas
5. _____parathyroid
6. _____ pineal
7. _____ pituitary
8. _____ testes
9. _____ thymus
10. _____ thyroid

a. testosterone
b. insulin
c. melatonin
d. parathormone
e. estrogen
f. somatotropin
g. thymosin
h. T_3, T_4
i. antidiuretic
j. glucocorticoid

Identification

Correctly label the illustration by writing the correct term on the line provided for each corresponding location.

adrenal   parathyroid   thymus
hypothalamus   pineal   thyroid
ovaries   pituitary
pancreas   testes

1. _____

2. _____

3. _____

4. _____

5. _____

6. _____

7. _____

8. _____

9. _____

10. _____

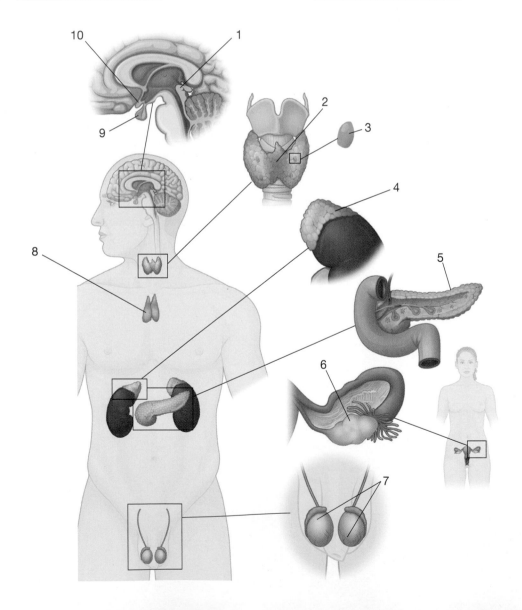

Abbreviations

Match the following abbreviations with their meanings.

1. _____ IDDM
2. _____ TSH
3. _____ FSH
4. _____ Na
5. _____ Ca
6. _____ ADH
7. _____ GH
8. _____ PTH
9. _____ MSH
10. _____ HVA

a. follicle-stimulating hormone
b. antidiuretic hormone
c. melanocyte-stimulating hormone
d. parathyroid hormone
e. insulin dependent diabetes mellitus
f. growth hormone
g. homovanillic acid
h. sodium
i. calcium
j. thyroid-stimulating hormone

Word-Building Challenge

Supply the word parts needed to complete each term, according to the definition provided.

1. endocrino_____ = disorder of an endocrine gland
2. melano_____ = black cell
3. _____lysis = breakdown of fats
4. _____ic = pertaining to the pancreas
5. _____thyroid_____ = decreased secretion of thyroid hormones
6. _____calcem_____ = condition of excessive calcium in the blood
7. _____diabetic agent = substance used to treat diabetes
8. _____thyroid = around or near the thyroid
9. _____kalemia = excessive amount of potassium in the blood
10. _____uria = increased glucose in the urine

Extension Activities

Complete the following activities as assigned by your instructor.

1. Search the Internet for common performance-enhancing drugs (steroids). What types of drugs are the most commonly used? Are these drugs readily available by prescription in the United States or are these drugs known to circulate in the black market? What pros/cons are discussed surrounding their use and misuse? Provide a specific example of how they been connected to the performance of any past or present professional athlete. What disciplinary actions were taken in response to the use of such substances? Create an informative article to share your findings with the class.

2. Find online articles that discuss scams and schemes related to human growth hormones. Read the article at http://MedTerm.ParadigmCollege.net/HGHScams. Write a one-page summary of your thoughts related to this sensitive subject and identify your sources.

3. Prevalence rates of type 2 diabetes are historically higher among minority populations. Use the Internet to obtain reliable statistical data concerning diagnoses among minority populations across the United States. Why are certain populations more likely to develop type 2 diabetes than members of other races and genders? What risk factors have been identified in reputable scientific research findings? Is this trend expected to continue? Be sure to cite all of your sources and present your findings to your class.

Student eResources

The Course Navigator learning management system that accompanies this textbook offers multiple opportunities to master chapter content, including end-of-chapter exercises, a glossary of key terms with audio pronunciations, games, pronunciation coach, and additional activities such as engaging with the BioDigital® Human.

14 The Male Reproductive System

> ❝A wise man should consider that health is the greatest of human blessings, and learn how by his own thought to derive benefit from his illnesses.❞
>
> **—Hippocrates, ancient Greek physician**

Translation Challenge

Read this excerpt from a medical record and try to answer the questions that follow.

Patient is to have testicular ultrasound, testicular scan, and left scrotal exploration with possible orchiectomy or bilateral orchidopexy. The complications were discussed, including bleeding, infection, and possibility of the need for future testicular prosthesis.

1. Orchiectomy and orchidopexy have the same root. What is the meaning of each medical term?

2. What is a bilateral orchidopexy?

3. What condition might require a patient to receive a testicular prosthesis?

Learning Objectives

14.1 List and define word parts most commonly used to create terms associated with the male reproductive system.

14.2 Identify and label structures of the male reproductive system.

14.3 Describe the role of the male reproductive organs in the process of fertilization.

14.4 Recognize diseases and disorders of the male reproductive system.

14.5 Identify diagnostic tests and treatments for disorders of the male reproductive system.

14.6 Define the abbreviations related to the male reproductive system.

14.7 Use male reproductive system vocabulary correctly in written and oral contexts.

14.8 Correctly spell and pronounce male reproductive system terminology.

COURSE NAVIGATOR

Access Additional Chapter Resources

This chapter focuses on the internal and external structures of the male reproductive system as well as the functions of the system. The diseases and disorders of the system will be briefly discussed along with treatment options. You will be introduced to the terminology associated with this system, including the word roots, prefixes, suffixes, and combining forms, as well as the abbreviations associated with the system.

In the Know: Male Reproductive System Specialties

The area of health care that focuses specifically on disease and conditions that affect men and the male reproductive system is called **andrology** (from the combining form *andr/o* meaning "male" and the suffix *-logy* meaning "study of"). Andrology is also known as "the science of men." Recall that *urology* is the branch of science that focuses on conditions affecting the urinary tract and male reproductive organs. Physicians who specialize in the diagnosis, treatment, and prevention of problems affecting the urinary system and male reproductive system are known as **urologists**. These physicians are trained in both surgical and non-surgical (medical) treatment methods.

Allied health professionals also play a variety of roles in the provision of health care for men. Ultrasound technicians, also known as *diagnostic medical sonographers*, are allied health professionals trained to use imaging equipment utilized to diagnose conditions of the male reproductive system. Medical assistants assist physicians with patient examinations and perform routine laboratory tests related to conditions associated with the male reproductive system. Phlebotomists are essential to laboratory procedures involving the collection and testing of blood.

Male Reproductive System Word Parts

As with other body systems, a core of combining forms serves as the source for most of the medical words associated with the male reproductive system. Table 14.1 lists the essential word parts for the male reproductive system.

TABLE 14.1 Word Parts Associated with the Male Reproductive System

Prefix	Meaning	Example
a-	no, not, without	aspermia (failure to produce sperm, absence of sperm in the semen)
circum-	around	male circumcision (surgical removal of the foreskin, the tissue around the head of the penis)
crypt-	hidden	cryptorchidism (congenital condition in which one or both testicles does not descend into the scrotum following birth)
epi-	upon, above	epispadias (congenital abnormality in which the urethral opening is on the topside of the penis)
hypo-	below, less	hypospadias (congenital abnormality in which the urethral opening is located below the head of the penis)
poly-	many	polyorchism (congenital abnormality in which an individual has more than 2 testicles)

Combining Form	Meaning	Example
andr/o	male, masculine	androgenous (giving birth to males)
balan/o	glans penis	balanoplasty (surgical reconstruction of the glans penis)
gamet/o	gamete	gametocyte (any germ cell capable of dividing to produce gametes; a spermatocyte or oocyte)
genit/o	genitals	genitalia (pertaining to the genitals)
gonad/o	gonad, seed	gonadal (relating to the gonad)
orchi/o	testis (testicle)	orchiocele (a testis retained in the inguinal canal)
orchid/o	testis (testicle)	orchidometer (caliper device used to measure the size of the testes)
pen/i	penis	penile (pertaining to the penis)
prostat/o	prostate	prostatectomy (removal of prostate gland)
scrot/o	scrotum	scrotal (pertaining to the sac containing the testes)
semin/i	semen	seminal (pertaining to the semen)
spermat/o	semen, spermatozoa	spermatogenesis (process by which spermatogonial stem cells divide and differentiate into sperm)
sperm/o	semen, spermatozoa	spermatic (relating to the sperm or semen)
test/o	testes, testicle	testicular (pertaining to the testes)
urethr/o	urethra	urethral (pertaining to the urethra)
vesicul/o	seminal vesicle	vesiculitis (inflammation of a vesicle, most commonly a seminal vesicle)
vas/o	vessel, ducts	vasectomy (excision of segment of vas deferens)

Suffix	Meaning	Example
-cele	hernia, protrusion	hydrocele (collection of fluid within the testis)
-ectomy	surgical removal	vasectomy (surgical removal of a portion of the vas deferens)

Continues

Suffix	Meaning	Example
-genesis	formation, production	aspermatogenesis (failure to produce sperm)
-itis	inflammation	orchitis (inflammation of the testicles)
-pathy	disease	orchiopathy (disease of a testis)
-pexy	surgical fixation	orchiopexy (surgical procedure to bring down an undescended testicle and suture in into the scrotum)
-plasia	formation	benign prostatic hyperplasia (enlarged prostate tissue causing pressure on the urethra)
-plasty	surgical repair	orchioplasty (surgical reconstruction of the testis)
-spadias	a tear	hypospadias (congenital condition in which the urethral opening is located below the head of the penis)
-stomy	new opening	vasovasostomy (surgical reunion of the vas deferens to create an opening to restore fertility, follows a previous vasectomy)

Anatomy and Physiology

The external organs of the reproductive systems are called **genitalia**. In the male reproductive system, genitals consist of the testicles, vas deferens, epididymis, seminal vesicles, prostate gland, and the penis. The **testes (testicles)** are egg-shaped glands that produce and store millions of tiny sperm cells. In adult men, the testicles can grow to measure approximately 2 inches in length and 1 inch in diameter. The testicle is composed of roughly a thousand long, coiled structures called **seminiferous tubules**, with special cells that secrete **testosterone**, the male sex hormone responsible for puberty and the stimulation of sperm production. Each testicle lies within a pouch-like sac known as the **scrotum**, that hangs outside the body. The scrotum is responsible for regulating the temperature of the testicles.

Sperm is stored in the **epididymis**, a structure located within the scrotal sac. Once matured, sperm travel from the epididymis to the vas deferens, also referred to as the ductus deferens. The vas deferens carry sperm from the testes toward the penis for ejaculation. The seminal vesicles and prostate are accessory glands within the male reproductive system. The **seminal vesicles** are located behind the urinary bladder in males. These glands are responsible for the production of seminal fluid (semen). The **prostate gland**, located between the urinary bladder and the penis, secretes the fluid that nourishes and protects sperm during and after ejaculation.

The **penis** is the male sex organ responsible for the excretion of sperm during ejaculation and for transporting urine outside the body.

Figure 14.1 shows the components of the male reproductive system. Table 14.2 identifies common anatomy and physiology terms related to the male reproductive system.

What's in a Word?

Prostate is a Greek word meaning "one who stands before," "protector," or "guardian."

FIGURE 14.1 Male Reproductive System

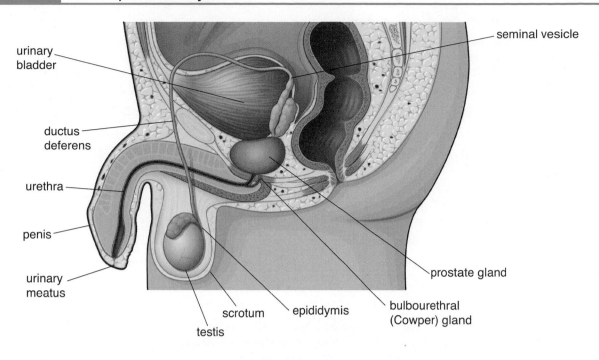

urinary bladder

ductus deferens

urethra

penis

urinary meatus

seminal vesicle

prostate gland

bulbourethral (Cowper) gland

epididymis

scrotum

testis

TABLE 14.2 Anatomy and Physiology Terms Associated with the Male Reproductive System

Term		Meaning	Word Analysis	
bulbourethral glands Cowper's glands	[**bul**-bO-yoo-**ree**-threl] [**kow**-perz]	pea-sized glands located under the prostate gland; assist the seminal vesicles in the production of semen	*bulb/o* *urethr/o* *-al*	bulb urethra pertaining to
corpus cavernosum	[**kor**-pus kav-er-**nO**-sum]	one of two columns of erectile tissue within the body of the penis, contains most of the blood in the penis during an erection	*corpus*	body
corpus spongiosum	[**kor**-pus spun-jee-**O**-sum]	one of two columns of erectile tissue within the body of the penis, inner portion surrounding the urethra	*corpus*	body
ejaculation	[ee-jak-yoo-**lay**-shun]	ejection of semen from the penis, generally following an orgasm		
ejaculatory ducts	[ee-**jak**-yoo-lah-tor-ee dukts]	tubes that are formed when the ducts of the seminal vesicles and vas deferens join; sperm travel along these tubes and pass through the prostate gland	*duct*	passage
epididymis	[ep-i-**did**-i-mis]	tube that connects to the testicle within the scrotum in which sperm is stored until maturity		
erection	[ee-**rek**-shin]	state in which the erectile tissue of the penis is filled with blood		
foreskin	[**for**-skin]	loosely folded tissue that covers the glans penis (tip of the penis), also known as *prepuce*	*fore* *prepuce*	before; in front Anglo Saxon term foreskin

Continues

Term		Meaning	Word Analysis	
gamete	[**gam**-eet]	male and female sex cells	*gamet/o*	to marry
genitals genitalia (sing.)	[**jen**-ih-telz] [jen-ih-**tay**-lee-ah]	male and female sex organs	*genitalia*	Latin, pertaining to generation or birth
glans penis	[glanz **pee**-nis]	the head of the penis, sensitive tip of the penis	*balan/o*	glans penis
gonad	[**gO**-nad]	organ that produces male and female sex cells	*gonad/o*	seed, sex organ
penis	[**pee**-nis]	male reproductive organ	*penis*	tail
prostate	[**pros**-tayt]	gland located between the urinary bladder and the penis, tasked with the secretion of fluid used to nourish and protect sperm as it travels outside the body during ejaculation	*prostat/o*	protector, guardian
scrotum	[**skrO**-tem]	sac that contains the testes; located below the penis	*scrot/o*	scrotum
semen	[**see**-men]	fluid containing the sperm	*semen*	seed
seminal vesicles	[**sem**-ih-nel **ves**-ih-kuls]	glands located behind the male urinary bladder responsible for the production of seminal fluid (semen)	*semin/i -al vesicul/o*	semen pertaining to small sac, seminal vesicle
sperm		male sex cell, has the ability to fertilize the female ovum to produce a zygote, also known as *spermatozoa*	*sperm/o spermat/o*	testes sperm
testes (pl)	[**tes**-teez]	male reproductive glands located within the scrotum; male gonads; testicles; testis (sing)	*test/o*	testes
testicle	[**tes**-tih-kul]	male reproductive organ	*test/o*	testes
testosterone	[tes-**tos**-tuh-rOn]	the sex hormone responsible for the growth and development of male sex characteristics	*test/o*	testis
urethra	[yoo-**ree**-thruh]	structure leading from the bladder to the urinary opening	*urethr/o*	urethra
vas deferens	[vas **def**-er-enz]	duct of the reproductive tract; carries sperm from the testes toward the penis for ejaculation; also known as *ductus deferens*	*vas defero*	a vessel to carry down
zygote	[**zI**-gOt]	cell that is the product of the joining of the ovum and the sperm	*zyg/o*	joining; yoked

The Penis

The **penis** is the male reproductive organ which serves as the gateway for the release of sperm during ejaculation and the excretion of urine. Chapter 16 provides a detailed overview of the reproductive process. The penis is made up of two main parts, the *shaft* or body, and the *glans penis*. The **shaft** of the penis encompasses the urethra and two columns of spongy tissue that fill with blood when the male is aroused. The first column is known as the corpus cavernosum and it houses a large portion of the blood stored in the penis during an erection. The inner column, called the corpus spongiosum, forms a layer of protection surrounding the urethra.

The **glans penis**, or head of the penis, contains the urethral opening and sensitive nerve endings. The glans is covered by loose skin known as the **foreskin** (also known as the *prepuce*). The foreskin may be removed shortly after birth for social, medical, or religious/cultural reasons. This procedure is called **circumcision** and will be discussed in the treatment section of this chapter. Figure 14.2 illustrates the structure of the penis.

FIGURE 14.2 Structure of the Penis

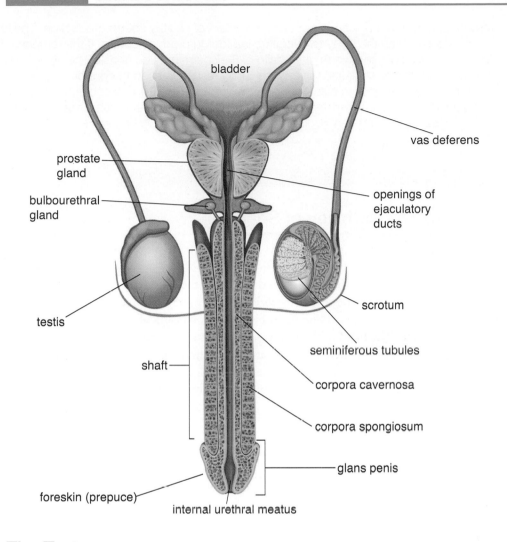

The Testes

The testes develop in the abdominal cavity of the male fetus. They descend along the inguinal canal in the groin into the scrotum before birth. Each testis is about 1/2 to 3/4 inches long by about 1/3 inch wide at birth and increases only slightly during childhood. With the onset of puberty, which can occur as early as age 9 or 10, testosterone initiates growth of the testes. Shortly thereafter, pubic hair appears and the penile size increases. Young men begin to develop hair under their arms and on the face. These changes in development are compared on a rating scale called **Tanner staging**. Recall that the Tanner Scale, also known as the *Normal Sexual Maturity Rating*, is a tool used to define physical measures of development based on external primary and secondary sex characteristics.

Male sexual development is completed in three to five years after the onset of puberty, and the system does not change significantly throughout the years of young and middle adulthood. Sperm production decreases around age 40, but an adult male may produce some sperm throughout his lifetime. In most men, testosterone begins to decline gradually after age 30, which produces physical changes such as decreased muscle tone and decreased energy levels. As the aging process continues, the amount of pubic hair decreases, and penile size and scrotal tone decline.

In the Know: Temperature Regulation

Temperature regulation is an important component of healthy sperm production. The testicles must be cooler than the body temperature in order to produce sperm. If the temperature inside the scrotum is too warm, the health of the sperm may be at risk. The nervous system is responsible for the facilitation of an involuntary response used to control temperature in the scrotum. When the body is cold, the scrotum shrinks in order to tighten around the testicles and hold in body heat. When the body is warm, the scrotum becomes larger in order to rid itself of extra heat. This is an involuntary response triggered and controlled by the nervous system.

Sperm and the Pathway of Sperm

The male reproductive cell, or **gamete**, is the sperm. Sperm are produced in both testicles. Sperm develop within the walls of the seminiferous tubules and are eventually released into the lumen of the tubules on their trip to the outside of the body. Although sperm are one of the smallest cells in the body, they are highly developed. The structure of the sperm, shown in Figure 14.3, consists of a head, a midpiece, and a tail. The **head** of the sperm contains genetic material (such as hair color, eye color, and any hereditary diseases or conditions). A covering on the head of the sperm contains special enzymes that break down the outside of the female's ovum. The **midpiece** of the sperm contains the **mitochondria**, the structures that produce energy to nourish the sperm. The **tail** propels the sperm during its journey.

> **To Note!**
>
> The reproductive cells (gametes) of females are ova (or eggs). In males, gametes are the sperm.

FIGURE 14.3 Sperm Structure

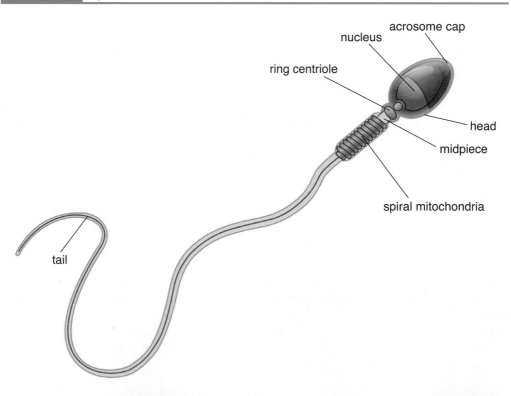

Sperm pass through many ducts as they move toward the outside of the body. The first is the **epididymis**, a long and twisted duct that stores the sperm for 10 to 20 days as they develop and mature. The epididymis lies along the top of and behind the testes.

The next structure through which the sperm pass is the **ductus deferens**, or **vas deferens**. This tube leads sperm from the epididymis, away from the scrotum, and into the abdominal cavity. The ductus deferens passes through the inguinal canal as part of the **spermatic cord**, over the top of and down the posterior surface of the bladder, and eventually joins the duct of the seminal vesicles. The spermatic cord is covered with connective tissue and muscle fibers, known as the cremaster muscle, to assist in the movement of the seminal fluid. The seminal vesicles are glands that create about 60 percent of the volume of **semen**, the thick, white fluid that contains sperm and other substances. Semen contains fructose, a type of sugar that provides a source of energy for the sperm. The seminal vesicles join to form the **ejaculatory duct**.

The ejaculatory duct passes through the walnut-shaped **prostate gland**, which is below the bladder. The prostate secretes a milky fluid that aids in the nourishment and mobility of the sperm and constitutes about 30 percent of semen. The journey of the sperm continues to the **bulbourethral**, or **Cowper's gland**, a pea-sized structure located under the prostate gland. The Cowper's gland secretes a mucus-like substance into the urethra to lubricate it, adding about 5 percent of the fluid volume of sperm.

The final fluid is **ejaculated** outside the body when a male reaches orgasm. **Ejaculation** is the rapid expulsion of the semen from the penis. About one teaspoon is ejaculated at one time, and this small amount of fluid contains about 100 million sperm. Sperm exits the body through the urethra. Recall that the urethra carries urine from the bladder to the outside of the body.

Figure 14.4 diagrams the journey of sperm through the ducts and glands of the male reproductive system. The combining forms for the names of the structures can be found in Table 14.1, and additional terms created from the combining forms are listed in Table 14.2.

> **What's in a Word?**
>
> Note that the word *ejaculate* can either be a noun meaning "the semen that is expelled" or a verb meaning "to suddenly expel."

FIGURE 14.4 Sperm Pathway through Ducts and Glands

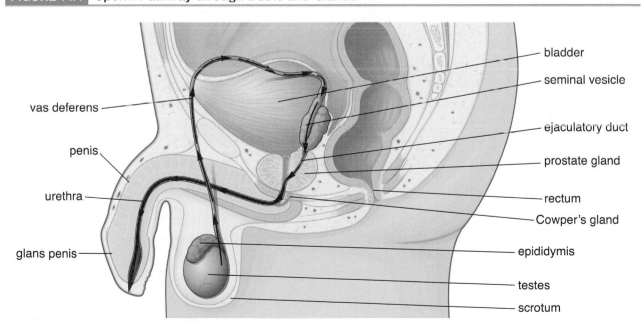

Checkpoint 14.1

Answer the following questions to identify any areas of the section that you may need to review.

1. What are the external organs of the male reproductive system called?

   _____

2. Sperm exits the testes through which duct?

   _____

3. Genetic material is located on which part of the sperm?

   _____

4. Approximately how many sperm are released with each ejaculate?

   _____

Exercise 14.1   Word Analysis

Separate the terms into their word parts using hyphens. Identify the parts by type, writing a letter above each word part (P = prefix, CF = combining form, S = suffix). Then define the term.

Term	Word Analysis	Definition
1. orchiocele	_____	_____
2. spermatic	_____	_____
3. aspermia	_____	_____
4. balanoplasty	_____	_____
5. gonadal	_____	_____

Exercise 14.2   Spelling Check

Each of the following sentences contains a misspelled term. Circle the misspelled term and then write it correctly on the line provided.

1. The patient's enlarged prostrate gland is preventing urine from passing through the urethra.   _____

2. The female ovum and the male sperm join to form the psygoat.   _____

3. Male and female sex cells are called gamites.   _____

4. A eurologist treats disorders of the male reproductive system.   _____

5. The scroteum is a pouch-like sac suspended from the body.   _____

Exercise 14.3 Matching

Match the terms or abbreviations in column 1 with the definitions in column 2. Write the letter of the definition on the line beside the correct term.

1. _____ mitochondria
2. _____ prepuce
3. _____ testosterone
4. _____ genitalia
5. _____ semen
6. _____ spermatic cord

a. loose-fitting tissue covering the glans penis
b. external organs of the male reproductive system
c. male sex hormone
d. extends through the inguinal canal and into the scrotum
e. structures that produce energy for the sperm, located in the midpiece
f. fluid containing sperm

Exercise 14.4 Word Building

Supply the missing word part or parts to complete each term.

1. _____/al means pertaining to the scrotum
2. oligo_____ia is a condition of scanty or deficient sperm
3. _____pexy means surgical fixation of a testicle
4. _____ectomy means removal of the epididymis
5. an_____ia means congenital absence of testes

Exercise 14.5 Comprehension Check

Circle the correct term from the pair in each sentence.

1. The male and female sex cells are called gametes/gonads.
2. The product of the joining of ovum and sperm is a prepuce/zygote.
3. At the tip of the penis is the corpus cavernosa/glans penis.
4. Sperm are released into the lumen/mitochondria of the tubules.
5. The first duct that sperm pass through is the epididymis/vas deferens.
6. Human reproductive organs are called ductus/gonads.

The following diagram depicts the journey of sperm from its origin in the testicle through the urethra. Complete the diagram by correctly placing the provided terms.

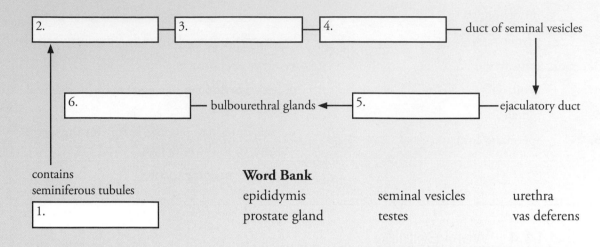

contains
seminiferous tubules

Word Bank

epididymis	seminal vesicles	urethra
prostate gland	testes	vas deferens

Conditions

A common problem for men is **impotence**, the inability to have an erection. Also known as **erectile dysfunction (ED)**, this condition can occur at any age, although it is more common in older men. The causes may be physical or psychological. Physical causes include chronic circulatory disease, excess alcohol intake, diabetes, paralysis, and certain medications. Psychological causes include stress, anxiety, and depression. Treatment for erectile dysfunction depends on the cause. Physicians may suggest making lifestyle changes prior to the use of medications.

Another problem in adult males is **sterility (infertility)**, a category of conditions related to diminished or absent sperm production. **Aspermatogenesis** is the inability to produce sperm; **aspermia** is the inability to produce semen; **oligospermia** is decreased sperm production. A man who is sterile is not necessarily impotent, and vice versa. Infertility is evaluated by a physician and treatment is based on the cause.

Common infections of the male reproductive organs include **balanitis**, inflammation of the glans penis; **orchitis**, inflammation of the testes; **epididymitis**, inflammation of the epididymis; and **prostatitis**, inflammation of the prostate gland. These inflammatory conditions are typically treated with antibiotics.

Phimosis is a narrow opening that prevents the foreskin from being drawn back over the head of the penis (glans), which may be congenital or caused by scarring from frequent infections. Surgery may be necessary to correct this condition.

Testicular carcinoma is found most commonly in the young adult population. It can affect one or both testicles and can be local or disseminated at diagnosis. It is treated by orchiectomy and chemotherapy.

Gynecomastia is a condition in which men develop an abnormal growth of fatty tissue in the breast. This is not a cause for concern except when the growth is excessive.

Table 14.3 lists terms and conditions relating to the male reproductive system that appear frequently in medical records and in other written and oral communications.

TABLE 14.3 Conditions Associated with the Male Reproductive System

Term		Meaning	Word Analysis	
aspermatogenesis	[ay-sper-mah-tO-**jen**-ah-sis]	failure of sperm production	*a-* *spermat/o* *-genesis*	no, not, without sperm formation, production
aspermia	[ah-**sper**-mee-ah]	ejaculation without seminal fluid or without sperm	*a-* *sperm/o* *-ia*	no, not, without sperm abnormal condition
balanitis	[bal-ah-**nI**-tis]	inflammation of the glans penis (head or tip of penis)	*balan/o* *-itis*	pertaining to the glans penis inflammation
benign prostatic hyperplasia	[bee-**nIn** pros-**tat**-ik hI-per-**play**-see-ah]	enlarged prostate tissue causing pressure on the urethra	*prostat/o* *hyper-* *-plasia*	protect increased formation
epididymitis	[ep-ih-did-ih-**mI**-tis]	inflammation of the epididymis	*-itis*	inflammation
hydrocele	[**hI**-drO-seel]	collection of fluid surrounding the testis within the scrotum	*hydr/o* *-cele*	pertaining to water hernia, protrusion
impotence	[**im**-pO-tens]	inability to achieve and/or maintain an erection of the penis, also known as *erectile dysfunction (ED)*		
oligospermia	[ol-ih-gO-**sper**-mee-ah]	decreased sperm in the ejaculate	*olig/o* *sperm/o*	too little sperm
orchitis	[or-**kI**-tis]	inflammation of the testis	*orchi/o* *-itis*	pertaining to the testes inflammation
Peyronie disease	[pah-rO-**nay**]	condition in which the penis is bent, curved during erection causing pain due to a decrease in blood flow to one side		
phimosis	[fI-**mO**-sis]	narrow opening that prevents the retraction of the foreskin over the head of the penis	*phimos*	muzzle
premature ejaculation		the rapid achievement of climax and ejaculation before or shortly after sexual penetration		
priapism	[**prI**-ah-piz-em]	prolonged erection	*Priapus*	Greek god of procreation
prostate cancer	[**prost**-ayt]	cancer within the prostate gland; most common cancer among men		
prostatitis	[pros-tah-**tI**-tis]	inflammation of the prostate	*prostat/o* *-itis*	protects inflammation
sterility	[stah-**ril**-ih-tee]	incapable of fertilization, also known as *infertility*	*sterilis*	barren
testicular torsion	[tes-**tik**-yoo-ler **tor**-shun]	rotation of the testis within the scrotum	*torsio*	twisting, rotation
testicular cancer		cancer of the testicles		
varicocele	[**vair**-ih-kO-seel]	varicose veins in the spermatic cord	*varic/o* *-cele*	dilated vein, varicosity hernia, protrusion
vesiculitis	[veh-**sik**-yoo-lI-tis]	inflammation of a vesicle, most commonly a seminal vesicle		

Infants

Abnormalities found in infancy include malposition of the urethral opening: **epispadias** (opening is on the top of the penis) and **hypospadias** (opening is on the underside of the penis). Other congenital anomalies of the male reproductive system include the following categories:

- Abnormalities of the testes, such as **anorchism** (congenital absence of testicles), **cryptorchism** (failure of one or both of the testicles to descend), and **polyorchism** (having more than two testicles);

- Abnormalities in the formation of the genitalia, such as **ambiguous genitalia** (the sex organs of the newborn are not completely developed and cannot be identified clearly) and **hermaphroditism** (the infant has both male and female sexual tissues).

Table 14.4 describes congenital anomalies of the male reproductive organs. Figure 14.5 illustrates some of these congenital malformations, as well as certain abnormalities that develop as a result of a disease process.

TABLE 14.4 Congenital Abnormalities of the Male Reproductive System

Term		Meaning	Word Analysis	
ambiguous genitalia	[am-**big**-yoo-us jen-ih-**tay**-lee-ah]	sex organs in a newborn that are not clearly male or female	*ambi- gen/i*	around, both sides being born, producing
anorchism	[an-**or**-kiz-em]	absence of the testes	*anorch/i*	without testes
cryptorchism	[krip-**tor**-kiz-em]	failure of one or both testicles to descend into the scrotal sac	*crypt/o orch/i*	hidden, concealed testes
epispadias	[ep-ih-**spay**-dee-as]	abnormality in which the urethral opening is on the dorsum of the penis	*epi- spadon*	on, above a tear, rip
hermaphroditism	[her-**maf**-rod-ih-tiz-em]	having both ovarian and testicular tissue; *pseudohermaphroditism* is the term used when the person displays either male or female sexual characteristics (e.g., male pseudohermaphrodite); also known as *hermaphrodism*	*Hermes* *Aphrodite* *pseud/o*	Greek god (Mercury), a male Greek goddess (Venus), a female false; denoting a resemblance
hypospadias	[hI-pO-**spay**-dee-as]	condition in which the urethral opening is located below the head of the penis)	*hypo spadias*	below; less a tear, rip
polyorchism	[pol-ee-**or**-kiz-em]	having more than two testicles, also known as *polyorchidism*	*poly orch/i (orchid/o)*	many testes

FIGURE 14.5 Abnormalities of the Male Reproductive Organs

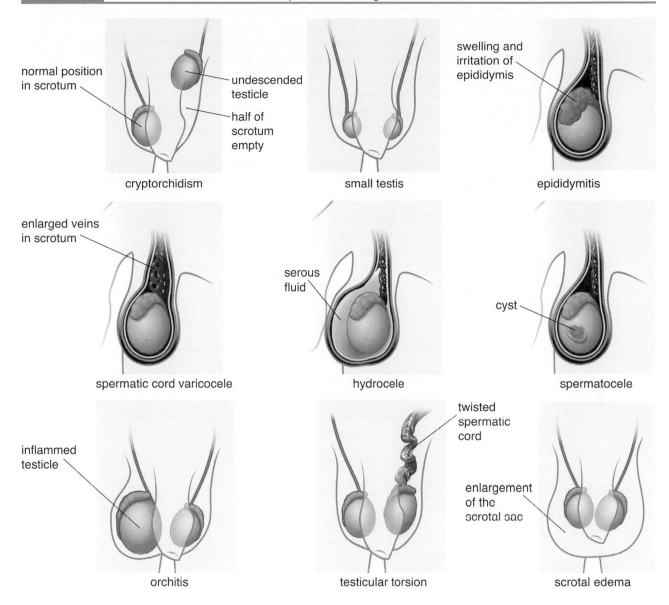

normal position in scrotum — undescended testicle — half of scrotum empty

cryptorchidism

small testis

swelling and irritation of epididymis

epididymitis

enlarged veins in scrotum

spermatic cord varicocele

serous fluid

hydrocele

cyst

spermatocele

inflammed testicle

orchitis

twisted spermatic cord

testicular torsion

enlargement of the scrotal sac

scrotal edema

Adolescents, Adults, and Seniors

Varicocele is a condition of varicose veins that form in the spermatic cord. The twisting and dilation of these vessels can decrease circulation to the testicle and decreased drainage into the spermatic cord. The scrotum can swell and take on the appearance of a "bag of worms" or a mass of varicose veins. A **hydrocele** is an accumulation of fluid surrounding the testicles that may cause swelling and discomfort.

A serious condition that often occurs in adolescence but that can also affect adults is **testicular torsion**. This occurs when the testicle twists, cutting off the blood supply to the testicle. Torsion is always an emergency and must be corrected surgically to prevent the testicular tissue from developing gangrene.

Problems associated with lack of or delayed maturation must be investigated and can indicate hormonal abnormalities or congenital malformation. Individuals pass through stages of puberty at different rates, according to their age at puberty.

Priapism, or prolonged erection, is a condition characterized by trapped blood in an erect penis. While it may be associated with sickle cell anemia or spinal cord injury, it may also occur with the use of drugs taken for erectile dysfunction. Immediate treatment is necessary to prevent residual damage. Depending on the cause, ice packs may relieve the condition, while more invasive procedures may be necessary in more severe cases.

Benign prostatic hyperplasia (BPH) occurs in men as they age. In this condition, the prostate gland becomes increasingly enlarged, squeezing the urethra that passes through it. The swollen prostate can cause painful, frequent, and/or difficult urination. BPH is often the reason older men will awaken several times during the night to urinate. Incomplete bladder emptying is often a problem.

Peyronie disease is the development of scar tissue that decreases blood flow to one side of the penis during an erection. It causes the penis to curve when erect rather than be straight. Intercourse may be not be possible depending on the direction and angle of the curve.

Prostate cancer is a malignant transformation within the prostate gland that is usually diagnosed in the older male. It can be treated with surgery (to remove the prostate), radiation (to shrink the tissue), medication, or a combination of all three. When diagnosed in more elderly patients it is often not treated. The rate of progression of prostate cancer is slow and in the very elderly, other age related illnesses are expected to be more of problem than this particular cancer.

Checkpoint 14.2

Answer the following questions to identify any areas of the section that you may need to review.

1. What condition describes a twisting of the testicle that requires emergency treatment?

   _____

2. Swelling due to an accumulation of fluid around the testicles within the scrotum is known as what condition?

   _____

3. What condition describes a child born with both male and female sex tissue?

   _____

Exercise 14.7   Word Analysis

Separate each word into its individual parts using hyphens. Identify the parts by type, writing a letter above each part (P = prefix, CF = combining form, S = suffix). Then define the term.

Term	Word Analysis	Definition
1. cryptorchism	_____	_____
2. polyorchism	_____	_____
3. anorchism	_____	_____
4. hydrocele	_____	_____
5. aspermia	_____	_____

Exercise 14.8   Comprehension Check

Select the correct medical term from the list to substitute for the underlined definition in each sentence. Write the correct term on the blank provided at the end of each sentence.

ambiguous genitalia	cryptorchism	phimosis
aspermia	epispadias	priapism
balanitis	circumcision	pseudohermaphroditism
benign prostatic hyperplasia	impotence	testicular torsion

1. The infant was born with <u>sex organs that are not clearly male or female</u>.

    _____

2. The child will require surgery for <u>failure of one or both of the testicles to descend into the scrotum</u>.

    _____

3. Surgery has already been scheduled for <u>condition where the urethral opening is on the upper side of the penis</u>.

    _____

4. The patient is a male <u>having both ovarian and testicular tissue, but displaying characteristics of only one gender</u>.

    _____

5. The <u>procedure to remove the foreskin from the penis</u> was performed several days after birth.

    _____

Exercise 14.9   Matching

Match the terms or abbreviations in column 1 with the definitions in column 2. Write the letter of the definition on the line beside the correct term.

1. _____ oligospermia

2. _____ balanitis

3. _____ hypospadias

4. _____ orchitis

5. _____ polyorchism

6. _____ aspermatogenic

7. _____ prostatitis

8. _____ hyperplasia

a. having more than two testicles

b. inflammation of the testicle or testicles

c. inflammation of the prostate

d. small or scanty amount of sperm

e. enlargement or excessive formation/development

f. inflammation of the glans penis

g. lacking formation of sperm

h. urinary meatus is displaced to the underside of the penis

Exercise 14.10   Word Building

Construct terms to match the definitions provided, using only suffixes *-itis*, *-ectomy*, and *-plasty*.

1. surgical repair of the vas deferens _____

2. inflammation of the epididymis _____

3. surgical repair of the glans penis _____

4. inflammation of the prostate _____

5. surgical removal of a portion of the vas deferens _____

Exercise 14.11   Spelling Check

Rewrite the misspelled terms, using the correct spelling, and then define the term. If the term is spelled correctly, write OK on the line beside the term and supply the definition.

1. _____ hydrocelle

_____

2. _____ phymosis

_____

3. _____ begnign prostetic hyperplasia

_____

4. _____ balanitis

_____

5. _____ oligiospermia

_____

Exercise 14.12   Word Maps

Complete the concept maps below by supplying the missing terms.

lack of production of sperm:

1.

term for male and female sex cells:

2.

deficient amount of sperm:

3.

male sex cell:

4.

female sex cell:

5.

absence of sperm:

6.

term for joined sex cells (fertilized egg):

7.

Diagnostic Tests and Examinations

During a physical examination, the physician palpates the testes to check for lumps or tenderness, inspects the urinary meatus (opening), and palpates the inguinal canal and prostate gland (in adults) to identify enlargement or other changes that may indicate disease. A **digital rectal exam (DRE)** is performed to evaluate the size, firmness, and nodularity of the prostate gland.

When physical examination of the prostate reveals an abnormality, it is important to test for prostate cancer with the **prostate-specific antigen (PSA)**. This blood test can help diagnose cancer of the prostate.

A blood test also can determine the amount of male hormones being secreted, for example, testosterone. **Semen analysis** calculates the amount of sperm that is ejaculated and evaluates sperm viability. Ultrasonography and CT scanning can identify structural abnormalities within the system. Table 14.5 lists common diagnostic procedures and tests for the male reproductive system.

TABLE 14.5 Diagnostic Tests and Procedures of the Male Reproductive System

Procedure	Description
digital rectal exam (DRE)	procedure performed to evaluate the size, firmness, and nodularity of the prostate gland
prostate-specific antigen (PSA)	blood test used to determine the presence of the antigen; its presence may be increased in both malignant or benign lesions of the prostate gland
semen analysis	seminal fluid examination that determines the number and viability of sperm in the semen; used during a fertility workup and after a vasectomy, also known as *sperm count*
testosterone levels test	blood test that measures the amount of testosterone secreted by the testes
ultrasonography or computed tomography (CT)	noninvasive diagnostic imaging test that uses high-frequency, inaudible sound waves to detect abnormalities in the prostate gland and the scrotum

Checkpoint 14.3

Answer the following questions to identify any areas of the section that you may need to review.

1. The PSA test may help diagnose benign or malignant lesions of which gland?

   _____

2. What noninvasive procedure is used to detect abnormalities of the prostate or scrotum?

   _____

3. What test is performed to help determine the cause of male infertility?

   _____

Treatments

Healthcare practitioners use predetermined guidelines to direct patient care. These guidelines, known as clinical practice guidelines and evidence-based practices, have been developed by the specialty societies based on past clinical research. They represent the treatment pathways that have achieved the best outcomes. Treatment decisions generally fall into three categories: surgical, clinical, and pharmacological.

Surgical treatments are generally invasive as they involve a puncture or an incision into the skin. *Clinical treatments* are generally noninvasive and involve nonsurgical techniques (e.g., physical therapy). *Pharmacological treatments* involve the utilization of medicines (drugs) to treat specific illnesses or diseases. Medication therapies are regulated by the Food and Drug Administration (FDA). To be approved by the FDA for use in the United States, every medicine must be backed by research studies that have shown the medication to be effective in its treatment of a given disease and has a tolerable safety profile. The following sections provide an overview of treatments common to the male reproductive system.

Surgical Treatments

One of the most common surgical procedures involving the male reproductive system is circumcision. **Circumcision** is the removal of all or part of the foreskin of the glans penis (see Figure 14.6). There are both benefits and risks to the circumcision procedure. The risks associated with the procedure include pain and a slight possibility of infection or continued bleeding. The American Academy of Pediatrics believes that having the procedure shortly after birth may decrease the risk of urinary tract infections and some sexually transmitted diseases. In recent years, the decision to have male babies circumcised has shifted to parents in consultation with a pediatrician. Parents base their decision on personal, religious, or cultural preferences.

An undescended testicle is repaired with a procedure called **orchidorrhaphy**, during which the testicle is affixed within the scrotum.

FIGURE 14.6 | Image of Penis, with and without Foreskin

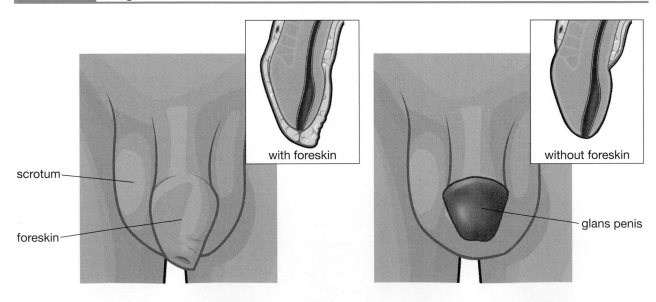

with foreskin

without foreskin

scrotum

foreskin

glans penis

A **vasectomy**, usually performed as a method of birth control, removes a section of the vas deferens to prevent sperm from exiting the body (thus preventing pregnancy). A **vesiculectomy** is the excision of all or part of the seminal vesicle. Table 14.6 lists common surgical procedures related to the male reproductive system.

TABLE 14.6 Surgical Treatments Associated with the Male Reproductive System

Treatment		Description
castration	[**kas**-tray-shun]	removal of both testes
circumcision	[sur-kum-**si**-shun]	removal of all or part of the foreskin
epididymotomy	[ep-ih-**did**-ih-**mot**-ah-mee]	incision into the epididymis to drain pus or other fluid
epididymovasostomy	[ep-ih-**did**-ih-mO-vahs-os-tah-mee]	surgical connection of the vas deferens to the epididymis
orchiopexy	[or-kee-O-**peck**-see]	procedure to bring down the undescended testicle and suture it into the scrotum, also known as *orchidopexy*
orchiectomy	[or-kee-**ek**-tah-mee]	removal of the testis (testes)
orchioplasty	[or-kee-O-**plas**-tee]	reconstruction of the testis
transurethral resection of the prostate (TURP)	[trans-yoo-**ree**-thral]	removal of all or part of the prostate gland; performed through the urethral opening
vasectomy	[vah-**sek**-tah-mee]	removal of a portion of the vas deferens
vasovasostomy	[vas-O-va-**sos**-tuh-mee]	surgical reunion of the vas deferens to create an opening to restore fertility, follows a previous vasectomy
vesiculectomy	[veh-sik-yoo-**lek**-tah-mee]	removal of the seminal vesicle

Pharmacological Treatments

Drugs used to treat problems of the male reproductive system include hormone replacement agents, erectile dysfunction therapy, and treatment for benign prostatic hyperplasia. Antibiotics are used when there is an infection in any of the organs or tissues of this system. Table 14.7 identifies common pharmacological treatments relating to the male reproductive system.

TABLE 14.7 Pharmacologic Agents Associated with the Male Reproductive System

Drug Class	Use	Generic Name	Brand Name
alpha blockers	treatment of BPH	doxazosin finasteride tamsulosin	Flomax
anti-impotence	assisting men with producing and/or maintaining an erection	tadalafil alprostadil (prostaglandin E$_1$) sildenafil vardenafil	Cialis Adcirca Caverject Injection MUSE Pellet Viagra Levitra
testosterone replacement hormone	replacement of the male hormone, testosterone	methyltestosterone testosterone transdermal patch testosterone transdermal gel	Android, Testred Androderm, Testoderm AndroGel

Soft Skills for Medical Professionals: Protecting Patient Privacy

Treating conditions and disorders of the male reproductive system can involve close contact with a patient's genital area. Maintaining a professional presence is extremely important to gain and keep the patient's trust. We must always remember to treat the patient with dignity and to respect their privacy. Proper draping and positioning can help protect that privacy. You want patients to be comfortable enough to ask any questions they have during treatment. Children should also be given the same respect. When possible, talk directly to the child rather than over the child to the parent.

Checkpoint 14.4

Answer the following questions to identify any areas of the section that you may need to review.

1. Why would a man undergo surgical removal of a portion of the vas deferens?

2. During a TURP procedure, which structure is all or partially removed?

3. What procedure removes the foreskin of the penis?

Abbreviations

In the medical field, information is generally recorded in medical charts and in electronic medical records and provided to healthcare workers in medical shorthand. It is important that healthcare professionals become familiar with the abbreviations utilized on a daily basis to successfully perform the duties assigned in a typical workday. Table 14.8 provides a list of common abbreviations used in reference to conditions, examinations, and treatments of the male reproductive system.

TABLE 14.8 Abbreviations Associated with the the Male Reproductive System

Abbreviation	Meaning
BPH	benign prostatic hyperplasia
DRE	digital rectal examination
ED	erectile dysfunction
PSA	prostate-specific antigen
STD	sexually transmitted disease
STI	sexually transmitted infection
TUR	transurethral resection
TURP	transurethral resection of the prostate gland; transurethral prostatectomy
VDRL	Venereal Disease Research Laboratory (test for syphilis, an STD)

Exercise 14.13 Word Analysis

Separate each word into its individual parts using hyphens. Identify the parts by type, writing a letter above each part (P = prefix, CV = combining form, S = suffix). Then define the term.

Term	Word Analysis	Definition
1. balanitis	_____	_____
2. spermatogenic	_____	_____
3. orchitis	_____	_____
4. vasectomy	_____	_____
5. hydrocele	_____	_____

Exercise 14.14 Comprehension Check

Read each sentence and select the most appropriate term from the two choices given. Underline your choice. You may need to use a medical dictionary for this exercise.

1. Mr. Masterson's testosterone/zygote level was evaluated.

2. A semen analysis/lumpectomy will be performed during the patient's fertility workup.

3. We will schedule a prostate-specific antigen test/circumcision on Mr. Smith to evaluate for prostate cancer.

4. Prostatic ultrasonography/orchidectomy will be performed in the morning to evaluate for BPH.

5. An epididymotomy/TURP will be necessary to remove the accumulated fluid.

Exercise 14.15 Matching

Match the abbreviations in column 1 with the meanings in column 2. Write the letter of the meaning on the line next to the abbreviation. You may need to use a medical dictionary.

1. _____ TURP

2. _____ BPH

3. _____ PSA

4. _____ STD

5. _____ VDRL

6. _____ TUR

a. benign prostatic hyperplasia

b. transurethral resection

c. Venereal Disease Research Laboratory (test for syphilis)

d. transurethral resection of the prostate

e. prostate-specific antigen

f. sexually transmitted infection

Exercise 14.16   Word Building

Supply the word parts to complete each term.

1. _____ectomy means surgical removal of the testes

2. _____ectomy means surgical removal of the prostate gland

3. _____ectomy means surgical removal of all or part of the seminal vesicle

4. _____urethral means through the urethra

5. _____ic means pertaining to the prostate

Exercise 14.17   Spelling Check

Check for misspelled terms and names in the list below. Make corrections by rewriting the word with the correct spelling. Then define it.

1. _____ transurthreal resetcion of the prostrate

   _____

2. _____ vassectomy

   _____

3. _____ orchioectomy

   _____

4. _____ semin alalysis

   _____

5. _____ doxasosine

   _____

Exercise 14.18   Word Maps

On the illustration below, identify the marked structures and write their names on the first line beside each item, then on the next lines write names of procedures performed on the structure.

structure: _____

procedures: _____

_____

_____ (abbreviation)

structure: _____

procedures: _____

_____

_____ (abbreviation)

structure: _____

procedures: _____

_____

_____ (abbreviation)

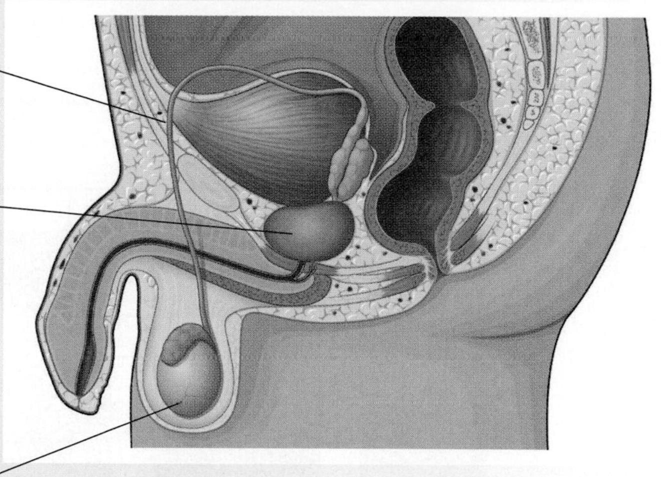

Chapter Review

After successfully completing this chapter, you should be able to correctly answer the following review questions. Answers are provided in the back of the text. Use this self-assessment opportunity to check your understanding of the content and determine whether you need to revisit any of the chapter's content.

Crossword Puzzle

Use the clues provided to fill in the puzzle with the correct terms. Enter one letter per square.

Across

1. tip of the penis
6. varicose veins in the spermatic cord
8. fluid containing secretions of male urogenital tract, including sperm
11. prefix meaning many
12. removal of vas deferens to prevent sperm from reaching the outside of the body
13. suturing of the testicle or testicles
15. semen

16. combining form meaning pertaining to the testes
18. corpus
21. procedure to remove the prepuce from the penis
22. word part meaning pouch, hernia
23. walnut-shaped gland that lies below the bladder

Down

2. male sex cell
3. andr/o
4. egg-shaped gland of male reproduction, source of sperm

5. tail
6. Latin for a vessel
7. undescended testicle or testicles
9. opening of the urinary meatus is on the dorsum of the penis
10. root meaning both
14. accumulation of fluid in the testicle or testicles
17. Latin for acorn
19. root meaning twin
20. scrotum

Matching

Match the following terms to their proper definitions.

1. _____ gonad
2. _____ fructose
3. _____ epididymis
4. _____ seminal vesicles
5. _____ prostate
6. _____ hydrocele
7. _____ scrotum
8. _____ sperm
9. _____ semen
10. _____ orchitis

a. glands that create a fluid containing sperm

b. walnut-shaped gland located below the bladder

c. inflammation of the testes

d. collection of fluid surrounding the testis within the scrotum

e. the sugar that provide energy for sperm

f. organ that produces male sex cells

g. male sex cell that fertilizes the ovum to produce a zygote

h. structure that matures, stores, and transports sperm

i. sac that contains testes

j. fluid that contains sperm

Identification

Correctly label the illustration by writing the correct terms on the lines provided.

1. _____
2. _____
3. _____
4. _____
5. _____
6. _____

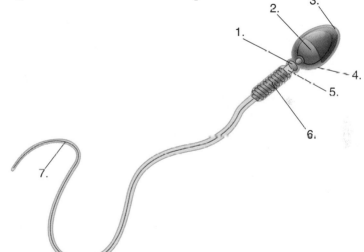

Abbreviations

Write out the meaning of each abbreviation on the line provided.

1. TURP _____
2. ED _____
3. TUR _____
4. PSA _____
5. BPH _____
6. DRE _____
7. STI _____
8. VDRL _____

Word-Building Challenge

Review the following list of terms. Apply your knowledge of the male reproductive system word parts to accurately identify the meaning of each new term. Write your answer on the line provided and then check your definition against the answer provided in the appendix.

1. epididymitis _____
2. ureterocele _____
3. hyperplasia _____
4. hyposecretion _____
5. prostatitis _____

Extension Activities

Complete the following activities as assigned by your instructor.

1. Research male infertility. Create a presentation that identifies at least three reasons for male infertility. For each, identify the cause and explain the available treatment options. What options are available to those who wish to conceive a child? Present your work to the class or as directed by your instructor.

2. Search the Internet for reputable medical journal articles discussing the link between the HCG hormone and the diagnosis of prostate cancer in men. What types of diagnostic examinations are used to assess HCG hormone levels in men? How are home pregnancy test kits being used? Is the use of a home pregnancy test an accepted method of diagnosis in the United States? Why or why not? Create an informational article to share your findings with the class.

3. Both quality and quantity of sperm production can be indicators of male infertility. Search the Internet to obtain three to five examples of conditions specifically associated with male infertility (e.g., congenital defects, absence of vas deferens, anti-sperm antibodies, retrograde ejaculation, duct obstruction, etc.). What types of fertility testing are generally used to identify the conditions selected? Create a PowerPoint presentation of five to ten slides outlining your findings.

4. Andropause, also known as *male menopause*, is a "debatable" condition among members of the medical community. Why is there controversy surrounding the validity of this condition in the healthcare arena? What types of signs and symptoms are documented to occur in men diagnosed with this condition? What hormone is said to be deficient? How is this condition generally diagnosed and treated? Share your findings with the class as directed by your instructor.

Student eResources

The Course Navigator learning management system that accompanies this textbook offers multiple opportunities to master chapter content, including end-of-chapter exercises, a glossary of key terms with audio pronunciations, games, pronunciation coach, and additional activities such as engaging with the BioDigital® Human.

The Female Reproductive System

> "A source of conflict for women everywhere is the pull between reproduction and production. Women worldwide have difficulty in balancing their dual roles as caregivers and providers."

—**Madeleine M. Kunin,** former Governor of Vermont

Translation Challenge

Read the following three excerpts from medical records and try to answer the questions that follow.

> This is a 25 y/o female, gravida 1, para 0, at 39 weeks.

> Endometriosis was causing dyspareunia and metrorrhagia.

> After having four children by natural childbirth, the woman had a uterine prolapse.

1. Define Gravida 1, para 0.

2. Endometriosis is an infectious condition. True or false?

3. Describe the symptoms associated with metrorrhagia.

4. What might be presenting symptoms in a patient with dyspareunia?

5. Define uterine prolapse.

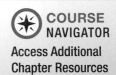
The female reproductive system is designed to produce the female egg cells (ova) and the hormones necessary for reproduction. The female reproductive system also includes the transportation system necessary for the fertilization and placement of the ova into the walls of the uterus. This chapter provides an overview of the main organs that make up the female reproductive system, explains the phases of the menstrual cycle, describes the conditions common to women's reproductive health, and identifies the tools used for diagnosis and treatment.

In the Know: Female Reproductive System Specialties

The medical care of the female reproductive system includes: **gynecology**, which includes the study of the organs, hormones, and diseases of the female reproductive system; **obstetrics**, the specialty that provides clinical care during pregnancy and the delivery of a baby; and **neonatology**, the study and treatment of the newborn infant, although today it usually refers to the premature infant. Family practitioners are also trained in obstetrics as it is an important part of family medicine. Some hospital systems permit family practitioners to oversee both vaginal and Cesarean deliveries.

Nurse midwives and doulas have also become an integral part of the reproductive process. Allied health professionals play a variety of roles in women's health. Ultrasound technicians, also known as *diagnostic medical sonographers*, are allied health professionals trained to use imaging equipment utilized to diagnose conditions of the female reproductive system. Medical assistants assist physicians with patient examinations and perform routine laboratory tests related to conditions associated with the male reproductive system. Phlebotomists are essential to laboratory procedures involving the collection and testing of blood.

Female Reproductive System Word Parts

As with other body systems, a core of combining forms serves as the source for most of the medical words associated with the female reproductive system. Table 15.1 lists common word parts, their meanings, and an example of each.

TABLE 15.1 Word Parts Associated with the Female Reproductive System

Prefix	Meaning	Example
an-	no, not, without	anovulation (condition in which the ovary fails to release an ovum [egg])
contra-	against	contraception (the prevention of pregnancy, conception)
dys-	painful	dysmenorrhea (painful menstruation, cramps)
hyper-	excessive, above	hypermenorrhea (excessively long or heavy menstrual bleeding lasting longer than 7 days)
hypo-	deficient, below	hypomenorrhea (extremely short or light menstrual bleeding)
neo-	new	neonatal (newborn)
pre-	before	prenatal (before birth)
poly-	many	polycystic ovary syndrome (endocrine system disorder in which ovaries are enlarged as a result of an accumulation of fluid)
pro-	forward	uterine prolapse (condition in which the uterus sags/falls into the vagina as a result of weakened pelvic muscles)
retro-	backward	retroverted uterus (condition in which the uterus tips backward toward the rectum as opposed to forward toward the belly)

Combining Form	Meaning	Example
cervic/o	cervix	cervical (pertaining to the lower part of the uterus)
colp/o	vagina	colposcopy (procedure to view the cervix, vagina, and vulva)
culd/o	rectouterine pouch	culdocentesis (medical procedure in which fluid is extracted from the rectouterine pouch to diagnose an abnormal condition, e.g., pelvic inflammatory disease and ectopic pregnancy)
cyst/o	bladder	oophorocystectomy (removal of an ovarian cyst)
embry/o	embryo	embryologist (one who specializes in the study of fertility and reproduction)
endometri/o	endometrium	endometrial (pertaining to the endometrium)
fibr/o	fiber	uterine fibroids (benign tumors that form on the walls of the uterus)
gyn/o, gynec/o	female	gynatresia (condition in which some part of the female genital tract is obstructed or occluded; could be a congenital defect)
hymen/o	hymen	hymenal (pertaining to the hymen)
hyster/o	uterus	hysteroscope (instrument used to view the inside of the uterus when abnormal bleeding is present and to assist with surgical procedures related to the uterus)
labi/o	lips	labia majora (the two folds of skin surrounding the opening of the vagina)
mast/o	breast	mastopexy (cosmetic procedure used to lift sagging breasts)
men/o, menstru/o	menses, menstruation	menstrual (pertaining to menstruation)
metr/o, metri/o	uterus	metrorrhagia (irregular vaginal bleeding)
o/o, ov/o	ovum, egg	oocyte (an immature egg cell produced in the ovary during the reproductive cycle)
olig/o	scanty, few	oligomenorrhea (abnormally light or infrequent menstrual flow)

Continues

oophor/o	ovary	oophoritis (inflammation of an ovary)
ovari/o	ovary	ovarian cyst (fluid-filled sac on the surface of an ovary)
papill/o	nipple	papillary adenoma (rare, benign breast tumor that arises under the nipple)
rect/o	rectum	rectal (pertaining to the rectum)
salping/o	fallopian tube	salpingitis (inflammation of the fallopian tubes)
thel/o	nipple	thelarche (the onset of breast development)
uter/o	uterus	uterine (related to the uterus)
vagin/o	vagina	vaginal (pertaining to the vagina)
vulv/o	vulva	vulvitis (inflammation of the vulva)

Suffix	Meaning	Example
-algia	pain	menorrhalgia (painful menstruation)
-arche	beginning	menarche (the first menstrual period)
-ation	process	menstruation (monthly process in which a woman's body sheds the lining of the uterus)
-cele	herniation, protrusion	cystocele (condition in which the bladder sags/falls into the vagina, which is weakened as a result of childbirth)
-dynia	pain	vulvodynia (condition in which chronic pain is present in the area around the vagina with no known cause)
-ectomy	removal, excision	mastectomy (removal of the breast)
-genesis	production, origin	oogenesis (development of a mature ovum)
-graphy	process of recording	mammography (imaging technique used to detect breast cancer, also known as a *mammogram*)
-itis	inflammation	cervicitis (inflammation of the cervix)
-ium	structure	perineum (in women, the area between the vagina and the rectum)
-lapse	fall	prolapse (the sinking of an organ of the body into another)
-lysis	freeing from adhesions	salpingolysis (surgical procedure in which scar tissue is removed from the fallopian tubes to increase the chances of fertility)
-osis	abnormal condition	endometriosis (painful condition in which the tissue that typically lines the inside of the uterus grows outside the uterus)
-pause	to stop, cease	menopause (the cessation of menstruation)
-pexy	fixation	colpopexy (surgical procedure used to correct vaginal prolapse)
-plasia	formation, development	endometrial hyperplasia (excessive buildup of cells in the lining of the uterus; can lead to uterine cancer)
-plasty	surgical repair	colpoplasty (surgical repair of the vagina)
-ptosis	drooping, falling	hysteroptosis (condition in which the uterus sags/falls into the vagina as a result of weakened pelvic muscles)
-rrhagia	bursting forth	menorrhagia (abnormally long or heavy menstrual periods)
-rrhea	discharge, flow	amenorrhea (an abnormal absence of menstruation)
-scopy	process of viewing	colposcopy (procedure used to biopsy the cervix/vagina)
-stomy	new opening	salpingostomy (surgical incision into a fallopian tube; often performed to remove an ectopic pregnancy)
-tomy	incision	episiotomy (an incision made in the perineum to enlarge the opening of the vagina during childbirth; also known as a *perineotomy*)
-tresia	opening	cervical atresia (mild form of agenesis in which the cervix is present but deformed and not functional)

Anatomy and Physiology

The female reproductive system includes structures that are both inside and outside the body. It is made up of the vagina, vulva, ovaries, fallopian tubes, uterus, and cervix (see Figure 15.1). The breasts also are considered part of the system, although they play no direct role in reproduction. Table 15.2 identifies anatomy and physiology terms related to the female reproductive system.

FIGURE 15.1 The Female Reproductive Organs

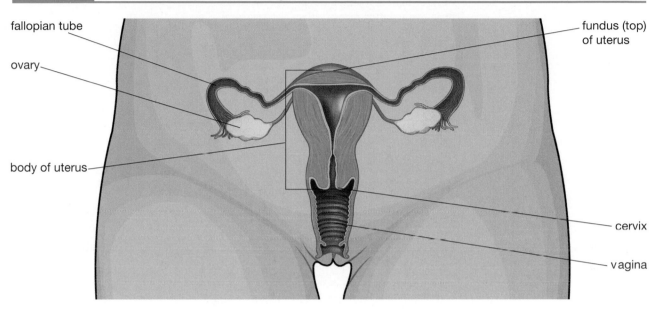

fallopian tube
ovary
body of uterus
fundus (top) of uterus
cervix
vagina

TABLE 15.2 Anatomy and Physiology Terms Associated with the Female Reproductive System

Term		Meaning	Word Analysis	
areola	[air-**ree**-O-lah]	small, darkened area around the nipple of each breast		
Bartholin's glands	[**bar**-tO-linz]	mucus-secreting glands that lubricate the vagina in preparation for and during intercourse	*Bartholin*	Danish anatomist Casper Bartholin
breasts		milk-secreting organs on the chest	*mamm/o, mast/o*	breast
cervix		lower part or neck of the uterus	*cervic/o*	neck, cervix
clitoris	[**klit**-uh-ris]	highly sensitive tissue located on the anterior surface of the vulva		
corpus albicans	[**kOr**-pus **al**-buh-kans]	a mass of scar tissue that develops once an ovum is not fertilized and the corpus luteum shrinks	*corpus* *albicans*	body white
corpus luteum	[**kOr**-pus **loo**-tee-um]	a mass of cells that forms following the release of a mature ovum; responsible for the secretion of estrogen and progesterone during pregnancy	*corpus* *luteum*	body yellow
endometrium	[en-dO-**mee**-tree-um]	the inner lining (layer) of the uterus	*endometri/o* *-um*	endometrium structure
estrogen	[**es**-trO-jen]	primary female sex hormone produced by the ovaries; important in reproduction		

Continues

Term		Meaning	Word Analysis	
fallopian tube	[ful-**loh**-pee-un]	ducts responsible for the transportation of ovum to the uterus	*fallopian*	Italian anatomist Gabriel Fallopius
fimbriae fimbria (sing.)	[**fim**-bree-ee]	fringes of tissue at the end of the fallopian tubes that help sweep a fertilized ovum into the uterus	*fimbria*	fringe
follicle		tiny sacs/glands found within an ovary that secrete hormones during menstruation		
follicle-stimulating hormone (FSH)		hormone secreted by the pituitary gland; stimulates the growth of ovarian follicles prior to the release of an ovum during menstruation; also regulates estrogen production		
fundus	[**fun**-dus]	the part of an organ farthest away from an opening	*fund/o*	fundus (base, bottom)
			-us	structure, thing
Graafian follicle	[**graf**-ee-an]	ripe or mature follicle that releases an ovum during the menstrual cycle	*Graafian*	Dutch physiologist Reijnier de Graaf
gynecology		the study of the female reproductive system	*gynec/o*	female
			-logy	study of
hymen	[**hI**-men]	membrane covering the external opening of the vagina	*hymen/o*	hymen
labia majora	[**lay**-bee-ah muh-**jor**-ah]	large, outer folds of skin surrounding the opening of the vagina	*labi/o*	labia, lips
			majora	large
labia minora	[**lay**-bee-ah muh-**nor**-ah]	small, inner folds of skin surrounding the opening of the vagina	*labi/o*	labia, lips
			minora	small
lactation	[**lak**-tay-shun]	milk production in response to hormonal secretion and the stimulation triggered by an infant sucking on its mother's nipples	*lacto*	milk
luteinizing hormone (LH)	[**loo**-tin-I-zing]	hormone secreted by the anterior pituitary gland; triggers ovulation (release of the ovum)		
menarche	[meh-**nar**-kee]	the first menstrual period	*men/o*	menstruation
			-arche	beginning
menses	[**men**-sis]	the monthly discharge of blood from the uterus; periodic shedding of the uterine lining that occurs approximately every 28 days	*men/o*	menstruation
menstrual cycle	[**men**-strahl]	female reproductive cycle; also known as a *period*		
mons pubis	[mahns **pew**-bis]	a pad of fatty tissue that lies over the pubic bones	*pub/o*	pubis, pelvic bone
myometrium	[mI-O-**mee**-tree-um]	the muscular layer of the uterus	*myometri/o*	myometrium
			-um	structure
neonate	[**nee**-O-nate]	newborn child, period lasting up to 4 weeks following birth	*neo-*	new
			nat/o	birth
obstetrics	[ahb-**steh**-triks]	study and treatment of pregnancy and childbirth		
oocyte	[**O**-uh-sIt]	immature ovum cell	*o/o*	egg, ovary
			cyt/o	cell
oogenesis	[**O**-uh-**jen**-ah-sis]	production of the female gametes (ova)	*o/o*	egg, ovary
			-genesis	production
ovulation	[ov-yoo-**lay**-shun]	phase of the menstrual cycle in which the ovum (egg) is released	*ov/o*	egg
			–ation	process

Continues

Term		Meaning	Word Analysis	
ovum	[**O**-vum]	egg, the female's reproductive cell	*ov/o, ov/i, o/o*	egg cell, ovary
perineum	[**pair**-ah-nee-um]	the area between the vagina and anus		
perimetrium	[pair-ah-**mee**-tree-um]	outer layer of the uterus; also called serosa	*perimetri/o -um*	perimetrium structure
progesterone	[prO-**jes**-tuh-rOn]	female sex hormone responsible for ovulation and menstruation		
salpinx	[**sal**-pinks]	fallopian tube	*salping/o*	fallopian tubes
symphysis pubis	[**sim**-fih-sis **pew**-bis]	joint between the pubic bones	*pub/o*	pubis, pelvic bone
urethra	[yoo-**ree**-thruh]	structure leading from the bladder to the urinary opening	*urethr/o*	urethra
uterus	[**yoo**-tuh-ris]	muscular organ in the pelvic cavity that houses the growing fetus	*uter/o, hyster/o*	uterus
vagina	[vah-**jI**-nah]	female sex organ, joins the cervix to the external genitals	*vagin/o*	vagina
vestibule	[**ves**-tih-byool]	the area between the labia minora and the opening of the vagina	*vestibul/o*	entrance
vulva	[**vul**-vah]	female external genitalia	*vulv/o*	vulva

External Genitalia and Vagina

The external genitalia (genitals) are a group of structures collectively known as the vulva (see Figure 15.2) and include the following:

- **mons pubis**, a pad of fatty tissue that lies over the **symphysis pubis** (the joint between the pubic bones);

- **labia majora** (translated as "large lips"), the large, outer folds of skin surrounding the opening of the vagina;

- **labia minora** ("small lips"), the small, inner folds of skin surrounding the opening of the vagina;

- **vestibule**, an area between the labia minora and the vaginal opening;

- **clitoris**, highly sensitive tissue located on the anterior surface of the vulva; and

- **Bartholin's glands**, located on either side of the vagina, whose function is to secrete a lubricating substance that prepares the vagina for intercourse.

The urethra, or urinary meatus, is located inferior to the clitoris and superior to the **vagina**, the female sex organ and birth canal that joins the cervix to the external genitals. The area between the vaginal opening and the anus is called the **perineum**. The opening to the vagina is sometimes covered by a membrane called the **hymen**. The vagina is located between the bladder and rectum, and extends inward about four inches.

Did You Know?

The hymen covers a portion of the vaginal opening and it can be torn during physical activity, cleansing of the vaginal area, or sexual intercourse.

FIGURE 15.2 The External Genitalia

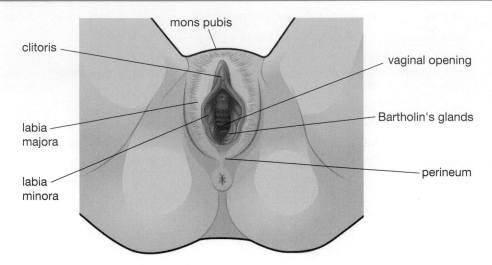

- mons pubis
- clitoris
- vaginal opening
- Bartholin's glands
- labia majora
- perineum
- labia minora

In the Know: pH Balance and Vaginal Health

Many are familiar with the pH scale from measuring the pH in swimming pools or reviewing the labels on bottles of shampoo. The body's pH is an indication of its health. While the organs throughout the body have varying pH levels, the body's overall pH should be 7 (that of healthy blood is 7.35). The pH scale measures acidity and alkalinity within an organism or substance and ranges from 0 (most acidic) to 14 (most alkaline). The ideal pH balance of a healthy vagina ranges between 3.5 and 4.7, quite similar to that of beer, soda, or orange juice. On the pH scale, this measurement is slightly acidic, as it serves as a defense mechanism to protect the vagina from infections. (A neutral pH level would be 7.) It is imperative to maintain the pH balance of the vagina to prevent vaginal issues, such as odor or discomfort, from occurring. Various factors can affect the pH of the vagina, ultimately affecting the balance of this environment. Blood from a woman's menstrual cycle, semen introduced during intercourse, and many hygiene products (such as soap) can raise the pH of the vagina to between 7.4 and 8.

Female Gonads

The actual organs of reproduction, or gonads, of the female are the **ovaries**, a pair of small oval-shaped glands located within the pelvic cavity on either side of the **uterus**, the organ that holds the fetus during pregnancy (see Figure 15.3). Ovaries are responsible for the production of the female's reproductive cell, which is called an **ovum**, or egg. The production of ova is called **oogenesis**. In addition to producing ova, the ovaries are responsible for the secretion of the hormones estrogen and progesterone beginning at puberty. Chapter 13 discussed the roles these particular hormones play in ovulation, menstruation, and reproduction.

To Note!

The female reproductive cell is called an ovum, or egg. The plural form of ovum is ova.

The two **fallopian tubes** are the transportation ducts for the ovaries, although they are not directly attached to the ovaries. The outer end of each fallopian tube is fan-shaped and has finger-like projections called **fimbriae** that are used to sweep fertilized eggs into the uterus to be implanted. The fertilization of an egg generally occurs in the fallopian tubes. The uterus is a small structure about the size of a pear that is composed mostly of muscle called the **myometrium**. The upper portion of the uterus is called the **body (corpus)**, and the lower portion is the **cervix**. The top of the uterus is called the **fundus**. The inside of the uterus is composed of a mucous membrane lining called the **endometrium**. It is in this membrane that a fertilized egg will implant itself and grow into a fetus. This lining is shed each month when a fertilized egg fails to implant. This is part of the menstrual cycle.

FIGURE 15.3 The Ovaries, Fallopian Tubes, and Uterus

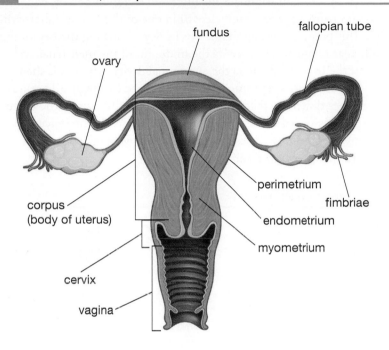

The Reproductive (Menstrual) Cycle

The reproductive cycle, also known as the *menstrual cycle*, is a repetitive sequence of hormonal activity that occurs in females who have reached puberty. This cycle repeats in approximately one-month intervals and is designed to prepare a woman's body for pregnancy.

Females are born with approximately one to two million **ovarian follicles** (large masses of cells that contain an immature female sex cell called an **oocyte**). As a girl grows to puberty, only about 400,000 follicles remain (called **primary follicles**). From this group 350 to 500 primary follicles develop fully to become mature follicles, or **Graafian follicles**. A Graafian follicle releases an egg during the ovulation phase of the menstrual cycle. All remaining eggs will die at menopause.

The average cycle takes place over 28 days and occurs in four phases.

Menses

Menses, also called the menstrual cycle, is the periodic shedding of the thickened uterine lining from the body through the vagina when pregnancy does not occur. Menstrual fluid is made up of blood and cells of the lining of the uterus. The average length of a menstrual period is between three days and one week.

Follicular Phase

The follicular phase starts on the first day of a woman's period. The pituitary gland in the brain stimulates the release of two hormones, follicle-stimulating hormone (FSH) and luteinizing hormone (LH). During the follicular phase, these hormones are responsible for stimulating the growth and maturation of approximately 20 eggs within the ovarian follicles and increasing the production of estrogen.

Ovulation Phase

Heightened levels of estrogen stimulate the increased secretion of LH, which triggers the release of an ovum from an ovarian follicle within one of the ovaries (alternating monthly). This phase starts approximately 14 days following the beginning of the follicular phase and represents the midpoint of the menstrual cycle. The ovum leaves the ovary and enters the abdominal cavity, where it is then captured by the fimbriae and swept into the fallopian tube (see Figure 15.4). The ovum continues down the fallopian tube and eventually rests in the uterus. If a woman has sexual intercourse during this phase, the presence of a thickened mucus produced by the cervix aids in the movement of the man's sperm toward the ovum for fertilization.

> **Did You Know?**
>
> The ovum is the largest cell in the body and can be seen with the naked eye.

FIGURE 15.4 Ovulation Phase

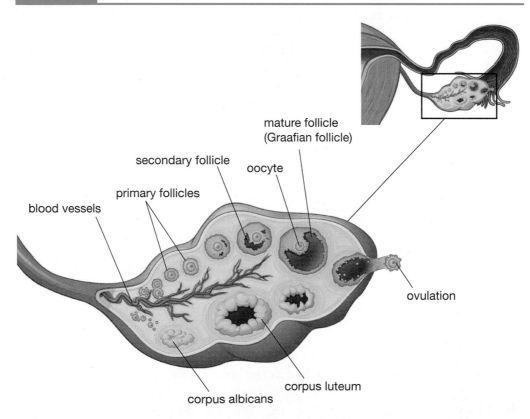

Luteal Phase

The luteal phase starts immediately following ovulation. Once an ovarian follicle has released its ovum, the empty shell shrinks to become the yellow-colored **corpus luteum**, the structure that secretes progesterone for about 11 days. Progesterone prepares the lining of the uterus for possible pregnancy, which will occur if the ovum is fertilized and implanted into the wall of the uterus. This process is called conception. If fertilization and implantation of the ovum are successful, then the corpus luteum continues to grow and secrete the various hormones needed for the pregnancy. The uterus will thicken and develop a rich blood supply to support fetal development. If conception does not occur within 13 days of ovulation, the corpus luteum shrinks and becomes the whitish structure called the **corpus albicans**. This transition results in the shedding of the uterine lining, also known as *menstruation*. The cycle of blood flow occurs approximately every 21 to 28 days and lasts from 3 to 7 days. Menstruation begins near the time of **puberty**, the onset of which varies from about age 10 to age 16. Menstruation continues monthly from the first period (**menarche**) until the time when estrogen and progesterone secretion diminishes (**menopause**), beginning at about age 50.

The 28-day menstrual cycle is divided into four phases, as shown in Figure 15.5.

What's in a Word?

The word *menarche* is formed by the word parts *men/o* (meaning "menses, menstruation") and *-arche* (meaning "beginning").

FIGURE 15.5 Phases of the Menstrual Cycle

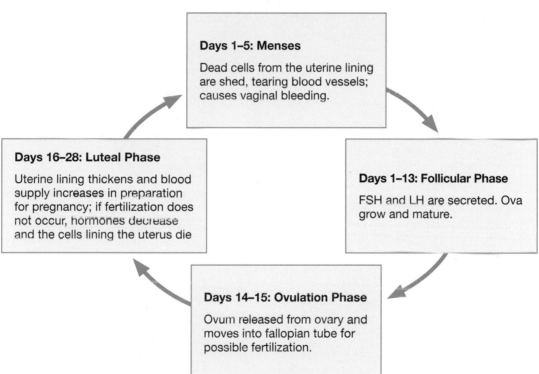

Days 1–5: Menses

Dead cells from the uterine lining are shed, tearing blood vessels; causes vaginal bleeding.

Days 1–13: Follicular Phase

FSH and LH are secreted. Ova grow and mature.

Days 14–15: Ovulation Phase

Ovum released from ovary and moves into fallopian tube for possible fertilization.

Days 16–28: Luteal Phase

Uterine lining thickens and blood supply increases in preparation for pregnancy; if fertilization does not occur, hormones decrease and the cells lining the uterus die

Breasts

The female breasts contain fatty tissue and specialized glands that produce milk during and after pregnancy. Milk production occurs in response to hormonal secretion and the stimulation triggered by the infant's sucking on the mother's nipples. The process is called lactation (from the Latin *lacto*, meaning "milk"). In addition to glandular tissue, the breasts (see Figure 15.6) contain **lactiferous sinuses**, which hold the milk, and **lactiferous ducts**, which carry the milk to openings in the **nipples** (the pigmented projection of the breast).

FIGURE 15.6 | Breast Structure

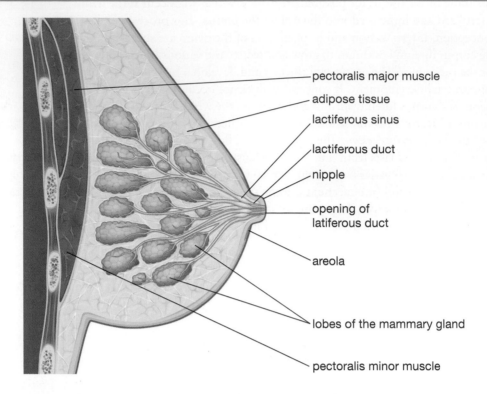

pectoralis major muscle

adipose tissue

lactiferous sinus

lactiferous duct

nipple

opening of
latiferous duct

areola

lobes of the mammary gland

pectoralis minor muscle

Checkpoint 15.1

Answer the following questions to identify any areas of the section that you may need to review.

1. During which phase of the menstrual cycle is the ovum released from the ovary and transported from the fallopian tube to the uterus for possible fertilization?

   _____

2. What is the medical term for the large, outer folds of skin surrounding the opening of the vagina?

   _____

3. What is the name of the small, darkened area around the nipple of each breast?

   _____

Exercise 15.1   Word Analysis

On the line beside each term, write the combining form that refers to the structure.

1. uterus _____

2. vagina _____

3. cervix _____

4. ovary _____

5. rectum _____

Exercise 15.2   Identification

Label the illustration by placing the corresponding letter (A–E) on the line provided beside each anatomical label.

1. _____ body of uterus

2. _____ fallopian tube

3. _____ vagina

4. _____ cervix

5. _____ ovary

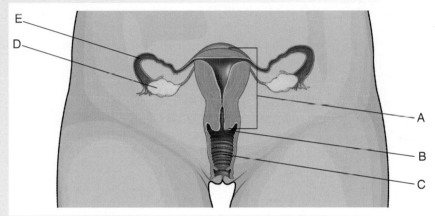

Exercise 15.3   Comprehension Check

Circle the correct term(s) to complete each sentence. Be sure to read the entire sentence and use the context of the sentence to make your selection.

1. The vestibule/vulva is the area between the labia minora and the opening of the vagina.

2. The mons pubis/pelvum lies just over the zygote/symphysis pubis.

3. Skin covering the labia majora/labia minora is pigmented and has hair on the outer surface.

4. Prior to their removal, the estrogens/ovaries were positively identified.

5. The gynecology/myometrium was intact, and the endometrium/puberty was undisturbed.

Exercise 15.4   Matching

Match the definition to the correct term. Write the correct term on the line next to the definition.

Bartholin's   corpus luteum   fimbriae
cervix   fallopian   hymen

1. _____ membranous skin fold that may cover the vagina

2. _____ mucus-secreting glands on either side of the vagina

3. _____ lower neck-like portion of the uterus

4. _____ tube that the ovum passes through to the uterus

5. _____ fringe-like structures at the end of the fallopian tubes

6. _____ yellow body formed in the ovary following the rupture of an ovarian follicle

Exercise 15.5   Word Building

Write the missing word parts in the blanks to create the correct term for the definition given.

1. _____ian means pertaining to the ovaries

2. _____al means pertaining to the cervix

3. _____itis means inflammation of the endometrium

4. _____rrhea means faulty, difficult or painful menstruation

5. a_____ means absence of menstruation

Exercise 15.6   Comprehension Check

Circle the correct word from the choices given.

1. The follicles/follicle had ruptured and the egg/eggs were/was released.

2. All of the fimbria/fimbriae were/was malformed.

3. The cervices/cervix of all the women were/was also of similar size.

4. The vulva/vulvae of both infants were/was atrophied.

5. Twelve ovums/ova were/was harvested and processed for freezing.

Exercise 15.7 Word Maps

The following diagram illustrates the development of an ovum and its ovarian follicle. Complete the diagram by supplying the missing terms.

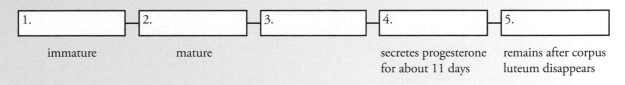

1.		2.		3.		4.		5.

immature   mature   secretes progesterone   remains after corpus
                                                                             for about 11 days   luteum disappears

Conditions

Breast cancer is the second-most common cancer in women in the United States; an average of 230,000 new cases are diagnosed annually. With early detection, attributable to the identification of a lump during a BSE (breast self-exam) or mammogram, the five-year survival rate is over 90 percent. **Ovarian cancer** is a type of cancer that begins in the ovaries. While ovarian cancer accounts for less than 3% of cancer diagnoses among women in the United States, it causes more deaths than any other cancer of the female reproductive system. This is attributable to the lack of early detection. Ovarian cancer is often undetected until it has spread from the ovaries to the pelvis and abdomen.

Endometriosis is a painful condition in which the tissue that typically lines the inside of the uterus grows outside the uterus (see Figure 15.7). Symptoms include severe menstrual pain (cramps), abnormal bleeding,

> **To Note!**
>
> Endometriosis can affect the ovaries, fallopian tubes, bowels, or the tissue lining the pelvis.

FIGURE 15.7 **Endometriosis**

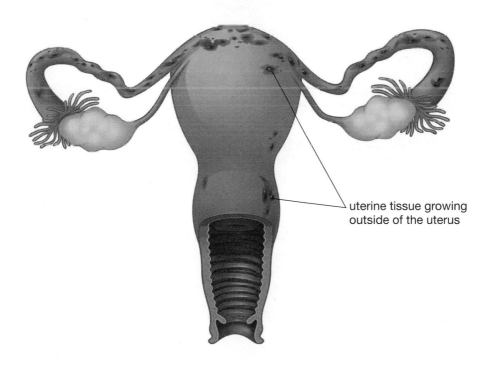

uterine tissue growing outside of the uterus

infertility, and painful intercourse (**dyspareunia**). Another common disorder is **pelvic inflammatory disease (PID)**, an infection of a woman's reproductive organs that often leads to infertility. PID can be a result of an untreated sexually transmitted infection (STI) and is often diagnosed in conjunction with acute salpingitis. **Salpingitis** is the inflammation and infection of the fallopian tubes. STIs are discussed in greater detail in Chapter 16.

Fibroids are firm, mobile, and painless nodules that form within the lining of a woman's uterus (see Figure 15.8). Fibroids are usually benign and are found most commonly in 30- to 45-year-old women. Symptoms of fibroids include heavy, prolonged menstrual bleeding and pelvic pain.

FIGURE 15.8 Fibroids

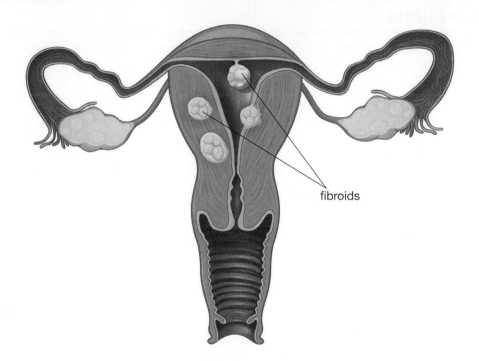

fibroids

Human papillomavirus (HPV) is an STI that is characterized by small growths on the genitalia. Certain types of HPV are associated with increased risk of cervical cancer; therefore, frequent Pap smears are recommended. The Gardasil vaccine is also recommended for adolescent girls and boys to aid in the prevention of four strands of HPV known to cause cervical cancer. Other common STIs include gonorrhea, syphilis, herpes, hepatitis, HIV, and chlamydial infections. Table 15.3 lists conditions pertaining to the female reproductive system.

TABLE 15.3 Conditions Associated with the Female Reproductive System

Term		Meaning	Word Analysis	
agenesis (vaginal)	[ay-**jen**-eh-sis]	absence of the vagina; failure of formation of the vagina	*a-*	without
			genesis	production
anovulation	[an-ov-yoo-**lay**-shun]	failure of an ovary to release an ovum	*an-*	not
			ovul/o	ovum
			-ation	process

Continues

Term		Meaning	Word Analysis	
atresia (cervical)	[ah-**tree**-zhah]	absence of the cervical opening	*a-*	without
			-tresia	an opening
breast cancer		cancer that forms in the cells of the breasts		
cervicitis	[sur-vih-**sI**-tis]	inflammation of the cervix	*cervic/o*	cervix
			-itis	inflammation
climacteric	[klI-**mak**-ter-ik/ klI-mak-**ter**-ik]	term for menopause		
cystocele	[**sis**-tO-seel]	condition involving a hernia of the bladder that pushes it into the vagina	*cyst/o*	relating to the bladder
			-cele	a hernia; swelling
dyspareunia	[dis-pah-**roo**-nee-ah]	pain during sexual intercourse	*dys-*	painful, difficult
endometrial cancer	[en-dO-**mee**-tree-ul]	most common type of uterine cancer, begins in the inner lining of the uterus, cause is unknown		
endometriosis	[en-dO-mee-tree-**O**-sis]	benign condition in which there is aberrant uterine tissue growing outside the uterine wall	*end/o*	within
			metr/o	uterus
			-osis	condition
endometritis	[en-dO-mee-**trI**-tis]	inflammation of the inner layer of the uterus	*endometri/o*	endometrium
			-itis	inflammation
endometrium	[en-dO-**mee**-tree-um]	mucous membrane layer of the uterine wall	*end/o*	within
			metr/o	uterus
			-ium	tissue or structure
fallopian tube adhesions		the presence of scar tissue binding the fallopian tubes together and resulting in infertility		
fibroids	[**fI**-broyds]	firm, mobile, nonmalignant nodules in the uterine wall, also known as *myomas*	*fibr/o*	pertaining to fibroid tissue
human papillomavirus	[pap-ih-**lO**-mah-vI-res]	a sexually transmitted disease that is associated with small growths on the genitalia	*papula*	pimple
			-oma	tumor
hysteroptosis (uterine prolapse)	[his-tur-op-**tO**-sis]	drooping of the uterus into the vagina	*hyster/o*	uterus
			-ptosis	drooping/sagging
leukorrhea	[loo-kuh-**ree**-uh]	white or yellow discharge of mucus from the vagina	*leuk/o*	white
			-rrhea	discharge, flow
mastitis	[mah-**stI**-tis]	inflammation of the breast	*mast/o*	breast
			-itis	inflammation
mastodynia	[mas-tO-**din**-ee-ah]	breast pain and tenderness, also known as *mastalgia*	*mast/o*	breast
			-dynia	pain
menarche	[men-**ar**-kee]	onset of menses (the first menstrual period)	*men/o*	pertaining to the menses
			-arche	first
menopause	[**men**-O-pawz]	period of time when a woman's hormones are decreasing, causing many changes	*men/o*	pertaining to the menses
ovarian cancer		cancer that forms in the ovaries, often goes undetected and spreads to the pelvis and abdomen		
ovarian cyst	[O-vair-ee-in]	a solid or fluid-filled sac or mass within or on the surface of an ovary	*ovari/o*	egg, ovum
			-an	pertaining to
oophoritis	[O-off-O-**rI**-tis]	inflammation of an ovary	*oophor/o*	ovary
			-itis	inflammation

Continues

Term		Meaning	Word Analysis	
myomas	[my-**O**-maz]	firm, mobile, nonmalignant nodules in the uterine wall, also known as *fibroids*	*myo-* *-oma*	muscle tumor
polycystic ovary syndrome (PCOS)		condition of the endocrine system affecting a woman's hormone levels, menstrual cycles, and ovulation	*poly-* *cyst/o* *-ic*	many cysts pertaining to
puberty	[**pyoo**-bur-tee]	onset of changes in the body that herald the physiologic maturity of the person		
rectocele	[**rek**-tO-seel]	prolapse of the rectum against the vaginal wall, bulge of tissue may protrude through the vaginal opening	*rect/o* *-cele*	pertaining to the rectum hernia; swelling
retroverted uterus (retroflexed, uterine displacement)		condition in which the uterus tips backward toward the rectum as opposed to forward toward the belly	*retro-* *uter/o*	backward uterus
salpingitis	[sal-pin-**jI**-tis]	inflammation of the fallopian tube(s)	*salping/o* *-itis*	a tube inflammation
sexually transmitted infection (STI)		viral or bacterial infections that are transmitted between sexual partners; also known as *sexually transmitted disease (STD)*		
speculum (sing.)	[**spek**-yoo-lem]	instrument that is inserted into an orifice to provide visualization		
thelarche	[thee-**lar**-kee]	beginning of breast development	*thel/o* *-arche*	nipple first
uterine prolapse	[**prO**-laps]	the sinking of an organ into another orifice	*pro-* *-lapse*	forward fall
vaginal prolapse	[**prO**-laps]	drooping, sagging of the vagina	*pro-* *-lapse*	forward fall
vaginitis	[va-jin-**nI**-tis]	inflammation of the vagina	*vagin/o* *-itis*	vagina inflammation
vulvitis	[vul-**vI**-tis]	inflammation of the vulva	*vulv/o* *-itis*	vulva inflammation
vulvodynia	[vul-vO-**din**-nee-ah]	chronic pain of the vulva	*vulv/o* *-dynia*	vulva pain
vulvovaginitis	[vul-vO-va-jin-**nI**-tis]	inflammation of the vulva and vagina	*vulv/o* *vagin/o* *-itis*	vulva vagina inflammation

Infants

Congenital anomalies that may be present in the newborn female include absence of the vagina (vaginal **agenesis**) and absence of the cervix (cervical **atresia**). A rare congenital defect is the presence of a double uterus (uterus didelphys). The uterus in a female fetus begins as two small tubes that generally join together during development. The failure of these tubes to join completely results in uterus didelphys. A female with this condition can have a single cervix that opens into one vagina or that can even develop two vaginas. **Ambiguous genitalia** is a rare condition in which the external genitals of an infant cannot be clearly identified as male or female. **Hermaphroditism** is a condition in which an individual possesses both male and female reproductive organs. Unless there is a congenital defect of the external genitalia, problems with the internal structures are rarely diagnosed until adolescence, when the girl does not develop appropriately during puberty, or adulthood, when the woman experiences problems with pregnancy and childbirth.

Adolescents

Puberty is marked by physical growth and sexual maturity. During puberty, young girls begin to develop secondary sex characteristics, beginning with breast development (called **thelarche**) and the appearance of pubic hair. For both males and females, a physical examination at this time includes an evaluation of sexual development according to the Tanner Scale. The **Tanner Scale**, also known as the *Normal Sexual Maturity Rating*, is a tool used to define physical measures of development based on external primary and secondary sex characteristics. Problems associated with lack of or delayed maturation must be investigated and can indicate hormonal abnormalities or congenital malformation. Individuals pass through Tanner's stages at different rates, according to the age at which puberty began. Recall that most adolescent girls reach menarche (the first menstrual period) between the ages of 10 and 16.

Several problems can occur with the menstrual period (see Table 15.4).

> **What's in a Word?**
>
> Most menstruation terms are formed by adding a prefix or suffix to the word parts *men/o* ("menses"), *-rrhagia* ("discharge"), and *-rrhea* ("flow").

TABLE 15.4 Abnormalities Pertaining to the Menstrual Period

Term		Meaning	Word Analysis	
amenorrhea	[ah-men-O-**ree**-ah]	absence of menses	*a-*	without
			men/o	menses (menstruation)
			-rrhea	flow
dysmenorrhea	[dis-men-O-**ree**-ah]	painful or difficult menstruation (period)	*dys-*	painful, difficult
			men/o	menses
			-rrhea	flow
hypermenorrhea	[hI-pur-men-O-**ree**-ah]	long or excessive bleeding during period	*hyper-*	increased
			men/o	menses
			-rrhea	flow
hypomenorrhea	[hI-pO-men-O-**ree**-ah]	short or decreased bleeding during period	*hypo-*	decreased
			men/o	menses
			-rrhea	flow
menometror-rhagia	[**men**-O-**meh**-trO-**rah**-zhah]	irregular or excessive bleeding during and between periods	*men/o*	menses
			metr/o	uterus
			-rrhagia	discharge
menorrhagia	[men-O-**rah**-zhah]	increased or excessive menstrual flow	*men/o*	menses
			-rrhagia	discharge
menorrhalgia	[men-O-**ral**-zhah]	painful menstruation	*men/o*	menses
			-rrhea	flow
			-algia	pain
metrorrhagia	[met-rO-**ray**-zhah] [met-rO-**rah**-zhah]	irregular bleeding between periods	*metr/o*	uterus
			-rrhagia	flow
oligomenorrhea	[ol-ih-gO-men-O-**ree**-ah]	abnormally light or infrequent menstrual flow	*olig/o*	little
			men/o	menses
			-rrhea	flow

Adults

The cervix of the female varies with the woman's age and the number of pregnancies she has had. Variations in the size, location, and texture of the cervix can be used to identify abnormalities due to menstruation, pregnancy, hormonal imbalance, and vulnerability to dysplasia (the development of precancerous cells).

What's in a Word?

The term *gravida* is pronounced "**grav**-ih-dah" and the term *para* is pronounced "**pair**-ah."

The term for pregnancy is *gravida*, which refers to the number of times a woman has been pregnant. *Para* (from the Latin word *pario*, meaning "to bring forth") refers to the number of births a woman has had. When caregivers refer to the number of pregnancies and births a woman has had, they use gravida and para to identify this information. For example, a medical report that reads "Patient is a 34 y/o female, gravida 1, para 0" indicates that the woman has been pregnant once before, but has had no live births. The statement "gravida II, para II" on a medical report indicates that the patient has been pregnant twice and has given birth twice.

See Table 15.5 for further explanation of these terms. Pregnancy and childbirth will be discussed in more detail in Chapter 16.

TABLE 15.5 Pregnancy and Birth Designations

Terminology for Pregnancies	Meaning
gravida I	1 pregnancy
gravida II	2 pregnancies
primigravida	first pregnancy
nulligravida	a woman who has never been pregnant
multigravida	two or more pregnancies
Terminology for Births	Meaning
para 0	no live births (may have experienced a miscarriage or stillbirth*)
para II	two live births
primipara	a woman who has delivered her first baby
nullipara	a woman who has never delivered a child
multipara	a woman who has delivered more than one baby

*Miscarriage is spontaneous abortion or pregnancy loss before the 20th week of pregnancy. It most often occurs prior to the 12th week of pregnancy. Stillbirth is when a baby is born dead after 20 weeks of pregnancy.

Seniors

As a woman ages, changes in the strength and durability of her pelvic muscles can cause **cystocele**, which is when the bladder pushes against or protrudes into the vagina; **uterine prolapse**, in which the uterus protrudes into the vagina; and **rectocele**, in which the rectum protrudes into the vagina. Weakness in musculature can be a result of age and/or a result of the strain of childbirth and delivery.

Many changes occur as a result of decreasing hormone levels in the aging female. This is known as **menopause** or **climacteric**. It is characterized by irregular periods that eventually cease altogether (the transition phase between regular menstrual periods and the absence of menstrual cycles is known as *perimenopause*). The ovaries stop producing progesterone and estrogen. Table 15.6 summarizes the changes associated with the menopause. Secondary symptoms include hot flashes, night sweats, and mood swings. Psychological effects of menopause include irritability, lack of motivation sadness, anxiety, fatigue, difficulty concentrating, aggressiveness, and changes in mood.

TABLE 15.6 Physiologic Changes Associated with Menopause

Anatomy	Change
external genitalia	decreased fat on mons pubis; decreased pubic hair; decrease in size of labia and clitoris
ovaries	decrease in size, leading to heavy and irregular bleeding that eventually ceases
uterus	prone to prolapse or protrusion due to weakened ligaments; shrinks in size as a result of decreased myometrium
vagina	decreased levels of estrogen and progesterone lead to vaginal dryness and discomfort during sexual intercourse; walls thin; becomes shorter and narrower

Checkpoint 15.2

Answer the following questions to identify any areas of the section that you may need to review.

1. What are two secondary sex characteristics developed during puberty?

   _____

   _____

2. What does the phrase "gravida II, para 1" indicate?

   _____

3. What condition is characterized by the decrease in hormone levels in the aging female?

   _____

Exercise 15.8 Word Analysis

In the following terms, identify the root by drawing a box around it. Write the definition for each root, and then the definition for the entire term.

Term	Root Word Definition	Term Definition
1. thelarche	_____	_____
2. metrorrhagia	_____	_____
3. oligomenorrhea	_____	_____
4. endometriosis	_____	_____
5. salpingitis	_____	_____

Exercise 15.9   Comprehension Check

Circle the correct term from the two choices in each sentence.

1. Cervical amenorrhea/atresia was noted at the time of the examination.

2. A speculum/rectocele was inserted into the vaginal opening.

3. Menopause/puberty is marked by increased physical growth.

4. The patient reports dysmenorrhea/dysmetrosis for the past three months.

5. The doctor prescribed pain medication to treat her menorrhagia/menorrhalgia.

Exercise 15.10   Matching

Select the term from column 1 to match the definition in column 2. Write the letter of your selection on the line beside the correct term.

1. _____ cystocele

2. _____ menarche

3. _____ salpingitis

4. _____ speculum

5. _____ vaginal agenesis

a. inflammation of the fallopian tubes

b. protrusion of the bladder into the vagina

c. onset of menses (the first menstrual period)

d. absence of the vagina

e. instrument used to visualize the vagina and cervix

Exercise 15.11   Word Building

Use prefixes, roots, combining vowels, and suffixes to create the medical term for each definition. Write the term in the space beside the definition.

1. painful or difficult menstruation   dys_____

2. increased or excessive bleeding during period   _____rrhea

3. irregular bleeding between periods   metro_____

4. radiological examination of the breasts   _____gram

5. process of ovulating   _____ion

Exercise 15.12   Spelling Check

From the choices given, circle the correct plural or singular form for each word.

1. The external genital/genitalia are/is normal.

2. Several fibroid/fibroids were/was palpable in the uterine wall.

3. There is one specula/speculum in the examining room.

4. Sexually transmitted infections/infection are/is on the increase.

5. The abdomen was opened and the left salpinx/salpinges were/was identified.

6. Both breasts/breast are palpated for lumps and other changes during the physical examination.

7. Sex hormones trigger the fimbriae/fimbria to sweep the ovary into the fallopian tubes.

8. Anovulation is the failure of the ovary to release ova/ovum over a period of three months or longer.

Diagnostic Tests and Examinations

Examination of adult female reproductive organs includes the breasts and internal and external genitalia. The physician may first perform a breast exam to check for the presence of any masses or tenderness within the breasts. Next, the woman is draped with a sheet and placed in lithotomy position. Recall that this is the position in which the patient is lying on her back with the hips and knees flexed and the thighs apart. The lithotomy position is often used for vaginal examinations (which can include Pap smears) and childbirth. The external genitalia are inspected and then an instrument called a **speculum** is inserted into the vaginal opening to allow visualization and palpation of the internal genitalia.

The examiner performs a bimanual ("two hands") examination of the vagina and cervix, inserting one or two fingers of a gloved and lubricated hand into the vagina and placing the other hand on the patient's abdomen. The examination allows the physician to assess the size, shape, and position of the uterus, and may aid in the discovery of any masses, abnormalities, or tenderness.

Laboratory tests of the female reproductive system include blood tests for measuring hormone levels. These tests can determine proper functioning at all stages of life, including childhood, adolescence, pregnancy, and menopause.

Procedures involve all the organs of the reproductive system, including the external genitalia and the internal structures. **Dilation and curettage (D&C)** is performed to obtain tissue from the inside of the uterus for examination. The D&C is most commonly performed to evaluate and treat abnormal uterine bleeding. In the procedure, the cervix is dilated and a curette is used to obtain uterine scrapings, which are then studied under the microscope to determine if diseased cells are present. A **colposcopy** is ordered when there is an abnormal Pap smear. Tissue is removed and a biopsy is performed.

The adult female should have an annual examination by a gynecologist, family practitioner, nurse midwife, or nurse practitioner. In addition to palpating and visualizing the reproductive organs, the physician performs an endocervical swab called the **Pap (Papanicolaou) smear** to screen for cervical cancer. A **mammogram** is an X-ray of the breasts to screen for cancer in women with no signs or symptoms of the disease. Mammograms are part of the routine examination for women. The American Cancer Society recommends the first mammogram screening at age 45, then annually through age 54, and dropping to every two years for women 55 and older. The American College of Obstetrics and Gynecologists and the American College of Radiology recommend annual mammograms starting at age 40. Note that a family history of breast cancer classifies women as high risk and warrants earlier screenings at more frequent intervals.

Table 15.7 summarizes the major tests and procedures relating to the female reproductive system.

TABLE 15.7 Female Reproductive System Tests, Examinations, and Diagnostic Tools

Test/Examination	Description
cervicography (cervigram)	imaging technique used to detect cervical cancer
colposcopy	diagnostic procedure used to perform a biopsy of the cervix and vagina
culdocentesis	laboratory tests in which fluid is extracted from the rectouterine pouch to detect dysplasia
culdoscopy	diagnostic tool used to perform a biopsy of the Douglas cul-de-sac
hormone levels	laboratory tests used to measure the presence of specific hormones in blood, urine, or body tissues; used to diagnose a variety of conditions common to the female reproductive system
hysterosalpingography (HSG)	X-ray in which a contrast dye is used to provide an image of the uterus and fallopian tubes
hysteroscopy	instrument used to view the inside of the uterus when abnormal bleeding is present (diagnostic) or when removing fibroids and polyps from the uterus
laparoscopy	diagnostic tool used to perform an ovarian biopsy
mammogram	X-ray of the breasts to screen for cancer in women with no signs or symptoms of the disease; part of the routine examination for women over the age of 40
Pap smear	procedure in which endocervical cells are collected and screened for cervical cancer
pelvic sonography (transvaginal)	use of high-frequency sound waves to create an image of the pelvic area, with or without the use of a probe

Soft Skills for Medical Professionals: Managing Conflicts

Your ability to work well with patients, coworkers, and supervisors is directly related to your career success. Excellent communication and self-management skills will help you navigate most conflicts. Consider these tips for handling conflict:

- Remain calm
- Avoid negative language
- Allow the other party to speak
- Ask questions
- Agree on the problem
- Brainstorm possible solutions
- Negotiate a solution

Through collaboration and compromise, a solution to conflict can usually be reached.

Breast Self-Exam

During a physical examination, a physician may check for lumps or other changes to the breast that may require further investigation. Patients are encouraged to perform breast self-examinations (BSEs) on a regular basis to familiarize themselves with their own breast tissue and to recognize changes that may require further investigation by a physician (see Figure 15.9). Breast self-exams are often recommended to be performed on a monthly basis (preferably at the same time each month). The exam should be performed using the methods of a physical and visual exam.

FIGURE 15.9 | **Breast Self-Examination**

LYING DOWN
Check your entire breast area with the finger pads of your left hand. Use small circles and follow an up and down pattern. Use light, medium, and firm pressure over each area of your breast. Gently squeeze the nipple for any discharge. Repeat these steps on your left breast.

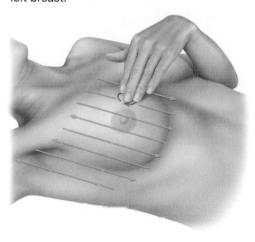

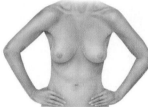

BEFORE A MIRROR
Check for any changes in the shape or look of your breasts.

IN THE SHOWER
Raise your right arm, With soapy hands and fingers flat, check your right breast. Use the method described in the "Lying Down" step. Repeat on your left breast.

Physical Self-Exam

Place a pillow under your shoulder. Put your right hand under your head. Check the entire area of your right breast using the fingertips of your left hand. Use small circles and follow an up-and-down pattern, keeping the fingers flat and together. Use light, medium, and firm pressure over each area of your breast. Gently squeeze the nipple and check for any discharge. Repeat these steps on your left breast. These steps can also be performed in the shower by raising each arm over your head as you examine your breasts using the techniques mentioned.

Visual Self-Exam

Using a mirror, check for any changes in the size, shape, color, and overall appearance of your breasts. Note skin dimpling, bulging, or nipple discharge. Inspect your breasts in four steps: arms at side, arms overhead, hands on hips, and bending forward.

In the Know: Menstrual Cycle Calculation

Why might the date of a woman's last menstrual period (LMP) be significant during examinations? This date is used to calculate a pregnancy and expected due date. This date can also be used to assist in the diagnosis of conditions related to irregularities in menstruation. A woman with a regularly occurring menstrual period will ovulate on day 14 of her cycle, and conception would take place approximately two weeks after day 1 of her LMP. A woman is therefore considered to be six weeks pregnant, two weeks following her missed period.

A woman can calculate the number of days in her menstrual cycle by recording day 1 of her LMP on a calendar and counting the number of days between day 1 of one menstrual period to day 1 of the next menstrual period. This number can vary drastically from woman to woman, but generally averages around 28 days.

Checkpoint 15.3

Answer the following questions to identify any areas of the section that you may need to review.

1. What diagnostic test is generally ordered following an abnormal Pap smear?

   _____

2. What diagnostic test takes an X-ray of the breasts and has become a part of the routine examination for women over the age of 40?

   _____

3. What diagnostic tool is used to perform the removal of fibroids or polyps within the uterus?

   _____

4. In which position does a patient most often maintain during vaginal examinations (Pap smears) and childbirth?

   _____

Treatments

Healthcare practitioners use predetermined guidelines to direct patient care. These guidelines, known as clinical practice guidelines and evidence-based practices, have been developed by the specialty societies based on past clinical research. They represent the treatment pathways that have achieved the best outcomes. Treatment decisions generally fall into three categories: surgical, clinical, and pharmacological.

Surgical treatments are generally invasive as they involve a puncture or an incision into the skin. *Clinical treatments* are generally noninvasive and involve nonsurgical techniques (e.g., physical therapy). *Pharmacological treatments* involve the utilization of medicines (drugs) to treat specific illnesses or diseases. Medication therapies are regulated by the Food and Drug Administration (FDA). To be approved by the FDA for use in the United States, every medicine must be backed by research studies that have shown the medication to be effective in its treatment of a given disease and has a tolerable safety profile. The following sections provide an overview of treatments common to the female reproductive system.

Surgical Treatments

A number of surgical procedures exist for the female reproductive system. Sterilization to prevent pregnancy is performed by cutting or cauterizing the fallopian tubes, known as **bilateral tubal ligation**. Although tubal ligation is intended to be a permanent form of birth control, in some women the ova find a way to enter the fallopian tube and pregnancy ensues. Patients may also regret their decision following a tubal ligation and later wish to become pregnant. A **salpingosalpingostomy** is a procedure in which previously cut fallopian tubes are reconnected, retied, or reopened in order to reverse a tubal ligation. A **hysterectomy** is a surgical procedure to remove the uterus. If the fallopian tubes and ovaries are removed, the procedure is known as a total hysterectomy with **bilateral salpingo-oophorectomy**. Table 15.8 describes additional surgical treatments.

TABLE 15.8 Surgical Treatments Associated with the Female Reproductive System

Treatment		Description
bilateral salpingo-oophorectomy	[sal-**ping**-O O-phOr-**ek**-tuh-mee]	removal of the fallopian tubes and ovaries
bilateral tubal ligation		procedure to prevent pregnancy by cutting or cauterizing the fallopian tubes
cervical conization	[kon-ih-**zay**-shun]	removal of cervical tissue
cervicectomy	[sur-vih-**sek**-tuh-mee]	removal of uterine cervix
clitoridectomy	[klih-tor-eh-**dek**-tuh-mee]	removal of all or part of the clitoris
colpopexy	[**kOl**-pO-peck-see]	fixation of the vagina to a structure to prevent prolapse
colpoplasty	[**kOl**-pO-plas-tee]	repair of the vagina, also known as *colporrhaphy*
endometrial ablation	[**en**-dO-mee-tree-uhl ab-**lay**-shun]	procedure in which lasers are used to destroy damaged endometrial tissue, used to treat dysmenorrhea
hymenectomy	[hI-meh-**nek**-tuh-mee]	removal of hymen to enlarge the vaginal opening, also known as *hymenotomy*
hysterectomy	[his-tur-**rek**-tuh-mee]	full or partial removal of the uterus
hysteropexy	[**his**-tur-rO-pek-see]	fixation of the uterus to a structure to prevent prolapse
loop electrocautery excision procedure (LEEP)	[ee-lek-trO-**kah**-tur-ee]	procedure used to remove abnormal cells caused by cervical dysplasia
lumpectomy	[lum-**pek**-tuh-mee]	removal of a tumor from the breast
mammoplasty	[**mam**-O-plas-tee]	surgical or cosmetic repair of the breast (e.g., augmentation or reduction)
mastectomy	[mah-**stek**-tuh-mee]	removal of one or both breasts
mastopexy	[**mas**-tO-pek-see]	reconstructive procedure used to lift the breasts
myomectomy	[my-O-**mek**-tuh-mee]	removal of fibroids from the uterus

Continues

Treatment		Description
oophorectomy	[oo-ah-for-**ek**-tuh-mee]	removal of one or both ovaries, also known as *ovariectomy*
oophorocystectomy	[oo-of-for-O-sis-**tek**-tuh-mee]	removal of an ovarian cyst
pelvic exenteration	[ek-sen-tuh-**ray**-shun]	removal of all or various parts of the pelvic cavity to prevent the spread of cancer
polypectomy	[pah-lee-**pek**-tuh-mee]	removal of polyps from the uterus
salpingectomy	[sal-pin-**gek**-tuh-mee]	removal of one or both fallopian tubes
salpingolysis	[sal-pin-**gah**-lI-sis]	procedure in which scar tissue is removed from the fallopian tubes to increase the chances of fertility
salpingo salpingostomy	[sal-**ping**-O sal-pin-**gos**-tuh-mee]	procedure to reconnect, retie, or reopen previously cut fallopian tubes to reverse a tubal ligation
theleplasty	[**thee**-leh-plas-tee]	repair of the nipple
uterine artery embolization (UAE)	[em-bO-lI-**zay**-shun]	blockage of blood supply to a uterine fibroid
vulvectomy	[vul-**vek**-tuh-mee]	complete or partial removal of the vulva, rare procedure to treat cancer of the vulva

In the Know: Clitoridectomies

A *clitoridectomy* is the surgical removal of the clitoris. There are two types of clitoridectomies. *Excision* is the removal of all or part of the clitoris. *Infibulation* (or radical circumcision) is excision plus the suturing of the vaginal opening, leaving only a small hole for menses and urination. Both procedures are also known as *female genital mutilation (FGM)*. The World Health Organization (WHO) has reported that an estimated 125 million women have had clitoridectomies as a form of FGM. Clitoridectomies are most common in Africa and the Middle East and are considered cultural and religious rituals that signal a rite of passage for young women and making them eligible for marriage. The term *female circumcision* is also used in reference to clitoridectomies, but the procedure is not comparable to male circumcision. Clitoridectomies are rarely used therapeutically in the United States. A small number of procedures have been performed to treat cancer that has spread to the clitoris.

Pharmacological Treatments

The list of pharmaceuticals used to treat conditions relating to the female reproductive system includes agents and devices used for contraception (the prevention of pregnancy); agents to increase fertility, to relieve menopausal symptoms, to manage endometriosis; and agents to induce labor. Lastly, there are drugs used for routine management after delivery of the placenta or to control vaginal bleeding. Chapter 16 will discuss all agents and devices used for contraception, sexually transmitted infections, fertility, and labor and delivery. Table 15.9 lists pharmaceutical agents used to treat conditions of the female reproductive system related to menopause and breast cancer. The generic and brand names are provided for each drug. Pharmaceutical agents associated with fertility, sexually transmitted infections, and childbirth will be discussed in Chapter 16.

Drug Class	Use	Generic Name	Brand Name
Gonadotropin-releasing hormone (synthetic)	breast cancer treatment	goserelin acetate injection	Zoladex
hormone replacement therapy	decrease symptoms of menopause, vaginal dryness	estrogen (conjugated/equine), estradiol transdermal (patch) system, estradiol vaginal cream	Premarin, Estraderm, Estrace

Checkpoint **15.4**

Answer the following questions to identify any areas of the section that you may need to review.

1. In which surgical procedure is scar tissue removed from the fallopian tubes to increase the chances of fertility?

_____

2. Which surgical procedure involves the fixation of the vagina to a structure to prevent recurring prolapse?

_____

3. Which procedure is referred to as a female circumcision?

_____

Abbreviations

In the medical field, information is generally recorded in medical charts and in electronic medical records and provided to healthcare workers in medical shorthand. It is important that healthcare professionals become familiar with the abbreviations used on a daily basis to successfully perform the duties assigned in a typical workday. Table 15.10 lists common abbreviations used in reference to conditions and treatments of the female reproductive system.

TABLE 15.10 Abbreviations Associated with the Female Reproductive System

Abbreviation	Meaning
AB, ab	abortion
BSE	breast self-exam
BSO	bilateral salpingo-oophorectomy
BTL	bilateral tubal ligation
D&C	dilation and curettage
DUB	dysfunctional uterine bleeding
ERT	estrogen replacement therapy

Continues

Abbreviation	Meaning
FSH	follicle-stimulating hormone
GC	gonorrhea
GYN	gynecology
HPV	human papilloma virus
HRT	hormone replacement therapy (usually refers to replacement at menopause)
HSG	hysterosalpingography
IUD	intrauterine device
LH	luteinizing hormone
LMP	last menstrual period
OB	obstetrics
PAP	pap test
PID	pelvic inflammatory disease
PMDD	premenstrual dysphoric disorder
PMP	previous menstrual period
PMS	premenstrual syndrome
Rh	rhesus factor
STI	sexually transmitted infection, also known as *sexually transmitted disease (STD)*
TAH	total abdominal hysterectomy
TAH/BSO	total abdominal hysterectomy with bilateral salpingo-oophorectomy
VH	vaginal hysterectomy

Exercise 15.13   Word Analysis

Using slashes, separate the terms into their individual word parts. Identify each word part by writing "P" for prefix, "CF" for combining form, and "S" for suffix above the word part. Then, supply the definition of the entire term.

Term	Word Analysis	Definition
1. amenorrhea	_____	_____
2. metrorrhagia	_____	_____
3. salpingectomy	_____	_____
4. lactogenesis	_____	_____
5. cervical	_____	_____

Exercise 15.14   Comprehension Check

Read each sentence and circle the better of the two terms given.

1. The patient experiences severe <u>mastodynia/cervical</u>.

2. A complex interaction of hormones causes <u>salpingectomy/lactogenesis</u>.

3. The patient will undergo the uterine treatment known as <u>polypectomy/theleplasty</u>.

4. The doctor recommended that a <u>cervicectomy/colpopexy</u> be performed to prevent prolapse.

5. Dilation and <u>curettage/salpingitis</u> was performed to obtain tissue samples.

Exercise 15.15   Abbreviations

Write the meaning for each definition in the space provided.

1. D&C _____

2. OB _____

3. TAH _____

4. GC _____

5. DUB _____

Exercise 15.16   Word Building

Construct terms to match the definitions provided, using only the suffixes *-cele*, *-ectomy*, and *-rrhaphy*.

1. herniation of the rectum into the vagina _____

2. herniation of the urethra into the vagina _____

3. surgical removal of the fallopian tubes and ovaries _____

4. suture of the vagina _____

5. suture of the vulva _____

Exercise 15.17 Spelling Check

Indicate whether each term is singular or plural by writing an S or a P after the term. Then use your knowledge of plural spellings to supply the opposite form (singular or plural) of the term.

Term	S/P	Opposite Form
1. oophorectomy	_____	_____
2. uterus	_____	_____
3. areola	_____	_____
4. fundus	_____	_____
5. cervix	_____	_____

Exercise 15.18 Identification

Define the following surgical procedures by indicating where on the figures these procedures would take place and then writing the definition of each term on the line provided.

Term	Location in Figure	Definition of Term
1. colposcopy	_____	_____
2. hysterectomy	_____	_____
3. mastectomy	_____	_____
4. oophorectomy	_____	_____
5. bilateral tubal ligation	_____	_____

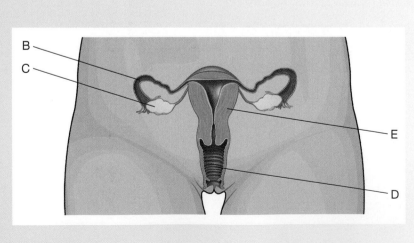

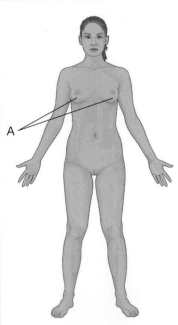

Chapter Review

After successfully completing this chapter, you should be able to correctly answer the following review questions. Answers are provided in the back of the text. Use this self-assessment opportunity to check your understanding of the content and determine whether you need to revisit any of the chapter's content.

Crossword Puzzle

Use the clues provided to fill in the puzzle with the correct terms. Enter one letter per square.

Across

2. difficult or painful menstruation
6. eggs
7. inflammation of the breast
9. combining form for cessation
11. pigmented area surrounding the nipple of the breast
12. removal of the ovary or ovaries
14. lateral
18. combining form for female
19. surgical removal of the uterus
21. surgical removal of the breast or breasts
22. absence of menstruation

Down

1. _____ follicles
3. inflammation of the fallopian tubes
4. largest cell in the body
5. combining form for vagina
8. fertilized ovum
9. endocervical swab; _____ smear
10. curettage
11. pertaining to inability to ovulate
13. type of STI
15. immature female sex cell
16. incapable of fertilization
17. prefix for against
20. -oma
23. abbreviation for abortion

Matching

Match the following terms to their proper definitions.

1. _____ areola
2. _____ cervix
3. _____ endometriosis
4. _____ fibroids
5. _____ fundus
6. _____ mammary glands
7. _____ menses
8. _____ mons pubis
9. _____ perineum
10. _____ puberty

a. firm, mobile, nonmalignant nodules in the uterine wall

b. onset of body changes that herald physiologic maturity of the person

c. milk-secreting organs on the chest

d. lower neck-like section of the uterus extending into the vagina

e. condition of the lining of the uterus

f. periodic shedding of the uterine lining

g. a pad of fatty tissue that lies over the bones of the pelvis

h. the area between the vaginal opening and the anus

i. the part of an organ farthest away from an opening

j. small, darkened area around the nipple of each breast

Identification

Correctly label the illustration by writing the correct term on the line provided for each of the corresponding locations in the figure.

body of uterus   fundus
cervix   ovary
fallopian tube   vagina

1. _____
2. _____
3. _____
4. _____
5. _____
6. _____

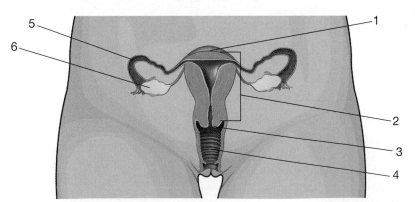

Abbreviations

Write the meaning of the abbreviation on the line provided.

1. BTL _____

2. D&C _____

3. GC _____

4. PMP _____

5. VH _____

6. GYN _____

7. HRT _____

8. TAH _____

9. HPV _____

10. PID _____

Word-Building Challenge

Review the following list of new terms. Apply your knowledge of female reproductive system word parts to accurately identify the meaning of each new term. Write your answer on the line provided and then check your definition against the answer provided in the appendix.

Term   **Definition**

1. hymenotomy _____
_____
_____

2. endometrial hyperplasia _____
_____
_____

3. pyosalpinx _____
_____
_____

4. hematosalpinx _____
_____
_____

5. colpoptosis _____
_____
_____

Extension Activities

Complete the following activities as assigned by your instructor.

1. Conduct an Internet search to find information on the relationship between toxic shock syndrome and tampon use. Using reliable sources, identify pertinent information such as the number of cases each year, the symptoms of the condition, risk factors, and how to avoid developing the condition. Be prepared to share your research with your instructor and class.

2. Research the statistical prevalence of a double vagina in women. Write a 250-word essay providing an overview of the condition and the statistical evidence you discovered.

3. There are many differing opinions on whether young women should receive the Gardasil vaccine. Go online and research the pros and cons of the vaccine, identifying the top concerns of both sides of the argument. What are some common misconceptions regarding the purpose of this vaccine? Is the vaccine currently recommended for both genders? Why or why not? Present your findings to the class using the method assigned by your instructor. Support your research using reliable sources.

Student eResources

The Course Navigator learning management system that accompanies this textbook offers multiple opportunities to master chapter content, including end-of-chapter exercises, a glossary of key terms with audio pronunciations, games, pronunciation coach, and additional activities such as engaging with the BioDigital® Human.

16 Pregnancy, Birth, and Postpartum

“One of the aims of sexual union is procreation—the creation by reproduction of an image of itself, of the union.”

—**Mortimer Adler,** author and philosopher

Translation Challenge

Read the following excerpts from a physician's report and try to answer the questions that follow.

DISCHARGE DIAGNOSES:
1. Intrauterine gestation at term.
2. History of two previous cesarean sections.
3. Delivered viable male infant.
4. Multiparity. Fertility. Desired sterilization.

PROCEDURES PERFORMED:
1. Repeat low transverse cesarean section.
2. Bilateral tubal ligation.

COMPLICATIONS: None.

PERTINENT FINDINGS/HISTORY AND PHYSICAL:
The patient is a 36 y/o gravida 6, now para 3-0-3-3 female, who was admitted at term for repeat cesarean section and sterilization. The patient had previous cesarean sections for labor arrest, for an infant weighing 9 pounds 12 ounces, and for elective repeat.

1. What does para 3-0-3-3 refer to?

2. What does gravida 6 mean?

3. What is a bilateral tubal ligation?

Learning Objectives

16.1 List and define word parts most commonly used to create terms related to pregnancy, birth, and postpartum.

16.2 Identify structures related to pregnancy, birth, and postpartum

16.3 Identify the normal stages of pregnancy and describe the changes in the female body during pregnancy and immediately after childbirth.

16.4 Define the stages of labor.

16.5 Recognize and describe common conditions of pregnancy, birth, and postpartum.

16.6 Describe the various tests and treatments used for major pregnancy, birth, and postpartum abnormalities.

16.7 Describe the various options available to assist in achieving or preventing conception.

16.8 State the meaning of abbreviations related to pregnancy, birth, and postpartum.

16.9 Correctly use the terms of pregnancy, birth, and postpartum in written and oral communication.

16.10 Correctly spell and pronounce pregnancy, birth, and postpartum terminology.

COURSE NAVIGATOR
Access Additional Chapter Resources

Body systems complete specific tasks to maintain homeostasis and ensure the survival of the individual. The reproductive systems (male and female) are unique in that they allow an individual to procreate. This chapter provides an overview of the stages of pregnancy and labor, describes the conditions common to pregnancy, fertility, and sexual health, and identifies the tools used for diagnosis and treatment.

In the Know: Pregnancy, Birth, and Postpartum Specialties

The medical care of the mother and child during and immediately following pregnancy is provided by gynecologists, obstetricians, neonatologists, and pediatricians. Many of the same clinicians are also involved in treating conditions related to the female reproductive system. Allied health professionals, like diagnostic medical sonographers, medical assistants, and phlebotomists, also assist in areas of human development. Embryologists are heavily involved in caring for conditions related to fertility and geneticists specialize in hereditary conditions and congenital malformations.

Nurse midwives and doulas have become an integral part of the reproductive and childbirth process. Although individual states may limit the scope of care for nurse midwives and doulas, midwives are generally permitted to perform annual gynecological exams, provide family planning, prenatal, and birthing care. The main purpose of a doula is to be an emotional support system and advocate for the mother and baby throughout pregnancy, delivery, and postpartum. Doulas may also provide homeopathic care, such as massage, for the mother.

Pregnancy, Birth, and Postpartum Word Parts

As with other body systems, a core of prefixes, suffixes, and combining forms serves as the source for most of the medical words associated with human development. Table 16.1 lists common word parts, their meanings, and an example.

TABLE 16.1 Word Parts Associated with Pregnancy, Birth, and Postpartum

Prefix	Meaning	Example
ecto-, ec-	out, outward	ectopic (pregnancy in which the fertilized ovum implants outside the uterus; tubal pregnancy)
meso-	middle	mesoderm (middle layers of cells during the embryonic phase of development; ultimately responsible for the development of the circulatory system, muscle, and bone)
multi-	many	multipara (a woman who has had more than one pregnancy resulting in a live birth)
neo-	new	neonatal (newborn)
nulli-	none	nullipara (a woman who has never given birth)
oxy-	rapid	oxytocia (an unusually rapid childbirth)
pre-	before	preterm labor (labor that occurs before the 37th week of pregnancy [term])
primi-	first	primigravida (first pregnancy)

Combining Form	Meaning	Example
amni/o	amnion	amniotic fluid (clear fluid that surrounds the unborn baby in the uterus during pregnancy)
cephal/o	head	cephalopelvic disproportion (a condition that exists when a baby's head or body is too large to fit through the mother's pelvis during delivery)
cervic/o	cervix	cervical (pertaining to the lower part of the uterus)
episi/o	vulva	episiotomy (an incision made in the perineum to enlarge the opening of the vagina during childbirth; also known as a *perineotomy*)
fet/o	fetus	fetal (pertaining to the fetus)
galact/o	milk	agalactia (failure of a mother to produce or secrete milk following childbirth; lactation failure)
hyster/o, metr/o, uter/o, metri/o	uterus	hysterectomy (surgical procedure in which all or part of the uterus is removed)
lact/o	milk	lactation (production or secretion of milk following childbirth)
leuk/o	white	leukorrhea (white or yellow discharge of mucus from the vagina)
ligat/o	tying	tubal ligation (sterilization procedure in which the fallopian tubes are tied, severed, or blocked to prevent a fertilized ovum from reaching the uterus)
mamm/o, mast/o	breast	mammary (relating to the breasts)
metr/o	womb, uterus	metrorrhagia (uterine/menstrual bleeding at irregular intervals)
nat/o	birth, born	postnatal (the period of time following childbirth)
oophor/o	ovary	oophorectomy (surgical removal of the ovaries)
placent/o	placenta	placenta previa (a pregnancy complication in which the placenta blocks all or part of the mother's cervix)
semin/i	semen	artificial insemination (mechanical injection of semen into the vagina or uterus with the intention of achieving pregnancy)
thel/o, papill/o	nipple	thelitis (inflammation of the nipple)
tub/o	tube	tubal pregnancy (pregnancy in which the fertilized ovum implants outside the uterus; ectopic)
vagin/o	vagina	vaginal (pertaining to the vagina)
umbilic/o	umbilicus (navel)	a flexible cord that connects from an opening in the baby's stomach, in the womb, to the mother's placenta for nourishment throughout pregnancy)

Continues

Suffix	Meaning	Example
-al, -ic	pertaining to	nuchal cord (a loop of umbilical cord found wrapped around the neck of the fetus at delivery)
-centesis	surgical puncture	amniocentesis (medical procedure in which amniotic fluid is removed from the uterus to diagnose fetal abnormalities)
-gravida	pregnancy	nulligravida (a woman who has never been pregnant)
-osis	abnormal condition	erythroblastosis fetalis (condition in which a mother is Rh negative and her fetus is Rh positive; antibodies are then produced that will attack future pregnancies with Rh-positive fetuses)
-para	delivery, birth	primipara (a woman who delivers her first baby)
-partum	delivery	postpartum (the period immediately following childbirth and extending about 6 weeks after)
-tocia	labor, delivery	fetal dystocia (abnormal fetal size or positioning resulting in difficult labor)

Anatomy and Physiology

Human development involves structures from multiple body systems, but mainly the male and female reproductive systems. These two systems work together to create and deliver offspring. The process begins when sperm from the male reproductive system encounters and fertilizes the female ovum (egg) and concludes roughly nine months later when an infant is born. The following sections and Table 16.2 identify the anatomy and physiology associated with pregnancy, birth, and postpartum.

TABLE 16.2 Anatomy and Physiology Terms Related to Pregnancy, Birth, and Postpartum

Term		Meaning	Word Analysis	
amnion	[**am**-nee-on]	fluid-filled sac that contains an embryo (inner)	amni/o -on	amnion structure
amniotic fluid	[am-nee-**ah**-tik]	the fluid that surrounds and protects the baby in the uterus during pregnancy	amni/o -tic	amnion pertaining to
alveolar glands	[al-**vee**-O-lur]	produces lactating milk		
blastocyst	[**blast**-O-sist]	a hollow ball of cells containing the fertilized embryo that implants itself in the wall of the uterus	blast/o -cyst	bud sac
blastocyte	[**blast**-O-sIt]	mass of cells that make up a fertilized ovum; will eventually implant into the wall of the uterus to initiate pregnancy	blast/o -cyte	bud, sprout, embryo cell
Braxton Hicks contractions		contractions that occur during pregnancy but do not lead to birth; named for the English physician John Braxton Hicks		
chorion	[**kore**-ee-on]	outermost membrane surrounding an embryo during pregnancy	chorion/o	chorion (outer layer of fetal sac)
embryo	[**em**-bree-O]	an organism in the early stages of development, from the fertilization of the ovum to week 8 of gestation		
embryonic phase	[**em**-bree-on-ik]	period of growth and development from week 9 of gestation to birth		
fetal phase	[**fee**-tul]	period of growth and development from the fertilization of the ovum to week 8 of gestation	fet/o —al	fetus pertaining to

Continues

Term		Meaning	Word Analysis	
fetus	[**fee**-tis]	a developing baby, more than 8 weeks of gestation	*fet/o* *—us*	fetus structure, thing
fraternal twins	[frah-**tur**-nul]	two individuals who developed from separate ova yet shared the same womb during development		
gestation	[jes-**tay**-shun]	pregnancy, the process of being carried in the womb, from the fertilization of the ovum to birth		
gravida	[**grav**-i-dah]	refers to the number of times a woman has been pregnant	*gravid/o*	pregnancy
identical twins		two individuals who developed from a single fertilized ovum and shared the same womb during development; also share the same appearance and genetic material		
labor	[**lay**-bur]	the process of giving birth		
lactiferous ducts	[lak-**tif**-ur-us]	responsible for the delivery of breast milk to the skin's surface and out of the mother's nipple	*lact/o* *-ferous* *duct/o*	milk pertaining to carrying carrying
lochia	[**lO**-kee-ah]	vaginal discharge present after the birth of a fetus		
meconium	[me-**kO**-nee-um]	the first feces of a newborn infant		
multigravida	[**mul**-tee-grav-i-dah]	a woman who has been pregnant at least two times	*multi-* *-gravida*	many pregnancy
multipara	[mul-**ti**-par-a]	a woman who has had at least two pregnancies resulting in live births	*multi-* *-para*	many delivery, birth
nulligravida	[nul-I-**grav**-i-da]	a woman who has never been pregnant	*nulli-* *—gravida*	none pregnancy
nullipara	[nul-I-par-**a**]	a woman who has never given birth	*nulli-* *-para*	none delivery, birth
parturition	[par-tur-**ri**-shun]	the process of giving birth	*part/o* *-tion*	delivery process of
parturient	[pahr-**chur**-ee-ent]	a woman in labor, about to give birth	*part/o*	delivery
placenta	[plah-**sen**-tah]	a highly vascular organ that provides for the exchange of gas and nutrients and the elimination of waste between mother and baby during pregnancy	*placent/o*	placenta
postpartum	[post-**pahr**-tum]	the period after the delivery of the placenta	*post-* *part/o* *-um*	after delivery structure, thing
relaxin	[**re**-lak-sin]	hormone responsible for the softening and loosening of the cervix, muscles, and joints during childbirth	*relaxo*	loosen
rectouterine pouch	[**rek**-tO-yoo-tur-in **powch**]	a space in the cavity between the uterus and the rectum; also called Douglas' cul-de-sac for the Scottish anatomist James Douglas	*rect/o* *uter/o* *-ine*	rectum uterus pertaining to
trimesters	[**trI**-mes-turz]	the three periods of three months, used to describe the duration of pregnancy	*tri-*	three
umbilical cord	[**um**-bil-ih-kul **kord**]	flexible cord that connects from an opening in the baby's stomach, in the womb, to the mother's placenta for nourishment throughout pregnancy	*umbilic/o* *-al*	umbilicus (navel) pertaining to
uterus	[**yoo**-tur-us]	female reproductive organ; also known as the *womb*; responsible for the development of the embryo and fetus during pregnancy	*uter/o* *-us*	uterus structure, thing
zygote	[**zI**-gOt]	a fertilized ovum (egg)		

Pregnancy

Pregnancy is a term used to describe the time between conception and birth. **Conception** occurs when the male's sperm meets and fertilizes the ovum. As discussed in Chapter 15, an ovum is released once a month from an ovary and swept into the fallopian tubes. During sexual intercourse, millions of sperm are ejaculated from the penis into the vagina. In just a few minutes, the sperm swim through the female's vagina, cervix, and uterus, and into one of the fallopian tubes. Ejaculated sperm race to reach the ovum, but only one sperm can enter and fertilize the ovum. Only a small fraction of sperm that began the race will actually complete the journey to reach the ovum. The fertilized ovum immediately divides into two cells as it makes its way to the uterus for implantation. This process of cell division is known as **mitosis**. After about three days, the fertilized ovum becomes a solid mass of cells called a **morula**. By the time the morula, which continues to divide, reaches the uterus, it contains the developing embryo and becomes a hollow ball of cells called a **blastocyst**, which implants itself in the wall of the uterus (see Figure 16.1). The uterus is known referred to as the womb. The process from fertilization to implantation takes about six days. The blastocyst develops into a structure with two cavities, the yolk sac and amniotic cavity. In humans, the yolk sac produces blood cells, and the amniotic cavity becomes the fluid-filled cavity in which the fetus floats while it develops.

The tiny zygote, barely as big as the period at the end of this sentence, grows about 200 billion times its size to become a fully-developed fetus. The entire process (from onset of last period to childbirth) averages about 9 months, or 280 days (40 weeks).

Gestational age is a term used to describe a pregnancy's progress and refers to the period between conception and the expected date of delivery or confinement (EDD or EDC). Dependent on the age of gestation, or development, different names are used to identify the fertilized ovum, which is immediately known as a **zygote**. During the first two months of gestation, the term **embryo** is used. From the third month of gestation to the time of birth, the developing baby is known as a **fetus**.

FIGURE 16.1 Implanted Blastocyst

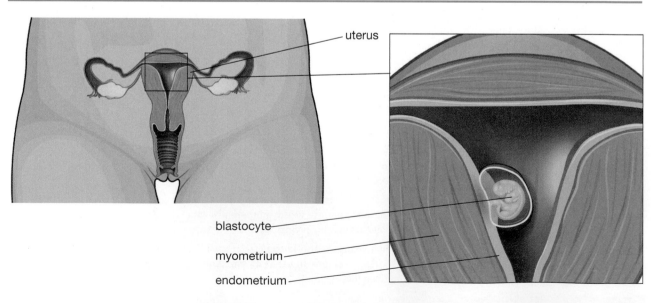

uterus

blastocyte

myometrium

endometrium

In the Know: Calculating the Due Date

Knowing when a baby is expected to be delivered is helpful for a number of reasons. Primarily, this date is used to monitor the growth and development of the fetus throughout the pregnancy. Prenatal care is designed to guide physicians and midwives through regular checkups to treat and prevent potential health problems for both mother and fetus. Specific tests and procedures are scheduled at various stages of gestation to monitor growth and development. Additionally, labor inductions and scheduled cesarean sections are generally scheduled around the expected date of delivery (EDD) to best predict an infant's ability to live independently of its mother (because, for example, developments such as lung maturity occur in specific weeks of gestation).

There are different ways to estimate the due date. One method uses the date of the patient's last menstrual period (LMP) and the other calculates the EDD based on the date of conception. The LMP method simply adds 280 days after the LMP, but may be miscalculated if the LMP date is misremembered or if the patient's ovulation cycle happens earlier or later than average.

The calculation method that uses the conception date assumes conception occurs near ovulation, or midway through the menstrual cycle, which is roughly 14 days after the first day of the last menstrual cycle. Thus, the pregnancy lasts 266 days, or 38 weeks.

Nägele's Rule

The following describes the quick method for calculating EDD (Nägele's Rule):

- Determine the first day of the last menstrual period (example: January 10)
- Add 7 days (January 17)
- Count back 3 months (October 17)
- Add 1 year

The resulting date is the EDD (October 17 of the next year).

Facts about Due Dates

- Due date calculations are only an estimate, as most babies are born between 38 and 42 weeks from the first day of their mother's LMP.
- Ninety percent of expectant mothers deliver within 2 weeks of their due date, but no more than 10 percent deliver on their due date.
- First pregnancies can have longer gestation (and longer labor), and mothers with several prior pregnancies often give birth earlier (and with shorter labor).

Placenta

After the blastocyte implants into the lining of the uterus, a support system composed of the placenta and umbilical cord begins to develop. These two structures are essential to sustaining a healthy pregnancy. The **placenta** is responsible for the exchange of oxygen, water, and nutrients from the mother to the baby. The placenta begins to develop (around the fifth week following fertilization) and is fully formed about 13 weeks after fertilization. With the help of the umbilical cord, the placenta also removes waste and carbon dioxide from the fetus and transports it to the mother for excretion from the body.

Umbilical Cord

The **umbilical cord** extends from the placenta to the navel (belly button) of the developing fetus (see Figure 16.2). It is often referred to as the lifeline between mother and baby. The umbilical cord contains a single vein, responsible for the transportation of oxygenated blood from mother to baby, and two arteries, responsible for returning deoxygenated blood, waste, and carbon dioxide from the baby to the mother for excretion. Conditions common to abnormalities of the placenta and umbilical cord will be discussed later in the chapter.

FIGURE 16.2 Placenta and Umbilical Cord in Early and Late Stages of Pregnancy

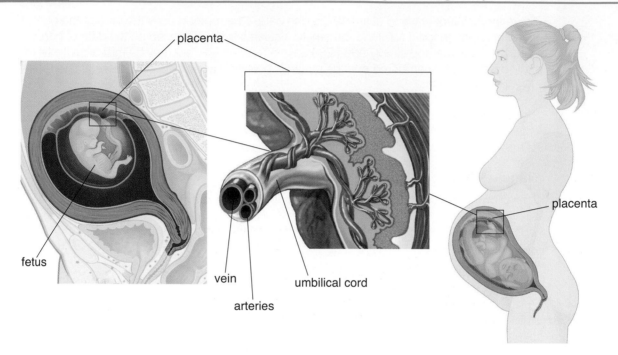

Growing Uterus (Womb)

Recall that once the blastocyte has planted itself into the lining of the uterus, the uterus is now referred to as the womb. Within the womb, an amniotic sac filled with amniotic fluid surrounds and protects the developing baby. The amniotic sac is known as the "bag of waters."

Amniotic fluid consists of 98 percent water and 2 percent salts and cells from the growing fetus. This fluid helps to keep the fetus warm, assists in lung development and movement inside the womb, and acts as a shock absorber by distributing any force penetrating the mother's uterus. The amniotic fluid ("waters") around the baby increases at about the midpoint of the pregnancy (20 weeks gestation). In the latter stages of development, the baby swallows up to 15 ounces of amniotic fluid per day to prepare its digestive and urinary systems for life outside the mother's womb.

> **Did You Know?**
>
> Prior to ICD-10, the first trimester was defined as weeks 0–12.

Embryonic Phase: First Trimester

Pregnancy is divided into three 3-month periods called **trimesters**. The first trimester of pregnancy, which ends at 14 weeks gestation, is crucial to normal development. While it is too early for the mother to show signs of pregnancy on the outside, all of the fetus's major organs and organ systems are rapidly forming on the inside. The embryonic phase makes up a large portion of the first trimester. This **embryonic phase** begins with fertilization and concludes at the end of the eighth week of gestation. The embryo resembles a tadpole up until the eighth week of gestation, when its tail is lost (see Figure 16.3). During this stage, nail beds are formed, bones begin to harden, and the fetal heartbeat can be heard during a prenatal exam.

FIGURE 16.3 Embryonic Phase Development

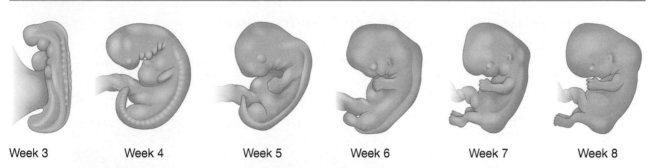

| Week 3 | Week 4 | Week 5 | Week 6 | Week 7 | Week 8 |

The embryonic phase is characterized by the development of three distinct layers of specialized cells, each of which eventually produces a definitive structure of the human body. These layers are known as the **endoderm**, or inside layer; **mesoderm**, or middle layer; and **ectoderm**, or outside layer. Table 16.3 identifies the structures that are formed by each of these layers. Any defects in the formation of a layer can cause an abnormality in the developing structures.

TABLE 16.3 The Embryonic Layers and Their Developing Structures

Term	Meaning	Word Analysis	
endoderm	digestive and respiratory systems	*endo-*	within
		derm	skin
mesoderm	skin and nervous system	*meso-*	middle
		derm	skin
ectoderm	musculoskeletal system	*ecto-*	outside
		derm	skin

During the embryonic phase, the risk of miscarriage and congenital abnormalities is high. The pregnant mother's exposure to infectious disease, alcohol, drugs, tobacco smoke, medications, and radiation can be detrimental to the development and survival of the developing embryo.

Although all organs and body systems are formed by the end of the first trimester, they are not completely functional and the fetus is unable to live independently of its mother.

Beyond Words: Population

Approximately 4 million babies are born in the United States each year. While the United States has ranked third as the world's most populous country (following China and India), it is projected to fall farther down the list by 2050. This decline has been attributed to trends in economic health, marriage, women's education, employment, and access to methods of contraception.

Fetal Phase: First, Second, and Third Trimester

The **fetal phase** extends from week 9 to birth, which means that it is included in the first, second, and third trimesters of development. This phase is characterized by the complete growth and development of all major organ systems. The fetus begins to look more and more human (see Figure 16.4). It forms sex organs, brain activity begins, and the organs prepare to function outside the womb. During this phase, the uterus expands to about 50–100 times its original size and occupies most of the mother's abdominal cavity. Table 16.4 traces the general development of the fetus from the embryonic phase to birth.

> **What's in a Word?**
>
> Note that the term *fetus* is used during the *fetal phase*, replacing *embryo* which is used in the *embryonic phase*.

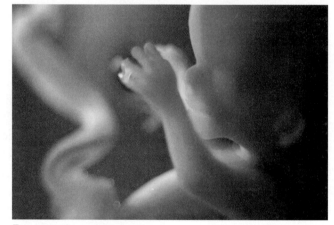

Fetus at 12 weeks gestation

FIGURE 16.4 Fetal Phase Development

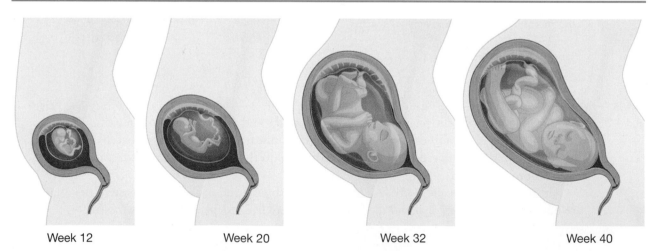

Week 12   Week 20   Week 32   Week 40

TABLE 16.4 | Fetal Development

Gestational Period	Average Length/Weight	Developing Characteristics
First Trimester (week 1 to the end of week 13)		
Weeks 1–3	~1/16th of an inch/~1 gram	Fertilized ovum is a ball of cells (blastocyst), DNA predetermined by parents (e.g., gender, eye color, hair color, etc.)
Weeks 4–7	~ the size of a sesame seed by the end of week 7	Officially an embryo. Facial features (eyes, nose, ears, and mouth) and all major organs begin to develop. Tiny heart begins to beat. Buds develop that will become arms and legs.
Weeks 8–10	~1 inch long/~1/2 ounce	Now a fetus. Begins to look more human with the loss of its "tail." Eyes shift to the front, although eyelids are fused shut. Vital organs begin to function (kidneys, intestines, brain, and liver).
Weeks 11–13	~3–4 inches long/~2/3 ounce	Fetus is almost fully formed. Bones begin to harden. Nail beds form. Heartbeat can be heard during a prenatal exam.
Second Trimester (week 14 to the end of week 27)		
Weeks 15–16	~7 inches long/~3 ounces	Fetus becomes active (mother feels movement). Fetus's kidneys begin to produce urine that is released into amniotic fluid. Facial expressions become prominent. Gender can generally be detected via ultrasound.
Weeks 17–20	~8 inches long/~10 ounces	Fetus can now hear mother's heartbeat and sounds that come from outside the body. Many are startled by loud noises. Vernix (waxy, protective coating on skin) and lanugo (fine, soft hair on body) begin to develop.
Week 24	~12 inches long/just over 1 pound	Fetus's taste buds begin to develop. Brain is growing quickly. Hair begins to grow. Skin appears wrinkled.
Third Trimester (week 28 to the end of pregnancy)		
Week 28	~14–15 inches long/~2¼ pounds	Fetus begins breathing by inhaling and exhaling amniotic fluid. Brain activity similar to that of a sleeping newborn. Some begin to dream while sleeping. Eyelashes form and eyesight improves. Eyes no longer fused shut, can open and close.
Week 32	~16–17 inches long/~3¾ pounds	Nails have grown to tips of fingers and toes. Creases begin to form on palms and soles of hands and feet.
Week 37	~19 inches long/~5½ pounds	Baby is now considered full term and most are in the head-down position. Brain and central nervous system are now functional. Weeks to follow are used to increase weight. Vernix and lanugo begin to disappear.
40 weeks (Term)	~20 inches long/~7½ pounds	Baby has reached estimated due date and is able to survive outside the womb. Labor may be induced if delivery does not occur within the next 1–2 weeks.

Note: The embryonic phase begins with fertilization and concludes at the end of week 8. Therefore, the first trimester of pregnancy includes components of both the embryonic and the fetal phases of growth and development.

In the Know: How Is Gender Determined?

Female DNA contains two X chromosomes (XX), and male DNA contains an X and a Y chromosome (XY). At the time of fertilization, each parent donates one sex chromosome. The female can only donate an X chromosome, so it's the male sperm that determines the sex of the embryo. If the X chromosome from the male is carried on the sperm that fertilizes the ovum, the embryo will have two Xs and be female. If the Y chromosome from the male is carried on the sperm that fertilizes the ovum, the embryo will be male with the X and Y sex chromosomes.

Pregnancy Milestones

Pregnancy results in numerous physical changes. Although many of these changes are short lived, others can extend beyond the birth of the child. These changes are a result of the mother's body adjusting to the growing fetus and preparing for birth.

The first time the mother feels the fetus move within her is called **quickening**. Quickening, or fetal movement, usually occurs by week 18 if the mother has not given birth before (is nulliparous) and week 16 if she has given birth two or more times (is multiparous). Early fetal movement is described as being similar to gas bubbles and is typically not painful. Later fetal movements may become more forceful and can be uncomfortable. These later movements can also be felt and seen from outside the body.

Braxton Hicks is a name given to the contractions performed by the uterus long before the body goes into labor. Often referred to as "false labor," these "practice" contractions occur throughout the pregnancy, but are usually not painful. They can be felt on the outside of the abdomen by about the 28th week of gestation. The contractions are not an indication that actual labor has begun or will soon begin.

At the end of the third trimester, the baby typically drops lower into the mother's pelvis. This action is known as **lightening** or dropping. Lightening is not a definitive indicator that labor will soon follow. Babies of first-time mothers generally drop between 2 and 4 weeks prior to delivery, while babies of those who have previously given birth may not drop until labor begins. Many mothers notice that breathing becomes easier and they experience less frequent heartburn after lightening occurs. This change in fetal position also leads to the mother's increased urge to urinate since the baby's location places greater pressure on the bladder.

Some pregnant women will experience a rupture in the amniotic sac later in pregnancy or during active labor. This rupture is known as the mother's "water breaking" and is followed by amniotic fluid leaking from the body in either small or large quantities.

Table 16.5 provides an overview of the physical changes common to the female body during pregnancy and shortly after childbirth.

TABLE 16.5 The Changing Female Body during Pregnancy

Change	Description
General	
fatigue	extreme tiredness
menstrual cycle suspended	menses is temporarily suspended during pregnancy and often postpartum
nausea	nausea and vomiting that generally occur during the first trimester, known as "morning sickness"; extreme cases are diagnosed as hyperemesis
urination frequency	increase in urination frequency due to pressure on the bladder from the growing fetus
Abdomen	
linea nigra	a dark line that appears vertically on the abdomen (belly) during pregnancy; also known as the pregnancy line
striae gravidarum	stripes or lines formed by the rapid stretching, tightening of skin; commonly called "stretch marks"
Breasts	
engorgement	active breast tissue fills with fluid and expands, leading to growth, enlargement, tenderness, and hypersensitivity
lactation	breasts may begin to secrete a thick, yellowish substance called colostrum; thin first milk can be expressed after 4th month of gestation; milk (lactation, or milk production) begins after delivery

Continues

Change	Description
Montgomery's tubercles	small glands that become raised bumps on the areola
nipples	grow larger and become more prominent
pigmentation	darkening of nipples and areolas due to increased secretion of hormones that affect pigmentation of the skin
striae gravidarum	stripes or lines formed by the rapid stretching, tightening of skin; commonly called "stretch marks"
Face	
chloasma	darkened patches that appear on the face during pregnancy (generally on the nose, forehead, and cheeks); also known as the "mask of pregnancy"
Genitalia	
Chadwick's sign	vagina, cervix, and labia appear cyanotic (bluish) as a result of increased blood flow, an early sign of pregnancy; named for James Read Chadwick, a 19th-century American gynecologist
Goodell's sign	cervix softens as an indication of pregnancy; named for William Goodell, a 19th-century American gynecologist
Hegar's sign	uterine isthmus softens, probable sign of pregnancy; named for Alfred Hegar, a 19th-century German gynecologist
Musculoskeletal System	
anterior cervical flexion	change in center of gravity causes head to protrude to maintain balance
back pain	pain in the back in 80% of pregnancies; can be attributed to elevated hormone levels loosening joints, and increased weight on muscular structures supporting the back
edema	swelling of ankles and feet during pregnancy as a result of fluid retention
peripartum pelvic pain	pain in the pelvic region, generally begins within 3 weeks of delivery; cause is unknown
waddling gait	change in center of gravity due to increased weight causes a widened stance and exaggerated side-to-side movement of the torso during walking

Fetal Positioning

Toward the end of pregnancy, the baby has very little room to move inside the womb. Fetal position plays a very important role in determining the course of labor, particularly in whether the baby will fit through the mother's birth canal. Fetal positioning that affects the labor process includes presentation, station, lie, and attitude.

Presentation

Presentation is the term used by health providers to describe the position of the fetus prior to delivery. Roughly 96 percent of babies will present (or be positioned) with the head down. This is known as *cephalic presentation*. The cephalic presentation is the most desired presentation. Other babies are in a position in which their shoulders or feet are presented first. The term **breech** is used to describe a baby who is positioned with the feet or buttocks first. A breech presentation occurs in approximately 4 percent of births. Breech deliveries are potentially dangerous because the baby's head could become trapped in the pelvic opening after the body has been delivered and the umbilical cord could be compressed, which would deprive the baby of oxygen.

Station

During the final month of pregnancy, physicians determine the descent of the baby's head into the mother's pelvis in a measurement referred to as **stations**. Stations are expressed using the numbers -3, 0, and +3 (see Table 16.6). Each number represents the relationship of the baby's head to the mother's pelvis. This relationship is also called **engagement**.

TABLE 16.6 Stations

Station	Description
-3	Head is above mother's pelvis
0	Head is at the bottom of the pelvis (fully engaged)
+3	Head is beginning to emerge from the birth canal (crowning)

Lie

Fetal **lie** refers to how the baby's spine lines up with the spine of its mother. Nearly all babies are positioned in a longitudinal lie, in which their spine is parallel to that of the mother. If the baby is sideways, the positioning is referred to as *transverse* lie as its spine is at a 90-degree angle to that of its mother.

Attitude

Fetal **attitude** refers to the relationship of the body parts of a fetus to one another. **Normal attitude** describes what most people call the "fetal position" in which the head, arms, and legs are tucked in (flexed) toward the center of the chest. An **abnormal attitude** describes a fetus with its head tilted back and its face presenting first. This is a potentially dangerous position during childbirth.

In the Know: Versions

A mother with a baby that is presenting in breech position in the last few weeks of pregnancy can undergo a procedure called **version**. This procedure involves the manual turning or repositioning of a baby into the head-down position. Versions are successful more than 50 percent of the time.

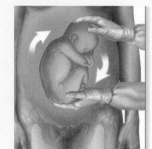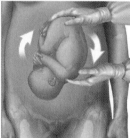

Manually correcting a breech presentation

Labor, Birth, and Postpartum

The process of labor and birth, also called **parturition**, is divided into three stages (see Figure 16.5). The first stage of labor describes the period of time that the woman's uterus contracts and the body prepares to deliver the baby. The second stage (also known as the "pushing stage") describes the period of time that a pregnant woman is pushing and giving birth to her baby. The third stage begins right after the baby and the placenta have been delivered.

First Stage of Labor: Early and Active

The first stage of labor is divided into two parts: early and active labor. **Early labor** begins when the uterus of the pregnant mother begins to contract. These contractions begin in an effort to move the baby along the birth canal. During early labor, the mother's cervix gradually thins out (**effaces**) and begins to dilate, or open in preparation to allow the baby to be born. Once labor begins, the secretion of the hormone oxytocin increases, which increases the frequency of contractions. The length of early labor varies by person. Some experience early labor for weeks, even months; others may experience early labor for only a few hours or may not notice these changes before active labor begins.

Active labor begins when labor contractions begin to grow progressively longer, stronger, and closer together. These contractions make the mother's cervix dilate faster than the contractions during early labor. Healthcare professionals refer to the final phase of active labor as transition. This is the period in which the mother's cervix dilates from 8 to 10 cm, leading into the second stage of labor. The cervix should dilate to 10 cm before the pregnant woman begins the second stage of labor.

Second Stage of Labor (Birth)

Once the mother's cervix is fully dilated, the second stage of labor has begun. This is commonly known as the "pushing stage," because this is the stage in which the mother pushes the baby out of the vaginal opening. The vagina expands with the aid of **relaxin**, which is a hormone produced by the placenta, corpus luteum, and uterus. As the baby moves through the birth canal and pushes on the cervix, the hormone oxytocin is produced. **Oxytocin** stimulates contractions and helps to push the baby further down the canal. This positive feedback loop (refer to Chapter 13 and Figure 13.3) causes the sequence of events that result in the baby's birth. Once the baby is delivered, this positive feedback loop stops. Childbirth is one of the few examples of a positive feedback system in the body, as the presence of oxytocin promotes the production of more oxytocin. Table 16.7 describes common signs of labor.

> **What's in a Word?**
>
> The term *parturient* (par-**toor**-ee-unt) refers to a woman about to give birth or in labor.

FIGURE 16.5 | The Stages of Labor

Stage 1:
The first stage of labor includes the dilation of the cervix, powerful contractions, and the rupture of the amniotic sac

Stage 2:
The second stage includes stronger contractions, and is usually when active pushing begins. The uterus presses the fetus against the cervix (which is now dilated to 10 cm).

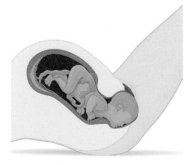

Stage 3:
The third stage starts when strong contractions push the baby through the cervix and the vagina.

After stage 3, the placenta pulls away from the uterine wall and passes through the cervix and the vagina.

TABLE 16.7 Signs of Labor (typically occurring 1–4 weeks before labor)

Sign	Description or Cause
"bag of water" ruptures	the rupture of the amniotic sac around the baby, also known as "water break"; can be either just a trickle or a gush of colorless, odorless fluid; this sign occurs in less than 15% of births
blood in vaginal discharge	also known as the bloody show, this vaginal discharge is the loss of the mucus plug (the seal between the vagina and cervix, which is lost as the cervix dilates)
contractions	becoming more regular, growing progressively stronger and lasting longer
diarrhea	due to the relaxation of muscles throughout the body in preparation for birth
dilated cervix	in preparation for birth, the cervix thins out (effaces) and begins to open (dilates)
lightening	baby begins its descent (drop) into the birth canal
loose joints	the hormone relaxin is being released into the mother's bloodstream in order to soften and loosen ligaments in preparation for birth
muscle pain	cramps and lower back pain are often attributed to the stretching and shifting of muscles and joints in preparation for birth
nesting	increased energy and/or inability to sleep; often described as an urge to clean and organize
weight loss	generally attributed to lower levels of amniotic fluid, frequent urination (due to lightening), and increased vaginal discharge

The Third Stage of Labor or the Postpartum Period

The third and final stage of labor begins immediately following the birth of the baby and results in the delivery of the placenta. The time after delivery is called the **postpartum period** (*post* means "after" and *partum* means "delivery"). The postpartum period begins immediately after the delivery of the placenta and lasts for about six weeks following the birth of the baby.

If the woman delivers her baby in a hospital or clinic setting, this third stage of labor would include the repairing of any tears or incisions that were made to the vaginal wall during the delivery process (such as an episiotomy). The mother is cleaned and covered to minimize cold and shaking from chills. The healthcare provider evaluates the position of the **fundus**, or base of the uterus, by palpating the abdomen and also by assessing the vaginal discharge, called **lochia**. Lochia generally lasts 4–6 weeks after childbirth.

At birth, the newborn requires immediate care. The first task is to establish and maintain the infant's airway. The airway (mouth and nose) must be cleared, and the infant must breathe on its own. The Apgar score, a rating system of a newborn's overall health, is completed immediately after the baby's birth. Once the Apgar scores are assessed and the baby is weighed, the newborn will be dried off and kept warm, usually by placing it on the mother's abdomen or chest and covering the newborn with a blanket. A cap may be placed on the baby's head to prevent heat loss.

The mother's postnatal care includes the close monitoring of bleeding, as well as bowel and bladder functions. Following a vaginal delivery, the mother can be released from the hospital as early as 1–2 days following childbirth. The average hospital stay for cesarean births is 3–4 days. Special attention should also be provided to the mother's mental well-being, as postpartum depression (PPD) requires the attention of a physician. PPD is described in greater detail in the "Conditions" section of this chapter.

Checkpoint 16.1

Answer the following questions to identify any areas of the section that you may need to review.

1. What two structures are responsible for exchanging oxygen and nutrients between the mother and the fetus?

   _____

   _____

2. What is the medical name given to describe early contractions known as "practice contractions"?

   _____

3. What term is used to describe the process of labor and birth?

   _____

Exercise 16.1   Word Analysis

Separate each term into its individual word parts using slashes, and indicate the type of word part using the letters P (prefix), S (suffix), and CF (combining form). Then write the definition of the term.

Term	Word Parts	Definition
1. amniotic	_____	_____
2. endoderm	_____	_____
3. ectoderm	_____	_____
4. mesoderm	_____	_____
5. oophorectomy	_____	_____

Exercise 16.2   Comprehension Check

Circle the correct term from the two choices provided in each sentence.

1. The process of conception/parturition is a miraculous event in which labor begins and the baby is delivered.

2. The ETC/EDD is the anticipated date of the baby's birth.

3. The date of the last gestational/menstrual cycle is used in calculating a woman's due date.

4. The placenta/endoderm is responsible for the exchange of nutrients and waste between the fetus and the mother.

5. Pregnancy is divided into three menarches/trimesters.

Exercise 16.3   Matching

Select the phase or stage in column 1 that matches the definition(s) in column 2. Write the letter of your answer on the line beside the phase or stage.

1. _____ embryonic phase

2. _____ fetal phase

3. _____ second stage of labor

4. _____ active labor

5. _____ postpartum period

a. describes the period of the second and third trimester

b. term used to describe the "pushing stage"

c. describes the period from conception to the eighth week

d. term used to describe "after delivery"

e. describes the period when labor contractions begin to grow progressively longer, stronger, and closer together.

Exercise 16.4   Word Building

Select a word part from the list in Table 16.1 to create the correct term for the definition provided. Note that not all items in the word part list will be used.

1. _____-al pertains to the lower part of the uterus.

2. _____-ic fluid surrounds the unborn baby in the uterus during pregnancy.

3. _____-ary means related to the breasts.

4. _____-ectomy is the surgical removal of all or part of the uterus.

5. _____-al pertains to the fetus.

Conditions

A wide variety of conditions exist that relate to human development. This variety is due to the nature of human development and conditions that can affect the mother, the father, the child, or all three. These include conditions that present during pregnancy, during the birth of the baby, and postpartum. Some of these conditions exist *only* during pregnancy and typically resolve once the baby has been delivered (such as gestational diabetes and preeclampsia). Other conditions, such as genetic defects, do not resolve on their own and require long-term treatment or care. Sexually transmitted infections (STIs), formerly known as sexually transmitted diseases (STDs), are caused by bacteria, viruses, or parasites. These infections can be passed from one person to another through unprotected sex or direct contact with one's genitalia. Table 16.8 identifies common sexually transmitted infections, while the sections that follow describe the conditions relating to pregnancy, labor and delivery, and the postpartum period.

TABLE 16.8 Sexually Transmitted Infections (STIs)

Type		Description
bacterial vaginosis	[bak-**teer**-ree-ohl vaj-ih-**nO**-sis]	vaginal discharge and odor caused by an overgrowth of bacteria in the vagina
chlamydia	[klah-**mih**-dee-ah]	bacterial infection spread by sexual contact that may be asymptomatic
gonorrhea	[gon-uh-**ree**-ah]	bacterial infection spread by sexual contact; often referred to as the clap or drip; results in burning sensation during urination and a discharge from the penis or vagina
herpes simplex virus (HSV-2)	[**hur**-peez]	viral infection that results in sores in the genital area, spread by skin-to-skin contact; also known as *genital herpes*
human immunodeficiency virus (HIV)		viral infection transmitted through body fluids that destroys the immune system of its host, leaving the host vulnerable to other infections and disease
human papillomavirus (HPV)	[pap-ih-**lO**-mah **vI**-rus]	an infection that causes warts in various parts of the body, dependent on the strain; also known as *genital warts*
pelvic inflammatory disease (PID)	[**pel**-vik in-**flam**-ah-tOr-ee]	infection of the reproductive organs that can result in infertility; often caused by untreated STIs
pubic lice	[**pew**-bik]	parasitic insects that infest the pubic area and lay eggs on the shaft of pubic hair; also known as "crabs"
syphilis	[**sif**-il-is]	bacterial infection usually spread by sexual contact; starts as a sore; generally treated with an antibiotic
trichomoniasis	[trik-ah-mah-**nI**-ah-sis]	a common, curable STI caused by a parasite; symptoms vary but can include itching of the genitals and vaginal discharge
urinary tract infection (UTI)/cystitis	[sih-**stI**-tis]	common infection in any part of the urinary system (kidneys, bladder, or urethra); not necessarily sexually transmitted, yet sexual intercourse increases risk factors; also known as a *bladder infection*

Conditions Associated with Pregnancy

Although proper prenatal care can assist most women in maintaining a healthy pregnancy, certain medical conditions may result in pregnancy complications. Roughly 10–20 percent of pregnancies are lost in the first 24 weeks as a result of **miscarriage**, the natural death of an embryo or fetus before it is able to live independently of its mother. Miscarriage is also known as a spontaneous abortion or pregnancy loss. Eighty percent of miscarriages occur in the first 12 weeks of gestation. Some feel that these early spontaneous abortions are due to the fetus having a significant defect. Often called the "all or none" effect," meaning that this particular birth defect was not survivable. Other, less severe problems can still be considered birth defects (club foot, cleft palate, etc), but would not cause the termination of pregnancy. Vaginal spotting and bleeding and abdominal cramps are considered early signs of miscarriage. **Stillbirth** is a condition in which a baby is born dead after 24 completed weeks of gestation. Although most stillbirths occur before a woman goes into labor, a small number occur during labor and delivery.

Ectopic pregnancy occurs when a fertilized ovum implants in a location other than the uterine lining. Most ectopic pregnancies occur in the fallopian tube (see Figure 16.6), but they can also occur in the ovary, abdominal cavity, or cervix. Ectopic pregnancies are not sustainable and can be life threatening if left untreated.

Gestational diabetes is a condition that occurs in approximately 4 percent of all pregnancies. **Gestational diabetes** occurs when insulin resistance develops in the pregnant mother, resulting in high concentrations of blood glucose in both mother and baby.

FIGURE 16.6 Ectopic Pregnancy

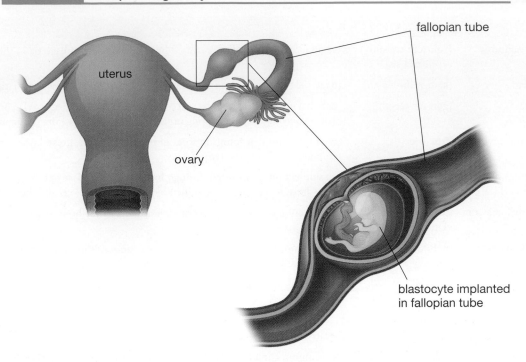

fallopian tube

uterus

ovary

blastocyte implanted
in fallopian tube

Mothers are screened for this condition between 24 and 28 weeks of pregnancy. Babies born to mothers with gestational diabetes are often susceptible to higher birth weights (10 pounds or more), premature delivery, and respiratory problems. This condition is generally resolved following delivery.

Preeclampsia is an abnormal condition in which a pregnant mother develops high blood pressure and increased levels of protein in the urine. This condition can lead to slowed fetal growth. Severe cases known as ecclampsia can lead to seizures and even the death of both mother and baby. This condition is the leading cause of bed rest and hospitalizations during pregnancy.

Fetal alcohol syndrome (FAS) is a group of signs and symptoms (birth defects) that appear in a newborn as a result of its mother's use of alcohol during pregnancy. Symptoms include small eyes, drooping eyelids, short, upturned nose, flattened cheeks, small jaw, and thin upper lip. While there is no evidence supporting a particular threshold of alcohol consumption leading to this outcome, most physicians are in agreement that the most detrimental effects occur when it is consumed in the first trimester of pregnancy.

References to "genes" typically relate to physical characteristics, personality traits, or talents shared with other members of our family. Although it is common knowledge that genes shape our physical appearance, it is equally important to understand the role genes play in overall health.

Sickle cell anemia is a genetic condition that is present at birth. It is inherited when a child receives two sickle cell genes, one from each parent. It is a blood disorder in which a person's red blood cells are shaped like sickles or crescent moons, as opposed to their usual round shape. The ideal shape for RBCs to effectively carry oxygen throughout the body is round. In the case of sickle cell anemia, RBCs often get trapped in smaller blood vessels and blood flow is compromised. These clogged blood vessels result in a condition known as sickle cell crisis, which usually requires hospitalization. Additionally, the body destroys these crescent-shaped RBCs faster than new ones can be replaced and this leads to anemia. Prenatal testing can be done to determine if a child will have sickle cell disease, be a carrier of sickle cell trait, or neither. While most people with sickle cell disease are of African descent, this condition also adversely affects those of Hispanic, southern European, Middle Eastern, and Asian Indian descent. If one parent is a carrier of the sickle cell gene (trait), the other should be tested prior to pregnancy.

In the Mediterranean population, parents may be tested for thalassemia, an inherited blood disorder in which the body produces an abnormal amount of hemoglobin.

Tay-Sachs disease is a rare, inherited disorder that destroys nerve cells in the brain and spinal cord, resulting in the loss of motor skills (such as sitting, turning over, and crawling), blindness, hearing loss, and possibly death. Individuals with this condition are missing an enzyme used to break down fatty substances. In the most common form, babies will begin to show symptoms around six months of age. Tay-Sachs disease occurs most frequently in individuals of Eastern and Central European Jewish descent. Prenatal genetic testing is recommended for parents with ancestors from these geographic areas.

One of the first prenatal tests given to a mother is a basic blood test to detect blood type and Rh factor. **Erythroblastosis fetalis** is a condition in which a mother's differing Rh factor could play a detrimental role in the baby's overall health and survival. Each of the four blood types (A, B, AB, and O) are further classified by the presence or absence of a protein on the surfaces of its red blood cells. The presence of this protein denotes an Rh-positive classification. Eighty-five percent of people carry this protein and are known as "Rh positive." Those who do not carry the protein are known as "Rh negative." An Rh-negative mother who conceives a child with an Rh-positive man may potentially produce a baby who is Rh positive. Rh incompatibility between the mother and baby is not a concern in a woman's first pregnancy because the baby's blood does not enter the mother's circulatory system during pregnancy. However, during delivery, there is a chance that the blood of mother and baby may come into contact. This interaction results in the mother's blood recognizing the baby's Rh protein as a foreign substance and beginning the creation of antibodies to offer protection against it. These antibodies are harmless until the mother has another pregnancy with an Rh-positive baby. When this occurs, the antibodies will attack the red blood cells of the fetus. See Figure 16.7.

FIGURE 16.7 **Rh Incompatibility**

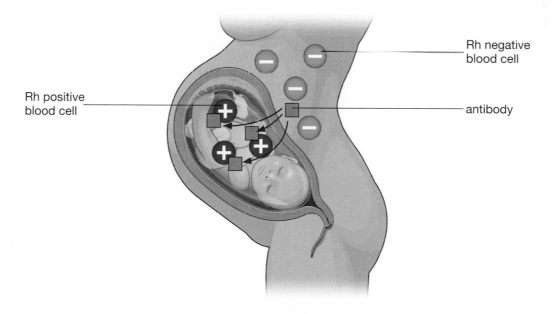

This attack may result in anemia, jaundice, brain damage, and heart failure in the newborn. Prenatal testing is imperative in detecting a mother who is Rh negative early in the pregnancy in order to offer preventive measures. Table 16.9 identifies these and other conditions related to pregnancy.

TABLE 16.9 Conditions Associated with Pregnancy

Term		Meaning	Word Analysis	
abruptio placentae	[ah-**brup**-she-O plah-**sen**-tee]	premature separation of the placenta from the uterus; also called placental abruption		
Down syndrome		genetic condition in which there is an extra copy of chromosome 21, causing a delay in a child's physical and mental development; also known as *trisomy 21*		
eclampsia	[e-**clamp**-see-ah]	life-threatening complication of pregnancy; preeclampsia (high blood pressure) that leads to seizures		
ectopic pregnancy	[ek-**tah**-pik]	implantation of the embryo in a location other than the uterus	*ec-* *top/o* *-ic*	out place pertaining to
erythroblastosis fetalis	[e-**rith**-rO-blas-tO-sis fe-**tal**-is]	condition in which an Rh-negative mother's red blood cells attack those of the baby she is carrying as if the baby is a foreign invader	*erythr/o* *blast/o* *-osis* *fet/o*	red blood cell immature abnormal condition fetus
fetal alcohol syndrome		a group of signs and symptoms that appear in a newborn as a result of the mother's use of alcohol during pregnancy		
gestational diabetes	[jes-**tay**-shun-uhl dI-ah-**bee**-teez]	condition in which insulin resistance (diabetes) develops during pregnancy; usually resolves after birth		
hemolytic disease of the newborn (HDN)		a blood disorder in which incompatible blood types between mother and fetus initiate the production of antibodies that attack the red blood cells of the developing fetus or infant	*hem/o*	blood
infertility		the inability to conceive or carry a pregnancy to term after 12 months of trying to conceive		
miscarriage		the natural death of an embryo or fetus before it is able to live independently of its mother; also known as a *spontaneous abortion* or *pregnancy loss*		
oligohydramnios	[O-lih-gO-hI-**dram**-nee-Os]	condition in which amniotic fluid is low; possible causes include high blood pressure, birth defects, and a rupture in the amniotic sac	*olig/o* *hydr/o* *-amnios*	scanty, few water, fluid amnion
polyhydramnios	[pah-lee-hI-**dram**-nee-Os]	condition in which there is an excessive amount of amniotic fluid present in the uterus surrounding the baby; usually serves as an indicator of other fetal conditions	*poly-* *hydr/o* *-amnios*	many, excessive water, fluid many, excessive
preeclampsia	[pree-eh-**clamp**-see-ah]	an abnormal condition in which a pregnant mother develops high blood pressure and increased levels of protein in the urine	*pre-*	before
sickle cell anemia		an inherited blood disorder in which irregularly shaped red blood cells fail to adequately circulate oxygen throughout the body		
stillbirth		condition in which a baby is born dead after 24 completed weeks of gestation		
Tay-Sachs disease	[**tay**-saks]	a rare inherited disorder that destroys nerve cells in the brain and spinal cord		
thalassemia	[**thal**-ah-se-mee-ah]	an inherited blood disorder in which the body produces an abnormal amount of hemoglobin		

Continues

Term	Meaning	Word Analysis
trisomy 18	condition in which a baby has three copies of chromosome 18 as opposed to two. The extra chromosome results in severe mental retardation and various physical deformities; 95% of children born with this condition die before their first birthday.	
Turner's syndrome	genetic condition in which a female is partially or completely missing an X chromosome; affects development and leads to infertility	

In the Know: Protecting a Fetus

A thin layer of placental tissue separates fetal blood from maternal blood and prevents toxins from reaching the fetus. Unfortunately, a variety of substances have the ability to penetrate this barrier. These include certain viruses and drugs (both legal and illegal). Drugs that can penetrate this barrier include alcohol, cocaine, and nicotine. Owing to the likelihood of this exchange from mother to baby, it is imperative that pregnant women refrain from the use of and exposure to these harmful substances. Caffeine can also penetrate this barrier, and excessive consumption of caffeine should be avoided during pregnancy.

Conditions Associated with Labor and Delivery

Occasionally, problems occur with labor and/or delivery. These difficulties include absence of contractions, or decreased labor, and difficult labor, called **dystocia**. Abnormalities with the placenta can occur, such as **placenta previa**, an abnormal placement of the placenta that causes hemorrhage, or **abruptio placentae**, a premature separation of the placenta from the uterine wall. These are emergency situations for the mother and the infant. Difficult labor, placental problems, and breech presentations usually require a **cesarean** birth (a surgical intervention also known as a C-section) to deliver the neonate. Table 16.10 identifies conditions related to labor and delivery.

TABLE 16.10 Conditions Associated with Labor and Delivery

Term		Meaning	Word Analysis	
breech presentation		a baby that is in a bottom- or feet-first position right before birth; most babies turn head down prior to birth		
cephalopelvic disproportion	[sef-fah-lO-**pel**-vik]	occurs when a baby's head or body is too large to pass through the mother's pelvis; often results in a cesarean section; also referred to as "failure to progress"	*cephal/o* *pelv/i* *-ic*	head pelvis pertaining to
dystocia	[dis-**tO**-sha]	difficult labor	*dys-* *-tocia*	difficult labor, delivery
nuchal cord	[**noo**-kul]	common occurrence in which the umbilical cord becomes wrapped around the neck of the fetus during labor and delivery	*nuch/o* *-al*	neck pertaining to
oxytocia	[ok-see-**tO**-sha]	rapid birth	*oxy-* *-tocia*	rapid labor, delivery
placenta previa	[plah-**sen**-tah **pree**-vee-ah]	condition in which the placenta partially or completely covers the mother's cervix		
premature infant		a baby that is born prior to the 37th week of pregnancy		

Conditions Associated with Postpartum

Postpartum depression (PPD) is a mental health condition that occurs in approximately three million women each year. Symptoms include mood swings, insomnia, loss of appetite, anxiety, crying episodes, irritability, and an inability to bond with the baby. Once diagnosed, PPD can be treated by a physician.

Postpartum depression is generally the most commonly recognized condition related to the postnatal period, but it is just one of the many conditions affecting the health and well-being of mother and newborn following delivery.

Agalactia, also called lactation failure, is the inability of the mother to produce milk following the birth of her child. This condition restricts a mother's ability to breastfeed and is usually a result of an insufficient secretion of the hormone prolactin from the pituitary gland.

Table 16.11 identifies conditions related to the postpartum period.

TABLE 16.11 Conditions Associated with Postpartum

Term		Meaning	Word Analysis	
agalactia	[a-gah-**lak**-tee-ah]	the inability of a mother to produce milk following childbirth	*a-*	not, without
			galact/o	milk
			-ia	condition
mastitis	[mas-**tI**-tis]	a painful infection of the breast tissue	*mast/o*	breast
			-itis	inflammation
mastoptosis	[mas-top-**tO**-sis]	drooping, sagging breasts	*mast/o*	breast
			-ptosis	drooping, sagging
postpartum depression (PPD)		mental health condition that occurs following childbirth with symptoms such as mood swings, anxiety, and insomnia	*post-*	after
			-partum	birth, delivery

In the Know: Infant Mortality

Infant mortality (defined as death within one year of birth) remains a problem all over the world. The 2013 infant mortality statistic for the United States is estimated to be 5.87 deaths per 1,000 live births. By one agency's ranking, this puts the United States at 167 out of 224 countries or locations, meaning that 57 countries had lower mortality. The infant mortality rate climbed (for the first time since the 1950s) from 6.8 in 2001 to 7.0 in 2002, possibly because of the increased incidence of females delaying childbearing into their late 30s and 40s. Some causes of infant mortality include birth defects, preterm delivery, and low birth weight. A large proportion of mothers still do not have access to prenatal care, which accounts for much of the mortality rate. The US Department of Health and Human Services has set particular objectives in the Healthy People 2020 initiative to promote national maternal and child health and decrease infant mortality disparities between ethnic and socioeconomic groups.[1] Healthcare personnel as well as consumers will work toward those goals.

[1] Healthy People 2020. http://MedTerm.ParadigmCollege.net/infantandchildhealth.

Checkpoint 16.2

Answer the following questions to identify any areas of the section that you may need to review.

1. What term is used to describe the condition when a baby's head or body is too large to pass through the mother's pelvis during delivery?

_____

2. What is the correct term to describe the premature separation of the placenta from the uterine wall?

_____

3. An excessive amount of amniotic fluid present in the uterus is known as what?

_____

Diagnostic Tests and Examinations

Prenatal care is essential for a healthy pregnancy. Regular doctor visits and examinations throughout pregnancy help by identifying any risk factors that might cause problems for the mother or the developing fetus. Prenatal examinations include weight and blood pressure monitoring, blood work to identify any risk factors, and urine analysis to test for protein in the urine (an indicator of preeclampsia). The healthcare provider may check the baby's heart rate with a Doppler fetal monitor, and ultrasounds may be provided to measure the baby and identify any risk factors. Mothers who are healthy and do not have any risk factors for pregnancy complications can expect to see their healthcare providers every four weeks through the 28th week of pregnancy. From week 28 through week 36, prenatal visits will occur every two weeks. From week 36 until delivery, visits are scheduled weekly.

Most prenatal visits will include the following: monitoring the mother's blood pressure and weight gain, measuring the abdomen to check the baby's growth, and checking the baby's heart rate. Other visits are focused on identifying risk factors for pregnancy complications. A **glucose tolerance test** is used to determine if a mother has developed gestational diabetes. During this test, the mother is given a sugary liquid to drink; this is followed by a blood glucose test to assess her body's ability to use insulin effectively. Blood is drawn approximately one hour after the drink is consumed.

A simple blood pressure test is important in determining whether the expectant woman has hypertension (high blood pressure). About 5 percent of pregnant women develop such high blood pressure that it becomes hazardous to them and the fetus. This is called preeclampsia (or toxemia). The high blood pressure leads to protein in their urine, which is detected by urinalysis. If the high blood pressure becomes severe, the mother and fetus are at high risk for stroke, coma, liver damage, and convulsions (eclampsia). The only real treatment is delivery of the baby.

Ultrasound imaging technology has many applications during pregnancy. Some of the common indications include verifying fetal age (fetal growth during the first trimester is highly predictable), determining whether twins, triplets (or more) are present, checking for ectopic pregnancy, screening for abnormalities, and more. Many companies advertise the creation of keepsake ultrasound images and videos of the unborn baby. While no studies have shown that having an ultrasound poses a risk to mother or fetus, many healthcare providers advise against using ultrasounds unless medically necessary.

A maternal blood sample can be used to screen for birth defects using the alpha-fetoprotein level (AFP), which can reveal a neural tube defect (for example, spina bifida), chromosomal abnormalities (including Down syndrome), and trisomy 18.

Amniocentesis (removal of a sample of fluid from the amniotic sac) is the most common test for ruling out birth defects. This procedure may be performed at 15–18 weeks and is between 99 and 100 percent accurate in detecting genetic abnormalities in the fetus. However, the risk of miscarriage is 2.6 percent when performed in the first trimester, and 0.8 percent when performed in the second trimester. This test is also used to test the maturity of an unborn baby's lungs in cases of elective delivery prior to 39 weeks gestation.

Chorionic villus sampling is 99 percent accurate in ruling out chromosomal abnormalities. This test can be done at week 10, earlier than amniocentesis. The test uses one of the tiny villi that attach the placenta to the uterine wall, and although there is a risk of miscarriage or fetal limb defects from performing this test, the risk is lower than that associated with early amniocentesis testing. Both amniocentesis testing and chorionic villus sampling can be used to provide DNA for paternity testing and to determine the gender of the fetus.

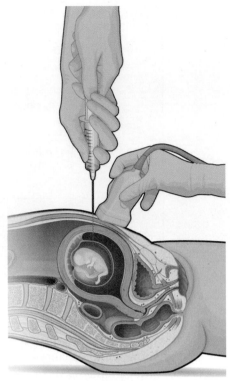

Amniocentesis

Fetal monitoring has become common during labor and delivery. Sensors measure the heart rate of the fetus, which is printed on strips of paper that eventually become part of the medical record. The information is important when the delivery team is determining the presence of fetal distress, or if an unplanned cesarean section (surgical delivery of the fetus) is indicated.

The **Apgar score** is a rating system of a newborn's overall health based on two brief assessments that occur immediately after the baby's birth. The first assessment is done one minute following birth and the second occurs five minutes after the birth. The test was developed in 1952 by an anesthesiologist named Virginia Apgar. This numerical value system indicates the infant's current state of health using the acronym APGAR: appearance (skin color), pulse (heart rate), grimace (reflexes), activity (muscle tone), and respiration (breathing rate and effort). A score of 7 points or above is normal. Scores that fall at 3 or below are regarded as critically low. Concerns regarding the first two Apgar scores can prompt a third score at 10 minutes after birth. Abnormalities related to the infant's cardiovascular and/or respiratory systems are addressed immediately. Table 16.12 displays the Apgar scoring system.

TABLE 16.12 Apgar Score

Apgar Points	0	1	2
appearance	blue or pale all over	blue extremities, body is normal color	hands and feet are pink; body is normal color
pulse	absent (no pulse)	below 100 beats/minute	normal; above 100 beats/minute
grimace	absent (no response to stimulation)	facial movement only	cries, sneezes, coughs, or pulls away with stimulation
activity	no movement, limp	arms and legs flexed with little movement	active movement
respiration	absent (no breathing)	weak, slow, irregular, gasping	normal rate and effort, good, strong cry

Table 16.13 identifies common tests and examinations performed during pregnancy, delivery, and postpartum.

TABLE 16.13 Tests and Examinations Associated with Pregnancy, Birth, and Postpartum

Procedure		Description
alpha-fetoprotein (AFP) test	[al-fah fee-tO-**prO**-teen]	maternal blood test performed between weeks 15 and 20 of gestation to check the levels of AFP in the blood; often used to detect abnormal conditions in the fetus (e.g., Down syndrome, spina bifida, and trisomy 18)
amniocentesis	[am-nee-O-sin-**tee**-sis]	diagnostic procedure in which a needle is inserted into the mother's abdomen in order to remove a sample of amniotic fluid; often used to diagnose fetal abnormalities and birth defects; also called *amniotic fluid test* or *AFT*
Apgar score	[**ap**-gar]	exam completed immediately following birth to assess the health status of a newborn; based on a numerical value system
biophysical profile (BPP)		test conducted in the third trimester that assesses the baby's breathing, movement, muscle tone, heart rate, and the amount of amniotic fluid present; generally involves an ultrasound and a nonstress test
chorionic villus sampling (CVS)	[kO-ree-**ah**-nik **vil**-us]	prenatal test used to detect birth defects, genetic diseases, and other conditions early in a pregnancy; a needle is used to remove a small sample of cells from the placenta for testing between 10 and 12 weeks gestation
contraction stress test (CST)		diagnostic tool used to ensure the baby is receiving an adequate supply of oxygen during labor, measures fetal heart rate during contractions of the uterus; also referred to as a *stress test*
fetal monitoring		diagnostic tool used during pregnancy, labor, and delivery to keep track of the baby's heart rate and strength/duration of uterine contractions
glucose tolerance test		analysis of the mother's fasting glucose followed by the consumption of a sugary drink to assess the ability to use insulin; conducted at 26–28 weeks gestation to detect gestational diabetes; also known as *maternal blood glucose*
group B streptococcus	[strep-tO-**cok**-us]	a swab is used to obtain cells from the vagina and rectum to detect the presence of bacteria that can cause pneumonia or serious illness in the newborn; generally done at 36–37 weeks of pregnancy
newborn screening tests		blood test for newborns used to screen for nearly 40 disorders, including congenital hypothyroidism, galactosemia, and phenylketonuria (PKU); hearing tests are also performed
nonstress tests (NST)		common prenatal test used to assess the health of a fetus; a belt is placed around the mother's abdomen and fetal heart rate is monitored following stimulation of the fetus to move about in utero; also known as *fetal heart rate monitoring*; generally conducted after 28 weeks
paternity test		the use of DNA profiling to determine whether an individual is the biological parent of a child
pelvimetry	[pel-**vi**-me-tree]	clinical measurement to assess the baby's progression along the birth canal
phenylketonuria (PKU)	[fee-nul-kee-tOn-**yoor**-ee-nah]	newborn screening used to detect the presence of an enzyme necessary for growth and development (phenylalanine); failure to treat can result in brain damage and mental retardation
pregnancy test		diagnostic tool used to detect hCG in urine or blood; used to determine if a woman is pregnant
Rh factor		screen to determine maternal-fetal blood incompatibility
sonohysterography	[sah-nO-his-tuh-rog-**raf**-ee]	diagnostic tool that uses ultrasound to view the fetus within the uterus
sterile vaginal exam		physical exam to check for cervix dilation and effacement
urine tests	[**yoor**-in]	a urine sample is collected in a sterile cup and test strips are dipped in to detect conditions such as urinary tract infections, diabetes, and preeclampsia

Soft Skills for Medical Professionals: Cultural Competence

Practicing cultural competency is essential when working in a healthcare setting. Healthcare providers need to provide consistent and supportive care to all of their patients and this includes awareness of cultural differences. Be mindful and conscious of the fact that others may regard family planning, pregnancy, infertility, birth, and postpartum very differently from you and your organization. For example, some religions and cultures do not support the use of birth control methods. Others may not approve of screening tests or routine prenatal care. It is also worth noting that not all pregnancies are expected (or welcome). The personal views and cultural values of healthcare providers should never influence the level of care they provide to their patients.

Parity

Knowing a patient's medical history is necessary for accurate exams. **Parity** is the number of times a woman has given birth. Females who have carried a single pregnancy to a minimum of 20 weeks gestation are considered primiparous (para 1), two total pregnancies are considered biparous (para 2), and three or more births are classified as multiparous (para 3 or more). The birth of multiples (e.g., twins, triplets) is considered only one pregnancy (not two, three, and so on). Note: Parity is not based on the number of babies born in a single pregnancy.

In the United States, women who reach 20 weeks of gestation in a pregnancy are considered to have given birth, to be "parous." Those who have not carried a pregnancy to a minimum of 20 weeks gestation are referred to as nulliparous (para 0), as they have never given birth.

Abortus is a term that describes the number of pregnancies that were lost. Loss includes miscarriages and induced abortions. **Miscarriage** is a term that means the baby died prior to 24 weeks gestation. **Induced abortions**, also known as therapeutic abortions, are the intentional termination of a pregnancy before the fetus can live independently. Abortus is equal to the number of pregnancies minus the number of times a woman has given birth. Abortus numbers do not include **stillbirths**, which are babies born dead after 24 completed weeks of gestation. These stillbirths are counted as pregnancies.

Note: Do not confuse gravida with parity. Gravida, which was discussed in Chapter 15, refers to the number of times a woman has become pregnant, regardless of whether the pregnancy was carried to term or resulted in a live birth.

To Note!

Do not confuse gravida (the number of times a woman has become pregnant) with parity (the number of times a woman has given birth).

In the Know: Documenting Pregnancy

TPAL is a common method used to provide a quick overview of a woman's obstetric history. In TPAL, the **T** refers to the number of births (after 37 weeks gestation); **P** to the number of premature births; **A**, the number of induced abortions and miscarriages reported prior to 20 weeks gestation; and **L**, the number of living children. For example, a woman who has carried two pregnancies to 36 weeks (one of which was stillborn), one pregnancy to 37 weeks, had one abortion at 10 weeks, and has two living children would have a TPAL annotation of T1, P2, A1, L2, or 1-2-1-2.

Checkpoint 16.3

Answer the following questions to identify any areas of the section that you may need to review.

1. Gravida and parity are used to describe what aspects of a woman's medical history?

   _____

   _____

2. High blood pressure and protein in the urine are both symptoms of what condition?

   _____

3. Which test involves aspirating fluid from the amniotic sac to determine whether a developing fetus has a birth defect?

   _____

Treatments

Healthcare practitioners use predetermined guidelines to direct patient care. These guidelines, known as clinical practice guidelines and evidence-based practices, have been developed by the specialty societies based on past clinical research. They represent the treatment pathways that have achieved the best outcomes. Treatment decisions generally fall into three categories: surgical, clinical, and pharmacological.

Surgical treatments are generally invasive as they involve a puncture or an incision into the skin. *Clinical treatments* are generally noninvasive and involve nonsurgical techniques (e.g., physical therapy). *Pharmacological treatments* involve the utilization of medicines (drugs) to treat specific illnesses or diseases. Medication therapies are regulated by the Food and Drug Administration (FDA). To be approved by the FDA for use in the United States, every medicine must be backed by research studies that have shown the medication to be effective in its treatment of a given disease and has a tolerable safety profile. The following sections provide an overview of treatments common to human development, pregnancy, labor and delivery, and postpartum conditions.

Birth control is the practice of preventing pregnancy. Contraception is a term that describes the use of artificial means to prevent pregnancy (e.g., condoms, birth control pills). Methods of birth control can be surgical, clinical, and pharmacological in nature. Methods that use the hormones estrogen and progesterone to prevent pregnancy include birth control pills, emergency contraception pills, hormonal injections, the patch, and some intrauterine devices. Estrogen tricks the female body into thinking it is already pregnant (thus stopping the release of the ovum) and progesterone or progestin options prevent pregnancy by making cervical mucus thicker (making it difficult for sperm to travel) and uterine lining thinner (making it difficult for an ovum to implant in the wall of the uterus). Table 16.14 identifies the various types of birth control methods available today.

> **Did You Know?**
>
> Progestin is the synthetic version of progesterone.

TABLE 16.14 Methods of Birth Control

Type	Description
abstinence	abstaining from sexual intercourse to prevent pregnancy
barrier methods	devices that block sperm from entering the uterus (male and female condoms, cervical cap, diaphragm, sponge)
bilateral tubal ligation	surgical procedure in which the fallopian tubes are blocked in order to prevent the fertilization of an ovum; can be blocked by cutting, burning, or removing sections of the fallopian tubes
emergency contraception pill (ECP)	pill containing high concentrations of progestin; also known as the *morning-after pill* (Plan B, Next Choice, RU 486, ellaOne); generally taken within 72 hours of unprotected sex
hormonal injection	injectable solution of progestin that prevents pregnancy for up to 3 months (Depo-Provera)
intrauterine device (IUD)	small, T-shaped device made of flexible plastic that inserts into the uterus and prevents pregnancy by damaging or destroying sperm; includes copper IUDs (Paragard) and hormonal IUDs (Liletta, Mirena, Skyla)
oral contraception or birth control pills	pill containing estrogen and/or progesterone taken daily
patch	thin, square patch that sticks to the skin and releases progesterone and estrogen hormones through the skin to the bloodstream; worn for three consecutive weeks (a new one is placed each week); no patch is worn during the fourth week and the menstrual cycle is present during this week
rhythm method	form of natural family planning in which the menstrual cycle is tracked to plan sexual intercourse during periods of ovulation
spermicide	foam or gel inserted inside a condom or into the vagina prior to intercourse to kill sperm and prevent pregnancy, also known as *spermatocide*
vasectomy	surgical procedure in which the vas deferens are cut and tied in order to prevent sperm from entering into semen, thus preventing fertilization

Did you Know: History of Birth Control Pills

The most common method of contraception is the use of oral contraceptives (birth control pills). The medical benefits of oral contraceptive use include decreased acne, cramping, and menstrual flow; decreased body hair; lower cancer risk; and protection against osteoporosis.

Did you know . . . ?:

- Margaret Sanger opened the first birth control clinic in the United States in 1916. Sanger's clinic was closed only 11 days after opening and Sanger was arrested.

- The birth control pill was approved in 1957 to treat severe menstrual problems. The pill came with a warning that it could prevent pregnancy. Within two years, half a million women were taking the pill for its "side effect."

- The FDA approved the pill for contraceptive use in 1960.

- In *Griswold v. Connecticut*, the US Supreme Court struck down state laws prohibiting married women from taking birth control pills (1960).

- Most oral birth control pills contain a 28-day regimen of pills to be taken daily. Each pack contains seven inactive, or placebo, pills. Women can elect to skip their periods if they begin the next month's pack on the first day of the placebo pills.

- The male birth control pill is currently in the early stages of research and development. Unlike the female birth control's role of stopping a single ovum from reaching its final destination, the male birth control pill is intended to stop approximately 1,500 sperm cells from reaching their destination.

Surgical Treatments

Recall that infertility is the inability to conceive a child despite having frequent, unprotected sexual intercourse over the course of a year. Among couples in the United States, 10–15 percent are infertile. Infertility can be the result of a single factor in the male, female, or a combination of both. Many safe and effective surgical treatments are available to significantly improve the probability of conception. Table 16.15 identifies the most common therapies used to treat infertility.

TABLE 16.15 Types of Infertility Treatments

Type	Description
artificial insemination (AI)	procedure in which semen is inserted into a woman's cervix, fallopian tubes, or uterus in order to treat infertility and conceive
gamete intrafallopian transfer (GIFT)	procedure in which the ova and sperm are mixed in a laboratory setting and immediately placed into a fallopian tube for fertilization
intracytoplasmic sperm injection (ICSI)	procedure in which a single sperm is injected directly into an ovum; generally used to treat male infertility
in vitro fertilization (IVF)	procedure in which the mother's ovum is fertilized outside the body and implanted into the uterus of the mother or surrogate
zygote intrafallopian transfer (ZIFT)	procedure in which the ovum and sperm are mixed in a laboratory setting; fertilization is confirmed prior to the ovum being transferred into the fallopian tubes

The surgical delivery of a baby is known as a **cesarean section** or **C-section** and involves incisions in the mother's abdomen and uterus to remove the baby. Although the majority of babies in the United States are delivered vaginally (vaginal delivery), some mothers either opt to deliver their children via C-section, or circumstances (such as placenta previa) require that they deliver via C-section.

Surgical treatments related to postpartum include methods to sterilize the mother and prevent future pregnancies. These include oophorectomies, tubal ligations, and hysterectomies. A **bilateral tubal ligation** is the procedure that

> **Did You Know?**
>
> The vaginal delivery of a baby following a previous C-section delivery is called "vaginal birth after cesarean (VBAC)."

FIGURE 16.8 Bilateral Tubal Ligation

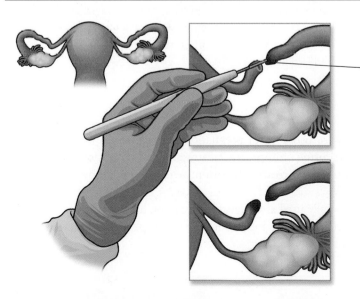

fallopian tube is cut and burned to prevent the fertilization of the ovum

> **What's in a Word?**
>
> The term *bilateral tubal ligation* includes the combining forms *later/o*, *tub/o*, and *ligat/o*, meaning "side," "tube," and "tying" (respectively).

prevents the fertilization of an ovum by blocking the fallopian tubes (via cutting, burning, or section removal).

Other surgical treatments are identified in Table 16.16.

TABLE 16.16 Surgical Treatments Associated with Pregnancy, Birth, and Postpartum

Treatment		Description
abortion	[ah-**bOr**-shun]	procedure in which a pregnancy is ended by removing an embryo or fetus from the womb before it has the ability to survive on its own
bilateral salpingo-oophorectomy	[sal-**pin**-gO-oo-ah-fOr-**ek**-tuh-mee]	surgical procedure to remove both ovaries and both fallopian tubes
castration	[kas-**tray**-shun]	removal of male (testes) and female (ovaries) gonads to cause sterilization; also known as a *gonadectomy*
cephalic version	[seh-**fal**-lik]	procedure in which the fetus is manually turned so that its head is in position for a vaginal delivery
cerclage	[sur-**klazh**]	surgical procedure in which the cervix is sutured closed to prevent preterm labor
cesarean section	[se-**sair**-ree-un]	surgical procedure used to deliver a baby through incisions in the mother's abdomen and uterus; commonly referred to as a C-section
endometrial ablation	[en-dO-**mee**-tree-al ah-**blay**-shun]	procedure in which a layer of tissue lining the uterus is permanently removed to stop or reduce abnormal or excessive bleeding following childbirth
episiorrhaphy	[e-**piz**-ee-or-ah-fee]	procedure to repair episiotomy
episiotomy	[e-pee-zee-**ah**-tuh-mee]	procedure in which an incision is made to the wall of the vagina in order to quickly enlarge the opening for the baby to pass through; also known as a *perineotomy*
forceps delivery		assisted vaginal delivery; forceps (an instrument shaped like a pair of large spoons or salad tongs) are applied to the baby's head to help guide the baby out of the birth canal
labor induction		procedure used to stimulate contractions of the uterus in order to initiate labor before it begins on its own (i.e., stripping of membranes in order to rupture the amniotic sac or break the water)
salpingo-salpingostomy	[sal-**pin**-gO-sal-pin-**gos**-tuh-mee]	procedure in which the fallopian tubes are rejoined in order to reverse a tubal ligation and reestablish a woman's ability to conceive
sterilization		procedure that intentionally leaves a person unable to reproduce
vacuum extraction		assisted vaginal delivery in which a vacuum (a cup with a handle and a vacuum pump) is applied to the baby's head to help guide the baby out of the birth canal
vasovasostomy	[vas-zoh-vuh-**sos**-tuh-mee]	procedure in which the ends of the vas deferens are reconnected to reverse sterilization

Clinical Treatments

A variety of clinical treatments are available for pregnant and postpartum mothers. Pain and discomfort can be managed using chiropractic treatments and relaxation techniques, such as yoga and Lamaze. Chiropractic treatments can provide pain relief by maintaining and realigning joints.

Prenatal yoga classes are generally used as outlets for relaxation and physical fitness during pregnancy. The benefits of prenatal yoga include improved sleep, stress relief, decreased lower back pain, and increased flexibility.

Lamaze has been a popular childbirth education resource for several decades and has evolved from basic breathing techniques into a comprehensive class aimed to increase a mother's confidence in her ability to give birth. Another growing trend in the clinical arena of labor and delivery is the use of hypnobirthing, also known as childbirth hypnosis programs. Hypnosis is a state of deep mental and physical relaxation that enables the hypnotized individual to block outside distractions by focusing on breathing and visualization techniques.

Water birth is the practice of laboring in a pool filled with warm water. This practice is another natural option for pain relief during labor and delivery and is offered by various birthing centers and nurse-midwives. Water births are not recommended once a mother enters stage two of labor and is completely dilated and prepared to push the baby out of the birth canal. Table 16.17 identifies various clinical techniques used during pregnancy, labor, and delivery.

TABLE 16.17 Clinical Treatments Associated with Pregnancy, Birth, and Postpartum

Treatment	Description
chiropractic	means to establishing pelvic balance and alignment during pregnancy to relieve pain
hypnobirth	birthing practice that assists mothers in replacing fear and expectations of pain with thoughts of safety and comfort; goal is to prevent the release of stress hormones leading to the "fight or flight" response
Lamaze	resource for methods of breathing, pain management, comfort, and relaxation during the birthing process
prenatal physical therapy	treats back pain caused by the additional weight, poor posture, and shift in the center of gravity during pregnancy
prenatal yoga	a source of relaxation and physical fitness during pregnancy
water birth	a natural option for mothers who are not interested in using medications for pain relief during labor and delivery; specific stages of labor occur in a warm pool of water

Pharmacological Treatments

Agents used for conditions related to human development include agents to support conception, such as anti-impotence drugs and ovulation stimulants. Agents used in pregnancy include antiviral and antibiotic drugs to treat infections such as STIs, UTIs, and group B strep. Other agents include those used for labor and delivery assistance, including pain relievers (epidurals) and labor inducers (cervical ripening agents). Table 16.18 describes the most common drugs used to treat problems during pregnancy, birth, and postpartum.

Did You Know?

Before modern antibiotics, the STI syphilis was treated by poisoning the patient with mercury. This led to very high body temperatures (up to 108) which killed the bacteria. Unfortunately the person being treated did not always fare well.

TABLE 16.18 · Pharmacological Agents for Pregnancy, Birth, and Postpartum

Drug Class	Use	Generic Name	Brand Name
antibiotics	treat group B strep, UTIs, and STIs during pregnancy	penicillin, ampicillin, tetracycline	
anti-impotence	treat impotence due to erectile dysfunction		Viagra, Cialis, Levitra
antivirals	treat genital herpes during pregnancy	acyclovir	Valtrex
cervical ripening	ripen cervix and encourage dilation during the induction of labor	prostaglandins: dinoprostone and misoprostol	Prepidil, Cervidil, Cytotec
labor inducing	induce labor by triggering the positive feedback loop to release the hormone oxytocin	oxytocin	Pitocin, Methergine, Ergotrate
labor inhibiting	stop or slow preterm labor by inhibiting contractions of the uterus	ritodrine	
local anesthetics	pain relief during labor and delivery	epidural block, spinal block, pudendal block bupivacaine, chloroprocaine, lidocaine	
opioids (narcotics)	pain relief during labor and delivery, and postpartum	fentanyl, sufentanil, clonidine, morphine,	Vicodin, Percocet
ovulation stimulants	stimulate the ovaries to release an ovum; also known as *fertility drugs*	clomifene citrate	Clomid, Serophene

Checkpoint 16.4

Answer the following questions to identify any areas of the section that you may need to review.

1. What type of birth control method involves refraining from sexual activity?

   _____

2. What is the name of the procedure in which an incision is made in the wall of the vagina to enlarge the vaginal opening during a vaginal delivery?

   _____

3. What procedure manually turns a fetus so that its head is in position for a vaginal delivery?

   _____

Abbreviations

In the medical field, information is generally recorded in medical charts and in electronic medical records and provided to healthcare workers in medical shorthand. It is important that healthcare professionals become familiar with the abbreviations used on a daily basis to successfully perform the duties assigned in a typical workday.

Table 16.19 lists common abbreviations used in reference to conditions and treatments of human development.

TABLE 16.19 Abbreviations Associated with Pregnancy, Birth, and Postpartum

Abbreviation	Meaning
AFP	alpha-fetoprotein test
AI	artificial insemination
AMN	anmiocentesis
CPD	cephalopelvic disproportion
CS, C-section, C/S	cesarean section
CST	contraction stress test
CVS	chorionic villus sampling
EDC	estimated date of confinement (due date)
EDD	estimated date of delivery
FECG	fetal electrocardiogram
FHR	fetal heart rate
FTND	full-term, normal delivery
FTNSVD	full-term, normal, spontaneous, vaginal delivery
GIFT	gamete intrafallopian transfer
grav I	first pregnancy
HCG	human chorionic gonadotropin
ICSI	intracytoplasmic sperm injection
IUD	intrauterine device
IUP	intrauterine pregnancy
IVF	in vitro fertilization
L&D	labor and delivery
LBW	low birth weight
LMP	last menstrual period
NB	newborn
NST	nonstress test
OCP	oral contraceptive pills
PI, para I	first delivery
PIH	pregnancy induced hypertension
SAB	spontaneous abortion
SB	stillbirth
STD	sexually transmitted disease
STI	sexually transmitted infection
TAH-BSO	total abdominal hysterectomy-bilateral salpingo-oophorectomy
TSS	toxic shock syndrome
TVS	transvaginal sonography
UC	uterine contractions
VBAC	vaginal birth after cesarean section
ZIFT	zygote intrafallopian transfer

Exercise 16.5   Comprehension Check

Select from the two terms to find a match for the definition provided, and circle the correct term.

1. hormone secretion increases after labor begins: oxytocin/testosterone

2. difficult labor: relaxin/dystocia

3. premature separation of the placenta from the uterine wall: abruptio placentae/distention

4. abnormal placement of the placenta, causing hemorrhage: zygote/placenta previa

5. screening tool for assessing newborn's condition: Apgar score/Braxton Hicks

Exercise 16.6   Matching

Select the term from column 1 that matches the definition in column 2. Write the letter of the answer on the line beside the term.

1. _____ blastocyst   a. pregnancy

2. _____ gestation   b. period after the delivery of the placenta

3. _____ mesoderm   c. hollow ball of cells

4. _____ mitosis   d. process whereby cells divide

5. _____ postpartum   e. forms nervous system and more

Exercise 16.7   Abbreviations

Read each sentence. Then write the appropriate abbreviation in the blank.

1. The fetal heart rate, or _____, was 160.

2. There were no complications, and Linda had a full term, normal, spontaneous, vaginal delivery, or a _____.

3. The newborn, _____, infant weighed 7 lbs., 6 oz.

4. Christie had a vaginal birth after a cesarean section, or a _____.

5. Louisa's urine was positive for human chorionic gonadotrophin, or _____.

Exercise 16.8   Word Analysis

Divide each word into its parts. Write the meaning of the parts on the line next to the word.

1. relaxin   _____

2. nulligravida   _____

3. dystocia   _____

4. postpartum   _____

5. amnion   _____

Chapter Review

After successfully completing this chapter, you should be able to correctly answer the following review questions. Answers are provided in the back of the text. Use this self-assessment opportunity to check your understanding of the content and determine whether you need to revisit any of the chapter's content.

Crossword Puzzle

Use the clues provided to fill in the puzzle with the correct terms. Enter one letter per square.

Across

3. prefix meaning after
5. nulla
6. Greek root for bent backward
8. Greek meaning of *amnio*
10. female who has never conceived a child
13. process of cell division
15. hormone that stimulates the flow of milk
16. Greek for a flat cake
20. female hormone
22. Greek for thread
24. walk
26. nutrient for the embryo that arises from the ovum

28. blastos
29. related to the neck

Down

1. myometrium
2. word part meaning turn
3. period following delivery of the placenta
4. yolk color
7. refers to number of pregnancies
8. hollow ball of cells
9. suffix meaning condition
11. vaginal discharge after delivery of a baby
12. puncture of the amniotic sac to remove sample of amniotic fluid

14. stripes
17. lining of the GI tract, epithelium of trachea, bronchi, lungs, liver, pancreas, urinary bladder
18. prefix meaning three
19. fertilized ovum
21. word part meaning acid
23. abbreviation for intrauterine device
25. score indicating infant's condition
27. dilate
29. abbreviation for cervix

Matching

Match the following terms to their proper definitions.

1. _____ castration
2. _____ cerclage
3. _____ amniocentesis
4. _____ Braxton Hicks
5. _____ pelvimetry
6. _____ trimesters
7. _____ presentation
8. _____ parturition
9. _____ zygote
10. _____ nullipara

a. removal of fluid from the amniotic sac
b. three periods of three months each, during a pregnancy
c. the position of the fetus prior to delivery
d. fertilized ovum
e. removal of male testes or female ovaries
f. a woman who has never given birth
g. known as practice contractions
h. clinical measurement to assess the baby's progression along the birth canal
i. surgical procedure in which the cervix is sutured closed
j. process of giving birth

Identification

Correctly label the illustration using the provided terms. Write the term's corresponding letter in the correct callout of the figure below.

1. _____ blastocyte
2. _____ falllopian tube
3. _____ ovary
4. _____ uterus

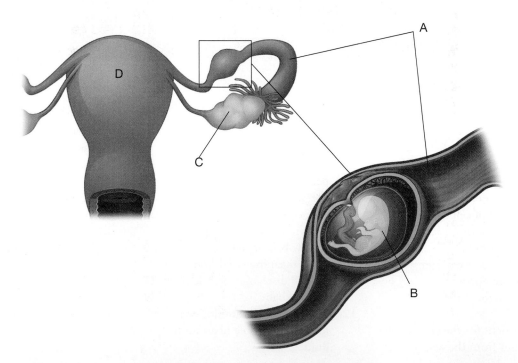

Abbreviations

Answer the following questions using abbreviations.

1. Terri had a C-section because of cephalopelvic disproportion, or _____.

2. Imaging revealed a _____, or normal intrauterine pregnancy.

3. The _____, or fetal electrocardiogram, revealed no abnormalities.

Word-Building Challenge

Review the following list of terms. Apply what you have learned in this chapter by identifying the meaning of the word parts within the term. Then write the likely definition of the term on the line provided.

1. amniochorial _____

2. embryopathy _____

3. placental dystocia _____

4. parturient canal _____

5. gravidic _____

Extension Activities

Complete the following activities as assigned by your instructor.

1. Conduct an Internet search for the most recent trends in male birth control methods (e.g., "clean sheets pill," Vaselgel, Gendarussa, anti-EPPIN agent). Provide an overview comparing and contrasting two to three of the methods identified. Discuss differences in medication administration, efficacy, cost, access, and mechanism (means) used to prevent pregnancy. Present your findings in a 5–10 slide PowerPoint presentation.

2. For many years, parents of stillborn children have rallied for an official, legal document that acknowledges the existence of their babies. Search the Internet for current legislation in your state of residence addressing the existence of vital records regarding stillbirths. Create a post in the discussion forum to share your findings with the class.

3. Follow the link, http://MedTerm.ParadigmCollege.net/humangeneticengineering to read the article on human genetic engineering. After reading the article, write a one-page summary of your thoughts regarding this sensitive subject.

Student eResources

The Course Navigator learning management system that accompanies this textbook offers multiple opportunities to master chapter content, including end-of-chapter exercises, a glossary of key terms with audio pronunciations, games, pronunciation coach, and additional activities such as engaging with the BioDigital® Human.

Answer Keys

Chapter 1: Word Structures

Translation Challenge

Responses will vary but should align with the following information: The office is contacting the patient regarding the treatment (Tx) of the son's circumcision, recommending she discontinue (D/C) the use of Neosporin. If the chief complaint (CC) of pain remains, she should give acetaminophen as long as no known allergies (NKA) exist. She should return to the office (RTO) if child becomes febrile in order to rule out (R/O) a possible urinary tract infection (UTI).

Checkpoint 1.1

1. root word: word part that forms basis of meaning, prefix: precedes the root and adds to or changes its meaning, suffix: follows root and adds to or changes its meaning, 2. Medical terms come from a couple of different languages, hence two root words can share the same meaning. Root words are not interchangeable because medical terms are fixed. 3. Greek and Latin

Exercise 1.1

1. c, 2. d, 3. a, 4. e, 5. b

Checkpoint 1.2

1. A combining form is a root word with a combining vowel attached.
2. Combining vowels make pronunciation easier.
3. o

Exercise 1.2

1. gynec = females, 2. leuko = white, cyto = cells, 3. tracheo = trachea, 4. cardio = heart, 5. hemato = blood, 6. gastro = stomach, entero = intestines, 7. cysto = sac or cyst, 8. cardio = heart

Checkpoint 1.3

1. Suffixes add information to the root word or combining form in order to describe something.
2. *–logy* indicates a specialty and *–logist* indicates the practitioner.
3. Two or more suffixes may have the same meaning such as *–ia* and *–ism*, which indicate a condition or process.

Exercise 1.3

1. carditis, itis = inflammation; 2. pulmonary, ry = pertaining to; 3. rheumatic, ic = pertaining to; 4. arthrosis, osis = condition; 5. cardiomegaly, megaly = enlargement; 6. renal, al = pertaining to; 7. anemia, emia = condition of the blood; 8. hypertrophy, trophy = development

Exercise 1.4

1. metry = process of measuring; 2. meter = measure or measurement; 3. scopy = process of viewing with an instrument; 4. gram = record; 5. graphy = process of recording; 6. iatric = treatment; 7. centesis = puncture to withdraw fluid, 8. desis = stabilization or binding

Exercise 1.5

1. osteoblasts, 2. erythrocyte, 3. hemostasis, 4. cephalalgia, 5. arthrodynia *or* arthralgia, 6. cystocele

Checkpoint 1.4

1. less than and under or below, 2. Answers will vary. Examples include: quadriplegia or unilateral. 3. Answers will vary. Examples include: distal and abduction.

Exercise 1.6

1. monochromatic, 2. bilateral, 3. ambidextrous, 4. trigeminy, 5. quadriplegia or tetraplegia, 6. polycythemia, 7. multidisciplinary, 8. megaloblasts

Exercise 1.7

1. hyper, 2. hypo, 3. sub, 4. super, 5. supra, 6. Ultra, 7. ad, 8. ab

Exercise 1.8

1. f, 2. e, 3. d, 4. c, 5. b, 6. a

Checkpoint 1.5

1. You drop the combining vowel.
2. You keep the combining vowel.
3. Responses will vary, but examples of eponyms include Lou Gehrig's disease, boycott, and Achilles heel.

Exercise 1.9

1. mastectomy, 2. cardiologist, 3. pericardial, 4. sarcoma, 5. dysphagia

Checkpoint 1.6

1. *s, es*
2. digiti
3. cortices

Exercise 1.10

1. correct, 2. tracheotomy, 3. cardiologist, 4. abdominocentesis, 5. tachycardia

Exercise 1.11

1. uro/logist; uro = urine, logist = someone who studies; a specialist in urology
2. thrombo/cyt/osis; thrombo = clot, cyt = cell, osis = condition; an increase in the number of circulating platelets
3. cephal/ic; cephal = head, ic = relating to; relating to the head
4. path/logy; path=disease, logy=study of; the study of disease
5. gastro/rrhaphy, gastro = stomach, rrhaphy = suturing; suture of a perforation of the stomach.

Exercise 1.12

1. f, 2. b, 3. d, 4. a, 5. h, 6. g, 7. e, 8. c

Chapter Review

Matching

1. f, 2. j, 3. h, 4. g, 5. c, 6. d, 7. a, 8. I, 9. b, 10. e

Abbreviations

1. pt, HTN; 2. CBC, pt, CC, r/o; 3. t.i.d.; 4. CC, CP, SOB, stat. 5. ♂, VS, WNL, PMH, Dx

Spell-Check

1. no change, 2. tracheotomy, 3. cardiologist, 4. amniocentesis, 5. tachycardia, 6. no change, 7. no change, 8. leukocytes, 9. cyanosis

Word-Building Challenge

1. pain of the joints, 2. excessive wordiness, 3. stubbornness (hard head), 5. excessive sleeping, 6. excessive salivating caused by increased eating

Chapter 2: Body Organization and Healthcare Terminology

Translation Challenge

Responses will vary slightly but should align with the following information:

The driver in vehicle 1 has several cuts to the front of the head. The airbag has also caused burns to the upper surface of the chest. The passenger in vehicle 2 was not wearing a seatbelt and has suffered injury to the upper neck due to the sudden backward and forward movement of the neck. The head and neck are held steady in a fixed position and the patients are taken to the hospital for medical images to be taken of the front to back view of their head and spine.

Checkpoint 2.1

1. cells, tissues, organs, body systems, organism; 2. skeletal or striated; 3. nucleus

Exercise 2.1

1. g, 2. a, 3. f, 4. h, 5. b, 6. c, 7. e, 8. d

Checkpoint 2.2

1. patient is standing, facing forward, arms at sides, palms facing forward, legs straight, feet flat on the floor with toes pointing forward
2. Answers will vary; an example could be "The wrist is distal in relation to the elbow."
3. eversion

Exercise 2.2

1. away from; 2. back; 3. medial, closer to the midline; 4. superficial, closer to the surface; 5. occurring on both sides; 6. farther from the point of attachment; 7. pertaining to the wall; 8. prone, lying horizontally and facing down

Checkpoint 2.3

1. pelvic cavity
2. Answer must include two of the following: right inguinal region, hypogastric region, left inguinal region
3. cervical vertebrae, 7

Exercise 2.3

1. c, 2. a, 3. d, 4. b, 5. f, 6. e

Exercise 2.4

1. D, 2. C, 3. E, 4. H, 5. F, 6. G, 7. A, 8. J, 9. B, 10. I

Exercise 2.5

right hypochondriac region	epigastric region	left hypochondriac region
right lumbar region	umbilical region	left lumbar region
right inguinal region	hypogastric region	left inguinal region

Checkpoint 2.4

1. fluoroscopy, 2. to monitor fetal growth and health status, 3. PET scans

Exercise 2.6

1. angiography, 2. bronchography, 3. echogram, 4. myelography, 5. radioimmunoassa

Exercise 2.7

1. urinalysis, 2. radioactive, 3. etiology, 4. inflammation, 5. radiogram, 6. pandemic, 7. roentgen, 8. culture

Checkpoint 2.5

1. the apothecary system and the metric system, 2. signa, 3. a route of administration in which a drug is placed under the tongue and is absorbed into the blood vessels there

Chapter Review

Crossword

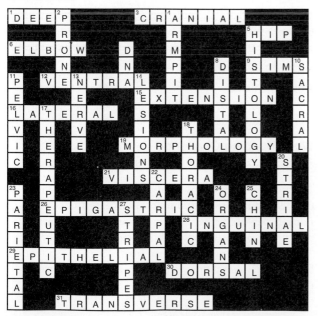

Matching

1. D, 2. E, 3. A, 4. C, 5. B

Identification

1. Trendelenburg position, 2. dorsal recumbent position, 3. supine position, 4. Sims' position, 5. knee-chest position, 6. sitting position, 7. prone position, 8. Fowler's position, 9. modified Trendelenburg position, 10. lithotomy position

Abbreviations

1. gt or gtt, 2. p.r.n., 3. stat, 4. fl oz, 5. AP, 6. Ⓑ

Word-Building Challenge

1. pertaining to the abdominal and pelvic regions of the body, 2. clavicle near front of rib cage, 3. between loin (adjoining the ribs to the hips) and lower back, 4. opposite side, 5. one side only

Extension Activities

1. Answers will vary.
2. Answers will vary.

Chapter 3: The Integumentary System

Translation Challenge

1. A comedo can either be a blackhead (open comedo) or a whitehead (closed comedo).
2. A pustular lesion contains pus.
3. The rash is erythematous, which means red. Erythe is the Latin root for "red."
4. A nevus is a beauty mark or a birthmark. Hyperpigmented means "having excessive pigment." So the statement is referring to a dark, raised beauty mark or birthmark.

Checkpoint 3.1

1. dermis, 2. melanin, 3. hair shaft

Exercise 3.1

1. seb/o, sebum; 2. cutane/o, skin; 3. dermat/o, skin; 4. derm/o, skin; 5. hidr/o, sweat glands

Exercise 3.2

1. adipose, 2. confluent, 3. intradermally, 4. apocrine, 5. Dermatology

Exercise 3.3

1. e, 2. b, 3. d, 4. a, 5. c

Exercise 3.4

1. cutane-ous, 2. dermato-logist, 3. epi-derm-is, 4. sub-cutane-ous, 5. lipo-lysis

Exercise 3.5

1. nevi, 2. follicles, 3. Melanocytes, 4. papillae, 5. Ephelides

Exercise 3.6

1. G, 2. F, 3. C, 4. B, 5. E, 6. H, 7. A, 8. D

Checkpoint 3.2

1. psoriasis, 2. basal cell carcinoma, 3. nevi

Exercise 3.7

1. melano = black, dark hue, cyte = cell, a pigment-producing cell; 2. ec = out of, chyme = juice, osis = condition, a condition of blood leaking from a vessel; 3. cyan = blue, osis = condition, blue appearance; 4. chron = time, ic =pertaining to, a condition through time; 5. pustul/ = pus, -e = noun, small pus-filled lesion

Exercise 3.8

1. Physiologic jaundice, 2. erythema toxicum, 3. nevus flammeus, 4. Striae, 5. sebaceous glands

Exercise 3.9

1. e, 2. c, 3. b, 4. d, 5. a

Exercise 3.10

1. dermatitis, dermat = skin, itis = inflammation; 2. seborrhea, sebo = oil, rrhea = flowing; 3. acrocyanosis, acro = tip, cyan = blue, osis = condition; 4. angioma, angi = vessel, oma = tumor; 5. carotenemia, carotene = orange pigment, emia = pertaining to blood

Exercise 3.11

1. xerosis, 2. purpura, 3. eczema, 4. linea nigra, 5. impetigo, 6. nodule, 7. pustule, 8. verruca, 9. xanthoma, 10. vitiligo

Exercise 3.12

1. macule, 2. papule, 3. ulcer, 4. plaque, 5. fissure

Checkpoint 3.3

1. Responses could include biopsies, patch tests, scratch tests, and intradermal injections; 2. a biopsy; 3. Wood's lamp

Checkpoint 3.4

1. microdermabrasion, 2. micropigmentation, 3. blepharoplasty

Exercise 3.13

1. adip-ose, fat tissue; 2. dermat-itis, inflammation of the skin; 3. cyanot-ic, bluish skin; 4. squam-ous, scaly cancer of the skin; 5. nevus, mole

Exercise 3.14

1. Dead tissue—debridement means removal of dead tissue, 2. Crust—eschar is a thick crust from a burn, 3. Separating—slough is the separation of dead tissue from live tissue, 4. Yes—a first degree burn is damage to the top layer of skin, 5. Area—the body is divided into regions of 9% each

Exercise 3.15

1. b, 2. a, 3. e, 4. d, 5. c

Exercise 3.16

1. dermatology, 2. anesthesia, 3. seborrhea, 4. intradermal, 5. dermabrasion

Exercise 3.17

1. angiomas, 2. keratoses, 3. comedones, 4. condylomata

Exercise 3.18

Newborns: acrocyanosis: blue extremities; milia: tiny epidermal cysts; erythema toxicum: self-limited rash

Pregnant women: chloasma: brown hyperpigmented patch; vascular spiders: tiny red lines; linea nigra: brownish-black line

Seniors: alopecia: loss or lack of hair; melanoma: malignancy of pigment cells; senile purpura: purple discoloration

Chapter Review

Crossword Puzzle

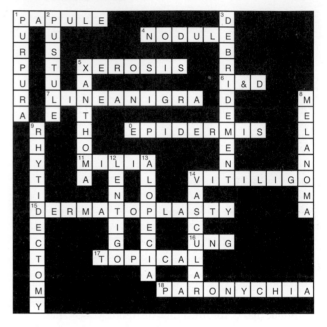

Matching

1. j 2. g 3. h 4. c 5. d 6. f 7. a 8. i, 9. e 10. b

Identification

1. sebaceous gland, 2. epidermis, 3. dermis, 4. subcutaneous (adipose) tissue, 5. sebum, 6. hair follicle, 7. arrector pili muscle, 8. stratum germinativum, 9. stratum corneum, 10. opening of sweat gland

Abbreviations

1. PPD test, 2. intradermal (ID) injection, 3. biopsy (bx), 4. incision and drainage (I&D), 5. ung

Word-Building Challenge

Answers may vary; the following are possible answers:

1. "through the skin" based on trans- (across/through), cutane/o (skin); -us (pertaining to); 2. "excessive perspiration", hyper- (excessive), hidr/o (sweat); -osis (abnormal condition); 3. "fatty tumor", lip/o (fat); -oma (tumor); 4. "softening of the nails", onych/o (nail), -malacia (softening); 5. "abnormal skin pigmentation/color", dys- (abnormal), chrom/o (color), -ia (condition)

Extension Activities

1. Answers will vary.
2. Answers will vary.
3. Answers will vary.

Chapter 4: The Musculoskeletal System

Translation Challenge

1. Chondromalacia patella, or runner's knee, is a condition in which the cartilage of the knee join deteriorates and softens.
2. Crepitus is a crackling or popping sound in a joint produced by friction between bone and cartilage.
3. X-rays are used to reveal injuries to the bones and skeleton; MRIs show soft tissues, such as muscles and tendons.

Checkpoint 4.1

1. diaphysis, 2. doctor of osteopathy (DO), 3. osteocytes

Exercise 4.1

1. G, 2. H, 3. D, 4. E, 5. B, 6. F, 7. C, 8. J, 9. I, 10. A

Exercise 4.2

1. e, 2. c, 3. d, 4. a, 5. b

Exercise 4.3

1. rheumato/logy, 2. ortho/ped/ics, 3. endo/scopy, 4. ossif/ication, 5. epi/phys/eal

Exercise 4.4

1. Ligaments, 2. vertebrae, 3. Osteoblasts, 4. scapulae, 5. phalanges

Checkpoint 4.2

1. origin, 2. Answers will vary., 3. fasciculi

Exercise 4.5

1. periosteum; 2. medullary cavity; 3. articular cartilage; 4. articulate; 5. synovial membrane, synovial fluid

Exercise 4.6

1. osteoarthritis, 2. fasciculus, 3. homeostasis, 4. tendon, 5. involuntary

Exercise 4.7

Muscle Type	skeletal	cardiac	smooth
Location	attached to skeleton	heart	intestine, GI system, uterus
Type of Nerve Control	voluntary	involuntary	involuntary

Exercise 4.8

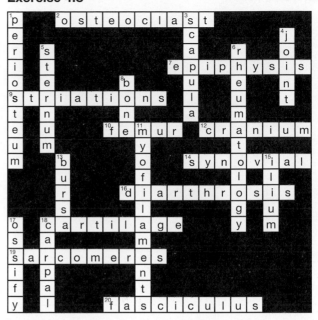

Checkpoint 4.3

1. lordosis, 2. fontanels, 3. carpal tunnel syndrome

Exercise 4.9

1. fibr/osis, reparative or reactive tissue, 2. arthr/itis, inflammation of a joint, 3. burs/itis, inflammation of a bursa, 4. necr/osis, death of tissue, 5. dis/location, separated from a place

Exercise 4.10

1. Carpal tunnel syndrome, 2. suture lines, 3. syndactyly, 4. Tibial torsion, 5. osteoporosis

Exercise 4.11

1. ankylosis, 2. bunion, 3. kyphosis, 4. osteoporosis, 5. calcaneus

Exercise 4.12

1. osteomyelitis, 2. femoral, 3. skeletal, 4. osteoma, 5. osteodynia

Exercise 4.13

1. biopsies, 2. antigen, 3. tibiae, 4. metatarsi, 5. fontanels

Exercise 4.14

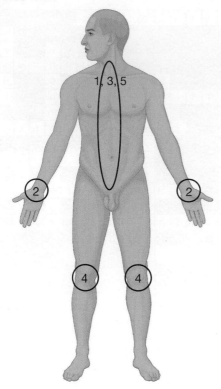

1. deformity of the thoracic spine—children/adolescents,
2. inflammation of tendon sheath or wrist caused by repetitive motion—adults/seniors
3. curvature of spine—children/adolescents,
4. inflammation of tibia tubercle—adolescents,
5. chronic, inflammatory disease of spine—adults

Checkpoint 4.4

1. arthrocentesis, 2. hypercalcemia, 3. arthrography

Checkpoint 4.5

1. internal fixation, 2. arthroscopy, 3. steroids

Exercise 4.15

1. logist, 2. scopy, 3. pathy, 4. chondr, 5. ar

Exercise 4.16

1. diagnostic test for muscle contractility; 2. physician who specializes in the musculoskeletal system; 3. thick fibrous membrane covering almost the entire surface of a bone, shaft of the bone; 4. living bone cells; 5. process of cartilage turning into bone

Exercise 4.17

1. c, 2. f, 3. e, 4. b, 5. d, 6. a

Exercise 4.18

1. osteo/logy, 2. a/vascul/ar, 3, necro/tic, 4. endo/chondr/al, 5. tendin/itis

Exercise 4.19

1. s, erythrocytes; 2. s, resections; 3. p, myofilament; 4. p, graft; 5. p, sprain

Exercise 4.20

1. feet: gout: arthrocentesis: allopurinol, 2. joints: JRA: ESR: immunosuppressants, 3. spine: osteoporosis: photon absorptiometry: calcium supplements

Chapter Review

Crossword Puzzle

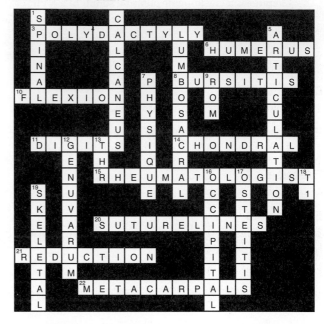

Matching

1. g, 2. f, 3. e, 4. h, 5. I, 6. j, 7. c, 8. b, 9. d, 10. a

Identification

1. deltoid, 2. biceps, 3. pectoralis major, 4. gastrocnemius, 5. adductor group, 6. hamstring group, 7. triceps brachii, 8. trapezius, 9. sternocleidomastoid, 10. gluteus maximus

Abbreviations

1. THR: total hip replacement, 2. NSAIDs: nonsteroidal anti-inflammatory agents, 3. RA: rheumatoid arthritis, 4. fx: fracture, 5. EMG: electromyogram

Word-Building Challenge

1. softening of cartilage, 2. creation of opening in a joint, 3. plastic repair of ligament, 4. reduced bone mass, 5. removal of meniscus

Extension Activities

1. Answers will vary.
2. Answers will vary.
3. Answers will vary.

Chapter 5: The Nervous System

Translation Challenge
1. stroke, 2. speech and walking, 3. transient ischemic attack.

Checkpoint 5.1
1. diencephalon, 2. central nervous system (CNS), 3. occipital lobe, 4. 31

Exercise 5.1
1. cephal/o, cephalagia; 2. electr/o, electroencephalogram; 3. kinesi/o, kinetic; 4. myel/o myelitis; 5. neur/o, nervous

Exercise 5.2
1. neurologist, 2. electroencephalogram, 3. meningitis, 4. ganglioneuroma, 5. astrocytes

Exercise 5.3
1. astrocyte, 2. olfactory, 3. cerebrum, 4. neurologist, 5. pons

Exercise 5.4
1. dyskinesic, 2. astrocyte, 3. neurotomy, 4. intracranial, 5. cephalic

Exercise 5.5
1. myelin–fatty sheath that surrounds, protects, and maintains axons of neurons; 2. cerebellar–pertaining to the cerebellum, which helps coordinate voluntary movements and maintains balance and posture; 3. craniotomy–surgical incision into the brain; 4. axons–part of a neuron that conducts nerve impulses between neurons; 5. encephalopathy–disease of the brain

Exercise 5.6
Line 1: central nervous system/peripheral nervous system; Line 2: somatic nervous system/autonomic nervous system; Line 3: sympathetic nervous system/parasympathetic nervous system

Checkpoint 5.2
1. ALS—Amyotrophic lateral sclerosis, 2. Tourette's syndrome, 3. hydrocephalus, 4. agraphia

Exercise 5.7
1. neur, pertaining to the nervous system; 2. cephal, head to foot; 3. mening, protrusion of spinal cord through the vertebrae; 4. cerebr, blood vessels of the brain; 5. myel, loss of insulating material between nerves

Exercise 5.8
1. nerves, 2. ventricles, 3. reflexes, 4. cortices, 5. dystrophies

Exercise 5.9
1. preictal, g; 2. hydrocephalus, j; 3. neural ,c; 4. ventricles, a; 5. cortex, b; 6. cephalocaudal, d; 7. paraplegia, i; 8. transient ischemic attack, e; 9. seizure, f; 10. paresis, h

Exercise 5.10
1. derma(tomes), 2. (glosso)pharyngeal nerve, 3. plant(ar reflex), 4. (infantile) automatisms, 5. plantar (grasp reflex)

Exercise 5.11
1. quadriplegia; 2. palsy; 3. decorticate; 4. ataxia, aphasia; 5. cerebrovascular

Exercise 5.12
Line 1: preictal/ictal/postictal; Line 2: aura

Exercise 5.13
1. acrophobia, 2. agoraphobia, 3. claustrophobia, 4. hemophobia, 5. allodoxaphobia

Exercise 5.14
1. ADHD, 2. acrophobia, 3. affective disorders, 4. mania and depression, 5. neurosis, 6. Phobia

Checkpoint 5.3
1. lumbar puncture, 2. Romberg test, 3. Thematic Apperception Test (TAT)

Checkpoint 5.4
1. antipsychotics, 2. depression caused by seasonal affective disorder, 3. anticonvulsants

Exercise 5.15
1. crani/o, cranium; 2. neur/o, nerve; 3. rhiz/o, nerve root; 4. lobe, subdivision

Exercise 5.16
1. CAT, 2. Romberg, 3. cerebrospinal, 4. EEG, 5. brain scan

Exercise 5.17
1. amyotrophic lateral sclerosis, 2. central nervous system, 3. deep tendon reflex, 4. cerebrospinal fluid, 5. multiple sclerosis

Exercise 5.18
1. cerebrovascular, 2. electroencephalogram, 3. neuromuscular, 4. neurosensory, 5. ataxia

Exercise 5.19
1. P, seizure; 2. S, palsies; 3. S, dermatomes; 4. P, neuroplasty; 5. S, ventriculotomies

Exercise 5.20
hemiplegia: paralyzed arm and leg; paraplegia: paralyzed legs; quadraplegia: paralyzed legs and arms

Chapter 5 Review

Crossword Puzzle

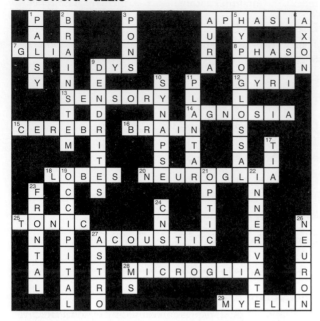

Matching

1. b, 2. d, 3.a, 4. c, 5. e

Identification

1. D, 2. C, 3. A, 4. B

Abbreviation

1. multiple sclerosis, 2. transient ischemic attack, 3. positron emission tomography, 4. central nervous system, 5. computerized axial tomography, 6. cerebrospinal fluid

Word-Building Challenge

1. neuroblastoma, 2. medullar, 3. demyelinate, 4. dysphagia, 5. subdural hematoma 6. myelocele, 7. epilepsy , 8. hydrocephalus, 9. astrocytoma, 10. hyperesthesia, 11. neurorrhaphy, 12. encephalopathy

Extension Activities

1. Answers will vary.
2. Answers will vary.
3. Answers will vary.

Chapter 6: The Special Senses

Translation Challenge

1. tinnitus; 2. oculus uterque, both eyes; 3. There is no cure for Ménière's disease; therefore, it is treated via the management of the presenting symptoms (e.g., medications to reduce fluid buildup in the inner ear and to reduce the symptoms of vertigo).

Checkpoint 6.1

1. normal vision or 20/20, 2. palpebral, 3. lacrimal

Exercise 6.1

1. ophthalm/o, ophthalmology; 2. blephar/o (or palpebr/o), blepharitis; 3. nyct/o, nyctalopia; 4. kerat/o (or corne/o, or cor/o), keratoplasty; 5. conjunctiv/o, conjunctivitis

Exercise 6.2

1. palpebrae, 2. nasolacrimal, 3. Extraocular, 4. retina, 5. refracted

Exercise 6.3

1. Extraocular, 2. Periorbital, 3. Conjunctivitis, 4. Intraocular, 5. Corneal

Exercise 6.4

1. ophthalmoscope, 2. ophthalmology, 3. corneal, 4. orbital, 5. pupillary

Exercise 6.5

1. Vision, 2. lenses, 3. ophthalmologist, 4. Laser, 5. optician

Exercise 6.6

Refer to Figure 6.1 for correct labeling.

Checkpoint 6.2

1. labyrinth; 2. malleus, incus, and stapes; 3. Eustachian tube

Exercise 6.7

1. tympano/o (CF) /scler (CF) /osis (S), hardening of the tympanic membrane; 2. peri (P) /auricul (CF) /ar (S), around the ear; 3. oto (CF) /scope (S), device for viewing the inside of the ear; 4. bi (P) /aur (CF) /al (S), pertaining to both ears; 5. salping/o eustachian tube -eal pertaining to, pertaining to the eustachian tube

Exercise 6.8

1. i, 2, g, 3. d, 4. f, 5. b, 6. j, 7. h, 8. e, 9. c, 10. a

Exercise 6.9

1. otoscope, 2. saccule, 3. tympanic, 4. periauricular, 5. vestibular

Exercise 6.10

1. prescription; 2. labyrinth, endolymph; 3. auditory; 4. canals, vestibule; 5. cochlea; 6. myringotomy

Exercise 6.11

Refer to Figure 6.4 for correct labeling.

Checkpoint 6.3

1. sweet, sour, bitter, salty; 2. smell; 3. the skin of the trunk

Exercise 6.12

1. olfactory bulb; 2. gustatory; 3. Dysgeusia; 4. Osmesis; 5. Anosmia

Checkpoint 6.4

1. diabetic retinopathy; 2. hypotropia; 3. esotropia

Exercise 6.13

Related terms and definitions will vary. 1. [irid]ectomy, pertaining to the iris; 2. [kerato]tomy, pertaining to the cornea; 3. [blepharo]ptosis, pertaining to the eyelid; 4. [ophthalmo]scope, pertaining to the eye; 5. eso[trop]ia, turning

Exercise 6.14

1. glaucoma; 2. chalazion; 3. ophthalmologists; 4. retinoblastoma; 5. esophoria

Exercise 6.15

1. c, 2. a, 3. f, 4. e, 5. d, 6. b

Exercise 6.16

1. blephar/o-plasty; 2. blephar/o-ptosis; 3. ophthalm-ic; 4. iritis; 5. kerat/o-tomy

Exercise 6.17

1. keratoplasty, surgical repair of the cornea; 2. ophthalmologist, specialist in diagnosis and treatment of eye disorders; 3. myopia, difficulty seeing distant objects; 4. conjunctivitis, inflammation of the conjunctiva; 5. vitreous, thick, clear, jelly-like substance within the eyeball

Exercise 6.18

Refer to Figure 6.8 for correct labeling.
myopia

Checkpoint 6.5

1. distance visual acuity, 2. tonometry, 3. phoropter

Checkpoint 6.6

1. corneal transplant, 2. cycloplegics, 3. cataract extraction

Exercise 6.19

1. blephar/o, eyelid, repair of the eyelid; 2. palpebr/o, eyelid, pertaining to the eyelid; 3. retin, retina, inflammation of the retina; 4. ophthalm/o, the eye, a device for viewing the interior of the eye; 5. lacrim, tears, pertaining to the tears

Exercise 6.20

1. ophthalmologist; 2. retina; 3. keratoplasty; 4. tonometry; 5. vitreous humor

Exercise 6.21

1. d, 2. a, 3. c, 4. e, 5. f, 6. b

Exercise 6.22

1. ocul-ar; 2. intra-ocul-ar; 3. conjunctiv-itis; 4. scler-al; 5. peri-orbit-al

Exercise 6.23

1. cataracts; 2. palpebrae; 3. sclerae ;4. sties or styes; 5. retinopathies

Exercise 6.24

Line 1: double vision; Line 2: myopia, hyperopia; Line 3: n/a; Line 4: esotropia or esophoria, exotropia or exophoria, amblyopia

Checkpoint 6.7

1. otitis media, 2. ear pain, 3. tinnitus

Checkpoint 6.8

1. otoscope, 2. UNHS, 3. audiometer

Checkpoint 6.9

1. cochlear implant, 2. myringotomy, 3. amoxicillin

Exercise 6.25

1. ot/o, ear, inflammation of the middle ear; 2. myring/o, tympanic membrane, incision into the tympanic membrane; 3. osse/o, bones of the middle ear, pertaining to the ossicles; 4. labyrinth, structure of the inner ear, removal of the labyrinth; 5. tympan, the tympanic membrane, a tube that opens the middle ear to the external ear

Exercise 6.26

1. tympanectomy; 2. AD; 3. vestibular; 4. Neuroplasty; 5. tinnitus

Exercise 6.27

1. Ménière's disease; 2. cholesteatoma; 3. tinnitus; 4. audiometry; 5. otoscopy; 6. tympanectomy

Exercise 6.28

1. oto-logy; 2. an-ot-ia; 3. labyrinth-itis; 4. mastoid-ectomy; 5. oto-rrhagia

Exercise 6.29

1. auricle; 2. cochlea; 3. endolymph; 4. meatus; 5. ossicle

Exercise 6.30

Line 1: External auditory meatus, Tympanic membrane; Line 2: Ossicular chain, Oval window; Line 3: Auditory nerve, Brain

Chapter Review

Crossword Puzzle

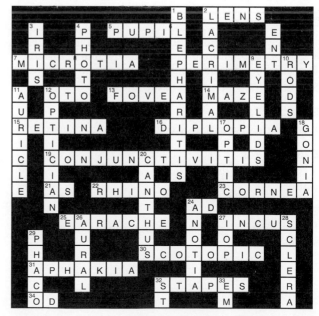

Matching

1. b; 2. h; 3. c; 4. d; 5. j; 6. e; 7. g; 8. f; 9. i; 10. a

Identification

Refer to Figure 6.4 for correct labeling.

Abbreviations

1. ENT, ear, nose, and throat specialist; 2. visual acuity (VA) assessment; 3. exotropia (XT); 4. pupil size, equal appearance, and reaction to light

Word-Building Challenge

1. blephar/o (eyelid), -ptosis (drooping); drooping of the upper eyelid
2. xer/o (dry), ophthalm/o (eye), -ia (condition); condition of dry eye
3. an- (not), is/o (equal), cor/o (pupil), -ia (condition); condition of unequally sized pupils
4. an- (no, not, without), -acusis (hearing); hearing loss or deafness
5. staped/o (stapes), -ectomy (removal); removal of the third ossicle/stape

Extension Activities

1. Answers will vary.
2. Answers will vary.
3. Answers will vary.

Chapter 7: The Respiratory System

Translation Challenge

1. False. The orthopneic position is sitting.
2. False. Cyanotic means the patient was bluish.
3. shortness of breath and difficulty breathing
4. False.

Checkpoint 7.1

1. cilia, 2. trachea, 3. inspiration and expiration (or inhalation and exhalation)

Exercise 7.1

1. pulmon/ary, relating to the lungs; 2. aero/phagia, swallowing of air; 3. pneumon/itis = inflammation of the lungs; 4. tracheo/stomy = creation of an opening into the throat; 5. pharyng/eal = pertaining to the throat

Exercise 7.2

1. epiglottis, 2. apnea, 3. alveolitis, 4. exhaled 5. apex

Exercise 7.3

1. diffusion, 2. carbon dioxide, 3. apex, 4. trachea, 5. nasal septum

Exercise 7.4

1. hypercapnia, 2. nasopharynx, 3. paranasal, 4. bronchial, 5. inhalation

Exercise 7.5

1. cilia, respiratory; 2. pharynx; 3. diaphragm, thoracic; 4. surfactant, alveoli; 5. diffusion

Exercise 7.6

Line 1: trachea; Line 2: bronchi; Line 3: bronchioles; Line 4: alveoli

Exercise 7.7

Upper: nares, oropharynx; Lower: alveoli, bronchioles, trachea; Not in the Respiratory Tract: astrocyte, myelin sheath, neurilemma

Checkpoint 7.2

1. tracheostenosis, 2. cystic fibrosis (CF), 3. upper respiratory infections (URI)

Exercise 7.8

1. pyr/o = pus - throrax = chest, pus in the chest; 2. cyan = blue, condition of blue skin; 3. pulmon/o = lungs, pertaining to the lungs; 4. glottis = mouth of windpipe, structure that closes on trachea; 5. bronchiol =bronchiole, inflammation of the bronchioles

Exercise 7.9

1. fibrosis, 2. RSV, 3. URI, 4. Atelectasis, 5. Pleurisy

Exercise 7.10

1. rhinitis, 2. tracheotomy, 3. thoracoplasty, 4. hemothorax, 5. pneumonectomy

Exercise 7.11

1. P, bronchus; 2. P, alveolus; 3. S, lungs; 4. P, cilium, 5. S, capillaries

Exercise 7.12

1. dys/pne, 2. eu/pnea, 3. tachy/pnea, 4. brady/pnea, 5. ortho/pnea, 6. hyper/pnea

Exercise 7.13

Fetus/Infant/Child: acute epiglottis, croup, cystic fibrosis, IRDS, respiratory syncytial virus
Adult/Senior: bronchitis, bronchogenic carcinoma, chronic obstructive, lung disease emphysema

Checkpoint 7.3

1. auscultation, 2. spirometer, 3. means instrument to listen

Checkpoint 7.4

Answer the following questions to identify any areas of the section that you may need to review.
1. endotracheal intubation, 2. tracheostomy, 3. bronchodilator

Exercise 7.14

1. laryngo-scope, instrument to view the larynx; 2. nas-al, pertaining to the nose; 3. pulmon-ologist, physician who specializes in the respiratory system; 4. spiro-metry, examination to measure breathing; 5. rhin-it is, inflammation of the nose

Exercise 7.15
1. COPD, 2. antitussive, 3. antipyretic, 4. Intubation, 5. ventilation

Exercise 7.16
1. b, 2. e, 3. d, 4. a, 5. c

Exercise 7.17
1. Laryngotracheobronchitis, 2. Dyspnea, 3. Respiratory, 4. lobectomy, 5. Endotracheal

Exercise 7.18
1. organism, 2, correct, 3. viruses, 4. inhalation, 5. correct

Exercise 7.19
Diagnostic Tests and Examinations: endoscopy, laryngoscopy, pulmonary function tests
Treatments: intubation, laryngectomy, laryngotomy, lobectomy, pulse oximetry

Chapter Review

Crossword Puzzle

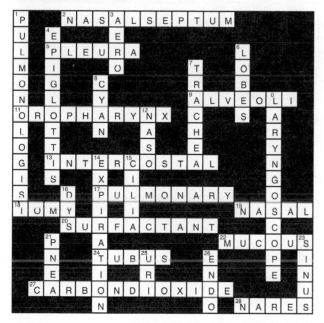

Matching
1. d, 2. f, 3. g, 4. h, 5. a, 6. e, 7. b, 8. c

Identification
1. nasal cavity, 2. pharynx, 3. larynx, 4. trachea, 5. bronchioles, 6. lungs, 7. diaphragm, 8. respiratory tract

Abbreviations
1. chest X-ray, tuberculosis; 2. chronic obstructive pulmonary disease, dyspnea on exertion; 3. multidrug-resistant tuberculosis; 4. coal worker's pneumoconiosis

Word-Building Challenge
1. dilation of the bronchi, 2. softening of the trachea, 3. incision of a sinus, 4. rapid breathing, 5. abnormally slow or shallow breathing

Extension Activities
1. Answers will vary.
2. Answers will vary.
3. Answers will vary.

Chapter 8 Cardiovascular System

Translation Challenge
1. placement of a catheter into the heart through a large vessel, 2. into the obstructed vessel, 3. Ischemia is a term used to describe decreased blood flow to the heart; without an adequate supply of oxygenated blood, the heart can lose muscle and eventually fail.

Checkpoint 8.1
1. SA node, AV node, AV bundle/bundle of HIS, Purkinje fibers; 2. mitral valve; 3. left and right atria

Exercise 8.1
1. C, 2. D, 3. B, 4. A, 5. F, 6. E

Exercise 8.2
1. cardiology, 2. thoracic, 3. visceral, 4. septum, 5. systole

Exercise 8.3
1. e, 2. a, 3. f, 4. c, 5. d, 6. b

Exercise 8.4
1. thrombosis, 2. myocarditis, 3. cardiomyopathy, 4. atrioventricular, 5. pericardium

Exercise 8.5
1. P, apex; 2. P, valve; 3. P, vena cava; 4. P, septum; 5. P, lumen

Exercise 8.6
Left—box 1: tricuspid valve; box 2: pulmonary valve; box 3: mitral or bicuspid valve; box 4: aortic valve

Checkpoint 8.2
1. ductus arteriosus, 2. bruit, 3. congestive heart failure

Exercise 8.7
1. pericard (CF) -itis (S): inflammation of the covering of the heart
2. pulmon (CF) - ic (S): relating to the lung
3. sten (CF) -osis (S): condition of narrowing
4. myocardi (CF) -al (S): relating to heart muscle
5. endocard (CF) - itis (S): inflammation of the lining of the heart

Exercise 8.8
1. palpitations, 2. ectopic, 3. congestive, 4. clubbing, 5. arrhythmias

Exercise 8.9
1. b, 2. d, 3. c, 4. a, 5. e

Exercise 8.10
1. stenosis, 2. sclerosis, 3. angiogram, 4. pericardial, 5. endocardium

Exercise 8.11
1. endocarditis, 2. embolism, 3. myocardial, 4. cardiomegaly, 5. hyperlipidemia

Exercise 8.12
1. mitral (bicuspid), tricuspid, pulmonic, aortic; 2. stenosis, regurgitation; 3. tricuspid stenosis: calcification impedes blood flow into right ventricle during diastole; tricuspid regurgitation: backflow of blood into right atrium; pulmonic regurgitation: backflow of blood from pulmonary artery into right ventricle; pulmonic stenosis: calcification restricts forward blood flow into the pulmonary artery; mitral regurgitation: backflow of blood into left ventricle; mitral stenosis: calcification prevents proper opening of valve; aortic stenosis: valve cusps restrict blood flow during systole; aortic regurgitation: backflow of blood from aorta into left ventricle during diastole

Checkpoint 8.3
1. lipid profile, 2. ECG or EKG, 3. thallium

Checkpoint 8.4
1. percutaneous transluminal coronary angioplasty (PTCA, or balloon angioplasty), 2. defibrillator, 3. antianginals (nitrates)

Exercise 8.13
1. cardi/o (CF) / logy (S): study of the heart
2. vascul (CF) / ar (S): pertaining to vessels
3. thromb (CF) / osis (S): condition of a blood clot
4. sept (CF) / al (S): pertaining to the septum
5. ventricul (CF) / ar (S): pertaining to a ventricle

Exercise 8.14
1. inferior vena cava; 2. lipid; 3. PTCA; 4. CABG; 5. cardiac enzymes

Exercise 8.15
1. c, 2. a, 3. e, 4. d, 5. b

Exercise 8.16
1. cardiology, 2. electrocardiogram, 3. atrial, 4. anticoagulant, 5. antianginal

Exercise 8.17
1. S, ventricles; 2. S, atria; 3. S, venae cavae; 4. S, angioplasties; 5. S, diuretics

Exercise 8.18
Responses will vary slightly. The procedure is known as a balloon angioplasty procedure or percutaneous transluminal coronary angioplasty (PTCA). In the balloon angioplasty, or PTCA, a catheter with a balloon tip is inserted into the obstructed vessel; the balloon is then inflated to open the vessel and allow the free flow of blood.

Chapter Review

Crossword Puzzle

Matching
1. g, 2. d, 3. f, 4. i, 5. j, 6. c, 7. b, 8. a, 9. e, 10. h

Identification
1. semilunar valves, 2. left atrium, 3. mitral valve, 4. chordae tendinae, 5. left ventricle, 6. apex, 7. inferior vena cava, 8. right ventricle, 9. tricuspid valve, 10. right atrium, 11. superior vena cava, 12. aorta

Abbreviations
1. left anterior descending coronary artery, 2. multigated acquisition (MUGA) scan, 3. coronary artery disease 4. coronary care unit 5. shortness of breath

Word-Building Challenge
1. inflammation of a vein caused by a blood clot
2. pain in the region of the heart
3. abnormality in a physiological rhythm
4. abnormally low blood pressure.
5. procedure that uses a needle to remove fluid from the pericardial sac
6. development of new blood vessels

Extension Activities
1. Answers will vary.
2. Answers will vary.
3. Answers will vary.

Chapter 9: Hematology

Translation Challenge

1. The patient is short of breath because she does not have enough hemoglobin molecules to carry sufficient oxygen to her tissues.
2. A CBC is a complete blood count; it will tell the physician the patient's hemoglobin and hematocrit values, red blood cell count, white blood cell count, and the platelet count.
3. Hypoxia means having too little oxygen
4. Iron is necessary for the production of hemoglobin.

Checkpoint 9.1

1. red blood cell, 2. platelet, 3. Neutrophils are white blood cells that seek, ingest, and kill bacteria that do not belong in the body.

Exercise 9.1

1. an- (P) / -emia (S): condition of decreased red blood cells; 2. micro- (P) / cyt (CF) / -ic (S): pertaining to a small cell; 3. hypo- (P) / chrom (R) / -ic (S): low or pale color; 4. splen (CF) / -ectomy (S): removal of the spleen; 5. hepat/o (CF) / megaly (S): enlargement of the liver

Exercise 9.2

1. Organomegaly, 2. Hypoxia, 3. Macrocytic, 4. Leukocytes, 5. Hematology

Exercise 9.3

1. d, 2. c, 3. a, 4. e, 5. b

Exercise 9.4

1. cyte, 2. leuko, 3. cyto, 4. Ser, 5. phil

Exercise 9.5

1. serum; 2. Plasma; 3. Albumin, globulins; 4. Oxyhemoglobin; 5. macrocytes, microcytes

Exercise 9.6

Line 2: plasma / cellular components; Line 3: serum / fibrinogen / RBCs / WBCs / thrombocytes

Checkpoint 9.2

1. hemophilia, 2. iron deficiency anemia, 3. spherocyte

Exercise 9.7

1. splen/o, spleen, enlargement of the spleen; 2. hem/o, blood, disease of the hemoglobin; 3. hem/o, blood, the destruction of red blood cells; 4. erythr/o red, cyt/o cell, -penia shortage/deficiency, deficiency of red blood cells in the body; 5. thromb/o, blood clot, cyt/o, cell, an abnormal decrease in the number of platelets

Exercise 9.8

1. anemia, 2. epistaxes, 3. menorrhagia, 4. splenomegaly, 5. occult

Exercise 9.9

1. e, 2. d, 3. a, 4. b, 5. c

Exercise 9.10

1. Intra, 2. rrhage, 3. sis, 4. emia, 5. logy

Exercise 9.11

1. hemosiderosis, accumulation of hemosiderin due to iron in the blood; 2. hemolysis, destruction of red blood cells; 3. infarction, obstruction of blood supply to tissue/organ; 4. hemoglobinopathy, disease related to hemoglobin; 5. hematologic, pertaining to the blood

Exercise 9.12

enlarged spleen	enlarged liver	pale lips, nail beds, pale inside mouth
splenomegaly	hepatomegaly	pallor
isolated blood cells, extramedullary hematopoiesis, hemolysis	hemolysis, congestive heart failure, extramedullary hematopoiesis	anemia

Checkpoint 9.3

1. RBC indices, 2. bone marrow aspiration and biopsy, 3. Coombs' test

Checkpoint 9.4

1. complete blood count, 2. posterior superior iliac crest, 3. thrombolytic

Exercise 9.13

Terms will vary. Examples are provided.

1. erythr/o, red, erythrocyte; 2. splen/o, spleen, splenectomy; 3. hem/o, blood, hemostasis; 4. thromb/o, blood clot, thrombosis; 5. cyt/o, cell, cytotoxic

Exercise 9.14

1. plasmapheresis, 2. hematologist, 3. prothrombin, 4. antibodies, 5. bone marrow

Exercise 9.15

1. c, 2. d, 3. b, 4. e, 5. a

Exercise 9.16

1. thromb; 2. cyte; 3. Hemo 4. poiesis; 5. morpho; 6. Anti

Exercise 9.17

1. hematocrit, 2. hemoglobin, 3. mean corpuscular hemoglobin, 4. monocyte, 5. polymorphonuclear neutrophils

Exercise 9.18

Drug Class	Use
anticoagulant (antithrombotic)	prevents blood from clotting
antihemophilic factors	promote clotting
biological response modifier: interferon	stimulates the body's own immune system
colony-stimulating factor	stimulates RBC production
granulocyte colony-stimulating factor	stimulates the formation of neutrophils

Chapter Review

Crossword Puzzle

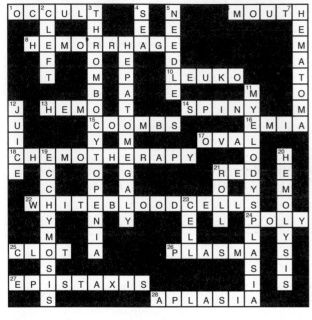

Matching

1. g; 2. f; 3. a; 4. h; 5. b; 6. j; 7. i; 8. c; 9. e; 10. d

Identification

1. blood type B, 2. blood type O, 3. blood type AB, 4. blood type A

Abbreviations

The patient presented at the physician's office with complaints of shortness of breath and loss of energy. She appears pale. A complete blood count with differential is ordered. Results show a decreased hemoglobin and hematocrit. Changes in the mean corpuscular hemoglobin, mean corpuscular volume, and mean corpuscular hemoglobin concentration show a nutritional anemia. Prothrombin time and partial thromboplastin time were within normal limits. The patient was crossmatched and prepared for a blood transfusion. The patient was given a prescription for iron supplements and was to return to the office in six weeks.

Word-Building Challenge

1. lympho, lymph, cyt, cell, osis, condition: a condition of abnormally high number of lymphocytes
2. erythro, red, cyt, cell, osis, condition: a condition of abnormally high number of red blood cell
3. phago, eating, cyt, cell, osis, condition: condition in which phagocytes eat solid particles
4. granulo, granular, cyte, cell: a cell containing granules in the cytoplasm
5. hypo, under, ox, oxygen, emia, blood condition: a condition of not having enough oxygen in the blood

Extension Activities

1. Answers will vary.
2. Answers will vary.
3. Answers will vary.

Chapter 10: The Lymphatic System

Translation Challenge

1. HIV is the abbreviation for human immunodeficiency virus.
2. AZT is a type of medication.
3. The lymph nodes mentioned are in the neck (cervical), under the arm (axillary), and in the groin (inguinal).

Checkpoint 10.1

1. passive acquired natural immunity, 2. spleen, 3. mediators

Exercise 10.1

Refer to Figure 10.1 for correct labeling. Related words will vary. Examples are provided.

1. axill/o, 2. tonsil/o, 3. inguin/o, 4. splen, 5. lymphat/o

Exercise 10.2

1. mediastinum, anterior portion of the chest; 2. pharyngeal tonsils, lymphatic tissue located in the posterior wall of the nasopharynx, sometimes called adenoids; 3. palatine tonsils, lymphatic tissue located on each side of the throat; 4. macrophages, mature white blood cells of the monocyte type; 5. antigen, substance that induces a state of sensitivity or immune response

Exercise 10.3

1. phagocytosis, 2. cellulitis, 3. lymphadenopathy, 4. autologous, 5. thymocyte

Exercise 10.4

1. b, 2. c. 3. a, 4. d, 5. e

Exercise 10.5

1. immunology, 2. immunoglobulin, 3. splenic, 4. monocyte, 5. humoral

Exercise 10.6

nonspecific immunity	specific immunity
mechanical barriers (e.g., skin, tears, and mucus membranes)	previous exposure to a disease
inflammatory response	vaccinations
	antibodies passed from mother to fetus

Checkpoint 10.2

1. anaphylactic shock, 2. lupus, 3. type 1 diabetes

Exercise 10.7

1. immun = immune (resistant), study of disease resistance;
2. splen/o = spleen, overactive spleen; 3. hemo = blood, erythrocyte destruction; 4. cyt/o = cell, white blood cell;
5. immun = immune (resistant), deficient immune response

Exercise 10.8

1. palpates, 2. immune, 3. lymphoid, 4. pernicious,
5. lympohoma

Exercise 10.9

1. d, 2. b, 3. e, 4. c, 5. a

Exercise 10.10

1. systemic, 2. lymphatic, 3. hepatic, 4. lymphoid 5. lymph-adenectomy

Exercise 10.11

1. immunologists, 2. macrophages, 3. involution, 4. antigen,
5. thoracic

Checkpoint 10.3

1. ELISA and Western blot, 2. gallium, 3. hematocrit (Hct)

Checkpoint 10.4

1. tonsillectomy, 2. biopsy, 3. antibiotics

Exercise 10.12

1. splenectomy, 2. angioplasty, 3. monocyte, 4. phagocytosis,
5. thymic

Exercise 10.13

1. tonsillectomy; 2. lymphocytes; 3. efferent; 4. autologous;
5. macrophages

Exercise 10.14

1. c, 2. e, 3. d, 4. a, 5. b

Exercise 10.15

1. hemolytic anemia, 2. lymphatic, 3. antibiotic, 4. lymphoid, 5. antiviral

Exercise 10.16

1. monocyte, 2. tonsils, 3. adenoid, 4. anemia, 5. immuno-deficiencies

Exercise 10.17

1. antihistamine, 2. antifungal, 3. inhibits viruses, 4. kills or inhibits fungus, 5. bacterial infection, 6. viral infection,
7. fungal infection, 8. acyclovir, 9. diphenhydramine

Chapter Review

Crossword Puzzle

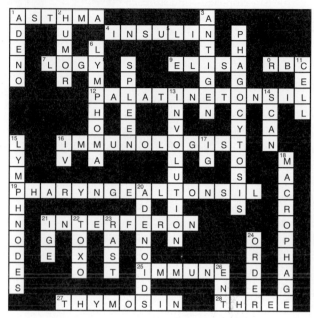

Matching

1. g, 2. e, 3. h, 4. f, 5. a, 6. d, 7. i, 8. j, 9. c, 10. b

Identification

1. tonsils, 2. cervical lymph nodes, 3. thoracic duct, 4. spleen,
5. cisterna chyli, 6. popliteal lymph nodes, 7. inguinal lymph nodes, 8. axillary lymph nodes, 9. right lymphatic duct, 10. submandibular lymph nodes

Abbreviations

1. bx, 2. ELISA, 3. Hct, 4. Ig, 5. SLE

Word-Building Challenge

1. pertaining to the thymus, 2. like or resembling lymph,
3. against a virus, 4. pertaining to bacteria, 5. surgical removal of the adenoid(s)

Extension Activities

1. Answers will vary.
2. Answers will vary.
3. Answers will vary.

Chapter 11: The Digestive System

Translation Challenge

1. A gastroenterologist is someone who studies structure, function, and diseases of digestive organs.

2. GERD is the condition in which contents in the stomach flow back to the esophagus due to the inability of the lower esophageal sphincter to function properly, resulting in a burning pain in the esophagus

3. An EGD is the abbreviation for esophagogastroduodenoscopy and it is a diagnostic procedure in which a scope is swallowed in order to view the back of the throat, esophagus, and stomach

Checkpoint 11.1
1. feces; 2. ingestion, digestion, absorption, and elimination; 3. bile

Exercise 11.1
1. col (CF) / itis (S): inflammation of the colon; 2. gastro (CF) / scopy (S): examination of the stomach through an instrument; 3. hepat (CF) / megaly (S): enlargement of the liver; 4. pancreat (CF) / ic (S): pertaining to the pancreas; 5. pyloro (CF) / plasty (S): surgical repair of the pylorus; 6. procto (CF) / logist (S): one who specializes in the study of the rectum

Exercise 11.2
1. cardiac sphincter, 2. hydrochloric, 3. ileum, 4. peristalsis, 5. hepatic, 6. amylase

Exercise 11.3
1. d, 2. e, 3. b, 4. a, 5. c, 6. f

Exercise 11.4
1. duodenal, 2. gastrectomy, 3. hypogastric, 4. hepatic, 5. sigmoidoscopy

Exercise 11.5
1. gastrointestinal, gastroenterology; 2. alimentary; 3. salivary; 4. deciduous; 5. stomach, rugae

Exercise 11.6
esophagus, stomach, duodenum, jejunum, ileum, cecum, ascending colon, transverse colon, descending colon, sigmoid colon, rectum

Checkpoint 11.2
1. achalasia, 2. a reducible hernia, 3. meconium

Exercise 11.7
1. gloss/o = tongue, absence of the tongue; 2. sten/o = narrowing, condition of narrowing; 3. chol/o = bile, presence of gallstones; 4. hepat/o = liver, inflammation of the liver; 5. stom/a = mouth or opening, inflammation of the lining of the mouth

Exercise 11.8
1. hypogastric, 2. cystic fibrosis, 3. T-E fistula, pyloric stenosis, 4. cholelithiasis, 5. intussusception

Exercise 11.9
1. e, 2. c, 3. d, 4. b, 5. a

Exercise 11.10
1. epigastric, 2. hepatitis, 3. colitis, 4. diarrhea, 5. aglossia

Exercise 11.11
1. diverticula, 2. quadrants, 3. proteins, 4. ducts, 5. villi

Exercise 11.12
Stomach: gastric ulcer, heartburn, hiatal hernia; Intestines: constipation, diverticulitis, inguinal hernia, intussusception, umbilical hernia; Rectum/Anus: hemorrhoids

Checkpoint 11.3
1. barium enema, 2. cholecystography, 3. colonoscopy

Checkpoint 11.4
1. ileostomy, 2. FDA, 3. hyperalimentation

Exercise 11.13
1. cholecyst-, gallbladder, removal of the gallbladder; 2. dent-, teeth, pertaining to the teeth; 3. sigmoido-, sigmoid colon, visualization of the sigmoid colon; 4. proct-, rectum, inflammation of the rectum; 5. enter-, intestines, pertaining to the intestines

Exercise 11.14
1. pancreas, 2. barium swallow, 3. GI series, 4. endoscopy, 5. hyperalimentation

Exercise 11.15
1. e, 2. a, 3. d, 4. b, 5. c

Exercise 11.16
1. after meals, 2. hydrochloric acid, 3. lower esophageal sphincter, 4. nausea and vomiting, 5. barium enema

Exercise 11.17
Responses will vary, but may include: 1. esophageal manometry or EGD, esophagitis; 2. gastroscopy, gastritis; 3. barium swallow, ileus or malabsorption syndrome; 4. colonoscopy, diverticulitis; 5. sigmoidoscopy, IBD, IBS, or diverticulitis; 6. proctoscopy, hemorrhoids

Chapter Review

Crossword Puzzle

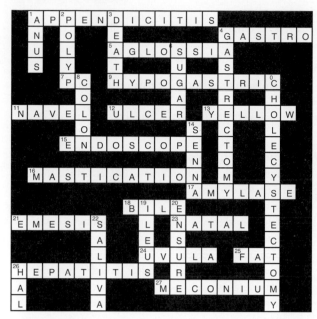

Matching

1. f, 2. h, 3. i, 4. e, 5. a, 6. d, 7. j, 8. g, 9. c, 10. b

Identification

1. transverse colon, 2. descending colon, 3. sigmoid colon, 4. rectum, 5. vermiform appendix, 6. cecum, 7. ascending colon

Abbreviations

1. NEC, 2. GI series, 3. HEV , 4. both GGT and LFT are possible answers

Word-Building Challenge

1. cholyecyst, 2. cholecyst, 3. cholangio, 4. colono, 5. colo, 6. gastr, 7. gastro, 8. procto, 9. ileo, 10. endo, 11. laparo, 12. append

Extension Activities

1. Answers will vary.
2. Answers will vary.
3. Answers will vary.

Chapter 12: The Urinary System

Translation Challenge

1. Pyelonephritis is inflammation of the internal structures of the kidney.
2. "Microscopic hematuria" refers to tiny amounts of blood.
3. Dysuria means painful urination. Remember that the prefix dys- refers to pain or difficulty.
4. CVA refers to the costovertebral angle.

Checkpoint 12.1

1. kidneys, ureters, bladder, and urethra, 2. to filter waste from the bloodstream and produce urine, 3. voiding, micturition

Exercise 12.1

1. cyst/o, bladder, removal of the bladder; 2. ren/i, kidney, pertaining to the kidney; 3. ureter/o, ureter, removal of the ureter; 4. urethr/o, urethra, inflammation of the urethra; 5. nephr/o, kidney, removal of the kidney

Exercise 12.2

1. urethra, 2. glomerulus, 3. nephron, 4. tubules, 5. Nephritis

Exercise 12.3

1. d, 2. b, 3. e, 4. c, 5. a

Exercise 12.4

1. pyelitis, 2. nephrectomy, 3. renal, 4. urinal, 5. cystitis

Exercise 12.5

1. medulla, inner portion of kidney; 2. renal pelvis, area at the upper end of the ureter that funnels urine to the ureters; 3. cystoscopy, examination of urethra and bladder using a cystoscope; 4. intravenous pyelogram, X-ray used to view kidneys using dye; 5. Bowman's capsule, structure that surround the glomerulus

Exercise 12.6

1. A, 2. E, 3. B, 4. H, 5. C, 6. D, 7. I, 8. G

Checkpoint 12.2

1. The female urethra is shorter. 2. kidney stone, 3. vesico-ureteral reflux

Exercise 12.7

1. urine, pyuria; 2. stone, nephrolithiasis; 3. kidney, nephrology; 4. bladder, cystitis; 5. tube that passes urine from the bladder to the outside, urethritis

Exercise 12.8

1. P,nephrons; 2. P; 3. P,tubules; 4. S,protein; 5. S,urethra

Exercise 12.9

1. e, 2. b, 3. d, 4. c, 5. a

Exercise 12.10

1. ureteritis, 2. pyuria, 3. urethritis, 4. pyelonephritis, 5. nephritis

Exercise 12.11

1. pyuria, pus in the urine; 2. hematuria, blood in the urine; proteinuria, protein in the urine; 3. systemic lupus erythematosus, an autoimmune disorder; 4. enuresis, bed-wetting; 5. glomerulus, capillary loops in Bowman's capsule

Exercise 12.12

1. d, 2. f, 3. e, 4. a, 5. b, 6. c, 7. d, 8. h

Checkpoint 12.3

1. urinalysis, 2. clean catch, 3. renal scan

Checkpoint 12.4

1. dialysis, 2. nephrectomy, 3. extracorporeal shock wave lithotripsy (ESWL)

Exercise 12.13

Terms will vary. Examples are provided. 1. kidney, nephritis; 2. urine, oliguria; 3. kidney, renal; 4. glomerulus, glomerulonephritis; 5. pus, pyuria

Exercise 12.14

1. nephr, kidney, a kidney specialist; 2. urin, urine, pertaining to urine; 3. ren, kidney, pertaining to the kidney; 4. glomeru, glomerulus, pertaining to the glomerulus; 5. cyst, bladder, inflammation of the bladder

Exercise 12.15

1. nephrectomy, 2. cystectomy, 3. peritoneal dialysis, 4. hemodialysis, 5. cystoscope

Exercise 12.16

1. kidneys, ureters, and bladder; 2. chronic kidney disease; 3. blood urea nitrogen; 4. glomerular filtration rate; 5. intravenous pyelogram

Exercise 12.17

1. ureteroplasty; 2. cystectomy; 3. nephrectomy; 4. cystocele; 5. lithotripsy; 6. ureterostomy

Exercise 12.18

1. P, cystectomy; 2. P, glomerulus; 3. P, catheterization; 4. S, urinalyses; 5. S, analgesics

Exercise 12.19

1. e, 2. c, 3. a, 4. d, 5. b

Chapter Review

Crossword Puzzle

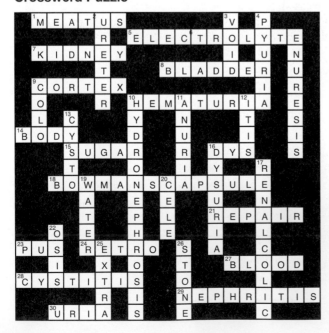

Matching

1. h, 2. b, 3. j, 4. a, 5. c, 6. d, 7. f, 8. g, 9. e, 10. i

Identification

1. calyces, 2. renal cortex, 3. renal medulla, 4. ureter, 5. renal pelvis

Abbreviations

1. acute glomerulonephritis; 2. acute renal failure; 3. cystoscopy; 4. glomerulonephritis; 5. hemodialysis; 6. extracorporeal shockwave lithotripsy; 7. urinalysis; 8. urinary tract infection; 9. intake and output; 10. peritoneal dialysis

Word-Building Challenge

1. transurethral: a medical procedure performed through the urethra; trans- (through), urethr/o (urethra), –al (pertaining to)
2. nephrosis: kidney disease; nephr/o (kidney), -osis (condition)
3. vesicoureteral: pertaining to the urinary bladder and ureter; vesic/o (urinary bladder), ureter/o (ureter), -al (pertaining to)
4. uremia: blood in the urine; ur/o (urine), -emia (blood)
5. hypoalbuminemia: lowered levels of albumin in the blood; hypo- (decreased, low), albumin/o (albumin), -emia (blood)

Extension Activities

1. Answers will vary.
2. Answers will vary.
3. Answers will vary.

Chapter 13: The Endocrine System

Translation Challenge

1. Polydipsia means "thirsty;" the patient would show signs of excessive thirst.
2. Polyphagia means "hungry;" Mrs. Smith is very hungry.
3. FBS is a fasting blood sugar test. It must be taken following a 12-hour fast in order to be used as an accurate diagnostic tool.

Checkpoint 13.1

1. hypothalamus, 2. tropic hormones, 3. adenohypophysis

Exercise 13.1

1. adren/al = pertaining to the adrenal glands; 2. pancreat/itis = inflammation of the pancreas; 3. glucos/uria = sugar in the urine; 4. hyper/glyc/emic = condition of excessive sugar in the blood; 5. endo/crine = to secrete within the body

Exercise 13.2

1. placenta, 2. hormones, 3. calcitonin, 4. hypothalamic, 5. testes

Exercise 13.3

1. d, 2. e, 3. b, 4. f, 5. a, 6. c

Exercise 13.4

1. antidiuretic hormone, 2. hypothalamus, 3. adrenal gland, 4. hypercalcemia, 5. metabolism

Exercise 13.5

1. Progesterone, steroid; 2. ovaries, reproductive; 3. mineralocorticoids, metabolism; 4. Melatonin, pineal; 5. islets, Langerhans, pancreas

Exercise 13.6

1. islets of Langerhans, 2. beta cells, 3. delta cells, 4. glucagons, 5. insulin, 6. somatostatin

Checkpoint 13.2

1. hypoglycemia, 2. myxedema, 3. polyphagia, 4. cretinism, 5. tetany

Exercise 13.7

3, 1, 4, 6, 2, 5

Exercise 13.8

1. hyperpituitarism, 2. polydipsia, 3. polyphagia, 4. aplasia, 5. diabetic ketoacidosis

Exercise 13.9

1. chromosomal, 2. dysfunction, 3. glycosuria, 4. dehydrated, 5. tachycardia

Exercise 13.10

1. e, 2. g, 3. j, 4. a, 5. b, 6. c, 7. d, 8. i, 9. f, 10. h

Exercise 13.11

1. thyrotoxicosis, 2. adrenal, 3. thymocyte, 4. thyroid carcinoma, 5. endocrine

Exercise 13.12

1. glucagon, 2. metabolic, 3. parathormone, 4. glucocorticoid, 5. medulla

Exercise 13.13

1. medulla, 2. corticosteroid hormones, 3. glucocorticoids, 4. sex hormones, 5. epinephrine, 6. adrenaline

Checkpoint 13.3

1. glucometer, 2. thyroid scan, 3. A1c

Checkpoint 13.4

1. type 1 diabetes, 2. corticosteroid hormones , 3. hypothyroidism

Exercise 13.14

Terms will vary. 1. adrenal glands, 2. gland, 3. thyroid, 4. secrete, 5. ketone

Exercise 13.15

1. disease in populations due to a deficiency of iodine; 2. low or insufficient sodium (salt) in the blood; 3. mineral salts in the body; 4. cavity in the skull that holds the pituitary gland; 5. hormone that stimulates secretion of gastric acid and stomach enzymes for digestion

Exercise 13.16

1. endocrinopathy, 2. melanocyte, 3. lipolysis, 4. hypercalcemia, 5. parathyroid

Exercise 13.17

1. triiodothyronine, 2. thyroxine, 3. luteinizing hormone, 4. fasting blood sugar, 5. glucose tolerance test

Exercise 13.18

1. hyperglycemia; 2. hypoglycemia; 3. polyuria, polydipsia, and weight loss; 4. sweating, palpitations, hunger, tachycardia, and headache; 5. insulin; 6. eat or drink something with sugar

Chapter Review

Crossword Puzzle

Matching

1. j, 2. i, 3. e, 4. b, 5. d, 6. c, 7. f, 8. a, 9. g, 10. h

Identification

1. pineal, 2. thyroid, 3. parathyroid, 4. adrenal, 5. pancreas, 6. ovaries (in female), 7. testes (in male), 8. thymus, 9. pituitary, 10. hypothalamus

Abbreviations

1. e, 2. j, 3. a, 4. h, 5. i, 6. b, 7. f, 8. d, 9. c, 10. g

Word-Building Challenge

1. endocrinopathy; 2. melanocyte; 3. lipolysis; 4. pancreatic; 5. hypothyroidism; 6. hypercalcemia; 7. antidiabetic agent; 8. parathyroid; 9. hyperkalemia; 10. glucosuria

Extension Activities
1. Answers will vary.
2. Answers will vary.
3. Answers will vary.

Chapter 14: The Male Reproductive System

Translation Challenge
1. Orchi/o or orchid/o means "testis" (testicle).
2. Orchidopexy is fixation by suturing the testicle into the scrotal sac. Bilateral means that the procedure is performed on both sides, that is, on both testicles.
3. Responses will vary, but could include testicular cancer, accidental injury, twisting or lack of normal development of the testis.

Checkpoint 14.1
1. genitalia, 2. epididymis, 3. the head, 4. 100 million

Exercise 14.1
1. orchio (CF) - cele (S): bulging of a testicle; 2. spermat (CF) - ic (S): pertaining to sperm; 3. a (P) - sperm (CF) - ia (S): lack of sperm production; 4. balano (CF) - plasty (S): surgical repair of the glans penis; 5. gonad (CF) - al (S): pertaining to the gonads

Exercise 14.2
1. prostate, 2. zygote, 3. gametes, 4. urologist, 5. scrotum

Exercise 14.3
1. e, 2. a, 3. c, 4. b, 5. f, 6. d

Exercise 14.4
1. scrotal, 2. oligospermia, 3. orchiopexy, 4. epididymectomy, 5. anorchia

Exercise 14.5
1. gametes, 2. zygote, 3. glans penis, 4. lumen, 5. epididymis, 6. gonads

Exercise 14.6
1. testes, 2. epididymis, 3. vas deferens, 4. seminal vesicles, 5. prostate gland, 6. urethra

Checkpoint 14.2
1. testicular torsion, 2. hydrocele, 3. hermaphroditism

Exercise 14.7
1. crypt (P) - orch/o (CF) - ism (S): undescended testicle(s); 2. poly (P) - orch/o (CF) - ism (S): more than two testicles; 3. an (P) - orch/o (CF) - ism (S): absence of testicles; 4. hydro (P) - cele (S): accumulation of fluid around the testicle; 5. a (P) - sperm/o (CF) - ia (S): ejaculation without seminal fluid or without sperm

Exercise 14.8
1. ambiguous genitalia; 2. cryptorchism; 3. epispadias; 4. pseudohermaphroditism 5. circumcision

Exercise 14.9
1. d, 2. f, 3. h, 4. b, 5. a, 6. g, 7. c, 8. e

Exercise 14.10
1. vasoplasty, 2. epididymitis, 3. balanoplasty, 4. prostatitis, 5. vasectomy

Exercise 14.11
1. hydrocele: collection of fluid around the testis; 2. phimosis: narrowness of the opening of the foreskin; 3. benign prostatic hyperplasia: enlarged prostate; 4. OK: inflammation of the glans penis; 5. oligospermia: scanty or deficient sperm

Exercise 14.12
Left: 1. aspermatogenesis, 3. oligospermia, 6. aspermia; Right: 2. gametes, 4. sperm, 5. ovum, 7. zygote

Checkpoint 14.3
1. prostate gland, 2. ultrasonography, 3. semen analysis

Checkpoint 14.4
1. as a method of birth control, 2. prostate gland, 3. circumcision

Exercise 14.13
1. balan (CF) - itis (S): inflammation of the glans penis; 2. spermat/o (CF) - genic (S): pertaining to the formation of sperm; 3. orch (CF) - itis (S): inflammation of the testicles; 4. vas (CF) - ectomy (S): removal of a portion of the vas deferens; 5. hydro (P) - cele (S): the accumulation of fluid in the scrotum

Exercise 14.14
1. testosterone, 2. semen analysis, 3. prostate-specific antigen test, 4. prostatic ultrasonography, 5. epididymotomy

Exercise 14.15
1. d, 2. a, 3. e, 4. f, 5. c, 6. b

Exercise 14.16
1. orchiectomy, 2. prostatectomy, 3. vesiculectomy, 4. transurethral, 5. prostatic

Exercise 14.17
1. transurethral resection of the prostate: removal of part or all of prostate gland through the urethra; 2. vasectomy: removal of all or part of vas deferens; 3. orchiectomy: removal of testis; 4. semen analysis: test to assess amount and viability of sperm; 5. doxazosin: generic drug to treat benign prostatic hyperplasia (BPH)

Exercise 14.18
Procedures will vary. Examples are provided.

Box 1: seminal vesicle, vesiculectomy; Box 2: prostate gland, prostatectomy, TURP; Box 3: testicle/testis: orchidorrhaphy, orchiectomy, orchiopexy

Chapter Review

Crossword Puzzle

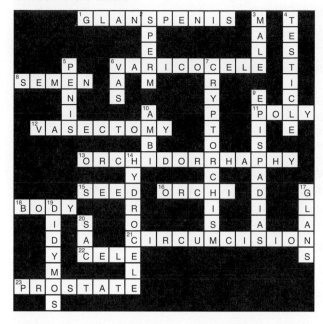

Matching

1. f, 2. e, 3. h, 4. a, 5. b, 6. d, 7. i, 8. g, 9. j, 10. c

Identification

1. ring centriole, 2. nucleus, 3. acrosome cap, 4. head, 5. midpiece, 6. spiral mitochondria, 7. tail

Abbreviations

1. transurethral resection of the prostate; 2. erectile dysfunction; 3. transurethral resection; 4. prostate-specific antigen; 5. benign prostatic hyperplasia; 6. digital rectal exam; 7. sexually transmitted infection; 8. Venereal Disease Research Laboratory

Word-Building Challenge

1. inflammation of the epididymis; 2. ureterocele: abnormality of the ureter; 3. hyperplasia: condition of excess growth; 4. hyposecretion: insufficient secretion (of hormones); 5. prostatitis: infection of the prostate

Extension Activities

1. Answers will vary.
2. Answers will vary.
3. Answers will vary.
4. Answers will vary.

Chapter 15: The Female Reproductive System

Translation Challenge

1. Gravida 1, para 0 means that the mother had one pregnancy and no births (at the time).
2. False
3. Metrorrhagia refers to irregular vaginal bleeding.
4. Dyspareunia refers to painful intercourse.

5. Uterine prolapse means the uterus fell from the pelvic cavity.

Checkpoint 15.1

1. ovulation phase, 2. labia majora, 3. areola

Exercise 15.1

1. uter/o, 2. vagin/o, 3. cervic/o, 4. oophor/o or ovari/o, 5. rect/o

Exercise 15.2

Refer to Figure 15.1 for correct labeling.
1. body of uterus, 2. fallopian tube, 3. vagina, 4. cervix, 5. ovary.

Exercise 15.3

1. vestibule; 2. mons pubis, symphysis pubis; 3. labia majora; 4. ovaries; 5. myometrium, endometrium

Exercise 15.4

1. hymen; 2. Bartholin's; 3. cervix; 4. fallopian; 5. fimbriae; 6. corpus luteum

Exercise 15.5

1. ovarian; 2. cervical; 3. endometritis; 4. dysmenorrhea; 5. amenorrhea

Exercise 15.6

1. follicle, egg, was; 2. fimbriae, were; 3. cervices, were; 4. vulvae, were; 5. ova, were

Exercise 15.7

1. primary follicle; 2. Graafian follicle; 3. ovulation; 4. corpus luteum; 5. corpus albicans

Checkpoint 15.2

1. breast development (called thelarche) and pubic hair; 2. two pregnancies but only one live birth; 3. menopause or climacteric

Exercise 15.8

1. thel/o: nipple, beginning breast development; 2. metr/o: uterus, irregular bleeding between periods; 3. men/o: menstruation, scant menstrual flow; 4. metr/o: uterus, uterine tissue growing outside the uterine wall; 5. salping/o: fallopian tube, inflammation of the fallopian tube

Exercise 15.9

1. atresia; 2. speculum; 3. puberty; 4. dysmenorrhea; 5. menorrhalgia

Exercise 15.10

1. b, 2. c, 3. a, 4. e, 5. d

Exercise 15.11

1. dysmenorrhea; 2. hypermenorrhea; 3. metrorrhagia; 4. mammogram; 5. ovulation

Exercise 15.12

1. genitalia, are; 2. fibroids, were; 3. speculum; 4. infections, are; 5. salpinx, was; 6. breasts; 7. fimbriae 8. ova

Checkpoint 15.3

1. colposcopy, 2. mammogram, 3. hysteroscopy, 4. lithotomy position

Checkpoint 15.4

1. salpingolysis, 2. colpopexy, 3. clitoridectomy

Exercise 15.13

1. a (P) – men/o (CF) - rrhea (S), absence of menses;
2. metr/o (CF) - rrhagia (S), irregular bleeding between periods; 3. salping (CF) - ectomy, removal of the fallopian tubes; 4. lact/o (CF) - gen (CF) - esis (S), milk production; 5. cervic (CF) - al (S), pertaining to the cervix

Exercise 15.14

1. mastodynia; 2. lactogenesis; 3. polypectomy; 4. colpopexy; 5. curettage

Exercise 15.15

1. dilation and curettage, 2. obstetrics, 3. total abdominal hysterectomy, 4. gonorrhea, 5. dysfunctional uterine bleeding

Exercise 15.16

1. rectocele, 2. urethrocele, 3. salpingo-oophorectomy, 4. colporrhaphy, 5. episiorrhaphy

Exercise 15.17

1. S, oophorectomies; 2. S, uteri; 3. S, areolae; 4. S, fundi; 5. S, cervices

Exercise 15.18

1. D, diagnostic procedure used to perform a biopsy of the cervix and vagina; 2. E, full or partial removal of the uterus; 3. A, removal of one or both breasts; 4. C, removal of one or both ovaries; 5. B, cutting or cauterizing the fallopian tubes

Chapter Review

Crossword Puzzle

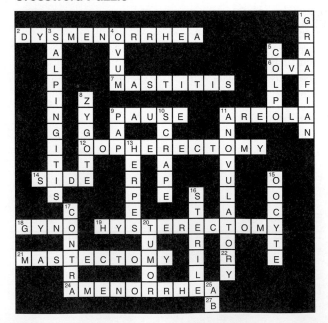

Matching

1. j, 2. d, 3. e, 4. a, 5. i, 6. c, 7. f, 8. g, 9. h, 10. b>

Identification

1. fundus, 2. body of uterus, 3. cervix, 4. vagina, 5. fallopian tube, 6. ovary

Abbreviations

1. bilateral tubal ligation, 2. dilation and curettage, 3. gonorrhea, 4. previous menstrual period, 5. vaginal hysterectomy, 6. gynecology, 7. hormone replacement therapy, 8. total abdominal hysterectomy, 9. human papilloma virus, 10. pelvic inflammatory disease

Word-Building Challenge

1. removal of hymen, 2. excessive buildup of cells in the lining of the uterus, 3. fallopian tube filled with pus, 4. bleeding into the fallopian tubes, 5. prolapse of the vaginal walls

Extension Activities

1. Answers will vary.
2. Answers will vary.
3. Answers will vary.

Chapter 16: Pregnancy, Birth, and Postpartum

Translation Challenge

1. three term births, zero preterm deliveries, zero abortions, three living children
2. This woman has been pregnant six times.
3. a sterilization procedure in which portions of the fallopian tubes are cauterized or cut to prevent the ovum (egg) from being fertilized

Checkpoint 16.1

1. placenta and umbilical cord, 2. Braxton Hicks, 3. parturition

Exercise 16.1

1. amni/o (CF) / ic (S), relating to amnion; 2. endo (P) / derm/o (CF), embryonic layer, "within skin"; 3. ecto (P) / derm/o (CF), embryonic layer, "outside skin"; 4. meso (P) / derm/o (CF), embryonic layer, "middle skin"; 5. oophor (CF) / ectomy (S), surgical removal of the ovaries

Exercise 16.2

1. parturition, 2. EDD, 3. menstrual, 4. placenta, 5. trimesters

Exercise 16.3

1. c, 2. a, 3. b, 4. e, 5. d

Exercise 16.4

1. cervical, 2. amniotic, 3. mammary, 4. hysterectomy, 5. fetal

Checkpoint 16.2

1. cephalopelvic disproportion, 2. abruptio placentae, 3. polyhydramnios

Checkpoint 16.3

1. The number of times a woman has given birth (parity) and the number of times a woman has become pregnant (gravida). 2. preeclampsia, 3. amniocentesis

Checkpoint 16.4

1. abstinence, 2. episiotomy or perineotomy, 3. cephalic version

Exercise 16.5

1. oxytocin, 2. dystocia, 3. abruptio placentae, 4. placenta previa, 5. Apgar score

Exercise 16.6

1. c, 2. a, 3. e, 4. d, 5. b

Exercise 16.7

1. FHR, 2. FTNSVD, 3. NB, 4. VBAC, 5. HCG

Exercise 16.8

1. relax/in, loosen, chemical; 2. nulli/gravida, none, pregnancy; 3. dys/tocia, difficult, labor or delivery; 4. post/part/um, after, delivery, structure or thing; 5. amni/on, amnion, structure

Matching

1. e, 2. i, 3. a, 4. g, 5. h, 6. b, 7. c, 8. j, 9. d, 10. f

Identification

1. b, 2. a, 3. c, 4. d

Abbreviations

1. CPD, 2. IUP, 3. FECG

Word-Building Challenge

1. relating to both amnion and chorion; 2. any disease developed in the embryo; 3. difficult delivery of the placenta; 4. birth canal; 5. relating to pregnancy or a pregnant woman

Extension Activities

1. Answers will vary.
2. Answers will vary.
3. Answers will vary.

Chapter Review

Crossword Puzzle

B Word Parts

a-	no, not, without, lack of, absence
ab-	away from
abdomin/o	abdomen
-ac	pertaining to
-ac	pertaining to
acous/o	hearing
ad-	toward, to, near, to administer (to give)
aden/o	gland
adenoid/o	adenoid
adip/o	fat
adren/o	adrenals
aer/o	air
-al	pertaining to
-algia	pain
alveol/o	hollow sac
ambi-	both
ambly/o	dull
amni/o	amnion
amyl/o	starch
an-	no, not, without
an/o	anus
ana-	back, away
andr/o	male, masculine
angi/o	vessel
anis/o	unequal
ankl/o	bent, fixed, stiffening, fusion
ante-	before
anti-	against, opposed to
aort/o	aorta
apic/o (apex/o)	apex
append/o	appendix
appendic/o	appendix
aque/o	water
-ar	relating to
-arche	beginning
arteri/o	artery
arteriol/o	artery
arthr/o	joint
articul/o	joint
-ary	pertaining to
-ase	enzyme
-asis	formation, presence of
asthen/o	loss of strength

astr/o	star-shaped
-ate	make, use, subject to
ather/o	deposit of pasty material
-ation	process
atri/o	atrium
audi/o	hearing, sound
aur/o	ear
auricul/o	ear
auto-	self
axill/o	armpit
bacteri/o	bacteria
balan/o	glans penis
bas/o	base, bottom
bi-	two, both
bio-	life
-blast	immature cell
blast/o	immature cell or tissue
blephar/o	eyelid
bol/o	bolus
brady-	slow
bronch/o	airway, bronchus
bronchiol/o	bronchiole
calc/o	calcium
capn/o	carbon dioxide
carcin/o	cancer
cardi/o	heart
-cardia	heart
cata-	down
cec/o	cecum
-cele	hernia, protrusion, pouch
celi/o	abdomen
-centesis	surgical puncture
cephal/o	head
cerebell/o	cerebellum
cerebr/o	cerebrum
cervic/o	cervix , neck
cheil/o (chil/o)	lips
-chezia	condition of stools
chol/o (chol/e)	bile
cholecyst/o	gallbladder
choledoch/o	common bile duct
chondr/o	cartilage
chord/o	cord
chrom/o	color
circum-	around, circular motion
-clasia	surgically break

-cle................... small	electr/o............. electric, electricity	gyn/o, gynec/o..... female
col/o................. colon	embry/o............. embryo	gynec/o............. woman; female
colon/o............. colon	-emesis.............. vomiting	hal/o................ breathe
colp/o............... vagina	-emia................ condition of the	hem/o............... blood
con-................. together, with	blood	hemat/o............. blood
conjunctiv/o....... conjunctiva	emmetr/o.......... correct measure, well	hemi-.............. half (usually right/left
contra-............. against, opposed to	proportioned	halves)
cord/o............... cord	en-................. inside or in	hepat/o............. liver
cor/o............... cornea	encephal/o........ related to the brain	herni/o............. rupture, hernia
corne/o............. cornea	endo-.............. inside, within, or in	hidr/o............. sweat glands
coron/o............ crown or circle	endocardi/o....... endocardium	hydr/o............. water
corp/.............. body	endometri/o....... endometrium	hymen/o........... hymen hymenal (per-
cost/o.............. rib	enter/o............. intestines	taining to the hymen)
crani/o............. head, cranium	epi-.............. upon, above	hyper-............. more, excessive,
crin/o............. secrete	episi/o............. vulva	increased, above
-crine............. to secrete	erythr/o............ red	hypo-............. less, deficient, below,
crypt-............. hidden	-esis............ state, condition	under
culd/o............. rectouterine pouch	esophagi/o........ esophagus	hyster/............. uterus
cut/o................ skin	esthesi/o............ feeling, sensation	hyster/o............ uterus
cutane/o........... skin	estr/o............ female	-ia................. condition, process, or
cyan/o.............. blue	eu-................. normal, healthy	state of
cyst/o................ bladder, pouch, sac,	-eum............... tissue or structure	-iasis................ condition, presence of
or cyst containing	ex-................. out, outside, away	-iatric............. treatment
fluid	exo-................ out, outside, away	-ic.................. pertaining to
cyt/o.................. cell	extra-............. out, outside, away	ichthy/o............ fish (scales) scaly
-cyte.................. cell	fet/o................. fetus	ile/o................ ileum
dacry/o............. tear	fibr/o................ fiber	ili/o................ ilium
dactyl/o............ fingers or toes	fibrin/o............. fiber	immun/o-........... immune
de-................. not, from, down	-flux.............. flow	in-................. inside, within, or in
dent/o.............. teeth	follicul/o............ follicle	infra-................ less than, under,
derm/o............. skin	-form............... shape or resembling	below
dermat/o-........... skin	galact/o............ milk	inguin/o............ groin
-desis................ stabilize, fuse, bind	gamet/o............ gamete	inter-.............. between
di-.................. through, complete	gangli/o............ swelling, collection	intra-.............. inside or in
di-.................. two	gastr/o-............. stomach	irid/o................ iris
dia-................ across or through	-gen .... producing	isch/o............... hold back
diaphragm/o..... diaphragm	-genesis............. origin, formation,	-ism................ condition, state of, or
diaphragmat/o.... diaphragm	production	process
dipl/o.............. double	-genic............. origin	-itis................ inflammation
-dipsia............. condition of thirst	genit/o............. genitals	-ium................ tissue or structure
dis-................. separate, apart	geus/o.............. taste	-ize................. make, use, subject to
diverticul/o........ diverticulum, pouch	gingiv/o............ gums	jejun/o............. jejunum
duoden/o.......... duodenum	glauc/o............ blue-gray	kary/o............. nucleus
-dynia.............. pain	gli/o................ gluey substance)	kerat/o............ cornea, horny tissue
dys-................. abnormal, bad, faulty,	-globin .... protein molecule	ket/o................ ketone
painful, difficult	glomerul/o........ glomerulus	kin/e................ motion, movement
e-.................. out, outside, away	gloss/o............ tongue	kinesi/o............ pertaining to move-
-e................... (noun marker)	gluc/o............... glucose (sugar)	ment
-eal.................. pertaining to	glyc/o............... sugar	labi/o............... lips
ec-................. out, outside, outward,	glycos/o............ sugar, glucose	labyrinth/o-....... inner ear
away	gonad/o............ gonad, seed, sex organ	lacrim/o........... tears
-ectasis.............. dilation	-gram................ record	lact/o................ milk
ecto-................. out, outside, outward	granul/o............ granular, granules	lapar/o............. abdomen
away	-graph............... record or instrument	-lapse............. fall
-ectomy .... surgical removal	used for making a record	laryng/o............ larynx
-edema.............. inflammation,	-graphy............. process of recording	leuk/o................ white
swelling	-gravida .... pregnancy	ligat/o.............. tying

lingu/o .... tongue
lip/ .... fat
lip/o .... fat, lipid
-lith .... stone, calcification
lith/o .... stone, calcification
lobl/o .... lobe
lumbl/o .... lower back
lumin/o .... lumen
lymph/o .... lymph
lymphat/o .... lymph
lymphaden/o ..... lymph gland
lymphangi/o ...... lymph vessel
-lysis .... breakdown, break up, dissolve, dissolution, or destruction
macro- .... large
mal- .... bad, abnormal
-malacia .... softening
mamm/o .... breast
mandibul/o .... jaw, lower jaw
mast/o .... breast
meat/o .... passageway or opening
mediastin/o .... mediastinum
medull/o .... medulla
mega- .... large, excessive
-megaly .... enlargement
melan/o .... black, dark
men/o .... menses, menstruation
menstru/o .... menses, menstruation
mening/o .... membrane covering brain and spinal column
meso- .... middle
meta- .... change, behind
-meter .... measure or measurement
metr/o .... womb, uterus
metri/o .... uterus
-metry .... process of measuring
mil/o .... less
micro- .... very small, tiny
mono- .... one
morph/o .... shape
muc/o .... mucus
multi- .... many, several
muscul/o .... muscle
my/o .... muscle
mydr/o .... widen
myel/o .... bone marrow, spinal cord
myocardi/o .... myocardium
myring/o .... tympanic membrane
nas/o .... nose
nat/o .... birth, born
necr/o .... death

neo- .... new
nephr/o- .... kidney(s)
neur/o- .... nerve
neutr/o .... neutral
nucle/o .... nucleus
nulli- .... none
nyctal/o .... night
o/o, ov/o .... ovum, egg
occipit/o .... occiput (back of the head)
ocul/o .... eye
odont/o .... tooth
-oid .... like, resembling
-ole .... small
olig- .... few, scant
olig/o .... scanty, few
-oma .... tumor, mass
onc/o .... tumor
onych/o .... nail
oophor/o .... ovary
ophthalm/o .... eye
opt/o .... eye, vision
or/o .... mouth
orchi/o .... testis (testicle)
orchid/o .... testis (testicle)
organ/o .... organ
orth/o .... straight
-ose .... pertaining to
-osis .... abnormal condition
osm/o .... sense of smell
osse/o .... bony
oste/o .... bone
-ostomy .... creation of an artificial opening
ot/o .... ear
-ous .... relating to
ovari/o .... ovary
ox/o .... oxygen molecule
oxy- .... rapid
pachy- .... thick
palpebr/o .... eyelid
pan- .... all
pancreat/o .... pancreas
papill/o .... nipple, papillary
par- .... near
para- .... alongside, beside, near, abnormal
-para .... delivery, birth
pariet/o .... wall
-partum .... delivery
path/o- .... disease
-pathy .... disease
-pause .... to stop, cease
pector/o .... chest
pelv/i .... basin, pelvis
pelv/o .... pelvis

pen/i .... penis
-penia .... abnormal reduction, shortage, deficiency, lack of
-pepsia .... digestive condition
per- .... through
peri- .... surrounding, around
pericardi/o .... pericardium
peritone/o .... peritoneum
-pexy .... surgical fixation, repair
phac/o .... lens of the eye
phag/o .... to eat
-phage .... eat, swallow
-phagia .... process of eating or related to eating
pharyng/o .... pharynx (throat)
phas/o .... speech
-phil .... attraction
-phile .... affinity for
phleb/o .... vein
-phobia .... fear
phon/o .... sound
phot/o .... light
phren/o
(diaphragm/o) .... diaphragm
pil/o .... hair
placent/o .... placenta
-plasia .... formation, development
plasm/o .... formed, plasma
-plasty .... surgical repair
pleur/o .... rib area
pne/o .... breath
-pnea .... breathing, related to breath
pneum/o .... lung, air
pod/o .... foot
-poiesis .... formation, production
poikil/o .... irregular
poly- .... many, frequent, excessive
post- .... after, behind
pre- .... before
presby/o .... old age
primi- .... first
pro- .... before, forward
proct/o .... rectum, anus
prostat/o .... prostate
prote/o .... protein
psych/o .... mental, the mind
-ptosis .... drooping, falling, prolapse
-ptysis .... spitting
pulmon/o- .... lung(s)

pupill/o .... pupil
py/o .... pus
pyel/o .... renal pelvis
pylor/o .... pylorus (gatekeeper)
quadri- .... four
radic/o .... nerve root, spinal nerve root
re- .... again, back
rect/o .... rectum
ren/o .... kidney
reticul/o .... reticulum
retin/o .... retina
retro- .... backward or behind
rhin/o .... nose
rhiz/o .... nerve root, spinal nerve root
rhythm/o .... rhythm
-rrhage .... bursting forth or rapid flow
-rrhagia .... bursting forth or rapid flow
-rrhaphy .... suturing
-rrhea .... drainage, discharge, flow
-ry .... relating to
sacr/o .... sacrum
salping/o .... fallopian tube
sarc/o .... flesh, tissue
scapul/o .... scapula
scler/o .... hardening
-sclerosis .... abnormal condition of hardening
-scope .... instrument used for viewing
-scopy .... process of viewing with an instrument
scot/o .... dark
scrot/o .... scrotum
seb/o .... pertaining to secretion from the sebaceous glands (sebum)
semi- .... part of a whole
semin/i .... semen
sept/o .... wall, partition
ser/o .... serum (fluid part of blood)
sial/o .... saliva
sigmoid/o .... sigmoid colon
sin/o .... sinus
sinus/o .... sinus
-sis .... process, action
somat/o .... body, relationship to the body
-spadias .... a tear
-spasm .... abrupt, forceful contraction

sperm/o .... semen, spermatozoa
spermat/o .... semen, spermatozoa
spher/o .... sphere-shaped
sphygm/o .... relating to the pulse
spir/o .... breathing
splen/o .... pertaining to the spleen
spondyl/o .... vertebrae
squam/o .... pertaining to scales
-stalsis .... contraction
-stasis .... stop, stand
sten/o .... narrowing, constriction
stern/o .... chest
steth/o .... chest
stom/a .... mouth
stomat/o .... mouth
-stomy .... new opening, surgical opening
sub- .... less than, under, below
sudor/o .... sweat
super- .... excessive, more, above
supra- .... above, excessive, outside, beyond
sym- .... with
syn- .... with, joined together
tachy- .... fast
tars/o .... tarsal bones in the foot
tempor/o .... temporal
tend/o .... tendon
tendin/o .... tendon
-tension .... process of stretching, pressure
test/o .... testes, testicle
tetra- .... four
thalam/ .... thalamus
thel/o .... nipple, papill
thorac/o .... chest
-thorax .... chest (pleural cavity)
-thrombin .... clotting substance
thrombocyt/o ...... clotting cell
thym/o .... thymus
thyr/o .... thyroid
-tic .... relating to
-tocia .... labor, delivery
-tomy .... cut or incision
tonsil/o .... tonsils
tox/o .... poison
trache/o .... windpipe, trachea
trans- .... across or through
-tresia .... opening, condition of an opening
tri- .... three

-tripsy .... crushing
trop/o .... turning toward, changing
-trophy .... development
tub/o .... tube
tympan/o .... drum
typhl/o .... cecum
-ula .... small
-ule .... small, little
ultra- .... excessive, beyond
umbilic/o .... umbilicus (navel)
ungu/o .... nail
uni- .... one, single
ur/e .... urea
ur/o .... urine
ureter/o .... ureter
urethr/o .... urethra
-uria .... urine
urin/o .... urine
uter/o .... uterus
uve/o .... uvea
vagin/o .... vagina
valvuv/o .... valve
varic/o .... twisted, swollen vein
vas/o .... vessel, ducts
vascul/o .... vessel
ven/o .... vein
ventricul/o .... ventricle
vertebr/o .... vertebra
vesic/o .... bladder
vesicul/o .... seminal vesicle
viscer/o .... internal organs, viscera
vitre/o .... glassy
vulv/o .... vulva
xanth/o .... yellow
xer/o .... dry
-y .... condition or process of
zyg/o .... a yoke; a type of joining

Abbreviations

♀	female	AML	acute myeloblastic leukemia (also known as acute myelogenous leukemia)
Ⓛ	left		
♂	male		
Ⓡ	right	AMN	anmiocentesis
↑	increased or increasing	amt.	amount
↓	decrease or decreasing	ANC	absolute neutrophil count
>	greater than	ANS	autonomic nervous system
<	less than	ant-	anterior
a	before	AOM	acute otitis media
A&P	auscultation and percussion	AP	anteroposterior *or* anterior posterior (used with X-ray views)
a.c.	before meals		
a.m.	before noon	APML	acute promyelocytic leukemia
A1c	average glucose level		
AB, ab	abortion	aq	water
ABG	arterial blood gas	ARDS	acute respiratory distress syndrome
ABR	auditory brainstem response		
		ARF	acute renal failure *or* acute respiratory failure
AC	air conduction		
Acc	accommodation	AROM	active range of motion
ACTH	adrenocorticotropic hormone	AS*	aortic stenosis *or* left ear (auris sinister)
ad lib	as desired	ASD	atrial septal defect
AD*	right ear (auris dexter)	ASHD	arteriosclerotic heart disease
ADH	antidiuretic hormone (vasopressin)		
		ASL	American Sign Language
ADHD	attention-deficit/hyperactivity disorder	ATN	acute tubular necrosis
		AU*	both ears (auris uterque)
ADL	activities of daily living	AV	atrioventricular; also abbreviated as A-V
AE/AEA	above-elbow amputation		
AF	atrial fibrillation	AZT	azidothymidine
AFB	acid-fast bacilli	B	bilateral
AFP	alpha-fetoprotein test	b.i.d.	twice a day
AGN	acute glomerulonephritis	BaE or BE	barium enema
AHF	antihemophilic factor VIII	baso	basophil
AHG	antihemophilic globulin factor VIII	BBB	bundle-branch block
		BC	bone conduction
AI	artificial insemination	BCC	basal cell carcinoma
AIDS	acquired immunodeficiency syndrome	BE/BEA	below-elbow amputation
		BG	blood glucose
AK/AKA	above-knee amputation	BiPAP	bilevel positive airway pressure
ALL	acute lymphoblastic leukemia		
		BK/BKA	below-knee amputation
ALS	amyotrophic lateral sclerosis	BM	bowel movement
		BMR	basal metabolic rate
AMI	acute myocardial infarction	BMT	bone marrow transplant

BP	blood pressure *or* bipolar disorder	CWP	coal worker's pneumoconiosis
BPH	benign prostatic hyperplasia	CX	circumflex (artery)
BS	bowel sounds	CXR	chest X-ray
BSE	breast self-exam	cysto	cystoscopy
BSO	bilateral salpingo-oophorectomy	D	diopter
BTL	bilateral tubal ligation	D&C	dilation and curettage
BUN	blood urea nitrogen	d.	day
bx	biopsy	D/C	discontinue or discharge
C	Celsius, centigrade	dB	decibel
c	with	DCR	dacryocystorhinostomy
C&S	culture and sensitivity test	derm.	dermatology
c/o	complains of (patient's report of a symptom)	DI	diabetes insipidus
C1, C2, etc.	cervical vertebrae (numbered according to area of the spine)	diff	differential
		DIP joint	distal interphalangeal joint
C1-C8	cervical nerves	DJD	degenerative joint disease
Ca	calcium	DKA	diabetic ketoacidosis
CA	chronological age	DM	diabetes mellitus
CAD	coronary artery disease	DNR	do not resuscitate
CAT	computerized axial tomography	DOE	dyspnea on exertion
cath	catheterization	dr	dram dr
CBC	complete blood count	DR, DRP	diabetic retinopathy
CC	chief complaint *or* clean-catch urine specimen	DRE	digital rectal examination
		DTR	deep tendon reflex
cc	cubic centimeter	DUB	dysfunctional uterine bleeding
CCU	coronary care unit	DVT	deep vein thrombosis
CDH	congenital dislocation of the hip	dx	diagnosis
CF	cystic fibrosis	EAC	external ear canal
CHF	congestive heart failure	ECCE	extracapsular cataract extraction
CHT	congenital hypothyroidism	ECG or EKG	electrocardiogram
CKD	chronic kidney disease	ECHO	echocardiogram
CLL	chronic lymphocytic leukemia	EchoEG	echoencephalography
cm	centimeter	ED	erectile dysfunction
CML	chronic myelogenous leukemia	EDC	estimated date of confinement (due date)
CNS	central nervous system	EDD	estimated date of delivery
CO	cardiac output	EEG	electroencephalogram or electroencephalography
CO$_2$	carbon dioxide		
COL	colonoscopy	EENT	eyes, ears, nose, and throat
COLD	chronic obstructive lung disease	EF	external fixation
COPD	chronic obstructive pulmonary disease	EGD	esophagogastroduodenoscopy
CP	chest pain *or* cerebral palsy	ELISA	enzyme-linked immunosorbent assay
CPAP	continuous positive airway pressure	Em	emmetropia
CPD	cephalopelvic disproportion	EMG	electromyography
CPR	cardiopulmonary resuscitation	ENT	ears, nose, and throat
CR	closed reduction	EOM	extraocular movements
CRF	chronic renal failure	eosin/eos	eosinophil
CS, C-section,		ERG	electroretinography
C/S	cesarean section	ERT	estrogen replacement therapy
CSF	cerebrospinal fluid	ERV	expiratory reserve volume
CST	contraction stress test	ESR	erythrocyte sedimentation rate
CT	computed tomography	ESRD	end-stage renal disease
CTA	clear to auscultation	ESWL	extracorporeal shock wave lithotripsy
cu mm	cubic millimeter	ETOH	ethyl alcohol (beverage alcohol)
CV	cardiovascular	F	Fahrenheit
CVA	cerebrovascular accident *or* costovertebral angle	FBS	fasting blood sugar
		FECG	fetal electrocardiogram
CVS	chorionic villus sampling	FEF	forced expiratory flow

FEF25–75	forced mid-expiratory flow during the middle half of the FVC		HGH	human growth hormone
FEV	forced expiratory volume		HHN	handheld nebulizer
FEV1	forced expiratory volume in 1 second		HIV	human immunodeficiency virus
FEV3	forced expiratory volume in 3 seconds		HLA	human leukocyte antigen
FHR	fetal heart rate		HNP	herniated nucleus pulposus (disk)
fl oz	fluid ounce fl oz		HP	hemipelvectomy
FS	frozen section		HPI	history of present illness
FSH	follicle-stimulating hormone		HPV	human papilloma virus
FTND	full-term, normal delivery		HRT	hormone replacement therapy
FTNSVD	full-term, normal, spontaneous, vaginal delivery		HSG	hysterosalpingography
			HTN	hypertension, high blood pressure
FVC	forced vital capacity		HVA	homovanillic acid
FVL	flow volume loop		hx	medical history
fx	fracture		i	one
g or gm	gram		I&D	incision and drainage
GAD	generalized anxiety disorder		I&O	intake and output
GAF Scale	Global Assessment of Functioning		IBD	inflammatory bowel disease
GB	gallbladder		IBS	irritable bowel syndrome
GC	gonorrhea		ICA	internal carotid artery
GD	Graves disease		ICCE	intracapsular cataract extraction
GERD	gastroesophageal reflux disease		ICP	intracranial pressure
GFR	glomerular filtration rate		ICSI	intracytoplasmic sperm injection
GGT	gamma-glutamyl transpeptidase		ID	intradermal
GH	growth hormone		IDDM	insulin-dependent diabetes mellitus
GHRH	growth hormone-releasing hormone		IF	internal fixation
GI	gastrointestinal		Ig	immunoglobulin
GIFT	gamete intrafallopian transfer		IH	inguinal hernia
GN	glomerulonephritis		ii	two
gr	grain gr		iii	three
grav I	first pregnancy		IM	intramuscular
gt	drop		IMA	internal mammary artery
gtt	drops		IMP	impression (related to diagnosis)
GTT	glucose tolerance test		inf-	inferior
GU	genitourinary		IO	intestinal obstruction
GYN	gynecology		IOL	intraocular lens
H	hypodermic		IOP	intraocular pressure
H&P	history and physical		IP	inpatient
H&P	history and physical		IP joint	interphalangeal joint
h.	hour		IPD	intermittent peritoneal dialysis
h.s.	hour of sleep		IPPB	intermittent positive pressure breathing
HAL	hyperalimentation		IQ	intelligence quotient
HAV	hepatitis A virus		IRDS	infant respiratory distress syndrome
HBV	hepatitis B virus		IRV	inspiratory reserve volume
HCG	human chorionic gonadotropin		IS	incentive spirometry or intracostal space
HCl	hydrochloric acid		ITP	immune thrombocytopenic purpura
HCT/Hct	hematocrit		IUD	intrauterine device
HCV	hepatitis C virus		IUP	intrauterine pregnancy
HD	hemodialysis or hip disarticulation		IV	intravenous or intravenously
HDL	high density lipoprotein		IVC	intravenous cholangiography
HDV	Hepatitis D virus		IVF	in vitro fertilization
HEENT	head, eyes, ears, nose, throat		IVP	intravenous pyelogram
HEV	Hepatitis E virus		IVU	intravenous urography
HF	heart failure		K	potassium
HG	hypoglycemia		KD	knee disarticulation
HGB/Hgb	hemoglobin		kg	kilogram
			KOH	potassium hydroxide

KUB	kidneys, ureters, bladder (X-ray)	NKDA	no known drug allergies
L	liter	NST	nonstress test
L&A	light and accommodation	O_2	oxygen
L&D	labor and delivery	OA	osteoarthritis
L1, L2, etc.	lumbar vertebrae	OB	obstetrics
L1-L5	lumbar nerves	OCD	obsessive-compulsive disorder
LA	left atrium	OCP	oral contraceptive pills
LAD	left anterior descending coronary artery	OD*	right eye (oculus dexter); doctor of optometry
Lap	laparoscopy		
LASIK	laser-assisted in situ keratomileusis	OM	otitis media
Lat	lateral	OP	outpatient
lb or #	pound	opim	other potentially infectious body fluids
LBW	low birth weight	OR	open reduction
LCA	left coronary artery	ortho	orthopedics
LDL	low-density lipoprotein	OS*	left eye (oculus sinister)
LES	lower esophageal sphincter	OSA	obstructive sleep apnea
LFT	liver function test	OT	oxytocin
LH	luteinizing hormone	Oto	otology
LIMA	left internal mammary artery	OU*	both eyes (oculus uterque)
LLL	left lower lobe of lung	oz	ounce
LLQ	left lower quadrant	p	after post *or* pulse
LMCA	left main coronary artery	p.c.	after meals
LMP	last menstrual period	p.m.	after noon
LP	lumbar puncture	p.o.**	by mouth
LPA	left pulmonary artery	p.p.	postprandial (after eating)
LUL	left upper lobe of lung	p.r.**	by rectum
LUQ	left upper quadrant	p.r.n**.	as needed
LV	left ventricle	PA	pernicious anemia, posterior anterior (used with X-ray views), *or* pulmonary artery
lymphs	lymphocytes		
MA	mental age		
MCH	mean corpuscular hemoglobin	PAC	premature atrial contraction
MCHC	mean corpuscular hemoglobin concentration	PAN	periodic alternating nystagmus
MCP joint	metacarpophalangeal joint	PAP	pap test *or* positive airway pressure
MCV	mean corpuscular volume	PAR	postanesthesia recovery
MDI	metered-dose inhaler	PAT	paroxysmal atrial tachycardia
MDRTB	multidrug-resistant tuberculosis	PCP	Pneumocystis carinii pneumonia
mg	milligram	PD	Parkinson's disease *or* peritoneal dialysis
MI	myocardial infarction	PDA	posterior descending artery; patent ductus arteriosus
mL	milliliter		
mm	millimeter	PE tubes	pressure-equalizing tubes
mono	monocyte	PEF	peak expiratory flow
MPA	main pulmonary artery	PEG	percutaneous endoscopic gastrostomy
MR	mitral regurgitation	per	by or through
MRI	magnetic resonance imaging	PERRLA	pupils equal, round, reactive to light and accommodation
MS	mitral stenosis *or* multiple sclerosis		
MSH	melanocyte-stimulating hormone	PET	positron emission tomography
MVP	mitral valve prolapse	PFT	pulmonary function test
my	myopia	PI, para I	first delivery
N&V	nausea and vomiting	PID	pelvic inflammatory disease
n.p.o.**	nothing by mouth	PIH	pregnancy induced hypertension *or* prolactin-inhibiting hormone
Na	sodium		
NB	newborn	PIP	joint proximal interphalangeal joint
NEC	neonatal necrotizing enterocolitis	PKD	polycystic kidney disease
Neut	neutrophils	plts/PLT	platelets
NIDDM	non-insulin dependent diabetes mellitus	PMDD	premenstrual dysphoric disorder
		PMH	past medical history
NKA	no known allergies	PMI	point of maximal impulse

PMN	polymorphonuclear neutrophil		RUL	right upper lobe of lung
PMP	previous menstrual period		RUQ	right upper quadrant
PMS	premenstrual syndrome		RV	residual volume *or* right ventricle
PND	paroxysmal nocturnia dyspnea		Rx	prescription
PNS	peripheral nervous system		s	without sine
polys	polymorphonuclear neutrophils		S1, S2, etc.	sacral vertebrae
Pos	posterior		S1-S5	sacral nerves
PP	postprandial		SA	sinoatrial node
PPD	puried protein derivative (utilized as a skin test for tuberculosis) **chapter 3		SAB	spontaneous abortion
			SAD	seasonal affective disorder
PPI	proton pump inhibitors		SARS	severe acute respiratory syndrome
PRH	prolactin-releasing hormone		SB	stillbirth
PRK	photorefractive keratectomy		SCA s	udden cardiac arrest
PRL	prolactin		SCC	squamous cell carcinoma
PROM	passive range of motion		SD	shoulder disarticulation
PSA	prostate-specific antigen		sed rate	sedimentation rate
pt	patient		segs	segmented neutrophils
PT	prothrombin time		SIADH	syndrome of inappropriate antidiuretic hormone
PTCA	percutaneous transluminal coronary angio-plasty			
			sig.	label; instructions
PTH	parathyroid hormone (parathormone)		SLE	systemic lupus erythematosus
PTSD	post-traumatic stress disorder		SNS	somatic nervous system
PTT	partial thromboplastin time		SOB	shortness of breath
PUD	peptic ulcer disease		SPECT	single-photon emission computed tomography
PV p	ulmonary vein			
PVC	premature ventricular contraction		ss	one-half
PVD	peripheral vascular disease		SSS	sick sinus syndrome
q.**	each or every		ST	esotropia
q.2h.	every two hours		stat	immediately
q.4h.	every four hours		stat.	at once, immediately
q.s.**	quantity sufficient		STD	sexually transmitted disease
qt	quart		STI	sexually transmitted infection
R	respirations		STSG	split-thickness skin graft
R/O	rule out		subq; SQ	subcutaneous
RA	rheumatoid arthritis *or* right atrium		Sup	superior
RAD	reactive airway disease		T	temperature
RBC	red blood cell		T&A	tonsillectomy and adenoidectomy
RCA	right coronary artery		t.i.d.**	three times a day
RDS	respiratory distress syndrome		T1, T2, etc.	thoracic vertebrae
REM	rapid eye movement		T1-T12	thoracic nerves
Rh	rhesus factor		T3	triiodothyronine
RIA	radioimmunoassay		T4	thyroxine
RIMA	right internal mammary artery		TAH	total abdominal hysterectomy
RLL	right lower lobe of lung		TAH/BSO	total abdominal hysterectomy with bilateral salpingo-oophorectomy
RLQ	right lower quadrant			
RML	right middle lobe of lung		TAH-BSO	total abdominal hysterectomy-bilateral salpingo-oophorectomy
ROJM	range of joint motion			
ROM	range of motion		TB	tuberculosis
ROP	retinopathy of prematurity		TBI	traumatic brain injury
ROS	review of systems		TCC	transitional cell carcinoma
RP	retrograde pyelogram		TENS	transcutaneous electric nerve stimulation
RPA	right pulmonary artery		TFT	thyroid function test
RRR	regular rate and rhythm (refers to heart)		THA	total hip arthroplasty
RSV	respiratory syncytial virus		THR	total hip replacement
RTC	return to clinic		TIA	transient ischemic attack
RTO	return to office		TKR	total knee replacement

TLC	total lung capacity	VA	visual acuity
TM	tympanic membrane	VBAC	vaginal birth after cesarean section
TPN	total parenteral nutrition (hyperalimentation)	VC	vital capacity
TRH	thyrotropin-releasing hormone	VCUG	voiding cystourethrography
TS	tricuspid stenosis	VDRL	Venereal Disease Research Laboratory (test for syphilis, an STD)
TSH	thyroid-stimulating hormone		
TSS	toxic shock syndrome	VF	ventricular fibrillation *or* visual field
TUR	transurethral resection	VH	vaginal hysterectomy
TURP	transurethral resection of the prostate gland; transurethral prostatectomy	VMA	vanillylmandelic acid
		VS	vital signs
TV	tidal volume *or* tricuspid valve	VSD	ventricular septal defect
TVS	transvaginal sonography	VT	ventricular tachycardia
Tx	treatment	WAIS	Wechsler Adult Intelligence Scale
UA, U/A	urinalysis	WBC	white blood cell
UC	ulcerative colitis, urine culture, *or* uterine contractions	WISC	Wechsler Intelligence Scale for Children
		wk	week
UGI	upper gastrointestinal	WNL	within normal limits
ung.	ointment	x	times or for
UNHS	universal newborn hearing screening test	XT	xotropia
URI	upper respiratory infection	yr	year
UTI	urinary tract infection	ZIFT	zygote intrafallopian transfer
UV	ultraviolet		

**Abbreviations pronounced letter-by-letter

*Note that some abbreviations have been used for multiple terms and could cause confusion in a medical setting. Healthcare providers may consider these abbreviations too dangerous to use.

Index

balloon angioplasty procedure, 351, 352t
bandage, meaning and word analysis, 77t
B antigen, 371
barbiturates, 222
bariatric surgery, 469t
barium enema, 467t
barium swallow, 467t
Barrett's esophagus, 458t
barrier methods (birth control), 650t
Bartholin's glands, 589t, 591
basal cell carcinoma, 104t
basophilia, 379t
basophils, 367t, 370, 372, 379t
B cells, 409, 410
beauty marks, 104t
bee stings, reactions to, 419f
behavior therapy, 222t
Bell's palsy, 203t, 209
belly button, 442t, 461, 465
benign prostatic hyperplasia (BPH), 567t, 570, 575
benzodiazepines, 222
beta-blockers, 353, 353t
beta cells, 529
bicuspid valve, 322, 323t
bilateral (directional term), 51t
bilateral salpingo-oophorectomy, 611, 611t
bilateral tubal ligation, 611, 611t, 650t, 651–652, 651f
bile, 440t, 449
bile duct, 440t, 449, 449f
bilevel positive airway pressure (BiPAP), 308
bilirubin, 381
bimanual examination, 607
biochemistry, 75
biological response modifier, 393t
biophysical profile (BPP), 647t
biopsy, 77t, 116, 169, 214, 425t, 467t, 501t
bipolar disorders, 214
birth
    abbreviations associated with, 654, 655t
    anatomy and physiology terms related to, 624–625t
    clinical treatments for, 652–653
    surgical treatments, 651–652
    word parts associated with, 623–624t
birth control, 649, 650t
birth control pills, 650t
birthmarks, 104t, 111
bitter taste, 249
Blackley, Charles Harrison, 419
bladder, 484t, 496, 500. See also Urinary bladder
bladder infections, 483
blastocyst, 624t, 626, 626f
blastocyte, 624t
bleeding time, 390
blepharectomy, 261t
blepharitis, 252t, 253
blepharoplasty, 119t, 261t
blepharoptosis, 252t
blindness, 251, 254, 255
blind spot, 259–260

blood, 327. See also Hematology
    circulation of, 329–332
    components of, 373f
    flow through the heart, 325, 326f, 327
    formed elements of, 369f
    types of, 371–372, 371f
    volume of, in human body, 369, 369f
blood-brain barrier, 198
blood cells
    abnormalities, 379, 380t
    during fetal life, 381
    red blood cells, 39, 370–371, 380t, 384
    three main types of, 370, 370t
    white blood cells, 372, 379t, 410
blood clotting, 373, 374f, 390
blood cultures, 424t
blood donation, 392
blood pressure (BP), 332, 343, 349t
blood smear, 389t
blood tests
    for GI tract conditions, 466
    for prostate cancer, 573, 573t
    for respiratory system, 302
blood transfusion, 372, 392t
blood type A, 371
blood types, 371–372, 371f, 372t
blood typing, 389t
blood urea nitrogen (BUN), 500, 501t
blood vessels, 318, 329–332
blood volume, by age, 369t
blushing, 94
B lymphocytes (B cells), 409
body
    planes of, 55, 56f
    terms describing movement of, 56–57t, 56–58, 57f
body (stomach), 445
body cavities, 59, 60t
body organization
    cells, 38–41
    key terms for, 37t
    levels of organization, 36–38, 37f
    tissues, 41–42
body positions, 51–52t, 52f, 53–55, 53–55f
body regions, 60–64, 63f, 64t
body systems. See also Individual body systems
    common root words associated with various, 6t
    root words associated with specific, 5t
bolus, 443
bone cells, 140, 141f
bone graft, 171
bone growth, 141, 142f
bone markings, 154, 156f, 156t
bone marrow, 137t, 139
bone marrow aspiration, 169, 169f, 389, 389t
bone marrow biopsy, 389, 389t
bone marrow donations, 391
bone marrow transplant, 391, 392t
bones
    fetal/infant, 161–162
    structure of long, 139, 140f

bony landmarks, palpable, 154, 156f, 156t
botulinum toxin type A, 120t
bovine collagen, 120t
bowel (abdominal) distension, 456t
bowels, 448
bowleg, 159t, 162
Bowman's capsule, 484t, 486, 486f
brachial artery, 323t
brachial body region, 63f
brachial region, 64t
bradycardia, 328, 336, 337t
bradypnea, 304t
brain scan, 220t
brainstem, 187t, 191f, 193
brain stem gliomas, 212t
brain, the, 186, 189
    lobes of, 192f
    meaning and word analysis, 187t
    meninges of, 190f
    parts of, 191–193, 191f
brain tumors, 212, 212t
Braxton Hicks contractions, 624t, 632
Brazilian butt lift, 119t
breast augmentation, 119t
breast cancer, 599
breast reduction, 119t
breast self-exam (BSE), 599, 609–610, 609f
breasts, female, 589t, 595, 596f
    changes in, during pregnancy, 632–633t
breathing. See Respiration
breech, 633
breech presentation, 643t
bronchi, 283f
bronchial tree, 284t, 288, 288f
bronchiectasis, 294t
bronchioles, 283f, 284t, 288f
bronchiolitis, 293, 294t, 298
bronchitis, 299
bronchodilators, 309t
bronchogenic carcinoma, 294t, 297
bronchogram, 304
bronchography, 72t
bronchophony, 303t
bronchoplasty, 307t
bronchoscopy, 304, 305t
bronchospasm, 294t
bronchus, 284t
Brudzinski reflex, 199t
bruises, 377
bruit (heart sound), 344t
buccal body region, 63f
buccal region, 64t
buckled fracture, 155t
bulbourethral (Cowper) gland, 559f, 559t, 561f, 563
bulimia nervosa, 213t, 215
bulla, 106t
bundle of His, 323t, 328
bunionectomy, 172t
bunions, 157, 158t
burns (skin), 104–105
    rule of nines, 105, 105f
    surgical treatments, 118

ciliary body, 239, 239*f*
circulatory system, 318. *See also* Cardiovascular system
circumcision, 560, 574, 574*f*, 575*t*
circumduction, 57*f*, 57*t*
circumscribed, 94*t*
cirrhosis, 460*t*
cistern chyli, 405*t*
claustrophobia, 214*t*
clean-catch urine sample, 500, 501*t*
cleft palate, 457*t*, 461
click (heart sound), 344*t*
climacteric, 601*t*, 604
clinical treatments
    associated with renal system, 504*t*
    for the ear(s), 269
    for the eye(s), 262
    musculoskeletal system, 171
    for pregnancy, birth, and postpartum, 652–653
    related to the eye(s), 262
    relating to the nervous system, 222*t*
    relating to the skin, 119–120, 120*t*
    for respiratory conditions, 307–308, 308*t*
clitoridectomies, 611*t*, 612
clitoris, 589*t*, 591
closed comedones (whiteheads), 112
closed fracture, 155*f*, 155*t*
closed reduction (CR), 171
clotting, 373, 374*f*
clubbing, 304*t*, 337*t*, 343
clubfoot, 162
coagulation, 367*t*
coarctation of the aorta, 341*f*, 341*t*
coccygeal region of the spinal column, 62, 62*f*, 62*t*
coccyx, 62, 62*f*, 62*t*
cochlea, 49, 242*t*, 245, 245*f*
cochlear duct, 246*f*
cochlear implant, 270*t*
cochlear nerve, 245*f*, 246*f*
cognitive therapy, 222*t*
colitis, 459*t*
collagen, 94*t*, 97
"collapsed lung," 299
collecting ducts, 486
collecting tubules, 486*f*, 488
colloid, 519*t*, 527
colonoscopy, 466, 467*t*
colony-stimulating factors, 370, 393*t*
colorectal, 440*t*
colorectal cancer, 455
colors, combining forms related to, 7, 8*t*
colostomy, 468, 469*t*
colpopexy, 611*t*
colpoplasty, 611*t*
colposcopy, 607, 608*t*
combining forms, 4, 7, 7*t*, 9–11. *See also* Word parts
    related to colors, 7, 8*t*
comedo/comedones, 109*t*, 112
comminuted fracture, 155*f*, 155*t*
common bile duct, 440*t*, 449
common cold, 293

common wart, 114
communication. *See also* Soft skills
    medical imaging and, 68
    value of, 3
complement, 405*t*
complete blood count (CBC), 75*t*, 388–389, 389*t*, 424*t*
computed tomography (CT) scans, 69, 70, 70*f*, 71, 304, 305*t*, 573, 573*t*
computerized axial tomography (CAT scan), 219, 220*t*
conception, 626
concha, 242*t*
conditions. *See also* Individual body systems
    common combining forms related to, 7*t*
    suffixes indicating, 11*t*
condyle, 137*t*
condyloid diarthroses, 143, 144*f*
condyloma acuminatum, 109*t*
confluent, 94*t*
congenital anomalies/disorders
    female reproductive system, 602–603
    infant neurological system, 210
    male reproductive system, 568, 568*t*, 569*f*
congenital heart defects, 340–342*t*
congenital malformations, skeletal, 161–162
congestive heart failure (CHF), 337*t*, 343, 344*t*
conjunctiva, 236*t*, 238, 239*f*
conjunctivitis, 251–252, 252*t*, 262
connective tissue, 41
constipation, 454, 456*t*
contact dermatitis, 104*t*
continuous positive airway pressure (CPAP), 308
contraction stress test (CST), 647
contrast dyes, 72
Coombs' test, 389*t*, 390
cordotomy, 222*t*
cornea, 236*t*, 238*f*, 239, 239*f*
corneal abrasions, 252, 252*t*
coronal plane, 56*f*
coronary arteries, 323*t*
coronary artery bypass grafts (CABG), 351, 352*t*
coronary artery disease (CAD), 337*t*, 343
coronary circulation, 325, 333
coronary stent, 352*t*
corpulmonale, 337*t*
corpus albicans, 589*t*, 595
corpus cavernosum, 559*t*, 560, 561*f*
corpus luteum, 589*t*, 594–595
corpus spongiosum, 559*t*, 560, 561*f*
corrective lenses, 262
cortex, 482–483, 483*f*, 484*t*, 528–529
cortical areas, 191
corticosteroids, 426*t*, 519*t*, 545*t*
coryza, 294*t*
costovertebral angle, 484*t*, 500
coughing, 294
counselors, 213

Cowper's glands, 559*f*, 559*t*, 563
coxal region, 64*t*
CPT (Current Procedural Terminology), 86
crackles, 303
cradle cap, 104*t*
cranial (directional term), 51*t*, 52*f*
cranial cavity, 59, 60*f*, 60*t*
cranial nerves, 186, 194, 194*t*, 195*f*, 206*f*
craniotomy, 222*t*
cranium, 64*t*
C-reactive protein (CRP) test, 168
creatinine, 500
creatinine clearance, 500, 501*t*
cremasteric reflex, 199*t*
crest, 137*t*
cretinism, 533*t*, 534*t*, 537
Crohn's disease, 455, 456*t*, 462
croup, 294*t*, 298
crural body region, 63*f*
crural region, 63*f*, 65*t*
cryoretinopexy, 261*t*
cryptorchism, 568, 568*t*, 569*f*
CT scans. *See* Computed tomography (CT) scans
cubital region, 64*t*
culdocentesis, 608*t*
cultural competence. *See* Soft skills
culture, defined, 75*t*
Current Procedural Terminology (CPT), 86
Cushing disease, 533, 535*t*
cutaneous, 95*t*
cuticle, 95*t*, 100, 101*f*
cyanosis, 295*t*, 304*t*, 337*t*
cyberknife, meaning and word analysis, 77*t*
cycloplegics, 262*t*
cystadenoma, 460*t*
cystectomy, 503, 503*t*
cystic fibrosis (CF), 295*t*, 298, 456*t*, 462
cystitis, 494*t*, 639*t*
cystocele, 493*t*, 496, 601*t*, 604
cystogram, 500, 501*t*
cystopexy, 503, 503*t*
cystoscopy, 500
cystourethroscopy, 501*t*
cysts, 106*t*
cytology, 38
cytomegalovirus (CMV), 420*t*, 423
cytoplasm, 38, 41

D

dacryocystorhinostomy, 261*t*
dacryoma, 252, 252*t*
dandruff, 120
D&C (Dilation and Curettage), 607
DEA (Drug Enforcement Administration), 80
deafness, 265
debridement, 118, 119*t*, 172*t*
decerebrate, 204*t*
deciduous teeth, 440*t*, 443, 444*f*
decongestants, 309*t*
decorticate, 204*t*

human chorionic gonadotropin (hCG), 530
human development. *See* Labor; Pregnancy
human immunodeficiency virus. *See* HIV (human immunodeficiency virus)
human leukocyte antigen (HLA) B-27, 169, 170*t*
human leukocyte antigen (HLA) tissue typing, 391
human papillomavirus (HPV), 600, 601*t*, 639*t*
humerus, 134, 138*t*
humor, 405*t*
humoral immunity, 409
humpback, 163
"hunger pangs," 530
hyaluronic acid, 120*t*
hydantoins, 222
hydrocele, 567*t*, 569, 569*f*
hydrocephalus, 204*t*, 210
hydrochloric acid, 445
hydrocortisone, 545
hydronephrosis, 493*t*
hydrophobia, 214*t*
hymen, 590*t*, 591
hymenectomy, 611*t*
hyoid bone, 287*f*
hyperalimentation, 469*t*
hyperbilirubinemia, 381
hypercalcemia, 169, 533*t*
hypercalciuria, 496*t*
hypercapnia, 304*t*
hyperglycemia, 519*t*, 529, 537
hyperinsulin (hypoglycemia), 533*t*
hyperinsulinism, 535*t*
hyperlipemia, 339*t*
hypermenorrhea, 603*t*
hyperopia, 253*t*
hyperparathyroidism, 535*t*
hyperplasia, meaning and word analysis, 76*t*
hyperpnea, 304*t*
hypertension, 332, 339*t*, 533*t*
hyperthyroidism, 535*t*, 538
hypertrophy, 336, 336*f*
hypertropia, 253*t*, 254
hyperventilation, 295*t*, 304*t*
hypnobirthing, 653, 653*t*
hypnotherapy, 222*t*
hypnotics, 223*t*
hypocalcemia, 533*t*
hypochromia, 380*t*
hypochromic, 368*t*
hypodermis layer, 97
hypoglycemia, 534, 537
hypoglycemic effect, 529
hypogonadism, 533*t*, 535*t*
hypolipidemics, 353*t*
hypomenorrhea, 603*t*
hyponatremia, 533*t*
hypoparathyroidism, 535*t*
hypophysectomy, 545*t*
hypophysis. *See* Hypothalamus
hypospadias, 493*t*, 568, 568*t*
hypotension, 332, 339*t*

hypothalamus, 188*t*, 192, 519*t*
hypothalamus abnormalities, 533*t*
hypothalamus gland, 518, 518*f*, 523, 524, 524*f*
hypothalamus hormones, 525*t*
hypothyroidism, 536*t*, 537, 538
hypovolemia, 378*t*
hypoxia, 304*t*, 370, 378*t*
hysterectomy, 611, 611*t*
hysteropexy, 611*t*
hysteroptosis (uterine prolapse), 601*t*
hysterosalpingography (HSG), 608*t*
hysteroscopy, 608*t*

I

ibuprofen, 172
ICD-9-CM (International Classification of Diseases-ninth version-Clinical Modification), 86
ICD-10, 86
ichthyosis, 49
ictal, 204*t*
ictal phase of seizures, 208
identical twins, 625*t*
idiopathic, 377
ileocecal valve, 447, 448*f*
ileostomy, 468, 469*t*
ileum, 441*t*
ileus, 454, 459*t*
illnesses. *See* Conditions
imaging. *See* Medical imaging
immobilization, for fractures, 171
immune system, 46*f*, 402. *See also* Lymphatic system
    assessing function of, 414–415
    major structures of, 46*f*
    medical field/specialists, 46*f*
    organs of, 406–408
    tests associated with, 424*t*
immune thrombocytopenic purpura (ITP), 377, 378*t*, 418*t*
immunity, 405*t*
    conditions associated with, 415–416*t*
    in infants, 416
    types of, 410, 410*t*
immunizations, 416, 417, 426*t*
immunodeficiency, 415*t*, 417
immunoglobulin E (IgE), 419
immunoglobulins (antibodies), 405*t*, 409, 419, 423
immunologists, 402
immunology, 402
immunosuppressants, 173, 173*t*, 426*t*
imperforate anus, 460*t*, 461
impetigo, 109*t*
impotence, 566, 567*t*
incision, meaning and word analysis, 77*t*
incontinence, urinary, 492, 493*t*, 496, 496*t*
incubation, 75*t*
incus, 243*t*, 244
indoor tanning, 117
induced abortions, 648
infantile automatisms, 210

infant mortality, 644
infant respiratory distress syndrome (IRDS), 297
infarct, 338*t*
infarction, 382, 383
infections
    bladder, 483
    in children, 417
    ear, 267
    meaning and word analysis, 76*t*
    upper respiratory infections (URIs), 296*t*, 298, 417
    urinary tract infections (UTIs), 483, 492, 493, 494*t*, 495, 500, 504
inferior (directional term), 51*t*, 52*f*
inferior lacrimal punctum, 238*f*
inferior palpebra, 238*f*
inferior venae cavae, 324*t*, 325. *See also* Vena cava
infertility, 566, 567*t*, 642*t*, 651
infibulation, 612
inflammation
    meaning and word analysis, 76*t*
    of nails and surrounding tissue, 108
inflammatory bowel disease (IBD), 455, 459*t*
inflammatory response, 405*t*, 410, 411*f*
influenza, 295*t*
ingestion, 442–443
inguinal hernia, 459*t*, 461
inguinal lymph nodes, 405*t*
inguinal region, 65*t*
inhalation, 280, 289, 289*f*
inhaled corticosteroids, 309*t*
innervate, 188*t*, 194
innervation, 194*t*
innocent heart murmurs, 343
insertion (skeletal muscle), 147*t*, 151
inspiration, 284*t*, 289
inspiratory reserve volume (IRV), 305
insulin, 529
insulin-dependent diabetes mellitus (IDDM). *See* Type 2 diabetes
integrity (skin), 95*t*
integument, 95*t*
integumentary system, 43*f*, 91–122. *See also* Hair; Nails; Skin
    abbreviations, 122*t*
    cancers of, 104*t*
    combining forms associated with, 93*t*
    major structures of, 43*f*
    medical field/specialists for, 43*f*
    pharmacological treatments, 120, 121*t*
    root words associated with, 5*t*
    terms related to conditions of, 108–110*t*
    word parts associated with, 92–93, 93*t*
intention tremor, 204*t*, 211
interatrial septum, 322
intercostal muscles, 284*t*, 289
interferon, 393*t*, 405*t*, 410
interferons, 410
internal (inner) ear, 244*f*, 245
internal fixation (IF), 171, 172*f*
internal urethral meatus, 561*f*

anatomy and physiology terms
associated with, 405–406*t*
cells of, 408–410
conditions associated with, 414–420
diagnostic tests and examinations, 423,
424*t*
practitioners for, 402
treatment for conditions of, 424–426
lymphatic vessels, 405*t*
lymph node filtering system, 408
lymph nodes, 405*t*, 408, 414–415
lymphocytes, 368*t*, 370, 379*t*, 404, 404*f*,
406, 408
lymphocytopenia, 379*t*
lymphocytosis, 379*t*
lymphomas, 385, 415*t*, 420*t*
lymph vessels, 408

M

macrocyte, 368*t*, 380*t*
macrocytic, 380*t*
macrophages, 405*t*
macrosomia, 537
macrotia, 265*t*, 266
macula lutea, 237*t*, 239*f*, 254
macular degeneration, 253*t*, 256
macule/macular, 106*t*
magnetic resonance imaging (MRI), 71,
71*f*, 220*t*, 304, 305*t*, 349*t*
malabsorption syndrome, 459*t*
male birth control pill, 650
male reproductive system, 556–576
abbreviations, 576, 576*t*
abnormalities of male reproductive
organs, 569*f*
anatomy and physiology, 558–563
anatomy and physiology terms
associated with, 559–560*t*
conditions associated with, 566–570
congenital abnormalities of, 568, 568*t*,
569*f*
diagnostic tests/examinations, 573,
573*t*
major structures of, 48*f*
medical field/specialists for, 48*f*
root words associated with, 5*t*
specialists, 556
treatment for conditions associated
with, 574–575
word parts associated with, 557–558*t*
malignant hypertension, 332
malignant melanomas, 104*t*
malleus, 243*t*, 244
malocclusion, 458*t*
mammary soufflé, 338*t*, 343
mammograms, 608, 608*t*
mammoplasty, 611*t*
mania, 213*t*
manic-depressive disorder, 214
Mantoux skin test, 305*t*
mast cells, 419
mastectomy, 611*t*
mastication (chewing), 441*t*, 443
mastitis, 601*t*, 644*t*

mastodynia, 601*t*
mastoiditis, 265*t*
mastopexy, 611*t*
mastoptosis, 644*t*
matrix, 138*t*, 141
maxillary sinus, 287
MCH concentration (MCHC), 388–389
mean corpuscular hemoglobin (MCH),
388
mean corpuscular volume (MCV), 388
measles, 416, 417
meatus, 138*t*, 243*t*, 561*f*
Meckel's diverticulum, 382
meconium, 461, 625*t*
meconium aspiration, 297
medial (directional term), 51*t*, 52*f*
mediators, 410
medical coding systems, 86
medical dictionaries, 28–29
medical imaging, 67–72, 73*t*
medical terminology/terms, 3–4, 85–86
origins of, 2–3
five ways to combine parts to create,
22–23
nondecodable, 23
pronouncing, 25–26
medical tourism, 121
medication
routes of administration, 83, 83*t*, 84*f*
terms related to administration of, 81,
82–83*t*
terms related to routes of, 83, 83*t*, 84*f*
medication administration terms, 81,
82–83*t*
medication orders, 79
medications. *See also* Pharmacological
treatments
digestive health and, 471
for the ear, 270
medulla, 483, 483*f*, 484*t*, 528
medulla oblongata, 188*t*, 193
medullary cavity, 138*t*, 139
medulloblastoma, 212*t*
megakaryocytes, 368*t*, 373
megaloblastic anemia, 377, 378*t*
meibomian glands, 238
melanin, 95*t*, 96
melanocytes, 96, 109*t*
melanocyte-stimulating hormone (MSH),
525*t*
melanoma, 109*t*, 112
melatonin, 520*t*, 524
melena, 457*t*
membrane (cell), 40
memory B cells, 409
menarche, 590*t*, 595, 601*t*
Ménière's disease, 265*t*, 267
meninges, 188*t*, 189, 190*f*
meningiomas, 212*t*
meningitis, 204*t*
meningomyelocele, 204*t*, 210
menometrorrhagia, 603*t*
menopause, 595, 601*t*, 604–605, 605*t*
menorrhagia, 378*t*, 384, 603*t*
menses, 590*t*, 593, 595*f*

menstrual cycle, 590*t*, 593–595
abnormalities pertaining to, 603*t*
last menstrual period (LMP) date, 610
mental body region, 63*f*
mental health, 212–215
disorders, 213–215
phobias, 215*t*
practitioners, 212–213
prevalence rates of mental illness, 215
terms, 213*t*
mental region, 64*t*
mental status assessment, 206
mesentery, 441*t*, 450
mesoderm, 629*t*
mesothelioma, 295*t*, 297
metabolism, 520*t*, 527
metaphysis, 139
metatarsus valgus, 159*t*, 161
metatarsus varus, 159*t*, 161
methylphenidates, 222
metric system, 77, 77*t*, 79*t*
metrorrhagia, 603*t*
microbiologist, 75
microbiology, 75
microcephaly, 205*t*, 210, 384
microcyte, 368*t*, 380*t*
microcytic, 380*t*
microdermabrasion, 120*t*
microglia, 188*t*, 198
microphthalmia, 253*t*, 384
micropigmentation, 119*t*
microscopic, 75
microtia, 266, 266*t*
microvilli, 441*t*
micturition. *See* Urination
midbrain, 188*t*, 193
middle ear, 244, 244*f*
midpiece (sperm), 562, 562*f*
midsagittal plane, 55
milia, 109*t*
mineralocorticoids, 520*t*, 529
miotic agents, 262, 262*t*
miscarriage, 604, 639, 642*t*, 646, 648
mitochondria (sperm), 562, 562*f*
mitosis (cell division), 39, 626
mitral regurgitation, 344*t*
mitral stenosis, 344*t*
mitral valve, 322–323, 324*t*
mitral valve prolapse (MVP), 344*t*
MMR vaccine, 417
modified Trendelenburg position, 55, 55*f*
Mohs technique, 118
Mongolian spot, 109*t*, 111
monocytes, 368*t*, 370, 379*t*, 406*t*
monocytosis, 379*t*
mononucleosis ("mono"), 415*t*
monospot, 424*t*
mons pubis, 590*t*, 591
Montgomery's tubercles, 633*t*
mood disorders, 533*t*
Moro's reflex, 210*t*
morphology, 75*t*, 378*t*
morula, 626
motor neurons, 198
mouth, 284*t*

conditions associated with, 457–458*t*
mouth, the, 443–444, 443*f*
MRI. *See* Magnetic resonance imaging (MRI)
mucolytic, 309*t*
mucosa, 284*t*
mucositis, 457*t*
mucus, 283
MUGA scan, 348
multiaxial ball and socket diarthroses, 144*f*
multigated acquisition (MUGA) scan, 348
multigravida, 625*t*
multipara, 625*t*
multiple myeloma, 385
multiple sclerosis (MS), 205*t*, 211, 418*t*
mumps, 416, 417
murmur (heart), 340, 343, 344*t*
muscle relaxants, 173, 173*t*, 223
muscles
    abnormal muscle movements, 209*t*
    anatomy and physiology terms relating to, 147, 147*t*
    within dermal layer, 100
    exercise and, 152
    naming of, 147
    skeletal, 147, 148–149*f*, 150
    word origin, 49
muscle tissue, 41
muscular dystrophy, 205*t*, 211
musculoskeletal system, 43*f*, 131–176
    abbreviations, 174, 174*t*
    anatomy and physiology of muscular system, 147–151
    anatomy and physiology of skeletal system, 134–144
    anterior view, 135*f*, 148*f*
    changes in, during pregnancy, 633*t*
    conditions of, 154–165
    diagnostic tests/procedures, 168–169, 170*t*
    major structures of, 43*f*
    medical fields/specialists, 43*f*
    overview, 132
    posterior view, 136*f*, 149*f*
    root words associated with, 5*t*
    skeleton, anatomy and physiology terms related to, 137–139*t*
    specialists of, 133
    treatment for conditions related to, 171–173
    word parts of, 133–134*t*
myasthenia gravis, 416*t*, 418*t*
Mycobacterium tuberculosis, 299
mydriatics, 262*t*
myelin, 188*t*, 196
myelinated nerve fibers, 194
myelodysplasia, 379*t*, 384
myelodysplastic syndrome, 384
myelofibrosis, 379*t*, 381
myelography, 73*t*
Myobacterium avium-intracellulare (MAI) complex, 420*t*
myocardial infarction, 338*t*
myocarditis, 338*t*
myocardium, 150, 320, 324*t*

myoclonic muscle movement, 209*t*
myoclonic seizures, 209*t*
myofilaments, 147*t*, 150
myomas, 602*t*
myomectomy, 611*t*
myometrium, 590*t*, 593*f*, 626*f*
myopia, 251, 253, 255
myorrhaphy, 172*t*
myringectomy, 270*t*
myringitis, 266*t*
myringoplasty, 270*t*
myringotomy, 267, 270*t*
myxedema, 533*t*, 536*t*, 538

N

Nägele's Rule, 627
nail bed, 100, 101*f*
nail biting, 100
nail body, 100, 101*f*
nail folds, 100, 101*f*
nail root, 101*f*
nails, 100, 101*f*, 108, 112
    anatomy and physiology terms relating to, 94*t*
    combining forms associated with, 93*t*
narcolepsy, 205*t*
nares (nostrils), 285
naris, 284*t*
nasal cavity, 283*f*, 285, 286*f*
nasal region, 64*t*
nasal septum, 284*t*, 285
nasogastric intubation, 469*t*
nasolacrimal, 237*t*
nasolacrimal duct, 238*f*
nasolacrimal sac, 238, 238*f*
nasopharynx, 283*f*, 285*t*, 286, 286*f*
natural (genetic) immunity, 410*t*
nausea, 457*t*
nearsightedness, 251
negative feedback, 520*t*, 522, 522*f*
neonatal necrotizing enterocolitis (NEC), 459*t*, 461
neonate, 590*t*
neonatologists, 622
neonatology, 586
nephrectomy, 503*t*
nephritis, 493*t*, 495
nephroblastoma, 495
nephrolith, 493*t*, 495
nephrolithiasis, 493*t*, 495–496
nephrolithotomy, 503*t*
nephrologists, 480
nephrology, 480
nephrons, 483, 484*t*, 486, 486*f*
nephropathy, 493*t*
nephropexy, 503*t*
nephroptosis, 493*t*
nephroscopy, 500
nephrostomy, 503, 503*t*
nephrotic syndrome, 493, 493*t*, 495
nephrotomography, 501*t*
nephrotomy, 503*t*
nerve conduction velocity, 220*t*
nerve impulse pathways, 198

nerve tissue, 42
nervous system, 44*f*, 184–225
    abbreviations, 224–225*t*
    anatomy and physiology of, 186–199
    anatomy and physiology terms relating to, 187–189*t*
    cancers of, 212
    combining forms related to, 184–185, 185*t*
    conditions of, 203–215
    diagnostic tests/procedures for, 219, 220*t*
    major structures of, 44*f*
    medical field/specialists for, 44*f*
    organization of, 186*f*
    overview, 184
    root words associated with, 5, 5*t*
    treatments for conditions related to, 220–223
neurilemma, 196
neuritis, 205*t*
neurofibromatosis, 111
neuroglia, 188*t*, 198
neurohypophysis lobes, 525
neurological disorders, assessment of, 206
neurology, 188*t*
neuromuscular blockers, 223*t*
neurons, 42, 188*t*, 196, 197*f*, 198
neuroplasty, 221, 222*t*
neuroses, 214
neurosis, 214
neurotransmitters, 188*t*, 196
neutropenia, 379*t*, 380*t*
neutrophilia, 379*t*
neutrophils, 368*t*, 370, 372, 379*t*, 406*t*
nevi/nevus, 95*t*, 104*t*
nevus flammeus, 110*t*, 111
nevus simplex, 111
newborns
    blood conditions in, 381
    cardiovascular system/defects in, 340–342*t*
    endocrine system conditions in, 537
newborn screening tests, 647*t*
nipples (breast), 595, 596*f*
nocturia, 492, 496*t*
nodes of Ranvier, 188*t*, 196
nodule/nodules, 106*t*, 110*t*
nondecodable terms, 23
nondisplaced fracture, 155*t*
non-Hodgkin lymphoma, 385
non-small cell lung cancer (NSCLC), 295*t*, 297
nonspecific immunity, 408, 410
nonsteroidal anti-inflammatory drugs (NSAIDs), 172–173, 173*t*, 223
nonsteroid hormones, 521
nonstress test (NST), 647*t*
nontropic hormones, 525*t*
norepinephrine, 198, 520*t*, 529
Normal Sexual Maturity Rating, 561, 603
normal sinus rhythm (NSR), 324*t*
nose, 285, 285*t*
nuchal cord, 643*t*
nuclear medicine, 67

76t
pathogens, 75t
pathologic fracture, 155f, 155t
pathology terms, 76, 76t
patient privacy. *See* Soft skills
pectoral body region, 63f
pectoralis major muscle, 596f
pectoralis minor muscle, 596f
pectoral region, 64t
pediatricians, 622
pediatrics, 586
pelvic cavity, 59, 60, 60f, 60t
pelvic exenteration, 612t
pelvic inflammatory disease (PID), 600,
    639t
pelvic sonography, 608t
pelvimetry, 647t
pelvis
    male *vs.* female, 165, 165f
    pregnant women, 164
    renal pelvis *vs.*, 483
penicillin, 426t
penis, 558, 559f, 560, 560t, 561f
pepsins, 445–446
percussing, 303, 349t
percutaneous transluminal coronary
    angioplasty (PTCA), 351, 351f, 352t
periauricular, 243t
pericardial fluid, 322
pericarditis, 338t
pericardium, 320, 322, 324t
perilymph, 243t, 245
perilymph space, 245f
perimenopause, 604–605
perimetrium, 591t
perimetry, 260t
perineal region, 65t
perineum, 591, 591t
periodontal disease/pyorrhea (gum
    disease), 458t
periosteum, 138t, 139
peripheral blood smear, 388, 389
peripheral iridectomy, 262t
peripheral nervous system (PNS), 186,
    189t, 194–198, 194–199
peripheral vascular disease (PVD), 339t
peristalsis, 441t, 446, 446t
peritoneal dialysis (PD), 503, 503t
peritoneum, 441t, 450
peritonitis, 457t
peritubular capillaries, 484t, 488
pernicious anemia, 377, 416t, 418
PERRLA, 259
"pertaining to," suffixes meaning, 11t
pertussis, 295t, 417
pes planus, 159t, 162
petechia, 110t
petit mal seizures, 208, 209t
PET scans, 70, 70f, 304
Peyronie disease, 567t, 570
phacoemulsification, 262t
phagocyte, 406t
phagocytosis, 406–407, 406t, 410
phalanges, 138t
pharmacological treatments, 425–426,

426t. *See also* Individual body systems.
pharmacology terms, general, 78–81
pharyngeal tonsils, 406t, 407, 407f
pharyngitis, 295t
pharynx (throat), 285t, 286, 286f, 445
    conditions associated with, 458t
pH balance, vaginal health and, 592
phenomenon syndrome, 339t
phenylketonuria (PKU), 647t
pheochromocytoma, 534, 536t
pheresis, 391, 392, 392t
phimosis, 566, 567t
phlebectomy, 352t
phlebitis, 339t
phlebotomists, 586
phobias, 214, 215t
phoropter, 260t
photon absorptiometry, 169
photopic vision, 239
physical examinations
    digestive system, 465
    of female reproductive organs, 607
    of musculoskeletal system, 154
Physician's Desk Reference (PDR), 27–28
physique
    of aging adult, 165
    meaning and word analysis, 160t
pia mater, 189–190, 189t
pigeon toes, 162
piles, 462
pineal body, 520t, 523, 524
pinealectomy, 545t
pineal gland, 518, 518f, 524f
pinna, 243t, 244
pituitary adenoma, 536t
pituitary gland (hypophysis), 518, 518f,
    520t, 523, 524–526, 524f
pituitary hormones, 525t, 526f
pivot diarthroses, 143, 144f
placenta, 520t, 530, 625t, 627, 628f
placenta previa, 643t
placing reflex, 210t
plantar body region, 63f
plantar flexion, 57t
plantar grasp, 210t
plantar reflex, 199t
plantar region, 63f, 65t
plaque, 458t
plaque/plaques, 106t
plasma, 368t
plasmapheresis, 391, 392t
plastic surgeons, 105
platelet count, 389t
plateletpheresis, 391, 392t
platelets, 368t, 370, 373
pleura, 285t, 288
pleural effusion, 295t
pleural rub, 303t
pleurisy, 296t
pleurodynia, 296t
plicae, 441t
plural forms, frequently used, 27t
plurals, formation of, 26–27
pneumoconiosis, 296t
pneumocystis, 420

Pneumocystis carinii pneumonia (PCP),
    420t
pneumonectomy, 307t
pneumonia, 296t, 298, 299
pneumothorax, 296t, 299
podagra, 160t, 164
podiatrists, 133
poikilocytosis, 380t
polio, 416
poliomyelitis, 205t, 209
polychromasia, 380t
polycystic kidney disease, 493t
polycystic ovary syndrome (PCOS), 602t
polycythemia, 379t
polycythemia vera, 384
polydactyly, 160t, 161
polydipsia, 542
polyhydramnios, 642t
polymorphonuclear, 368t
polymorphonuclear leukocytes, 372
polyorchism, 568t
polyotia, 266, 266t
polypectomy, 470t, 612t
polyphagia, 542
polyps, 459t, 462
polyuria, 492, 497t, 533t, 538, 542
pons, 189t, 193
popliteal body region, 63f
popliteal region, 65t
population, 630
portwine stain, 111, 111f
position/direction, prefixes related to, 18t,
    19t
positions/positional terms, 51
    analogies used to remember, 53
    anatomical, 51
    anatomical position, 51
    of the human body, 51–52t, 53–55,
        53–55f
positive feedback, 520t, 522, 523f
positron emission tomography (PET) scan,
    70, 70f, 220t, 349t
posterior (directional term), 51t, 52f
posterior pituitary hormones, 525t, 545t
postictal phase of seizures, 208
postpartum, 625t, 636
    abbreviations associated with, 654,
        655t
    anatomy and physiology terms related
        to, 624–625t
    conditions associated with, 644
    word parts associated with, 623–624t
postpartum depression (PPD), 636, 644,
    644t
postprandial (PP) test, 543
post-traumatic stress syndrome disorder
    (PTSD), 214
posture, 151, 162–163, 164
practice algorithms, 221
practitioners/specialists. *See also* Individual
    body systems
    ear conditions, 243
    suffixes used in the names of, 10t
    vision, 240
precocious puberty, 533t, 536t

vesicle, 106*t*
vesicotomy, 504*t*
vesicoureteral reflux, 495*t*, 496
vesicourethral suspension, 504*t*
vesiculectomy, 575, 575*t*
vesiculitis, 567*t*
vestibular nerve, 245*f*, 246*f*
vestibule, 243*t*, 245*f*, 591, 591*t*
villi, 442*t*
visceral (directional term), 52*t*
visceral organs, 42
visceral (inner) pericardium, 322
visceral/visceral layer (digestive system), 442*t*, 450
viscosity, 384
vision. *See* Eye(s)
vision system, practitioners for, 240
vital capacity (VC), 305
Vitamin B$_{12}$, 377
vitamin supplements, 471*t*
vitiligo, 110*t*, 418*t*
vitreous humor, 237*t*
vocal cords, 286, 287*f*
voice box. *See* Larynx
voiding. *See* Urination
voiding cystourethrograph (VCUG), 501*t*
voluntary muscles, 147, 147*t*, 148*f*
voluntary muscle tissue, 41
volvulus, 457*t*, 462
vomiting, 454, 456*t*

von Willebrand's disease, 382*t*, 384
vulva, 591*t*
vulvectomy, 612*t*
vulvitis, 602*t*
vulvodynia, 602*t*
vulvovaginitis, 602*t*

W

Wallace rule of nines, 105, 105*f*
warts, 114
waste elimination, 40
water births, 653, 653*t*
WBCs. *See* White blood cells (WBCs)
Weber's test, 268*t*
Weschler Adult Intelligence Scale (WAIS), 220*t*
Western blot, 423, 424*t*
wheals, 106*t*
wheeze, 303, 303*t*
white blood cell count, 410, 424
white blood cell count with differential, 388
white blood cells (WBCs), 372, 379*t*, 410
Wilm's tumor, 495, 495*t*
Wiskott-Aldrich syndrome, 416*t*, 417
womb, 628
Wood's lamp, 117
word parts, 2. *See also* Individual body systems

explained, 3–4
five ways to combine, 22–23
word play, 24
World Health Organization (WHO), 86, 612
wrinkles, clinical treatments for, 119–120, 120*t*

X

xanthoma, 110*t*
X chromosomes, 631
xenograft, 119*t*
xenophobia, 214*t*
xerosis, 110*t*, 113
X-rays, 67, 68, 71, 304, 466, 500, 608

Y

Y chromosomes, 631
young adults. *See also* Adolescents
 neurological development and conditions in, 211
 respiratory system conditions in, 299

Z

zidovudine, 425
zygote, 560*t*, 625*t*, 626

Photo Acknowledgments

Cover: © iStock.com/iLexx; © wawritto/Shutterstock.com;

4 FreeImages.com/Jean Scheijen; **53-55** Electronic Illustrators Group; **70** (bottom image) © iStock.com/wenht; **84, 88-89, 106-107** Electronic Illustrators Group; **112** (top image) © iStock.com/aniaostudio, (bottom image) © iStock.com/Suze777; **113** (left image) © iStock.com/banarfilardhi; (middle image) © iStock.com/Agnieszka_M; (right image) © iStock.com/napatcha; **116** (top images) Electronic Illustrators Group; (bottom image) © Goodluz | Dreamstime.com; **150** (top of image) A.D.A.M.; (bottom of image) Electronic Illustrators Group; **162** © stihii/Shutterstock; **255** Public Domain; **373** (left half of image) A.D.A.M. (right half of image) Electronic Illustrators Group; **423** © James Gathany / Public Health Image Library (PHIL); **461** © iStock.com/tshortell; **500** Cancer Research UK / Wikimedia Commons; **630** (top image) © DOPAMINE/SCIENCE PHOTO LIBRARY

  All other images courtesy of A.D.A.M. a business unit of Ebix, Inc. All rights reserved. Images may not be reproduced in any manner without express written consent of A.D.A.M., a business unit of Ebix, Inc.; 1 Ebix Way, Johns Creek, GA 30097 USA

Notes

Notes

Notes

Notes

Notes

Notes

Medical
Terminology

Connecting through Language

Enrich Your Program with Paradigm

Paradigm Education Solutions is committed to equipping educators and students with innovative courseware for success in today's classroom, at work, and in life.

We believe students learn most effectively through a combination of print and digital tools, so we accompany our textbooks with exceptional digital resources that help students master core content and strengthen their skills.

Explore our learning solutions at **ParadigmCollege.com**.

**COURSE
NAVIGATOR**

The Course Navigator learning management system that accompanies this textbook provides students with a robust, interactive program to help them master content and provides instructors with tools to support successful instruction and assessment.

ISBN 978-0-76386-826-0

9 780763 868260

PARADIGM
EDUCATION SOLUTIONS

Learn drug names and medical terms faster with additional study tools from Paradigm.

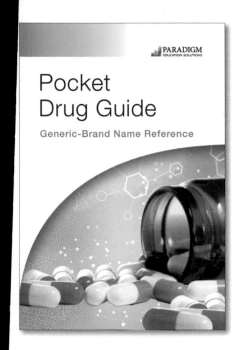

Paradigm's Pocket Drug Guide

Now offered in 3 formats, including an app!

The *Pocket Drug Guide* provides a quick, convenient reference for learning nearly 1,000 generic and brand-name drugs. A full alphabetic listing by brand and generic names allows you to easily locate drugs, with the most commonly prescribed drugs highlighted.

Choose the format that works best for you:

1 Booklet!
©2017 | 100 pages

2 eBook!
©2017 | 100 pages

Access the *Pocket Drug Guide* anywhere and on any device!

3 App!
The *Paradigm Health Careers Drugs & Terms* app incorporates the information from the *Pocket Drug Guide* and essential medical terminology. This app identifies more than 1,000 drugs and 2,000 medical terms. You are able to:

- Search the terms database by drug class or body system.
- Master pronunciation of medical terminology with audio functionality.
- Create your own flash cards to practice identifying drugs and medical terms.

The app is available for purchase from iTunes and Google Play for only $5.95!

PARADIGM
EDUCATION SOLUTIONS

WWP206624

ParadigmEducation.com | 800-535-6865

Rely on Paradigm for Superior, Personalized Support

U.S. Based

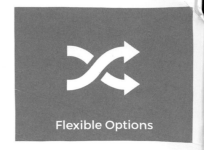

Flexible Options

Available 24/7

Personalized Service

Superior Technical Support

Paradigm Education Solutions offers unparalleled technical support for students and instructors. Our specialists are based in our home office in St. Paul, Minnesota. They find answers, explain features and functionality, and follow up quickly to ensure everyone can easily access and navigate Paradigm's courseware.

Flexible Options that Fit Your Schedule

Instructors and students have the option to live chat, call, or email questions to a technical specialist, who will provide quick and thorough responses to inquiries.

Live Chat Available 24/7

 Visit support.emcp.com to view FAQs, user guides, training videos, or to start a live chat with a technical specialist.

Phone

Available Monday through Sunday 8AM – 10PM (CST).

☎ 800-535-6865 (press 2)

Email

✉ support@emcp.com

Personalized Customer Service

Paradigm's Customer Service Department can provide additional information about courseware and the order process.

Our representatives are available Monday through Friday, 8AM – 5PM (CST).

✉ educate@emcp.com   ☎ 800-535-6865

PARADI
EDUCATION SO